G000091385

BED &

BREAKFAST

GUIDE

Mary Winget

FODOR'S TRAVEL PUBLICATIONS, INC.
New York & London

ISBN 0-679-01719-4

Fodor's Bed & Breakfast Guide

Editor: Alice Thompson
Illustrations: Paul Verga
Maps: Jon Bauch Design
Cover Photograph: Will Faller

Cover Design: Vignelli Associates

MANUFACTURED IN THE UNITED STATES OF AMERICA
10 9 8 7 6 5 4 3 2 1

Contents

CANADA   511

MEXICO   561

Foreword

The bed & breakfast phenomenon, once found almost exclusively abroad, has hit Norrth America in full force. From private homes in the rural midwest to small New England inns, from contemporary California condos to sophisticated New York high rises, B&B accommodations branch out into areas previously unknown to prospective guests. Canada and Mexico, too, offer an incredible variety of choices to the traveler seeking a more personalized, less standardized stay than one to be found in the nearest branch of a large motel chain.

Fodor's *Bed & Breakfast Guide* is designed to help you plan your own trip based on your schedule, your budget, your energy, and your idea of what the trip should be. After reading this guide, you'll have some new ideas.

This guide is a selected list of B&Bs throughout the United States, Canada, and Mexico. Obviously, Fodor's could neither include every such establishment, nor personally inspect each one. However, each one listed either belongs to a reputable reservation service organization with its own evaluation procedures, or is a licensed inn and as such is subject to local regulations governing such establishments. Every effort was made to protect you, the reader.

Errors are bound to creep into any travel guide, however. Much change can and will occur even while the book is on press, and also during the year that this edition is on sale.

We sincerely welcome letters from our readers on these changes, or from those whose opinions differ from ours, and we are ready to revise our entries for the next edition when the facts warrant it.

Send your letters to the editors at Fodor's Travel Publications, 201 East 50th Street, New York, NY 10022. European or British Commonwealth readers may prefer to write to Fodor's Travel Publications, 30–32 Bedford Square, London, WC1B 3SG, England.

HOW TO USE THIS BOOK

This book's listings are organized by country. Within each country, entries are listed by state. The state's name appears only once, at the beginning of each section, so if you find a listing in a state you cannot identify, simply turn back to the beginning of the chapter to learn the state in which it is located. The city name also appears only once, with a rule underneath it, so if you see a listing with a rule and no copy above it, you simply need to turn to the beginning of that city's listings to locate a particular establishment. The following information will help you understand how each listing works:

ID Number: Appears in the upper right-hand corner of the rule at the top of each listing. Give that number to the *Reservation Contact* when reserving your guest room.

Nearby Attractions: Anything in the vicinity that may interest you—from museums, universities, and zoos to activities such as fishing, boating, etc. Appears directly under the rule at the top of each listing.

Nearby Routes: Appear in italics directly below *Nearby Attractions*. Lists nearby highways, routes, interstates, and major thoroughfares.

The text follows and is self-explanatory.

Singles and **Doubles:** Both words appear in boldface type in the left-hand column under the text. They refer to the sleeping capacity of each room and also tell you whether the bath will be private or shared. For example, if, under *Singles,* the notation "2 sb" appears, you can understand that two rooms, each of which sleeps one, and each with a shared bath, are available.

Type: This allows you to categorize the accommodations. Will you be staying in a private home, a small inn, or a high-rise apartment complex?

Breakfast: See *Introduction* for a complete explanation of *Full, Continental,* and *Continental Plus.*

S-Rates and D-Rates: These notations explain how much it will cost to stay in a double or single room (distinguishing between those that offer private and those that offer shared baths if both are available) and differentiates, rate-wise, between one and two people staying in the same room.

Bldg: Type of structure (e.g., Victorian, 1950s split-level) was identified when such information was available.

Reservation Contact: This tells you who to contact when making your reservation. It will almost always be the name of a registry, UNLESS the particular establishment is listed under its own name, which is rarely the case.

Introduction

Welcome to the world of Bed & Breakfast! These accommodations have enjoyed a long and pleasant history in Great Britain and many other European countries. Travelers have used them as comfortable and economical places to stop for a good night's rest, a hearty breakfast, good conversation, and useful travel tips about the local area. B&Bs have obviously passed the test of time abroad. Now they're creating a travel revolution on this continent.

In Europe visitors walk down the street until they find a bed & breakfast or *zimmer frei* sign. But most American bed & breakfast homes operate through an RSO, a reservation service organization. The RSO represents the host homes and generally takes care of the business end of the B&B. RSOs differ in size. Although most of them operate with one or two people from an office at home, some do maintain separate offices and a staff. They can represent host homes in an individual city, throughout a state or region, or throughout the country; a few are even international. Likewise, host homes can be represented by several RSOs—by local, state, and national services. Names and addresses of individual host homes and most of the small inns listed are not stated; instead ID numbers are given. Every effort was made to avoid duplication in this book.

The RSO checks a host's references, and host homes are inspected by at least one of the RSOs that represents them. It is not unusual for an RSO to ask guests for references, too, since they act as a screening device for the hosts they represent.

Why the elaborate system? Many hosts don't want to "go public." Most do not offer bed & breakfast accommodations on a full-time basis and do not want people arriving on their doorsteps unannounced. The RSO takes care of that. It also collects deposits and sends reservation confirmations, leaving hosts free to do what they do best—take care of their guests.

Most RSOs have brochures that they are happy to send to prospective guests. When requesting material by mail, please enclose a stamped, self-addressed envelope.

It should also be noted that there are some bed & breakfast inns that register with RSOs, and they, too, are described in this guide. Also listed are some licensed inns that are not affiliated with any reservation service organization. These inns are inspected as part of the licensing procedure and can provide promotional material. In addition, their references have been checked.

Making Reservations

Reservations can be made by calling or writing to the reservation service organization (RSO) listed at the bottom of each description. Independent inns can be contacted directly.

Whoever you call will want to know the identification number of the host home or inn (or the name, if it's given), the number in your party, arrival and departure dates, and your approximate time of arrival. If it's a private home you're contacting, you may also be asked for the name of your employer and for references. If you're calling an RSO and the B&B of your choice is not available, an alternative might be suggested for your consideration.

If you are placing a reservation by mail, be sure to include a stamped, self-addressed envelope and your telephone number. If possible, provide several alternative B&Bs with their identification numbers. Let the RSO know whether a comparable B&B would be acceptable even though it is not listed in this guide and, above all, allow extra time for mail reservations.

In almost all cases, a deposit will be necessary. The amount required varies widely; a few RSOs might even require prepayment in full. Each listing states whether or not credit cards are accepted. If so, the deposit can be taken care of by telephone. Be sure to ask about cancellation policies so the deposit is not lost if a change in plans occurs. If you're staying at a B&B registered with an RSO, after the deposit is received, the RSO will send you written confirmation with the name, address, and telephone number of your host as well as directions to the front door. The balance of the bill should be paid to your host on arrival after you inspect the accommodations. Remember that the majority of host homes do not accept and cannot process credit cards, so the balance of the payment should be made in cash or traveler's checks. Many hosts also accept personal checks. And please note that although the prices listed in this guide were accurate at press time, some rates are subject to change; it is important, therefore, to confirm the cost when making your reservation.

It is absolutely essential to explain what *you* want when you place your reservation. Don't be afraid to ask questions. If you want a romantic weekend away from the kids, you're probably not interested in the spare room of a house with three resident children; if you're a family type away on business, you might just love it! If you're picturing a place with antiques, lace curtains, and a canopy bed, say so. If total privacy is very important, ask where the rooms are located. Some homes afford more privacy than others because of the layout; many even have separate guest wings or private entrances. Some people feel uncomfortable in a private home and prefer an inn, others feel that private homes are the only authentic bed & breakfast accommodations.

In many B&Bs guests share a bath or baths. If that is not acceptable, be sure to state when reserving the room that you want a private bath. The descriptions in this book state whether baths are private or shared; frequently there are both types in one location.

If you are allergic to cats, dogs, or smoke, mention it to the RSO. Likewise, if you must smoke, be sure it is permitted in the home or inn at which you are making reservations.

Finally, if there is any change in you projected time of arrival, be sure to contact your host. It is a courteous gesture to call ahead in any case, but if you arrive later or earlier than stated there may be no one to let you in.

What to Expect

Guests can expect clean, comfortable accommodations, good hospitality, and breakfast. Aside from that the variety of hosts and host homes—or inns— is almost infinite. Accommodations can be a modest home with a spare room, a carriage house overlooking a lake, a room in a condo or apartment building, a dairy farm or cattle ranch, a hilltop cottage in San Francisco or a stone cottage in Missouri, a houseboat, a former stagecoach station, a picturesque New England inn, a villa, an antebellum plantation. Most, however, are just nice private homes. Some are furnished with heirloom antiques while others are strictly contemporary. Most are probably eclectic. Some were built in the 1700s; some were built just last year.

With one or two exceptions, all the locations listed in this book serve—or at least provide the ingredients for—breakfast. Breakfast can mean anything from a hot drink and a roll to a sumptuous meal of several courses. The three breakfast types are Continental (hot beverage plus roll or muffin), Continental Plus (same but with more elaborate ingredients or juice), and Full (traditional several courses, usually including an egg-based dish). Many hosts try to make breakfast an occasion and the table is set with the best crystal, china, and silver. Other hosts, however, have simpler lifestyles or schedules that don't allow much time for breakfast. In addition, there are often state or local ordinances that restric hosts from preparing a full breakfast without installing a commercial kitchen and obtaining a special license to serve food. If you have any special dietary needs or restrictions, mention them when making your reservation so the RSO can let your host know in advance of your arrival.

Bed & breakfast hosts want to be hospitable and help you with directions and suggestions; they also respect your privacy and take cues from you. Many hosts and guests become lifelong friends and correspondents. However, if all you desire is a quiet, private place to sleep, that's fine, too.

The doors of the guest rooms in most of the smaller B&Bs are generally unlocked. In most cases these are private homes, and the hosts are not full-time innkeepers. In general, a bed & breakfast experience is more like visiting a friend than like staying at a motel or hotel, and usually there is no daily maid service. The exception to this rule is the small inn, which usually offers most of the standard hotel amenities.

Staying at a B&B is generally less expensive than staying in a hotel or motel. The range of bed & breakfast rates reflects the range of accommodations. Rates also vary from one area of the country to another. When you read about $25 nightly bed & breakfast rates, they're probably not in New York City! But if bed & breakfast rates reflect geographic locale, so do the B&Bs themselves: You'll remember where you stayed in Boston, and it won't look like the place you stayed in San Francisco. You'll also remember your hosts.

Other amenities vary widely. In many places you will be greeted with a glass of wine or a soft drink and a light snack. You will often find fresh flowers in your rooms, a carafe of wine or a liqueur on the bedside table, fancy soaps in the bath, chocolates on the pillow, and/or turn-down service. Some hosts serve tea or sherry in the afternoon or evening. This affords you a pleasant opportunity to mingle with other guests and compare notes on local attractions and activities. You are usually invited to use other areas of the house, such as the living room, game room, deck, patio, or pool; don't assume this is always the case, however. Extras, such as bikes, canoes, fishing equipment, and tennis racquets, are often at your disposal. Arrival/departure transportation, additional meals, child care, area tours, and boat rides are frequently available, sometimes free, sometimes for a small charge.

The RSOs contributing to this guide were asked to submit their best B&Bs. Best in this case does not necessarily mean the most elegant or most expensive but rather the overall quality of the host home or inn. Most RSOs have some evaluation process and know which of their hosts consistently get rave reviews. These are the homes and inns that we sought to include in this guide.

Almost half of the homes and inns in this book were built before 1900 and around one out of every eight is Victorian in style. Many locations are included in the National Register of Historic Places, and over 300 have antique furnishings. Cumulatively, the RSOs in this guide represent more than 6,500 bed & breakfast locations with almost 13,000 guest rooms. All 50 states are represented as well as the District of Columbia, six Canadian provinces, and Mexico. If you can't find the exact location you need in this book, contact an RSO. They represent many more locations than are included here and a bed & breakfast home or inn may very well be there waiting to welcome you.

Bed & Breakfast Registry

Founded in 1982, the Bed & Breakfast Registry is a North American service that has helped popularize European-style bed & breakfast travel throughout the continent. In the years since its founding, the Bed & Breakfast Registry has introduced thousands of North American travelers to the joys of bed & breakfast travel.

Reservations Network

The following Reservation Service Organizations (RSOs) have formed a reservations network for the purpose of this book. Every bed & breakfast traveler booking a reservation with one of these RSOs has access to the combined listings of all of their accommodations and is offered a satisfaction guarantee; full refund of the deposit if, upon inspection of the accommodations, the guest is dissatisfied and submits the reasons for the dissatisfaction in writing to the pertinent RSO.

> **Greater Boston Hospitality**
> Box 1142
> Brookline, MA 02146
> 617–277–5430

> **City Lights Bed & Breakfast, Ltd.**
> Bos 20355, Cherokee Station
> New York, NY 10028
> 212–737–7049

> **Bed & Breakfast Registry Ltd.**
> Bos 8174
> St. Paul, MN 55108
> 612–646–4238

ALABAMA

BIRMINGHAM

ID: BIR–DDDWLHT

RED MOUNTAIN.

Near I–65, I–59, I–20.

This massive, three-story frame house sits on the side of Red Mountain. From the porch guests have a view of the city. The front entrance has imposing double doors; inside you'll find dark wood floors, a huge living room with fireplaces at either end, and a broad stairway that leads to the guest rooms. One room has a king-sized bed, and the other three have double beds. The rooms have working fireplaces, ceiling fans, antique wooden beds covered with period quilts and linens, and settees; three have private baths. In the rear of the house there is a deck, swimming pool, and off-street parking.

1

No. Rooms: 4		**Breakfast:** Continental	
Singles: None		**S-Rates:** $65 pb, $65 sb	
Doubles: 3 pb, 1 sb		**D-Rates:** $65 pb, $65 sb	
Type: Private home		**Bldg:** 1910 Craftsman	

Minimum Stay: none. **Credit Card(s) Accepted:** MC, V. **Open:** all year. No resident dogs. No dogs please. No resident cats. No cats please. Non-smoking host. Guests may smoke in designated areas. Children welcome with prior notice. **Discounts:** weekly.

Reservation Contact: Bed & Breakfast Birmingham, Inc., Bill Shaw & Larry Hanson, Box 31328, Birmingham, AL 35222; 205–933–2487.

ID: BIR–DTWAL

QUIET RETREAT, 20 MINUTES FROM BIRMINGHAM.

Near I–20, I–59, I–65.

Twenty minutes from the city, this contemporary split-level is set on five wooded acres. Various animals, including chickens, dogs, cats, and geese, roam the property. There are two guest rooms, one with twin beds, one with a double bed, that share a bath. Your hosts enjoy gardening and collecting clocks.

No. Rooms: 2	**Breakfast:** Continental
Singles: None	**S-Rates:** $40 sb
Doubles: 2 sb	**D-Rates:** $40 sb
Type: Private home	**Bldg:** Contemporary

Minimum Stay: none. **Credit Card(s) Accepted:** MC, V. **Open:** all year. Resident dog. No dogs please. Resident cat. No cats please. Nonsmoking host. Guests may not smoke in residence. Children welcome with prior notice. **Discounts:** weekly.

Reservation Contact: Bed & Breakfast Birmingham, Inc., Bill Shaw & Larry Hanson, Box 31328, Birmingham, AL 35222; 205–933–2487.

ID: BIR–QQTXHS

SLOSS MUSEUM, SYMPHONY.

Near I–65, I–20, I–59, Highland Ave.

Located in the historic Highland Avenue section of Birmingham, the craftsmanship and design of this home is apparent in the ten-foot ceilings and picture moldings in the formal downstairs rooms. Guests are welcome to use the living room with fireplace. The four guest rooms, all with TVs and private baths, are named after Alabama towns and cities: Montgomery is done in dusty rose and slate blue with an oriental carpet; Mobile has a port-city theme with nautical red and blue; Fort Payne has country maple furniture and a peach and hunter green color scheme; and Birmingham is decorated in burnt orange and has modern furniture.

Three rooms have queen-sized beds and one has twin beds. A Full breakfast is served. This location is convenient to the downtown area, the Sloss Museum, art museums, and the symphony. Your host is a retired businessman.

No. Rooms: 4	**Breakfast:** Full
Singles: None	**S-Rates:** $45 pb
Doubles: 4 pb	**D-Rates:** $55 pb
Type: Private home	**Bldg:** 1916 Craftsman

Minimum Stay: none. **Credit Card(s) Accepted:** MC, V. **Open:** all year. No resident dogs. No dogs please. No resident cats. No cats please. Nonsmoking host. Guests may smoke in designated areas. Children welcome with prior notice. **Discounts:** weekly.

Reservation Contact: Bed & Breakfast Birmingham, Inc., Bill Shaw & Larry Hanson, Box 31328, Birmingham, AL 35222; 205–933–2487.

ID: BIR–QTCHLD

HISTORIC FOREST PARK AREA.

Near I–65, I–20, I–59.

This rustic split-level home is located in a quiet residential area near the historic Forest Park area. The living room has a fireplace and french doors that lead to a deck overlooking the backyard. A recreation room in the basement offers color cable TV. The two guest rooms, one with a double bed and one with twin beds, have contemporary furnishings and share a bath. The house, which has central heat, air-conditioning, and off-street parking, is close to restaurants.

No. Rooms: 2	**Breakfast:** Continental
Singles: None	**S-Rates:** $35 sb
Doubles: 2 sb	**D-Rates:** $35 sb
Type: Private home	**Bldg:** Ranch

Minimum Stay: none. **Credit Card(s) Accepted:** MC, V. **Open:** all year. No resident dogs. No dogs please. No resident cats. No cats please. Nonsmoking host. Guests may smoke in designated areas. Children welcome with restrictions. **Discounts:** weekly.

Reservation Contact: Bed & Breakfast Birmingham Inc., Bill Shaw & Larry Hanson, Box 31328, Birmingham, AL 35222; 205–933–2487.

CRANE HILL
ID: BIR–CRANEH

WILLIAM BANKHEAD NATIONAL FOREST.

Near Cullman, I–65, U.S. 31.

Located in a very secluded wooded area on a lake, this rustic cedar-shingled ranch-style home is a wonderful spot for getting away from it all—the nearest traffic is seventeen miles away. The lake offers fishing and swimming, but swimmers are warned that it does have an irregular mud bottom. Rafts and floats are provided. There is a pleasant screened porch and indoor and outdoor eating facilities. This unhosted cottage sleeps four comfortably. There are two bedrooms, one with a double bed and the other with a queen-sized bed. There are two baths with showers and an air-conditioning and heating unit. Breakfast items are provided.

No. Rooms: 2	**Breakfast:** Continental
Singles: None	**S-Rates:** None
Doubles: 2 pb	**D-Rates:** $80 pb
Type: Private cottage	**Bldg:** Ranch-style

Minimum Stay: none. **Credit Card(s) Accepted:** MC, V. **Open:** all year. No resident dogs. No dogs please. No resident cats. No cats please. Nonsmoking host. Guests may smoke in designated areas. Children welcome with prior notice. **Discounts:** weekly.

Reservation Contact: Bed & Breakfast Birmingham, Inc., Bill Shaw & Larry Hanson, Box 31328, Birmingham, AL 35222; 205–933–2487.

DECATUR
ID: BIR–VDDDDAND

POINT MALLARD, BALLOON RACES, HUNTSVILLE SPACE CENTER, HELEN KELLER'S HOME.

Near U.S. 31, U.S. 20, I–65.

This three-story Palladian home, listed on the National Register, is located in the heart of old Decatur on the Tennessee River. Nearby are Point Mallard with its wave pool, hot-air balloon races, fishing, and boating. The Huntsville Space Center is twenty-seven miles away, and Helen Keller's home is forty miles away at Tuscumbia. Built in 1829, the Federal-style house has four-foot wide doorways, built to accommodate the ladies' wide hoop skirts, the fashion of the day. The house was headquarters for the Ohio regiment during the Civil War. The current owners are involved in an ongoing, very accurate restoration. The house is furnished with antiques, most of which are for sale. There are two third-floor guest rooms with double beds, antique furnishings, and a shared guest bath. A Continental breakfast is served. Arrival/departure transportation and area tours are available. Your hosts, members of the Alabama Historical Society, are knowledgeable about local and state history and have many stories to tell about their home.

No. Rooms: 2	**Breakfast:** Continental
Singles: None	**S-Rates:** $40 sb
Doubles: 2 sb	**D-Rates:** $45 sb
Type: Private home	**Bldg:** 1829 Palladian

Minimum Stay: none, but there is a $5 surcharge for one-night stays. **Credit Card(s) Accepted:** MC, V. **Open:** all year. No resident dogs. No dogs please. No resident cats. No cats please. Nonsmoking host. Guests

may smoke in designated areas. Children welcome with prior notice. **Discounts:** weekly.

Reservation Contact: Bed & Breakfast Birmingham, Inc., Bill Shaw & Larry Hanson, Box 31328, Birmingham, AL 35222; 205–933–2487.

MILLBROOK ID: MONT–HI

SHAKESPEARE FESTIVAL, HISTORIC SITES.

Near I–65, I–85, rtes. 143, 80.

This contemporary home on thirteen acres in the heart of Millbrook offers complete privacy with many beautiful trees, a creek, patio, courtyard, and glassed-in porch. The three guest rooms have private baths and are furnished with double beds and antiques. One room also has a sitting room with TV, refrigerator, and private entrance. A Full breakfast is served. Your host is a retired teacher who enjoys swimming and travel.

No. Rooms: 3	**Breakfast:** Full
Singles: None	**S-Rates:** $36 pb
Doubles: 3 pb	**D-Rates:** $40 pb
Type: Private home	**Bldg:** Contemporary

Minimum Stay: none. **Credit Card(s) Accepted:** none. **Open:** all year. Resident dog. No dogs please. Resident cat. No cats please. Nonsmoking host. Guests may smoke. Children welcome with restrictions. **Discounts:** for stays of more than three nights.

Reservation Contact: Bed & Breakfast Montgomery, Helen Maier, Box 886, Millbrook, AL 36054; 205–285–5421.

MONTGOMERY

ID: MONT–WA

COTTAGE HILL DISTRICT, SHAKESPEARE FESTIVAL, STATE CAPITOL, FIVE MINUTES FROM DOWNTOWN.

Near I–65, I–85, U.S. 80, Madison Ave. & Commerce St.

Situated in a neighborhood of 19th-century cottages and homes in the historic Cottage Hill District, this home, in the style of a raised cottage, takes advantage of the beautiful views: the plain and the river can be seen from one side, downtown and the state capitol from the other. Guests will enjoy relaxing on the porch, in the gazebo, or in the garden. There is a family room with a fireplace and a music room complete with harpsichord. The eclectic furnishings include many interesting pieces such as a 1735 Chinese chest, a plantation desk, and a 1798 grandfather clock. There are four guest rooms on the ground floor, each with a private bath: Granny's Room has a Queen Anne desk and a three-quarter bed with a spread crocheted by the host's grandmother; the River Room is furnished with a double bed, Chippendale table, Victorian washstand, and an overstuffed chair; the Garden Room has twin beds and a rocking chair; and the Gazebo Room, the largest room, has twin beds. An adjacent children's room is also available with a single bed or crib, wooden blocks, and books. Guests are served a Full breakfast either in the dining room or on the large porch overlooking the river plain. Your hosts are graduates of the College of William and Mary. They have a wide range of interests including church and community activities, travel, music, gardening, and theater.

No. Rooms: 4	**Breakfast:** Full
Singles: 1 pb	**S-Rates:** $45 pb
Doubles: 3 pb	**D-Rates:** $50 pb
Type: Private home	**Bldg:** Raised cottage

Minimum Stay: none. **Credit Card(s) Accepted:** none. **Open:** all year. Resident dog. No dogs please. No resident cats. No cats please. Nonsmoking hosts. Guests may smoke. Children welcome. **Discounts:** special rates for 5 or more days.

Reservation Contact: Bed & Breakfast Montgomery, Helen Maier, Box 886, Millbrook, AL 36054; 205–285–5421.

CAPITOL, SHAKESPEARE FESTIVAL.

Near hwys. 143 & 14, I–65N.

This restored raised cottage, circa 1840, is filled with antiques. There is one guest room with twin beds and private bath. A Full breakfast is served. The house is about fifteen minutes from downtown Montgomery and located next to an antebellum church. Your hosts, a retired colonel and his wife, have interests in home restoration, antiques, and music. They have traveled both in the United States and abroad.

No. Rooms: 1   **Breakfast:** Full
Singles: None   **S-Rates:** $36 pb
Doubles: 1 pb   **D-Rates:** $40 pb
Type: Private home   **Bldg:** 1840 raised cottage

Minimum Stay: none. **Credit Card(s) Accepted:** none. **Open:** all year, except Christmas. No resident dogs. No dogs please. Resident cats. No cats please. Host smokes. Guests may smoke. Residence not appropriate for children. **Discounts:** none.

Reservation Contact: Bed & Breakfast Montgomery, Helen Maier, Box 886, Millbrook, AL 36054; 205–285–5421.

SHAKESPEARE FESTIVAL, DOG RACING TRACK.

Near I–85E.

This attractively furnished contemporary home is on a sixty-acre farm just outside the city. There are four guest rooms with private baths built around a covered pool, each with private entrance, kitchenette, and dining space; each has a different decor—Oriental, nautical, Americana, and contemporary. Three rooms have queen-sized beds, and one is furnished with twin beds. A Full breakfast is served and other meals are available if requested ahead of time. Other amenities include air-conditioning, TV, patio, and laundry privileges. Your gracious hosts, a retired colonel and an interior decorator, are widely traveled. They enjoy antiques, decorating, and playing the guitar.

No. Rooms: 4   **Breakfast:** Full
Singles: None   **S-Rates:** $36 pb
Doubles: 4 pb   **D-Rates:** $40 pb
Type: Private home   **Bldg:** 1983 contemporary

Minimum Stay: none. **Credit Card(s) Accepted:** none. **Open:** all year, except Christmas. No resident dogs. No dogs please. No resident cats. No cats please. Nonsmoking host. Guests may smoke. Children welcome. **Discounts:** weekly.

Reservation Contact: Bed & Breakfast Montgomery, Helen Maier, Box 886, Millbrook, AL 36054; 205–285–5421.

PIKE ROAD

20 MINUTES FROM MONTGOMERY.

Near I–85E.

This delightful restored farmhouse is located on 120 acres of land just outside Montgomery. It is also near an antebellum Episcopal church with an English garden. The house has two guest rooms, one with double bed, one with twin beds, both with shared guest bath. Both rooms are not rented at the same time except to members of the same party. A Full breakfast is served, and you can use the yard and TV. Your host, a retired social worker, enjoys antiques.

No. Rooms: 2	**Breakfast:** Full
Singles: None	**S-Rates:** $34–$36 sb
Doubles: 2 sb	**D-Rates:** $36–$40 sb
Type: Private home	**Bldg:** 1900s farmhouse

Minimum Stay: none. **Credit Card(s) Accepted:** none. **Open:** all year, except Christmas. No resident dogs. No dogs please. No resident cats. No cats please. Nonsmoking host. Guests may not smoke in guest rooms. Children welcome with restrictions. **Discounts:** none.

Reservation Contact: Bed & Breakfast Montgomery, Helen Maier, Box 886, Millbrook, AL 36054; 205–285–5421.

TRUSSVILLE

30 MINUTES NORTHEAST OF BIRMINGHAM.

Near Rockridge Ave., Chalkville Rd., I–59, I–20, I–78, I–459.

This cozy red brick house is located on a well-kept lot surrounded by trees and flowers. You are welcome to use the living room, den, kitchen, and patio. There is one guest room with twin beds and adjacent private bath. A Continental breakfast is served on the patio surrounded by azaleas and dogwoods. Your hosts' interests include travel, music, drama, and gardening. Arrival/departure transportation from the airport is available.

No. Rooms: 1	**Breakfast:** Continental
Singles: None	**S-Rates:** $40 pb
Doubles: 1 pb	**D-Rates:** $40 pb
Type: Private cottage	**Bldg:** 1948 red brick

Minimum Stay: none. **Credit Card(s) Accepted:** MC, V. **Open:** all year. No resident dogs. No dogs please. No resident cats. No cats please. Nonsmoking host. Guests may smoke in designated areas. Children welcome with advance notice. **Discounts:** weekly.

Reservation Contact: Bed & Breakfast Birmingham, Inc., Bill Shaw & Larry Hanson, Box 31328, Birmingham, AL 35222; 205–933–2487.

ALASKA

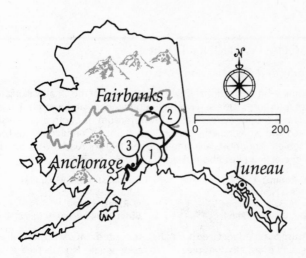

FAIRBANKS

ID: FAIRBANKS–1

HISTORIC DISTRICT.

Near Cowles, Airport Rd., George Parks Hwy.

Located in a quiet, historic area, this two-story frame house is reminiscent of the gold-mining era of Fairbanks. The house is about eight blocks from the town center, and public transportation is available. There are three guest rooms, one with private bath. One room has twin beds, a nightstand with light, plus an overhead light, dresser, chair, and towel stand. A second room has an antique iron double bed and coordinated furnishings. Both rooms look out on the large backyard and share a guest bath. The third room, overlooking the front yard, is furnished with a queen-sized bed, easy chair and ottoman, dresser, color TV, nightstand, lamps, and wall-to-wall carpeting and has a private bath with shower. A Continental Plus breakfast is served. Your hosts' interests, besides their home, include art and gardening, and they have traveled extensively.

No. Rooms: 3	**Breakfast:** Continental Plus
Singles: None	**S-Rates:** $36 pb, $36 sb
Doubles: 1 pb, 2 sb	**D-Rates:** $48–$68 pb, $48–$58 sb
Type: Private home	**Bldg:** 1981 contemporary

Minimum Stay: none. **Credit Card(s) Accepted:** none. **Open:** all year. No resident dogs. No dogs please. No resident cats. Guests may bring cat. Nonsmoking host. Guests may not smoke in guest rooms. Children welcome with restrictions. **Discounts:** none.

Reservation Contact: Fairbanks Bed & Breakfast, Barb & Greg Neub-
auer, Box 74573, Fairbanks, AK 99701; 907–452–4967.

ON LOCAL WALKING TOUR.

Near Cowles Rd. and Airport Hwy.

This home is on the National Register and is part of the local walking tour.
It offers four guest rooms. Two have double beds and another has twin
beds. These rooms share a bath. A fourth room has both a queen-sized
brass bed and a single bed, and a private bath. A Continental Plus breakfast is served. Your hosts are long-time residents of Alaska who can share
many interesting tales about Alaska and gold mining.

No. Rooms: 4	**Breakfast:** Continental Plus
Singles: None	**S-Rates:** $25
Doubles: 3 sb, 1 pb	**D-Rates:** $35
Type: Private home	**Bldg:** 1904 two-story frame

Minimum Stay: none. **Credit Card(s) Accepted:** MC, V. **Open:** all year.
No resident dogs. No dogs please. No resident cats. No cats please. Nonsmoking host. Guests may smoke in restricted areas. Residence is not appropriate for children. **Discounts:** none.

Reservation Contact: Fairbanks Bed & Breakfast, Barb & Greg Neub-
auer, Box 74573, Fairbanks, AK 99701; 907–452–4967.

ARIZONA

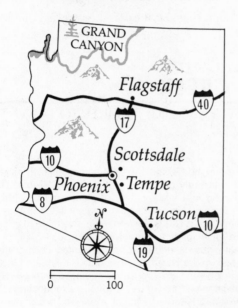

AJO

ID: 85321MAN

ORGAN PIPE CACTUS NATIONAL MONUMENT; TWO HOURS FROM ROCKY POINT, MEXICO.

Near AZ 85 & AZ 86.

This house, which once belonged to the local mine manager, is set on the area's highest hill overlooking the town on one side and the mine on the other. The terraced grounds are planted with fruit trees and vegetable and flower gardens, and there is also a fish pond with a waterfall and a horseshoe course for guests' use. A restored 1940 Packard is available to take guests on a tour of the town. There are five guest rooms with private baths, each individually furnished. Among the rooms are Perseus, with private entrance, two queen-sized beds plus a single hide-a-bed, and a view of the old mine; and the Early American Suite, which boasts a queen-sized bed, a sitting room with a queen-sized hide-a-bed, maple floors, and a panoramic view of the mine and town. A Continental Plus breakfast is served in the dining room.

No. Rooms: 5	**Breakfast:** Continental Plus
Singles: None	**S-Rates:** $19–$79 pb
Doubles: 5 pb	**D-Rates:** $49–$79 pb
Type: Private home	**Bldg:** 1919 Craftsman

Minimum Stay: none. **Credit Card(s) Accepted:** MC, V. **Open:** Sept. 1–July 4. Dog in residence. No dogs please. No resident cats. No cats please. Nonsmoking host. Guests may not smoke in residence. Residence not appropriate for children. **Discounts:** none.

Reservation Contact: Bed & Breakfast Registry Ltd., Gary Winget, Box 8174, St. Paul, MN 55108; 612–646–4238.

CAVE CREEK
ID: JCC–1–AZ

LUSH DESERT SETTING; 35 MILES TO DOWNTOWN SCOTTSDALE.

Near I–17 & Carefree Hwy.

This contemporary home, ideal for the nature lover, is situated on ten acres of land, with only one or two other homes visible. The hills and mountains abound in a wide variety of plants, trees, wildflowers, and wildlife. Guests can hike to their hearts' content in this lush desert setting, four miles from a rustic 1800s western town, five miles to exclusive Carefree, and thirty-five miles to downtown Scottsdale. The one spacious guest suite with private entrance has a vaulted ceiling, pine interior, queen-sized bed, and private bath. The suite is decorated in printed blue chintz with thick beige carpeting and is equipped with a wet bar and refrigerator. The large picture window provides a mountain view. A Continental Plus breakfast is served. One of your hosts has an intimate knowledge of Indian culture and artifacts, does beadwork, has an interest in archaeology, and has traveled extensively through the south and northwest. Your other host, an amateur botanist and photographer, is extremely knowledgeable about flora and fauna and enjoys travel and people.

No. Rooms: 1	**Breakfast:** Continental Plus
Singles: None	**S-Rates:** $50 pb
Doubles: 1 pb	**D-Rates:** $50 pb
Type: Private home	**Bldg:** 1980 contemporary

Minimum Stay: 2 nights. **Credit Card(s) Accepted:** none. **Open:** all year. No resident dogs. No dogs please. No resident cats. No cats please. Nonsmoking host. Guests may not smoke in residence. Children welcome. **Discounts:** 10% for 7 + days.

Reservation Contact: Bed & Breakfast Scottsdale and the West, George & Joyce Thomson, Box 3999, Prescott, AZ 86302; 602–776–1102.

FLAGSTAFF
ID: MICASA–100

GRAND CANYON; HORSEBACK RIDING, SKIING.

Near Humphreys & Beale, I–40, I–17.

This two-story ranch-style house is located in what is said to be the prettiest neighborhood in Flagstaff. Guests are welcome to use the recreation room equipped with TV, VCR, and fireplace. The two guest rooms are ten steps down from the entrance, while the family quarters are on the second floor. Both rooms have king-sized beds; one is a waterbed. The two guest rooms share a bath. A Full breakfast is served. Your hosts, a marketing manager and a teacher, take pleasure in outdoor activities, including hiking, skiing, golf, tennis, and travel.

No. Rooms: 2	**Breakfast:** Full
Singles: None	**S-Rates:** $30 sb
Doubles: 2 sb	**D-Rates:** $40 sb
Type: Private home	**Bldg:** 1970 ranch

Minimum Stay: none. **Credit Card(s) Accepted:** none. **Open:** all year. Dog in residence. No dogs please. No resident cats. No cats please. Non-smoking host. Guests may not smoke in residence. Children welcome. **Discounts:** weekly.

Reservation Contact: Mi Casa-Su Casa Bed & Breakfast, Ruth Young, Box 950, Tempe, AZ 85281; 602–990–0682.

FOUNTAIN HILLS   ID: 85268VIL

MCDOWELL MOUNTAIN PARK, MAYO CLINIC, SAGUARO LAKE, SCOTTSDALE, ART FESTIVALS, GOLF.

Near AZ 87 & Shea Blvd.

This luxurious, resort-style villa offers spectacular views from an elegant setting. Guests may use the private tennis court, exercise machines, and the fifty-foot pool with water jets. The nearby golf course is one of the most challenging in the area. Guests may browse in the extensive library, or enjoy the grand piano and organ in the living room. The lower-level guest room offers a queen-sized bed, sofa, desk, chair, walk-in closet, private bath, and a private patio that leads to the tennis court. This room is ideal for a honeymoon couple. The upper-level guest room, which overlooks the courtyard and pool, has a queen-sized bed, private bath, walk-in closet, and original batiks on the walls. The Full breakfast might consist of french toast with apricot sauce, scrambled eggs with herb tomatoes, pecan and wild-rice waffles, or eggs benedict with sausage, along with muffins or coffee cake, fresh juice, and fresh-ground coffee. The house is in a quiet community with scenic mountain beauty and fresh air. Major arts and crafts festivals take place in February and November. Other points of interest include the McDowell Mountain Park, Saguaro Lake, the Mayo Clinic, the McDonnel Douglas/Hughes Helicopter plant, and fashionable Scottsdale. The hosts enjoy good food and wine, entertaining, art, travel, and architecture.

No. Rooms: 2	**Breakfast:** Full
Singles: None	**S-Rates:** $85–$100 pb
Doubles: 2 pb	**D-Rates:** $95–$110 pb
Type: Private home	**Bldg:** 1983 Spanish contemporary

Minimum Stay: 2 nights. **Credit Card(s) Accepted:** none. **Open:** all year. No resident dogs. No dogs please. Cat in residence. No cats please.

Nonsmoking host. Guests may not smoke in residence. Residence not appropriate for children. **Discounts:** none. German spoken.

Reservation Contact: Bed & Breakfast Registry Ltd., Gary Winget, Box 8174, St. Paul, MN 55108; 612–646–4238.

PHOENIX
ID: MICASA–82

FINE RESTAURANTS, EXCLUSIVE SHOPPING.

Near 24th & Camelback, I–10, I–17.

An oversized yard with fruit trees and flowering bushes sets this handsome ranch house back from the busy street. One of the guest rooms has a private entrance, private bath, sitting area, and king-sized bed. The other smaller room has a double bed and shared bath. A Continental Plus breakfast is served. Guests are invited to use the pool, patio, and yard. The house, located near the famous Biltmore, is also within walking distance of exclusive shops and fine restaurants. Your host, a retired restauranteur, enjoys horses, antiques, travel, art, gourmet cooking, and volunteer work.

No. Rooms: 2	**Breakfast:** Continental Plus
Singles: None	**S-Rates:** $50 pb, $40 sb
Doubles: 1 pb, 1 sb	**D-Rates:** $60 pb, $40 sb
Type: Private home	**Bldg:** 1957 ranch

Minimum Stay: 2 nights. **Credit Card(s) Accepted:** none. **Open:** all year. Dog in residence. No dogs please. No resident cats. No cats please. Nonsmoking host. Guests may not smoke in residence. Children welcome with restrictions. **Discounts:** none.

Reservation Contact: Mi Casa-Su Casa Bed & Breakfast, Ruth Young, Box 950, Tempe, AZ 85281; 602–990–0682.

ID: MICASA–125

GOLF, TENNIS, HIKING.

Near Lincoln, Tatum, I–10, I–17.

Your hosts have refurbished a little inn where many well-known people are reputed to have stayed. It is in a quiet, scenic area surrounded by handsome neighborhood homes, close to a large shopping mall, tennis, and golf. Both the main and guest houses are furnished with quaint 1930s-style furniture. The guest house, near Squaw Peak Mountain Preserve, opens to a large courtyard and pool, and offers eight guest rooms, six with private baths, and a living room with fireplace and piano. Double, queen-, and king-sized beds are available. The rooms have separate entrances, TVs, and telephones, and most have refrigerators and some other kitchen appliances. Refrigerators are stocked for the first morning's breakfast. A Full breakfast is available in the main house for an additional charge of $5; otherwise a Continental breakfast is served. The hosts, a potter and a realtor, enjoy travel, fine arts, and church activities.

No. Rooms: 8   **Breakfast:** Continental
Singles: None   **S-Rates:** $40–$65 pb, $40–$65 sb
Doubles: 6 pb, 2 sb   **D-Rates:** $40–$65 pb, $40–$65 sb
Type: Private home   **Bldg:** 1930s Spanish

Minimum Stay: 2 nights. **Credit Card(s) Accepted:** none. **Open:** all year. Dog in residence. No dogs please. No resident cats. No cats please. Nonsmoking host. Guests may not smoke in residence. Children welcome with restrictions. **Discounts:** weekly.

Reservation Contact: Mi Casa-Su Casa Bed & Breakfast, Ruth Young, Box 950, Tempe, AZ 85281; 602–990–0682.

ID: MICASA–137

Near I–10 & Peoria Ave., I–17.

This townhouse, in a quiet residential area, is within walking distance of a very large mall, theaters, and restaurants. It has one guest room with a queen-sized bed, contemporary European-style furniture, a covered balcony, and shared bath. A Full German breakfast is served. Guests may use the pool and tennis court. Nearby is a lake with a complete walkway around it, beautified by tall jacaranda and orchid trees, flowering shrubs, and grassy areas. Your host enjoys travel, gardening, and cooking.

No. Rooms: 1   **Breakfast:** Full
Singles: None   **S-Rates:** $35 pb
Doubles: 1 pb   **D-Rates:** $40 pb
Type: Private home   **Bldg:** 1978 Canadian

Minimum Stay: 2 nights. **Credit Card(s) Accepted:** none. **Open:** all year. No resident dogs. No dogs please. No resident cats. No cats please. Nonsmoking host. Guests may not smoke in residence. Residence not appropriate for children. **Discounts:** weekly. German spoken.

Reservation Contact: Mi Casa-Su Casa Bed & Breakfast, Ruth Young, Box 950, Tempe, AZ 85281; 602–990–0682.

ID: MICASA–155

CIVIC CENTER; RESTAURANTS.

Near Central & Fifth aves., I–17, I–10.

The beamed ceiling in the living room and the arched doorways lend a quaint charm to this Spanish-style home with two guest rooms. One of them, a bright, cheerful room with a southern exposure and view of the backyard and gazebo, has antique furnishings and a queen-sized bed. The other has a single bed with brass headboard, rocking chair, hump-backed trunk, and handmade rug. The two rooms share a guest bath. Guests are also invited to share the patio, yard, and sitting room with TV. A Full breakfast is served. The house, in a quiet, older, yet well preserved area of Phoenix, is five minutes from the Civic Center and within walking distance of restaurants, churches, and a shopping mall. Your hosts' interests include sailing, travel, dancing, handcrafts, cooking, dining out, and entertaining.

No. Rooms: 2	**Breakfast:** Full
Singles: 1 sb	**S-Rates:** $40 pb
Doubles: 1 pb	**D-Rates:** $45 pb
Type: Private home	**Bldg:** 1937 Spanish

Minimum Stay: none. **Credit Card(s) Accepted:** none. **Open:** all year. No resident dogs. No dogs please. No resident cats. No cats please. Nonsmoking host. Guests may not smoke in residence. Children welcome. **Discounts:** none.

Reservation Contact: Mi Casa-Su Casa Bed & Breakfast, Ruth Young, Box 950, Tempe, AZ 85281; 602–990–0682.

ID: MICASA–165

MOUNTAIN VIEWS.

Near Shea & 32d sts., I–10, I–17.

This comfortable Spanish-style house, on a quiet cul-de-sac at the foot of a mountain, is beautifully decorated with American Indian and Oriental art. There are two air-conditioned guest rooms. One has extra-long brass twin beds, private entrance, and private bath; the other has a round king-sized bed and shares the bath across the hall. A Continental Plus breakfast is served. Your host is an educational consultant with an interest in art, Indian history, and travel.

No. Rooms: 2	**Breakfast:** Continental Plus
Singles: None	**S-Rates:** $50 pb, $40 sb
Doubles: 1 pb, 1 sb	**D-Rates:** $50 pb, $40 sb
Type: Private home	**Bldg:** 1974 Spanish

Minimum Stay: 2 nights. **Credit Card(s) Accepted:** none. **Open:** all year. Dog in residence. No dogs please. No resident cats. No cats please. Nonsmoking host. Guests may not smoke in residence. Residence not appropriate for children. **Discounts:** weekly.

Reservation Contact: Mi Casa-Su Casa Bed & Breakfast, Ruth Young, Box 950, Tempe, AZ 85281; 602–990–0682.

ID: SCOTWEST-A

BILTMORE FASHION PARK; GOLF, RESTAURANTS.

Near Camelback & 24th St., I–17.

This two-story townhouse is quiet despite its central location near a busy downtown intersection. The airport is ten minutes away, and shopping and golf are nearby. There is one guest room with a queen-sized bed, private bath, and a balcony overlooking the golf course fairway. A Continental Plus breakfast is served. Your host is a semi-retired real estate broker.

No. Rooms: 1	**Breakfast:** Continental Plus
Singles: None	**S-Rates:** $55 pb
Doubles: 1 pb	**D-Rates:** $55 pb
Type: Private home	**Bldg:** Contemporary

Minimum Stay: None, but $5 charge for one-night stays. **Credit Card(s) Accepted:** none. **Open:** all year. No resident dogs. No dogs please. No resident cats. No cats please. Host smokes. Guests may smoke. Residence not appropriate for children. **Discounts:** none.

Reservation Contact: Bed & Breakfast Scottsdale and the West, George & Joyce Thomson, Box 3999, Prescott, AZ 86302; 602–776–1102.

ID: 85022SPE

MOUNTAIN PRESERVE, MUSEUMS, INDIAN RUINS, ZOO; GOLF, STABLES, HOT-AIR BALLOONING, UNIQUE SHOPS.

Near Thunderbird & 7th sts., I–17.

Phoenix Mountain Preserve provides the views for this contemporary, air-conditioned, ranch-style home. There's an interesting mix of desert and traditional garden plantings, complete with fragrant roses and bearing almond, lemon, and tangelo trees. Guests can make themselves at home on the covered patio or in the comfortable living and dining areas with interior greenery. There are two air-conditioned guest rooms with a shared guest bath. One room has a double bed and color TV; the other has a single bed and black and white TV. A Full breakfast is served in the dining room or on the patio. Your hosts will be happy to direct you to the many area attractions including nearby horseback riding stables. For golf enthusiasts, there's the Phoenix Open, the Turquoise Classic, and the Arizona Classic, and bring your clubs along for the nearby new par seventy-two course. If you enjoy walking, you'll love this spot and shouldn't be surprised if a cottontail, jack rabbit, or covey of quail cross your path. Your hosts love to travel and are especially knowledgeable about Arizona. Escorted sightseeing is available.

No. Rooms: 2	**Breakfast:** Full
Singles: 1 sb	**S-Rates:** $30 sb
Doubles: 1 sb	**D-Rates:** $40 sb
Type: Private home	**Bldg:** 1981 ranch

Minimum Stay: none. **Credit Card(s) Accepted:** none. **Open:** all year. Dog in residence. No dogs please. Cat in residence. No cats please. Non-smoking host. Guests may not smoke in residence. Children welcome with restrictions. **Discounts:** none.

Reservation Contact: Bed & Breakfast Registry Ltd., Gary Winget, Box 8174, St. Paul, MN 55108; 612–646–4238.

ID: 85310WES

THEATER, CONCERTS, HEARD MUSEUM, PHOENIX ART MUSEUM; SHOPPING, SPORTS.

Near Bell Rd. & 59th Ave., I–17.

This mini-resort, conveniently located in northwest Phoenix, has been designed for comfort. Interior furnishings include leather and oak in the sunken living room with fireplace, antiques in the Victorian-style dining room, and rattan and oak in the Arizona-style leisure room with big-screen TV, VCR, table games, stereo, ping-pong, library, and fireplace. A snack center in the kitchen is stocked with soft drinks, mixers, and snacks. Outside the courtyard has comfortable outdoor furniture and beautiful plantings. Grass borders the twenty-by-forty-foot diving pool and adjacent whirlpool, and there are lounge chairs and umbrella tables for outdoor dining. Other amenities include horseshoe pits, a campfire pit, and a fitness shed complete with exercise bike, weights, and other equipment. Guests may also use ten-speed touring bikes, tennis racquets, and golf clubs. Each of the six uniquely decorated guest rooms (or casitas) has a double or queen-sized bed, AM/FM clock radio, color TV, reading chair, and appropriate bureaus and closets. The baths (two private) feature mounted hair dryers, automatic shoe polishers, personal grooming kits, and an abundance of thick towels. A Full breakfast that includes fruit and the pastry creation of the day is served in the kitchen or on the patio. Weekly guests enjoy a complimentary steak barbeque with all the fixings. Both hosts have traveled widely and have had previous experience in the hospitality industry.

No. Rooms: 7	**Breakfast:** Full
Singles: 1 sb	**S-Rates:** $66–$90 pb, $66 sb
Doubles: 2 pb, 4 sb	**D-Rates:** $78–$102 pb, $78 sb
Type: Private inn	**Bldg:** 1982 Spanish Mediterranean

Minimum Stay: 2 days over holidays. **Credit Card(s) Accepted:** AE, D, MC, V. **Open:** all year. No resident dogs. No dogs please. Cat in residence. No cats please. Host smokes. Guests may smoke in designated areas. Children are welcome with restrictions. **Discounts:** June–Sept. French and Spanish spoken.

Reservation Contact: Bed & Breakfast Registry Ltd., Gary Winget, Box 8174, St. Paul, MN 55108; 612–646–4238.

SCOTTSDALE

ID: AP108–AZ

CANYON HIKING.

Near Tatum Blvd. & Lincoln Dr., I–17.

This historic adobe was built in the canyon in the 1930s and has provided a relaxing haven for many famous movie stars and politicians. Four guest rooms and a guest cottage feature private baths. The first room, with private entrance, opens onto the rooftop terrace overlooking the valley. From here, guests can watch the moon rise over the mountains. The room, with a cozy country atmosphere, has a queen-sized bed, wet bar, and refrigerator. Another room, also with private upstairs entrance and wet bar, overlooks the courtyard and is furnished with antiques and a double bed. The third and fourth rooms are at the front of the main entrance just off the courtyard. They are simply decorated and have king-sized waterbeds. The cottage, accessible through a private screened porch, provides a king-sized bed and country decor. A Continental Plus breakfast is served. Your hosts, an investment counselor and a potter are interested in real estate and church activities.

No. Rooms: 8	Breakfast: Continental Plus
Singles: None	S-Rates: $40–$125 pb
Doubles: 8 pb	D-Rates: $40–$125 pb
Type: Private home	Bldg: 1930s Santa Fe adobe

Minimum Stay: 3 days. **Credit Card(s) Accepted:** none. **Open:** all year. Dog in residence. No dogs please. No resident cats. No cats please. Nonsmoking host. Guests may smoke. Children welcome. **Discounts:** 10% for 7+ days.

Reservation Contact: Bed & Breakfast Scottsdale and the West, George & Joyce Thomson, Box 3999, Prescott, AZ 86302; 602–776–1102.

ID: LS101–1AZ

FISHING, TENNIS, GOLF, BIKING, ART GALLERIES; IN HEART OF SCOTTSDALE.

Near Scottsdale Rd. & Lincoln Dr.

This cozy, informal home, located in the heart of Scottsdale, has a cottage look and relaxed atmosphere. A five-minute walk brings you to a park with fishing, jogging, tennis, golf, and biking, and a five-minute drive offers access to fine dining, shopping, art galleries, and Old Town Scottsdale. The living room, dining room, and kitchen are open to guests as is the pool and patio. A charming guest suite with private entrance is reached via the patio. It is furnished in a southwestern decor of soft rose, beige, and brown, with wicker, plants, a sitting area, corner fireplace, wet bar, table and chairs, Mexican tiled floor, and private bath. A Continental Plus breakfast, including fruit freshly picked from the trees, is served. One of your hosts is an artist who enjoys travel and people; the other writes poetry and likes carpentry and restoring cars.

No. Rooms: 1 suite	Breakfast: Continental Plus
Singles: none	S-Rates: $60 pb
Doubles: 1 pb	D-Rates: $60 pb
Type: Private home	Bldg: 1968 contemporary

Minimum Stay: 2 nights. **Credit Card(s) Accepted:** none. **Open:** all year. No resident dogs. No dogs please. Cat in residence. Guests may bring cats. Host smokes. Guests may smoke. Children welcome. **Discounts:** 10% after 7+ days.

Reservation Contact: Bed & Breakfast Scottsdale and the West, George & Joyce Thomson, Box 3999, Prescott, AZ 86302; 602–776–1102.

CAMELBACK MOUNTAIN, BOTANICAL GARDENS, ZOO, ARIZONA STATE UNIVERSITY; ART GALLERIES.

Near McDowell & Oak, I–17, I–10.

This ranch-style house, near the canal, Botanical Gardens, zoo, Arizona State University, art galleries, and restaurants, has one guest room with a double bed and private bath. A Full breakfast is served. Guests also have use of the den with TV and telephone. The house is decorated with small antique glass, china, and silver collections. Your host enjoys travel, needlepoint, knitting, reading, and entertaining.

No. Rooms: 1	**Breakfast:** Full
Singles: None	**S-Rates:** $35 pb
Doubles: 1 pb	**D-Rates:** $35 pb
Type: Private home	**Bldg:** 1958 ranch

Minimum Stay: none. **Credit Card(s) Accepted:** none. **Open:** all year. No resident dogs. No dogs please. No resident cats. No cats please. Nonsmoking host. Guests may not smoke in residence. Residence not appropriate for children. **Discounts:** weekly.

Reservation Contact: Mi Casa-Su Casa Bed & Breakfast, Ruth Young, Box 950, Tempe, AZ 85281; 602–990–0682.

PARKS, GOLF, SHOPPING, RESTAURANTS, HORSEBACK RIDING, MOUNTAIN TRAILS.

Near McDonald & Scottsdale Rd.

This Spanish-style home with a red tile roof offers use of a heated pool, sauna, patio, and lighted tennis court. Because it is in the heart of some of Scottsdale's finest resorts, parks, golf, horseback riding, mountain trails, and shopping are just minutes away. The decor of the house blends antiques with contemporary furniture. A vaulted ceiling, an antique English dresser, decorator drapes and wallpaper, and a queen-sized bed enhance the guest room with private bath. A Continental Plus breakfast is served, and complimentary wine and cheese are offered in the afternoon. Your host, a realtor, enjoys music, literature, antiques, and sports.

No. Rooms: 1	**Breakfast:** Continental Plus
Singles: None	**S-Rates:** $30–$40 pb
Doubles: 1 pb	**D-Rates:** $30–$45 pb
Type: Private home	**Bldg:** Spanish

Minimum Stay: none, but a surcharge for stays of only one night. **Credit Card(s) Accepted:** none. **Open:** all year. No resident dogs. No dogs please. Resident cat. No cats please. Nonsmoking host. Guests may smoke. Residence is not appropriate for children. **Discounts:** 7th night free.

Reservation Contact: Mi Casa-Su Casa Bed & Breakfast, Ruth Young, Box 950, Tempe, AZ 85281; 602–990–0682.

RESORT AREA, MAYO CLINIC, FRANK LLOYD WRIGHT CENTER.

Near Shea Blvd. & 110th St.

This contemporary two-story home is located in northeast Scottsdale only six miles from the new Mayo Clinic. Guests will find jogging and biking paths just behind the house. The two guest rooms, one with a queen-sized bed and the other with a king-sized bed, have private baths. Both rooms overlook the pool and both have private entrances. Other amenities include air-conditioning, off-street parking, and use of telephone, TV, and pool table. A Continental breakfast is served during the week and a Full breakfast is served on weekends. Your host is a business executive who enjoys entertaining and traveling.

No. Rooms: 2
Singles: None
Doubles: 2 pb
Type: Private home

Breakfast: Continental (Full on weekends)
S-Rates: $50–$58
D-Rates: $50–$58
Bldg: Contemporary

Minimum stay: $5 surcharge for one night only. **Credit Card(s) Accepted:** none. **Open:** all year. No resident dogs. No dogs please. No resident cats. No cats please. Nonsmoking host. Guests may not smoke. Children over 12 welcome. **Discounts:** none.

Reservation Contact: Bed & Breakfast Scottsdale and the West, George Thomson, Box 3999, Prescott, AZ 86302–3999; 602–776–1102.

SCOTTSDALE/ PARADISE VALLEY

SCOTTSDALE RESORTS ATTRACTIONS.

Near Scottsdale Rd., Lincoln Dr., I–17, Rte. 87.

Located in the Scottsdale resort area, this luxurious, Spanish colonial single-story home is adjacent to a golf course. The house boasts a lush pool and lounge area and an expansive lawn with many palm trees and other greenery. In this beautifully furnished house are two guest rooms, both with private baths, dressing rooms, TVs, and telephones. One has a king-sized bed and direct access to the pool; the other is furnished with a queen-sized bed and two twin beds. A Full breakfast is served. Your host is a business person who enjoys the arts, travel, tennis, and golf.

No. Rooms: 2	**Breakfast:** Full
Singles: None	**S-Rates:** $45–$65 pb
Doubles: 2 pb	**D-Rates:** $55–$75 pb
Type: Private home	**Bldg:** Spanish colonial

Minimum Stay: additional charge for stays of only one night. **Credit Card(s) Accepted:** none. **Open:** all year. No resident dogs. No dogs please. Resident cat. No cats please. Host smokes. Guests may smoke. Residence not appropriate for children. **Discounts:** none. Italian spoken.

Reservation Contact: Bed & Breakfast Scottsdale and the West, George & Joyce Thomson, Box 3999, Prescott, AZ 86302; 602–776–1102.

SEDONA

ID: MICASA–211

RED ROCK PALISADES.

Near 89A, 279, I–17.

Nestled in an evergreen forest, this large country French home provides views of the Red Rock Palisades. The two guest rooms, which share a bath, are only rented to one party at a time. Both rooms have remote cable TV and private entrances to the patio. One room is furnished with Victorian antiques and the other with Norwegian antiques. A Full gourmet breakfast is served in the Great Room or on the deck. Your hosts enjoy hiking, fishing, golf, antiques, classical music, and flower gardening.

No. Rooms: 2	**Breakfast:** Full
Singles: None	**S-Rates:** $70–$80 sb
Doubles: 2 sb	**D-Rates:** $75–$85 sb
Type: Private home	**Bldg:** Country French

Minimum Stay: none. **Credit Card(s) Accepted:** none. **Open:** all year. No resident dogs. No dogs please. No resident cats. No cats please. Non-smoking hosts. Guests may not smoke in residence. Residence not appropriate for children. **Discounts:** none.

Reservation Contact: Mi Casa-Su Casa Bed & Breakfast, Ruth Young, Box 950, Tempe, AZ 85281; 602–990–0632.

TEMPE

ID: MICASA–221

BOATING, SWIMMING, GOLF.

Near I–10, I–17, rtes. 60, 89, Base Line Rd. & Rural Rd.

This spacious house is on a man-made lake in a community of attractive homes with well-kept yards. Guests will enjoy their own living room, and also a mini-kitchen with a microwave, refrigerator, and coffee maker. The balcony overlooks the lake. There are three guest rooms, one with a king-sized bed and another with two double beds that share a bath, and a third with a queen-sized bed and private bath. A Full breakfast is served.

Your hosts' interests include gourmet cooking, fishing, tennis, travel, and art.

No. Rooms: 3	**Breakfast:** Full
Singles: None	**S-Rates:** $40
Doubles: 1 pb, 2 sb	**D-Rates:** $45–$60
Type: Private home	**Bldg:** Mission style

Minimum Stay: none. **Credit Card(s) Accepted:** none. **Open:** all year. No resident dogs. No dogs please. No resident cats. No cats please. Non-smoking host. Guests may not smoke. Children welcome with restrictions. **Discounts:** 7th night free. French, Italian, Spanish, and Arabic spoken.

Reservation Contact: Mi Casa-Su Casa Bed & Breakfast, Ruth Young, Box 950, Tempe, AZ 85281; 602–990–0682.

ID: 85281VAL

PHOENIX ZOO, SUN DEVIL STADIUM, PUEBLO GRANDE RUINS MUSEUM, PHOENIX AREA, COLLEGE AREA.

Near Curry & College sts., U.S. 60.

A large yard and L-shaped patio with colorful lawn furniture grace this contemporary ranch-style home. The two air-conditioned guest rooms share a bath. One has a blue, yellow, and white color scheme, a brass double bed, a black and white TV, and large closet. There is also a large colorful map of the area on the back of the door. The other room, furnished with a wicker daybed that has a trundle, is decorated in pastel blue with white lace curtains and has a stereo and TV. A Full breakfast is served in the dining room. Nearby, guests will find the Phoenix Zoo and Sun Devil Stadium. This home is ideally located in the college area of Tempe and is close to Scottsdale shops and restaurants.

No. Rooms: 2	**Breakfast:** Full
Singles: None	**S-Rates:** $25 sb
Doubles: 2 sb	**D-Rates:** $35 sb
Type: Private home	**Bldg:** Ranch style

Minimum Stay: none. **Credit Card(s) Accepted:** none. **Open:** all year. No resident dogs. No dogs please. Resident cat. No cats please. Non-smoking host. Guests may not smoke in residence. Residence is not appropriate for children. **Discounts:** none.

Reservation Contact: Bed & Breakfast Registry Ltd., Gary Winget, Box 8174, St. Paul, MN 55108; 612–646–4238.

TUCSON

SONORA DESERT MUSEUM, SABINO CANYON, COLOSSAL CAVE.

Near Grant & Country Club, I–10, I–19.

This ranch home with a casual, hospitable atmosphere is within easy walking distance of the bus and a pool. Its quiet locale features neatly tended homes and yards. The three guest rooms share a guest bath. The first room has a southwestern decor with twin beds, the second, a single bed and honey maple furniture, and the third, a double hide-a-bed. A Full breakfast is served, and guests have light kitchen and laundry privileges. Your hosts, a realtor and a university administrator, like sports, camping, sailing, reading, genealogy, biking, and music.

No. Rooms: 3	**Breakfast:** Full
Singles: 1 sb	**S-Rates:** $30 sb
Doubles: 2 sb	**D-Rates:** $35–$40 sb
Type: Private home	**Bldg:** 1950 ranch

Minimum Stay: 2 nights. **Credit Card(s) Accepted:** none. **Open:** all year. Dog in residence. No dogs please. No resident cats. No cats please. Nonsmoking host. Guests may not smoke in residence. Children welcome. **Discounts:** weekly for seniors.

Reservation Contact: Mi Casa-Su Casa Bed & Breakfast, Ruth Young, Box 950, Tempe, AZ 85281; 602–990–0682.

SAN XAVIER DEL BAC, SONORA DESERT MUSEUM, KITT PEAK OBSERVATORY.

Near First Ave. & Ina Rd., I–10, I–19.

This expansive one-of-a-kind ranch home in the foothills of the Catalina Mountains welcomes guests to its natural desert setting. Wildlife abounds, but there are also beautiful night views of the city lights. It is an easy drive to the University of Arizona, well-known golf courses, and mountaintop. The pool, patio, and yard are available for guests' use. The two guest rooms, in a separate wing of the house with their own cooling and heating system, have twin beds and private baths. One of the two guest rooms is an extra large room with a sitting area. A Full breakfast is served. Your hosts enjoy gardening, travel, and Arizona tours.

No. Rooms: 2	**Breakfast:** Full
Singles: None	**S-Rates:** $35–$40 pb
Doubles: 2 pb	**D-Rates:** $40–$45 pb
Type: Private home	**Bldg:** 1978 ranch

Minimum Stay: none. **Credit Card(s) Accepted:** none. **Open:** all year. No resident dogs. No dogs please. Resident cat. No cats please. Host smokes. Guests may smoke. Children welcome with restrictions. **Discounts:** 10% for seniors.

Reservation Contact: Mi Casa-Su Casa Bed & Breakfast, Ruth Young, Box 950, Tempe, AZ 85281; 602–990–0682.

ID: MICASA142

SONORA DESERT MUSEUM, CATALINA MOUNTAINS, PLANETARIUM.

Near Ina Rd. & First Ave., I–10, I–19.

This ranch-style home in a garden setting next to 127 acres of natural desert is ideal for walking. Quail, great horned owls, and other wildlife inhabit the area, and there are both mountain and city views to enjoy. Guests are invited to use the pool, patio, and yard. There is one guest room with a queen-sized hide-a-bed in the main house, and a guest house with living room, dining area, bedroom with twin beds, kitchen, and bath. A Continental Plus breakfast is served for guest-room residents. The refrigerator in the guest house is stocked for the first morning, but guests serve themselves. Shopping, theaters, churches, restaurants, and the university are an easy drive away. The hosts take pleasure in entertaining, reading, collecting art, wildlife, gardening, travel, cooking, and their Moluccan cockatoo.

No. Rooms: 2	**Breakfast:** Continental Plus
Singles: None	**S-Rates:** $30–$60 pb
Doubles: 2 pb	**D-Rates:** $35–$60 pb
Type: Private home	**Bldg:** 1970 ranch

Minimum Stay: 3 nights. **Credit Card(s) Accepted:** none. **Open:** all year. Dog in residence. No dogs please. No resident cats. No cats please. Nonsmoking host. Guests may smoke. Children welcome with restrictions. **Discounts:** weekly.

Reservation Contact: Mi Casa-Su Casa Bed & Breakfast, Ruth Young, Box 950, Tempe, AZ 85281; 602–990–0682.

ID: MICASA–169

UNIVERSITY OF ARIZONA, SAGUARO NATIONAL PARK, SABINO CANYON, COLOSSAL CAVE, MT. LEMMON, KITT PEAK, OLD TUCSON, SAN XAVIER MISSION.

Near 22nd St. & Camino Seco.

This comfortable Mediterranean-style townhouse is in a quiet suburban neighborhood convenient to many attractions. Two guest rooms are available. One has a queen-sized bed, large closet area, TV, radio, telephone, and adjacent private bath. The other is a suite with two queen-sized beds, TV, telephone, radio, and private bath, and overlooks an oasis of trees, shrubs, and grass. A Full breakfast is served. Your hosts, a retired air force pilot and his wife, enjoy travel, sports, hiking, golf, cooking, and meeting new people. Arrival/departure transportation and area tours are available.

No. Rooms: 2	**Breakfast:** Full
Singles: None	**S-Rates:** $35–$40 pb
Doubles: 2 pb	**D-Rates:** $45–$50 pb
Type: Private home	**Bldg:** Mediterranean-style

Minimum Stay: none. **Credit Cards Accepted:** none. **Open:** all year. No resident dogs. No dogs please. Resident cat. No cats please. Nonsmoking host. Guests may smoke in designated areas. Children over 14 welcome. **Discounts:** 7th night free.

Reservation contact: Mi Casa-Su Casa Bed & Breakfast, Ruth Young, Box 950, Tempe, AZ 85281; 602–990–0682.

ID: MICASA–223

SAN SABINO CANYON, MT. LEMMON, SAGUARO NATIONAL MONUMENT.

Near I–10, I–19, Catalina Hwy., Tanque Verde.

Imagine being able to ski on Mt. Lemmon in the morning and sunbathe by the pool in the afternoon! This Spanish-style home is on a hilltop with panoramic mountain and city views and is surrounded by eighteen acres with birds, rabbits, and ground squirrels. All the guest rooms open onto the courtyard which is accented by a fountain. The living room, which guests are welcome to use, has a high, beamed ceiling. The three guest rooms have twin beds, original art, and shared baths. A separate guest house with a sunken living room, fireplace, complete kitchen, TV, and large bedroom is also available. Breakfast in the guest house is self-serve, but a Full breakfast is served in the main house. Your hosts' interests include art, books, and travel.

No. Rooms: 4	**Breakfast:** Full
Singles: None	**S-Rates:** $75 sb
Doubles: 4 sb	**D-Rates:** $75 sb
Type: Private home	**Bldg:** Spanish

Minimum Stay: 3 nights in main house, 5 nights in guest house. **Credit Card(s) Accepted:** none. **Open:** all year. No resident dogs. No dogs please. No resident cats. No cats please. Nonsmoking hosts. Guests may not smoke in residence. Children welcome with restrictions. **Discounts:** for guest house only.

Reservation Contact: Mi Casa-Su Casa Bed & Breakfast, Ruth Young, Box 950, Tempe, AZ 85281; 602–990–0632.

CATALINA MOUNTAINS, UNIVERSITY OF ARIZONA.

Near I–10, Houghton & Prince.

Located on 20 desert acres, this hacienda offers western charm in a quiet, peaceful setting. All the rooms open onto a lovely courtyard and there are views of the distant mountains and the city of Tucson, and patio and pool are pleasant places to relax. In the main house there are two guest rooms with private baths, TVs, and clock radios. One has twin beds and the other a queen-sized bed. Also available is a guest cottage that consists of a living room with fireplace, a kitchen, a tile bath with double sinks, a bedroom with a queen-sized bed, and a private, enclosed patio. A Full breakfast is served. One of your hosts is an artist and collector of rare books; the other knits and gardens. Both have traveled extensively.

No. Rooms: 3	**Breakfast:** Full
Singles: None	**S-Rates:** $75–$95 pb
Doubles: 3 pb	**D-Rates:** $75–$95 pb
Type: Private home	**Bldg:** Adobe hacienda

Minimum Stay: none. **Credit Card(s) Accepted:** none. **Open:** all year. No resident dogs. No dogs please. No resident cats. No cats please. Non-smoking host. Guests may not smoke in residence. Residence is not appropriate for children. **Discounts:** none.

Reservation Contact: Rimrock West, Mae & Val Robbins, 3450 N. Drake Pl., Tucson, AZ 85749; 602–749–8774.

UNIVERSITY OF ARIZONA, STATE MUSEUM, HERITAGE CENTER, MUSEUM OF ART, EL PRESIDIO HISTORIC AREA.

Near Broadway & Alvernon, I–10.

This comfortable home features a private patio, screened porch, and tasteful traditional furnishings. There is a large family room with an Indian art collection, library, color TV, and pool table. Two guest rooms are available with a shared bath. One is a paneled room with Navajo rugs, a queen-sized bed that can be made up as twin beds, and a desk. The second room is carpeted and done up in blue and white, with twin beds and a desk. A Continental Plus breakfast is served in the dining area Monday through Friday, and a Full breakfast is served on weekends. The house, in an attractive residential area, is close to a large city park and shopping mall. Off-street parking and city bus service are available to the University of Arizona and downtown Tucson. Your gracious hosts, both teachers, are available to share their extensive knowledge about the Southwest and northern Mexico, and they sometimes even provide personal tours. Their interests include Indian culture, literature of the Southwest, and travel.

No. Rooms: 2
Singles: None
Doubles: 2 sb
Type: Private home

Breakfast: Continental Plus
   (weekdays); Full (weekends)
S-Rates: $25 sb
D-Rates: $35 sb
Bldg: 1951 ranch

Minimum Stay: none. **Credit Card(s) Accepted:** none. **Open:** all year. No resident dogs. A dog is allowed with restrictions. No resident cats. A cat is allowed with restrictions. Nonsmoking host. Guests may not smoke in residence. Children welcome. **Discounts:** none. Spanish spoken.

Reservation Contact: Bed & Breakfast Registry Ltd., Gary Winget, Box 8174, St. Paul, MN 55108; 612–646–4238.

ARKANSAS

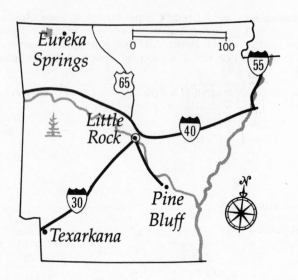

EUREKA SPRINGS

ID: 72632SIN

FOOTHILLS OF THE OZARKS.

Near U.S. 62, Rte. 23.

This small country Victorian home is located on an old, narrow street at the edge of the historic district on a ridge above Eureka's unique shops and cafés. You can walk the scenic wooded path two blocks to the main shopping area and to one of the sixty-two springs for which the town is known. Open antique trolleys take you through the historic district. The house is decorated with an eclectic collection of folk art, comfortable antiques, and unexpected treasures. The garden features stone paths winding through arches, arbors covered with morning glories, and surprises at every turn. The four light and airy guest rooms have romantic touches, such as fresh flowers, ceiling fans, handmade quilts, and brass and iron bedsteads. The rooms feature double or twin beds and shared or private baths. A Continental Plus breakfast is served on the balcony. Your host, a former interior designer, invites you to accompany her on a walking tour to meet the locals and explore the shops, springs, and landmarks that reflect the true charm and history of this quaint artist's colony. Beaver Lake and other popular attractions are nearby.

No. Rooms: 4
Singles: None
Doubles: 2 pb, 2 sb
Type: Private home

Breakfast: Continental Plus
S-Rates: $60 pb, $50 sb
D-Rates: $65 pb, $55 sb
Bldg: 1900s country Victorian

Minimum Stay: none. **Credit Card(s) Accepted:** MC, V. **Open:** all year, except major holidays. Dog in residence. No dogs please. No resident cats. No cats please. Nonsmoking host. Guests may not smoke in guest rooms. Children welcome. **Discounts:** after 4th night.

Reservation Contact: Bed & Breakfast Registry Ltd., Gary Winget, Box 8174, St. Paul, MN 55108; 612–646–4238.

CALIFORNIA

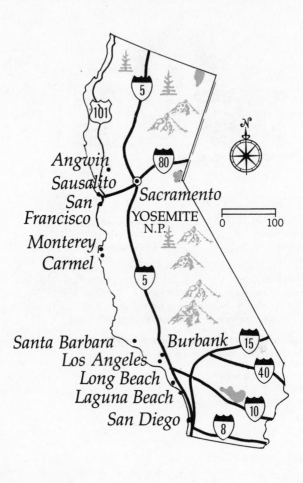

ANAHEIM

ID:92802ANA

DISNEYLAND, KNOTTS BERRY FARM, ANAHEIM
CONVENTION CENTER.

Near I–5 & Ball St., Rte. 57.

John Cook, prominent landowner and former Anaheim mayor, built this
beautiful Princess Anne-style home in 1910. The house is now an elegant
little inn graced with leaded glass windows, lace curtains, and charming
turn-of-the-century furnishings. The inn is set on spacious grounds in the

midst of a quiet residential neighborhood. Guests may relax in the quiet upstairs reading area, the comfortable Victorian living room, or on one of the airy porches, or wander through the garden and under the avocado trees. There are nine guest rooms. The first, formerly the bedroom of John and Anna Cook, is a large, comfortable room with a queen-sized bed and private bath. The second has a queen-sized bed, balcony with a view, and a shared bath. The third is a quiet traditional room with twin

beds and shared bath. Others include a picturesque corner room with a double bed; a cheerful room with a single bed and windows along the south and east walls to capture the morning sun; a quaint ground-floor room that features a double spool bed and an old-fashioned sewing machine; a bright corner room furnished with a nautical theme and a brass and iron double bed; a pretty, high-ceilinged room with a white iron double bed; and a spacious room with rattan furniture, queen-sized and double beds, private bath, and private outside entrance to the garden. A hearty breakfast is served in the sunny country dining room. Before dining in one of the fine local restaurants, guests are invited for light appetizers during the social hour in the parlor. The host will gladly help you select a restaurant and make reservations. The inn is near Disneyland and the convention/tourist area. There is ample off-street parking.

No. Rooms: 9	**Breakfast:** Full
Singles: 1 sb	**S-Rates:** $50–$85 pb, $40–$65 sb
Doubles: 4 pb, 4 sb	**D-Rates:** $50–$85 pb, $40–$65 sb
Type: Small inn	**Bldg:** 1910

Minimum Stay: none. **Credit Card(s) Accepted:** AE, MC, V. **Open:** all year. No resident dogs. No dogs please. No resident cats. No cats please. Nonsmoking host. Guests may not smoke in residence. Children welcome with restrictions. **Discounts:** 10% for 7+ days, 25% Dec.–Feb.

Reservation Contact: Bed & Breakfast Registry Ltd., Gary Winget, Box 8174, St. Paul, MN 55108; 612–646–4238.

ANGWIN   ID: 11–AMFAM

NAPA VALLEY, WINE COUNTRY.

Near Hwy. 29, Rte. 128.

This colonial-style home, near many of California's early historic sites, is in the heart of the Napa Valley wine country, and though it has a tranquil country setting, it is close to many exciting tourist attractions. The large, very nicely furnished guest suite features a fireplace, paneled walls, sofa, coffee table, rocking chair, piano, TV, and air-conditioning. Off-street parking is offered as is private deck for sunning, private entrance, and private bath. Two queen-sized beds plus a rollaway and a child's cot are in the bedroom loft. Either a Full or Continental Plus breakfast with homemade items is served. A light evening meal is also available. Your hosts, a nurse and a building contractor, enjoy travel and photography.

No. Rooms: 1	**Breakfast:** Full or Continental Plus
Singles: None	**S-Rates:** $55 pb
Doubles: 1 pb	**D-Rates:** $65 pb
Type: Private home	**Bldg:** 1945 early colonial

Minimum Stay: 2 weekend nights. **Credit Card(s) Accepted:** none. **Open:** all year. No resident dogs. A dog is allowed with restrictions. Cat in residence. A cat is allowed with restrictions. Nonsmoking host. Guests may not smoke in residence. Children welcome with restrictions. **Discounts:** none.

Reservation Contact: American Family Inn/B&B San Francisco, Susan & Richard Kreibich, Box 349, San Francisco, CA 94101; 415–931–3083.

BALBOA   ID: L–DAHLH

ONE BLOCK FROM WATER.

Near Ocean Blvd., Newport Fwy. 55.

This home, located in a residential neighborhood on the quiet side of the famous Balboa Peninsula, is one block from the water and eight blocks to the pier and tourist activities, boats to Catalina, public transportation, and restaurants. Two guest rooms are available. The loft room overlooking the living area has two queen-sized beds, private bath, and roof deck with mini-kitchen and sea views. For more magnificent views, guests can climb to the crow's nest. The downstairs guest room has a double bed, antique furnishings, and private bath. Guests also have access to the TV and fireplace. A Continental breakfast is served. Your hosts are artists who make stained glass for various local customers.

No. Rooms: 2
Singles: None
Doubles: 2 pb
Type: Private home

Breakfast: Continental
S-Rates: $50 pb
D-Rates: $50 pb
Bldg: European cottage

Minimum Stay: 2 nights. **Credit Card(s) Accepted:** MC, V. **Open:** all year. No resident dogs. No dogs please. No resident cat. No cats please. Nonsmoking host. Guests may smoke. Children welcome. **Discounts:** none.

Reservation Contact: Bed and Breakfast of Los Angeles, Peg Marshall & Angie Kobabe, 32074 Waterside Ln., Westlake Village, CA 91361; 818–889–8870.

BEVERLY HILLS   ID: L–BEVERLYHIL

EXCELLENT SHOPPING.

Near Maple, Burton Way, 405 San Diego Fwy.

The ultimate in luxury living, this contemporary condo is near shopping and public transportation. The remodeled ground-floor condominium offers everything a guest could want, including a pool, spa, and private gardens. The eclectically furnished apartment features lots of mirrors and off-white carpeting and walls. The beautifully decorated guest room has twin beds, TV, a private bath, and a view of the garden. A Continental breakfast is served. Arrival/departure transportation is available.

No. Rooms: 1
Singles: None
Doubles: 1 pb
Type: Private apartment

Breakfast: Continental
S-Rates: $40 pb
D-Rates: $45 pb
Bldg: Contemporary condominium

Minimum Stay: none. **Credit Card(s) Accepted:** MC, V. **Open:** all year. Dog in residence. No dogs please. No resident cats. No cats please. Nonsmoking host. Guests may not smoke. Children welcome. **Discounts:** weekly.

Reservation Contact: Bed and Breakfast of Los Angeles, Peg Marshall & Angie Kobabe, 32074 Waterside Ln., Westlake Village, CA 91361; 818–889–8870.

BURBANK   ID: 91505BEL

LOS ANGELES AREA, U.C.L.A., UNIVERSAL & NBC STUDIOS, HOLLYWOOD.

Near Chandler Blvd. & Buena Vista, I–5.

This contemporary two-story home with tropical landscaping is in a quiet residential neighborhood and convenient to Universal and NBC studios, Hollywood, downtown LA (one block from the LA bus), and coast and mountain areas. This home has two guest rooms, one double with shared bath and one triple with private bath. Guests can choose either a Full or Continental Plus breakfast. Transportation from Burbank Airport is available. Your host is a retired teacher with interests in music, world travel, and art.

No. Rooms: 3	**Breakfast:** Full or Continental Plus
Singles: 1 sb	**S-Rates:** $35 pb, $30–$35 sb
Doubles: 1 pb, 1 sb	**D-Rates:** $45 pb, $40–$45 sb
Type: Private home	**Bldg:** Contemporary design

Minimum Stay: none. **Credit Card(s) Accepted:** none. **Open:** all year. No resident dogs. No dogs please. No resident cats. No cats please. Nonsmoking host. Children welcome. Guests may smoke. **Discounts:** none.

Reservation Contact: Bed & Breakfast Registry Ltd., Gary Winget, Box 8174, St. Paul, MN 55108; 612–646–4238.

CALISTOGA   ID: 94515QUA

NAPA VALLEY WINERIES; BALLOONING, HIKING, BIKING.

Near CA–29, CA–128.

This secluded little inn, furnished with antiques and fine works of art, is located on 26 forested acres 300 feet above the Napa Valley. You'll find splendid specimens of redwood, douglas fir, madrona, oak, and manzanity on the grounds in addition to dogwood, wild lilac, ferns, berries, wildflowers, and wildlife such as deer, raccoons, squirrels, and numerous species of birds. There are three guest rooms, all with private baths, down comforters and pillows, handmade quilts, and private decks that overlook the forest. Two rooms have king-sized beds and one has twin beds. One room has an attached sitting room. A Full gourmet breakfast is served in the solarium. Your well traveled hosts have interests in art, gardening, tennis and cooking. Bus transportation is available from San Francisco to Calistoga; arrival/departure transportation available.

No. Rooms: 3	**Breakfast:** Full
Singles: None	**S-Rates:** $65 pb
Doubles: 3 pb	**D-Rates:** $80–$90 pb
Type: Private home	**Bldg:** 1984 contemporary

Minimum Stay: none. **Credit Card(s) Accepted:** none. **Open:** all year except Christmas. Dog in residence. No dogs please. Cat in residence. No cats please. Nonsmoking host. Guests may not smoke in residence. Children welcome with restrictions. **Discounts:** none.

Reservation Contact: Bed & Breakfast Registry Ltd., Gary Winget, Box 8174, St. Paul, MN 55108; 612–646–4238.

CAMBRIA

HEARST CASTLE; 30 MINUTES TO MORRO BAY.

Near Rte. 1.

This contemporary townhouse consists of a bedroom with queen-sized bed and stereo; a living room with fireplace, TV, and a spectacular ocean view; kitchen; and a deck with private hot tub. A Full breakfast is served. Your host is a wine merchant originally from England.

No. Rooms: 1	**Breakfast:** Full
Singles: None	**S-Rates:** $85 pb
Doubles: 1 pb	**D-Rates:** $85 pb
Type: Private townhouse	**Bldg:** 1975 modern

Minimum Stay: none. **Credit Card(s) Accepted:** none. **Open:** all year. No resident dogs. No dogs please. No resident cats. No cats please. Nonsmoking host. Guests may not smoke in residence. Children welcome with restrictions. **Discounts:** none.

Reservation Contact: Bed & Breakfast Homestay, Jack & Ginny Anderson, Box 326, Cambria, CA 93428; 805–927–4613.

HEARST CASTLE, SEA OTTER PRESERVE, COASTAL CLIFFS OF BIG SUR.

Near Rte. 1, Rte. 46.

This high quality, modern cedar-sided home with a view of the ocean is in a quiet residential area surrounded by pines and oak trees. Just seven miles away are Hearst Castle, the Sea Otter Preserve, and picturesque Cambria Village, with its unique shops and fine dining. The two-story home features two guest rooms on the lower level, one with a double bed and one with twin beds. Both have carpets, tables and chairs, night lights, and TVs. A Full breakfast is served. Your hosts enjoy traveling.

No. Rooms: 2	**Breakfast:** Full
Singles: None	**S-Rates:** $60 pb
Doubles: 2 pb	**D-Rates:** $68 pb
Type: Private home	**Bldg:** Contemporary

Minimum Stay: 2 nights. **Credit Card(s) Accepted:** none. **Open:** all year. No resident dogs. No dogs please. No resident cats. No cats please. Nonsmoking host. Guests may smoke. Children welcome. **Discounts:** 10% weekly.

Reservation Contact: Bed & Breakfast International, Jean Brown, 1181-B Solano Ave., Albany, CA 94706; 415–525–4569.

ID: 93428OLA

SAN LUIS OPISPO AREA, HEARST CASTLE; SURFING, ROCK HUNTING, SURF FISHING.

Near Main St., Rte. 1.

This completely restored Greek Revival house, built in the 1870s, is registered with the Historical House Association of America. The six guest rooms are decorated with antiques, and the honeymoon suite features a canopy bed and a sunken bath. Continental breakfast is served in the white wicker "gathering room," and complimentary wine and cheese are served in the parlor each evening. Guests may take advantage of this opportunity to mingle and look over the menus of the many fine restaurants within walking distance. Shops and galleries are also only a few blocks away. Cambria has miles of beaches for surf fishing, rock hunting (jade and moonstone), wet suit diving, and surfing. Also nearby are wineries, bicycle paths, tennis, lawn bowling, and deep-sea fishing.

No. Rooms: 6	**Breakfast:** Continental
Singles: None	**S-Rates:** $70–$90 pb
Doubles: 6 pb	**D-Rates:** $70–$90 pb
Type: Inn	**Bldg:** 1871 Greek Revival

Minimum Stay: none. **Credit Card(s) Accepted:** MC, V. **Open:** all year. No resident dogs. No dogs please. No resident cats. No cats please. Guests may not smoke in guest rooms. Children are welcome with restrictions. **Discounts:** none.

Reservation Contact: Bed & Breakfast Registry Ltd., Gary Winget, Box 8174, St. Paul, MN 55108; 612–646–4238.

CARLSBAD
ID: 92008PEL

BEACH, WATER SPORTS, THEATER, CONCERTS, MISSIONS, OBSERVATORY, SAN DIEGO ZOO, DEL MAR RACE TRACK, WILD ANIMAL PARK, GOLF, RESTAURANTS, SHOPPING.

Near Carlsbad Blvd. & Walnut Ave., I–5, CA–78.

Carlsbad is a delightful vacation spot without crowds or congested streets. This little inn is only two hundred yards from the ocean and an easy stroll from the fine restaurants and pleasant shops of the village. A porch, from which guests enter their rooms, wraps around three sides of the inn. The four guest rooms feature private baths, fireplaces, optional Scandia feather beds, down comforters, TVs, and a pleasing blend of antique and contemporary furnishings. The Balboa Room has twin brass beds and an armoire; the Laguna Room has a queen-sized brass bed, an antique chest, and a French chaise; the Carlsbad Suite has a king-sized bed and armoire; and the Newporter Room features a queen-sized bed, circular ceiling, armoire, and a beautiful Victorian chair. A Continental Plus breakfast and afternoon wine are served. Bicycles, beach chairs, towels, and picnic baskets are available for use by guests. Your hosts enjoy golf, tennis, bridge, crossword puzzles, sailing, and Chinese cooking.

No. Rooms: 4	**Breakfast:** Continental Plus
Singles: None	**S-Rates:** $75–$115 pb
Doubles: 4 pb	**D-Rates:** $85–$125 pb
Type: Inn	**Bldg:** 1960 beach house

Minimum Stay: none. **Credit Card(s) Accepted:** none. **Open:** all year. Dog in residence. No dogs please. No resident cats. No cats please. Host smokes. Guests may smoke. Children over 12 welcome. **Discounts:** 10% weekly.

Reservation Contact: Bed & Breakfast Registry Ltd., Gary Winget, Box 8174, St. Paul, MN 55108; 612–646–4238.

CARMEL   ID: INTNAT14

CARMEL MISSION, MONTEREY PRESIDO, AQUARIUM, BEACH.

Near Hwy. 1.

Located in an area of modern townhouses, this home is five minutes from the beach, Carmel Mission, the historic Monterey Presidio, and the new aquarium. There is one large, sunny guest room with a queen-sized bed, sitting area, original art, contemporary furnishings, and private bath. A Full breakfast is served. Other amenities include a heated swimming pool. The host's studio is in the house and guests will enjoy seeing the work of this well-known cartoonist.

No. Rooms: 1	**Breakfast:** Full
Singles: None	**S-Rates:** $68 pb
Doubles: 1 pb	**D-Rates:** $68 pb
Type: Private home	**Bldg:** Townhouse

Minimum Stay: 2 nights. **Credit Card(s) Accepted:** AE, MC, V. **Open:** all year. No resident dogs. No dogs please. No resident cats. No cats please. Nonsmoking host. Guests may smoke on deck. Children welcome. **Discounts:** 10% weekly.

Reservation Contact: Bed & Breakfast International, Jean Brown, 1181-B Solano Ave., Albany, CA 94706; 415–525–4569.

ID: 93921COB

MISSION; BEACH, SHOPS, RESTAURANTS.

Near Ocean Ave. & Juniper, Rte. 1.

The lavish living room of this traditional Carmel inn—with its soft rose carpeting, comfortable chairs and sofas, country antiques, fresh flowers, and large stone fireplace—is the perfect place for enjoying the pleasure of new friends. All twenty-four guest rooms have private baths. Each room is furnished with English country antiques, a soft cozy quilt, fresh fruit and garden flowers, refrigerator, color TV, and wall-to-wall carpeting. A Continental Plus breakfast is served as are afternoon tea or sherry and hors d'oeuvres in front of the fire. Shops, restaurants, the beach, and mission are within walking distance, and it is only two blocks from the center of town. Also, Pt. Lobos State Reserve is two miles to the south, and beyond that is the Big Sur coastline.

No. Rooms: 24	**Breakfast:** Continental Plus
Singles: None	**S-Rates:** $95–$180 pb
Doubles: 24 pb	**D-Rates:** $95–$180 pb
Type: Public inn	**Bldg:** 1950 traditional Carmel

Minimum Stay: 2 nights. **Credit Card(s) Accepted:** none. **Open:** all year. No resident dogs. No dogs please. No resident cats. No cats please. Nonsmoking host. Guests may not smoke in residence. Children welcome. **Discounts:** none.

Reservation Contact: Bed & Breakfast Registry Ltd., Gary Winget, Box 8174, St. Paul, MN 55108; 612–646–4238.

ID: 93921STO

CARMEL BEACH, PT. LOBOS STATE RESERVE, COASTAL AREAS; TENNIS, GOLF.

Near Monte Verde & 8th sts., Rte. 1.

This luxurious stone country house is on a quiet street only three blocks from the beach and has a glass-enclosed front porch with wicker furniture. Wine is served every afternoon around the large stone fireplace in the living room. There is a cozy sunroom for reading and relaxing. A Full breakfast is served in the dining room with a view of the garden. The six light and airy guest rooms, some with ocean views, have ruffled curtains and twin, double, king-, or queen-sized beds with wood or metal bedsteads. You will find fresh fruit in your room and other special touches. Bicycles are available for guests who want to explore the area.

No. Rooms: 6	**Breakfast:** Full
Singles: None	**S-Rates:** $80–$105 sb
Doubles: 6 sb	**D-Rates:** $80–$105 sb
Type: Inn	**Bldg:** 1906 Stone house

Minimum Stay: none. **Credit Card(s) Accepted:** MC, V. **Open:** all year. No resident dogs. No dogs please. No resident cats. No cats please. Nonsmoking host. Guests may not smoke in residence. Children welcome with restrictions. **Discounts:** none.

Reservation Contact: Bed & Breakfast Registry Ltd., Gary Winget, Box 8174, St. Paul, MN 55108; 612–646–4238.

CLOVERDALE

RUSSIAN RIVER WINE COUNTRY.

Near Rte. 128, U.S. 101.

This fully renovated private ranch features a comfortable sitting area in the main house. Between the house and pool is an outdoor living area around which strut peacocks, llamas, and chickens. Quarter horses and black Angus cattle are also at home on the premises. Vineyards, rolling hills, and rangeland surround the building. The two guest rooms, grouped around the central living area, are simply yet artistically furnished. One has a double bed and private bath; the other has a single bed and shared bath. A Full breakfast is served. Laundry facilities and fishing equipment are available. The ranch is one mile from both the spot where canoeing commences down the Russian River and from Asti, the location of Italian Swiss Colony, one of the first California wineries. Many other wineries are within a few miles. Your hosts are a physician and a lighting manufacturer.

No. Rooms: 2	**Breakfast:** Full
Singles: 1 sb	**S-Rates:** $62 pb, $52 sb
Doubles: 1 pb	**D-Rates:** $68 pb
Type: Private home	**Bldg:** 1800 ranch

Minimum Stay: 2 nights. **Credit Card(s) Accepted:** none. **Open:** all year. A cat is allowed with restrictions. Children welcome with restrictions. **Discounts:** 10% weekly. German & Spanish spoken.

Reservation Contact: Bed & Breakfast International, Jean Brown, 1181-B Solano Ave., Albany, CA 94706; 415–525–4569.

CULVER CITY

WEST LOS ANGELES.

Near Overland, Washington, & Culver, I–10, I–405.

This two-story Spanish-style house features a large enclosed front yard with a patio landscaped with shrubs, and fruit trees. The location is convenient to shopping, public transportation, and tourist areas. The guest room has a trundle bed, dresser, desk and chair, upholstered chair, TV, private bath, and glass patio doors that open onto the yard. A Continental Plus breakfast is served. Discount tickets to restaurants, Disneyland, and other attractions are offered to guests, and both child care and arrival/departure transportation are available.

No. Rooms: 1	**Breakfast:** Continental Plus
Singles: None	**S-Rates:** $40 pb
Doubles: 1 pb	**D-Rates:** $50 pb
Type: Private home	**Bldg:** 1979 Spanish-style

Minimum Stay: none. **Credit Card(s) Accepted:** none. **Open:** all year. Dog in residence. No dogs please. No resident cats. No cats please. Non-

,smoking host. Guests may smoke. Children welcome. **Discounts:** 10% after 7 days. Spanish spoken.

Reservation Contact: Bed & Breakfast Registry Ltd., Gary Winget, Box 8174, St. Paul, MN 55108; 612–646–4238.

CYPRESS   ID: RENTROOM6

LONG BEACH AREA.

Near Chapman & Knott aves., I–405, I–605.

This large home features three guest rooms on the second floor, with a stairway near the front entrance. Two of the rooms have double beds, one offers a TV and pool table as well, and the third room has a single bed. All three share a guest bath. A Continental Plus breakfast is served. The house is about thirty minutes from all major tourist attractions. Both hosts enjoy travel, sports, and photography.

No. Rooms: 3	**Breakfast:** Continental Plus
Singles: 1 sb	**S-Rates:** $25 sb
Doubles: 2 sb	**D-Rates:** $35 sb
Type: Private home	**Bldg:** 1972 contemporary

Minimum Stay: none. **Credit Card(s) Accepted:** none. **Open:** all year. No resident dogs. No dogs please. No resident cats. Guests may bring cat. Nonsmoking host. Guests may smoke. Children welcome. **Discounts:** none.

Reservation Contact: Rent-A-Room International B&B, Esther MacLachlan, 11531 Varna St., Garden Grove, CA 92640; 714–638–1406.

FOUNTAIN VALLEY   ID: 0–14

CLOSE TO ANAHEIM AND DISNEYLAND.

Near Brookhurst & I–405.

Mirrors reflect the entry fountain in this immaculate home. There are four guest rooms with private baths. The two downstairs rooms have a king and a queen-sized bed, while the upper rooms offer twin or king-sized beds. A Continental breakfast is served. Guests may use the patio, yard with barbecue, private neighborhood pool, and tennis court.

No. Rooms: 4	**Breakfast:** Continental
Singles: None	**S-Rates:** $45 pb
Doubles: 4 pb	**D-Rates:** $45 pb
Type: Private home	

Minimum Stay: none. **Credit Card(s) Accepted:** none. **Open:** all year. Resident dogs. No dogs please. No resident cats. No cats please. Nonsmoking host. Guests may not smoke. Children welcome with restrictions. **Discounts:** none.

Reservation Contact: Bed and Breakfast of Los Angeles, Peg Marshall & Angie Kobabe, 32074 Waterside Ln., Westlake Village, CA 91361; 818–889–8870.

GARDEN GROVE   ID: RENTROOM1

DISNEYLAND, ANAHEIM CONVENTION CENTER, HUNTINGTON BEACH STATE PARK, G.G. CRYSTAL CATHEDRAL.

Near Orangewood & Euclid sts., I–5.

Located in a suburban neighborhood, this contemporary one-story home has a sunny patio for pleasant outdoor dining, a yard, and a swimming pool. The one guest room has a double bed, dresser, and private bath with tub and shower. A den with a double sofa bed can be used in conjunction with the guest room for additional adults or children in the same party. A Continental Plus breakfast is served, and guests are permitted to use the kitchen for other meals if they wish. The house is within walking distance of restaurants and shops, and since it is only 1 ½ miles from Disneyland, guests often come back to the house to swim or rest before returning to the amusement park in the evening. It is the same distance to the Anaheim Convention Center, and your thoughtful host provides transportation to guests attending conventions. The G.G. Crystal Cathedral (Glory of Christmas and Glory of Easter) is three miles away. Your host, a seasoned traveler, first experienced Bed & Breakfast in Great Britain. She has been a B&B host for six years. Besides travel, she enjoys gardening, reading, and needlepoint.

No. Rooms: 1	**Breakfast:** Continental Plus
Singles: None	**S-Rates:** $25 pb
Doubles: 1 pb	**D-Rates:** $35 pb
Type: Private home	**Bldg:** 1963 contemporary

Minimum Stay: 2 nights. **Credit Card(s) Accepted:** none. **Open:** all year. No resident dogs. Guests may bring dog. No resident cats. Guests may bring cat. Nonsmoking host. Guests may not smoke in residence. Children welcome. **Discounts:** none.

Reservation Contact: Rent-A-Room International B&B, Esther MacLachlan, 11531 Varna St., Garden Grove, CA 92640; 714–638–1406.

GEYSERVILLE

ID:95441ISI

SONOMA VALLEY, WINERIES, MINI-ZOO, THEATER, HIKING TRAILS, HISTORIC BUILDINGS.

Near U.S. 101, Rte. 128.

This B&B lodge, located on 10 acres of lush grounds, offers guests many diversions, including various cultural events, a sauna, a pool with a dramatic tile mural portraying the cosmos, a game room, secluded garden, vineyards, and hiking trails. Several of the 16 guest rooms are furnished with bamboo, greenery, and Egyptian wall hangings. A new addition includes a restored farmhouse that can accommodate 15 people. It has a kitchen, decks, hot tub, and fireplace. There is also a three-room cottage with a fireplace and private hot tub. Guests receive a complimentary bottle of wine upon arrival, and a Full country breakfast is served daily. There is a resident cat and dog, plus a menagerie of other animals, including peacocks, ocelots, and a black swan. Arrival/departure transportation and area tours are usually available. Your host is a former San Francisco art gallery owner. Her interests include art, yoga, and Egyptology.

No. Rooms: 16	**Breakfast:** Full
Singles: None	**S-Rates:** $35 sb, $50–$90 pb
Doubles: 12 sb, 4 pb	**D-Rates:** $50 sb, $65–$90 pb
Type: Inn	**Bldg:** 1932 chalet

Minimum Stay: none. **Credit Card(s) Accepted:** MC, V. **Open:** all year. Host's dog resides outside the house. A dog is allowed with restrictions. Host's cat resides outside the house. A cat is allowed with restrictions. Nonsmoking host. Guests may not smoke in residence. Children welcome with restrictions. **Discounts:** group rates.

Reservation Contact: Bed & Breakfast Registry Ltd., Gary Winget, Box 8174, St. Paul, MN 55108; 612–646–4238.

GUALALA

ID: 95445ANC

OCEAN VIEW, REDWOODS.

Near Rte. 1.

This lovely contemporary California-style home overlooks the Pacific Ocean and is surrounded by redwood trees. There is one guest suite with twin beds, skylight, TV, private entrance, private bath, and a deck with ocean view. One host says the seals' barking can be heard. "It makes guests feel as though they were in a tree house with the ocean below." There is a fireplace in the living room where your hosts like to share wine, cheese, and stories with guests. A TV is available. A Full breakfast is served in the dining room. This is a wonderful escape from crowded tourist areas. Guests can stroll along the beaches, walk among the redwoods, or explore the shops of local artisans. Your hosts, who have traveled Europe and the Orient, enjoy tennis, horticulture, beachcombing, fishing, and Oriental cooking.

No. Rooms: 1	**Breakfast:** Full
Singles: None	**S-Rates:** $45 pb
Doubles: 1 pb	**D-Rates:** $50 pb
Type: Private home	**Bldg:** 1976 California style

Minimum Stay: none. **Credit Card(s) Accepted:** none. **Open:** all year. Dog in residence. No dogs please. Cat in residence. No cats please. Nonsmoking host. Guests may not smoke in residence. Residence not appropriate for children. **Discounts:** none.

Reservation Contact: Bed & Breakfast Registry Ltd., Gary Winget, Box 8174, St. Paul, MN 55108; 612–646–4238.

JAMUL
ID: 92035LIO

SAN DIEGO AREA, ZOO, SEA WORLD, BALBOA PARK, WILD ANIMAL PARK, SEAPORT VILLAGE.

Near CA 94 & Lyons Valley Rd.

This imposing Spanish villa provides expansive views of the Pacific, San Diego, Mexico, and El Cajon. There is a walking path on the eight surrounding acres. A grand piano, big screen TV, and a thousand movies are available for guests' leisure hours. The nine-hundred-square-foot living room features open beams, a fireplace, and views of sunsets over the water. There are two guest rooms plus an apartment and a guest house. One of the guest rooms has a corner fireplace and a queen-sized bed with lots of fluffy pillows. The other has a brass king-sized bed. Both have private entrances and private decks. The two-story apartment is furnished with a king-sized bed, a queen-sized bed, a hide-a-bed, many antiques, a TV, VCR, and telephone. It has a fireplace, private entrance, and private balcony. The guest house boasts a four-poster double bed, antique dresser, sofa, and coffee table, kitchenette, TV, and a roof-top deck that overlooks the valley. A Full breakfast is served and guests will find complimentary wine in their rooms. Arrival/departure transportation, child care, laundry service, additional meals, and area tours are available.

No. Rooms: 4	**Breakfast:** Full
Singles: None	**S-Rates:** $40–$50 pb
Doubles: 4 pb	**D-Rates:** $50–$70 pb
Type: Private home	**Bldg:** 1980 Spanish stucco

Minimum Stay: none. **Credit Card(s) Accepted:** none. **Open:** all year. Dog in residence. A dog is allowed with restrictions. Cat in residence. A cat is allowed with restrictions. Nonsmoking host. Guest may not smoke in residence. Children welcome. **Discounts:** 10% senior and student. Italian and Spanish spoken.

Reservation Contact: Bed & Breakfast Registry Ltd., Gary Winget, Box 8174, St. Paul, MN 55108; 612–646–4238.

LAGUNA BEACH

LOCATED AT TOP OF LAGUNA'S HIGHEST PEAK; VIEW OF OCEAN.

Near Temple Hills Dr., Pacific Coast Hwy.

Located at the "Top of the World," Laguna's highest peak, this warm and comfortable ranch-style home offers a 180-degree view of the beautiful blue Pacific and Mystic Hills. On a clear day you can see San Clemente Island, Catalina Island, and Long Beach. The sole guest room features a double bed and nicely appointed private bath. In warm weather, the Full breakfast is served on the patio overlooking the ocean, and the hosts often try to make guests feel at home by offering the patio and lounge for an evening barbecue. One of your hosts is a former pianist and singer, so naturally music is a primary interest of your hosts.

No. Rooms: 1	**Breakfast:** Full
Singles: None	**S-Rates:** $40 pb
Doubles: 1 pb	**D-Rates:** $45 pb
Type: Private townhouse	**Bldg:** 1963 ranch style

Minimum Stay: none. **Credit Card(s) Accepted:** none. **Open:** all year. No resident dogs. No dogs please. No resident cats. Guests may bring cat. Nonsmoking host. Guests may not smoke in residence. Children welcome. **Discounts:** none.

Reservation Contact: Rent-A-Room International B&B, Esther MacLachlan, 11531 Varna St., Garden Grove, CA 92640; 714–638–1406.

LOS ANGELES AREA, DISNEYLAND, KNOTTS BERRY FARM.

Near Cress St., Rte. 1.

This New Orleans colonial-style home, built in 1920, encloses a brick courtyard filled with plants, a large tiered fountain, and a huge tree dripping with moss. All the suites in this small inn consist of a sitting room and bedroom furnished with antiques and family memorabilia. All have private baths and TV. Most have kitchen facilities. All accommodate two to four people. One suite is done in cranberry and lilac tones and contains antiques, an old brass bed, and French doors opening onto the courtyard. Another has white wicker furniture and a bay window opening onto the courtyard. Another has an English country feeling with dark blue and yellow—two bedrooms, sitting room, complete kitchen, and dining area. The other three suites have similar facilities. Guests are greeted in their suites with a complimentary bottle of California wine and a bowl of fresh fruit. A decanter of sherry is available for late-night get-togethers. The interests of your exceptional hosts include jogging, theater, and cooking.

No. Rooms: 6	**Breakfast:** Continental Plus
Singles: None	**S-Rates:** $85–$125 pb
Doubles: 6 pb	**D-Rates:** $85–$125 pb
Type: Inn	**Bldg:** 1920 colonial

Minimum Stay: 2 nights on weekends. **Credit Card(s) Accepted:** none. **Open:** all year. No resident dog. No dogs please. Cat in residence. No cats please. Nonsmoking host. Guests may smoke. Children welcome. **Discounts:** none.

Reservation Contact: Bed & Breakfast Registry Ltd., Gary Winget, Box 8174, St. Paul, MN 55108; 612–646–4238.

ID: 92651CAS

OCEAN VIEW, ARTS FESTIVAL, WINTER FESTIVAL, MOULTON PLAYHOUSE, MUSEUM OF ART, HORTENSE MILLER GARDEN; ANTIQUES AND ART GALLERIES.

Near Nyes Pl., CA 1.

This extraordinary little inn is a pleasing combination of California Mission and Spanish revival architectural styles. The bedrooms and suites have been lovingly decorated and furnished with American and European antiques to create a warm, comfortable atmosphere. The original Mission House and cottage were built in the early 1930s as guest facilities. The *casitas,* consisting of sixteen courtyard and balcony bedroom suites, were added in the 40s to accommodate visitors to the growing artist colony of Laguna. It was recently purchased by the current hosts who have painstakingly converted it to a distinctive country inn. Guests are invited to relax in the living room of the historic Mission with a glass of wine or cup of tea, in the library, or on one of the several pool or garden patios surrounded by hanging baskets and colorful pots of flowers. There are twenty guest rooms, each individually decorated in pleasing colors with comfortable beds (twin and double) and a blend of antique and contemporary furnishings. All rooms have color TV, refrigerator, and private bath. Some rooms open onto the lovely shaded Spanish patio with colorful hibiscus, bougainvillea, and impatients plants. Others open onto a terrace with a panoramic view of the Pacific. There are four suites with living rooms, dining rooms, and fully equipped kitchens. There is also a deluxe cottage beautifully furnished and fully equipped, ideal for a first or second honeymoon. A Continental breakfast buffet is served in the dining room or on the garden patios. Guests can spend their days sunning and swimming at beautiful Victoria Beach. Deep-sea fishing, golf, tennis, horseback riding, shops, restaurants, and galleries are also nearby.

No. Rooms: 20	**Breakfast:** Continental Plus
Singles: None	**S-Rates:** $100–$190 pb
Doubles: 20 pb	**D-Rates:** $100–$190 pb
Type: Inn	**Bldg:** 1930s Spanish revival

Minimum Stay: 2 nights on weekends. **Credit Card(s) Accepted:** AE, DC, Discover, MC, V. **Open:** all year. Host's dog is not allowed in guest areas. No dogs please. No resident cats. No cats please. Host does not smoke in guest areas. Guests may smoke. Children welcome. **Discounts:** weekdays Oct.–May.

Reservation Contact: Bed & Breakfast Registry Ltd., Gary Winget, Box 8174, St. Paul, MN 55108; 612–646–4238.

LAKE ARROWHEAD   ID: 92352BLU

SKIING, SWIMMING, BOATING.

Near Rte. 18.

In a 1950s Bavarian-style home, you can relax in the casual elegance of an Alpine setting. In the parlor, with English floral carpet, lace curtains, antique crystal, cozy sofas, and fireplace, you will find books, puzzles, checkers, works of art, and good music. There is also a deck for bird-watching and a hammock for napping. Four of the six guest rooms are on the main floor and share two baths. All rooms sleep at least two. A Continental Plus breakfast is served on the shaded deck or in the dining room between 8:30 and 10 A.M. during the week and at 9 A.M. on Sundays. Wine and cheese are served in the late afternoon. Lake Arrowhead offers a beach, arcade, shops, restaurants, and entertainment. You can rent a fishing boat, enjoy the *Arrowhead Queen* excursion boat, ice skate in nearby Blue Jay, or swim and sun at a private beach. Winter sports are less than thirty minutes away.

No. Rooms: 5	**Breakfast:** Continental Plus
Singles: None	**S-Rates:** $75–$95 pb, $60–$65 sb
Doubles: 3 pb, 2 sb	**D-Rates:** $75–$95 pb, $60–$65 sb
Type: Private home	**Bldg:** 1950s Bavarian

Minimum Stay: 2 nights weekends. **Credit Card(s) Accepted:** none. **Open:** all year, except Christmas. Dog in residence. No dogs please. No resident cats. No cats please. Nonsmoking host. Guests may not smoke in residence. Residence not appropriate for children. **Discounts:** weekdays Feb.–May, and for senior citizens all year.

Reservation Contact: Bed & Breakfast Registry Ltd., Gary Winget, Box 8174, St. Paul, MN 55108; 612–646–4238.

LOS ANGELES   ID: G–5

FAIRFAX DISTRICT.

Near La Cienega & Melrose.

This two-bedroom apartment is done in California-style with wicker, plants, and pretty prints. The guest room has a double bed, TV, and shared bath. A Continental breakfast is served. Shopping and public transportation are one block away.

No. Rooms: 1   Breakfast: Continental
Singles: None   S-Rates: $40 sb
Doubles: 1 sb   D-Rates: $45 sb
Type: Private home   Bldg: Apartment

Minimum Stay: none. **Credit Card(s) Accepted:** none. **Open:** all year. No resident dogs. No dogs please. Resident cats. No cats please. Nonsmoking host. Guests may smoke. Children welcome. **Discounts:** 7th night free.

Reservation Contact: Bed and Breakfast of Los Angeles, Peg Marshall & Angie Kobabe, 32074 Waterside Ln., Westlake Village, CA 91361; 818–889–8870.

ID: INTNAT44

CHEVIOT HILL AREA.

Near Motor Ave., San Diego Fwy.

Cheviot Hills, one of the fine upper-middle-class neighborhoods of Los Angeles, is centrally located in relation to many tourist attractions. This 1950s ranch-style house features an artist's studio, and her work is displayed. The rear patio is set in an exceptional garden combining Japanese and original design. One carpeted guest room offers a double bed, bedside tables, chairs, desk, small table, original paintings, and private bath. An adjoining den with TV, bookcases, table, and single bed could accommodate an additional guest of the same party. A Full breakfast is served. Your hosts, a school psychologist and an artist, enjoy photography, hiking, biking, and golf.

No. Rooms: 2   Breakfast: Full
Singles: 1 sb   S-Rates: $48 pb, $38 sb
Doubles: 1 pb   D-Rates: $58 pb
Type: Private home   Bldg: 1950 ranch style

Minimum Stay: 2 nights. **Credit Card(s) Accepted:** none. **Open:** all year. No resident dogs. No dogs please. No resident cats. No cats please. Nonsmoking host. Guests may not smoke in guest rooms. Children welcome with restrictions. **Discounts:** none.

Reservation Contact: Bed & Breakfast International, Jean Brown, 1181-B Solano Ave., Albany, CA 94706; 415–525–4569.

ID: RENTROM10

MOVIE & TV STUDIOS, MUSEUMS, GALLERIES, HISTORIC HOMES; SHOPPING; HANCOCK PARK AREA.

Near Wilshire & LaBrea.

This Italianate home, built in 1925, is furnished with antiques and has two stained-glass ceilings. Centrally located and with good public transportation, this house is also in one of the outstanding neighborhoods in southern California. Hancock Park is one of the most posh areas of Los Angeles, comparable to Beverly Hills. Shops, museums, galleries, historic homes, and movie and TV studios are all easily accessible. Disneyland is thirty miles away. The two guest rooms feature double beds, antique furnishings, and TV. One has a day bed that could accommodate a third person, and a private bath; the other has a shared bath. A Full breakfast is served. Your host, with degrees in languages and international relations, has visited over one hundred countries. Interests include architectural preservation, history, gardening, entertaining, and travel. Arrival/departure transportation and area tours are available. No reservations will be accepted during the Christmas or Thanksgiving periods.

No. Rooms: 2	**Breakfast:** Full
Singles: None	**S-Rates:** $40 pb, $40 sb
Doubles: 1 pb, 1 sb	**D-Rates:** $50 pb, $50 sb
Type: Private home	**Bldg:** 1925 Italianate

Minimum Stay: none. **Credit Card(s) Accepted:** none. **Open:** all year, except Christmas. Dog in residence. No dogs please. No resident cats. No cats please. Nonsmoking host. Guests may not smoke in guest rooms. Children welcome with restrictions. **Discounts:** weekly.

Reservation Contact: Rent-A-Room International B&B, Esther MacLachlan, 11531 Varna St., Garden Grove, CA 92640; 714–638–1406.

ID: 90004HER

HOLLYWOOD, LARCHMONT VILLAGE, GRIFFITH PARK, BEVERLY HILLS.

Near Vine St. & Melrose Ave., U.S. 101, Rte. 2.

This comfortable two-story home is a wonderful place to relax after a hectic day of sightseeing or business meetings. You can barbeque on the patio near the fountain and watch the hummingbirds or spend the evening conversing by the fireplace. Guests will find plants and bouquets throughout the house. There are two guest rooms. The Rose Room is decorated with a garden-trellis motif and has twin beds, a cozy alcove seat, and a balcony overlooking the garden. The Blue Room has a queen-sized bed, two Queen Anne chairs, and small dressing room. The two rooms share one full and one half bath. A Continental breakfast is served in the formal dining room or the cozy breakfast nook. Guests have full kitchen

privileges, and a washing machine is available. The neighborhood has a variety of restaurants within walking distance. La Cienega's Village, a tree-lined block of interesting shops, grocery stores, and cafés, is an easy walk. Only two miles down the street is LA's newest "trendy" shopping district, where you can get everything from Italian gelati to punk clothing. The house is close to the Hollywood Freeway (U.S. 101), so it is convenient to major tourist attractions and business districts. Your host, a research specialist, enjoys folk dancing, sewing, and, most of all, gardening. She has traveled to Europe and Egypt and plans to visit Australia.

No. Rooms: 2	**Breakfast:** Continental
Singles: None	**S-Rates:** $30 sb
Doubles: 2 sb	**D-Rates:** $40 sb
Type: Private home	**Bldg:** 1930s two-story

Minimum Stay: none. **Credit Card(s) Accepted:** none. **Open:** all year. No resident dogs. A dog is allowed with restrictions. No resident cats. No cats please. Nonsmoking host. Guests may not smoke in residence. Children welcome. **Discounts:** weekly. German spoken.

Reservation Contact: Bed & Breakfast Registry Ltd., Gary Winget, Box 8174, St. Paul, MN 55108; 612–646–4238.

MALIBU

ID: L–MALIBU

BEACH, RESTAURANTS.

Near Winding Way, Rte. 1.

Malibu, world famous for its delightful restaurants and lovely beaches, is the scene of this perfect getaway spot. A little guest cottage built behind the garage offers complete privacy and a view of the ocean down through the canyon. Guests enter down a garden path to find a full kitchen, bedroom with queen-sized bed, living room with double hide-a-bed, and private bath. A Continental breakfast is served. Your hosts, a teacher and her husband, have two teenage sons.

No. Rooms: 1	**Breakfast:** Continental
Singles: None	**S-Rates:** $50 sb
Doubles: 1 pb	**D-Rates:** $60 sb
Type: Private home	**Bldg:** 1984 cottage

Minimum Stay: none. **Credit Card(s) Accepted:** MC, V. **Open:** all year. Dog in residence. No dogs please. No resident cats. No cats please. Non-smoking host. Guests may smoke in residence. Children welcome. **Discounts:** none.

Reservation Contact: Bed and Breakfast of Los Angeles, Peg Marshall & Angie Kobabe, 32074 Waterside Ln., Westlake Village, CA 91361; 818–889–8870.

MANHATTAN BEACH

ID: L–BEACHSUITE

½ BLOCK FROM BEACH.

Near Ocean & Fourth, 405, San Diego Fwy.

This completely redecorated home is just one-half block from the ocean in an area excellent for seeing all the attractions of Los Angeles. The three-level house has plush carpeting and high ceilings. The entire entry level, which consists of a living room with fireplace, wet bar, and TV, is for guests' use. The guest room, just down the hall, has twin beds and a private bath. A Continental breakfast is served. Your host is interested in real estate.

No. Rooms: 1	**Breakfast:** Continental
Singles: None	**S-Rates:** $50 pb
Doubles: 1 pb	**D-Rates:** $50 pb
Type: Private home	**Bldg:** Modern

Minimum Stay: none. **Credit Card(s) Accepted:** MC, V. **Open:** all year. Dog in residence. No dogs please. No resident cats. No cats please. Non-smoking host. Guests may not smoke in residence. Children welcome with restrictions. **Discounts:** none.

Reservation Contact: Bed and Breakfast of Los Angeles, Peg Marshall

& Angie Kobabe, 32074 Waterside Ln., Westlake Village, CA 91361;
818–889–8870.

MONTARA

ID: 94037MON

MONTARA STATE BEACH, MCNEE RANCH STATE PARK, FITZGERALD MARINE RESERVE, 30 MINUTES FROM SAN FRANCISCO.

Near CA 1 & 2nd St.

This inviting contemporary home is located in the coastal hamlet of Montara, a semi-rural area 30 minutes from San Francisco. Local attractions include Montara State Beach, hiking trails at McNee Ranch State Park, Fitzgerald Marine Reserve in Moss Beach, historic Half Moon Bay, horseback riding on Miramar Beach, whale watching and deep-sea fishing, Point Montara Lighthouse, and numerous seafood and ethnic restaurants. The guest room, with private bath and private entrance, has a trundle

bed which can be made into a queen-sized bed or two twin beds. A connecting sitting room with a fireplace provides an ocean view and opens onto a redwood deck overlooking a flower garden. A Full breakfast (which features honey from your hosts' beehives) is served in the solarium. Your hosts enjoy jewelry design, hiking, and camping. They have spent many years exploring San Francisco and the greater Bay Area, and are eager to share their intimate knowledge with visitors.

No. Rooms: 1	**Breakfast:** Full
Singles: None	**S-Rates:** $55 pb
Doubles: 1 pb	**D-Rates:** $65 pb
Type: Private home	**Bldg:** 1965 contemporary

Minimum Stay: none. **Credit Card(s) Accepted:** none. **Open:** all year. Dog in residence. No dogs please. No resident cats. No cats please. Non-

smoking host. Guests may not smoke in residence. Residence not appropriate for children. **Discounts:** 7th night free. German and Spanish spoken.

Reservation Contact: Bed & Breakfast Registry Ltd., Gary Winget, Box
8174, St. Paul, MN 55108; 612–646–4238.

MONTEREY   ID: INTNAT50

VIEW OF BAY.

Near Mar Vista, Rte. 1.

This modern ranch-style house with wood-shingle roof is set amongst
trees and has a sweeping view of Monterey Bay. The first of two available
guest rooms has a queen-sized bed, dresser, chairs, Oriental rugs, and
private bath. The furnishings and art are a tasteful blend of old and new,
reflective of the local style. The second guest room, with twin beds and
shared bath, has similar decor. A patio and laundry facilities are also
available to guests. A Full breakfast includes sourdough pancakes. Your
host, a retired teacher, goes out of her way to help you feel at home in
this beautiful area. A world traveler and opera buff, she also enjoys
beachcombing.

No. Rooms: 2	**Breakfast:** Full
Singles: None	**S-Rates:** $62 pb, $52 sb
Doubles: 1 pb, 1 sb	**D-Rates:** $68 pb, $58 sb
Type: Private home	**Bldg:** 1950 ranch

Minimum Stay: 2 nights. **Credit Card(s) Accepted:** none. **Open:** all
year. No resident dogs. No dogs please. No resident cats. No cats please.
Nonsmoking host. Guests may not smoke in residence. Children welcome. **Discounts:** 10% weekly, family discount. Spanish spoken.

Reservation Contact: Bed & Breakfast International, Jean Brown,
1181-B Solano Ave., Albany, CA 94706; 415–525–4569.

MORAGA   ID: 94556HAL

SAN FRANCISCO AREA, MT. DIABLO, MARINE
WORLD, UNIVERSITY OF CALIFORNIA BERKELEY.

Near Moraga Way & Canyon Rd., Rte. 24.

This attractive contemporary home is located in beautiful Moraga Valley,
30 minutes from downtown San Francisco. You can take a refreshing dip
in the pool, relax in the hot tub (Apr.–Oct.), or lounge on the patio after
a busy day in the city. There are two guest rooms, one with Victorian
furnishings, the other contemporary. Both have comfortable queen-sized
beds and shared guest bath. Full breakfast is served on the terrace or in
the dining room. Public transportation to San Francisco is available two

blocks from the house. Your hosts' interests include computers, solar energy, sewing, gardening, and swimming.

No. Rooms: 2	**Breakfast:** Full
Singles: None	**S-Rates:** $45 sb
Doubles: 2 sb	**D-Rates:** $55 sb
Type: Private home	**Bldg:** 1970 California contemporary

Minimum Stay: none. **Credit Card(s) Accepted:** none. **Open:** all year. No resident dogs. No dogs please. Cat in residence. No cats please. Nonsmoking host. Guests may not smoke in guest rooms. Children welcome with restrictions. **Discounts:** weekly & family.

Reservation Contact: Bed & Breakfast Registry Ltd., Gary Winget, Box 8174, St. Paul, MN 55108; 612–646–4238.

MUIR BEACH   ID: 13–AMFAM

ON OCEAN.

Near Rte. 1, U.S. 101.

This fabulous contemporary country home, surrounded by hills and hiking paths, overlooks the ocean. It has large windows and open beams, a fireplace, huge library, and balcony overlooking the water. Muir Beach is just below the house, and Muir Woods is five minutes away. The guest quarters consist of a sitting room with picture window overlooking San Francisco and the Pacific, a fireplace, and a trundle under a window seat that forms two twin beds. The other room has a single bed. There is a private entrance and private bath, and a Full breakfast is served. Your host, a graduate of Smith College and Hastings College of Law, is an attorney and world traveler, with interests in art, reading, and the stock market.

No. Rooms: 1	**Breakfast:** Full
Singles: None	**S-Rates:** $95 pb
Doubles: 1 pb	**D-Rates:** $95 pb
Type: Private home	**Bldg:** 1977 California style

Minimum Stay: 2 weekend nights. **Credit Card(s) Accepted:** none. **Open:** all year. Dog in residence. No dogs please. No resident cats. No cats please. Nonsmoking host. Guests may not smoke in guest rooms. Children welcome with restrictions. **Discounts:** none.

Reservation Contact: American Family Inn/B&B San Francisco, Susan & Richard Kreibich, Box 349, San Francisco CA 94101; 415–931–3083.

NEWPORT BEACH   ID: 92663VIL

L.A. AREA, DISNEYLAND, KNOTTS BERRY FARM, HARBOR.

On Lido Isle, Rte. 1.

This contemporary two-story villa with tropical decor on Lido Isle offers a brick terrace on the bay with a sensational view. There are two spacious double guest rooms, with sun decks, ample closet space, TV, and private baths. One of the rooms has a queen-sized bed and the other has twin beds. Continental breakfast is served in the dining room. The area offers fishing, sailing, surfing, swimming, cycling, harbor cruises, whale watching, and art festivals. The house is one-and-a-half blocks from Lido Village, where you will find tree-lined brick streets, boutiques, and fine waterfront restaurants. Your hosts' interests include golf, travel, and people.

No. Rooms: 2	**Breakfast:** Continental Plus
Singles: None	**S-Rates:** $86 pb
Doubles: 2 pb	**D-Rates:** $86 pb
Type: Private home	**Bldg:** Contemporary

Minimum Stay: none. **Credit Card(s) Accepted:** none. **Open:** Sept.–May. Dog in residence. No dogs please. No resident cats. No cats please. Nonsmoking host. Guests may not smoke in guest rooms. **Discounts:** none. Spanish spoken.

Reservation Contact: Bed & Breakfast Registry Ltd., Gary Winget, Box 8174, St. Paul, MN 55108; 612–646–4238.

OAKHURST/YOSEMITE   ID: INTNAT65

YOSEMITE NATIONAL PARK.

Near rtes. 41, 635, 99.

This spacious, contemporary home of rock and wood is at the gateway to Yosemite National Park and overlooks a stream. After a day of sightseeing guests may relax in the pool or try a game of pool in the recreation room. A golf course is also nearby. The two guest rooms, one with twin beds and one with a double bed, are decorated with pine furniture and country prints. A hide-a-bed in the recreation room can accommodate extra people in the same party. A Full breakfast is served. TV and laundry facilities are available. Your retired hosts enjoy needlework, gardening, and travel.

No. Rooms: 2	**Breakfast:** Full
Singles: None	**S-Rates:** $42–$52 pb
Doubles: 2 pb	**D-Rates:** $48–$58 pb
Type: Private home	**Bldg:** Contemporary alpine-style

Minimum Stay: 2 nights. **Credit Card(s) Accepted:** MC, V. **Open:** all year. No resident dog. No dogs please. No resident cat. No cats please.

Nonsmoking host. Guest may smoke in residence. Children welcome with restrictions. **Discounts:** weekly and family rates.

Reservation Contact: Bed & Breakfast International, Jean Brown, 1108-B Solano Ave., Albany, CA 94706; 415–525–4569.

ORANGE
ID: 92669COU

DISNEYLAND, KNOTT'S BERRY FARM, BEACH, ANGEL STADIUM, ANAHEIM CONVENTION CENTER, SOUTH COAST REPERTORY THEATRE, ORANGE COUNTY CENTER FOR PERFORMING ARTS.

Near CA 55 & CA 22, I–5.

This home is noted for its unique glass architecture. Guests are welcome to relax in the large family room with cable TV and VCR with many popular movies. The south wall of the living room faces the hills and guests may sit in front of the fireplace while having some evening refreshment. After a day of sightseeing guests will also enjoy the pool and spa. There are four nicely furnished guest rooms. The quaint Blue Room has a king-sized bed with a brass headboard, and an antique chifforobe. The Rust Room has a queen-sized bed, rocking chair, and Victorian decor. The Library Room, furnished with a Queen Anne brass day bed, is hunter green with white eyelet and displays a large collection of books. The Peach Room is also decorated with white eyelet and has a TV and private bath. The other three rooms share two baths. A Full farm-style breakfast is served. Bicycles (including a tandem) are available. Local attractions include Disneyland, Knott's Berry Farm, and, of course, the beach. Nearby Angel Stadium and the Anaheim Convention Center host many exciting events. Local theaters include the South Coast Repertory and the new Orange County Center for Performing Arts. Nearby Long Beach is home to the *Queen Mary,* the *Spruce Goose,* and Ports o' Call.

No. Rooms: 4	**Breakfast:** Full
Singles: None	**S-Rates:** $63 pb, $48 sb
Doubles: 1 pb, 3 sb	**D-Rates:** $68 pb, $53 sb
Type: Private home	**Bldg:** 1960s Executive Eichler

Minimum Stay: none. **Credit Card(s) Accepted:** none. **Open:** all year. No resident dogs. No dogs please. No resident cats. No cats please. Nonsmoking host. Guests may not smoke in residence. Children welcome. **Discounts:** none.

Reservation Contact: Bed & Breakfast Registry Ltd., Gary Winget, Box 8174, St. Paul, MN 55108; 612–646–4238.

OROSI

ID: 93647VAL

SEQUOIA NATIONAL PARK, KINGS CANYON NATIONAL PARK, CAVES.

Near Ave. 416, Rte. 99.

This lovely California citrus ranch offers a beautiful view, gracious hospitality, and a unique vacation environment. There are four guest rooms, one with twin beds, one with a queen-sized bed, and two with king-sized beds; two have private baths, and two share a bath. All are air-conditioned. A Full breakfast of your choice is served in the gazebo, weather permitting. Tennis court, barbeque, picnic tables, garden, and TV are available for guests' enjoyment. Sequoia and Kings Canyon National Parks are nearby. Your hosts' interests include fishing, art, and gardening.

> **No. Rooms:** 4
> **Singles:** None
> **Doubles:** 2 pb, 2 sb
> **Type:** Private home
>
> **Breakfast:** Full
> **S-Rates:** $42 pb, $42 sb
> **D-Rates:** $45 pb, $45 sb
> **Bldg:** 1964 Spanish ranch style

Minimum Stay: none. **Credit Card(s) Accepted:** none. **Open:** all year. Two resident dogs. A dog is allowed with restrictions. Resident cat. No cats please. Nonsmoking host. Guests may smoke. Children welcome. **Discounts:** family rate.

Reservation Contact: Bed & Breakfast Registry Ltd., Gary Winget, Box 8174, St. Paul, MN 55108; 612–646–4238.

OROVILLE

ID: 95965JEA

FEATHER RIVER, PLUMAS NATIONAL FOREST, TAHOE NATIONAL FOREST.

Near Rte. 70, Rte. 162.

This attractive contemporary home is nestled under the trees on the bank of the Feather River. You can use canoes to explore the river, swim, fish, or picnic. During cooler weather, you can sit in front of the fire and watch the ducks, squirrels, pheasant, heron, and quail on the five acres of grounds. The history of Oroville, a town that sprang up during the gold-rush era, is preserved in a local museum. All seven guest rooms have private baths. Some have private entrances, decks, and four-poster beds. A Continental Plus breakfast is served. Your host's interests include golf, furniture refinishing, and travel. Additional meals, arrival/departure transportation, and area tours are usually available.

> **No. Rooms:** 7
> **Singles:** None
> **Doubles:** 7 pb
> **Type:** Private home
>
> **Breakfast:** Continental Plus
> **S-Rates:** $35–$60 pb
> **D-Rates:** $45–$80 pb
> **Bldg:** 1948 natural cedar

Minimum Stay: 2 nights. **Credit Card(s) Accepted:** V. **Open:** all year. No resident dogs. A dog is allowed with restrictions. No resident cats. A cat is allowed with restrictions. Nonsmoking host. Guests may not smoke in residence. Children welcome with restrictions. **Discounts:** 10% after 5 days. French spoken.

Reservation Contact: Bed & Breakfast Registry Ltd., Gary Winget, Box 8174, St. Paul, MN 55108; 612–646–4238.

PACIFIC GROVE

ID: 93950GOS

MONTEREY AREA, NATIONAL REGISTER OF HISTORIC PLACES, MIGRATING WHALES, SEALS; TENNIS, GOLF.

Near Forest Ave., Rte. 1.

Tastefully restored, this 1880 Victorian mansion has rounded corner tower and bay windows, and is furnished with many antiques. A large parlor, as well as an old-fashioned garden with winding brick path, tables, and chairs, are available to you for breakfast, reading, or relaxing. The front porch has wicker furnishings. Guest rooms are carpeted and decorated with pastel floral wallpaper, ruffled curtains, lace pillows, quilts, and antique bedsteads. Some have fireplaces and small kitchens, and most have private baths. Guests will find fresh fruit and flowers in their rooms.

No. Rooms: 22
Singles: None
Doubles: 20 pb, 2 sb
Type: Inn

Breakfast: Continental Plus
S-Rates: $110–$125 pb, $90–$105 sb
D-Rates: $110–$125 pb, $90–$105 sb
Bldg: 1880s Victorian

Minimum Stay: 2 nights. **Credit Card(s) Accepted:** none. **Open:** all year. No resident dogs. No dogs please. No resident cats. No cats please. Nonsmoking host. Guests may not smoke in residence. Children welcome. **Discounts:** none.

Reservation Contact: Bed & Breakfast Registry Ltd., Gary Winget, Box 8174, St. Paul, MN 55108; 612–646–4238.

ID: 93950GRE

CANNERY ROW, MONTEREY BAY AQUARIUM.

Near Ocean Blvd. & 5th St., CA 1.

This Queen Anne-style mansion was built in 1888 and is considered one of the most elegant on the Monterey Peninsula. Set on the Pacific Grove shoreline, it provides a panoramic view of Monterey Bay. The living room features large window alcoves facing the bay, a lovely collection of antique furnishings, and a unique fireplace framed by stained-glass panels. There are five guest rooms plus a two-room suite in the main house, and five more guest rooms in the carriage house across the courtyard. Guests will find flowers, fresh fruit, cozy quilts and pillows, and antiques in their rooms. Four of the guest rooms share two baths while the fifth room and the suite have private baths. Each of the guest rooms in the carriage house has a private bath and a sitting area with a fireplace. A Full country-style breakfast is served in the dining room or in the alcoves of the living room which face the sea. In the late afternoon a simple tea is available in front of the fire. Near the inn is a public beach perfect for swimming and scuba diving. A shoreline trail for jogging or strolling continues to the Fishermen's Wharf, and it is a short walk to both Cannery Row, with its myriad of shops and restaurants, and to the Monterey Bay Aquarium.

No. Rooms: 11	**Breakfast:** Full
Singles: None	**S-Rates:** $125–$140 pb,
Doubles: 7 pb, 4 sb	$90–$115 sb
Type: Inn	**D-Rates:** $125–$140 pb,
	$90–$115 sb
	Bldg: 1888 Queen Anne Victorian

Minimum Stay: none. **Credit Card(s) Accepted:** AE, MC, V. **Open:** all year. No resident dogs. No dogs please. No resident cats. No cats please. Nonsmoking host. Guests may not smoke in residence. Children are welcome with restrictions. **Discounts:** none.

Reservation Contact: Bed & Breakfast Registry Ltd., Gary Winget, Box 8174, St. Paul, MN 55108; 612–646–4238.

PALO ALTO   ID: 94301VIC

STANFORD UNIVERSITY, MUSEUMS, THEATER; RESTAURANTS & CAFÉS.

Near University & Middlefield, Rte. 101.

This lovely Victorian inn is located in one of California's most charming cities, home of Stanford University and neighbor to San Francisco and Silicon Valley. You will find fine restaurants, cafés, theater, and shops only a few blocks away. Originally built in 1895, the house was fully restored ninety years later and turned into an inn. Each room is named for Queen Victoria or one of her nine children, and each has a separate sitting parlor, telephone, and private bath. Most of the rooms have a canopy or four-poster king- or queen-sized bed. The "Princess Royal," done in beige, cream and green, has a king-size canopy bed, lace curtains and table covers, extra-plump pillows and a bear-claw tub in the bathroom. "Princess Christian" has a peach color scheme, traditional furniture, antiques, and a king-sized bed. "King Edward" is done in gray and white with similar furnishings. "Queen Victoria," in olive green and navy, has a queen-sized canopy bed, armoire, desk, many antiques, and a skylight. A Continental Plus breakfast is served in the guest room or on the patio. In the evening, fellow guests meet over a glass or sherry or port in the parlor. Your hosts enjoy art, classical music, and European travel.

No. Rooms: 10
Singles: None
Doubles: 10 pb
Type: Inn

Breakfast: Continental Plus
S-Rates: $90 pb
D-Rates: $135 pb
Bldg: 1895 Victorian

Minimum Stay: none. **Credit Card(s) Accepted:** AE, MC, V. **Open:** all year. No resident dogs. No dogs please. No resident cats. No cats please. Nonsmoking host. Guests may not smoke in residence. Children welcome with restrictions. **Discounts:** corporate.

Reservation Contact: Bed & Breakfast Registry Ltd., Gary Winget, Box 8174, St. Paul, MN 55108; 612–646–4238.

PALOS VERDES
ID: L–WHALER

ACROSS STREET FROM BEACH.

Near Palos Verdes Dr., Harbor Fwy.

Palos Verdes Peninsula is a rural area, yet close to Los Angeles. With the Pacific Ocean and private beach just across the street and below the cliffs, this is a delightful place from which to escape the heat and crowds. This traditional home, on the tip of the peninsula, provides sweeping views of the water and Catalina Island. Guests might even be able to catch a glimpse of the migrating whales. One of the two guest rooms, which share a guest bath, has a double bed and ocean view, while the other has twin beds. Guests can enjoy the fireplace, TV, and patio. A Full breakfast is served.

No. Rooms: 2
Singles: None
Doubles: 2 sb
Type: Private home

Breakfast: Full
S-Rates: $40 sb
D-Rates: $50 sb
Bldg: Traditional

Minimum Stay: none. **Credit Card(s) Accepted:** MC, V. **Open:** all year. Dog in residence. No dogs please. No resident cats. No cats please. Nonsmoking host. Guests may not smoke. Children welcome. **Discounts:** none.

Reservation Contact: Bed and Breakfast of Los Angeles, Peg Marshall & Angie Kobabe, 32074 Waterside Ln., Westlake Village, CA 91361; 818–889–8870.

PHILO
ID: 95466PHI

MENDOCINO COUNTY, WINERIES, PARKS, ANDERSON VALLEY; GOURMET RESTAURANTS.

Near Rte. 128.

Nestled in the lush green Anderson Valley, this former nineteenth-century stagecoach stop is high-ceilinged and cool in summer. There are four

guest rooms; two have private baths and two share a bath. All but one room can accommodate three people. A Continental Plus breakfast is served in the formal dining room. Your hosts are prominent regional artists whose gallery and studio, located behind the main house, are open to guests. A flower and vegetable garden, including one of the largest blackberry patches in Mendocino County, completes the rural setting.

No. Rooms: 4
Singles: None
Doubles: 2 pb, 2 sb
Type: Private home

Breakfast: Continental Plus
S-Rates: $55–$65 pb, $45–$50 sb
D-Rates: $60–$65 pb, $50–$55 sb
Bldg: 1880s redwood

Minimum Stay: 2 nights. **Credit Card(s) Accepted:** none. **Open:** all year. Dog in residence. No dogs please. Cat in residence. No cats please. Nonsmoking host. Guests may not smoke in residence. Children welcome with restrictions. **Discounts:** none.

Reservation Contact: Bed & Breakfast Registry Ltd., Gary Winget, Box 8174, St. Paul, MN 55108; 612–646–4238.

RANCHO BERNARDO   ID: RENTROOM2

SAN DIEGO ZOO, SEA WORLD, OLD TOWN, WILD ANIMAL PARK.

Near Pomerado & Rancho Bernardo rds., I–15.

A large covered patio, with pleasant garden and beautiful flowers, lends an aura of restful relaxation to this two-story stucco home. The first-floor guest room is done in pale yellow and has papered walls, two twin beds, a wicker nightstand with lamp and clock radio, a closet, a large window to view the flowered back yard, and a private bath with shower. The second-floor room features a green and white motif, with a single bed, and large window facing east. A built-in desk and book shelves enhance its comfortable atmosphere. A Continental Plus breakfast is served. The attractive neighborhood is fourteen years old, and the town of Rancho Bernardo boasts thirteen golf courses. The Swim and Tennis Club is also available to guests, with three swimming pools, a Jacuzzi, sauna, shuffleboard and tennis courts, and a playground. Within twenty-five miles, guests will encounter the ocean, mountains, and lakes, as well as the San Diego Zoo, Sea World, Old Town, the Wild Animal Park, and even a side trip to Mexico. The combined interests of your two hosts include boating, camping, fishing, art, music, flowers, and church activities. Arrival/departure transportation and child care are available, and guests have kitchen and laundry privileges.

No. Rooms: 2	**Breakfast:** Continental Plus
Singles: 1 sb	**S-Rates:** $35 pb, $25 sb
Doubles: 1 pb	**D-Rates:** $40 pb
Type: Private home	**Bldg:** 1971 two-story stucco

Minimum Stay: none. **Credit Card(s) Accepted:** none. **Open:** all year. Dog in residence. No dogs please. Cat in residence. No cats please. Non-smoking host. Guests may not smoke in residence. Children welcome. **Discounts:** none.

Reservation Contact: Rent-A-Room International B&B, Esther MacLachlan, 11531 Varna St., Garden Grove, CA 92640; 714–638–1406.

RANCHO PALOS VERDES

ID: RENTROOM8

MARINELAND, LOS ANGELES HARBOR, ANTIQUES, OCEAN FRONT.

Near Schooner, Rte. 1, I–110.

This exceptional colonial ranch-style house with private beach fronting the ocean is located in a cove called Portuguese Bend, which, at one time, was a Portuguese whaling station. It is a lovely, quiet residential area with beautiful cliffs and scenic beaches. The house has many unusual antique accessories, including some two-hundred-year-old furnishings. The lit candles in the windows add an extra-special touch. There are cozy and comfortable common rooms with a double fireplace, and dining areas in the garden and front porch overlooking the ocean. The two guest rooms offer large private baths and an unlimited number of towels. Colonial furnishings grace the first room, with double bed, lamp table, writing desk, chest of drawers, chairs, blanket chest, color TV, and two large closets. The second room is decorated in a Spanish motif, with twin beds, rocking chair, chest of drawers, color TV, and stereo. Both rooms have wall-to-wall carpeting. A Full breakfast is served, including such favorites as quiche, pancakes, waffles or French toast with ham, sausage or bacon and eggs, a platter of fresh fruit, and freshly squeezed orange juice. In addition, there is a complimentary cocktail hour with snacks. A beach car, complete with beach chairs, mats, and paddle-tennis equipment is available. Your host is very attentive to your needs yet respects her guests' privacy. Many honeymooners have returned here to celebrate wedding anniversaries because of the serenity of the area, the gorgeous sunsets, and the moonlit walks along the ocean. Your host can provide discount tickets for all major southern California tourist attractions, and direct you to the area's free public tennis and golf courses. Also nearby are riding stables, deep-sea fishing, harbor cruises, and excellent restaurants. Your host has traveled throughout the U.S., Europe, Canada, and Mexico. She has been a B&B host for more than five years and enjoys graduate courses, reading, needlework, cooking, and gardening. Arrival/departure transportation, additional meals, child care, and bicycles are available.

No. Rooms: 2	**Breakfast:** Full
Singles: None	**S-Rates:** $35 pb
Doubles: 2 pb	**D-Rates:** $50 pb
Type: Private home	**Bldg:** 1958 colonial

Minimum Stay: none. **Credit Card(s) Accepted:** none. **Open:** all year. Dog in residence. Guests may bring dog. No resident cats. No cats please. Nonsmoking host. Guests may not smoke in residence. Children welcome. **Discounts:** seniors.

Reservation Contact: Rent-A-Room International B&B, Esther MacLachlan, 11531 Varna St., Garden Grove, CA 92640; 714–638–1406.

ROUND MOUNTAIN   ID: 578–NW

MT. SHASTA, BURNEY FALLS, LASSEN NATIONAL PARK.

Near Hwy. 299, Terry Miller Rd.

Formerly a hunting lodge, this large log home in the foothills of the Cascades provides a lovely retreat with mountain views. Cattle, turkeys, and peacocks are raised on 30 acres of land. Special features of this home include a comfortable country kitchen, knotty pine dining room, and many mementos and early Americana such as an antique Edison Victrola. Four guest rooms are available. One has twin beds with children's pictures imaginatively made into quilts and pillows. Lemon-colored wallpaper and carpeting the color of daffodils brighten the second room, furnished with a double bed with antique quilts and spreads and a wicker rocker. The third room features knotty-pine walls, a collection of antique hats, antique furniture, and a queen-sized bed with a plum-colored spread. These three second floor rooms share a bath. On the first floor there is one guest room with knotty-pine walls, fireplace, queen-sized bed, antique furniture, carpeting, and private bath. A Full breakfast is served. The hobbies of your hosts include gardening, reading, bridge, and hosting a radio program.

No. Rooms: 4
Singles: None
Doubles: 1 pb, 3 sb
Type: Private home

Breakfast: Full
S-Rates: $45 pb, $45 sb
D-Rates: $55 pb, $55 sb
Bldg: 1940s log house

Minimum Stay: none. **Credit Card(s) Accepted:** none. **Open:** all year. No resident dogs. Well-trained dogs allowed. No resident cats. No cats please. Nonsmoking host. Guests may not smoke in residence. Children welcome. **Discounts:** none.

Reservation Contact: Northwest Bed & Breakfast, Inc., L. Friedman & G. Shaich, 610 SW Broadway, #606, Portland, OR 97205; 503–243–7616.

ST. HELENA   ID: 94574INK

NAPA VALLEY, WINE COUNTRY, HOT-AIR BALLOONS.

Near Rte. 128, Rte. 29.

This Italianate Victorian home, built in 1884, has an encircling veranda and a sunny, high-ceilinged interior furnished with antiques. The parlor is an inviting spot, where guests can relax and visit. There is no TV, however, games are available. Nearby are many excellent restaurants, shops, and wineries. There are four guest rooms, all with private baths. A home-made Continental breakfast is served. There is a two-night minimum stay required on weekends. Check-in time is 4–6 P.M.; check-out time by 11 A.M.

No. Rooms: 4
Singles: None
Doubles: 4 pb
Type: Private home

Breakfast: Continental
S-Rates: $70–$90 pb
D-Rates: $70–$90 pb
Bldg: 1884 Victorian

Minimum Stay: 2 days on weekends. **Credit Card(s) Accepted:** none. **Open:** all year, except Christmas. No resident dogs. No dogs please. No resident cats. No cats please. Nonsmoking host. Guests may not smoke in residence. Residence is not appropriate for children. **Discounts:** none.

Reservation Contact: Bed & Breakfast Registry Ltd., Gary Winget, Box 8174, St. Paul, MN 55108; 612–646–4238.

ID: 94574JUD

NAPA VALLEY, WINERIES, GLIDER FLIGHTS, MINERAL BATHS, CANDLE FACTORY.

Near Rte. 128, Rte. 29.

Although this attractive, ranch-style home is within walking distance of town, it has a quiet country atmosphere and is surrounded by vineyards.

The one guest room, with private entrance and private bath, is furnished with antiques and a queen-sized brass bed. You are greeted with a warm welcome and a complimentary bottle of wine. There is a swimming pool for your use. A freshly baked Continental breakfast is served in your room or by the pool. Your hosts are interested in sports, grape growing, wine, cooking, sewing, and gardening.

No. Rooms: 1	**Breakfast:** Continental
Singles: None	**S-Rates:** $65 pb
Doubles: 1 pb	**D-Rates:** $75–$85 pb
Type: Private home	**Bldg:** Ranch style

Minimum Stay: 2 nights. **Credit Card(s) Accepted:** none. **Open:** all year. No resident dogs. No dogs please. Cat in residence. No cats please. Nonsmoking host. Guests may not smoke in residence. Children are welcome with restrictions. **Discounts:** none. Italian spoken.

Reservation Contact: Bed & Breakfast Registry Ltd., Gary Winget, Box 8174, St. Paul, MN 55108; 612–646–4238.

ID: 94574RAN

WINERIES, RESTAURANTS, SHOPPING, CONN VALLEY.

Near Silverado Trail & Pope St., CA 128; CA 29.

This ranch-style inn provides a great place to relax after a day of touring and has a magnificent view of the Conn Valley. The location gives access to wineries, mud baths, balloon rides, glider flights, restaurants, and shops. Guests may unwind in the Jacuzzi while watching the cattle, deer, and quail in the neighboring pasture. Each of the three guest rooms has a queen-sized bed and a private bath. The Blue Room and the Rose Room are furnished with white wicker, antique wash stands, and color-coordinated wallpaper and comforters. The Fireplace Room features a wood-burning stove, a skylight, and French doors that open onto a deck overlooking the garden. A Continental breakfast is served and complimentary wine is offered in the afternoon or evening.

No. Rooms: 3	**Breakfast:** Continental
Singles: None	**S-Rates:** $65 pb
Doubles: 3 pb	**D-Rates:** $85–$95 pb
Type: Private home	**Bldg:** 1947 Ranch house

Minimum Stay: 2 days on weekends. **Credit Card(s) Accepted:** none. **Open:** all year. No resident dogs. No dogs please. No resident cats. No cats please. Nonsmoking host. Guest may not smoke in residence. Children are welcome with restrictions. **Discounts:** 10% after 4 days.

Reservation Contact: Bed & Breakfast Registry Ltd., Gary Winget, Box 8174, St. Paul, MN 55108; 612–646–4238.

SAN DIEGO

ZOO, SEA WORLD, BEACH.

Near I–5, I–8, Friars Rd. & Via Las Cumbres.

This townhouse is located within five miles of the zoo, the beach, and Sea World. It has a private downstairs apartment with a bedroom with a queen-sized bed, a sitting room with a queen-sized hide-a-bed, and a private bath. A Full breakfast is served.

No. Rooms: 1	**Breakfast:** Full
Singles: None	**S-Rates:** $45 pb
Doubles: 1 pb	**D-Rates:** $55 pb
Type: Private home	**Bldg:** Townhouse

Minimum Stay: none. **Credit Card(s) Accepted:** none. **Open:** all year. No resident dog. No dogs please. No resident cats. No cats please. Nonsmoking host. Guests may smoke. Children welcome with restrictions. **Discounts:** none.

Reservation Contact: Rent-A-Room International B&B, Esther MacLachlan, 11531 Varna St., Garden Grove, CA 92640; 714–638–1406.

SAN FRANCISCO

PACIFIC HEIGHTS.

Near Octavia & California sts., U.S. 101.

This twenty-two-room Italianate Victorian mansion is one of the great "Painted Ladies" of the city. It was built in 1876 and has a red, white, and blue skylight to commemorate the Centennial. (It was saved from the 1906 fire because it had a water tank and the owners put wet rugs on the roof.) The house is completely furnished with museum-quality antiques. The guest rooms consist of two suites, both with bedroom and sitting room, queen-sized bed, antique furnishings, comfortable upholstered chairs, table, and TV; one has a shared bath and one has a private bath. Pacific Heights is a fine neighborhood near the city center and very convenient for tourists. The house is on a slight incline, permitting a view from the guest room window that extends all the way to the ocean. A Full breakfast is served. Your hosts collect classic films. They also have the largest collection of miniatures in the U.S. and manufacture miniature furniture.

No. Rooms: 2	**Breakfast:** Full
Singles: None	**S-Rates:** $82 pb, $82 sb
Doubles: 1 pb, 1 sb	**D-Rates:** $88 pb, $88 sb
Type: Private home	**Bldg:** 1876 Italianate Victorian

Minimum Stay: 2 nights. **Credit Card(s) Accepted:** none. **Open:** all year. No resident dogs. No dogs please. No resident cats. No cats please. Host smokes. Guests may smoke. Residence not appropriate for children. **Discounts:** 10% weekly.

Reservation Contact: Bed & Breakfast International, Jean Brown, 1181-B Solano Ave., Albany, CA 94706; 415–525–4569.

RUSSIAN HILL, FISHERMAN'S WHARF, NORTH BEACH.

Near Union St. & Green St.

This charming Victorian home, furnished with country antiques, provides wonderful views of the city. The house is within walking distance of Fisherman's Wharf and North Beach. The guest room, with fireplace and twin trundle beds, is decorated with American pine antiques, country print fabrics, and braided rugs. The Full breakfast might include waffles with strawberries and whipped cream, omelets with pesto sauce, or other special treats. Your host, a real estate agent, enjoys travel, cooking, and music.

No. Rooms: 1	**Breakfast:** Full
Singles: None	**S-Rates:** $62 sb
Doubles: 1 sb	**D-Rates:** $68 sb
Type: Private home	**Bldg:** Victorian

Minimum Stay: 2 nights. **Credit Cards Accepted:** MC, V. **Open:** all year. No resident dogs. No dogs please. Resident cat. No cats please. Nonsmoking host. Guests may smoke in living room. Residence not appropriate for children. **Discounts:** 10% weekly.

Reservation Contact: Bed & Breakfast International, Jean Brown, 1181-B Solano Ave., Albany, CA 94706; 415–525–4569.

GHIRARDELLI SQUARE, FISHERMAN'S WHARF.

Near Bay St., U.S. 101.

This California craftsman-style home, built in 1924, is one block from Fisherman's Wharf and the cable car. There are three guest rooms, each with private bath. The Garden Room and the Fuchsia Room are separated from the common rooms by a hall, offering a sense of privacy. The Garden Room has a king-sized bed, bedside phone, cable TV, table, and easy chairs. Because it is in the back of the house, it has a garden view, and street noise is eliminated. The Fuchsia Room is smaller and has a similar decor. The Redwood Room has been newly constructed and may be entered from Bay Street. It has redwood paneling, chairs and table, and garage parking is available. A Full breakfast is served. The exceptional quality of the home lies not so much in the furnishings as in the quality of hospitality. A lifetime resident of the area, your host is skilled at helping people plan where to go and how to get there. *Cordon Bleu* trained, he is one of the culinary authorities in the Bay area. Free parking, very unusual for this area, is offered.

No. Rooms: 3	**Breakfast:** Full
Singles: None	**S-Rates:** $62–$82 pb
Doubles: 3 pb	**D-Rates:** $68–$88 pb
Type: Private home	**Bldg:** 1924 California Craftsman

Minimum Stay: 2 nights. **Credit Card(s) Accepted:** none. **Open:** all year. Dog in residence. No dogs please. No resident cats. No cats please. Host smokes. Guests may smoke. Children welcome with restrictions. **Discounts:** 10% weekly. German & Italian spoken.

Reservation Contact: Bed & Breakfast International, Jean Brown, 1181-B Solano Ave., Albany, CA 94706; 415–525–4569.

ID: INTNAT164

PACIFIC HEIGHTS, JAPAN CENTER.

Near U.S. 101, Washington & Filmore sts.

The San Francisco fire stopped just short of this 1876 house, sparing it and many other Victorian homes on this street. The location is close to the Japan Center and many interesting restaurants. The house, which boasts marble fireplaces, has furnishings not easily categorized since your host collects antiques, fine modern art, and displays her own work as a silk screen designer. The guest quarters consist of a two-room suite with fifteen-foot ceilings, a fireplace, a deck, antique furnishings, twin beds in one room and a single bed in the other, and private bath. Guests also have access to a small kitchen for preparing light snacks. A two-room cottage is also available at the rear of the house. It has a queen-sized bed, full kitchen, enclosed patio, private entrance, and private bath. Television, telephone, and laundry facilities are available. A Full breakfast is served. Your host is interested in antiques and historic preservation.

No. Rooms: 2	**Breakfast:** Full
Singles: None	**S-Rates:** $62–$82 pb
Doubles: 2 pb	**D-Rates:** $68–$88 pb
Type: Private home	**Bldg:** 1876 Italianate Victorian

Minimum Stay: none. **Credit Card(s) Accepted:** MC, V. **Open:** all year. No resident dogs. No dogs please. No resident cats. No cats please. Host smokes. Guests may smoke in residence. Children welcome. **Discounts:** weekly 10%; family 20%.

Reservation Contact: Bed & Breakfast International, Jean Brown, 1181-B Solano Ave., Albany, CA 94706; 415–525–4569.

Near 5th & California sts. U.S. 101.

Although this turn-of-the-century home does not conform to any one style, everything in it is distinctly beautiful. Registry Service Organization manager Jean Brown claims it's the most interesting and tastefully decorated of all the homes she's visited. The fragrance of eucalyptus leaves in the entryway greets guests when they arrive. The grand piano in the living room is always in tune and frequently in use. Fine original art adorns the walls, and prize collections of candelabra, antique glass paperweights, and snuff boxes are found throughout. The library is overflowing, and a wooden deck in the backyard is perfect for sunbathing. The second-floor guest room, with double bed, down quilt, and private bath, has two large windows from which to view the colorful Victorian houses lining the street. The sleeping area has bookshelves along one wall, many fine prints, and a rocking chair. The sitting area has a nonworking fireplace, small antique sofa, tables, and chairs. The two third-floor rooms, which share a guest bath, are entered from a central hall. One room has a double bed; the other has both a double and a single. Each has a table, chairs, dressers, and luggage racks. One has a street view, while the other looks out on the exquisite back garden. A Full gourmet breakfast is served. This conveniently located home offers easy access to moderately priced fine restaurants, Golden Gate Park, and the downtown area. The Presidio jogging path is a block away, and public transportation is good. Your hosts, a retired architect and a graphic artist, enjoy showing visitors around the city. Their interests include music, literature, public affairs, and gourmet cooking.

No. Rooms: 3
Singles: None
Doubles: 1 pb, 2 sb
Type: Private home

Breakfast: Full
S-Rates: $56 pb, $44 sb
D-Rates: $68 pb, $48 sb
Bldg: 1906 turn-of-the-century

Minimum Stay: 2 nights. **Credit Card(s) Accepted:** none. **Open:** all year. Dog in residence. No dogs please. No resident cats. No cats please. Host smokes. Guests may smoke. Children welcome. **Discounts:** none.

Reservation Contact: Bed & Breakfast International, Jean Brown, 1181-B Solano Ave., Albany, CA 94706; 415–525–4569.

MONTEREY HEIGHTS/SUNSET DISTRICT, ZOO, GOLDEN GATE PARK.

Near CA Hwy. 1, Monterey Blvd.

Located in the Monterey Heights/Sunset District, this Mediterranean-style home is easily accessible for those driving to the city since there are no steep hills to negotiate. The home is near the beach, zoo, and Golden Gate Park. There is a two-room guest suite with a private deck and private entrance. The living room has a bar with refrigerator, sink, microwave, and coffee maker. Furnishings include a piano, bookshelves, sofa, table and chairs, and queen-sized bed. Guests have a panoramic view of the ocean and Golden Gate Park. Telephone, TV, and area tours are available. Breakfast might include an asparagus-and-mushroom omelet or spinach quiche, muffins, juice, and coffee. The host is a realtor who likes opera, art, and archaeology. She is also in a volunteer city-guide program.

No. Rooms: 1	**Breakfast:** Full
Singles: None	**S-Rates:** $62 pb
Doubles: 1 pb	**D-Rates:** $68 pb
Type: Private home	**Bldg:** Mediterranean

Minimum Stay: none. **Credit Card(s) Accepted:** MC, V. **Open:** all year. No resident dogs. No dogs please. No resident cats. No cats please. Non-smoking host. Guest may smoke in residence. Children welcome. **Discounts:** 10% weekly.

Reservation Contact: Bed & Breakfast International, Jean Brown, 1181-B Solano Ave., Albany, CA 94706; 415–525–4569.

ID: #01–AMFAM

NOB HILL.

Near Manson & Sacramento sts., U.S. 101.

This small Victorian "doll house" on Nob Hill is near the cable cars, Fisherman's Wharf, and Union Square. Downtown San Francisco is a five-minute walk from here. Two guest rooms, with a shared guest bath, are available. One has an antique double bed and antique chair and dresser; the other, with twin beds, has wicker furniture as well as some antique pieces. A Full breakfast is served. Your host spent twenty years in the foreign service in Australia, France, England, and Germany.

No. Rooms: 2	**Breakfast:** Full
Singles: None	**S-Rates:** $50 sb
Doubles: 2 sb	**D-Rates:** $60 sb
Type: Private home	**Bldg:** 1890 Victorian

Minimum Stay: 2 weekend nights. **Credit Card(s) Accepted:** none. **Open:** all year. No resident dogs. No dogs please. No resident cats. No cats please. Nonsmoking host. Guests may not smoke in guest rooms. Children welcome with restrictions. **Discounts:** none. French spoken.

Reservation Contact: American Family Inn/B&B San Francisco, Susan & Richard Kreibich, Box 349, San Francisco, CA 94101; 415–931–3083.

HAIGHT AREA.

Near Baker St., U.S. 101.

This Queen Anne home, built in 1895 on three city lots, is one of San Francisco's most beautiful and most loved buildings, located in the area known as Haight Ashbury in the 60s. Your host traveled to London to purchase original patterns for the lace net curtains, chintz, linens, and perfume bottles. Each room is unique, with specially selected items. Three of the six rooms have private baths, with three sharing a bath. One of the rooms has chintz padded walls, velvet drapes, lace curtains, an Oriental rug, queen-sized bed, antique furniture, and private bath, as well as a view of the park. The other rooms, one done in yellow, one with an old rose print, and one in aqua, have similar decor. Three have double beds, and one has twin beds with a king-sized headboard. A Full breakfast is served in the grand dining room with an ornate ceiling. The living-room, with walls padded in silk, is decorated for guests' comfort. The entire house is done in a gracious old-world manner and perfect for guests celebrating that special occasion. Because your hosts are wine merchants and import French copper cookware, they travel to France quite often. One of your hosts is a horseback-riding enthusiast, and both enjoy cooking and entertaining.

No. Rooms: 6
Singles: None
Doubles: 3 pb, 3 sb
Type: Private home

Breakfast: Full
S-Rates: $135 pb, $85 sb
D-Rates: $135 pb, $85 sb
Bldg: 1895 Queen Anne tower

Minimum Stay: 2 weekend nights. **Credit Card(s) Accepted:** none.

Open: all year. Dog in residence. No dogs please. Cat in residence. No cats please. Nonsmoking host. Guests may not smoke in residence. Residence not appropriate for children. **Discounts:** none. Some French spoken.

Reservation Contact: American Family Inn/B&B San Francisco, Susan & Richard Kreibich, Box 349, San Francisco, CA 94101; 415–931–3083.

ID: 05–AMFAM

DIAMOND HEIGHTS AREA.

Near Diamond Hts. Blvd., I–280.

This contemporary home, located in a quiet neighborhood on the western slope of Diamond Heights, is only one mile from the famous Twin Peaks. Near the geographical center of the city, it offers a panoramic view that is both urban and rustic. The house is within walking distance of a shopping center, restaurants, tennis courts, and two playgrounds. It is also near public transportation, including the BART and Muni Metro, one mile from I–280, and twenty minutes from the airport. Three guest rooms share two full baths. The first is a charming room with queen-sized bed, double dresser with mirror, TV, wall-to-wall carpeting and large window, framing Glen Canyon Park with its eucalyptus grove, and Mt. Davidson, the city's highest point. The second room, with twin beds, is similarly furnished and shares the same view. Excellent for families of up to four, the third large cheerful room has a double bed and two single beds. It contains a sitting area with two love seats, TV, piano, and books for relaxation. A Full gourmet breakfast is served. A crib, high chair, ice, telephone, maps, and tourist information are all available. Your hosts, a research analyst and an attorney, though European born, are long-time residents of San Francisco. One of your hosts was instrumental in saving the city's cable-car system several years ago. Both have traveled widely, are active in community organizations, enjoy spoiling their grandchildren, and take pleasure in discussing the world with their guests.

No. Rooms: 3	**Breakfast:** Full
Singles: None	**S-Rates:** $50 sb
Doubles: 3 sb	**D-Rates:** $60 sb
Type: Private home	**Bldg:** 1967 contemporary

Minimum Stay: 2 nights. **Credit Card(s) Accepted:** none. **Open:** all year. No resident dogs. No dogs please. No resident cats. No cats please. Nonsmoking host. Guests may not smoke in guest rooms. Children welcome. **Discounts:** none. German & Swedish spoken.

Reservation Contact: American Family Inn/B&B San Francisco, Susan & Richard Kreibich, Box 349, San Francisco, CA 94101; 415–931–3083.

ID: 06–AMFAM

PALACE OF FINE ARTS, GOLDEN GATE BRIDGE, MARINA AREA.

Near Lombard & Divisidero, U.S. 101.

Although part of old San Francisco, this charming flat, just two blocks from the Palace of Fine Arts and three blocks from the Marina, is well-maintained. Visitors can walk along the bay to Golden Gate Bridge, a scenic and charming route. Conveniently located near all transportation, shopping, and many tourist sights, these accommodations offer a two-room guest suite overlooking an Italian garden. The sitting room has two chairs draped in French antique fabric, a sofa, TV, and telephone. The spacious bedroom features a French antique brass double bed, ferns, and a large closet. A Full breakfast is served. Your host is a psychologist interested in people, travel, fashion design, and good conversation.

No. Rooms: 1	**Breakfast:** Full
Singles: None	**S-Rates:** $60 sb
Doubles: 1 sb	**D-Rates:** $65 sb
Type: Private home	**Bldg:** 1940 marina flat

Minimum Stay: 2 nights. **Credit Card(s) Accepted:** none. **Open:** all year. No resident dogs. No dogs please. No resident cats. No cats please. Nonsmoking host. Guests may not smoke in residence. Residence not appropriate for children. **Discounts:** 7th night free.

Reservation Contact: American Family Inn/B&B San Francisco, Susan & Richard Kreibich, Box 349, San Francisco, CA 94101; 415–931–3083.

ID: 08–AMFAM

FISHERMAN'S WHARF, TELEGRAPH HILL, CHINATOWN, COIT TOWER, NORTH BEACH AREA.

Near Bay & Columbus, U.S. 101, I–80.

This Victorian stucco home is in the area in which San Francisco was first settled. Fisherman's Wharf, Telegraph Hill, North Beach, Chinatown, Coit Tower, and the cable cars are all within walking distance. The two guest rooms share a bath with the host. One of the rooms has a king-sized bed, fireplace, and sitting area, with bay window and comfortable wing chairs. The other room has a double bed, dresser, and cuddly teddy bear collection. You will find fresh flowers, a fruit basket, water, ice, TV, and a telephone in your room, and there is also a bicycle available for your use. A Full breakfast is served at a table in front of the window in the guests' room. Your host, a flight attendant with an international airline for twenty years, owns an art gallery and an antique shop.

No. Rooms: 2	**Breakfast:** Full
Singles: None	**S-Rates:** $45–$55 sb
Doubles: 2 sb	**D-Rates:** $55–$65 sb
Type: Private home	**Bldg:** 1920 Victorian stucco

Minimum Stay: 2 nights. **Credit Card(s) Accepted:** none. **Open:** all year. No resident dogs. No dogs please. No resident cats. No cats please. Nonsmoking host. Guests may not smoke in residence. Residence not appropriate for children. **Discounts:** none. Greek spoken.

Reservation Contact: American Family Inn/B&B San Francisco, Susan & Richard Kreibich, Box 349, San Francisco, CA 94101; 415–931–3083.

ID: 09–AMFAM

SYMPHONY HALL, OPERA HOUSE, CIVIC CENTER, CITY HALL, UNION SQUARE; ALAMO SQUARE HISTORIC DISTRICT.

Near Grove, U.S. 101.

Perhaps the most photographed house in America, this Queen Anne Victorian is now a designated landmark, as are all the other houses in Alamo Square, an area of rapid gentrification. The house has appeared in three movies, thirty TV commercials, and on magazine covers, book jackets, and postcards. Conveniently located, it is six blocks from Symphony Hall, the Opera House, City Hall, and the Civic Center, and a mere fifteen-minute walk to Union Square. This house, as well as the other houses in the row, were built by Matthew C. Kavanagh, a carpenter/builder. Scheduled for demolition in 1975, the residence was saved and has been almost totally restored by its current owners. The interior includes a stained-glass skylight in the central hall, plus seven other stained-glass windows. The gilded mirror in the main parlor was purchased by the Fulton family in New York City in 1872 and shipped to their home in San Francisco, where it remained until purchased for this house in 1975. All the light fixtures on the main floor are working gaslights. The two-room guest suite consists of a front bedroom with a four-window view overlooking Alamo Square Park, a working fireplace, a handmade (by owner) custom steel four-poster bed, Chinese, Korean, and English antiques, and private bath. The library, a smaller side room, has twin beds that can be made into a double. A Full breakfast is served. Your hosts are a photographer-turned-furniture manufacturer and a doctor.

No. Rooms: 1	**Breakfast:** Full
Singles: None	**S-Rates:** $85 pb
Doubles: 1 pb	**D-Rates:** $85 pb
Type: Private home	**Bldg:** 1890 Victorian

Minimum Stay: 2 weekend nights. **Credit Card(s) Accepted:** none. **Open:** all year. Dog in residence. No dogs please. Cat in residence. No cats please. Nonsmoking host. Guests may not smoke in residence. Children welcome with restrictions. **Discounts:** none.

Reservation Contact: American Family Inn/B&B San Francisco, Susan & Richard Kreibich, Box 349, San Francisco, CA 94101; 415–931–3083.

ID: 10–AMFAM

DOLORES PARK AREA, COUNTRY COTTAGE.

Near Dolores & Market sts., U.S. 101.

Located on a quiet street away from the city noise, this cozy country cottage home, built in 1900, is in an historic area of the city, close to Mission Dolores, San Francisco's oldest building. All four guest rooms have private entrances but share two baths. The Patio Room is decorated in peach and blue tones, with an antique brass double bed, antique furnishings, and French doors, which open out to a fragrant flower-filled patio. The Brass Room is a large bedroom, done in rose tones, with a queen-sized brass bed and antique dresser. The Blue Room has French windows on all sides that open out to a patio, a queen-sized oak bed, and antique furniture. A fourth room has a large pine bed. A Full breakfast is served in the sunny kitchen, and complimentary wine is available for guests. Your hosts, retired professional ice skaters, are experts on San Francisco and enjoy helping guests get to know their city. Both are world travelers who enjoy sailing, biking, and restaurants.

No. Rooms: 3	**Breakfast:** Full
Singles: None	**S-Rates:** $50 sb
Doubles: 3 sb	**D-Rates:** $60 sb
Type: Private home	**Bldg:** 1900 country cottage

Minimum Stay: 2 weekend nights. **Credit Card(s) Accepted:** AE, MC, V. **Open:** all year. No resident dogs. No dogs please. No resident cats. No cats please. Nonsmoking host. Guests may not smoke in residence. Children welcome with restrictions. **Discounts:** none. German & Russian spoken.

Reservation Contact: American Family Inn/B&B San Francisco, Susan & Richard Kreibich, Box 349, San Francisco, CA 94101; 415–931–3083.

ID: 18–AMFAM

RUSSIAN HILL.

Near Lombard and Hyde sts.

Guests thoroughly enjoy this unit located on Russian Hill, half a block away from the Hyde Street cable car and the Alice Marble Tennis Courts. For those who enjoy walking, Fisherman's Wharf, North Beach, Chinatown, and Union Street are easily reached. This cottage, built in 1908, is situated in a quiet area on Lombard Street, "the crookedest street in the world." Guests stay in a separate, recently remodeled apartment with private entrance, living room, bedroom, kitchen, bath, gas-burning fireplace, private garden, and a view of Coit Tower and North Beach. Furnishings include a brass bed with a down comforter, wicker furniture, color TV, and a clock radio. A Full breakfast is served. Other amenities include a bottle of wine, fresh fruit, fresh-ground coffee, and premium teas. The hosts have traveled extensively in the United States, Europe, and Asia.

No. Rooms: 1	**Breakfast:** Full
Singles: None	**S-Rates:** $110 pb
Doubles: 1 pb	**D-Rates:** $110 pb
Type: Private home	**Bldg:** Cottage

Minimum Stay: none. **Credit Card(s) Accepted:** AE, MC, V. **Open:** all year. No resident dog. No dogs please. No resident cat. No cats please. Hosts smoke. Guests may smoke. Residence not appropriate for children. **Discounts:** none. German spoken.

Reservation Contact: American Family Inn/B&B San Francisco, Susan & Richard Kreibich, Box 349, San Francisco, CA 94101; 415–931–3083.

ID: 19–AMFAM

U. OF C. MEDICAL SCHOOL, GOLDEN GATE PARK, DE YOUNG MUSEUM, JAPANESE TEA GARDEN.

Near Judah & Kirkham sts.

Adjacent to the University of California Medical School and two blocks from Golden Gate Park, this Edwardian-style home is within easy walking distance of restaurants, tennis courts, and a children's playground with a vintage 1912 carousel. The house boasts fine antique furniture, stained-glass entry windows, Edwardian architectural details, and beautiful views. It offers a penthouse apartment, fully carpeted, with fireplace, private deck, kitchen, queen-sized hide-a-bed sofa, king-sized bed, private bath, and views of the Golden Gate Bridge and the Marin headlands. Supplies for a Full breakfast are provided. Your hosts enjoy music, reading, antiquing, and travel.

No. Rooms: 1	**Breakfast:** Full
Singles: None	**S-Rates:** $70 pb
Doubles: 1 pb	**D-Rates:** $70 pb
Type: Private home	**Bldg:** Edwardian

Minimum Stay: none. **Credit Card(s) Accepted:** AE, MC, V. **Open:** all year. Resident dog. No dogs please. No resident cat. No cats please. Non-smoking hosts. Guests may not smoke. Children welcome. **Discounts:** 7th night free.

Reservation Contact: American Family Inn/B&B San Francisco, Susan & Richard Kreibich, Box 349, San Francisco, CA 94101; 415–931–3083.

DOLORES HEIGHTS; SPECTACULAR CITY VIEWS.

Near Noe & Sanchez sts.

This contemporary home offers fantastic views of the city and was designed by the owner/architect. It is located on a steep hill known as Dolores Heights, just southwest of the oldest building in San Francisco, Dolores Mission. It overlooks the historical Mission District to the east, the Castro District to the west, and the Noe Valley to the south. The two guest rooms have private baths. The first is a large, well-furnished room with a panoramic view of downtown San Francisco, the Bay, Oakland, and Berkeley. It has a large bay window, sofa, easy chair, small refrigerator, and separate dressing area. The fireplace can be enjoyed from the two-person Jaccuzzi set into one wall. The other, smaller room is attractively furnished with antiques and also has a good view of the Bay. A Full English-style breakfast is served. Your hosts are an interesting couple who enjoy travel, the out-of-doors, classical music, and good food.

No. Rooms: 2	**Breakfast:** Full
Singles: None	**S-Rates:** $60–$95 pb
Doubles: 2 pb	**D-Rates:** $65–$100 pb
Type: Private home	**Bldg:** Contemporary

Minimum Stay: none. **Credit Card(s) Accepted:** AE, MC, V. **Open:** all year. Resident dog. A dog is allowed with restrictions. No resident cats. No cats please. Nonsmoking hosts. Guests may not smoke. Children welcome. **Discounts:** none.

Reservation Contact: American Family Inn/B&B San Francisco, Susan & Richard Kreibich, Box 349, San Francisco, CA 94101; 415–931–3083.

ALAMO SQUARE.

Near hwys. 101, 280.

Located in the historic district of Alamo Square, this Victorian home, with five guest rooms, affords a postcard view. Two of the rooms have queen-sized brass beds and private baths. Another room has willow furniture, queen-sized bed, fireplace, and private bath. Two other rooms, one with a queen-sized bed and one with twin beds, share a bath. A Full breakfast is served. Guests are welcome to use the common areas of the house. Your hosts are former ice skaters whose current hobbies include photography, video, travel, and sailing.

No. Rooms: 5	**Breakfast:** Full
Singles: None	**S-Rates:** $65 pb, $60 sb
Doubles: 3 pb, 2 sb	**D-Rates:** $75 pb, $65 sb
Type: Private home	**Bldg:** Victorian

Minimum Stay: none. **Credit Card(s) Accepted:** AE, MC, V. **Open:** all year. No resident dogs. No dogs please. No resident cats. No cats please.

Nonsmoking host. Guests may not smoke in residence. Residence not appropriate for children. **Discounts:** none. German spoken.

Reservation Contact: American Family Inn/B&B San Francisco, Susan & Richard Kreibich, Box 349, San Francisco, CA 94101; 415–931–3083.

ID: 94108PET

NOB HILL AREA, UNION SQUARE, THEATER DISTRICT, CHINATOWN, CIVIC CENTER.

Near Taylor & Bush sts., U.S. 101.

Conveniently located, this elegant little 1900s Baroque inn offers romantic comfort with French country-style decor. Each room is beautifully decorated with antiques, pastel wall coverings, fluffy quilts, handmade pillows, and fresh fruits and flowers. Most rooms have fireplaces; all have private baths. There is turn-down service every evening, as well as afternoon tea and hors d'oeuvres. Your hosts will be happy to light the fireplace, polish your shoes, or arrange for theater tickets. A generous country breakfast is served in a cheerful room with garden view.

No. Rooms: 26	**Breakfast:** Full
Singles: None	**S-Rates:** $105–$195 pb
Doubles: 26 pb	**D-Rates:** $105–$195 pb
Type: Inn	**Bldg:** 1919 Baroque

Minimum Stay: none. **Credit Card(s) Accepted:** AE, Discover, MC, V. **Open:** all year. No resident dogs. No dogs please. No resident cats. No cats please. Nonsmoking host. Guests may not smoke in common areas. Children welcome. **Discounts:** none. French & Cantonese spoken.

Reservation Contact: Bed & Breakfast Registry Ltd., Gary Winget, Box 8174, St. Paul, MN 55108; 612–646–4238.

ID: 94108SWA

NOB HILL, CHINATOWN, CIVIC CENTER.

Near Taylor & Bush sts., U.S. 101.

The charming serenity of an English guesthouse and the graceful sophistication of cosmopolitan San Francisco are tastefully combined at this elegant country inn. You are greeted with curved bay windows, fresh flowers, cozy quilts, handsome antiques, overstuffed chairs, fresh fruit, and a refreshing garden retreat. All the rooms, including the living room, dining room, conference room, and library are tastefully appointed in rich warm woods. The twenty-six guest rooms are individually decorated; each has a fireplace, refrigerator, private bath, telephone, and color TV. A Continental Plus breakfast is served in the dining room or in the garden room. In the afternoon, tea and hors d'oeuvres are served in the library and living room where you may gather in front of the welcoming fire.

Sherry is served in the evening. Your hosts will gladly make dinner, theater, or symphony reservations, see that your shoes are polished, and
make sure that the morning newspaper waits outside your door.

No. Rooms: 26	**Breakfast:** Full
Singles: None	**S-Rates:** $145–$250 pb
Doubles: 26 pb	**D-Rates:** $145–$250 pb
Type: Inn	**Bldg:** 1908 English design

Minimum Stay: none. **Credit Card(s) Accepted:** AE, Discover, MC, V.
Open: all year. No resident dogs. No dogs please. No resident cats. No
cats please. Nonsmoking host. Guests may smoke in guest rooms. Children welcome. **Discounts:** none. French & Cantonese spoken.

Reservation Contact: Bed & Breakfast Registry Ltd., Gary Winget, Box
8174, St. Paul, MN 55108; 612–646–4238.

ID: 94122MIC

GOLDEN GATE PARK, DE YOUNG MUSEUM, STEINHART AQUARIUM, JAPANESE TEA GARDENS.

Near Judah & Irving sts., Rte. 1.

This charming Edwardian-era house with leaded stained-glass cabinets
has three guest rooms. The first is a light and airy room done in shades
of mint and cream, and furnished with an English armoir, fully equipped
adjoining kitchen, outside deck, and double bed. The second is a regal-
looking blue room, with double bed and cherry flower-filled window
box. The spacious third guest room is done in dusty rose and has a
custom-made king-sized bed. You will find fresh flowers in the hallway
and guest rooms, and down comforters on the beds. A split bath is
shared. A Continental breakfast of fresh juice, hot croissants and/or
scones, muffins, freshly ground coffee or tea is served. A variety of shops
and excellent restaurants are nearby. Your delightful English hosts are interested in soccer, travel, calligraphy, architecture, and music.

No. Rooms: 3	**Breakfast:** Continental
Singles: None	**S-Rates:** $35 sb
Doubles: 3 sb	**D-Rates:** $45 sb
Type: Private home	**Bldg:** Edwardian

Minimum Stay: none. **Credit Card(s) Accepted:** none. **Open:** all year.
Dog in residence. No dogs please. No resident cats. No cats please. Nonsmoking host. Guests may not smoke in residence. Children are allowed
with restrictions. **Discounts:** none. French spoken.

Reservation Contact: Bed & Breakfast Registry Ltd., Gary Winget, Box
8174, St. Paul, MN 55108; 612–646–4238.

ID: 94122MOF

GOLDEN GATE PARK AREA, SHOPPING.

Near Lincoln Way & 7th Ave., CA 1.

This 1910 Edwardian home is in a pleasant neighborhood near Golden Gate Park and the University of California Medical Center. Public transportation is excellent and pleasant shops are nearby. There are four guest rooms with twin, double, or queen-sized beds. One of the rooms can accommodate four people. Baths are shared. A self-serve Continental breakfast is provided.

No. Rooms: 4	**Breakfast:** Continental
Singles: 1 sb	**S-Rates:** $30 sb
Doubles: 3 sb	**D-Rates:** $50 sb
Type: Private home	**Bldg:** 1910 Edwardian

Minimum Stay: none. **Credit Card(s) Accepted:** none. **Open:** all year. No resident dogs. No dogs please. Resident cat. No cats please. Non-smoking host. Guests may not smoke in residence. Children welcome. **Discounts:** none. Spanish and French spoken.

Reservation Contact: Bed & Breakfast Registry Ltd., Gary Winget, Box 8174, St. Paul, MN 55108; 612–646–4238.

ID: 94123ARA

PACIFIC HEIGHTS, FISHERMAN'S WHARF, GHIRARDELLI SQUARE, AQUATIC PARK, UNION STREET SHOPS.

Near Union & Van Ness sts., U.S. 101.

This lovely Victorian home is located in the Pacific Heights area near Fisherman's Wharf, Ghirardelli Square, the Aquatic Park, and the Palace of Fine Arts. A block away visitors will find the unique shops of Union Street as well as a bus that takes them to North Beach. The three guest rooms share a bath. The first has a king-sized bed, antique furnishings including a loveseat, hardwood floors, an area rug, TV, and a bright window facing the street. The second has a double bed and French provincial furnishings, while the third, also with a double bed, is smaller and is used only as a single room. A Continental breakfast is served.

No. Rooms: 3	**Breakfast:** Continental
Singles: 1 sb	**S-Rates:** $50–$55 sb
Doubles: 2 sb	**D-Rates:** $70 sb
Type: Private home	**Bldg:** 1890 Victorian

Minimum Stay: none. **Credit Card(s) Accepted:** none. **Open:** all year. No resident dogs. No dogs please. No resident cats. No cats please. Non-smoking host. Guests may not smoke in residence. Children welcome. **Discounts:** none. Spanish spoken.

Reservation Contact: Bed & Breakfast Registry Ltd., Gary Winget, Box 8174, St. Paul, MN 55108; 612–646–4238.

ID: 94123ART

FISHERMAN'S WHARF, MARITIME MUSEUM, TEN MINUTES TO DOWNTOWN.

Near Lombard St. & Van Ness Ave., US 101.

This unique B&B caters to artists, although non-artists are certainly welcome. It offers four suites with private baths. One is a three-room apartment with living room, bedroom with queen-sized bed, and kitchen. There are two two-room apartments with queen-sized beds, extra single beds, fireplaces, and kitchens. There is also a large studio apartment with a double bed, coffee bar, and private street entrance. All suites have color TV, radio, and use of the garden and patio. A Continental Plus breakfast is served. Within a block there is a public parking garage and city bus service to all points. One of your hosts is an artist who offers Saturday classes; the other is a printer and publisher. Their other interests include history, the Bible, travel, and boating.

No. Rooms: 4	**Breakfast:** Continental Plus
Singles: None	**S-Rates:** $65–$115 pb
Doubles: 4 pb	**D-Rates:** $65–$115 pb
Type: Inn	**Bldg:** 1857 townhouse

Minimum Stay: none. **Credit Card(s) Accepted:** AE, DC, MC, V. **Open:** all year. Dog in residence. No dogs please. No resident cats. No cats please. Nonsmoking host. Guests may not smoke in residence. Children welcome. **Discounts:** none. Finnish spoken.

Reservation Contact: Bed & Breakfast Registry Ltd., Gary Winget, Box 8174, St. Paul, MN 55108; 612–646–4238.

ID: 94127CAS

FOREST HILL AREA, UNIVERSITY OF CALIFORNIA MEDICAL CENTER, GOLDEN GATE PARK.

Near Portola & Claremont, Rte. 1.

This cozy cottage, perched high on a hill, provides a lovely view of the city. It has a fireplace, alcove with desk, two twin beds, kitchen furnished with all necessary condiments, dining area, and private bath.

No. Rooms: 1	**Breakfast:** Continental
Singles: None	**S-Rates:** $65 pb
Doubles: 1 pb	**D-Rates:** $70 pb
Type: Private home	**Bldg:** Cottage

Minimum Stay: 2 nights. **Credit Card(s) Accepted:** none. **Open:** all year. Host's dog resides in a separate area. No dogs please. Host's cat resides in a separate area. **Discounts:** none. Spanish spoken.

Reservation Contact: Bed & Breakfast Registry Ltd., Gary Winget, Box 8174, St. Paul, MN 55108; 612–646–4238.

SANTA ANA   ID: 92706CRA

L.A. AREA, DISNEYLAND, KNOTT'S BERRY FARM, NEWPORT BEACH, MARINELAND, BOWERS MUSEUM.

Near Main & 17th sts., I–5, Rte. 22.

This craftsman-style home, built in 1910, has two guest rooms. Both have double beds, TVs, telephones, and a shared bath. One is furnished in Danish pine antiques, the other in American oak. There is a large yard and deck area, where guests can enjoy meals or just relax. You are also welcome to use the living and dining rooms. Staying at this handsomely restored home puts you close to many local attractions. Arrival/departure transportation and additional meals are available. Your cordial hosts are interested in old homes, antiques, computers, travel, sewing, and cooking.

No. Rooms: 2	**Breakfast:** Continental Plus
Singles: None	**S-Rates:** $40 pb, $40 sb
Doubles: 2 sb	**D-Rates:** $65 pb, $65 sb
Type: Private home	**Bldg:** 1910 craftsman-style

Minimum Stay: 2 nights. **Credit Card(s) Accepted:** none. **Open:** all year. No resident dogs. No dogs please. No resident cats. No cats please. Nonsmoking host. Guests may not smoke in residence. Children are welcome with restrictions. **Discounts:** none. Danish & Swedish spoken.

Reservation Contact: Bed & Breakfast Registry Ltd., Gary Winget, Box 8174, St. Paul, MN 55108; 612–646–4238.

SANTA BARBARA   ID: INTNAT155

GOLETA BEACH, U.C. SANTA BARBARA.

Near Turnpike Rd./Cathedral Oaks, U.S. 101.

This luxurious ranch-style home is in a peaceful neighborhood on a hill north of downtown Santa Barbara. The house is surrounded by a flower-filled patio and oak trees, and it has a panoramic view of the Santa Ynez Mountains and the ocean. Guests can watch the sun set over the Pacific. Each of the two guest rooms opens onto the patio and therefore has a private entrance. In addition to the full bath, which the rooms share, each room has a walk-in dressing room with a sink, fine contemporary furnishings, and double beds. There is also an office with a bed which could be used for an extra person. Only members of the same party are accommodated. Breakfast includes gourmet omelets and homemade bread. Your hosts are active in community affairs.

No. Rooms: 2	**Breakfast:** Full
Singles: None	**S-Rates:** $52–$62 sb
Doubles: 2 sb	**D-Rates:** $58–$68 sb
Type: Private home	**Bldg:** Spanish-style

Minimum Stay: 2 nights. **Credit Card(s) Accepted:** AE, MC, V. **Open:** all year. No resident dogs. No dogs please. No resident cats. No cats please. Nonsmoking host. Guests may not smoke in residence. Children welcome. **Discounts:** 10% weekly, 20% families.

Reservation Contact: Bed & Breakfast International, Jean Brown, 1181-B Solano Ave., Albany, CA 94706; 415–525–4569.

ID: 93101BLU

MUSEUMS, SANTA BARBARA MISSION, WHARF.

Near Bath & Mission sts., U.S. 101.

This small B&B inn, set back from the street, is composed of a main house and several cottages that surround two private garden areas. The furnishings are early American. Single rooms and suites are available with private or shared baths. Hot apple cider is served each evening in the living room. Bikes and arrival/departure transportation are available. The inn is located one mile from downtown and three miles from the beach, an easy bike ride. Your well-traveled host is interested in sewing, dining, travel, and wines.

No. Rooms: 8	**Breakfast:** Continental Plus
Singles: None	**S-Rates:** $55–$85 pb, $65–$80 sb
Doubles: 6 pb, 2 sb	**D-Rates:** $55–85 pb, $65–$80 sb
Type: Inn	**Bldg:** 1915 California bungalow

Minimum Stay: 2 nights on weekends. **Credit Card(s) Accepted:** MC, V. **Open:** all year, except Christmas. Dog in residence. No dogs please. No resident cats. No cats please. Nonsmoking host. Guests may not smoke in residence. Children welcome with restrictions. **Discounts:** none.

Reservation Contact: Bed & Breakfast Registry Ltd., Gary Winget, Box 8174, St. Paul, MN 55108; 612–646–4238.

ID: 93101VIL

BEACH, ZOOLOGICAL GARDENS; OCEAN VIEWS.

Near Cabeillo Blvd., U.S. 101.

This half-century-old Spanish Mediterranean building has been completely renovated and transformed into an intimate little B&B inn. Some guest rooms enjoy a mountain view, while others overlook the harbor. The inn features fireplaces, sunken baths, plantation shutters, and French doors. Suites with sitting rooms and dinettes are available. All rooms have private baths and telephones. Guests may use the outdoor heated pool and Jacuzzi. Continental breakfast is served in your room, outdoors, or in the lounge area. Complimentary sherry and port are served 9–11 P.M. Beds are turned down in the evening, with a rose and a mint left on your pillow. The inn is 84 steps to the beach and within walking distance to shops and restaurants.

No. Rooms: 18	**Breakfast:** Continental
Singles: None	**S-Rates:** $90–$185 pb
Doubles: 18 pb	**D-Rates:** $90–$185 pb
Type: Inn	**Bldg:** 1930s Mediterranean

Minimum Stay: 2 nights. **Credit Card(s) Accepted:** AE, MC, V. **Open:** all year. No resident dogs. No dogs please. No resident cats. No cats please. Nonsmoking host. Guests may smoke. Children welcome with restrictions. **Discounts:** none.

Reservation Contact: Bed & Breakfast Registry Ltd., Gary Winget, Box 8174, St. Paul, MN 55108; 612–646–4238.

ID: 93108VAL

COASTAL AREA, SANTA BARBARA MISSION, UNIVERSITY OF CALIFORNIA, MOUNTAINS, BEACHES.

Near Olive Mill & Sycamore Canyon, U.S. 101.

This contemporary ranch-style house features fireplace, grand piano, sunny decks, garden, and mountain view. There are two guest rooms. The first is charmingly furnished, with coordinated drapes, double bed, antique dresser, highboy, and accent table. The other guest room has been professionally decorated and has queen-sized bed and designer drapes. There is a large master bath with sunken tub and separate shower that overlooks the fenced fern garden. Sliding glass doors provide a private entrance. The home is located near beaches, mountains, golf courses, and tennis courts. Arrival/departure transportation and child care are available if prearranged. A Full breakfast is served. Evenings, enjoy a cup of Cafe Mocha or a glass of wine in the living room. Your host has traveled throughout Europe, Egypt, Israel, and Mexico. Her interests include art, travel, reading, boating, gardening, decorating, swimming, and gourmet cooking.

No. Rooms: 2	**Breakfast:** Full
Singles: None	**S-Rates:** $55 pb
Doubles: 2 pb	**D-Rates:** $75 pb
Type: Private home	**Bldg:** 1980 Contemporary

Minimum Stay: 2 nights on weekends. **Credit Card(s) Accepted:** none. **Open:** all year. No resident dogs. No dogs please. No resident cats. No cats please. Nonsmoking host. Guests may not smoke in guest rooms. Children welcome. **Discounts:** none.

Reservation Contact: Bed & Breakfast Registry Ltd., Gary Winget, Box 8174, St. Paul, MN 55108; 612–646–4238.

SANTA MONICA   ID: L–PINES

MINUTES TO BEACH OR TOWN.

Near Montana, 20th, I–405.

This country-style home on a corner lot is in a quiet, pleasant residential area, just minutes from the beach or town. The guest wing has a private entrance leading into a mini-kitchen with a dining area. To the left is the first guest room, with queen-sized bed, antique furnishings, and doors that open out onto to a brick patio. The second room has a double hide-a-bed. This room may be used as a sitting room or as a second bedroom. A shared guest bath connects the guest rooms. A Continental breakfast is served. TV is available. Your host is in real estate.

No. Rooms: 2	**Breakfast:** Continental
Singles: None	**S-Rates:** $45 sb
Doubles: 2 sb	**D-Rates:** $50 sb
Type: Private home	**Bldg:** Bungalow

Minimum Stay: none. **Credit Card(s) Accepted:** MC, V. **Open:** all year. No resident dogs. No dogs please. No resident cats. No cats please. Non-smoking host. Guests may not smoke in residence. Children welcome. **Discounts:** none.

Reservation Contact: Bed and Breakfast of Los Angeles, Peg Marshall & Angie Kobabe, 32074 Waterside Ln., Westlake Village, CA 91361; 818–889–8870.

SANTA MONICA CANYON   ID: INTNAT190

WILL ROGERS STATE BEACH.

Near Entrada Dr., Rte. 1.

This fine villa, built in the California-mission style with high vaulted beamed ceiling in the living room, tiled floors, and Oriental rugs, is accented with striking Mexican-Indian wall tapestries. The kidney-shaped swimming pool is completely surrounded by semi-tropical plants and trees, and there is also a badminton court on the premises. All three guest rooms are furnished with fine wood furniture, mostly quality Spanish-style antiques to complement the architecture of the home. Each room has a dresser and table and chairs, and guests will find a decanter of sherry and a bowl of fruit in their rooms. Two of the rooms have queen-sized beds, while the other has twin beds. One has a private bath; the other two share a bath. Your hosts have studied cooking in Mexico and enjoy preparing and eating a Full breakfast with their guests. One of your hosts is an engineer; the other is an anthropologist with a special interest in Central and South America. They share an interest in Mexican folk arts and crafts. From the house, guests can cross the street, go down a flight of stairs to the coast highway overpass, and find themselves at Will Rogers State Beach. Superior restaurants are nearby, and Wilshire Boulevard is only five minutes away.

No. Rooms: 3	**Breakfast:** Full
Singles: None	**S-Rates:** $70 pb, $70 sb
Doubles: 1 pb, 2 sb	**D-Rates:** $76 pb, $76 sb
Type: Private home	**Bldg:** 1939 California mansion

Minimum Stay: 2 nights. **Credit Card(s) Accepted:** none. **Open:** all year. No resident dogs. No dogs please. Cat in residence. No cats please. Nonsmoking host. Guests may not smoke in residence. Children welcome. **Discounts:** weekly. Spanish spoken.

Reservation Contact: Bed & Breakfast International, Jean Brown, 151 Ardmore Rd., Kensington, CA 94707; 415–525–4569.

SAUSALITO
ID: INTNAT285

HOUSEBOAT AREA.

Near U.S. 101, Bridgeway.

The quiet houseboat area in Sausalito is a world apart from San Francisco, yet close to the city's fine restaurants and sights. Sausalito is connected to the city by jet-propelled ferries. This luxurious houseboat is berthed in deep water and is on a cement base so there is little or no movement. The boat is at the end of the dock, which means that it offers expansive water views from its floor-to-ceiling windows and private deck. A telescope affords views of sea birds, sea mammals, and sailboats. There is one sunny guest room with a queen-sized bed, and a loft with a single futon bed. The furnishings are tasteful, and amenities include a fireplace, Jacuzzi, TV, telephone, fishing equipment, and off-street parking. A Full breakfast is served. Your hosts enjoy travel, boating, and camping.

No. Rooms: 2	**Breakfast:** Full
Singles: 1 sb	**S-Rates:** $92 pb, $72 sb
Doubles: 1 pb	**D-Rates:** $98 pb, $78 sb
Type: Private home	**Bldg:** Houseboat

Minimum Stay: 2 nights. **Credit Card(s) Accepted:** AE, MC, V. **Open:** all year. Resident dog. No dogs please. No resident cats. No cats please. Hosts smoke. Guests may smoke. Children welcome with restrictions. **Discounts:** 10% weekly, 20% families.

Reservation Contact: Bed & Breakfast International, Jean Brown, 1181-B Solano Ave., Albany, CA 94706; 415–525–4569.

SEAL BEACH

ID: 90740SEA

L.A. AREA, DISNEYLAND, KNOTTS BERRY FARM, UNIVERSAL STUDIOS.

Near Pacific Coast Hwy. & Ocean Blvd., Rte. 1, I–405.

This French Mediterranean-style country inn has a charming old-world feel. You can enjoy the pool, surrounded by a colorful garden or the shore, which is only 300 yards away. Old Town, the marina, and eighteen restaurants are within easy walking distance. There are 23 pleasant, antique-furnished guest rooms, all with private baths. Area tours are usually available. Your host's interests include skiing and antiques.

No. Rooms: 23	**Breakfast:** Full
Singles: None	**S-Rates:** $88–$155 pb
Doubles: 23 pb	**D-Rates:** $88–$155 pb
Type: Inn	**Bldg:** 1923 Mediterranean

Minimum Stay: none. **Credit Card(s) Accepted:** AE, MC, V. **Open:** all year. No resident dogs. No dogs please. No resident cats. No cats please. Nonsmoking host. Guests may not smoke in residence. Children welcome. **Discounts:** none.

Reservation Contact: Bed & Breakfast Registry Ltd., Gary Winget, Box 8174, St. Paul, MN 55108; 612–646–4238.

SOUTH LAGUNA BEACH

ID: Q–15

OCEAN VIEWS, TWO BLOCKS TO BEACH.

Near Pacific Coast Hwy. & Monterey.

The guest quarters in this home include a living room with a private entrance, fireplace, TV, and ocean views. The two guest rooms, decorated with antiques and wicker, have queen-sized beds and private baths. A Full breakfast is served. The beach is two blocks away.

No. Rooms: 2	**Breakfast:** Full
Singles: None	**S-Rates:** $75 pb
Doubles: 2 pb	**D-Rates:** $75 pb
Type: Private home	

Minimum Stay: 2 nights. **Credit Card(s) Accepted:** MC, V. **Open:** all year. No resident dogs. No dogs please. Resident cat. No cats please. Nonsmoking host. Guests may not smoke. Residence not appropriate for children. **Discounts:** none.

Reservation Contact: Bed & Breakfast of Los Angeles, Peg Marshall & Angie Kobabe, 32074 Waterside Ln., Westlake Village, CA 91361; 818–889–8870.

STUDIO CITY

MOVIE STUDIOS.

Near Ventura Blvd., Coldwater Canyon, Ventura Fwy. 101.

Studio City is convenient to all of Los Angeles, since it is only minutes from the studios, with easy access to town and tourist attractions. This house is in a pleasant residential neighborhood of well-maintained homes on a quiet street. Bus lines and restaurants are only a few blocks away. The air-conditioned guest room has twin beds and a private bath. A Continental breakfast is served. Guests can enjoy a glass of sherry or a cup of tea amid the country decor of this delightful home with stained glass and skylights. The enclosed garden with brick patio is a wonderful spot for relaxing, and there is also a swimming pool available to guests.

No. Rooms: 1	**Breakfast:** Continental
Singles: None	**S-Rates:** $45 pb
Doubles: 1 pb	**D-Rates:** $50 pb
Type: Private home	**Bldg:** European cottage

Minimum Stay: none. **Credit Card(s) Accepted:** none. **Open:** all year. No resident dogs. No dogs please. No resident cats. No cats please. Non-smoking host. Guests may not smoke in residence. Children welcome. **Discounts:** weekly.

Reservation Contact: Bed and Breakfast of Los Angeles, Peg Marshall & Angie Kobabe, 32074 Waterside Ln., Westlake Village, CA 91361; 818–889–8870.

TAHOMA

LAKE TAHOE, SUGAR PINE STATE PARK, MEEKS BAY BEACH STATE PARK, EMERALD BAY; POOL, SKIING.

Near Rte. 89, Rte. 28.

This Alpine-style country inn is situated on one-and-a-half acres of park-like grounds on Lake Tahoe. There are seven fresh and airy guest rooms with twin and double beds; one has a queen-sized bed and large deck overlooking the pool. All have private baths, hand-painted pine head-boards, and cozy comforters. In addition, there are six two-bedroom cottages. They have living rooms with fireplaces, kitchens, and private baths. In this lovely setting, you can enjoy the large heated pool, volleyball, hiking, biking, horse shoes, table tennis, and lake access. Ski areas are two minutes away. Guests staying in the B&B rooms are served a Full breakfast. Other meals are available at the excellent restaurant with Swiss/Austrian decor—one of the best in the area—and a warm, friendly atmosphere. There is also a lounge with rock fireplace for guests' relaxation.

No. Rooms: 15	**Breakfast:** Full
Singles: None	**S-Rates:** $65–$95 pb
Doubles: 15 pb	**D-Rates:** $65–$95 pb
Type: Inn	**Bldg:** 1948 old Tahoe

Minimum Stay: none. **Credit Card(s) Accepted:** AE, MC, V. **Open:** all year. No resident dogs. No dogs please. No resident cats. No cats please. Nonsmoking host. Guests may smoke. Children welcome with restrictions. **Discounts:** none.

Reservation Contact: Bed & Breakfast Registry Ltd., Gary Winget, Box 8174, St. Paul, MN 55108; 612–646–4238.

THOUSAND OAKS   ID: L–RETIREMENT

40 MILES NORTHWEST OF LOS ANGELES.

Near Erbes, Los Arboles, Rte. 23.

This beautiful new condominium forty miles northwest of central Los Angeles offers sports facilities, hiking trails, and spectacular views. Malibu is just over the mountains, and Santa Barbara is but an hour away. The unit is decorated with elegant traditional furnishings and features a shady patio with a view of the hills beyond. The guest room is just off the entry hall and has a double bed, antique furnishings, private bath, and sliding doors that open onto a small enclosed patio. The hide-a-bed in the den can be used to accommodate a child. Guests are welcome to share the hosts' TV. A Continental breakfast is served. Your hosts are a retired educator and his wife.

No. Rooms: 2	**Breakfast:** Continental
Singles: None	**S-Rates:** $40 pb, $40 sb
Doubles: 1 pb, 1 sb	**D-Rates:** $40 pb, $40 sb
Type: Private home	**Bldg:** 1982 contemporary

Minimum Stay: none. **Credit Card(s) Accepted:** MC, V. **Open:** all year. No resident dogs. No dogs please. No resident cats. No cats please. Nonsmoking host. Guests may smoke. Children welcome. **Discounts:** weekly.

Reservation Contact: Bed and Breakfast of Los Angeles, Peg Marshall & Angie Kobabe, 32074 Waterside Ln., Westlake Village, CA 91361; 818–889–8870.

VENICE

SANTA MONICA AREA.

Near Hwy. 90, Lincoln, San Diego Fwy. 405.

This large family home is in a residential neighborhood bordering Santa Monica and offers easy access to the beaches or town, with the bus line two blocks away. The home has a spacious living room with stone fireplace, and guests can share the TV with the family in the den. The two guest rooms are in a private hallway with private entrance. One has twin beds; the other is a single. A Continental breakfast is served, and child care and area tours are available. Your charming Hungarian hosts, parents of two school-aged children, want guests to feel at home and will help you find your way around the area.

No. Rooms: 2	**Breakfast:** Continental
Singles: 1 sb	**S-Rates:** $30 sb
Doubles: 1 sb	**D-Rates:** $35 sb
Type: Private home	

Minimum Stay: none. **Credit Card(s) Accepted:** MC, V. **Open:** all year. Dog in residence. No dogs please. No resident cats. No cats please. Nonsmoking host. Guests may not smoke in residence. Children welcome with restrictions. **Discounts:** weekly & monthly. Hungarian, German, & Swedish spoken.

Reservation Contact: Bed and Breakfast of Los Angeles, Peg Marshall & Angie Kobabe, 32074 Waterside Ln., Westlake Village, CA 91361; 818–889–8870.

WEST LOS ANGELES

U.C.L.A., HOLLYWOOD, BEVERLY HILLS; SANTA MONICA AREA.

Near Wilshire & Sunset blvds.

This home is a peaceful oasis in the midst of a fast-paced metropolis. There is a large lawn in back of the residence with an abundance of flowers and fruit trees. There are two guest rooms available with shared bath. One has twin beds, the other has a double bed and private entryway. Both rooms can be closed off from the rest of the house for complete privacy. There is a fireplace and TV for your use. Additional meals are available. Public transportation is good, and there is door-to-door shuttle bus service from Los Angeles Airport.

No. Rooms: 2	**Breakfast:** Continental Plus
Singles: None	**S-Rates:** $35 pb
Doubles: 2 pb	**D-Rates:** $50 pb
Type: Private home	**Bldg:** 1945

Minimum Stay: none. **Credit Card(s) Accepted:** none. **Open:** all year. No resident dogs. No dogs please. No resident cats. No cats please. Nonsmoking host. Guests may not smoke in residence. Children welcome. **Discounts:** none. French & Spanish spoken.

Reservation Contact: Rent-A-Room International B&B, Esther MacLachlan, 11531 Varna Street, Garden Grove, CA 92640, 714–638–1406.

WESTWOOD   ID: H–5

CENTURY CITY, U.C.L.A.

Near Santa Monica Blvd. & Beverly Glen.

This luxury apartment, within walking distance of Century City, offers one guest room with twin beds and private bath. Amenities include underground parking, pool, sauna, and spa; there is handicapped access and bus lines are nearby. Your host is a social worker.

No. Rooms: 1	**Breakfast:** Continental
Singles: None	**S-Rates:** $45 pb
Doubles: 1	**D-Rates:** $45 pb
Type: Private home	**Bldg:** Apartment

Minimum Stay: none. **Credit Card(s) Accepted:** MC, V. **Open:** all year. No resident dogs. No dogs please. No resident cats. No cats please. Nonsmoking host. Guests may smoke. Residence not appropriate for children. **Discounts:** none.

Reservation Contact: Bed and Breakfast of Los Angeles, Peg Marshall & Angie Kobabe, 32074 Waterside Ln., Westlake Village, CA 91361; 818–889–8870.

COLORADO

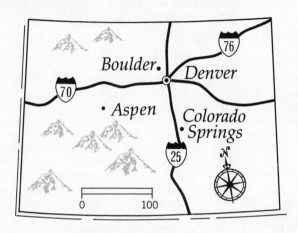

ASPEN

ID: ROC–LOGHOUSE

SKIING, HIKING, HORSEBACK RIDING.

Hwy. 82, I–70.

Built in 1865, this renovated log home offers two large guest rooms with queen-sized beds, writing desks, and shared or private bath. The house is located in a quiet, rural area 20 miles from Aspen, Glenwood, and Snowmass. Other amenities include a wood burning stove and use of telephone, laundry facilities, and refrigerator. Skiing, golf, river rafting, and horseback riding are nearby. Your host has hiked extensively in the area and also enjoys reading, cooking, skiing, and biking.

No. Rooms: 2	**Breakfast:** Continental
Singles: None	**S-Rates:** $35–$50
Doubles: 1 pb, 1 sb	**D-Rates:** $40–$65
Type: Private home	**Bldg:** Log house

Minimum Stay: none. **Credit Card(s) Accepted:** none. **Open:** all year. No resident dogs. No dogs please. Resident cat. No cats please. Non-smoking host. Guests may not smoke in residence. Children welcome.

Reservation Contact: Bed & Breakfast-Rocky Mountains, Kate Peterson Winters, Box 804, Colorado Springs, CO 80901; 719–630–3433.

BEULAH

ROYAL GORGE, INDIAN PETROGLYPHS HISTORIC
SITE, SAN ISABEL NATIONAL FOREST; 25 MILES
SOUTHWEST OF PUEBLO.

Near Mountain Park Rd., Rte. 78.

Located on a working ranch next to a six-hundred-and-fifty-acre mountain park, is this nineteenth-century farmhouse with log siding. There are
thirteen resident horses and a carriage museum on the premises. The
house is totally furnished with choice antiques, many sculptures, and *ob-
jets d'art.* Of the four charming guest rooms, the first has a fireplace, rocking chair, reading lamp, double brass bed with attractive quilted spread,
an antique desk, chair, slipper stool, and commode and wash stand. The
second room, with double bed and quilts, is furnished with antique dresser, commode, Morris chair, luggage rack, and a corner desk and chair;
the walls are adorned with oil paintings. A third room has a wood-burning
stove, iron double bed, youth bed and crib with antique quilts, a commode, and trunks. These three rooms share a guest bath. The fourth
room, with private bath, is furnished with twin beds, commode, dresser,
sewing machine, rocker, and cricket chair. A Continental Plus breakfast
is served. Your host, a retired naval officer, has traveled extensively and
enjoys raising horses and restoring antique carriages and sleighs.

No. Rooms: 4	**Breakfast:** Continental Plus
Singles: None	**S-Rates:** $32 pb, $32 sb
Doubles: 1 pb, 3 sb	**D-Rates:** $38 pb, $38 sb
Type: Private home	**Bldg:** 1878 log-siding farmhouse

Minimum Stay: none. **Credit Card(s) Accepted:** MC, V. **Open:** all year.
Dog in residence. Guests may bring dog. Cat in residence. Guests may
bring cat. Nonsmoking host. Guests may smoke. Children welcome. **Discounts:** none.

Reservation Contact: Bed & Breakfast Colorado, Jim & Kate Carey, Box
6061, Boulder, CO 80306; 303–494–4994.

BOULDER

UNIVERSITY OF COLORADO, ROCKY MOUNTAINS.

Near Broadway, Pine, rtes. 119, 36, 93.

This home, on a cul-de-sac in a quiet, established neighborhood eight
blocks from downtown Boulder, overlooks the city. The guest room offers twin beds, sitting area with fireplace, private bath, and private entrance. The large windows have eastern and southern exposures. A Full
breakfast is served. Your hosts, a retired meteorologist and his wife, are
active in city planning and other civic affairs. They enjoy bicycling and
are tour guides for the National Center for Atmospheric Research.

No. Rooms: 1	**Breakfast:** Full
Singles: None	**S-Rates:** $32 pb
Doubles: 1 sb	**D-Rates:** $40 pb
Type: Private home	**Bldg:** 1953 traditional

Minimum Stay: none. **Credit Card(s) Accepted:** MC, V. **Open:** all year. No resident dogs. No dogs please. Cat in residence. No cats please. Nonsmoking host. Guests may not smoke in residence. Children welcome with restrictions. **Discounts:** none.

Reservation Contact: Bed & Breakfast Colorado, Jim & Kate Carey, Box 6061, Boulder, CO 80306; 303–494–4994.

ID: DT3–BOULDER

HISTORIC DISTRICT.

Near Pearl St., 9th Ave., rtes. 119, 36, 93.

This Victorian home, built in 1900, has a large yard with lovely trees, a creek running through the property, and an interior with fine furnishings and paintings. Guests can relax on the east-side deck. The guest room offers a double bed, contemporary furniture, TV, telephone, and private bath. A Continental Plus breakfast is served. One of your hosts is an architect and the other is a weaver. They are well-traveled and enjoy tennis and biking.

No. Rooms: 1	**Breakfast:** Continental Plus
Singles: None	**S-Rates:** $32 pb
Doubles: 1 pb	**D-Rates:** $40 pb
Type: Private home	**Bldg:** 1900 Victorian

Minimum Stay: none. **Credit Card(s) Accepted:** MC, V. **Open:** all year. No resident dogs. No dogs please. No resident cats. No cats please. Nonsmoking host. Guests may not smoke in residence. Children welcome with restrictions. **Discounts:** none.

Reservation Contact: Bed & Breakfast Colorado, Jim & Kate Carey, Box 6061, Boulder, CO 80306; 303–494–4994.

ID: LL1–BOULDER

ROCKY MOUNTAINS.

Near 97th, Arapahoe, I–25, Rte. 36.

This colonial brick house in a lovely country setting offers an excellent view of the front range. The two guest rooms have private baths. One has a double bed, maple-wood furnishings, carpeting, and mountain view; the other has twin beds. A Full breakfast is served in the greenhouse, after which guests are free to take a dip in the pool. Your hosts, a retired engineer and a homemaker, have traveled extensively and are especially interested in Scotland. They enjoy golf and cross-country and downhill skiing.

No. Rooms: 2	**Breakfast:** Full
Singles: None	**S-Rates:** $30 pb
Doubles: 2 pb	**D-Rates:** $38 pb
Type: Private home	**Bldg:** 1968 brick colonial

Minimum Stay: none. **Credit Card(s) Accepted:** MC, V. **Open:** all year. Dog in residence. No dogs please. No resident cats. No cats please. Host smokes. Guests may not smoke in residence. **Discounts:** weekly.

Reservation Contact: Bed & Breakfast Colorado, Jim & Kate Carey, Box 6061, Boulder, CO 80306; 303–494–4994.

ID: U3–BOULDER

UNIVERSITY OF COLORADO.

Near Baseline, 9th Ave., rtes. 36, 119, 93.

This private home is located in a quiet neighborhood two blocks from a park, with hiking, biking, and cross-country skiing nearby. The University of Colorado is less than a mile away. A garden-level guest room has its own entrance, queen-sized bed, clock radio, carpeting, and private bath. A Continental Plus breakfast is served. Your host, with a law degree, is an outdoors enthusiast who has traveled extensively throughout South America and the highlands of Asia.

No. Rooms: 1	**Breakfast:** Continental Plus
Singles: None	**S-Rates:** $32 pb
Doubles: 1 pb	**D-Rates:** $40 pb
Type: Private home	**Bldg:** 1920 style

Minimum Stay: none. **Credit Card(s) Accepted:** MC, V. **Open:** all year. No resident dogs. No dogs please. No resident cats. No cats please. Non-smoking host. Guests may not smoke in residence. Residence not appropriate for children. **Discounts:** none.

Reservation Contact: Bed & Breakfast Colorado, Jim & Kate Carey, Box 6061, Boulder, CO 80306; 303–494–4994.

BRECKENRIDGE
ID: SUMMIT–CO

SKIING, HIKING, MOUNTAIN CLIMBING, GOLF, FISHING, BOATING; 80 MILES WEST OF DENVER.

Near Rte. 9 & Tiger Rd., I–70.

Breckenridge, an old mining town, is on the National Register of Historic Places. It offers many outstanding restaurants, shops, and activities for visitors. Many good trails for hiking and mountain climbing are nearby, and five major ski areas and bike and boat rentals are within a ten-minute drive. An eighteen-hole championship golf course is less than a quarter of a mile away. This contemporary house is warmly paneled and furnished with many antiques. The carpeted living room has a large stone fireplace and comfortable chairs for reading or watching TV. In the basement, guests will find a piano, table tennis, and a sauna. The hot tub is nestled in a corner of the sun room, with its many plants and lovely mountain views. One of the two guest rooms has a king-sized bed, bureau, two bedside tables with lamps, a rocking chair, large closet, and private bath. The other room is furnished with twin beds, a nightstand with a lamp, an easy chair, bureau, and small table. In the sun room, guests choose a Full breakfast from a menu. Bird feeders in the trees just outside the window attract over thirty different species of birds. Your hosts, who recently traveled to Europe, Kenya, and the Bahamas, enjoy skiing, hiking, gardening, music, and stamp collecting.

No. Rooms: 2	**Breakfast:** Full
Singles: None	**S-Rates:** $55 pb, $55 sb
Doubles: 1 pb, 1 sb	**D-Rates:** $55 pb, $55 sb
Type: Private home	**Bldg:** 1980 mountain contemporary

Minimum Stay: none. **Credit Card(s) Accepted:** MC, V. **Open:** all year. No resident dogs. No dogs please. Cat in residence. No cats please. Non-smoking host. Guests may not smoke in residence. Children welcome with restrictions. **Discounts:** none.

Reservation Contact: Bed & Breakfast Colorado, Jim & Kate Carey, Box 6061, Boulder, CO 80306; 303–494–4994.

ID: 80424TRA

VAIL SKI AREA; DOWNHILL & CROSS-COUNTRY SKIING, HIKING, HORSEBACK RIDING, FISHING.

Near Rte. 9, I–70.

This quiet chalet with its spectacular view and exceptional location has a woodburning stove in the living room, new interior furnishings, tele-

phone and kitchen privileges, and a large deck. There are three guest rooms with a shared bath. Your host's interests include skiing, outdoor activities, and travel.

No. Rooms: 3	**Breakfast:** Continental Plus
Singles: None	**S-Rates:** $45–$65 sb
Doubles: 3 sb	**D-Rates:** $45–$65 sb
Type: Private home	**Bldg:** Chalet

Minimum Stay: 2 nights. **Credit Card(s) Accepted:** none. **Open:** all year. No resident dogs. No dogs please. No resident cats. No cats please. Nonsmoking host. Guests may not smoke in residence. Children welcome. **Discounts:** none.

Reservation Contact: Bed & Breakfast Registry Ltd., Gary Winget, Box 8174, St. Paul, MN 55108; 612–646–4238.

COLORADO SPRINGS ID: MANIT–SPG

MANITOU SPRINGS.

Near CO 24, Manitou Ave., I–25.

Built in 1889, this two-story Victorian home in the historic district makes a very romantic setting. The guest room has a separate entrance and is in a separate wing so privacy is guaranteed. Furnishings include antiques, queen-sized bed, and a wood burning stove. It has a private bath, and a hot tub under the stars is available by appointment. The host, an architect, enjoys outdoor activities. A Continental breakfast is served.

No. Rooms: 1	**Breakfast:** Continental
Singles: None	**S-Rates:** $65–$75 pb
Doubles: 1 pb	**D-Rates:** $65–$75 pb
Type: Private home	**Bldg:** Victorian

Minimum Stay: 2 nights. **Credit Card(s) Accepted:** none. **Open:** all year. No resident dogs. No dogs please. No resident cats. No cats please. Nonsmoking host. Guests may not smoke in residence. Children welcome. **Discounts:** none.

Reservation Contact: Bed & Breakfast-Rocky Mountains, Kate Peterson Winters, Box 804, Colorado Springs, CO 80901; 719–630–3433.

ID: ROC–54

OLYMPIC TRAINING CENTER, PIKE'S PEAK, CAVE OF THE WINDS, U.S. AIR FORCE ACADEMY.

Near W. Pike's Peak Ave., I–25.

This spacious 1902 Victorian home located in the historic area of the city is filled with family heirlooms. Built by Isabel Holden, the widow of a wealthy businessman, the residence features three guest rooms, each with private bath. The Cripple Creek, a spacious room with a queen-sized brass bed and antique quilts, is decorated in soft blue and cream and provides a mountain view. The Leadville room is done in pastel prints; its double bed is adorned with an antique quilt, and the bath with a claw-foot tub. The Silverton room, decorated in crisp blue and yellow, has a double bed with satin comforter and mirror-topped dressing table. A Full breakfast is served on the veranda when weather permits. Fine restaurants, unique gift shops, and many other attractions are nearby, some within walking distance. Your hosts, who have energetically restored their house, enjoy tennis, hiking, needlework, crafts, and golf.

No. Rooms: 3	**Breakfast:** Full
Singles: None	**S-Rates:** $40–$46 pb
Doubles: 3 pb	**D-Rates:** $40–$46 pb
Type: Private home	**Bldg:** 1902 Victorian

Minimum Stay: none. **Credit Card(s) Accepted:** none. **Open:** all year. No resident dogs. No dogs please. Cat in residence. No cats please. Non-smoking host. Guests may not smoke in residence. Children welcome with restrictions. **Discounts:** none.

Reservation Contact: Bed & Breakfast-Rocky Mountains, Kate Peterson Winters, Box 804, Colorado Springs, CO 80901; 719–630–3433.

DENVER

ID: MALS–CO

ELITCH GARDENS, SLOAN LAKE, U.S. MINT, STATE CAPITOL, UNIVERSITY OF DENVER, WHEAT RIDGE AREA.

Near 38th St., Sheridan Blvd., I–70.

This Cape Cod-style house in the Denver suburb of Wheat Ridge is about twenty minutes from the center of the city and five minutes from Elitch Gardens, home of the oldest summer theater west of the Mississippi. Also nearby is Sloan Lake, with boating, fishing, and wildlife. Some of the city's top free attractions include the U.S. Mint, and the State Capitol with its mile-high view of the city, as well as a sampling tour at Coors Brewery. The house, filled with antiques, family heirlooms, and many hand-crafted items, has two guest rooms. The first room, with an early-American decor, has a double bed, maple-wood dressers, and a braided wool rug; a civil-war vintage quilt hangs on the wall. The room also has a private bath. The other guest room, also with double bed, is done in pink and green, with antique dresser and throw rugs. A Full breakfast of the guest's choice is served. One of your hosts is a golf enthusiast; the other enjoys cooking, sewing, and antiques.

No. Rooms: 2	**Breakfast:** Full
Singles: None	**S-Rates:** $30 pb, $30 sb
Doubles: 1 pb, 1 sb	**D-Rates:** $39 pb, $39 sb
Type: Private home	**Bldg:** 1968 Cape Cod

Minimum Stay: none. **Credit Card(s) Accepted:** MC, V. **Open:** all year. No resident dogs. No dogs please. No resident cats. No cats please. Non-smoking host. Guests may smoke. Children welcome. **Discounts:** weekly.

Reservation Contact: Bed & Breakfast Colorado, Jim & Kate Carey, Box 6061, Boulder, CO 80306; 303–494–4994.

ID: QUILTS–CO

MUSEUM OF NATURAL HISTORY, GATES PLANETARIUM, ZOO, DENVER ART MUSEUM.

Near Colorado Blvd., E. Colfax, I–70, U.S. 40.

Built in 1909, this large, attractive home is located in one of Denver's oldest, most prestigious neighborhoods, a lovely area for walking. City Park, which contains the Museum of Natural History, the seventh largest museum in the country and one of the great centers of its kind in the world, is two blocks away. Visitors will also find Gates Planetarium, the Denver Zoo, a lake with paddleboats, and a night-time fountain display. The sunny, colorfully decorated house is only one block from public transportation and ten minutes from the city center. The furnishings and accessories include family heirlooms, period antiques, and garage-sale finds. Heirloom quilts and needlework are displayed alongside new ma-chine-made quilts. Guests are encouraged to make use of all the living areas, both indoor and out. Because there is just one spare room, guests receive very personal attention. The room has a queen-sized quilt-covered bed, comfortable chairs, table, overhead lighting and reading lamp, nightstands, a clock radio, rag rugs atop the hardwood floor, and private bath. A typical Full breakfast might consist of eggs cooked in En-glish porcelain coddlers with cheese or meat and fresh herbs from the garden, juice or fresh fruit, homemade jelly and bran muffins wrapped in their own little quilts to keep them warm, and coffee or tea. Weather permitting, breakfast is served in the garden; otherwise, it is served in the dining room. Your host is a custom quiltmaker, designer, and teacher, whose interests include archeology, anthropology, Indian art, gardening, and travel. Arrival/departure transportation and city tours are available.

No. Rooms: 1	**Breakfast:** Full
Singles: None	**S-Rates:** $38 pb
Doubles: 1 pb	**D-Rates:** $42 pb
Type: Private home	**Bldg:** 1909

Minimum Stay: none. **Credit Card(s) Accepted:** MC, V. **Open:** all year.

Dog in residence. No dogs please. No resident cats. No cats please. Non-smoking host. Guests may not smoke in residence. Children welcome with restrictions. **Discounts:** none.

Reservation Contact: Bed & Breakfast Colorado, Jim & Kate Carey, Box 6061, Boulder, CO 80306; 303–494–4994.

ID: QUEENANNE

DOWNTOWN, U.S. MINT, STATE CAPITOL, HERITAGE CENTER, ART MUSEUM, CENTER FOR PERFORMING ARTS.

Near Colfax & 16th St.

Four blocks from the heart of Denver's business district, this three-story 1879 home is exemplary of the Queen Anne-style of Victorian architecture. It is situated among other meticulously restored homes and gardens in the Clements Historic District, Denver's oldest continuously occupied residential neighborhood. The ten guest rooms have private baths. A sampling includes the Fountain Room with a queen-sized canopy bed, antique writing desk, comfortable sofa, sunken tub, and views of the fountain and park; the Skyline Room, with views of the city and mountains, an antique queen-sized brass bed, and carved walnut loveseat and armchair; and the Tower Room the largest of the ten, is furnished with a carved king-sized bed, antique cherry armoire, loveseat, chair, and leather-topped desk. A Continental breakfast and afternoon wine and tea are served.

No. Rooms: 10	**Breakfast:** Continental
Singles: 1 pb	**S-Rates:** $54–$89 pb
Doubles: 9 pb	**D-Rates:** $69–$99 pb
Type: Inn	**Bldg:** Queen Anne Victorian

Minimum Stay: none. **Credit Card(s) Accepted:** MC, V. **Open:** all year. No resident dog. No dogs please. No resident cats. No cats please. Non-smoking hosts. Guests may not smoke in residence. Residence is not appropriate for children. **Discounts:** none.

Reservation Contact: Bed & Breakfast Registry, Gary Winget, Box 8174, St. Paul, MN 55108; 612–646–4238; or Bed & Breakfast Rocky Mountains, Kate Peterson Winters, Box 804, Colorado Springs, Co 80901; 719–630–3433.

DURANGO

MESA VERDE NATIONAL PARK, CLIFF DWELLINGS.

Near hwys. 160 & 140.

This Victorian farmhouse, in a farming and ranching community, is about twenty minutes from Durango and offers spectacular views and gardens. Previous guests say the home is reminiscent of the Cotswolds or southern France. It is elegantly furnished with an eclectic collection of antiques. The Rose Room, with queen-sized bed, down quilt, antique gilt armoire, jade carpeting, and private bath, has an all-encompassing view of the lake, mountains, and gardens. The Victorian Room, decorated in a floral print, has a four-poster Civil War bed, antique dresser, primitive paintings, and a separate entrance. The Mexican Room, decorated with colorful Mexican folk art, and with a single hand-painted Mexican bed, is suitable for a child, and it shares a bath with the Victorian Room. The large Blue Room, with its pale blue walls, has a double and a queen-sized bed, sitting area, and private bath with tub and shower. A Full breakfast, consisting of fresh orange juice, a fruit dish, omelet or French toast, homemade muffins, and freshly ground coffee, is served. One of your hosts is a published writer who enjoys cooking; the other has traveled to the Far East and Africa, and has a passion for gardening. Child care and arrival/departure transportation are available. Reservations are not accepted between October 12 and May 1.

> **No. Rooms:** 5
> **Singles:** 1 sb
> **Doubles:** 2 pb, 1 sb
> **Type:** Small inn
>
> **Breakfast:** Full
> **S-Rates:** $55–$95 pb, $55–$95 sb
> **D-Rates:** $75–$125 pb, $75–$125 sb
> **Bldg:** Victorian farmhouse

Minimum Stay: none. **Credit Card(s) Accepted:** none. **Open:** May 1 to October 12. No resident dogs. No dogs please. No resident cats. No cats please. Nonsmoking host. Guests may not smoke in residence. Children welcome with restrictions. **Discounts:** none. Spanish spoken.

Reservation Contact: Bed & Breakfast Colorado, Jim & Kate Carey, Box 6061, Boulder, CO 80306; 303–494–4994.

ESTES PARK

ROCKY MOUNTAIN NATIONAL PARK; HIKING, FISHING.

Near CO–7, County Rd. 82.

This modified A-frame is on three-and-one-half acres of open forest, ideal for hiking and fishing. Hikes start from your door or from any number of trailheads in or out of Rocky Mountain National Park. The trailhead to Long's Peak (14,255 feet) is three miles away. Wildflowers abound, and there are many interesting rock outcroppings. Bird-watching opportunities are excellent. Horseback riding is nearby. Rocky Ridge Music Camp, a summer experience for talented young people, is three miles away, and there are concerts each Friday and Saturday. The house has two guest rooms that share a bath with the hosts. The Wildflower Room is colorful, with an antique walnut double bed, commode, and reading lamps. The Travel Room has twin beds and an antique oak commode with marble top. Guests find fresh flowers in their rooms. A Full breakfast of daily specialties is served. Previous menus have offered German apple pancakes, corned beef hash with poached eggs, and eggs with sausage or bacon. All this is provided with juice or fruit in season, cereal, home-made breads and sweet rolls. Your hosts are a physician and a home economist, and their interests include hiking, cross-country skiing, nature photography, and travel.

No. Rooms: 2	**Breakfast:** Full
Singles: None.	**S-Rates:** $30 sb
Doubles: 2 sb	**D-Rates:** $40 sb
Type: Private home	**Bldg:** 1979 modified A-frame

Minimum Stay: none. **Credit Card(s) Accepted:** MC, V. **Open:** June 16 to Sept. 30. Dog in residence. No dogs please. No resident cats. No cats please. Nonsmoking host. Guests may not smoke in guest rooms. Children welcome with restrictions. **Discounts:** none.

Reservation Contact: Bed & Breakfast Colorado, Jim & Kate Carey, Box 6061, Boulder, CO 80306; 303–494–4994.

ID: ROC–TERRA

ROCKY MOUNTAIN NATIONAL PARK.

Near hwys. 36 & 34.

This Tudor-style home is located at the edge of Rocky Mountain National Park and offers four guest rooms and a Full breakfast. One of the rooms has a queen-sized bed and private bath. The other three, with queen, twin, or double beds, share a bath. Amenities include a fireplace, off-street parking, TV, patio, yard, laundry facilities, and beautiful views. Your host enjoys skiing, hiking, cooking, sewing, and travel.

No. Rooms: 4	**Breakfast:** Full
Singles: None	**S-Rates:** $45 pb, $28–$35 sb
Doubles: 1 pb, 3 sb	**D-Rates:** $45 pb, $32–$38 sb
Type: Private home	**Bldg:** Tudor

Minimum Stay: none. **Credit Card(s) Accepted:** none. **Open:** all year. No resident dogs. No dogs please. No resident cats. No cats please. Non-smoking host. Guests may not smoke in guest rooms. Children welcome. **Discounts:** none.

Reservation Contact: Bed & Breakfast-Rocky Mountains, Kate Peterson Winters, Box 804, Colorado Springs, CO 80901; 719–630–3433.

FRISCO

ID: 80443TWI

BRECKENRIDGE, COPPER MOUNTAIN, KEYSTONE, ARAPAHOE BASIN & VAIL SKI AREAS, LAKE DILLON, ARAPAHOE NATIONAL FOREST.

Near I–70 & CO 9.

Although this attractive little inn is newly constructed, it was designed and furnished to reflect Frisco's earlier years. Frisco is centrally located in Summit County so all activities are within a pleasant stroll or a short drive, and the inn is near a variety of restaurants and shops. The twelve guest rooms are furnished with early 1900s dressers, rockers, tables, and several have unusual antique beds. Two of the first-floor rooms open onto a private courtyard through sliding glass doors. Eight of the rooms have private baths and four other rooms share two baths. A sun deck offers a hot tub, and a view of downtown Frisco against a backdrop of Buffalo Mountain. There is also a steam room. A Continental Plus breakfast is served buffet-style in the first-floor Fireside Room.

No. Rooms: 12	**Breakfast:** Continental Plus
Singles: None	**S-Rates:** $41–$65 pb, $31–$41 sb
Doubles: 8 pb, 4 sb	**D-Rates:** $55–$69 pb, $45–$55 sb
Type: Inn	**Bldg:** 1987 log

Minimum Stay: none. **Credit Card(s) Accepted:** AE, MC, V. **Open:** all year. Dog in residence. A dog is allowed with restrictions. No resident cats. Guests may bring cat. Host smokes. Guests may smoke. Children welcome. **Discounts:** 10% after 5 nights.

Reservation Contact: Bed & Breakfast Registry Ltd., Gary Winget, Box 8174, St. Paul, MN 55108; 612–646–4238.

GOLDEN

ID: 80401DOV

COLORADO SCHOOL OF MINES, BUFFALO BILL'S GRAVE, HERITAGE SQUARE, COORS BREWERY TOURS; QUAINT SHOPS AND RESTAURANTS; ROCKY MOUNTAIN REGION.

Near Washington & 14th sts., I–70, U.S. 6.

This delightful little Victorian inn, located in the foothills just west of Denver, has beautifully landscaped grounds, decks, walkways, and huge trees. The inn was built in 1889 has six guest rooms, all with decorative wallpaper, Victorian decor, and bay or dormer windows. One room has a separate entry with a small private patio, queen-sized bed with brass headboard, hide-a-bed, and private bath. A sunny corner room, also with queen-sized bed, has an old-fashioned decor and dormer windows. The bathroom has a clawfoot tub. Another room is done in Wedgewood blue, with twin beds, a built-in chest of drawers and vanity counter, a large closet, half bath, and a view of Golden. The fourth room, done in grasscloth wallpaper, is furnished with a queen-sized bed, double hide-a-bed, antique dresser, and writing table; bay windows offer a view of Golden and there is a private half bath. A Full breakfast is served. Because of its proximity to Denver, this romantic inn is a wonderful spot for weekend getaways, anniversaries, and honeymoons. Historic downtown Golden is nearby, and Denver is only twenty minutes away. Other local attractions include the Coors Brewery tours, Colorado School of Mines, Colorado Railroad Museum, Buffalo Bill's grave, and Heritage Square. Your hosts, an interior decorator and a pilot, enjoy theater and bridge.

No. Rooms: 6	**Breakfast:** Full
Singles: None	**S-Rates:** $34–$54 pb, $34–$49 sb
Doubles: 4 pb, 2 sb	**D-Rates:** $39–$59 pb, $39–$44 sb
Type: Private inn	**Bldg:** 1889 Victorian

Minimum Stay: none. **Credit Card(s) Accepted:** AE, DC, MC, V. **Open:** all year. No resident dogs. No dogs please. No resident cats. No cats please. Nonsmoking host. Guests may not smoke. Children welcome with restrictions. **Discounts:** 10% weekly. Spanish spoken.

Reservation Contact: Bed & Breakfast Registry Ltd., Gary Winget, Box 8174, St. Paul, MN 55108; 612–646–4238.

LAKEWOOD   ID: LAKEWOOD

SUBURBAN DENVER.

Near I–70, I–25, Wadsworth & Yale.

This two-story suburban home in a quiet residential area offers two guest rooms with double beds and shared bath. A Full breakfast is served, and other amenities include a large yard with hot tub, barbecue grill, and patio. Your host enjoys collecting china, travel, gardening, and antiques.

No. Rooms: 2	**Breakfast:** Full
Singles: None	**S-Rates:** $27–$38 sb
Doubles: 2 sb	**D-Rates:** $27–$38 sb
Type: Private home	**Bldg:** 2-story suburban

Minimum Stay: none. **Credit Card(s) Accepted:** none. **Open:** all year. No resident dog. No dogs please. No resident cats. No cats please. Nonsmoking hosts. Guests may not smoke in residence. Children welcome. **Discounts:** none.

Reservation Contact: Bed & Breakfast Rocky Mountains, Kate Peterson Winters, Box 804, Colorado Springs, CO 80901; 719–630–3433.

MANITOU SPRINGS   ID: NIPPER–CO

PIKE'S PEAK, CRIPPLE CREEK HISTORICAL AREA, U.S. AIR FORCE ACADEMY, NATIONAL CARVERS MUSEUM, CAVE OF THE WINDS, GARDEN OF THE GODS.

Near Hwy. 24, Manitou Ave., I–25.

Manitou Springs is a hundred-and-ten-year-old community located at the foot of Pike's Peak, five minutes from the Garden of the Gods, Cave of the Winds, two mountainside cog railroads, and many little specialty shops in their original turn-of-the-century condition. It is ten minutes from Colorado Springs and thirty minutes from the U.S. Air Force Academy. The twelve-room Queen Anne Victorian home is in a quiet residential area at the top of a hill, surrounded by vintage homes, an artists' colony, and quaint shops. From a balcony, there is a view across the valley to other mountains, including Pike's Peak, and the village of Manitou. The home was totally restored in the late 1970s and is decorated with period antiques, award-winning photographs of Colorado, collections of antique mustache cups, vintage dolls, miniatures, paintings, salty stained glass, clocks, and dishes. Each of the three guest rooms has a private sitting room, with TV and comfortable furnishings. The Queen Anne Room has a queen-sized cannonball bed, ceiling fan, lush cream-colored carpeting, and a view of the valley below and the front garden. The Queen Palmer Room is furnished with a queen-sized canopy bed and has a private entrance and private shower and vanity. The Princess Kathleen Room is an elegant but somewhat smaller room, with two antique double beds, handmade spreads, antique dresser, and vanity and a view of the village below. All three rooms share a bath. A Full breakfast of juice, fresh fruit, assorted egg and meat dishes, and breads and rolls is served. One of your hosts is a school psychologist who enjoys photography, golfing, and computers; the other, an elementary-school teacher, is an antiques and gardening enthusiast. Reservations are not accepted weekdays during the school year or during the weeks of Christmas and New Year's.

No. Rooms: 3	**Breakfast:** Full
Singles: None	**S-Rates:** $38 sb
Doubles: 3 sb	**D-Rates:** $44 sb
Type: Private home	**Bldg:** 1885 Queen Anne

Minimum Stay: none. **Credit Card(s) Accepted:** MC, V. **Open:** daily, summer; weekends Sept.–June. No resident dogs. No dogs please. No resident cats. No cats please. Host smokes. Guests may smoke. Children welcome with restrictions. **Discounts:** none. Spanish spoken.

Reservation Contact: Bed & Breakfast Colorado, Jim & Kate Carey, Box 6061, Boulder, CO 80306; 303–494–4944.

PAONIA
ID: 81428ETS

ROCKY MOUNTAINS, BLACK CANYON, SKIING, HUNTING, FISHING.

Near Rte. 133, Rte. 92.

Contemporary ranch-style home offers a relaxed easygoing atmosphere in a lovely mountainous area. The house has attractive traditional furnishings, a fireplace in the dining room, and a wood-burning stove in the living room. You are welcome to use the barbeque, TV, patio, deck, kitchen, and laundry facilities. The two guest rooms share a guest bath. The first room has a queen-sized bed, and beautiful view; the second has a double bed and similar furnishings. A Continental breakfast is served in the morning. With advance notice, your hosts can make arrangements for you to attend the Aspen Music Festival or Thunder Mountain Theater, or set up a date for horseback riding or river rafting. Other area activities include hunting, fishing, and skiing. Your hosts like to travel and are involved in church activities.

No. Rooms: 2	**Breakfast:** Continental
Singles: None	**S-Rates:** $35 sb
Doubles: 2 sb	**D-Rates:** $45 sb
Type: Private home	**Bldg:** Ranch style

Minimum Stay: none. **Credit Card(s) Accepted:** none. **Open:** all year. Dog in residence. No resident cats. Nonsmoking host. Guests may not smoke in guest rooms. Children welcome. **Discounts:** none.

Reservation Contact: Bed & Breakfast Registry Ltd., Gary Winget, Box 8174, St. Paul, MN 55108; 612–646–4238.

TELLURIDE
ID: SAN–SOPHIA

SKIING, HANG GLIDING, CHAMBER MUSIC & FILM FESTIVALS.

Near CO 145.

Established as a mining town in the 1880s, Telluride has a long and colorful history. Today it is primarily a resort area featuring skiing in winter and various festivals during the summer months. This inn offers 16 guest rooms with private baths. The rooms are divided into three categories: exclusive, select, and standard. Exclusive rooms have brass queen-sized, double, or twin beds and views of the waterfalls at the east end of the valley; some rooms also have private decks. Select rooms have queen-sized beds and views of Cornet Creek and the San Sophia Ridge. Standard rooms also have queen-sized brass beds and bay windows that face west for viewing spectacular sunsets. All rooms have handmade quilts and armoires with built-in cable TV. Other amenities include covered parking and concierge service. A Full, gourmet breakfast is served buffet-style. Both hosts enjoy hiking and downhill and cross-country skiing. The main hobby of one of your hosts is black-and-white photography and many of his photographs can be seen in the guest rooms.

No. Rooms: 16	**Breakfast:** Full
Singles: None	**S-Rates:** $60–$170 pb
Doubles: 16 pb	**D-Rates:** $60–$170 pb
Type: Inn	**Bldg:** Clapboard

Minimum Stay: none. **Credit Card(s) Accepted:** AE, MC, V. **Open:** all year. No resident dogs. No dogs please. No resident cats. No cats please. Nonsmoking host. Guests may not smoke in residence. Children welcome with restrictions. **Discounts:** 15% for 7 night stay.

Reservation Contact: The San Sophia, Gary & Dianne Eschman, 330 West Pacific Ave., Box 1825, Telluride, CO 81435; 800–537–4781.

CONNECTICUT

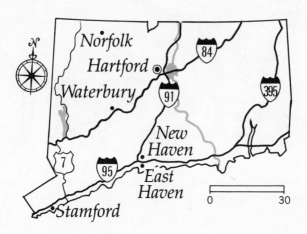

COLCHESTER

ID: 06415HAY

CONNECTICUT RIVER, MYSTIC SEAPORT.

Near CT 2, CT 85, CT 11.

This 1776 Federal-style home, listed on the National Register of Historic Places, has eight fireplaces and raised panel walls. Located on the Colchester town green, the house is close to Eash Haddam, the Connecticut River, Mystic Seaport, and the shore line. There are three guest rooms with private baths. The first has a queen-sized bed, antique furnishings, and a sitting room with a day bed. The second features a king-sized bed, chaise lounge, and an alcove with a table. The last is a two-room suite with a king-sized and a double bed and a Jacuzzi. A Continental Plus breakfast is served. Your hosts' interests include flying, skiing, historic houses, and herb gardening.

No. Rooms: 3	**Breakfast:** Continental Plus
Singles: None	**S-Rates:** $113 pb
Doubles: 3 pb	**D-Rates:** $125–$200 pb
Type: Inn	**Bldg:** 1776 Georgian Federal

Minimum Stay: 2 nights on weekends. **Credit Card(s) Accepted:** none. **Open:** all year. No resident dogs. No dogs please. No resident cats. No cats please. Host smokes. Guests may smoke. Children welcome. **Discounts:** none.

Reservation Contact: Bed & Breakfast Registry Ltd., Gary Winget, Box 8174, St. Paul, MN 55108; 612–646–4238.

EAST HAVEN

ID: 06512NEA

YALE UNIVERSITY, TROLLEY MUSEUM, THEATERS, MUSEUMS, BEACHFRONT.

Near Rte. 142, I–95, U.S. 1.

This spacious shoreline home, with beautiful Long Island Sound at its doorstep, is only 15 minutes from downtown New Haven. There is a family room with cable TV, porch, large yard with lawn table and chairs for lounging and sunbathing, and a private beach. Of the two single and two double guest rooms, two have views of the water and share a bath. Continental breakfast is served. A sailboat and rowboat are available, as is off-street parking. Your hosts' interests include reading, public relations, homemaking, and beach activities.

No. Rooms: 4	**Breakfast:** Continental
Singles: 2 sb	**S-Rates:** $35–$45 sb
Doubles: 2 sb	**D-Rates:** $65–$70 sb
Type: Private home	**Bldg:** 1920s beach house

Minimum Stay: none. **Credit Card(s) Accepted:** none. **Open:** all year. Dog in residence. No dogs please. No resident cats. No cats please. Host smokes. Guests may smoke. Children welcome. **Discounts:** none. Some French spoken.

Reservation Contact: Bed & Breakfast Registry Ltd., Gary Winget, Box 8174, St. Paul, MN 55108; 612–646–4238.

MERIDEN

ID: 06450SAU

Near Rte. 15, Rte. 66, I–91.

This spacious home, with two lakes on the surrounding property, offers guests hiking, canoeing, cross-country skiing, bicycling, and bird-watching. There are also decks and a screened porch for relaxing. There are two guest rooms available, one with twin beds, and one with double bed and private bath. Both offer a mountain country view. A Continental Plus breakfast is served. Your hosts are interested in tennis, racquetball, reading, singing, and volunteer work.

No. Rooms: 2	**Breakfast:** Continental Plus
Singles: None	**S-Rates:** $45 pb, $40 sb
Doubles: 1 pb, 1 sb	**D-Rates:** $55 pb, $50 sb
Type: Private home	

Minimum Stay: none. **Credit Card(s) Accepted:** none. **Open:** all year. No resident dogs. No dogs please. Cat in residence. No cats please. Non-smoking host. Guests may not smoke in residence. Children welcome. **Discounts:** none.

Reservation Contact: Bed & Breakfast Registry Ltd., Gary Winget, Box 8174, St. Paul, MN 55108; 612–646–4238.

NEW BRITAIN

ID: 06052VAN

MYSTIC AND STURBRIDGE VILLAGE 1 HOUR AWAY.

Near Corbin St., I–84.

This lovely home in a tree-lined residential community allows easy access to most points in the state. Guests may use the family room, with large fireplace and TV, the game room with pool table, and the outdoor deck for sunning. There is one air-conditioned guest room, recently redecorated with many antiques, two double beds, rocker, and wingback chair, private bath. A Continental breakfast is served. Your hosts' interests include golf, sailing, camping, tennis, and writing.

No. Rooms: 1	**Breakfast:** Continental
Singles: None	**S-Rates:** $35 sb
Doubles: 1 sb	**D-Rates:** $40 sb
Type: Private home	**Bldg:** Contemporary

Minimum Stay: 2 nights. **Credit Card(s) Accepted:** none. **Open:** all year. No resident dogs. No dogs please. No resident cats. No cats please. Nonsmoking host. Guests may smoke. **Discounts:** none.

Reservation Contact: Bed & Breakfast Registry Ltd., Gary Winget, Box 8174, St. Paul, MN 55108; 612–646–4238.

NEW HARTFORD   ID: CT16–COVBR

BERKSHIRE FOOTHILLS.

Near rtes. 44 & 219.

This Colonial home is situated in a country setting. Guests can stroll down a country road, swim in the spring-fed pond, or relax in the terraced yard with huge old trees and lovely gardens. The Hen & Rooster Room has chestnut-plank floors, braided rugs, a double bed with canopy, comfortable chairs, an antique chest, and a private bath. The walls of the Barnyard Room have a border of stenciled animals and the bed is a step-up bed with many pillows and a fluffy comforter. This room has a private bath with a tub (no shower). The Calico Cat Room has twin beds, and the Gooseberry Room has a queen-sized canopy bed with lace sides curtains, a loveseat, and a view of the garden. A child's room is also available. The host serves a Full breakfast which might include melon, pumpkin bread, bacon or sausage, and french toast with raspberry filling.

No. Rooms: 4	**Breakfast:** Full
Singles: None	**S-Rates:** $85 sb, $95 pb
Doubles: 4	**D-Rates:** $85 sb, $95 pb
Type: Private home	**Bldg:** Colonial

Minimum Stay: 2 nights on weekends. **Credit Card(s) Accepted:** none. **Open:** Apr.–Jan. Resident dog. No dogs please. Resident cat. No cats please. Nonsmoking hosts. Guests may not smoke in residence. Children welcome with restrictions. **Discounts:** none.

Reservation Contact: Covered Bridge Bed & Breakfast, Diane Tremblay, Box 447, Norfold, CT 06058; 203–542–5944.

NORFOLK   ID: C15–COVBR

NORFOLK HISTORICAL MUSEUM, YALE SUMMER SCHOOL OF MUSIC AND ART, TANGLEWOOD, MUSIC MOUNTAIN, RIDING STABLES, LIME ROCK PARK; SKIING, HIKING.

Near Rte. 8, U.S. 44.

In the 1800s Norfolk was a resort for the very wealthy, and that influence is still seen in the neighboring homes and grounds. This elegant Victorian inn was built in 1898 by Charles Spofford, architect of London's subway system and son of Ainsworth Rand Spofford, Abraham Lincoln's Librarian of Congress. The inn is completely furnished with antiques and features a six-foot fireplace. Guests step into the cherry-paneled foyer and are surrounded by old-world refinement in the baronial living and breakfast rooms with Tiffany and leaded-glass windows. Guests ascend the handsomely carved cherry staircase to the eight guest rooms, six with private baths. Great care was taken in the decoration of each of the rooms, each with its own distinct charm. The Morgan Room is furnished with a queen-sized bed with antique cherry headboard, built-in dresser, reading chair, and small table and chairs. The private bath has both a tub and shower, and there is also a private balcony. The Spofford Room has a king-sized bed with an antique lace canopy, a built-in dresser, and table and chairs for dining. A sofa and rocking chair surround a beautiful Victorian fireplace. The private bath features a shower and marble sink. The furnishings of the Lincoln Room include an antique sleigh bed with an ornately carved headboard, mahogany dressing table, dining table, Victorian couch, fireplace, and a private bath with shower. La Chambre has an antique brass double bed, mahogany dresser, easy chairs, and a very large Art-Deco bath with claw-foot tub. In the English Room, the twin beds can be converted to a king-sized bed, and a dressing table and large sitting area with sofa and easy chair are featured. The bath, with brass fixtures, has a shower. Guests are pampered with breakfast in bed or served on the sunlit porch or in the elegant dining room. A typical breakfast might consist of eggs, bacon, blueberry pancakes, orange waffles, French toast stuffed with seasonal berries, and homemade breads and muffins, all served with steaming pots of coffee, fine teas, and juice. Complimentary champagne is provided for honeymoons and anniversaries, and there are even horse-drawn sleigh or carriage rides during the winter months. Guests then return for mulled cider and popcorn in front of the fire. Norfolk Historical Museum and the Yale Summer School of Music and Art, which hosts the annual Summer Chamber Music Series, are within walking distance of the inn. Nearby, guests will find Tanglewood and Music Mountain, alpine and cross-country skiing, hiking, biking, horseback riding, antique and craft shops, vineyards, theater, golf, and water sports. Your hosts are both college graduates who left executive positions to become innkeepers. They have traveled extensively and enjoy racquetball, hiking, biking, antiquing, gardening, water sports, and cross-country skiing.

No. Rooms: 8	**Breakfast:** Full
Singles: None	**S-Rates:** $65–$130 pb, $45–$65 sb
Doubles: 6 pb, 2 sb	**D-Rates:** $65–$120 pb,
Type: Inn	$65–$90 sb
	Bldg: 1898 English Tudor

Minimum Stay: 2 days over holidays. **Credit Card(s) Accepted:** AE, MC, V. **Open:** all year. No resident dogs. No dogs please. Cat in residence. No cats please. Nonsmoking host. Guests may not smoke in guest rooms. Children welcome with restrictions. **Discounts:** midweek. French spoken.

Reservation Contact: Covered Bridge Bed & Breakfast, Diane Tremblay, Box 447, Norfolk, CT 06058; 203–542–5944.

DELAWARE

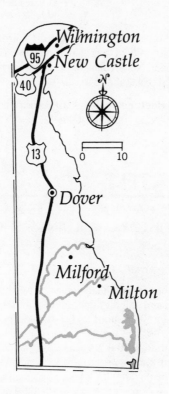

MILTON

ID: 19968MIL

REHOBOTH AND LEWES BEACHES, CANOEING,
BIKING, ANTIQUING.

Near MD 1 & Rte. 5, US 113, US 9.

This charming Federal-style inn is close to ocean beaches. The four air-
conditioned guest rooms are simply but comfortably furnished. A Continental Plus breakfast is served. From this location guests may walk or bike
around Wagamon's Pond and historic Milton (which has some of the finest surviving concentration of 19th-century architecture in the county),
go antiquing or bargain hunting at garage sales and auctions, or take a
canoe ride through Prime Hook Wildlife Refuge. Your host is a former

Madison Avenue accountant, credit consultant, and realtor who decided to seek a simpler life in this historic little town.

No. Rooms: 4	**Breakfast:** Continental Plus
Singles: 1 sb	**S-Rates:** $30–$35 sb
Doubles: 3 sb	**D-Rates:** $45–$50 sb
Type: Small inn	**Bldg:** 1900 Federal

Minimum Stay: 2 days July–Aug. **Credit Card(s) Accepted:** none. **Open:** all year. No resident dogs. Guest may bring dog. No resident cats. Guest may bring cat. Nonsmoking host. Guest may smoke. Children welcome. **Discounts:** 10% after 3 days.

Reservation Contact: Bed & Breakfast Registry Ltd., Gary Winget, Box 8174, St. Paul, MN 55108; 612–646–4238.

NEW CASTLE   ID: 19720JEF

LONGWOOD GARDENS, HAGLEY & WINTERTHUR MUSEUMS, HISTORIC BUILDINGS, SHOPS, RESTAURANTS.

Near Stant at the Wharf, U.S. 40, U.S. 13.

Located only an hour from Philadelphia and two hours from Washington, New Castle's quaint cobblestone streets, museums, historic Colonial buildings, and interesting shops and restaurants make it an ideal spot for a get-away weekend. This two-hundred-year-old home stands at the foot of the wharf near an official "William Penn landed here . . ." historical marker. There are three guest rooms with private baths. The first is an efficiency apartment with full kitchen. The second, on the first floor, features an original working fireplace, and the third boasts a screened porch with a view of the Delaware River. The rooms are tastefully furnished either with antiques or in a country motif, and all have private entrances and air-conditioning. A Full breakfast or Sunday brunch is served in an affiliated restaurant.

No. Rooms: 3	**Breakfast:** Full
Singles: None	**S-Rates:** $65 pb
Doubles: 3 pb	**D-Rates:** $65 pb
Type: Private home	**Bldg:** 1700s Georgian

Minimum Stay: none. **Credit Card(s) Accepted:** none. **Open:** all year. No resident dogs. No dogs please. No resident cats. No cats please. Children welcome. **Discounts:** off season.

Reservation Contact: Bed & Breakfast Registry Ltd., Gary Winget, Box 8174, St. Paul, MN 55108; 612–646–4238.

WILMINGTON

ID: 19803SMA

COLONIAL NEW CASTLE, LONGWOOD GARDENS, WINTERTHUR MUSEUM & GARDENS, HAGLEY MUSEUM, NEMOURS.

Near Marsh Rd., I–95, I–295, I–495.

This modified Cape Cod home features traditional furnishings, award-winning landscaping, in-ground pool (May-Sept.), year-round hot tub, and air-conditioning. In addition to the living room with fireplace, den, study, recreation, and music rooms, there are three guest rooms, one with private bath, two with shared bath. The first is a large sunny room, with dormer windows, walnut furniture, twin beds, desk, and reclining rocker. The Oak Nest Room has a king-sized bed and Art-Deco mahogany furniture, and adjoins a study with console TV and queen-sized sofa bed. A third room, overlooking the pool and garden, has birch furniture and a double bed. A Full breakfast of your choice is served until 9:30 A.M. Your congenial hosts are native to the area and are thus informed guides to local history and the many surrounding attractions. Their hobbies include music, theater, travel, gardening, history, and cooking. (For more detailed information about area attractions, see Kennett Square, PA.)

No. Rooms: 3	**Breakfast:** Full
Singles: None	**S-Rates:** $55 pb, $45 sb
Doubles: 1 pb, 2 sb	**D-Rates:** $65 pb, $60 sb
Type: Private home	**Bldg:** 1950 modified Cape Cod

Minimum Stay: none. **Credit Card(s) Accepted:** MC, V with fee. **Open:** all year. No resident dogs. No dogs please. No resident cats. No cats please. Nonsmoking host. Guests may not smoke in residence. Children welcome with restrictions. **Discounts:** weekly & monthly.

Reservation Contact: Bed & Breakfast Registry Ltd., Gary Winget, Box 8174, St. Paul, MN 55108; 612–646–4238.

DISTRICT OF
COLUMBIA

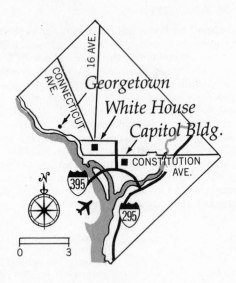

ID: BB,LTD100

LOGAN CIRCLE.

Near Rhode Island Ave., Vermont Ave.

The one-hundred-year-old Victorian mansion built by John Shipman as his personal residence has been carefully and extensively restored by its present owners. Exterior landscaping, gardens, a terrace, and fountains have been added to the original townhouse. The house features the original wood paneling, stained glass, chandeliers, Victorian lattice porch, and Victorian and art-nouveau antiques and decorations. It is on the Logan Circle House Tour and has appeared in local magazines. In addition to air-conditioned guest rooms with color TVs, there is a fully equipped one-bedroom apartment for longer stays or family groups. A crib and laundry facilities are available. The house adjoins the Logan Circle Historic District, with excellent transportation and easy parking. It is located ten blocks from the White House and seven blocks from the Metro, with two major bus lines to take guests to the Mall, Capitol, or Georgetown only a block away. One of your hosts is a lawyer and a partner in a real-estate development and syndication firm; the other has studied interior design and was involved in real-estate development prior to becoming a bed-and-breakfast host.

No. Rooms: 6	**Breakfast:** Continental
Singles: None	**S-Rates:** $50–$60
Doubles: 5 sb, 1 pb	**D-Rates:** $60–$70
Type: Townhouse	**Bldg:** 1880s Victorian

Minimum Stay: none. **Credit Card(s) Accepted:** AE, MC, V. **Open:** all year. Children welcome. **Discounts:** none. French spoken.

Reservation Contact: Bed 'n' Breakfast Ltd. of Washington, DC, Lisa Stofan, Box 12011, Washington, DC 20005; 202–328–3510.

ID: BB,LTD111

DUPONT CIRCLE.

Near Massachusetts Ave., Connecticut Ave.

In 1880, when the federal government did not have enough funds to give pensions to the Union generals, it built a row of townhouses and gave them to the victors in lieu of cash payments. Today this group of dwellings is aptly known as Generals' Row. Located just three blocks from Dupont Circle, the area boasts excellent restaurants, bookstores, and boutiques. This house offers three guest rooms, one with twin beds and shared bath, one with a double bed and shared bath, and one with double bed and private bath. Your host, an artist, is the brains behind many of the city's art auctions and benefit galas. Guests just might arrive to find people stuffing flyers into envelopes or addressing invitations. Occasionally an informal showing by some new local artist is held at the house. Your host also does catering and is known for her delicious breakfasts.

No. Rooms: 3	**Breakfast:** Continental Plus
Singles: None	**S-Rates:** $35 sb, $40 pb
Doubles: 2 sb, 1 pb	**D-Rates:** $45 sb, $50 pb
Type: Private townhouse	**Bldg:** 1880s

Minimum Stay: none. **Credit Card(s) Accepted:** AE, MC, V. **Open:** all year. No resident dogs. No dogs please. Resident cats. No cats please. **Discounts:** none.

Reservation Contact: Bed 'n' Breakfast Ltd. of Washington, DC, Lisa Stofan, Box 12011, Washington, DC 20005; 202–328–3510.

ID: BB,LTD119

CLEVELAND PARK, WASHINGTON CATHEDRAL.

Near Wisconsin Ave., Connecticut Ave.

This spacious frame/stucco home, in one of Washington's most distinguished neighborhoods, has one large guest room with twin beds, private bath, air-conditioning, color TV, and large walk-in closet. Weather permitting, breakfast is served on an outdoor porch overlooking the flower and vegetable garden. The house is located in Cleveland Park, midway between Wisconsin and Connecticut avenues. The Metro stop is six blocks away, and a connecting bus stop is one block away. Shops and restaurants are within walking distance, and six blocks away is Washington Cathedral. One of your hosts is a journalist who writes for agricultural journals in several countries, and a economic development consultant.

No. Rooms: 1	**Breakfast:** Continental
Singles: None	**S-Rates:** $45 pb
Doubles: 1 pb	**D-Rates:** $55 pb
Type: Private home	**Bldg:** Frame stucco

Minimum Stay: none. **Credit Card(s) Accepted:** none. **Open:** all year. No resident dogs. No dogs please. No resident cats. No cats please. Nonsmoking host. Guests may smoke. Children welcome. **Discounts:** none.

Reservation Contact: Bed 'n' Breakfast Ltd. of Washington, DC, Lisa Stofan, Box 12011, Washington, DC 20005; 202–328–3510.

ID: BB,LTD126

TENLEY CIRCLE, AMERICAN UNIVERSITY.

Near Wisconsin & Nebraska aves.

Just one block from the Tenleytown Metro station and major bus routes, this Georgian-style brick Colonial with slate roof offers easy access to downtown business areas, tourist attractions, and embassies. Within two blocks are restaurants, shops, movie theaters, tennis courts, and an indoor swimming pool. There are two large guest rooms with wall-to-wall carpeting, color TVs, and private baths, and each has a small dining table and sitting area. The rooms are tastefully furnished with antiques and reproductions. One room has a maple-and-pine four-poster double bed with canopy, a full-sized sofa, and a view of the garden. The second room has a queen-sized bed and a private balcony overlooking the garden.

No. Rooms: 2	**Breakfast:** Continental
Singles: None	**S-Rates:** $45 pb
Doubles: 2 pb	**D-Rates:** $55 pb
Type: Private home	**Bldg:** Georgian colonial

Minimum Stay: none. **Credit Card(s) Accepted:** AE, MC, V. **Open:** all year. No resident dogs. No dogs please. Resident cat. No cats please. Nonsmoking hosts. Guests may not smoke in residence. Children welcome. **Discounts:** none.

Reservation Contact: Bed 'n' Breakfast Ltd. of Washington, DC, Lisa Stofan, Box 12011, Washington, DC 20005; 202–328–3510.

ID: BB,LTD129

GALLERIES, FINE RESTAURANTS, SHOPS; DUPONT CIRCLE.

Near Massachusetts Ave., Connecticut Ave.

This freestanding single-family dwelling was designed by Washington architect Ferdinand J. Schneider and built in 1903 by Thomas C. Henderson. It reflects the Romanesque Revival style, popular during the Victorian era. Stones for the massive front door jamb and balustrade were hewn from the same quarry as the stones used to build the original Smithsonian building. The house retains its original oak woodwork, pocket shutters and doors, red Georgia pine floors, gas fireplaces with their ornate mantles, a walk-in silver safe, and speaking tubes connecting the servants' quarters with the upper floors. The five double guest rooms with private baths are tastefully decorated with authentic Victorian furnishings, period reproduction wallpapers, antique chandeliers, intricately carved furniture, and lace curtains. Dupont Circle, in the heart of Washington, is midway between the National Cathedral and the Capitol dome, and just minutes by Metro to the downtown business district, the White House, and Capitol Mall. For evening entertainment, Georgetown and the Kennedy Center are a short drive away. Specialty shops, cafés, and galleries are within walking distance. Both hosts are attorneys, originally from New Jersey. One is a member of a local choral group; the other enjoys woodworking. Members of the Victorian Society, both like to cook and hunt for antiques.

No. Rooms: 5	**Breakfast:** Continental
Singles: None	**S-Rates:** $45–$55 pb
Doubles: 5 pb	**D-Rates:** $55–$65 pb
Type: Private home	**Bldg:** 1903 Romanesque revival

Minimum Stay: none. **Credit Card(s) Accepted:** none. **Open:** all year. No dogs please. No cats please. Guests may not smoke in residence. Residence not appropriate for children. **Discounts:** none.

Reservation Contact: Bed 'n' Breakfast Ltd. of Washington, DC, Lisa Stofan, Box 12011, Washington, DC 20005; 202–328–3510.

ID: BB,LTD131

FRIENDSHIP HEIGHTS.

Near Wisconsin Ave., Military Rd.

This Federal-style brick house, custom-designed by the owners, features a lovely stained-glass window, several fireplaces, antiques, a walled-in garden, and heated outdoor swimming pool. There is also a game room with pool table, pinball machine, game table, and stereo. The two guest rooms each offer a private bath. The room on the lower level is large, with a double bed and a hide-a-bed, TV, and fireplace. The other, on the upper level, has a double bed and antique furnishings. There is an adjacent sitting room with TV. The house is on a quiet tree-lined street just inside the District of Columbia border. Located midway between Wisconsin and Connecticut avenues, this dwelling is convenient to numerous restaurants, movie theaters, and the Mazza Gallery, where guests can browse through shops, like Neiman Marcus, or dine in lovely cafés. A ten-minute walk brings you to the Metro, and there are buses at both Wisconsin and Connecticut avenues. One of your hosts is an attorney who has had a Pentagon appointment and a foreign-service assignment in Brazil; the other runs her own consulting business and enjoys decorating and cooking. Both have traveled extensively.

No. Rooms: 2	**Breakfast:** Continental
Singles: None	**S-Rates:** $50 pb
Doubles: 2 pb	**D-Rates:** $61 pb
Type: Private home	**Bldg:** 1982 brick Federal

Minimum Stay: none. **Credit Card(s) Accepted:** none. **Open:** all year. Guests may not smoke in guest rooms. **Discounts:** none.

Reservation Contact: Bed 'n' Breakfast Ltd. of Washington, DC, Lisa Stofan, Box 12011, Washington, DC 20005; 202–328–3510.

ID: BB,LTD137

KALORAMA AREA.

Near Connecticut Ave., Columbus Ave.

Built in the early 1900s by Harry Wardman, this apartment building is now on the Register of Historic Buildings. Wardman also built the Wardman Park—now the Sheraton Washington Hotel—and many other distinguished buildings in the Kalorama area. This bright and sunny apartment, with all the rooms facing the outside, has a unique blend of Oriental and English furniture and artifacts. Twenty-four-hour security and a wonderful roof garden with a spectacular view of the city are other special features. The sunny guest room has a large picture window, double bed, and private bath. Guests are welcome to use the adjacent den with color TV. The building is located between the Sheraton Washington and the Washington Hilton hotels. Two Metro stations are within a ten-minute walk, and the building is on a direct bus line to all downtown locations. Fine restaurants and shops are nearby along Connecticut Avenue. Your host, a seventh-generation Washingtonian who lived in England and Ireland for almost fifteen years, was press secretary to Mrs. Nixon. In addition to her five years at the White House, she was executive secretary for eighteen years to three bureau chiefs at the New York Daily News and served as assistant information officer at the American Embassy in London for three years.

No. Rooms: 1	**Breakfast:** Continental
Singles: None	**S-Rates:** $61 pb
Doubles: 1 pb	**D-Rates:** $72 pb
Type: Private apartment	**Bldg:** 1900s

Minimum Stay: none. **Credit Card(s) Accepted:** none. **Open:** all year. **Discounts:** none.

Reservation Contact: Bed 'n' Breakfast Ltd. of Washington, DC, Lisa Stofan, Box 12011, Washington, DC 20005; 202–328–3510.

WOODLEY PARK, ZOO, NATIONAL CATHEDRAL

Near Connecticut Ave. & Woodley Rd.

This spacious house was designed by Harry Wardman who developed the elegant, tree-lined district adjacent to Rock Creek Park. All three guest rooms have private baths; one has twin beds and a sitting room while the other two have single beds. There is an enclosed garden in the back where parking is available. The home is ten minutes from the Woodley Park-Zoo subway station, the National Zoo, the National Cathedral, and numerous restaurants. The host is a native Washingtonian who is active in the arts.

No. Rooms: 3		**Breakfast:** Continental	
Singles: 2 pb		**S-Rates:** $50 pb	
Doubles: 1 pb		**D-Rates:** $60 pb	
Type: Private home		**Bldg:** Georgian	

Minimum Stay: none. **Credit Card(s) Accepted:** AE, MC, V. **Open:** all year. Resident cat. No cats please. Resident dog. No dogs please. Host smokes. Guests may smoke. Children welcome. **Discounts:** none.

Reservation Contact: Bed 'n' Breakfast Ltd. of Washington, DC, Lisa Stofan, Box 12011, Washington, DC 20005; 202–328–3510.

CAPITOL HILL, SUPREME COURT, LIBRARY OF CONGRESS.

Near Mass. Ave. and 10th St.

This townhouse is in a prestigious, tree-lined district on Capitol Hill. The elegantly restored and appointed thirteen-room residence is a fine example of Colonial Revival architecture. There are three guest rooms with shared bath, and a one-bedroom apartment available. Two of the rooms have double beds and one has twin beds. The house is twelve blocks from the Capitol, Supreme Court, and the Library of Congress. It is near Capitol Hill's shopping hub with boutiques, antique shops, restaurants, and pubs. The subway is five blocks away and major bus lines are nearby. The host is consultant and a partner in a catering firm and is active in community affairs and the arts.

No. Rooms: 4		**Breakfast:** Continental	
Singles: None		**S-Rates:** $50 sb, $60 pb	
Doubles: 3 sb, 1 pb		**D-Rates:** $60 sb, $65 pb	
Type: Private home		**Bldg:** Townhouse	

Minimum Stay: none. **Credit Card(s) Accepted:** AE, MC, V. **Open:** all year. No resident dogs. No dogs please. Resident cats. No cats please. Nonsmoking host. Guests may smoke. Children welcome. **Discounts:** none.

Reservation Contact: Bed 'n' Breakfast Ltd. of Washington, DC, Lisa Stofan, Box 12011, Washington, DC 20005; 202–328–3510.

ID: SWE–BECKER

AMERICAN UNIVERSITY/WESLEY HEIGHTS AREA.

Near New Mexico & Cathedral, NW; Nebraska Ave., rtes. 495, 50, 66.

This Colonial brick townhouse in the Wesley Heights area is a five-minute walk from American University and a five-minute drive from Georgetown. Guests may avail themselves of the fireplace, TV, and patio. One small guest room features twin beds and private bath. A Full breakfast is served.

No. Rooms: 1	**Breakfast:** Full
Singles: None	**S-Rates:** $45 pb
Doubles: 1 pb	**D-Rates:** $55 pb
Type: Private townhouse	**Bldg:** 1979 colonial brick

Minimum Stay: 2 nights. **Credit Card(s) Accepted:** none. **Open:** all year. Dog in residence. No dogs please. No resident cats. No cats please. Nonsmoking host. Guests may not smoke in residence. Children welcome. **Discounts:** none.

Reservation Contact: The Bed & Breakfast League/Sweet Dreams & Toast, Millie Groobey, Box 9490, Washington, DC 20008; 202–363–7767.

ID: SWE–CLINTON

AMERICAN UNIVERSITY PARK.

Near I–95, I–495.

This typical single-family colonial brick structure is located in a quiet residential neighborhood called American University Park. The nearby Metro assures easy access to all major monuments, museums, and art galleries in the nation's capital. Two guest rooms share a bath with the family. One has twin beds, desk, and black and white TV; the other, in the library, is furnished with a hide-a-bed, two cushioned chairs, several thousand books, and a color TV. A Continental breakfast is served. Your friendly, casual hosts, winners of *Washingtonian* magazine's "How Well Do You Know Washington?" contest, are anxious to make guests comfortable and your stay memorable. They offer a personalized tour built around the wishes of their guests. One host is a director at the Depart-

ment of D.C. Energy; the other is a director of nursing. They enjoy sports and travel.

No. Rooms: 2
Singles: 1 sb
Doubles: 1 sb
Type: Private home

Breakfast: Continental
S-Rates: $40–$43 sb
D-Rates: $50–$53 sb
Bldg: 1939 brick colonial

Minimum Stay: 2 nights. **Credit Card(s) Accepted:** none. **Open:** all year. Dog in residence. No dogs please. No resident cats. No cats please. Nonsmoking host. Guests may not smoke in residence. Children welcome. **Discounts:** none.

Reservation Contact: The Bed & Breakfast League/Sweet Dreams & Toast, Millie Groobey, Box 9490, Washington, DC 20008; 202–363–7767.

ID: SWE–CRAIG

NATIONAL CATHEDRAL, ZOO, WOODLEY PARK.

Near Connecticut & Cathedral aves., Capital Beltway.

Just across the Connecticut Avenue Bridge from Dupont Circle, Woodley Park is a neighborhood with lots of greenery, restaurants, shops, pubs, and entertainment. Within walking distance are the National Cathedral, the Zoo, fine dining and ethnic bistros, and Rock Creek Park. The subway is three blocks away. This large, Federal-style brick townhouse was designed and built in 1911 by architect Harry Wardman. Except for the modernized baths and kitchen, the house retains its original character, with decorative moldings, brass fixtures, columns, and chandeliers. Furnishings are an eclectic blend of antique and contemporary. An extensive library, including resources on Washington, is available to guests. There are three guest rooms, two with private bath. The Blue Room, a two-room suite, has queen-sized bed, Eastlake-style furniture with marble tops, a desk, sitting room, and private bath. The third-floor Yellow Room has twin beds and a shared bath. The Executive Suite, a small lower-level apartment, features kitchen facilities, TV, air-conditoning, desk, double bed, private bath, and private entrance. A Continental breakfast is served in the cheery breakfast room or on the terrace; both overlook the garden. One of your hosts is a management consultant and the other is a self-employed lobbyist. They collect antiques and like to explore out-of-the-way country towns and inns. She enjoys gourmet cooking and is active in the women's movement.

No. Rooms: 3	**Breakfast:** Continental
Singles: None	**S-Rates:** $45–$50 pb, $35–$40 sb
Doubles: 2 pb, 1 sb	**D-Rates:** $55–$60 pb, $45–$50 sb
Type: Private townhouse	**Bldg:** 1911 Federal

Minimum Stay: 2 nights. **Credit Card(s) Accepted:** none. **Open:** all year. No resident dogs. No dogs please. No resident cats. No cats please. Nonsmoking host. Guests may not smoke in residence. Children welcome with restrictions. **Discounts:** none.

Reservation Contact: The Bed & Breakfast League/Sweet Dreams & Toast, Millie Groobey, Box 9490, Washington, DC 20008; 202–363–7767.

ID: SWE–MILLER

MUSEUMS, HISTORIC SITES, RESTAURANTS, SHOPPING; DUPONT CIRCLE.

Near 19th St., Florida Ave.

Dupont Circle is an area of historic homes, convenient to all attractions. This large Georgian home, built in 1908, has been beautifully restored and furnished with antiques and Oriental rugs. Guests have the use of two living rooms and access to the library, garden, and patio. Four guest rooms share a guest bath. One room has a double bed, easy chair, lamps, bureau, mirror, and a wall lined with bookcases. The second is furnished with a queen-sized bed, desk, easy chair, and bureau. The two third-floor rooms have twin beds and furnishings similar to the second-floor rooms. Third-floor guests also have a private deck. A Continental Plus breakfast is served. Your hosts, who lived in Brazil for over five years, have traveled extensively. One is a psychiatric social worker; the other is a published writer.

No. Rooms: 4	**Breakfast:** Continental Plus
Singles: None	**S-Rates:** $50 sb
Doubles: 4 sb	**D-Rates:** $60 sb
Type: Private home	**Bldg:** 1908 Georgian

Minimum Stay: 2 nights. **Credit Card(s) Accepted:** none. **Open:** all year. No resident dogs. No dogs please. No resident cats. No cats please. Nonsmoking host. Guests may not smoke in guest rooms. Children welcome with restrictions. **Discounts:** none.

Reservation Contact: The Bed & Breakfast League/Sweet Dreams & Toast, Millie Groobey, Box 9490, Washington, DC 20008; 202–363–7767.

ID: 20008WOO

WOODLEY PARK, ZOO, NW WASHINGTON.

Near Connecticut & Cathedral aves.

This turn-of-the-century house, in a residential neighborhood with tree-lined streets and old-fashioned lamp posts, is one block from outdoor cafés and convenience stores. There are nineteen guest rooms, twelve with private baths. One very large room, with private bath and two double beds, has the original marble fireplace, period furnishings and artwork, and a built-in bookcase. One of the suites is furnished with a camel-back hide-a-bed that faces an elaborately carved fireplace mantle. The bedroom has a queen-sized bed, empire dresser, 1920s sewing stand, a separate dressing room, and a private bath. A third room is furnished with a double bed, an English armoire, and an antique tile wood-burning stove. It, too, has the original fireplace mantle and private bath. There is a sunny corner room in which antique charcoal portraits hang over twin beds. It has an empire dresser, turn-of-the-century bric-a-brac, and large private bath with the original tiles. Another room has a queen-sized bed, antique oak dresser and desk, sewing stand, and private porch. This room shares a bath. You are welcome to use the TV and the telephone for local calls. The house is air-conditioned and is near public transportation. A Continental breakfast is served, as is afternoon sherry.

No. Rooms: 19	**Breakfast:** Continental
Singles: None	**S-Rates:** $60–$85 pb, $45–$65 sb
Doubles: 12 pb, 7 sb	**D-Rates:** $65–$90 pb, $45–$65 sb
Type: Inn	**Bldg:** 1903 turn-of-the-century

Minimum Stay: none. **Credit Card(s) Accepted:** AE, MC, V. **Open:** all year. No resident dogs. No dogs please. No resident cats. No cats please. Nonsmoking host. Guests may smoke. Children welcome with restrictions. **Discounts:** none.

Reservation Contact: Bed & Breakfast Registry Ltd., Gary Winget, Box 8174, St. Paul, MN 55108; 612–646–4238.

ID: 20009KAL

WALK TO RESTAURANTS & SHOPS; NW WASHINGTON.

Near Connecticut Ave., Columbia.

These three cozy Victorian townhouses are situated in a quiet residential neighborhood. The main house has a parlor and dining area with fireplace, where you can chat, eat breakfast, or enjoy an afternoon sherry.

The decor in each of the guest rooms differs, but the cozy old-fashioned charm stays the same with brass beds, plush comforters, Oriental carpets, green plants, and turn-of-the-century artwork. The houses are air-conditioned and within walking distance of the subway.

No. Rooms: 31	**Breakfast:** Continental
Singles: 2 pb, 2 sb	**S-Rates:** $50–$75 pb, $40–$60 sb
Doubles: 16 pb, 11 sb	**D-Rates:** $55–$80 pb, $45–$65 sb
Type: Inn	**Bldg:** 1890s Victorian townhouse

Minimum Stay: none. **Credit Card(s) Accepted:** AE, MC, V. **Open:** all year. No resident dogs. No dogs please. No resident cats. No cats please. Nonsmoking host. Guests may smoke. Children welcome with restrictions. **Discounts:** none.

Reservation Contact: Bed & Breakfast Registry Ltd., Gary Winget, Box 8174, St. Paul, MN 55108; 612–646–4238.

FLORIDA

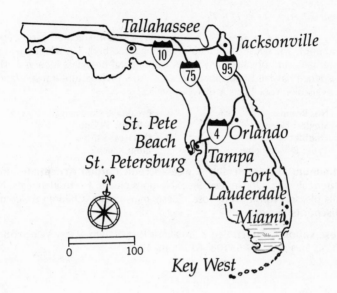

Tallahassee
Jacksonville
10
75 95
St. Pete
Beach
4 Orlando
St. Petersburg
Tampa
Fort
Lauderdale
Miami
N
0   100
Key West

FORT LAUDERDALE

ID: TROP.FL#213

OCEAN, SHOPS, RESTAURANTS.

Near Sunrise Blvd. & A1A.

This contemporary ranch-style home offers proximity to both the ocean and the shops and restaurants along Sunrise. The two guest rooms share a bath. One room has twin beds and the other has a double bed. A Continental breakfast is served. Amenities include off-street parking and use of the TV, telephone, and yard.

No. Rooms: 2
Singles: None
Doubles: 2 sb
Type: Private home

Breakfast: Continental
S-Rates: $30–$35 sb
D-Rates: $35–$40 sb
Bldg: Ranch-style

Minimum Stay: $5 surcharge for stays of 1–2 nights. **Credit Card(s) Accepted:** AE, MC, V. **Open:** all year. No resident dogs. No dogs please. No resident cats. No cats please. Nonsmoking host. Guests may not smoke in residence. Children welcome. **Discounts:** monthly.

Reservation Contact: Bed & Breakfast Co.—Tropical Florida, M. Schaible, Box 262, So. Miami, FL 33243; 305–661–3270.

ID: 33305WAR

EVERGLADES, BEACH; SHOPS, RESTAURANTS.

Near 21 Ave., U.S. 1, I–95.

This contemporary ranch-style house has a well-manicured yard, patio, and pool. The guest room features a king-sized bed, TV, telephone, private bath, and private entrance. A Continental breakfast is served. The residence has fair handicapped access. Arrival/departure transportation is available. Your hosts are well-traveled.

No. Rooms: 1	**Breakfast:** Continental
Singles: None	**S-Rates:** $45 pb
Doubles: 1 pb	**D-Rates:** $45 pb
Type: Private home	**Bldg:** Ranch

Minimum Stay: preferably a week. **Credit Card(s) Accepted:** none. **Open:** all year. Dog in residence. No dogs please. No resident cats. No cats please. Nonsmoking host. Guests may smoke. Children welcome. **Discounts:** none.

Reservation Contact: Bed & Breakfast Registry Ltd., Gary Winget, Box 8174, St. Paul, MN 55108; 612–646–4238.

HOLLEY   ID: TROP.FL#201

PENSACOLA BEACH, FT. WALTON BEACH.

Near U.S. 98, 87, I–10.

This contemporary ranch home is located on East Bay between Pensacola and Fort Walton Beach. Landscaped grounds surround the patio and pool, and guests can relax in a hammock under the trees. There are two guest rooms with private baths. One is a glassed-in room with a double studio bed, and the other has a conventional double bed. An apartment is also available that offers a living room with a hide-a-bed, a king-sized bed in the bedroom, kitchen, private bath, skylight, elegant contemporary furnishings, and a private entrance onto the pool and garden area. Your hosts are a retired contractor and an artist.

No. Rooms: 3	**Breakfast:** Continental
Singles: None	**S-Rates:** $30–$55 pb
Doubles: 3 pb	**D-Rates:** $35–$60 pb
Type: Private home	**Bldg:** Contemporary ranch-style

Minimum Stay: Surcharge for 1–2-night stays. **Credit Card(s) Accepted:** AE, MC, V. **Open:** all year. No resident dogs. No dogs please. No resident cats. No cats please. Nonsmoking hosts. Guests may smoke. Children welcome with restrictions. **Discounts:** monthly rates.

Reservation Contact: Bed & Breakfast Co.—Tropical Florida, M. Schaible, Box 262, So. Miami, FL 33243; 305–661–3270.

JACKSONVILLE
ID: TROP.FL#207

HISTORIC AREA, RIVERFRONT.

Near I–95, I–10.

This Federal-style clapboard house, built in 1912, is in the Jacksonville historic area. It sits beside the St. Johns River surrounded by flowering shrubs and towering trees. Three of the four guest rooms are suites with adjacent sitting rooms. Two have twin beds, one a double bed, and one a queen-sized bed. Two have private baths. A Full breakfast is served. Guests can walk to interesting shops and restaurants and the downtown area is a short drive. Your hosts are active in civic activities and enjoy travel and antiques.

No. Rooms: 4	**Breakfast:** Full
Singles: None	**S-Rates:** $50 pb, $50 sb
Doubles: 2 pb, 2 sb	**D-Rates:** $55 pb, $55 sb
Type: Private home	**Bldg:** Federal clapboard

Minimum Stay: Surcharge for 1 or 2-night stays. **Credit Card(s) Accepted:** AE, MC, V. **Open:** all year. Resident dog. No dogs please. No resident cats. No cats please. Nonsmoking hosts. Guests may smoke. Children welcome with restrictions. **Discounts:** monthly rates.

Reservation Contact: Bed & Breakfast Co.—Tropical Florida, M. Schaible, Box 262, So. Miami, FL 33243; 305–661–3270.

KEY WEST
ID: TROP.FL.#108

OLD TOWN AREA.

Near Duval, U.S. 1.

This modest, air-conditioned room with private entrance has a double bed, chest, cable TV, refrigerator, and private bath, and is located in the Old Town section of Key West. There is also a rollaway bed available for an extra guest. Just outside the door is a patio and small pool. It is within walking distance of all attractions and only two blocks to the public beach, shopping, and restaurants. Your hosts are a retired couple who enjoy gardening and telling guests about Key West.

No. Rooms: 1	**Breakfast:** Continental
Singles: None	**S-Rates:** $35–$40 pb
Doubles: 1 pb	**D-Rates:** $40–$45 pb
Type: Private home	

Minimum Stay: surcharge for 1 or 2-night stays. **Credit Card(s) Accepted:** AE, MC, V. **Open:** all year. Dog in residence. No dogs please. No resident cats. No cats please. Nonsmoking host. Guests may not smoke in guest rooms. Children welcome. **Discounts:** none. Spanish spoken.

Reservation Contact: Bed & Breakfast Co.–Tropical Florida, M. Schaible, Box 262, So. Miami, FL 33243; 305–661–3270.

LACOOCHEE

ID: TROP.FL#200

WITHLACOOCHEE RIVER, STATE FOREST; HIKING, FISHING, CANOEING.

Near I–75, FL 61.

Nature lovers will relish the wooded setting of this attractive, three-story cedar home. The house is on the Withlacoochee River and is adjacent to a large state forest so hiking and fishing are nearby. Tampa, Orlando, and gulf beaches are a forty-five-minute drive. The two guest rooms share a bath and have country furnishings; one has twin beds and the other has a double bed. A Full breakfast is served with fresh eggs from the chickens on the premises. Your hosts' hobbies include restoring classic cars, ham radio, genealogy, roses, nature photography, and travel.

No. Rooms: 2	**Breakfast:** Full
Singles: None	**S-Rates:** $35–$40 sb
Doubles: 2 sb	**D-Rates:** $40–$45 sb
Type: Private home	**Bldg:** Contemporary

Minimum Stay: Surcharge for 1 or 2-night stays. **Credit Card(s) Accepted:** AE, MC, V. **Open:** all year. Resident dog. No dogs please. Resident cat. No cats please. Host smokes. Guests may smoke. Children welcome. **Discounts:** monthly rates.

Reservation Contact: Bed & Breakfast Co.—Tropical Florida, M. Schaible, Box 262, So. Miami, FL 33243; 305–661–3270.

LONGBOAT KEY

ID: 33548BRU

SARASOTA JUNGLE GARDENS, MARIE SELBY BOTANICAL GARDENS, RINGLING ART AND CIRCUS MUSEUM; NEAR SARASOTA, ON WATER.

Near Gulf of Mexico Dr., Rte. 41.

Longboat Key is a twelve-mile island with public beaches and a bike path the entire length of the island. The house is contemporary Spanish-style, situated on a quiet dead-end street. Surrounded by orange and grapefruit trees, the house is on the water and has a beautiful view of the intracoastal waterway. The guest room also overlooks the water, has a king-sized bed, large dresser, full closet, and private adjoining bath. A Continental Plus breakfast with freshly squeezed juice is served. Your host enjoys sailing.

No. Rooms: 1	**Breakfast:** Continental Plus
Singles: None	**S-Rates:** $40 pb
Doubles: 1 pb	**D-Rates:** $50 pb
Type: Private home	**Bldg:** 1968 Spanish

Minimum Stay: none. **Credit Card(s) Accepted:** none. **Open:** October through April. No resident dogs. No dogs please. No resident cats. No cats please. Host smokes. Guests may smoke. **Discounts:** none.

Reservation Contact: Bed & Breakfast Registry Ltd., Gary Winget, Box 8174, St. Paul, MN 55108; 612-646-4238.

MIAMI
ID: TROP.FL.#106

COCONUT GROVE AREA, BISCAYNE BAY; BOATING, FISHING, SHOPS, RESTAURANTS.

Near Ingram & Douglas sts., U.S. 1.

This beautiful air-conditioned two-story stone home with historic designation is located in Coconut Grove, an exclusive residential area with dense foliage and trees overhanging the walkways. Nearby are excellent shops and restaurants, a twenty-mile bicycle path, and day fishing boats and sailboat rentals on Biscayne Bay. The house, a well-known landmark in the village, was formerly an inn. The guest room is large and has a fireplace. Although the kitchen was modernized, its antique stove and ice box remain. One of the two garden/patio areas is used for *al fresco* dining, while the other functions as an organic garden, where vegetables for the table are grown. The guest room is furnished with antiques and a king-sized bed. Your hosts, an attorney and an office manager, enjoy traveling, cooking, entertaining, theater, and music.

No. Rooms: 1	**Breakfast:** Continental
Singles: None	**S-Rates:** $55 pb
Doubles: 1 pb	**D-Rates:** $60 pb
Type: Private home	**Bldg:** Stone

Minimum Stay: surcharge for 1- or 2-night stays. **Credit Card(s) Accepted:** AE, MC, V. **Open:** all year. Dog in residence. No dogs please. Cat in residence. No cats please. Nonsmoking host. Guests may not smoke in residence. Children welcome with restrictions. **Discounts:** none.

Reservation Contact: Bed & Breakfast Co.—Tropical Florida, M. Schaible, Box 262, So. Miami, FL 33243; 305-661-3270.

ID: TROP.FL#214

COCONUT GROVE AREA, ARTS FESTIVAL, RENAISSANCE FESTIVAL, SHAKESPEARE FESTIVAL, SHOPPING, OUTDOOR CAFES, THEATER, WATER SPORTS.

Near I-95, U.S. 1 & Douglas.

Coconut Grove is a little village on Biscayne Bay that is only ten minutes from downtown Miami. It features exquisite shops, theaters, restaurants,

outdoor cafes, all sorts of water sports, and various seasonal festivals. This beautiful little cottage sets behind the main house in an exclusive residential area. Guests are welcome to use the pool and tropical, landscaped gardens which separate the guest quarters from the main house. The cottage consists of a studio, bedroom with queen-sized bed, kitchen, and bath. Attractive furnishings and accessories enhance its charm. Your hosts enjoy community activities, travel, art, music, and skiing.

No. Rooms: 1	**Breakfast:** Continental
Singles: None	**S-Rates:** $70–$80 pb
Doubles: 1 pb	**D-Rates:** $70–$80 pb
Type: Private home	**Bldg:** Frame cottage

Minimum Stay: Surcharge for 1 or 2-night stays. **Credit Card(s) Accepted:** AE, MC, V. **Open:** all year. No resident dogs. No dogs please. No resident cats. No cats please. Nonsmoking hosts. Guests may smoke. Children welcome with restrictions. **Discounts:** monthly rate.

Reservation Contact: Bed & Breakfast Co.—Tropical Florida, M. Schaible, Box 262, So. Miami, FL 33243; 305–661–3270.

MIAMI BEACH

ID: TROP.FL.#100

PRIVATE RESIDENTIAL ISLAND.

Near Rte. 195 & Alton Rd., I-95.

This air-conditioned house is on a private residential island in Biscayne Bay, an exclusive area with many mansions and estates. Close to golf and many Miami Beach attractions, the dwelling features a huge living room with fireplace, fourteen-foot windows that overlook the bay, a natural, ecologically balanced pool with fish and plants, an unusual fountain, and a hot tub. The furnishings reflect the old-world charm of your Danish hosts. The three large guest rooms, with private baths, are decorated with a comfortable mixture of antiques, handloomed fabrics, and quilts. One of the rooms has a double and single bed, another has a queen-sized and a double bed, and the third is furnished with a double bed plus a trundle bed. Your hosts enjoy sailing and have a twenty-eight-foot boat at their dock. They are well-traveled people whose interests encompass tatting, weaving, ballet, and music.

No. Rooms: 3	**Breakfast:** Continental
Singles: None	**S-Rates:** $50–$55 pb
Doubles: 3 pb	**D-Rates:** $60–$65 pb
Type: Private home	**Bldg:** Mediterranean art deco

Minimum Stay: none. **Credit Card(s) Accepted:** none. **Open:** all year. Resident dog. No dogs please. Cat in residence. No cats please. Nonsmoking host. Guests may not smoke in guest rooms. Children welcome. **Discounts:** none. Danish & German spoken.

Reservation Contact: Bed & Breakfast Co.—Tropical Florida, M. Schaible, Box 262, So. Miami, FL 33243; 305–661–3270.

ID: TROP.FL.#215

GOLF, OCEAN, RESTAURANTS, SHOPPING.

Near I-95, A1A.

Across from the public golf course, this attractive home is in a residential area of older, Spanish-style homes. Guests can walk to restaurants and shops, and the ocean is one mile away. The carriage house has been transformed into a cozy apartment with a living room, dining area, bedroom with double bed, kitchen, bath, private entrance, and yard. The host is a professional who enjoys skiing, entertaining, and travel.

No. Rooms: 1	**Breakfast:** Continental
Singles: None	**S-Rates:** $45–$50 pb
Doubles: 1 pb	**D-Rates:** $45–$50 pb
Type: Private home	**Bldg:** Spanish-style carriage house

Minimum Stay: surcharge for 1- or 2-night stays. **Credit Card(s) Accepted:** AE, MC, V. **Open:** all year. No resident dogs. No dogs please. No resident cats. No cats please. Nonsmoking host. Guests may smoke. Children welcome. **Discounts:** monthly rates. Spanish spoken.

Reservation Contact: Bed & Breakfast Co.—Tropical Florida, M. Schaible, Box 262, So. Miami, FL 33243; 305–661–3270.

ORLANDO

DISNEY WORLD, EPCOT CENTER, SEA WORLD, KENNEDY SPACE CENTER.

Near Church & Magnolia, I–4.

This attractive apartment is located downtown near the newly refurbished Eola Park with its lighted fountain, swan-shaped paddle boats, and lakeside walks. The spacious apartment is beautifully furnished and guests are invited to relax in the comfortable living room. The guest room, with a private bath and twin beds, has a large balcony from which to view the city. The location is perfect for downtown meetings and convenient to I–4, which takes guests to Disney World, Epcot Center, Sea World, Circus World, and other area attractions. Your host, a native of Orlando, can offer many suggestions on things to see and do in the area.

No. Rooms: 1	**Breakfast:** Continental Plus
Singles: None	**S-Rates:** $45 pb
Doubles: 1 pb	**D-Rates:** $55 pb
Type: Private apartment	**Bldg:** 1980s modern

Minimum Stay: none. **Credit Card(s) Accepted:** none. **Open:** all year. Dog in residence. No dogs please. No resident cats. No cats please. Non-smoking host. Guests may not smoke in residence. Residence not appropriate for children. **Discounts:** none.

Reservation Contact: Bed & Breakfast Registry Ltd., Gary Winget, Box 8174, St. Paul, MN 55108; 612–646–4238.

ORMOND BEACH

INTERNATIONAL SPEEDWAY, SPACE NEEDLE, TOMOKA STATE PARK, LIGHTHOUSE MUSEUM; CHARTER FISHING.

Near I–95, rtes. A1A & 1.

The east central coast of Florida is noted for its balmy temperatures and golden sunshine. In Ormond Beach, visitors can enjoy 914 acres of salt-water marsh and forests that provide a pleasant sojourn with nature, or visit Ponce de Leon Inlet and the Lighthouse Museum, also in the area. Daytona, just to the south, has larger crowds and even more excitement. The boardwalk is lined with cafés, souvenir shops, and arcades. Daytona is also known for its rock-hard beach; the firm, packed sand is appealing to sun-worshipers and sand-castle builders alike. Daytona, however, is most famous for its International Speedway, with racing events scheduled throughout the year—the two biggest ones on July third and fourth. Bus tours are available when there are no races. The home in Ormond Beach has one air-conditioned guest room with private bath and Continental Plus breakfast. It is an easy walk to the ocean from here. Your hosts are a retired policeman and his wife, both of whom enjoy traveling.

No. Rooms: 1
Singles: None
Doubles: 1 pb
Type: Private home

Breakfast: Continental Plus
S-Rates: $30–$40 pb
D-Rates: $40–$55 pb

Minimum Stay: none. **Credit Card(s) Accepted:** none. **Open:** all year. No resident dogs. No dogs please. No resident cats. No cats please. Non-smoking host. Guests may not smoke in guest rooms. Children welcome. **Discounts:** none.

Reservation Contact: B&B Suncoast Accommodations, Danie Bernard, 8690 Gulf Blvd., St. Pete Beach, FL 33706; 813–360–1753.

PALMETTO   ID: 9–SUNCOAST

BETWEEN ST. PETERSBURG AND SARASOTA.

Near Gillette Rd., U.S. 301, Rte. 41, I–75.

Palmetto is located near Bradenton, about halfway between St. Petersburg and Sarasota. This log house in a picturesque setting is on a brook, with botanical gardens surrounded by woods. The air-conditioned dwelling has a fireplace, pool, patio, and yard available for guests' use. One of the two second-floor guest rooms is decorated with a safari motif and has a queen-sized screened bed and private bath. The other room, also nicely appointed, has twin beds and a shared bath. A Continental Plus breakfast of homemade scones is served, and additional meals are available. One of your hosts does some farming, while the other is a ceramics teacher.

No. Rooms: 2
Singles: None
Doubles: 1 pb, 1 sb
Type: Private home

Breakfast: Continental Plus
S-Rates: $35–$50 pb, $30–$45 sb
D-Rates: $45–$60 pb, $40–$50 sb
Bldg: Log home

Minimum Stay: 2 days. **Credit Card(s) Accepted:** none. **Open:** all year. Dog in residence. No dogs please. No resident cats. No cats please. Non-smoking host. Guests may not smoke in residence. Children welcome with restrictions. **Discounts:** none.

Reservation Contact: B&B Suncoast Accommodations, Danie Bernard, 8690 Gulf Blvd., St. Pete Beach, FL 33706; 813–360–1753.

POMPANO BEACH

WATER SPORTS.

Near U.S. 1, A1A, I–95.

It's just a ten-minute walk to the beach from this contemporary ranch-style house situated in a pleasant residential area. The pool area is screened and equipped with solar heating for comfort in winter months. There are two guest rooms with private baths and small refrigerators. One has a double bed and the other a single bed plus a double hide-a-bed. Guests will get a taste of British hospitality here as the hosts hail from London.

No. Rooms: 2	**Breakfast:** Continental
Singles: None	**S-Rates:** $40–$50 pb
Doubles: 2 pb	**D-Rates:** $45–$55 pb
Type: Private home	**Bldg:** Ranch-style

Minimum Stay: surcharge for 1 or 2-night stays. **Credit Card(s) Accepted:** AE, MC, V. **Open:** all year. Resident dog. No dogs please. No resident cats. No cats please. Host smokes. Guests may smoke. Children welcome with restrictions. **Discounts:** monthly.

Reservation Contact: Bed & Breakfast Co.—Tropical Florida, M. Schaible, Box 262, So. Miami, FL 33243; 305–661–3270.

ST. PETE BEACH

LONDON WAX MUSEUM, ECKERD COLLEGE; TENNIS, SHUFFLEBOARD, NIGHTCLUBS, RESTAURANTS.

Near Pinellas Bayway, Pasadena Ave., U.S. 19, I–275.

This contemporary Spanish-style house has a deck overlooking the water, and is located on the north end of a six-mile-long, one-quarter-mile-wide island. The island has several restaurants and nightclubs, tennis and shuffleboard courts, and a Wax Museum. The air-conditioned house, with an atmosphere that is both comfortable and informal, has two guest rooms. The Blue Room has a queen-sized bed, private bath and entrance, TV, and refrigerator. Hand-carved swans decorate a brass double bed in the Gold Room which has a shared bath. A serve-yourself Continental Plus breakfast is provided. Guests are free to use the patio, dock, hot tub, gas barbeque grill, and phone, and have kitchen and laundry privileges. Beaches are nearby; Disney World is two hours away, and guests can even avoid the traffic and arrive by boat. Your host enjoys the beach, politics, and civic affairs.

No. Rooms: 2	**Breakfast:** Continental Plus
Singles: None	**S-Rates:** $40–$60 pb, $25–$45 sb
Doubles: 1 pb, 1 sb	**D-Rates:** $45–$65 pb, $40–$55 sb
Type: Private home	**Bldg:** 1956 Spanish

Minimum Stay: none. **Credit Card(s) Accepted:** none. **Open:** all year. No resident dogs. A dog is allowed with restrictions. No resident cats. No cats please. Host smokes. Guests may not smoke in guest rooms. Children welcome with restrictions. **Discounts:** 7th night free.

Reservation Contact: B&B Suncoast Accommodations, Danie Bernard, 8690 Gulf Blvd., St. Pete Beach, FL 33706; 813–360–1753.

ST. PETERSBURG
ID: TROP.FL#216

SALVADOR DALI MUSEUM, SUNKEN GARDENS, WATER SPORTS, TAMPA BAY.

Near I–295, I–92, 22nd Ave. S.

This lovely Victorian house in one of St. Petersburg's oldest sections has a wraparound porch that overlooks Lassing Park and Tampa Bay. Furnishings include many antiques such as marble-topped tables, gas lights, rockers, wicker, cut-glass pieces, and a player piano. The three guest rooms with private baths are also furnished with antiques and interesting accessories. The rooms have twin, double, or queen-sized beds. Guests can walk to the beach for swimming, fishing, and crabbing, or relax on the veranda and enjoy the breeze across the bay. Your hosts are teachers with interests in antiques and restoration.

No. Rooms: 3	**Breakfast:** Continental
Singles: None	**S-Rates:** $65 pb
Doubles: 3 pb	**D-Rates:** $65 pb
Type: Private home	**Bldg:** Victorian

Minimum Stay: surcharge for 1- or 2-night stays. **Credit Card(s) Accepted:** AE, MC, V. **Open:** all year. No resident dog. No dogs please. No resident cats. No cats please. Nonsmoking hosts. Guests may smoke on veranda. Residence is not appropriate for children. **Discounts:** monthly.

Reservation Contact: Bed & Breakfast Co.—Tropical Florida, M. Schaible, Box 262, So. Miami, FL 33243; 305–661–3270.

ID: 4–SUNCOAST

GULF BEACHES, SUNKEN GARDENS, MGM'S BOUNTY EXHIBIT.

Near Park St., U.S. 19, I–275.

St. Petersburg has a wealth of Floridian attractions, year-round fishing, and a tempting beachfront. Next to St. Pete Pier is MGM's *Bounty* exhibit, a painstakingly authentic reproduction of the original British sailing ship. This is the ship Clark Gable strode upon in *Mutiny on the Bounty*. One of Florida's oldest attractions, the Sunken Gardens, is also nearby. Built on the site of a former sinkhole, a breathtaking array of over seven-thousand different varieties of flowers and shrubs are displayed, along with a zoo and trained bird collection. There is also a biblical wax museum exhibit. For shoppers, Isle of Nations is a cluster of fascinating pierside boutiques from countries all around the world. The contemporary air-conditioned B&B home offers guests a suite consisting of a bedroom with twin beds, TV, private bath, and private entrance. It is in a quiet neighborhood only a few miles from the beaches. There is ample off-street parking, with arrival/departure transportation available, too. Public transportation in the area is also good. A Continental breakfast is served.

No. Rooms: 1	**Breakfast:** Continental
Singles: None	**S-Rates:** $40–$45 pb
Doubles: 1 pb	**D-Rates:** $45–$50 pb
Type: Private home	**Bldg:** Modern

Minimum Stay: 2 days. **Credit Card(s) Accepted:** none. **Open:** all year. No resident dogs. No dogs please. No resident cats. No cats please. Non-smoking host. Guests may not smoke in guest rooms. Children welcome with restrictions. **Discounts:** none.

Reservation Contact: B&B Suncoast Accommodations, Danie Bernard, 8690 Gulf Blvd., St. Pete Beach, FL 33706; 813–360–1753.

SARASOTA
ID: TROP.FL#204

ST. ARMAND'S KEY, BOUTIQUES, SPECIALTY SHOPS.

Near rtes. 41 & 780.

This contemporary ranch-style home is located in a residential area of St. Armand's Key, ten minutes from Sarasota. A short walk brings guests to St. Armand's Circle, an area of specialty shops and boutiques. Private beaches along the Gulf of Mexico are two blocks away. The house has one spacious guest room with twin beds, private entrance, and private bath, and another room with a queen-sized bed and a shared bath. Situated on the shore of Sarasota Bay, the house affords lovely views of the waterway and the city of Sarasota.

No. Rooms: 2
Singles: None
Doubles: 1 pb, 1 sb
Type: Private home

Breakfast: Continental
S-Rates: $40–$45 pb, $35–$40 sb
D-Rates: $45–$50 pb, $40–$45 sb
Bldg: Contemporary ranch-style

Minimum Stay: none. **Credit Card(s) Accepted:** AE, MC, V. **Open:** all year. No resident dogs. No dogs please. No resident cats. No cats please. Nonsmoking host. Guests may smoke. Children welcome with restrictions. **Discounts:** monthly. Yugoslavian and Croatian spoken.

Reservation Contact: Bed & Breakfast Co.—Tropical Florida, M. Schaible, Box 262, So. Miami, FL 33243; 305–661–3270.

SOUTH MIAMI   ID: TROP.FL.#105

UNIVERSITY OF MIAMI; ON LAKE.

Near US–1 & Red Rd., Rt. 826.

Separate from the main house, this cozy air-conditioned cottage is situated on an inland lake suitable for swimming and fishing. It is in an older residential area convenient to public transportation and the University of Miami. The newly decorated air-conditioned cottage consists of a bedroom with a high-rise bed (two singles), adjoining sitting room with TV, and bath. Your hosts enjoy tennis, travel, and entertaining.

No. Rooms: 1
Singles: None
Doubles: 1 pb
Type: Private cottage

Breakfast: Continental
S-Rates: $35–$40 pb
D-Rates: $40–$45 pb
Bldg: Lakeside cottage

Minimum Stay: surcharge for 1- or 2-night stays. **Credit Card(s) Accepted:** AE, MC, V. **Open:** all year. No resident dogs. No dogs please. No resident cats. No cats please. Nonsmoking host. Guests may not smoke in guest rooms. Children welcome with restrictions. **Discounts:** none.

Reservation Contact: Bed & Breakfast Co.—Tropical Florida, M. Schaible, Box 262, So. Miami, FL 33243; 305–661–3270.

SUMMERLAND KEY

ID: TROP.FL#202

FLORIDA KEYS, 20 MINUTES FROM KEY WEST; BAHIA HONDA STATE PARK, SWIMMING, BOATING, FISHING.

Near U.S. 1.

Although within an easy drive of the restaurants and night life of Key West, this location offers quiet privacy and ocean views in a neighborhood of single family homes. The guest accommodation consists of a ground-floor apartment with a screened porch that overlooks the garden, pool, and hot tub. There is a bedroom with twin beds, living room, kitchenette, barbecue area, television, telephone, air-conditioning, and private bath. Windows and glass doors on two sides of the apartment offer guests a magnificent view of the water. There is also a private dock for boaters. Your hosts' living quarters are on a separate floor. A Continental breakfast is served and champagne is provided for honeymoon and anniversary couples. Nearby Bahia Honda Recreation Area has one of the best swimming beaches in the Keys. The hosts enjoy fishing, boating, gardening, and travel and are active in community activities.

No. Rooms: 1	**Breakfast:** Continental
Singles: None	**S-Rates:** $70 pb
Doubles: 1 pb	**D-Rates:** $75 pb
Type: Private home	**Bldg:** Ground-level apartment

Minimum Stay: none. **Credit Card(s) Accepted:** none. **Open:** all year. No resident dogs. No dogs please. No resident cats. No cats please. Non-smoking host. Guest may smoke in residence. Children welcome. **Discounts:** none.

Reservation Contact: Bed & Breakfast Co.—Tropical Florida, M. Schaible, Box 262, So. Miami, FL 33243; 305–661–3270.

TAMPA

ID: TROP.FL.#101

BUSCH GARDENS, UNIVERSITY OF SOUTH FLORIDA, TAMPA STADIUM.

Near Buffalo Ave., I–275.

This cozy older home in the heart of Tampa is located on a quiet street that runs along the Tampa River, in a residential area bordering commercial properties and close to Tampa Stadium, shopping malls, medical offices, and a hospital. The major expressways are easily accessible. The quiet guest room, just off the family room, has twin beds and private bath. Your hosts, long-time Tampa residents, can advise guests about all the area attractions and events. They are a retired couple who enjoy gardening, auto racing, and travel. Arrival/departure transportation is available.

No. Rooms: 1	**Breakfast:** Continental
Singles: None	**S-Rates:** $30–$35 pb
Doubles: 1 pb	**D-Rates:** $35–$40 pb
Type: Private home	**Bldg:** 1940 One-story frame

Minimum Stay: surcharge for 1 or 2-night stays. **Credit Card(s) Accepted:** AE, MC, V. **Open:** all year. No resident dogs. No dogs please. No resident cats. No cats please. Nonsmoking host. Guests may not smoke in guest rooms. Children welcome with restrictions. **Discounts:** none.

Reservation Contact: Bed & Breakfast Co.—Tropical Florida, M. Schaible, Box 262, So. Miami, FL 33243; 305–661–3270.

ID: 33629SAA

BUSCH GARDENS, BEACHES.

Near I–275 & Westshore Blvd., I–4.

With courtyard in front and patio in rear, this handsome white brick house is located in the Westshore area, one of the most exclusive areas of Tampa. The home is large, and its design offers great privacy to guests. There are two guest rooms with double beds. One is done in earth tones with a floral decor; the other is done up in blue and red. Arrival/departure transportation and area tours are often available. Your charming host is well-traveled and enjoys water sports, watercolor painting, and gourmet cooking.

No. Rooms: 2	**Breakfast:** Continental Plus
Singles: None	**S-Rates:** $30 pb, $30 sb
Doubles: 1 pb, 1 sb	**D-Rates:** $35 pb, $35 sb
Type: Private home	**Bldg:** 1960 New Orleans

Minimum Stay: 2 nights. **Credit Card(s) Accepted:** none. **Open:** all year. No resident dogs. No dogs please. No resident cats. No cats please. Nonsmoking host. Guests may not smoke in guest rooms. Children welcome with restrictions. **Discounts:** none.

Reservation Contact: Bed & Breakfast Registry Ltd., Gary Winget, Box 8174, St. Paul, MN 55108; 612–646–4238.

TAVARES
ID: TROP.FL#210

ORLANDO AREA, LAKE DORA, BOATING, FISHING.

Near U.S. 27, S.R. 19, I–4.

This stately three-story Georgian colonial is surrounded by landscaped grounds and shaded by towering oak trees. Inside, guests will find period furnishings, leaded-glass windows, inlaid mahogany floors, and a hand-carved French balustrade. A pool, gardens, and cabana are at the rear of the house and the yard reaches down to Lake Dora, the second largest

inland lake in Florida. Two of the three guest rooms have twin beds and share a bath. The third has a double hide-a-bed and private bath. About 30 minutes from Orlando, this location provides a quiet retreat after a day at Disney World. The hosts have interests in gardening, travel, and boating.

No. Rooms: 3
Singles: None
Doubles: 1 pb, 2 sb
Type: Private home

Breakfast: Continental
S-Rates: $45–$55 pb, $45–$55 sb
D-Rates: $50–$60 pb, $50–$60 sb
Bldg: Colonial mansion

Minimum Stay: surcharge for 1- or 2-night stays. **Credit Card(s) Accepted:** AE, MC, V. **Open:** all year. No resident dogs. A dog is allowed with restrictions. No resident cats. No cats please. Nonsmoking hosts. Guests may smoke outside. Children welcome. **Discounts:** monthly.

Reservation Contact: Bed & Breakfast Co.—Tropical Florida, M. Schaible, Box 262, So. Miami, FL 33243; 305–661–3270.

TREASURE ISLAND
ID: 3–SUNCOAST

TIKI GARDENS, LOUIS TUSSAND LONDON WAX MUSEUM, WATER SPORTS.

Near Central Ave., I–275, U.S. 19.

This contemporary bay-front home offers many amenities, including air-conditioning, fireplace, pool, and patio, all in a beautiful setting. The house has a guest suite with sitting area, bedroom with double bed, and private bath. A Continental Plus breakfast is served. Among the area's attractions are the Tiki Gardens, a strange and enchanting world of pagan customs and South Sea island beauty. In the London Wax Museum, over one hundred life-sized wax figures from England are exhibited in authentic settings. Your hosts are a retired couple.

No. Rooms: 1	**Breakfast:** Continental Plus
Singles: None	**S-Rates:** $50–$60 pb
Doubles: 1 pb	**D-Rates:** $55–$70 pb
Type: Private home	**Bldg:** Modern

Minimum Stay: 2 days. **Credit Card(s) Accepted:** none. **Open:** all year. No resident dogs. No dogs please. Resident cat. No cats please. Nonsmoking host. Guests may not smoke in residence. **Discounts:** 7th night free.

Reservation Contact: B&B Suncoast Accommodations, Danie Bernard, 8690 Gulf Blvd., St. Pete Beach, FL 33706; 813–360–1753.

WEST PALM BEACH   ID: TROP.FL.#104

LAKE PARK AREA.

Near Military Trail and Blue Heron Blvd., I–95.

This home, located in the suburban area of West Palm Beach called Lake Park, is nestled among pine and citrus trees and surrounded by a wooden fence and gates. The air-conditioned guest cottage is directly behind the main house. It has a bedroom with twin beds, private bath, and an adjoining sitting area with refrigerator and TV. The pool and patio are for swimming and sunning. Although guests can walk to a local convenience store, this is a country setting, and a car is advisable. Your hosts, both in business in the city, have two riding horses and several friendly dogs. While feeding carrots to the horses is permitted, riding is not. However, riding stables are nearby.

No. Rooms: 1	**Breakfast:** Continental
Singles: None	**S-Rates:** $40–$45 pb
Doubles: 1 pb	**D-Rates:** $45–$50 pb
Type: Private home	**Bldg:** Cottage

Minimum Stay: surcharge for 1- or 2-night stays. **Credit Card(s) Accepted:** AE, MC, V. **Open:** all year. Dog in residence. No dogs please. No resident cats. No cats please. Guests may not smoke in guest rooms. Residence not appropriate for children. **Discounts:** none. German & Danish spoken.

Reservation Contact: Bed & Breakfast Co.—Tropical Florida, M. Schaible, Box 262, So. Miami, FL 33243; 305–661–3270.

ID: TROP.FL.#107

FLAGLER MUSEUM, NORTON ART GALLERY, AUDITORIUM; EL CID SECTION.

Near Belvedere Rd., I–95.

El Cid is an older area of the city, with many homes designed by a prominent architect who also planned large areas of Palm Beach. Your host recently restored and renovated this lovely old home and garden. It is only two houses away from the Intercoastal Waterway, where there is a pleasant walkway along the water's edge. The house is close to the famous Norton Art Gallery, Auditorium, and Flagler Museum. It affords easy access to the causeway leading to Palm Beach and the ocean. Close to the center of the city, guests can walk to shopping, restaurants, and public transportation. The comfortable air-conditioned guest room offers a double bed and shared bath. Your host is an educator interested in travel, photography, music, and gardening.

No. Rooms: 1	**Breakfast:** Continental
Singles: None	**S-Rates:** $35 sb
Doubles: 1 sb	**D-Rates:** $38 sb
Type: Private home	**Bldg:** Traditional

Minimum Stay: surcharge for 1- or 2-night stays. **Credit Card(s) Accepted:** AE, MC, V. **Open:** all year. No resident dogs. No dogs please. No resident cats. No cats please. Nonsmoking host. Guests may not smoke in residence. Children welcome with restrictions. **Discounts:** none.

Reservation Contact: Bed & Breakfast Co.—Tropical Florida, M. Schaible, Box 262, So. Miami, FL 33243; 305–661–3270.

GEORGIA

ATLANTA

ID: ATLANTA–28

INMAN PARK.

Near I–20, I–85, I–75, Waverly Way & Euclid.

Inman Park, Atlanta's first suburb, was developed in the 1880s and is characterized by Victorian mansions and smaller craftsman-style cottages. This house, built in 1916, boasts restored moldings, wood floors, Oriental rugs, and a forty-foot central hall which displays an art collection. There are three guest rooms. The first features a double bed, Laura Ashley wallpaper, Dhurri rugs, Victorian oak furniture, an ornamental fireplace, and the original pedestal sink and clawfoot tub. The second room has a king-sized brass bed, Oriental rug, a Victorian chest and armoire, fireplace, and private bath. The third room has a double sleigh bed, Laura Ashley wallpaper and bedding, dormers, and a view of the park. A Continental Plus breakfast is served. Your host is interested in historic preservation, collecting antiques, and reading. She has traveled throughout the world.

No. Rooms: 3	**Breakfast:** Continental Plus
Singles: None	**S-Rates:** $60–$70 pb, $52 sb
Doubles: 2 pb, 1 sb	**D-Rates:** $60–$70 pb, $52 sb
Type: Private home	**Bldg:** 1916 brick with slate roof

Minimum Stay: none. **Credit Card(s) Accepted:** AE, MC, V. **Open:** all year. No resident dogs. No dogs please. Resident cats. No cats please. Host smokes. Guests may smoke in residence. Children welcome. **Discounts:** none.

Reservation Contact: Bed & Breakfast Atlanta, Madalyn Eplan, 1801 Piedmont Ave. NE, Suite 208, Atlanta, GA 30324; 404–875–0525.

ATLANTA–46

SHOPPING, RESTAURANTS, COUNTRY CLUB.

Near I–85, I–75, Peachtree Rd. & Lenox Rd.

Just blocks from the largest shopping mall in the South is a lovely and historic residential neighborhood surrounding the Capital City Country Club. This attractive, air-conditioned house has a large yard and deck accented with brightly colored flowers. One of the two guest rooms has a private bath, overlooks the garden, and is furnished with twin beds, desk, upholstered wing chair, and foot stool. Regional folk art adds to the charm of the room. The second room, also with twin beds, has an antique dresser and chair, an adjoining sun porch, and shared bath. A Full breakfast is served. The host has lived in various parts of the country and likes to travel, garden, knit, and sew.

No. Rooms: 2	**Breakfast:** Full
Singles: None	**S-Rates:** $56 pb, $48 sb
Doubles: 1 pb, 1 sb	**D-Rates:** $64 pb, $56 sb
Type: Private home	**Bldg:** Ranch-style

Minimum Stay: none. **Credit Card(s) Accepted:** AE, MC, V. **Open:** all year. Resident dog. No dogs please. Resident cat. No cats please. Non-smoking host. Guest may smoke. Children welcome with restrictions. **Discounts:** none.

Reservation Contact: Bed & Breakfast Atlanta, Paula Gris and Madalyne Eplan, 1801 Piedmont Ave. NE, Suite 208, Atlanta, GA 30324; 404–875–0525.

ID: ATLANTA–50

MIDTOWN, ANSLEY PARK.

Near I–85, I–75, Piedmont Ave. & Peachtree St.

Ansley Park, once a historic suburb, is now situated in the midst of mid-town Atlanta, close to public transit, shopping, restaurants, and art and theater attractions. This 1919 Tudor cottage reflects your hosts' interests in folklore and pottery, and the gardens, both front and back, demonstrate their love of the outdoors. There are two guest rooms with private baths. The first is a basement apartment with a private entrance, a kitchen with a small refrigerator and small appliances, a double hide-a-bed, and TV. The second guest room is a library with a double hide-a-bed, fireplace, and Oriental rug. Guests may choose the type of breakfast they prefer. The hosts, native Atlantans, enjoy literature, history, sports, gardening, and travel.

No. Rooms: 2	**Breakfast:** Choice
Singles: None	**S-Rates:** $48 pb
Doubles: 2 pb	**D-Rates:** $48 pb
Type: Private home	**Bldg:** 1919 Tudor cottage

Minimum Stay: none. **Credit Card(s) Accepted:** none. **Open:** all year. No resident dogs. No dogs please. Resident cat. No cats please. Nonsmoking host. Guests may smoke in residence. Children welcome with restrictions. **Discounts:** none.

Reservation Contact: Bed & Breakfast Atlanta, Paula Gris and Madalyne Eplan, 1801 Piedmont Ave. NE, Suite 208, Atlanta, GA 30324; 404–875–0525.

ID: ATLANTA–56

EMORY UNIVERSITY, FERNBANK SCIENCE CENTER, CENTERS FOR DISEASE CONTROL.

Near Houton Mill & Clairmont Rd., I–85.

This air-conditioned traditional two-story house with swimming pool is located in a well-tended residential neighborhood in northeastern Atlanta. Situated on sixteen beautifully wooded acres overlooking a neighborhood park, it is within easy walking distance of the V.A. Hospital and Emory University. Two guest rooms offer double beds. One room is done in yellow, with handmade quilts, an antique doll collection, and private bath. The other provides a wonderful view of the pool, woods, and flowers, with a shared bath. A Continental Plus breakfast is served. One of your hosts, a retired engineer, builds beautiful reproduction furniture; an impressive silver chest in the front entry is evidence of his skill. The other host specializes in baking and showering genuine southern hospitality on her guests.

No. Rooms: 2	**Breakfast:** Continental Plus
Singles: None	**S-Rates:** $44 pb, $44 sb
Doubles: 1 pb, 1 sb	**D-Rates:** $52 pb, $52 sb
Type: Private home	**Bldg:** Traditional

Minimum Stay: none. **Credit Card(s) Accepted:** none. **Open:** all year. No resident dogs. No resident cats. No cats please. Nonsmoking host. Guests may smoke. Residence is not appropriate for children. **Discounts:** none.

Reservation Contact: Bed & Breakfast Atlanta, Paula Gris and Madalyne

Eplan, 1801 Piedmont Ave. NE, Suite 208, Atlanta, GA 30324;
404–875–0525.

WOODRUFF ARTS CENTER, HIGH MUSEUM, COLONY SQUARE; ANSLEY PARK AREA.

Near Peachtree & 15th sts., I–75.

The Ansley Park area is one of lovely winding parks and turn-of-the-century homes. From here, it is only a short walk to Peachtree Street, Woodruff Arts Center, High Museum, and Colony Square. The park itself is across the street and the botanical gardens are just around the corner. A large, screened back porch overlooks the park, and there is a deck and patio tucked into a wooded setting—a great location for birdwatching. There are two guest rooms. One is done with rose patterned paper and furnished with twin beds and antique furniture, including a night table, dresser, Jacobean arm chair, and oak secretary. The other room, which is extremely spacious, has a contemporary walnut king-sized bed, night tables, and a double dresser. There is also a sitting area. A Continental Plus breakfast is served. One of your hosts, a native of Atlanta, is a city planner; the other is in business. They both enjoy travel, good food, and conversation.

No. Rooms: 2	**Breakfast:** Continental Plus
Singles: None	**S-Rates:** $70 pb, $60 sb
Doubles: 1 sb, 1 pb	**D-Rates:** $70 pb, $60 sb
Type: Private home	**Bldg:** Lodge

Minimum Stay: none. **Credit Card(s) Accepted:** none. **Open:** all year. Dog in residence. No dogs please. No resident cats. No cats please. Non-smoking host. Guests may not smoke in residence. Children welcome with restrictions. **Discounts:** none.

Reservation Contact: Bed & Breakfast Atlanta, Paula Gris and Madalyne Eplan, 1801 Piedmont Ave. NE, Suite 208, Atlanta, GA 30324; 404–875–0525.

NORTHWEST ATLANTA, HISTORICAL SOCIETY, CIVIL WAR BATTLE SITES.

Near I–75, Peachtree Rd. & Peachtree Battle Ave.

This attractive New England-style house is located in a beautiful, older neighborhood near public transportation, shopping, restaurants, and jogging and biking trails. The guest room, with private bath, has a private entry off the pool and patio. It has traditional furniture including two three-quarter beds, dressing table, and dormer windows. A Continental Plus breakfast is served poolside, in the guest room, or in the dining room.

The interests of your hosts include education, gardening, and floral design.

No. Rooms: 1	**Breakfast:** Continental Plus
Singles: None	**S-Rates:** $56 pb
Doubles: 1 pb	**D-Rates:** $64 pb
Type: Private home	**Bldg:** New England clapboard

Minimum Stay: none. **Credit Card(s) Accepted:** AE, MC, V. **Open:** all year. Resident dog. No dogs please. Resident cat. No cats please. Nonsmoking host. Guests may not smoke in residence. Children welcome. **Discounts:** none.

Reservation Contact: Bed & Breakfast Atlanta, Paula Gris and Madalyne Eplan, 1801 Piedmont Ave. NE, Suite 208, Atlanta, GA 30324; 404–875–0525.

ID: 30308SHE

CULTURAL DISTRICT, FOX THEATER; THEATER, RESTAURANTS.

Near Piedmont & North aves., I–75, I–85, I–20.

Built in 1891, this colonial-revival Victorian house, now on the National Register of Historic Places, has been painstakingly restored to its former splendor. The current owners have been able to replicate colors, wallpaper patterns, and even the original stenciling. You will find many special touches, including lace-trimmed sheets, large fluffy towels, and specialty soaps; wine or soft drinks, fruit, and chocolates are left in the rooms each evening. Newspapers and a pot of coffee are brought to the upstairs landing each morning, so you can take them back to bed before breakfast if you like. Two lounges, a dining room, and a little library of Moorish design, dubbed the Turkish Corner, are available. Guests can choose from among three guest rooms and the carriage house, all with private baths. All the rooms have central heat and air-conditioning. Full concierge services are available. The inn is located in a residential neighborhood, about one mile from Atlanta's central business district and within the theater, restaurant, and cultural district. For theater buffs, the Fox Theater, built in 1929 and now designated as a National Landmark, is only five blocks away. Live performances and classic films are featured, but there are also guided tours. Your hospitable hosts' interests include antiques and historic sites and preservation.

No. Rooms: 4	**Breakfast:** Continental Plus
Singles: None	**S-Rates:** $75–$95 pb
Doubles: 4 pb	**D-Rates:** $80–$105 pb
Type: Public inn	**Bldg:** 1891 colonial revival

Minimum Stay: none. **Credit Card(s) Accepted:** AE, MC, V. **Open:** all year. No resident dogs. No dogs please. Cat in residence. No cats please. Nonsmoking host. Guests may smoke. Children welcome with restrictions. **Discounts:** 8th day, AARP.

Reservation Contact: Bed & Breakfast Registry Ltd., Gary Winget, Box 8174, St. Paul, MN 55108; 612–646–4238.

DECATUR
ID: ATLANTA–22

TWENTY MINUTES TO METRO ATLANTA; MARTIN LUTHER KING CENTER, LENOX SQUARE MALL, EMORY UNIVERSITY, CARTER LIBRARY.

Near I–285, I–20, I–85, Ponce de Leon Ave. & Clairmont Rd.

This comfortable home is within walking distance of excellent public transportation and many restaurants. It has a large deck overlooking the heavily wooded lot, a screened porch, and a fireplace—all good spots for curling up with a good book. The guest room has an antique iron double bed with masses of down pillows, a handmade quilt, a rocking chair, and a basket of current magazines and newspapers. A collection of matted and framed dried flowers adorn the walls. The Continental Plus breakfast includes regional cuisine. Decatur is about twenty minutes from downtown Atlanta and less than five miles from Emory University. Your hosts enjoy travel, gourmet cooking, gardening, and beekeeping.

No. Rooms: 1	**Breakfast:** Continental plus
Singles: None	**S-Rates:** $44 pb
Doubles: 1 pb	**D-Rates:** $52 pb
Type: Private home	**Bldg:** 1940

Minimum Stay: none. **Credit Card(s) Accepted:** AE, MC, V. **Open:** all year. No resident dogs. No dogs please. Resident cat. No cats please. Nonsmoking host. Guests may not smoke in residence. Children welcome with restrictions. **Discounts:** none.

Reservation Contact: Bed & Breakfast Atlanta, Paula Gris and Madalyne Eplan, 1801 Piedmont Ave. NE, Suite 208, Atlanta, GA 30324; 404–875–0525.

MC DONOUGH

ID: ATLANTA–34

STONE MOUNTAIN, SIX FLAGS.

Near U.S. 23, Rte. 81, I–75.

McDonough is a typical small southern town on the periphery of Atlanta. The local square has been beautifully restored and offers many shopping options. The air-conditioned turn-of-the-century Victorian-style home in the historic section of town provides old-fashioned southern hospitality. Two guest rooms are offered, each with private bath. The first has a queen-sized rice bed, mahogany furnishings, a recliner chair, walk-in closet, and ceiling fan. The other, a beautifully decorated Victorian room, is furnished with a double bed, loveseat, restored traveling trunk, small rocker, and comfortable chair by the fireplace. A Continental breakfast is served, and arrival/departure transportation and area tours are available. Your host's interests include antiques, restoration, politics, community affairs, and art collecting.

No. Rooms: 2	**Breakfast:** Continental
Singles: None	**S-Rates:** $60–$70 pb
Doubles: 2 pb	**D-Rates:** $60–$70 pb
Type: Private home	**Bldg:** 1900 turn-of-century

Minimum Stay: none. **Credit Card(s) Accepted:** none. **Open:** all year. No resident dogs. No dogs please. No resident cats. No cats please. Guests may not smoke in guest rooms. Children welcome with restrictions. **Discounts:** none.

Reservation Contact: Bed & Breakfast Atlanta, Paula Gris and Madalyne Eplan, 1801 Piedmont Ave. NE, Suite 208, Atlanta, GA 30324; 404–875–0525.

SAVANNAH

ID: 31401LIB

CIVIC CENTER; WATERFRONT, MUSEUMS, HISTORIC HOMES, SHOPS AND RESTAURANTS.

Near Liberty and Barnard sts., I–16.

This three-story home has been restored to its original grandeur, with brass beds, antiques, fireplaces, artwork, and floral arrangements. There is a large garden with a spa, patio, and gas grill for your enjoyment. Settled by the British in 1733, Savannah is rich in history, and this home is right in the center of it all. There are four guest suites available, all of which have private bath, private entrance, telephone, color cable TV, and air-conditioning. The first is a three-room suite with a queen-sized bed in each of the two bedrooms. Each bedroom has an adjoining bath, and one has a sitting area with TV. This lovely suite is complete with a family room and a garden entrance. It is suitable for one or two couples, or a family of four. The second is a three-room suite with two queen-sized beds in one bedroom and one queen-sized bed in the second. Each has an adjoining bath. Family-room furnishings include a queen-sized sofa bed and TV. Enter by the front door or the garden entrance. The third

and fourth are two-room suites also with queen-sized beds, adjoining baths, and family rooms. Entrances are through the garden or mini court-yard. One accommodates four, the other, six. Laundry facilities are available, and there is good handicapped access. Guests are greeted with sherry or cocktails upon arrival.

No. Rooms: 5	**Breakfast:** Continental
Singles: None	**S-Rates:** $90–$105 pb
Doubles: 5 pb	**D-Rates:** $90–$105 pb
Type: Public inn	**Bldg:** 1834 Federal

Minimum Stay: none. **Credit Card(s) Accepted:** AE, MC, V. **Open:** all year. No resident dogs. No dogs please. No resident cats. No cats please. Host smokes. Guests may smoke. Children welcome. **Discounts:** none.

Reservation Contact: Bed & Breakfast Registry Ltd., Gary Winget, Box 8174, St. Paul, MN 55108; 612–646–4238.

HAWAII

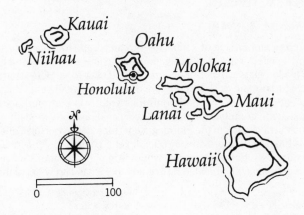

Kauai

Niihau

Oahu

Honolulu

Molokai

Lanai

Maui

Hawaii

N

0   100

Hawaii

HONAUNAU

ID: HAW–H25

PLACE OF REFUGE.

Near Kailuakona Hwy.

This Kona-style home located on the slopes above the Place of Refuge offers a panoramic view of the ocean. The house is eighteen miles south of Kailua, and a half acre of gardens make it a cool, quiet, and private retreat. There is one garden level guest room with a king-sized bed, private bath, small refrigerator, and wonderful view. Breakfast is served upstairs on the fifty-foot lanai. The hosts are avid fishermen and scuba divers.

No. Rooms: 1
Singles: None
Doubles: 1 pb
Type: Private home

Breakfast: Continental Plus
S-Rates: $45 pb
D-Rates: $45 pb
Bldg: Contemporary

Minimum Stay: 2 nights. **Credit Card(s) Accepted:** none. **Open:** all year. No resident dogs. No dogs please. No resident cats. No cats please. Nonsmoking host. Guest may not smoke in residence. Children welcome. **Discounts:** none.

Reservation Contact: Bed & Breakfast Hawaii, Evie Warner & Al Davis, Box 449, Kapaa, HI 96746; 808–822–7771.

KAILUA KONA

WATER ACTIVITIES.

Near Rte. 19, Rte. 190.

On the peaceful hillside of Kailua, guests can escape to this custom-built home. The interior is meticulously furnished in fine koa wood, and hand-made leaded-glass cabinet doors grace the dining room. Guests are encouraged to use the deck and hot tub; the view is magnificent. The guest apartment consists of two bedrooms (one with twin beds and one with a double bed), complete kitchen and living area, and private bath. Since your hosts leave early in the morning, items for a do-it-yourself Continental Plus breakfast are provided. You will get a chance to get acquainted with your hosts, however, one of whom is in public relations, while the other is a designer and builder. Both enjoy the ocean and water activities.

No. Rooms: 2	**Breakfast:** Continental Plus
Singles: None	**S-Rates:** $55 sb
Doubles: 2 sb	**D-Rates:** $55 sb
Type: Private home	**Bldg:** 1983 contemporary

Minimum Stay: 2 nights. **Credit Card(s) Accepted:** none. **Open:** all year. No resident dogs. A dog is allowed with restrictions. No resident cats. A cat is allowed with restrictions. Nonsmoking host. Guests may not smoke in guest rooms. Children welcome with restrictions. **Discounts:** none.

Reservation Contact: Bed & Breakfast Hawaii, Evie Warner & Al Davis, Box 449, Kapaa, HI 96746; 808–822–7771.

NAALEHU

VOLCANO NATIONAL PARK, PUNALU'U BLACK SAND BEACH.

Hwy. 11.

Halfway between Kailua-Kona and Hilo on the "Big Island" of Hawaii, this is the perfect location for touring the island. This home is on two acres of land and guests approach by way of a palm-lined drive. The house was built by your host and has many windows with pleasant views, high ceilings, and ceiling fans that add to the tropical flavor. The dining room overlooks the swimming pool and outdoor Jacuzzi, and the living room has comfortable furnishings, oriental rugs, and views of the ocean on one side and the Maura Loa volcano on the other. The guest room has a queen-sized bed, private bath, private entrance, Oriental rugs, oak furniture, paintings, prints, and a ceiling fan. A Continental Plus breakfast is served as well as wine and *pupus* (Hawaiin hors d'oeuvres) in the evening. Your hosts, originally from Seattle, enjoy music, travel, and dance.

No. Rooms: 1
Singles: None
Doubles: 1 pb
Type: Private home

Breakfast: Continental Plus
S-Rates: $55 pb
D-Rates: $60 pb
Bldg: Contemporary

Minimum Stay: none. **Credit Card(s) Accepted:** none. **Open:** all year. No resident dogs. No dogs please. No resident cats. No cats please. Non-smoking hosts. Guests may not smoke in residence. Residence not appropriate for children. **Discounts:** none.

Reservation Contact: Bed & Breakfast Registry, Gary Winget, Box 8174, St. Paul, MN 55108; 612–646–4238.

PEEPEKEO

ID: HAW–H3

AKAKA FALLS STATE PARK.

This modern Hawaiian-style home, in a park-like setting, is located on an oceanfront bluff with a panoramic view of beautiful Wailea Bay. The house provides a peaceful haven, yet it is close enough to everything to be convenient. A tennis court and municipal beach are within walking distance, and the world-famous Akaka Falls State Park is just a short drive away. A one-bedroom apartment, with fully equipped kitchenette, large living room with cable TV, radio, and piano, dining room, and private bath, is available. There is also a double room with private bath in the main house. A Continental Plus breakfast is provided. Your hosts, a real-estate broker and an insurance agent, have lived in Hawaii all their lives and offer guests invaluable sightseeing information.

No. Rooms: 2
Singles: None
Doubles: 2 pb
Type: Private townhouse

Breakfast: Continental Plus
S-Rates: $55 pb
D-Rates: $55 pb
Bldg: 1982 Hawaiian

Minimum Stay: 2 nights. **Credit Card(s) Accepted:** none. **Open:** all year, except New Year's Eve. Dog in residence. No dogs please. Cat in residence. No cats please. Host smokes. Guests may not smoke in guest rooms. Residence not appropriate for children. **Discounts:** none.

Reservation Contact: Bed & Breakfast Hawaii, Evie Warner & Al Davis, Box 449, Kapaa, HI 96746; 808–822–7771.

Kauai

HANALEI

HANALEI BAY.

Near Hwy. 56.

Guests have the use of the entire lower level of this two-story home located one hundred yards from Hanalei Bay. There is a living room with TV, bedroom with queen-sized bed, and a private bath. Guests may also use the kitchen to prepare snacks or picnic lunches. A one-bedroom apartment with a garden view is also available. It consists of a tastefully decorated living room, a kitchenette, bedroom with queen-sized bed, and private bath. A Continental Plus breakfast is served. Everything in Hanalei Town is within walking distance from here. One of your hosts is a photographer and the other works in the tourist industry.

No. Rooms: 2	**Breakfast:** Continental Plus
Singles: None	**S-Rates:** $55–$70 pb
Doubles: 2 pb	**D-Rates:** $55–$70 pb
Type: Private home	**Bldg:** Contemporary

Minimum Stay: 3 day minimum for apartment. **Credit Card(s) Accepted:** none. **Open:** all year. No resident dogs. No dogs please. No resident cats. No cats please. Nonsmoking host. Guest may not smoke in residence. Residence not appropriate for children. **Discounts:** none.

Reservation Contact: Bed & Breakfast Hawaii, Evie Warner & Al David, Box 449, Kapaa, HI 96746; 808–822–7771.

KALAHEO

OCEAN VIEW.

This custom-designed dwelling is elegantly finished in koa wood, one of Hawaii's most beautiful hardwoods, and the richness of its color enhances the beauty of this comfortable home. A large living area offers a panoramic view of the ocean, and there are two patios, one with a hot tub. The two guest rooms share a bath. One has a queen-sized bed, and the other has two double beds and an island decor. A Continental Plus breakfast is served. The house is a short drive from the main highway and close to the Kukuiolono golf course.

No. Rooms: 2	**Breakfast:** Continental Plus
Singles: None	**S-Rates:** $40 sb
Doubles: 2 sb	**D-Rates:** $45 sb
Type: Private home	**Bldg:** 1975 plantation style

Minimum Stay: 2 nights. **Credit Card(s) Accepted:** none. **Open:** all year. No resident dogs. No dogs please. No resident cats. No cats please. Nonsmoking host. Guests may not smoke in guest rooms. Children welcome with restrictions. **Discounts:** none.

Reservation Contact: Bed & Breakfast Hawaii, Evie Warner & Al Davis, Box 449, Kapaa, HI 96746; 808–822–7771.

KAPAA
ID: 96746MAK

BEACHES, SNORKELING, KAYAKING, FISHING, HELICOPTER TOURS.

Near Kuhio Hwy., Rte. 580

This romantic guest house is on a half acre of landscaped grounds, with mango, avocado, lychee, and lilikoi trees, Norfolk pines, birds of paradise, plumeria, and wild birds. It is located on a cliff overlooking the north fork of Wailua River in a quiet neighborhood, historically an area where hundreds of alii (Hawaiian royalty) lived. The guest house can accommodate a party of four. It has a living room with two studio couches (called punees in Hawaiian), a bedroom with a king-sized bed, two chests of drawers, bedside tables, a veranda with an ice-cream table and chairs, private bath (shower only), small refrigerator, and cooking appliances. There is a three-night minimum stay. For visits of one week or more, the seventh night is free. There is no public transportation. Your hosts have interests in travel, gardening, golf, and education.

No. Rooms: 1	**Breakfast:** Continental Plus
Singles: None	**S-Rates:** $50 pb
Doubles: 1 pb	**D-Rates:** $50 pb
Type: Private cottage	**Bldg:** 1971

Minimum Stay: 3 nights. **Credit Card(s) Accepted:** none. **Open:** all year. No resident dogs. No dogs please. No resident cats. No cats please. Nonsmoking host. Guests may not smoke in residence. Residence not appropriate for children. **Discounts:** 7th night free. Japanese spoken.

Reservation Contact: Bed & Breakfast Registry Ltd., Gary Winget, Box 8174, St. Paul, MN 55108; 612–646–4238.

POIPU
ID: 96756GLO

OCEANFRONT, SPOUTING HORN; SWIMMING, FISHING, SURFING, SAILING, SNORKELING.

Near Hwy. 50.

This little inn is one of the few remaining completely restored "sugar shacks," a beach house on the perimeter of the cane fields on the sunny side of the island of Kauai. In addition to its charmingly furnished interior, it boasts a breathtaking location on the ocean. The eighty-foot oceanfront property is flanked by four coconut trees with inviting hammocks overlooking the pounding surf. You are free to lounge on the spacious lanai, hike the volcanic cliffs on the shore of the island, shell on the black-sand beach, or swim, snorkel, surf, fish, and sail in the surrounding waters. A small boat harbor is within view, where you can be accommodated on catamarans for snorkeling and sunset sails. The more adventurous can try a trip on a zodiac. The inn is within walking distance of Poipu's many fine dining spots and minutes away from Old Koloa Town, a restored sugar plantation center. Two guest rooms share a bath and three have private baths. A favorite room for honeymooners is the Japanese Tea House with oceanfront deck, sitting area overlooking the Japanese koi pond, and a bath featuring a Japanese-style soaking tub. The Continental breakfast consists of fresh tropical fruit, guava juice, pastry, and tea or coffee. Coolers, beach mats, and towels are provided. One of your hosts is an accountant; the other is a psychotherapist.

No. Rooms: 5	**Breakfast:** Continental
Singles: None	**S-Rates:** $75 pb, $45–$65 sb
Doubles: 3 pb, 2 sb	**D-Rates:** $80 pb, $50–$70 sb
Type: Public inn	**Bldg:** 1943 beach house

Minimum Stay: none. **Credit Card(s) Accepted:** none. **Open:** all year. No resident dogs. No dogs please. No resident cats. No cats please. Nonsmoking host. Guests may not smoke in residence. Residence not appropriate for children. **Discounts:** none.

Reservation Contact: Bed & Breakfast Registry Ltd., Gary Winget, Box 8174, St. Paul, MN 55108; 612–646–4238.

POIPU BEACH
ID: HAW–K22

BEACH, GOLF, TENNIS, SNORKELING, BOATING, WIND SAILING.

This large fifty-year-old plantation home is situated on an acre of beautifully landscaped property. Three guest rooms offer private baths. One room has twin beds, one has a queen-sized bed, and one has a king-sized bed and dressing room. There are also some rental cottages available, each with bedroom, fully equipped kitchen, living room, and dining area. Since your hosts occupy a garden-level apartment, the guests are free to use the entire main house. A Continental Plus breakfast is served. Your hosts provide beach equipment, such as snorkels and fins. One of your hosts is a retired school principal; the other has been involved in both teaching and real estate. Both enjoy golf, tennis, swimming, cards, and travel.

No. Rooms: 3	**Breakfast:** Continental Plus
Singles: None	**S-Rates:** $45 pb
Doubles: 3 pb	**D-Rates:** $45 pb
Type: Private home	**Bldg:** 1930 plantation style

Minimum Stay: none. **Credit Card(s) Accepted:** none. **Open:** all year. No resident dogs. No dogs please. No resident cats. No cats please. Non-smoking host. Guests may not smoke in guest rooms. Children welcome with restrictions. **Discounts:** none.

Reservation Contact: Bed & Breakfast Hawaii, Evie Warner & Al Davis, Box 449, Kapaa, HI 96746; 808–822–7771.

Maui

HAIKU

ID: HAW–M18A

OCEAN VIEW.

Near HI–36.

This creatively designed house, perched on the edge of a deep gulch filled with tropical greenery, is a romantic hideaway. The two guest rooms have private baths. The deluxe master suite, with king-sized bed, is nestled in the trees overlooking a lush Maui valley, with an unobstructed view to the ocean. For the more adventurous, there is the Moon Room, an all-glass tower, with a bed that rotates 360 degrees. A Continental Plus breakfast is served near the stream that runs through the center of the house or on one of the decks. After a day on the island, guests can relax in the hot tub with a glass of champagne. Your host is an architect whose hobbies include photography and tropical fish.

No. Rooms: 2	**Breakfast:** Continental Plus
Singles: None.	**S-Rates:** $85 pb
Doubles: 2 pb	**D-Rates:** $85 pb
Type: Private home	**Bldg:** 1986 modern

Minimum Stay: none. **Credit Card(s) Accepted:** none. **Open:** all year. No resident dogs. No dogs please. No resident cats. No cats please. Non-smoking host. Guests may not smoke in residence. Residence not appropriate for children. **Discounts:** weekly.

Reservation Contact: Bed & Breakfast Hawaii, Evie Warner & Al Davis, Box 449, Kapaa, HI 96746; 808–822–7771.

KIHEI
ID: HAW–M19

MAUI MEADOWS SUBDIVISION.

Near Rte. 31, Rte. 350.

These two large studio apartments have black and white TV, small refrigerators, and private baths, as well as a private entrance and *lanai* (screened porch). One of the apartments has a queen-sized bed, and the other has twin beds. There is a connecting door between the units for use by family or friends, but it can be locked for complete privacy. Breakfast, with fresh fruit from the tropical gardens, is served on the large *lanai*. The subdivision of Maui Meadows is one-and-a-half miles from swimming, tennis, and golf, and there is a magnificent view of the West Maui mountains, the ocean, and the islands of Lanai and Kahoolawe. Your hosts, originally from Hungary, can assist guests with information about Maui.

No. Rooms: 2	**Breakfast:** Continental Plus
Singles: None	**S-Rates:** $45–$50 pb
Doubles: 2 pb	**D-Rates:** $45–$50 pb
Type: Private home	**Bldg:** 1984

Minimum Stay: none. **Credit Card(s) Accepted:** none. **Open:** all year. No resident dogs. No dogs please. No resident cats. No cats please. Non-smoking host. Guests may smoke. Residence not appropriate for children. **Discounts:** none. Hungarian spoken.

Reservation Contact: Bed & Breakfast Hawaii, Evie Warner & Al Davis, Box 449, Kapaa, HI 96746; 808–822–7771.

Molokai

KAUNAKAKAI
ID: HAW–MO3

16 MILES EAST OF KAUNAKAKAI.

Near Rte. 46, Rte. 450.

Enjoy a peaceful, relaxing vacation at this home located sixteen miles east of Kaunakakai. It is situated on a three-and-a-half-acre mini-farm and offers a fully furnished apartment with kitchen, living room with a queen-sized hide-a-bed, bedroom with twin beds, and private bath. Because it is just a few steps from the beach, there is almost no need to leave the grounds. No breakfast is provided at this location. Your hosts are involved in real estate and one has also written two cookbooks.

No. Rooms: 1   Breakfast: None
Singles: None   S-Rates: $50 pb
Doubles: 1 pb   D-Rates: $50 pb
Type: Private apartment

Minimum Stay: none. Credit Card(s) Accepted: none. Open: all year.
No dogs in residence. No dogs please. No cats in residence. No cats
please. Nonsmoking host. Guests may smoke. Residence not appropriate
for children. Discounts: none.

Reservation Contact: Bed & Breakfast Hawaii, Evie Warner & Al Davis,
Box 449, Kapaa, HI 96746; 808–822–7771.

Oahu

AIEA

HAW–01A

VIEW OF HONOLULU; PEARL CITY AREA.

Near H–1.

Located just eight miles from Honolulu International Airport and a mile
from the Pearl City golf course, this home offers a garden-level apartment. The house is located at the end of a cul-de-sac which creates a
quiet, private setting. The guest apartment has a separate entrance, private bath, kitchenette, double bed, TV, and opens onto a large pool
which guests are welcome to use. From this vantage point guests can
view all of Honolulu and the entire south coast of Oahu. A Continental
breakfast is served.

No. Rooms: 1   Breakfast: Continental
Singles: None   S-Rates: $50 pb
Doubles: 1 pb   D-Rates: $50 pb
Type: Private home   Bldg: Contemporary

Minimum Stay: 2 nights. Credit Card(s) Accepted: none. Open: all
year. No resident dogs. No dogs please. Resident cats. No cats please.
Guests may smoke. Children welcome with restrictions. Discounts:
weekly.

Reservation Contact: Bed & Breakfast Hawaii, Evie Warner & Al Davis,
Box 449, Kapaa, HI 96746; 808–822–7771.

HONOLULU

ID: HAW–019

SWEEPING VIEW.

Near Rte. 61, Rte. 1.

In this home there are two guest rooms, one with a queen-sized bed and the other with a double bed. Both have private baths. A Continental Plus breakfast is served in the dining room or on the lanai. Guests may use the swimming pool. Your hosts, from England, own a small importing business. Their interests include playing bridge and mahjong.

No. Rooms: 2
Singles: None
Doubles: 2 pb
Type: Private home

Breakfast: Continental Plus
S-Rates: $35 pb
D-Rates: $45 pb
Bldg: Oceanfront

Minimum Stay: none. **Credit Card(s) Accepted:** none. **Open:** all year. Dog in residence. No dogs please. No resident cats. No cats please. Non-smoking host. Guests may not smoke in guest rooms. Children welcome. **Discounts:** none.

Reservation Contact: Bed & Breakfast Hawaii, Evie Warner & Al Davis, Box 449, Kapaa, HI 96746; 808–822–7771.

KAILUA

ID: DOW–16

NEAR BEACH.

Hwy. 61.

This bright and cheerful cottage, attached to the main house, has a tropical motif. It consists of a living room/kitchen, bedroom with king-sized bed, private bath, private entrance, and covered lanai. It is just steps away from Kailua Beach. No breakfast is served. Guests may use the pool, patio, yard, TV, and laundry facilities. Your hosts, who have lived in France and Japan, enjoy bowling, golf, and swimming.

No. Rooms: 1
Singles: None
Doubles: 1 pb
Type: Private home

Breakfast: None
S-Rates: $65 pb
D-Rates: $65 pb
Bldg: Cottage

Minimum Stay: 3 nights. **Credit Card(s) Accepted:** none. **Open:** all year. Resident dog. No dogs please. No resident cats. No cats please. Nonsmoking host. Guest may smoke. Children welcome. **Discounts:** none.

Reservation Contact: Pacific-Hawaii Bed & Breakfast, Ruth Winson & Eileen Palmer, 19 Kai Nani Pl., Kailua, Oahu, HI 96734; 808–262–6026.

ID: EP–5

WHITE SAND BEACH, WINDSURFING, GOLF.

Near Likelike & Pali hwys.

This contemporary Spanish-style house has a large yard and patio area and offers a white-sand beach ideal for swimming. Guest quarters consist of a two-room suite suitable for a family or two couples traveling together. One room has a king-sized bed and the other has a double and a single bed. Other furnishings include a color TV, desk, small table, refrigerator, hot plate, micro-toaster, dishes, and telephone. The two rooms share a bath. Each of the rooms has a private entrance. A Continental breakfast is served. Your hosts' hobbies are golf, reading, and walking.

No. Rooms: 2	**Breakfast:** Continental
Singles: None	**S-Rates:** $85 sb
Doubles: 2 sb	**D-Rates:** $85 sb
Type: Private home	**Bldg:** Contemporary Spanish

Minimum Stay: 3 nights. **Credit Card(s) Accepted:** none. **Open:** all year. Resident dog. No dogs please. No resident cats. No cats please. Nonsmoking host. Guests may smoke. Children welcome. **Discounts:** weekly and monthly.

Reservation Contact: Pacific Hawaii Bed & Breakfast, Ruth Winson & Eileen Palmer, 19 Kai Nani Pl., Kailua, Oahu, HI 96734; 808–262–6026.

IDAHO

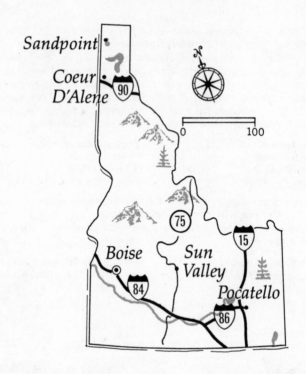

Sandpoint
Coeur
D'Alene
90

Boise
84

75

Sun
Valley

15

Pocatello
86

0 — 100

COEUR D'ALENE

ID: 83814GRE

SWIMMING, BOATING, FISHING, SKIING,
SNOWMOBILING, SUMMER THEATER.

Near Sherman & 4th sts., I–90, I–95.

The interior of this 1908 house, now on the National Register, boasts
winding mahogany staircases, arched passageways and windows, high
ceilings, and handcrafted cabinetry. The guest rooms on the third floor
are both cozy and spacious, with dormer window seats overlooking the
maples. On the second floor there are four guest rooms plus a library
and TV room. The guest rooms have king-sized, queen-sized, or double
beds with imported down comforters. Two rooms have additional single
beds to accommodate a third person. The decor is unmistakably influ-
enced by your host's love of elegant simplicity and comfort. All the rooms
are furnished with antique furniture, sheer white curtains, prints, and
flower bouquets. There is a shared guest bath on each floor. The breakfast
menu at this little inn is mouth-watering: fluffy cream puffs filled with

thyme-flavored eggs and topped with Swiss cheese and sliced almonds; cheese strata, a cheddar and jack cheese with a sausage, egg, and bread mixture baked to a delicate puffiness and followed by pecan Belgian waffles; cheese souffle; Swedish pancakes topped with pecans and accompanied by a sausage/ham roll. The host also packs delectable picnic lunches for those desiring them. Try cheese and salami calzones; curried rice and chicken salad with fresh tomatoes, mushrooms, and broccoli; or huge cream puffs filled with cheeses and fresh vegetables. Other amenities include a hot tub, and canoe and bike rentals. Guests can relax on the front porch or walk to the nearby waterfront. Lake Coeur d'Alene is well known as one of the most pristinely beautiful lakes in the United States. Fishermen love the abundance of land-locked salmon, trout, and bass. Other water sports abound as well. There is also summer theater and a dinner-dance boat that departs each evening. During the winter months hunting, skiing, and snowmobiling are only a few miles away. Child care and additional meals are frequently available. Your hosts love travel, art, and music.

No. Rooms: 7	**Breakfast:** Full
Singles: None	**S-Rates:** $35–$45 sb
Doubles: 7 sb	**D-Rates:** $45–$55 sb
Type: Inn	**Bldg:** 1908 Early American

Minimum Stay: none. **Credit Card(s) Accepted:** MC, V. **Open:** all year. No resident dogs. No dogs please. No resident cats. No cats please. Non-smoking host. Guests may not smoke in residence. Children welcome. **Discounts:** weekly, groups. Some French spoken.

Reservation Contact: Bed & Breakfast Registry Ltd., Gary Winget, Box 8174, St. Paul, MN 55108; 612–646–4238.

SANDPOINT

ID: 83864CHA

SCHWEITZER SKI AREA; HUCKLEBERRIES, HIKING.

Near Boyer Ave., N, U.S. 95, U.S. 2.

With the look of a Swiss chalet, this new condo unit offers a delightful and romantic setting, with rustic lofted and beamed ceilings, fireplace, snowy landscape view, ski runs, and lake. During August and September huckleberries are in abundance. There are four guest rooms, two with double beds, one with three single beds, and one with two single beds and shared bath. Guest rooms are attractively decorated with imported weavings, decorator pillows, carpets, and one has clerestory windows. A Full breakfast is served, including huckleberry pancakes in season. Sandpoint has excellent restaurants and shopping malls, and is situated on the shore of Pend Oreille Lake. Your hosts are former professional ski instructors and avid game players who enjoy showing guests around. Their other interests include waterskiing, boating, racquetball, swimming, and reading.

No. Rooms: 4	**Breakfast:** Full
Singles: None	**S-Rates:** $20–$30 sb
Doubles: 4 sb	**D-Rates:** $30–$40 sb
Type: Private condo	**Bldg:** 1981 chalet

Minimum Stay: 2 nights. **Credit Card(s) Accepted:** none. **Open:** all year. Dog in residence. No dogs please. No resident cats. No cats please. Nonsmoking host. Guests may not smoke in residence. Children welcome. **Discounts:** none.

Reservation Contact: Bed & Breakfast Registry Ltd., Gary Winget, Box 8174, St. Paul, MN 55108; 612–646–4238.

ILLINOIS

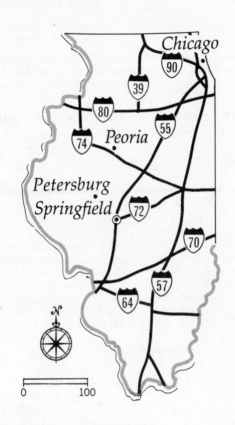

CHICAGO

ID: 2–CHICAGO

ART INSTITUTE, MERCHANDISE MART, GRANT PARK, DOWNTOWN BUSINESSES, MICHIGAN AVENUE SHOPS.

Near State St., Wacker Dr., I–95, I–55, I–90.

This unhosted luxury high-rise apartment, on the Chicago River in the downtown area, provides wonderful views of the city from the thirty-first floor. The building complex contains a grocery, restaurants, and shops. This studio apartment has a double bed and a queen-sized hide-a-bed. A sliding door separates the living room and bedroom. A self-serve Continental breakfast is provided. From this location, guests can walk to the Art Institute, Merchandise Mart, Grant Park, downtown businesses, and

Michigan Avenue shops. Transportation to other parts of the city is excellent. Your host is a marketing director.

No. Rooms: 1	**Breakfast:** Continental
Singles: None	**S-Rates:** $75 pb
Doubles: 1 pb	**D-Rates:** $85 pb
Type: Private apartment	**Bldg:** 1970 high rise

Minimum Stay: 3 days. **Credit Card(s) Accepted:** AE, MC, V. **Open:** all year. No resident dogs. No dogs please. No resident cats. No cats please. Guests may smoke. Children welcome with restrictions. **Discounts:** none.

Reservation Contact: Bed & Breakfast/Chicago, Inc., Mary Shaw, Box 14088, Chicago, IL 60614; 312–951–0085.

ID: 3–CHICAGO

OLD TOWN, NEAR NORTH SIDE.

Near North Ave. & Wells St., I–90, I–94.

The Old Town area, now on the Historic Register, is filled with boutiques and restaurants. Public transportation to and from downtown is excellent. Although this self-contained studio apartment has its own entrance, guests also have access to the host's quarter upstairs. The apartment is decorated in peach and green and has pine furnishings and a four-poster double bed as well as a queen-sized hide-a-bed, TV, telephone, and air-conditioning. A Full, self-serve breakfast is provided. Other amenities include use of the yard and bicycles. Your hosts, a TV reporter and an RSO manager, are very familiar with the city.

No. Rooms: 1	**Breakfast:** Full
Singles: None	**S-Rates:** $75 pb
Doubles: 1 pb	**D-Rates:** $75 pb
Type: Private home	**Bldg:** 1890s frame

Minimum Stay: 3 nights. **Credit Card(s) Accepted:** AE, MC, V. **Open:** all year. No resident dogs. No dogs please. No resident cats. No cats please. Nonsmoking host. Guests may smoke in residence. Children welcome. **Discounts:** none.

Reservation Contact: Bed & Breakfast/Chicago, Inc., Mary Shaw, Box 14088, Chicago, IL 60614; 312–951–0085.

ID: 9–CHICAGO

MAGNIFICENT MILE.

Near Oak St., Michigan Ave., I–94, I–90.

This downtown apartment is located across from Oak Street Beach and at the beginning of Chicago's Magnificent Mile, the city's premier shopping area. Off-street parking is available for $4.50 a day, a real bargain in downtown Chicago, and access to public transportation is excellent. The guest room has twin beds, air-conditioning, TV, telephone, and private bath. A Continental Plus breakfast is served. Your host is a marketing executive who enjoys photography, literature, music, writing, and sports.

No. Rooms: 1	**Breakfast:** Continental Plus
Singles: None	**S-Rates:** $60 pb
Doubles: 1 pb	**D-Rates:** $65 pb
Type: Private apartment	**Bldg:** 1970

Minimum Stay: 2 nights. **Credit Card(s) Accepted:** none. **Open:** all year. No resident dogs. No dogs please. No resident cats. No cats please. Host smokes. Guests may not smoke in residence. Residence not appropriate for children. **Discounts:** none.

Reservation Contact: Bed & Breakfast/Chicago, Inc., Mary Shaw, Box 14088, Chicago, IL 60614; 312–951–0085.

ID: 28–CHICAGO

DOWNTOWN.

Near Ohio St. & Lake Shore Dr., I–90, I–94, I–55.

This extremely convenient location is downtown, three blocks east of Michigan Avenue. The self-contained unhosted studio apartment offered is in a prime high-rise building complex, complete with restaurants, shops, grocery store, and theater. The air-conditioned apartment has TV and telephone. You can walk to business appointments, excellent shopping, and the wonderful lakefront. The owner is a musician whose primary residence is not in Chicago.

No. Rooms: 1	**Breakfast:** Continental
Singles: None	**S-Rates:** $65 pb
Doubles: 1 pb	**D-Rates:** $75 pb
Type: Private apartment	**Bldg:** Contemporary

Minimum Stay: 3 days. **Credit Card(s) Accepted:** none. **Open:** all year. No resident dogs. No dogs please. No resident cats. No cats please. Nonsmoking host. Guests may smoke. Children welcome. Discounts: none.

Reservation Contact: Bed & Breakfast/Chicago, Inc., Mary Shaw, Box 14088, Chicago, IL 60614; 312–951–0085.

ID: 47A–CHICAGO

OLD TOWN.

Near Wells, North, I–90, I–94.

This self-contained garden apartment is in a renovated frame building in historic Old Town, a mile-and-a-half from the downtown area, with excellent access to public transportation. The unit consists of a bedroom with queen-sized bed, sitting room with hide-a-bed, kitchen, and private bath. A Continental breakfast is provided. Your host is a banker.

No. Rooms: 1	**Breakfast:** Continental
Singles: None	**S-Rates:** $65 pb
Doubles: 1 pb	**D-Rates:** $75 pb
Type: Private home	**Bldg:** 1890s frame

Minimum Stay: 3 nights. **Credit Card(s) Accepted:** none. **Open:** all year. No resident dogs. No dogs please. No resident cats. No cats please. Nonsmoking host. Guests may not smoke in guest rooms. Children welcome. **Discounts:** none.

Reservation Contact: Bed & Breakfast/Chicago, Inc., Mary Shaw, Box 14088, Chicago, IL 60614; 312–951–0085.

ID: 55–CHICAGO

OLD TOWN.

Near North, Wells, I–90, I–94.

This house, originally built in the 1920s as a chauffeur's garage, was recently converted to an architecturally contemporary home. A catwalk on the second level allows open space between the first and second floors. The furnishings are antique. There are two air-conditioned guest rooms, one with twin beds and one with double bed, both with private baths. A Continental breakfast is served in the garden, weather permitting. The Old Town area is full of interesting shops and restaurants and is only minutes from the city center. It also borders Lincoln Park, with its zoo, beach, and miles of lakefront jogging and biking trails. Your host is a marketing writer.

No. Rooms: 2	**Breakfast:** Continental
Singles: None	**S-Rates:** $55 pb
Doubles: 2 pb	**D-Rates:** $65 pb
Type: Private apartment	**Bldg:** 1920s contemporary

Minimum Stay: 2 nights. **Credit Card(s) Accepted:** none. **Open:** all year. No resident dogs. No dogs please. No resident cats. No cats please. Nonsmoking host. Guests may not smoke in guest rooms. Residence not appropriate for children. **Discounts:** weekly.

Reservation Contact: Bed & Breakfast/Chicago, Inc., Mary Shaw, Box 14088, Chicago, IL 60614; 312–951–0085.

ID: 58–CHICAGO

NORTH SIDE, WRIGLEY FIELD.

Near I–94, Addison Ave. & Clark St.

Excellent public transportation makes this totally renovated Victorian house an ideal base for downtown business and sightseeing. The guest room is done in red and black and has a double futon bed, fireplace, beautiful wood floors, contemporary furnishings, and a private bath. A Continental Plus breakfast is served. Other amenities include telephone, sauna, laundry facilities, patio, and off-street parking. Your hosts, both in marketing, are well traveled and knowledgeable about Chicago.

No. Rooms: 1	**Breakfast:** Continental Plus
Singles: None	**S-Rates:** $60 pb
Doubles: 1 pb	**D-Rates:** $65 pb
Type: Private home	**Bldg:** Victorian

Minimum Stay: none. **Credit Card(s) Accepted:** AE, MC, V. **Open:** all year. No resident dogs. No dogs please. No resident cats. No cats please. Nonsmoking host. Guests may not smoke in residence. Residence is not appropriate for children. **Discounts:** none.

Reservation Contact: Bed & Breakfast Chicago, Inc., Mary Shaw, Box 14088, Chicago, IL 60614; 312–951–0085.

ID: 60614BUR

LINCOLN PARK AREA, ZOO, CONSERVATORY, LAKE MICHIGAN SHORE, BOUTIQUES; 10 MINUTES TO DOWNTOWN.

Near Fullerton & Halstead, I–90, I–94.

This picturesque Victorian brownstone, circa 1890, features original stained glass and an elaborate oak staircase. Guests have use of an upstairs living room, an outside deck, and a stocked kitchen for light meals. The two guest rooms share a bath. The first, done in tones of silver-gray and rose, has an ornate brass-and-iron queen-sized bed, period dresser, night stand, and chair. The second has extra-long twin beds, cream-colored walls, sea-green carpeting, and period furnishings. A Continental Plus breakfast is served. This is a wonderful location for visitors to the "windy city," convenient to downtown by bus or elevated train. The upscale neighborhood, bordered on the east by Lincoln Park and the beautiful shore of Lake Michigan, has tree-lined streets and elegant apartment buildings and townhouses. Restaurants and shops are within walking distance; parking is usually available on the street. Your hosts' interests include travel and sailing.

No. Rooms: 2	**Breakfast:** Continental Plus
Singles: None	**S-Rates:** $55 sb
Doubles: 2 sb	**D-Rates:** $70 sb
Type: Private home	**Bldg:** 1888 Victorian brownstone

Minimum Stay: 2 nights. **Credit Card(s) Accepted:** MC, V. **Open:** all year. No resident dogs. No dogs please. No resident cats. No cats please. Nonsmoking host. Guests may not smoke in guest rooms. Children welcome. **Discounts:** 15% weekly.

Reservation Contact: Bed & Breakfast Registry Ltd., Gary Winget, Box 8174, St. Paul, MN 55108; 612–646–4238.

COLLINSVILLE

ID: 62234MAG

ST. LOUIS AREA, MISSISSIPPI RIVER.

Near IL 159 & Belt Line Rd., I–55, I–70, I–64.

Formerly the home of a mining superintendent, this house, surrounded by trees, is in a quiet, country setting but only fifteen minutes from St. Louis. The house is tastefully furnished with antiques, collectibles, and art objects from around the world. On the lower level guests will find a room with games, a comfortable seating area, cable TV, and a hot tub. Four guest rooms share two baths. The Yellow Room is furnished with a single bed covered with a handmade quilt, chest of drawers, chair, and wall-to-wall carpeting. Convenient for families, the Blue Room features a queen-sized bed and two single beds with handmade quilts and antiques. A Full breakfast is served. Arrival/departure transportation, child care, and additional meals are available. Your host is a retired teacher who enjoys travel, antiques, sewing, knitting, and bridge.

No. Rooms: 4
Singles: 1 sb
Doubles: 3 sb
Type: Private home

Breakfast: Full
S-Rates: $25 sb
D-Rates: $35 sb

Minimum Stay: none. **Credit Card(s) Accepted:** none. **Open:** all year. No resident dogs. A dog is allowed with restrictions. No resident cats. No cats please. Nonsmoking host. Guest may smoke. Children welcome. **Discounts:** none.

Reservation Contact: Bed & Breakfast Registry Ltd., Gary Winget, Box 8174, St. Paul, MN 55108; 612–646–4238.

PETERSBURG

ID: 62675CAR

NEW SALEM AREA, 15 MINUTES FROM SPRINGFIELD, HOME AND TOMB OF ABRAHAM LINCOLN.

Near IL 97 IL 123, IL 97.

Built in 1874 by Robert Frackelton, this lovely Italianate home overlooks historic Petersburg, home of Edgar Lee Masters. The house features double parlors with fresco ceiling medallions, marble fireplace mantels, and original woodwork. Three guest rooms share two baths. The Ann Rutledge Suite is furnished with attached twin beds with a king-sized brass headboard, two chairs, an antique dresser, and a wicker sofa. Twin brass beds with embroidered spreads adorn the Edgar Lee Masters Room; other furnishings include an antique dresser and mirror, a rocker, night stands, and lamps. The Mentor Graham Room features a high, antique walnut bed with a hand-made spread, a library table, and lace curtains. A Full breakfast is served in the formal dining room between 7:30 and 9 A.M. Guests can also gather for wine and cheese in the parlor between 5 and 6 P.M. Your hosts have traveled extensively.

No. Rooms: 3   **Breakfast:** Full
Singles: None   **S-Rates:** $35 sb
Doubles: 3 sb   **D-Rates:** $45 sb
Type: Inn   **Bldg:** 1873 Italianate Victorian

Minimum Stay: none. **Credit Card(s) Accepted:** none. **Open:** all year. Dog in residence. No dogs please. No resident cats. No cats please. Non-smoking host. Guests may not smoke in residence. Children are welcome with restrictions. **Discounts:** two or more rooms.

Reservation Contact: Bed & Breakfast Registry Ltd., Gary Winget, Box 8174, St. Paul, MN 55108; 612–646–4238.

INDIANA

BATESVILLE

ID: 1–IND–OHIO

ANTIQUING, COVERED BRIDGES, FOSSIL
COLLECTING, 45 MINUTES FROM CINCINNATI.

Near I–74.

Near historic Metamora, the Batesville area appeals to those who enjoy
antiquing, viewing historic homes and covered bridges, and fossil collecting. This beautiful country home is situated on more than six landscaped
acres with flowering trees and shrubs. It features three fireplaces, custom-
made furniture, and a kitchen built for a gourmet chef. The four guest
rooms have private baths, TVs, and telephones. Two have queen-sized
beds, one has a king-sized bed, and one has two queen-sized beds. The
rooms have mahogany wood and are done in browns, greens, and ma-
roon. One has a fireplace. Amenities include off-street parking, laundry
facilities, and use of the yard and terrace. There is also a card room with
a stereo. A Full buffet breakfast is served. Your hosts enjoy golf, cooking,
and crafts and have an excellent knowledge of the area's history.

No. Rooms: 4	**Breakfast:** Full
Singles: None	**S-Rates:** $75–$95 pb
Doubles: 4 pb	**D-Rates:** $75–$95 pb
Type: Inn	**Bldg:** Country house

Minimum Stay: none. **Credit Card(s) Accepted:** MC, V. **Open:** all year. No resident dogs. No dogs please. Resident cat. No cats please. Non-smoking host. Guests may smoke in residence. Children welcome. **Discounts:** none.

Reservation Contact: Ohio Valley Bed & Breakfast, Nancy Cully, 6876 Taylor Mill Rd., Independence, KY 41051; 606–356–7865.

INDIANAPOLIS

ID: 46202STE

DOWNTOWN INDIANAPOLIS, OLD NORTHSIDE AREA, ART GALLERIES, RESTAURANTS.

Near Meridian & 16th sts., I–65, I–70, I–74.

Within walking distance to all downtown attractions, this three-story brick mansion, built in 1870, is a beautiful example of Victorian Italianate architecture. Among its features are massive woodwork with pocket doors, carved mantels, parquet floors, working gaslight chandeliers, and antique furnishings. The four guest rooms have private baths. The Master Suite has an ornately carved fireplace, a double bed, and the bath has a clawfoot tub. Grandma's Room is furnished with an antique double bed and matching dressing table. The Skylight Studio has an antique iron bed and is enhanced by a skylight that provides a view of the city. Rosetta's Room also has a city view. A Continental Plus breakfast is served. Your hosts enjoy jazz, art, water sports, and travel.

No. Rooms: 4	**Breakfast:** Continental Plus
Singles: None	**S-Rates:** $50–$100 pb
Doubles: 4 pb	**D-Rates:** $50–$100 pb
Type: Inn	**Bldg:** 1870 Victorian Italianate

Minimum Stay: none. **Credit Card(s) Accepted:** MC, V. **Open:** all year. No resident dogs. No dogs please. No resident cats. No cats please. Non-smoking host. Guest may smoke. Children welcome. **Discounts:** none.

Reservation Contact: Bed & Breakfast Registry Ltd., Gary Winget, Box 8174, St. Paul, MN 55108; 612–646–4238.

WASHINGTON   ID: WA02

HOOSIER NATIONAL FOREST.

Near IN Hwy. 57, U.S. 150 & 50.

Situated on a city block, this house was designed by a Wisconsin architect and is a classic example of early Frank Lloyd Wright prairie style. Shallow urns grace either side of the front entrance, and the interior is paneled in lavish woods with murals adorning several walls. Six guest rooms are available. The Knute Rockne Room is a large room with twin beds, early twentieth-century French furniture including comfortable chairs and a desk, and private bath. The Colonel Robuck Room, also with twin beds and private bath, is a cozy room with a fireplace. Although small, Darnall's Room easily accommodates a double bed and other early twentieth-century furniture, and the Sewing Room has a single bed and a door to the porch. The other two rooms have bunk beds. A Full breakfast is served. The home is in a scenic, hilly section of Indiana near Hoosier National Forest and about 60 miles from Evansville. Your hosts are college graduates who are active in civic and community affairs.

No. Rooms: 6	**Breakfast:** Full
Singles: 1 sb	**S-Rates:** $65–$70 pb, $40–$60 sb
Doubles: 2 pb, 3 sb	**D-Rates:** $70–$75 pb, $45–$65 sb
Type: Private home	**Bldg:** Brick prairie

Minimum Stay: none. **Credit Card(s) Accepted:** AE, MC, V. **Open:** all year. No resident dogs. No dogs please. No resident cats. No cats please. Host smokes. Guests may smoke in residence. Residence is not appropriate for children. **Discounts:** $5 per night for 2 or more nights.

Reservation Contact: Kentucky Homes Bed & Breakfast, John Dillehay, 1431 St. James Court, Louisville, KY 40208; 502–635–7341.

IOWA

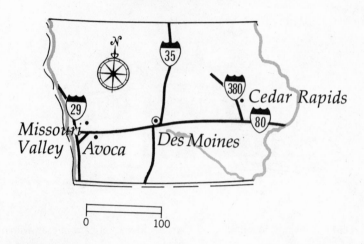

AVOCA

ID: 51521VIC

CARSTENS MEMORIAL FARM, DE SOTO NATIONAL
WILDLIFE REFUGE, ELK HORN DANISH WINDMILL,
WESTERN IOWA COUNTRY MUSIC CONTEST,
ANTIQUES; 40 MILES EAST OF OMAHA.

Near U.S. 59, I–80.

Built in 1904 by the prominent contractor Fred Thiessen as his family
home, this Queen Anne Victorian was one of the finest residences in the
community in its day. The golden-pine woodwork is an outstanding feature, and the open staircase and entry hall provide a welcoming atmosphere for guests. The five guest rooms have antique furnishings and lace
curtains. The Apple Blossom Room has queen-sized bed with a handmade quilt, Eastlake furnishings, and an Oriental rug. Elizabeth's Room
is done in a delicate rose color and has a walnut double bed with a hand-
crocheted canopy and a sitting area, complete with table, chairs, and Oriental rug. The spacious Wild Rose Room is furnished with a queen-sized
iron-and-brass bed, walnut chest, and wardrobe. The sitting area has a
marble-top table and ice-cream chairs. The elegant Jasmine Room has
a queen-sized brass bed and an oak wardrobe, secretary, and dresser.
In the Parlor guests will find a Murphy bed that folds into a beautiful oak
cabinet, and Eastlake furnishings. A Full breakfast is served in the dining
room, which has a large window with window seat, ornately carved columns, and antique oak furnishings. Complimentary wine is also served.
The town of Avoca, just off I–80, hosts the annual National Old Time
Country Music Contest and the Pottawattamie County Fair. There is a
nine-hole golf course and a park with a restored one-room country
schoolhouse dating from 1858. Just to the east is the town of Walnut,
which boasts 14 antique shops. The DeSoto National Wildlife Refuge,

Elk Horn Danish Windmill, and Carstens Memorial Farm are all within an hour's drive.

No. Rooms: 5		**Breakfast:** Full	
Singles: None		**S-Rates:** $38–$44 sb	
Doubles: 5 sb		**D-Rates:** $38–$44 sb	
Type: Private home		**Bldg:** 1904 Victorian	

Minimum Stay: none. **Credit Card(s) Accepted:** V, MC. **Open:** all year. No resident dogs. No dogs please. No resident cats. No cats please. Non-smoking host. Guests may not smoke in guest rooms. Children welcome with restrictions. **Discounts:** none.

Reservation Contact: Bed & Breakfast Registry Ltd., Gary Winget, Box 8174, St. Paul, MN 55108; 612–646–4238.

MISSOURI VALLEY

ID: GP101IA

DE SOTO BEND NATIONAL WILDLIFE REFUGE, BERTRAND MUSEUM, HARRISON COUNTY HISTORICAL VILLAGE & VISITOR'S CENTER, LOESS HILLS.

Near U.S. 30, I–29.

This comfortable farmhouse, located on an apple orchard in the rich apple land of Iowa, overlooks the beautiful Boyer River valley. The home is decorated in a 1930s style with original paintings and handcrafted articles. Guests can relax in the hot tub, and Harrison County Historical Village is just a short walk. The three guest rooms share a bath. The Full country breakfast includes delicious homemade baked goods; gourmet dinners by candlelight are available if prearranged. The hosts learned about bed and breakfast when they traveled to Ireland.

No. Rooms: 3
Singles: None
Doubles: 3 sb
Type: Private home

Breakfast: Full
S-Rates: $30 sb
D-Rates: $35 sb
Bldg: Farmhouse

Minimum Stay: none. **Credit Card(s) Accepted:** V. **Open:** all year. No resident dogs. No dogs please. No resident cats. No cats please. Non-smoking host. Guests may smoke in designated areas. Children welcome. **Discounts:** corporate.

Reservation Contact: Bed & Breakfast of the Great Plains, Rose Ann Foster, Box 2333, Lincoln, NE 68502; 402–423–3480.

KANSAS

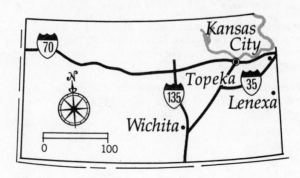

LENEXA

ID: KS–MO79

SWIMMING POOL, TENNIS.

Near I–35.

This handsome condominium features a lavish master bedroom with king-sized bed and private bath with double vanity, and private balcony. A Full breakfast is served in the dining room or on the shaded patio. Swimming pool and tennis courts are available. Your host is a magazine editor.

No. Rooms: 1	**Breakfast:** Full
Singles: None	**S-Rates:** $30 pb
Doubles: 1 pb	**D-Rates:** $45 pb
Type: Private home	**Bldg:** Contemporary

Minimum Stay: none. **Credit Card(s) Accepted:** none. **Open:** all year. No resident dogs. No dogs please. No resident cats. No cats please. Nonsmoking host. Guests may not smoke in residence. Residence not appropriate for children. **Discounts:** none.

Reservation Contact: Kansas City Bed & Breakfast, Edwina Monroe, Box 14781, Lenexa, KS 66215; 913–888–3636.

WICHITA

ID: 67218MAX

THE MAX PAUL

WICHITA ART MUSEUM, WICHITA STATE UNIVERSITY, COLISEUM, MC CONNEL AIR FORCE BASE.

Near Kellogg & Bluff, I–135, U.S. 54.

The Max Paul is on the edge of College Hill, one of Wichita's oldest and most interesting neighborhoods. The homes here, dating from the turn of the century, are in a variety of architectural styles, with winding shaded streets. Many border College Hill Park, Wichita's first country club, which is perfect for jogging, walking, or picnicking. It is also the site of "Shakespeare in the Park" during the summer months. The inn is convenient to all the city's major attractions. The zoo, Cowtown, art and American Indian museums, shopping centers, and major industries are only minutes away. All fourteen guest rooms are furnished with eighteenth-and-nineteenth-century European antiques, and all have feather beds atop extra-firm mattresses. The TVs are concealed in armoires or radio cabinets. Wardrobes substitute for closets and are combined with claw-foot chests and overstuffed chairs to give each room its own antique charm. All the rooms have private baths and clock-radio telephones. Most of the rooms overlook the inn's private garden, pond, and decks. Many of the suites have comfortable work/dining areas and wood-burning fireplaces, private balconies, hardwood floors, and skylights. The Windsor, an elegant two-room suite, is done in a pale caramel color. The living room, complete with fireplace and bay window, is ideal for relaxing or entertaining. French doors to the bedroom provide additional privacy. Under the dramatic angles and skylights of the bedroom's cathedral ceiling is the queen-sized bed with down comforter and pillows. A crystal chandelier and an eighteenth-century Portuguese armoire add to the decor. The living-room sofa also opens to a queen-sized bed, and the bath has a claw-foot tub as well as a separate shower. The Charbonneaux Room is done in rich shades of brown. Racks of horns and game heads hang high above the suite's sitting room, and shuttered windows open onto a private balcony. The massive platform bed, with padded headboard, has a view of the woodburning fireplace. The oversized bath has a wood-lined shower, a "tub for two," antique sink, and suede claw-foot loveseat. The light and airy Belgrave Suite has a sitting room with a daybed and writing desk. Through the open archway is the bedroom with pastel floral linens, burled wardrobe, king-sized bed, and Queen Anne wingback chairs at the breakfast table for two. Needlepoint adorns the walls. The Garden Room has an excellent view of the gardens and a private entrance that opens onto one of the inn's many decks. Floral carpet and drapes complement the English Art-Deco wardrobe and breakfast table. This room has a double bed. The East Room, with a dormer ceiling, is cozy and comfortable. It has a double and single bed, and an adjoining nook is perfect for reading or sleeping. A Continental breakfast is served in the dining room, but on weekends guests may enjoy breakfast in bed or in the gardens. The inn has meeting rooms for business conferences. For relaxing there is a library, gallery, exercise room, and Jacuzzi. Your hosts are two sisters whose backgrounds include managing restaurant, retail, and catering establishments; and experience in TV and radio sales, and copy writing.

No. Rooms: 14	**Breakfast:** Continental
Singles: None	**S-Rates:** $50–$95 pb
Doubles: 14 pb	**D-Rates:** $60–$105 pb
Type: Inn	**Bldg:** English Tudor

Minimum Stay: none. **Credit Card(s) Accepted:** AE, DC, MC, V. **Open:** all year. No resident dog. No dogs please. Cat in residence. No cats please. Host smokes. Guests may smoke. Children welcome with restrictions. **Discounts:** none.

Reservation Contact: The Max Paul, Roberta Eaton, 3910 E. Kellogg, Wichita, KS 67218; 316–689–8101.

KENTUCKY

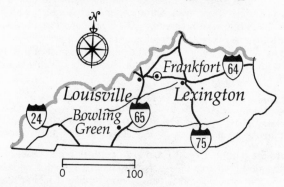

BOWLING GREEN

ID: 42101BOW

W. KENTUCKY UNIVERSITY.

Near US–31W & 12th St., I–65, U.S. 231.

This very attractive custom-built house, with side porch, landscaped yard, and picnic area, is located on a corner lot. There are three guest rooms, two with double beds and one with a queen-sized hide-a-bed; one room has a private bath. A Continental Plus breakfast is served. Additional meals and arrival/departure transportation are often available. Your hosts, a nurse/teacher and a chemistry professor, are interested in travel, antiques, antique autos, photography, music, theater, and writing.

No. Rooms: 3	**Breakfast:** Continental Plus
Singles: None	**S-Rates:** $32 pb, $32 sb
Doubles: 1 pb, 2 sb	**D-Rates:** $45 pb, $45 sb
Type: Private home	**Bldg:** 1939 custom built

Minimum Stay: none. **Credit Card(s) Accepted:** none. **Open:** all year. No resident dogs. No dogs please. No resident cats. No cats please. Non-smoking host. Guests may not smoke in residence. Children welcome with restrictions. **Discounts:** weekly, monthly.

Reservation Contact: Bed & Breakfast Registry Ltd., Gary Winget, Box 8174, St. Paul, MN 55108; 612–646–4238.

COVINGTON

ID: 2–OHIO

5 MINUTES TO DOWNTOWN CINCINNATI.

Near I–75, I–71, I–275, I–471.

This one-hundred-year-old restored brick row house features a second-floor efficiency apartment. The building is conveniently located near public transportation, scenic attractions, and excellent restaurants, and is just five minutes from downtown Cincinnati. The apartment has a double and single bed, fireplace, kitchen, color TV, reading lights, closet and drawer space, air-conditioning, private entrance, and private bath with a claw-foot tub. A Full breakfast is served, and arrival/departure transportation and area tours are available. One of your hosts is an artist, with a gallery attached to the house, which is open to guests. Your hosts' other interests include computers, historic restoration, ballroom dancing, gardening, and cats.

No. Rooms: 1	**Breakfast:** Full
Singles: None	**S-Rates:** $50 pb
Doubles: 1 pb	**D-Rates:** $55 pb
Type: Private townhouse	**Bldg:** 1880s brick row house

Minimum Stay: none. **Credit Card(s) Accepted:** none. **Open:** all year. No resident dogs. No dogs please. No resident cats. A cat is allowed with restrictions. Nonsmoking host. Guests may smoke. Children welcome with restrictions. **Discounts:** none.

Reservation Contact: Ohio Valley Bed & Breakfast, Nancy Cully, 6876 Taylor Mill Rd., Independence, KY 41051; 606–356–7865.

LOUISVILLE   ID: LU11

THEATER, OPERA, BALLET, CHURCHILL DOWNS.

Near Lexington & Alta Vista, I–64, I–71, I–65.

In 1912 this elaborate, Georgian house was built for Louisville's best known hotelier, Louis Seelbach. When guests enter they are transported to a world of luxury and elegance. The entrance hall leads into an immense salon with sun porches on either end. The colonnaded porch overlooks a green yard sloping down to Beals Branch Creek and a rocky cliff opposite. Two very private guest rooms are available with private baths. The first is a large, sunny, corner room with a cozy sitting area. It is tastefully decorated with English country-style furniture and has a double bed. The second room has a king-sized brass bed. A Full breakfast is served in the formal dining room or in one of the two glassed-in porches that grace the ends of the house. Guests are also welcome to use the billiard room. This has become a popular spot to spend the wedding night since the hosts provide chilled champagne in the guest room and serve a champagne breakfast before departure for the honeymoon. The interests of your hosts include golf, music, gardening, and architecture. Both have traveled widely.

No. Rooms: 2	**Breakfast:** Full
Singles: None	**S-Rates:** $75 pb
Doubles: 2 pb	**D-Rates:** $80 pb
Type: Private home	**Bldg:** Georgian

Minimum Stay: none. **Credit Card(s) Accepted:** AE, MC, V. **Open:** all year. Resident dog. No dogs please. No resident cats. No cats please. Nonsmoking host. Guests may smoke. Residence is not appropriate for children. **Discounts:** $5 discount for 2 or more nights.

Reservation Contact: Kentucky Homes Bed & Breakfast, Inc., John Dillehay, 1431 St. James Ct., Louisville, KY 40208; 502–635–7341.

RUSSELLVILLE

ID: RU–1

PERRYVILLE AREA, LAKE MALONE, SWIMMING, FISHING, BOATING.

Near KY Hwy. 100, I–24, I–65.

Although this is a relatively new house (1976), old logs, stones, and bricks were used in its construction wherever possible and it is furnished with antiques and auction finds. A two-story log studio used for spinning and weaving classes connects to the south end of the main house. A large solarium with a hot tub runs across the back of the house, and the covered second-floor porch has swings and chairs in which guests can relax. All four guest rooms have private baths. The large fireplace and exposed log walls of the first room create the ambience of pioneer life. It has a double bed. A second room is furnished with a four-poster double bed and a cedar blanket chest. The corner room, with a painted, iron double bed, has exposed logs on two walls and a cozy sitting area with a sofa and chairs. The fourth room has both a single and a double bed. A Full breakfast is served. One of your hosts is a textile design graduate from Wales who is also interested in antiques; the other host is a businessperson who also pilots his own plane. Both have traveled extensively.

No. Rooms: 4	**Breakfast:** Full
Singles: None	**S-Rates:** $55 pb
Doubles: 4 pb	**D-Rates:** $60 pb
Type: Private home	**Bldg:** Log house

Minimum Stay: none. **Credit Card(s) Accepted:** AE, MC, V. **Open:** all year. No resident dogs. No dogs please. Resident cat. No cats please. Host smokes. Guests may smoke in residence. Children welcome. **Discounts:** $5 per night for 2 or more nights.

Reservation Contact: Kentucky Homes Bed & Breakfast, John Dillehay, 1431 St. James Court, Louisville, KY 40208; 502–635–7341.

SPRINGFIELD

ID: SP01

PERRYVILLE BATTLEFIELD, LINCOLN'S BOYHOOD HOME.

Near U.S. Hwy. 15, KY Bluegrass Pkwy.

This historic area of Kentucky has several early pioneer settlements. This house is similar to the first brick house ever built in the state. The bricks, laid in a Flemish bond pattern, are capped with a simple cornice under the gabled roof. Set on a gently sloping hill, the house overlooks a long, narrow valley that provides a lovely, serene setting. The six mantels, chair rails, and base boards inside are original; the small entrance porch appears to be a later addition but it is still very early. All four guest rooms have working fireplaces. The first-floor room is in the oldest part of the house (circa 1785) and is furnished with antiques, a double bed, and a daybed available for a third person; the private bath is down the hall. One of the second-floor rooms has twin, empire-style, four-poster beds made by your host; another has an antique double bed plus a single bed, and a third has an antique double bed. These three rooms share a bath. A Full breakfast is served. One of your hosts is a retired education administrator interested in music, painting, and furniture making. The other is a marketing consultant who collects antiques and does needle work.

No. Rooms: 4	**Breakfast:** Full
Singles: None	**S-Rates:** $55 pb, $55 sb
Doubles: 1 pb, 3 sb	**D-Rates:** $60 pb, $60 sb
Type: Private home	**Bldg:** 1785 colonial

Minimum Stay: none. **Credit Card(s) Accepted:** AE, MC, V. **Open:** all year. No resident dogs. No dogs please. No resident cats. No cats please. Host smokes. Guests may smoke in residence. Children welcome. **Discounts:** $5 per night for 2 or more nights.

Reservation Contact: Kentucky Homes Bed & Breakfast, John Dillehay, 1431 St. James Court, Louisville, KY 40208; 502–635–7341.

WILLIAMSTOWN   ID: 2–KENTUCKY

MIDWAY BETWEEN CINCINNATI, OHIO, AND LEXINGTON, KY; KENTUCKY HORSE PARK, WILLIAMSTOWN LAKE.

Near I–75, I–71.

Guest accommodations here consist of a complete apartment in a ranch house situated on twenty-four acres with a view of surrounding woodlands and wildlife. The apartment includes a living room, dining room, fully equipped kitchen, three bedrooms, and a bath. The entire apartment may be rented or just a single room. A Full breakfast is served. Your hosts love to travel, refinish antique furniture, and meet new people.

No. Rooms: 3	**Breakfast:** Full
Singles: None	**S-Rates:** $40 sb
Doubles: 3 sb	**D-Rates:** $45 sb
Type: Private home	**Bldg:** Ranch-style

Minimum Stay: none. **Credit Card(s) Accepted:** MC, V. **Open:** Apr. 15–Dec. 20. Resident dog. A dog is allowed with restrictions. Resident cat. A cat is allowed with restrictions. Nonsmoking host. Guests may smoke in residence. Children welcome with restrictions. **Discounts:** none.

Reservation Contact: Ohio Valley Bed & Breakfast, Nancy Cully, 6876 Taylor Mill Rd., Independence, KY 41051; 606–356–7865.

LOUISIANA

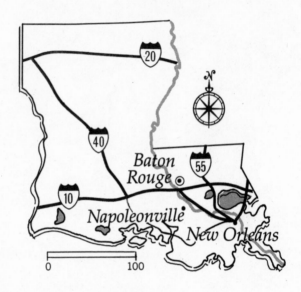

BATON ROUGE

ID: LBR–2–SOUTH

LOUISIANA STATE UNIVERSITY, SOUTHERN UNIVERSITY, STATE CAPITOL.

Near U.S. 61, I–10, I–12.

This two-story stucco home has a mid-city location, close to shopping, the interstate, and Louisiana State University. The house has a second-floor guest suite with sitting room, complete with TV, VCR and tapes, a full kitchen with microwave and refrigerator, and two bedrooms with double beds, antique furnishings, and private baths. There is also a first-floor room with a double bed and shared bath. This is available for single occupancy only. The Full breakfast is one of your host's many specialties. Arrival/departure transportation and area tours are available. Guests may also use the tennis court and laundry facilities. Your host enjoys tennis and cooking.

No. Rooms: 3	**Breakfast:** Full
Singles: 1 sb	**S-Rates:** $38 pb
Doubles: 2 pb	**D-Rates:** $48 pb
Type: Private home	**Bldg:** 1925 two-story stucco

Minimum Stay: none. **Credit Card(s) Accepted:** none. **Open:** all year, except Christmas. Dog in residence. No dogs please. No resident cats. No cats please. Nonsmoking host. Guests may smoke. Children welcome with restrictions. **Discounts:** none.

Reservation Contact: Southern Comfort Bed & Breakfast Reservations, Susan Morris & Helen Heath, 2856 Hundred Oaks, Baton Rouge, LA 70808; 504–346–1928 or 504–928–9815.

FRANKLIN

CAJUN COUNTRY, ANTEBELLUM MANSIONS.

Near U.S. 90, LA 182.

Cajun country offers delightful sights, interesting music, and wonderful Cajun food. The area has many beautiful antebellum mansions and is in the heart of sugarcane country. The area also boasts colorful camelias in December and January, azaleas in March, and moss-draped oaks year-round. In the main house there are two air-conditioned guest rooms with antique double beds and private baths. A semi-detached suite with private entrance, living area, kitchen, bedroom, and bath, furnished with antiques, is also available. A Full breakfast is served. Tennis, swimming, fishing, and golf are nearby. Your hosts speak French, have traveled widely, and are knowledgeable about the history and customs of the area.

No. Rooms: 3	**Breakfast:** Full
Singles: None	**S-Rates:** $75–$125 pb
Doubles: 3 pb	**D-Rates:** $75–$125 pb
Type: Private home	**Bldg:** 1880 raised cottage

Minimum Stay: none. **Credit Card(s) Accepted:** none. **Open:** all year. No resident dogs. No dogs please. No resident cats. No cats please. Non-smoking host. Guests may smoke in designated areas. Children welcome with restrictions. **Discounts:** none. French spoken.

Reservation Contact: Southern Comfort Bed & Breakfast Reservations, Susan Morris, 2856 Hundred Oaks, Baton Rouge, LA 70808; 504–346–1928 or 504–928–9815.

JEANERETTE

ON THE BAYOU.

Near Rte. 182, U.S. 90.

This contemporary air-conditioned guest house on the bayou offers one large room with private bath and kitchenette, dining table, TV, comfortable chairs, and beds that sleep up to four. The beautiful grounds, with large oaks and cypress trees with Spanish moss, roll to the bayou. Items for a Continental Plus breakfast are provided. Your hosts, a sugar-cane farmer and his wife, are well-educated and knowledgeable about the area's attractions.

No. Rooms: 1
Singles: None
Doubles: 1 pb
Type: Private cottage

Breakfast: Continental Plus
S-Rates: $40 pb
D-Rates: $45 pb
Bldg: Contemporary

Minimum Stay: none. **Credit Card(s) Accepted:** none. **Open:** all year, except holidays. No resident dogs. No dogs please. No resident cats. No cats please. Nonsmoking host. Guests may smoke. Children welcome. **Discounts:** none. French spoken.

Reservation Contact: Southern Comfort Bed & Breakfast Reservations, Susan Morris & Helen Heath, 2856 Hundred Oaks, Baton Rouge, LA 70808; 504–346–1928 or 504–928–9815.

KENNER   ID: NEWORLE10

LAKE PONCHARTRAIN.

Near I–10, Williams Blvd.

In this West Indies-style home on Lake Ponchartrain, the entire second floor is for guests. The stair wells hold beautifully displayed Mardi Gras souvenirs which your hosts have accumulated. Two guest rooms, each with a private bath, are done in period plantation style. Each morning the host places a fresh pot of coffee on a hot plate outside the door. A Full breakfast is served later in the family dining room downstairs. Your hosts enjoy gardening and restoration.

No. Rooms: 2
Singles: None
Doubles: 2 pb
Type: Private home

Breakfast: Full
S-Rates: $85–$125 pb
D-Rates: $85–$125 pb
Bldg: West Indies-style

Minimum Stay: none. **Credit Card(s) Accepted:** none. **Open:** all year. No resident dog. No dogs please. No resident cat. No cats please. Nonsmoking host. Guests may not smoke in residence. Residence is not appropriate for children. **Discounts:** none.

Reservation Contact: New Orleans Bed & Breakfast, Sarah Margaret Brown, Box 8163, New Orleans, LA 70182; 504–822–5038.

NAPOLEONVILLE   ID: LNAP1–SOUTH

BAYOU LAND.

Near Rte. 1, Rte. 308.

Located on the banks of one of Louisiana's major bayous, this magnificently restored 1846 Greek Revival mansion is considered one of the finest in the South. It was restored by its present owners as a labor of love and is now filled with period antiques and works of art. There are six guest rooms in the main house, one located on the first floor and five on the second floor. Four rooms have double beds, one has two double beds, and one has twin beds. Five rooms have private baths. There is also a restored slave cottage and a riverboat captain's house on the grounds. The cottage has a bedroom with a double bed plus another small room with a single bed which can be used for a child or third member of the party, and private bath. The restored captains house features two guest suites and one guest room, all with private baths. A Full or Continental breakfast is served as well as a plantation dinner with wine and candle-light. Child care and area tours are available. Your host, a Rhodes scholar, owns a large business in New Orleans and is active in civic affairs, the arts, and historic preservation.

No. Rooms: 10
Singles: None
Doubles: 9 pb, 1 sb
Type: Private home

Breakfast: Full or Continental
S-Rates: $85–$115 sb, $125 pb
D-Rates: $85–$135 sb, $150 pb
Bldg: 1846 Greek Revival

Minimum Stay: none. **Credit Card(s) Accepted:** none. **Open:** all year. No resident dogs. No dogs please. No resident cats. No cats please. Non-smoking host. Guests may not smoke in residence. Children welcome with restrictions. **Discounts:** none.

Reservation Contact: Southern Comfort Bed & Breakfast Reservations, Susan Morris & Helen Heath, 2856 Hundred Oaks, Baton Rouge, LA 70808; 504–346–1928 or 504–928–9815.

NEW ORLEANS   ID: LA–INC–#01

GARDEN DISTRICT.

Near St. Charles & Louisiana aves., Hwy. 90, I–10.

Built in 1880, this Victorian home is one-half block from historic St. Charles Avenue in the Garden District. Five air-conditioned guest rooms share four guest baths. All have TVs, and three have an additional bed to accommodate a third person. Your host has an interest in historic reno-vation, music, travel, painting, antiques, theater, and art exhibits.

No. Rooms: 5
Singles: None
Doubles: 5 sb
Type: Private home

Breakfast: Continental
S-Rates: $40–$45 sb
D-Rates: $50–$55 sb
Bldg: 1880 Victorian

Minimum Stay: none. **Credit Card(s) Accepted:** none. **Open:** all year. No resident dogs. No dogs please. No resident cats. No cats please. Non-smoking host. Guests may smoke. Children welcome. **Discounts:** bi-weekly.

Reservation Contact: Bed & Breakfast Inc., Hazell Boyce, 1360 Moss St., New Orleans, LA 70152; 504–525–4640, or 800–228–9711, dial tone, 184.

NEAR THE GARDEN DISTRICT.

Near St. Charles & Napoleon aves., I–10.

This beautifully restored Victorian dwelling, in a lovely residential area of nineteenth-century homes, is just a short streetcar ride from the French Quarter. The hand-painted ceilings and lush draperies add to the formal atmosphere and reflect some of your hosts' talent for fine craftsmanship. Guests can relax in the elegant double parlors, furnished with antiques and a grand piano. Four guest rooms feature double beds and private baths. The first room, furnished with antiques, has a sitting area with sofa, tables, and color TV. Because the sofa opens into a double bed, the room can accommodate four persons. Fully draped floor-to-ceiling windows open onto a large second-floor porch. Additional guest rooms have queen- or king-sized beds and private baths. A Continental breakfast is served. Your hosts, an architect and a furniture designer, can assist guests in planning tours. Their hobbies include collecting antiques and antique prints, painting, renovation, cooking, and travel.

No. Rooms: 4	**Breakfast:** Continental
Singles: None	**S-Rates:** $50–$60 pb
Doubles: 4 pb	**D-Rates:** $60–$75 pb
Type: Private home	**Bldg:** 1840 Greek Revival

Minimum Stay: none. **Credit Card(s) Accepted:** none. **Open:** all year. Dog in residence. No dogs please. Cat in residence. No cats please. Host smokes. Guests may not smoke in guest rooms. Children welcome with restrictions. **Discounts:** bi-weekly.

Reservation Contact: Bed & Breakfast Inc., Hazell Boyce, 1360 Moss

St., New Orleans, LA 70152; 504–525–4640, or 800–228–9711, dial tone, 184.

ID: LA–INC–#03

UNIVERSITIES, ZOO, AUDUBON PARK.

Near St. Charles & S. Carrollton aves., I–10.

This home, which has been in the family for two generations, is conveniently located on the St. Charles streetcar line near the university area. Two guest rooms offer twin beds and shared bath. A Continental breakfast is served. Your host's interests encompass gardening, Creole and Cajun cooking, antiques, and tennis.

No. Rooms: 2	**Breakfast:** Continental
Singles: None	**S-Rates:** $50 sb
Doubles: 2 sb	**D-Rates:** $50 sb
Type: Private home	**Bldg:** 1900 Victorian

Minimum Stay: none. **Credit Card(s) Accepted:** none. **Open:** all year. Dog in residence. No dogs please. No resident cats. No cats please. Non-smoking host. Guests may not smoke in residence. Children welcome with restrictions. **Discounts:** none. Spanish spoken.

Reservation Contact: Bed & Breakfast Inc., Hazell Boyce, 1360 Moss St., New Orleans, LA 70152; 504–525–4640, or 800–288–9711, dial tone, 184.

ID: LA–INC–#07

GARDEN DISTRICT, AUDUBON PARK.

Near St. Charles Ave., I–10.

These charming little guest cottages are off the main house, built in 1870. They are in a historic neighborhood three blocks from the Mardi Gras parades, a fifteen-minute ride from the French Quarter, and a ten-minute streetcar ride to the zoo, Audubon Park, and Tulane and Loyola universities. Guests enter each romantic cottage through French doors from the courtyard to find slate-and-hardwood floors and lace curtains. A Continental breakfast is served in the cottage or the intimate courtyard. Your hosts are college graduates who have lived in the Middle East and traveled throughout Europe. Their hobbies include sailing, windsurfing, cooking, gardening, entertaining, reading, computers, film, theater, music, and dance.

No. Rooms: 3	**Breakfast:** Continental
Singles: None	**S-Rates:** $50–$60 pb
Doubles: 3 pb	**D-Rates:** $60–$70 pb
Type: Private cottage	**Bldg:** Cottages

Minimum Stay: none. **Credit Card(s) Accepted:** none. **Open:** all year.

No resident dogs. A dog is allowed with restrictions. No resident cats.
A cat is allowed with restrictions. Nonsmoking host. Guests may smoke.
Children welcome. **Discounts:** bi-weekly. French & Arabic spoken.

Reservation Contact: Bed & Breakfast Inc., Hazell Boyce, 1360 Moss
St., New Orleans, LA 70152; 504–525–4640, or 800–228–9711, dial
tone, 184.

ID: LA–INC–#08

FRENCH QUARTER.

Near Canal & Bourbon sts., I–10, I–610.

This Creole-style guest cottage is ideally located in the historic French
Quarter, five blocks from the central business district. It is close to public
transportation, the convention center, shopping, famous restaurants, and
entertainment. The free-standing two-story cottage, a former slaves'
quarters, features a living/sitting area with a double hide-a-bed and kitch-
en on the first floor. There is also a balcony off the bedrooms with a view
of the courtyard. Ingredients for a Continental breakfast are stocked. Your
hosts have traveled throughout the United States, Europe, Canada, and
Mexico. They enjoy biking, jogging, walking, swimming, reading, and
gardening.

No. Rooms: 1	**Breakfast:** Continental
Singles: None	**S-Rates:** $75–$85 pb
Doubles: 1 pb	**D-Rates:** $75–$85 pb
Type: Private cottage	**Bldg:** 1820s Creole

Minimum Stay: 2 nights. **Credit Card(s) Accepted:** none. **Open:** all
year. No resident dogs. No dogs please. No resident cats. No cats please.
Nonsmoking host. Guests may not smoke in guest rooms. Children welcome with restrictions. **Discounts:** bi-weekly.

Reservation Contact: Bed & Breakfast Inc., Hazell Boyce, 1360 Moss
St., New Orleans, LA 70152; 504–525–4640, or 800–228–9711, dial
tone, 184.

ID: LA–INC.#11

FRENCH QUARTER.

Near I–10, I–610, Rampart & Esplanade aves.

This Creole cottage is secluded and quiet (the courtyard has ten-foot
walls), yet it is just a few minutes from Royal and Bourbon streets. One
of the three air-conditioned guest rooms is in the main house. It has a
four-poster double bed, ceiling fan, wingback chair, private bath, and is
adjacent to a sitting-kitchen area off the courtyard. The other two guest
rooms share a bath and are located on the second level in the historic
slave quarters and kitchen, a detached structure across the planted court-

yard with fountain. There is also a living room and kitchen in the structure. A continental breakfast is served. Your host, an architect, is interested in renovation, city planning, horticulture, carpentry, and travel.

No. Rooms: 3
Singles: None
Doubles: 1 pb, 2 sb
Type: Private home

Breakfast: Continental
S-Rates: $50–$75 pb, $75–$100 sb
D-Rates: $60–$75 pb, $75–$100 sb
Bldg: Creole cottage

Minimum Stay: none. **Credit Card(s) Accepted:** none. **Open:** all year.
No resident dogs. Guests may bring dog with restrictions. No resident
cats. No cats please. Nonsmoking host. Guests may smoke. Children welcome. **Discounts:** weekly rates.

Reservation Contact: Bed & Breakfast Inc., Hazell Boyce, 1360 Moss
St., New Orleans, LA 70152; 504–525–4640, or 800–228–9711, dial
tone, 184.

ID: LA–INC.#12

FRENCH QUARTER.

Near I–10, Dumaine & St. Philip sts.

This home, located in a residential section of the French Quarter, is convenient to restaurants, shops, and museums. It dates back to 1775 and
has beautiful French doors, lovely brick walls, attractive furnishings, and
a spacious, plant-filled patio. The guest room is furnished with antiques
and has twin four-poster beds, dresser, chest, coat rack, and private bath.
A Continental breakfast is served. Your host enjoys travel and gardening.

No. Rooms: 1
Singles: None
Doubles: 1 pb
Type: Private home

Breakfast: Continental
S-Rates: $60 pb
D-Rates: $70 pb
Bldg: French-style

Minimum Stay: none. **Credit Card(s) Accepted:** none. **Open:** all year.
No resident dogs. No dogs please. No resident cats. No cats please. Nonsmoking host. Guests may not smoke in residence. Residence is not appropriate for children. **Discounts:** none.

Reservation Contact: Bed & Breakfast Inc., Hazell Boyce, 1360 Moss
St., New Orleans, LA 70152; 504–525–4640, or 800–228–9711, dial
tone, 184.

ID: LA–INC.#14

CONVENTION CENTER, FRENCH QUARTER.

Near I–10, Claiborne Ave. & Broad St.

This spacious raised cottage with a large veranda combines Old-world
charm with modern convenience. It is located on a boulevard lined with

eighty-year-old trees and old family homes. Conveniently located, it is one block from the famous Rex Parade on Mardi Gras Day. One of the four guest rooms has a small balcony, French windows, and a private bath. It is done in dark green with white trim. Another is furnished with a queen-sized brass bed and Eastlake antiques. A third is done in cornflower blue and has jazz posters, a fireplace, and a queen-sized bed. The fourth room can sleep three with an antique Eastlake bed and a single bed. Your hosts enjoy travel, skiing, and their two children.

No. Rooms: 4	**Breakfast:** Continental
Singles: None	**S-Rates:** $50–$60 pb, $35–$50 sb
Doubles: 1 pb, 3 sb	**D-Rates:** $60–$65 pb, $45–$55 sb
Type: Private home	**Bldg:** Raised Cottage

Minimum Stay: none. **Credit Card(s) Accepted:** none. **Open:** all year. Resident dog. No dogs please. No resident cat. No cats please. Nonsmoking host. Guests may smoke. Children welcome. **Discounts:** none.

Reservation Contact: Bed & Breakfast Inc., Hazell Boyce, 1360 Moss St., New Orleans, LA 70152; 504–525–4640, or 800–228–9711, dial tone, 184.

ID: NEWORLE1

FRENCH QUARTER.

Near Royal & Dumaine, I–10.

Enter this cottage, in the heart of the French Quarter, through the brick courtyard with shade trees, blooming flowers, and table and chairs. There is a pleasant living/dining area on the first floor and a bedroom with twin beds and adjoining bath on the second floor. Your hosts are talented, knowledgeable, and well-traveled.

No. Rooms: 1	**Breakfast:** Continental
Singles: None	**S-Rates:** $85 pb
Doubles: 1 pb	**D-Rates:** $85 pb
Type: Private home	**Bldg:** Cottage

Minimum Stay: none. **Credit Card(s) Accepted:** AE, MC, V. **Open:** all year. No resident dogs. No dogs please. No resident cats. No cats please. Nonsmoking host. Guests may not smoke in residence. Residence not appropriate for children. **Discounts:** none.

Reservation Contact: New Orleans Bed & Breakfast, Sarah Margaret Brown, Box 8163, New Orleans, LA 70182; 504–822–5038.

GENTILLY AREA.

Near I–10, Franklin Ave.

In the attractive Gentilly area guests can walk, jog, bicycle, or just relax in the back gardens. Three guest rooms are available in this Spanish-style brick home. In the first room ivory moiré taffeta draperies and bedspread are accented with rose and give the ivory, lacquered modern furniture an art deco look; the private bath is done in burgundy. Another room off the upstairs balcony is done in blue and has a double bed. This room has a large tile bath with a separate soaking tub and shower which is private unless the adjoining room is rented as a suite. The adjoining room has twin beds and a bay window that overlooks the boulevard. All the rooms are air-conditioned and have ceiling fans. The sun room serves as a TV and common room. Continental breakfast is served in the dining room. Your host, a retired teacher, is interested in travel and gardening.

No. Rooms: 3	**Breakfast:** Continental
Singles: None	**S-Rates:** $40–$55 pb, $40–$55 sb
Doubles: 1 pb, 2 sb	**D-Rates:** $40–$55 pb, $40–$50 sb
Type: Private home	**Bldg:** Spanish-style

Minimum Stay: none. **Credit Card(s) Accepted:** AE, MC, V. **Open:** all year. No resident dogs. No dogs please. No resident cats. No cats please. Nonsmoking host. Guests may smoke in room. Children welcome with restrictions. **Discounts:** none.

Reservation Contact: New Orleans Bed & Breakfast, Sarah Margaret Brown, Box 8163, New Orleans, LA 70182; 504–822–5038.

GENTILLY DISTRICT.

Near Gentilly Blvd., Franklin Ave., I–10.

This typical 1920s New Orleans-style raised bungalow sits on a quiet tree-lined street. Although far enough away from the noisy party of the city, the air-conditioned house is on a direct bus line to the French Quarter and other parts of the city. The Gentilly District is notable for its quiet charm. Two guest rooms and three apartments are available, all with private baths. One of the guest rooms is done in Art-Deco style. All the bedrooms except one have double beds; the other has twin beds. The apartments consist of living room, bedroom, and kitchenette and can accommodate up to four people. A Continental breakfast is served. Your host, a retired school teacher, is an authority on the history and locales of New Orleans and will gladly advise visitors about the many free and moderately priced activities going on throughout the city. Child care and area tours are available.

No. Rooms: 5	**Breakfast:** None
Singles: None	**S-Rates:** $30–$40 pb
Doubles: 5 pb	**D-Rates:** $35–$45 pb
Type: Private home	**Bldg:** 1920 raised bungalow

Minimum Stay: none. **Credit Card(s) Accepted:** none. **Open:** all year. No resident dogs. A dog is allowed with restrictions. No resident cats. Guests may bring cat. Nonsmoking host. Guests may not smoke in guest rooms. Children welcome. **Discounts:** weekly.

Reservation Contact: New Orleans Bed & Breakfast, Sarah-Margaret Brown, Box 8163, New Orleans, LA 70182; 504–822–5038.

ID: NEWORLE4

FRENCH MARKET, NEW ORLEANS MUSEUM OF ART, FRENCH QUARTER, ESPLANADE RIDGE.

Near Esplanade & Royal, I–10, I–610, U.S. 90.

This is the home for the lover of ambiance, art, antiques, and quiet elegance. This Greek Revival townhouse was built in 1873 on what was then called the Commons or Military Esplanade. Today Esplanade Ridge is known for its historic homes and events. Esplanade Avenue runs from the river to the city park and the New Orleans Museum of Art. Oak trees line the median, and the sedate homes radiate an aura of quiet charm. The air-conditioned house is near the mint, the French Market, park, and museum. The French Quarter is across the street. Two guest suites offer private baths. The living room of the first, overlooking Esplanade Avenue, is done up in forest green, with a double bed. There is another double bed in the bedroom furnished with antiques, a fireplace, and framed posters. The second has a spacious living rooms with a fireplace and opens to a side gallery. The bedroom has a double four-poster bed. A Continental breakfast is served. One of your hosts is from Germany; the other from New York. Both are avid antique and art collectors and enthusiastic members of the Spring Fiesta.

No. Rooms: 2	**Breakfast:** Continental
Singles: None	**S-Rates:** $75–$85 pb
Doubles: 2 pb	**D-Rates:** $85–$95 pb
Type: Private townhouse	**Bldg:** 1800 Greek Revival

Minimum Stay: none. **Credit Card(s) Accepted:** none. **Open:** all year. No resident dogs. No dogs please. No resident cats. No cats please. Nonsmoking host. Guests may not smoke in guest rooms. Residence not appropriate for children. **Discounts:** weekly. German spoken.

Reservation Contact: New Orleans Bed & Breakfast, Sarah-Margaret Brown, Box 8163, New Orleans, LA 70182; 504–822–5038.

UPTOWN, UNIVERSITY, AUDUBON ZOO.

Near St. Charles Ave. & Jefferson, I–10.

This stately home, built in the early years of the century, is entered through elaborate double beveled-glass doors. On the left are the living, dining, and sun rooms. To the right is the original library. Up the wide stairway are the four air-conditioned guest rooms. The two largest form a suite if needed, and share a large tiled bath. All the beds are four-posters, twin in one room and double in the other. A smaller room is across the hall with a private bath and double bed. On the third floor is a "garden" room with private bath and windows on three sides that look onto the tops of great oak trees and the street below. A white wicker double bed, settee, and other garden-style appointments give this room a cozy feeling. There is an elevator to the third floor.

No. Rooms: 4	**Breakfast:** Continental
Singles: None	**S-Rates:** $85 pb, $65 sb
Doubles: 2 pb, 2 sb	**D-Rates:** $85 pb, $65 sb
Type: Private home	**Bldg:** Turn-of-the-century

Minimum Stay: none. **Credit Card(s) Accepted:** AE, MC, V. **Open:** all year. No resident dogs. No dogs please. Resident cat. No cats please. Children welcome. Host smokes. Guests may smoke. **Discounts:** none.

Reservation Contact: New Orleans Bed & Breakfast, Sarah Margaret Brown, Box 8163, New Orleans, LA 70182; 504–822–5038.

ESPLANADE RIDGE.

Near Esplanade Ave. & Broad St., I–10.

This raised, center-hall home is located in Esplanade Ridge, an area known for its architectural diversity. A three-room, eclectically furnished apartment accommodates four. Continental breakfast is provided in the refrigerator. The garden surrounds the home on three sides and is filled with many old-fashioned flowers. Across the street visitors can board the Esplanade bus for the French Quarter, downtown, or the City Park Museum area. Your hosts are both artists who make sure to answer all of their guests' questions before leaving for their downtown gallery.

No. Rooms: 1	**Breakfast:** Continental
Singles: None	**S-Rates:** $85 pb
Doubles: 1 pb	**D-Rates:** $85 pb
Type: Private home	**Bldg:** Apartment

Minimum Stay: none. **Credit Card(s) Accepted:** AE, MC, V. **Open:** all year. No resident dogs. No dogs please. No resident cats. No cats please. Nonsmoking host. Guests may not smoke in residence. Children welcome with restrictions. **Discounts:** none.

Reservation Contact: New Orleans Bed & Breakfast, Sarah-Margaret Brown, Box 8163, New Orleans, LA 70182; 504–822–5038.

ID: NEWORLE8

UPTOWN AREA.

Near St. Charles Ave., I–10.

This huge home, in the lush Uptown area of New Orleans, was built in the 1840s as a plantation. Historic Uptown is a veritable trip into the past, with homes restored to their original splendor on every street. Uptown is bisected by legendary St. Charles Avenue, which still boasts the country's oldest continuously running streetcar. The area is directly connected to all of the attractions for which New Orleans is famous. The house, completely renovated by the owners, features fifty rooms of antiques and original rich woods and banisters. There are four guest rooms plus an efficiency apartment, with double bed, full kitchen with utensils, and private bath. The first guest room is very large, elegantly furnished, and has access to the upper balcony. It is done in soft hues of rose and green and has a queen-sized bed with a magnificent carved-wood headboard and footboard. A sitting area offers a queen-sized hide-a-bed, fireplace, tables, and lamps. The second room, done in dark green and white, has a king-sized brass bed with fluffy white spread and dust ruffle. The third room, done in pink, has a similar bed, and a fireplace with a gilt mirror over the mantle. This room has access to a side balcony. The fourth room, done in a brown and beige with floral draperies and pillows, has twin beds and can form a suite with the previous room. All but the last room have private baths, and there is an additional bath in the hall for guests' use. A Continental breakfast is served. Your hosts, a designer and a renovator of historic buildings, have varied interests and are well-traveled.

No. Rooms: 5	**Breakfast:** Continental
Singles: None	**S-Rates:** $55–$65 pb, $50–$55 sb
Doubles: 4 pb, 1 sb	**D-Rates:** $60–$75 pb, $50–$55 sb
Type: Private home	**Bldg:** 1840 old New Orleans

Minimum Stay: none. **Credit Card(s) Accepted:** none. **Open:** all year. Dog in residence. A dog is allowed with restrictions. Cat in residence. A cat is allowed with restrictions. Host smokes. Guests may smoke. Children welcome with restrictions. **Discounts:** weekly.

Reservation Contact: New Orleans Bed & Breakfast, Sarah-Margaret Brown, Box 8163, New Orleans, LA 70182; 504–822–5038.

ID: NEWORLE9

FRENCH QUARTER, JACKSON SQUARE.

Near Decatur & S. Peter sts., I–10, I–12.

Conveniently located in the heart of the French Quarter, this home makes car rentals and cab fares unnecessary; the entire area is within walking distance of Jackson Square, four blocks away is the famous French market complex, where guests can purchase fresh fruits and vegetables. The house, built in 1843, has two guest suites. Both are elegantly furnished in a contemporary style and can accommodate four persons. Each has a living room, bedroom, full kitchen, and private bath. Guests will find the brick walls and floor-to-ceiling windows typical of the area's architecture. In the living room of one suite, there is a double hide-a-bed, tables, lamps, and dining table and chairs. The other suite has seating at the breakfast bar. The bedrooms have double brass beds with fluffy floral spreads. A Continental breakfast is provided.

No. Rooms: 2	**Breakfast:** Continental
Singles: None	**S-Rates:** $75–$95 pb
Doubles: 2 pb	**D-Rates:** $75–$95 pb
Type: Private inn	**Bldg:** 1843 French-Quarter style

Minimum Stay: 2 nights. **Credit Card(s) Accepted:** MC, V. **Open:** all year. No resident dogs. No dogs please. No resident cats. No cats please. Host smokes. Guests may not smoke in guest rooms. Children welcome. **Discounts:** none.

Reservation Contact: New Orleans Bed & Breakfast, Sarah-Margaret Brown, Box 8163, New Orleans, LA 70182; 504–822–5038.

ID: 70116LAF

FRENCH QUARTER, SHOPS, MUSEUMS, WORLD-FAMOUS RESTAURANTS.

Near Bourbon & St. Philip sts., I–10.

The spacious entrance parlor of this fine old French manor greets you with the elegance and tradition of a bygone era, yet the house has been meticulously restored to afford every modern convenience. Fine antique pieces and reproductions from around the world lend unsurpassed authenticity in the *Vieux Carre* area. Located in the heart of the French Quarter, the inn (on the National Register of Historic Places) offers easy access to antique shops, museums, and restaurants. You will also enjoy a quiet stroll through the rows of colorful Creole and Spanish cottages and, of course, the nightlife of Bourbon Street. All fourteen guest rooms are carpeted and have either queen- or king-sized beds, private baths, central heat, and air-conditioning. Each room is individually decorated with period furnishings that differ in detail. Some rooms have wet bars and refrigerators; some have fireplaces. A Continental breakfast of freshly squeezed orange juice, delicate pastries, and coffee is served on private wrought-iron balconies or in the more intimate setting of the beautiful

courtyard. Wine is served in the front parlor at five o'clock. The inn also provides complimentary champagne to honeymooners and those celebrating birthdays and anniversaries. Child care, room service, arrival/departure transportation, and area tours are available.

No. Rooms: 14
Singles: None
Doubles: 14 pb
Type: Inn

Breakfast: Continental
S-Rates: $65–$105 pb
D-Rates: $75–$115 pb
Bldg: 1849 French manor

Minimum Stay: during Mardi Gras. **Credit Card(s) Accepted:** AE, Discovery, MC, V. **Open:** all year. No resident dogs. No dogs please. No resident cats. No cats please. Nonsmoking host. Guests may smoke. Children welcome. **Discounts:** none.

Reservation Contact: Bed & Breakfast Registry Ltd., Gary Winget, Box 8174, St. Paul, MN 55108; 612–646–4238.

ID: 70130TER

FRENCH QUARTER, GALLERIES, TULANE AND LOYOLA UNIVERSITIES, ZOO.

Near Magazine & Melpomene sts., I–10, U.S. 90.

Built in 1858 by a prominent New Orleans cotton merchant, this charming antebellum mansion has been faithfully restored. Located in the Garden District, one of the city's first major American residential neighborhoods, the house offers antique furnishings and modern conveniences. The twin parlors and formal dining room with gas chandeliers, gold mirrors, marble mantles, and period furnishings, capture the grace and elegance of days gone by. There are six guest rooms in the mansion and four in the carriage house. All are tastefully furnished and open onto balconies and a large landscaped courtyard. All have double beds, private baths, telephones, color TV, central air-conditioning, and heat. Continental breakfast is served in the dining room, and an evening cocktail is served in the parlors or courtyard. This little B&B inn is conveniently located, with good public transportation to the Business District and the French Quarter.

No. Rooms: 10	**Breakfast:** Continental
Singles: 1 pb	**S-Rates:** $55–$70 pb
Doubles: 9 pb	**D-Rates:** $65–$90 pb
Type: Inn	**Bldg:** 1858 Greek Revival

Minimum Stay: During Mardi Gras only. **Credit Card(s) Accepted:** AE, MC, V. **Open:** all year. No resident dogs. No dogs please. No resident cats. No cats please. Nonsmoking host. Guests may smoke. Children welcome. **Discounts:** weekly.

Reservation Contact: Bed & Breakfast Registry Ltd., Gary Winget, Box 8174, St. Paul, MN 55108; 612–646–4238.

PONCHATOULA

ID: LPNT1–SOUTH

LAKE PONTCHARTRAIN, ALLIGATOR FARM, SWAMP TOUR, SOUTHEASTERN LOUISIANA UNIVERSITY, CRAFT SHOPS, ANTIQUES.

Near I–55, U.S. 51, LA 22.

Reminiscent of a European *gasthaus,* this home offers a delightful country atmosphere and proximity to your host's Bavarian bakery. Although in a quiet, rural area, the house is close to a number of attractions. There are two guest rooms with private baths and TVs. One of the rooms also has a king-sized hide-a-bed and another hide-a-bed in the den available for children. A Full, European-style breakfast is served in the bakery.

No. Rooms: 2   **Breakfast:** Full
Singles: None   **S-Rates:** $40 pb
Doubles: 2 pb   **D-Rates:** $50 pb
Type: Private home   **Bldg:** Country-style brick

Minimum Stay: none. **Credit Card(s) Accepted:** none. **Open:** all year. No resident dogs. No dogs please. Resident cats. No cats please. Non-smoking host. Guests may not smoke in residence. Children welcome. **Discounts:** 10% senior citizens.

Reservation Contact: Southern Comfort Bed & Breakfast Reservations, Susan Morris, 2856 Hundred Oaks, Baton Rouge, LA 70808; 504–346–1928 or 504–928–9815.

ST. FRANCISVILLE   ID: LSF01–SOUTH

JOHN JAMES AUDUBON COUNTRY, ANTEBELLUM PLANTATIONS.

Near U.S. 61, LA 10.

The Feliciana Parishes of Louisiana were settled in the late eighteenth century, primarily by the English. Six miles from the historic district of St. Francisville and close to numerous antebellum plantations, this is a convenient location for touring the surrounding area. This carriage house is on the grounds of an antebellum home with beautifully landscaped grounds and a pond at which Canadian geese live and deer come to drink. The guest apartment includes a living room with a queen-sized hide-a-bed, dining room, kitchen, bedroom with queen-sized bed, and a full bath. Items for a Full breakfast are provided. Your host, a retired military officer, is a native and an authority on the history of the area.

No. Rooms: 1   **Breakfast:** Full
Singles: None   **S-Rates:** $80 pb
Doubles: 1 pb   **D-Rates:** $80 pb
Type: Private home   **Bldg:** Carriage house

Minimum Stay: none. **Credit Card(s) Accepted:** none. **Open:** all year. No resident dogs. No dogs please. No resident cats. No cats please. Non-smoking host. Guests may not smoke in residence. Children welcome with restrictions. **Discounts:** none.

Reservation Contact: Southern Comfort Bed & Breakfast Reservations, Susan Morris, 2856 Hundred Oaks, Baton Rouge, LA 70808; 504–346–1928 or 504–928–9815.

MAINE

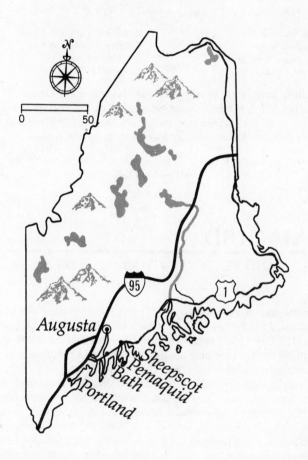

BATH

ID: 04530GLA

POPHAM BEACH, REID STATE PARK, L.L. BEAN,
MARITIME MUSEUM, BOWDOIN COLLEGE.

Near Washington & North sts., U.S. 1.

This Victorian house, located in the historic section of Bath, has received
rave reviews from previous guests. You are invited to use the parlors, with
TV, stereo, games, and grand piano. Three guest rooms, two with twin
beds, one with a double bed, share two guest baths. A Continental Plus
breakfast is served in the dining room or on the screened porch. Bath

is a ship-building town of 10,000 on the Kennebec River, and this home is about one-and-a-half blocks from a fine maritime museum. Also nearby are lovely shops and a small theater. Your charming host has traveled extensively and enjoys music, cooking, gardening, and needlework.

No. Rooms: 3	**Breakfast:** Continental Plus
Singles: None	**S-Rates:** $40–$45 sb
Doubles: 3 sb	**D-Rates:** $40–$45 sb
Type: Private home	**Bldg:** 1851 Victorian

Minimum Stay: none. **Credit Card(s) Accepted:** none. **Open:** all year. Dog in residence. No dogs please. No resident cats. No cats please. Non-smoking host. Guests may not smoke in residence. Children welcome with restrictions. **Discounts:** none. Spanish & French spoken.

Reservation Contact: Bed & Breakfast Registry Ltd., Gary Winget, Box 8174, St. Paul, MN 55108; 612–646–4238.

PEMAQUID   ID: 04558LIT

WHITE SAND BEACH, LIGHTHOUSE, FORT STONE.

Near Rte. 130, U.S. 1.

This one-hundred-and-forty-year-old Cape Cod-style house is located on the banks of the Pemaquid River, which cascades out of a blue spruce forest. The home has a large yard, library, piano, and games. There are nine rustic guest rooms with antique furnishings and double beds; two have private baths while the others share baths. Most have a view of the river, forest, and salt cover, and guests fall asleep to the soothing sound of the waterfalls. Many rooms have the original high beamed ceilings. One has a fireplace; others have skylights. A Full breakfast is served in the dining room overlooking the river and forest. Pemaquid offers a beautiful crescent-shaped white-sand beach, a majestic lighthouse perched on jagged rock ledges, and a rebuilt stone fort and museum, with ongoing archeological digs. This area features both rustic and gourmet restaurants and a scattering of tasteful shops and galleries.

No. Rooms: 9	**Breakfast:** Full
Singles: None	**S-Rates:** $55 pb, $45–$55 sb
Doubles: 2 pb, 7 sb	**D-Rates:** $60 pb, $50–$60 sb
Type: Inn	**Bldg:** 1840s Cape Cod farmhouse

Minimum Stay: none. **Credit Card(s) Accepted:** MC, V. **Open:** all year. Dog in residence. No dogs please. No resident cats. No cats please. Non-smoking host. Guests may smoke. Children welcome. **Discounts:** none.

Reservation Contact: Bed & Breakfast Registry Ltd., Gary Winget, Box 8174, St. Paul, MN 55108; 612–646–4238.

WALDOBORO

ID: 04572OLD

CONCERTS, THEATER, FESTIVALS, SAILING,
RESTAURANTS, ANTIQUES, GALLERIES.

Near U.S. 1, Rte. 220.

This charming little midcoastal inn is located near the Medomak River.
You are invited to use the living room, TV, piano, and decks. There are
five guest rooms which share three full baths. All have double or twin
beds. A Full breakfast is served in the dining room or spacious kitchen
with fireplace. Tea and sherry are served at 5 P.M. You will find tea, cookies, and baskets of fruit at bedtime. Bikes are available for your enjoyment
and tennis is nearby. Area tours, art workshop weeks, and candlelight
gourmet dinners are available by reservation. Your well-traveled hosts,
retired artists, enjoy painting, theater, opera, and ballet.

No. Rooms: 5	**Breakfast:** Full
Singles: None	**S-Rates:** $40–$65 sb
Doubles: 5 sb	**D-Rates:** $45–$70 sb
Type: Private home	**Bldg:** 1830 colonial

Minimum Stay: 2 days in Aug. **Credit Card(s) Accepted:** MC, V. **Open:**
all year. Dog in residence. No dogs please. No resident cats. No cats
please. Host smokes. Guests may not smoke in guest rooms. Children
welcome with restrictions. **Discounts:** off season, senior citizens. Some
French spoken.

Reservation Contact: Bed & Breakfast Registry Ltd., Gary Winget, Box
8174, St. Paul, MN 55108; 612–646–4238.

WELLS BEACH

ID: 04090BAY

OCEAN FRONT.

Near U.S. 1.

This historic 1890s carriage house is completely restored to its original
charm. This oceanfront home offers five cozy guest rooms with a view
of the ocean, double or twin beds, and two shared guest baths. The
homemade Continental breakfast is served in the sitting room overlooking
the beach. Here you can visit, watch cable TV, read, or watch the seals
cavort on the rocks at low tide. Shops, restaurants, excellent fishing, and
a harbor, with virtually every type of boat available, are easily accessible.

No. Rooms: 5	**Breakfast:** Continental Plus
Singles: None	**S-Rates:** $50–$105 sb
Doubles: 5 sb	**D-Rates:** $50–$105 sb
Type: Inn	**Bldg:** 1890s carriage house

Minimum Stay: 2 nights. **Credit Card(s) Accepted:** none. **Open:** all
year. No dogs please. No resident cats. No cats please. Guests may
smoke in guest rooms. Children welcome with restrictions. **Discounts:**
none.

Reservation Contact: Bed & Breakfast Registry Ltd., Gary Winget, Box 8174, St. Paul, MN 55108; 612–646–4238.

YORK BEACH
ID: 03903CAN

HISTORIC AREA, AMUSEMENT PARK, BEACHES, MT. AGAMENTICUS; ANTIQUES, SHOPS, RESTAURANTS.

Near U.S. 1, I–95.

This large Victorian home offers a touch of lavender and old lace—on bed linens, gracing tabletops, pillowcases, even some windows. Located on a quiet street, this house allows you to hear the roar of the ocean, not the sound of traffic. There are ten guest rooms, all wallpapered and furnished with treasured collectibles. The rooms have twin or double beds, accommodate one to five persons, and share baths. Homemade Continental breakfast is served. In the living room, you can gather for conversation, TV, reading, or games, or else enjoy the sun deck, and front porch. A refrigerator for your use is also available. The area has attracted visitors since the mid-1800s. Although there are many things to do and sights to see, the pace is relaxed and leisurely. Your hosts' interests include skiing, biking, hunting, fishing, crafts, and cars.

No. Rooms: 10	**Breakfast:** Continental
Singles: None	**S-Rates:** $50–$65 sb
Doubles: 10 sb	**D-Rates:** $55–$65 sb
Type: Inn	**Bldg:** 1902 Victorian

Minimum Stay: none. **Credit Card(s) Accepted:** none. **Open:** July 1–Sept. 5. Dog in residence. No dogs please. No resident cats. No cats please. Nonsmoking host. Guests may smoke. Children welcome. **Discounts:** none.

Reservation Contact: Bed & Breakfast Registry Ltd., Gary Winget, Box 8174, St. Paul, MN 55108; 612–646–4238.

MARYLAND

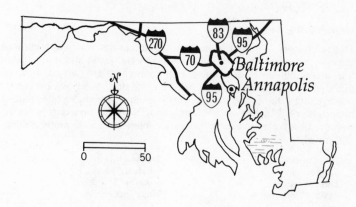

ANNAPOLIS

ID: 21401CHA

U.S. NAVAL ACADEMY, HARBOR, ST. JOHN'S COLLEGE; HISTORIC AREA.

Near Duke of Glouester & Cathedral sts., U.S. 50.

Built in 1860, this delightful Federal-style inn offers a unique way to visit historic Annapolis. The home is a five-minute walk to the harbor and a ten-minute walk to the naval academy. Because the inn is located on the water, many guests arrive by water taxi, while others arrive in their yachts. There is, however, off-street parking for those using more conventional modes of transportation. The inn has five guest rooms, all with wall-to-wall carpeting and air-conditioning. All rooms offer queen-sized or double beds. A Continental breakfast is served. Your hosts, both brokers, have interests in sailing, travel, wines, and gourmet cooking.

No. Rooms: 5	**Breakfast:** Continental
Singles: None	**S-Rates:** $95 pb, $60 sb
Doubles: 1 pb, 4 sb	**D-Rates:** $95 pb, $60 sb
Type: Inn	**Bldg:** 1860 Federal

Minimum Stay: none. **Credit Card(s) Accepted:** none. **Open:** all year. No resident dogs. No dogs please. No resident cats. No cats please. Non-smoking host. Guests may not smoke in guest rooms. Children welcome. **Discounts:** none.

Reservation Contact: Bed & Breakfast Registry Ltd., Gary Winget, Box 8174, St. Paul, MN 55108; 612–646–4238.

BALTIMORE

ID: 21313PAU

NORTHEAST SECTION OF BALTIMORE, CLOSE TO DOWNTOWN.

Near Harford Rd. & Erdman Ave.

This three-story, Tudor-style home is located in the Mayfield section of the city, a lovely neighborhood bounded by two parks and a small lake. It is fifteen minutes to downtown Baltimore. There are two guest rooms that share a bath. One has twin beds, a chest of drawers, wicker chairs, reading lamps, table, and large mirror. The other room has a queen-sized bed, desk, chair, white wicker lamp, and TV. A Full breakfast is served with the best coffee in town. Your hosts' interests include music, sailing, and travel.

No. Rooms: 2	**Breakfast:** Full
Singles: None	**S-Rates:** $50 sb
Doubles: 2 sb	**D-Rates:** $55 sb
Type: Private home	**Bldg:** Tudor-style

Minimum Stay: none. **Credit Cards Accepted:** none. **Open:** all year. No resident dogs. No dogs please. Resident cat. No cats please. Non-smoking host. Guests may not smoke indoors. Children welcome. **Discounts:** 10% senior citizens and weekly.

Reservation Contact: Bed & Breakfast Registry, Gary Winget, Box 8174, St. Paul, MN 55108; 612–646–4238.

ID: 21201MUL

HARBOR PLACE, CONVENTION CENTER, SCIENCE CENTER, NATIONAL AQUARIUM, PEABODY CONSERVATORY OF MUSIC; DOWNTOWN BALTIMORE.

Near Cathedral St., I–95, I–70, U.S. 40.

This elegant house was originally built in the 1800s on land purchased from a former officer in Washington's army. A three-story building, attached to the rear of the house, is now your hosts' residence. The main house was painstakingly restored in every detail. You are invited to enjoy the living room with fireplace, grand piano, crystal chandelier, comfortable chairs, and sofa. There are four large deluxe guest rooms on the second and third floors, with a shared bath on each floor. All the rooms have double beds with down comforters, fireplaces, antique armoires, comfortable chairs, brass chandeliers, carpets, and air-conditioning. The house is located in the Cathedral Hill area of downtown Baltimore so you can walk to many attractions, including Harbor Place, Mount Vernon Place Convention Center, and the Science Center. Off-street parking and arrival/departure transportation are available. Your hosts, a former teacher and a former engineer, are always available to guests for tour direction, restaurant suggestions, or just friendly conversation.

No. Rooms: 4 **Breakfast:** Full
Singles: None **S-Rates:** $65 sb
Doubles: 4 sb **D-Rates:** $65 sb
Type: Private home **Bldg:** 1830 Federal

Minimum Stay: none. **Credit Card(s) Accepted:** none. **Open:** all year. No resident dogs. No dogs please. No resident cats. No cats please. Host smokes. Guests may not smoke in guest rooms. Children welcome with restrictions. **Discounts:** none. German spoken.

Reservation Contact: Bed & Breakfast Registry Ltd., Gary Winget, Box 8174, St. Paul, MN 55108; 612–646–4238.

ID: 21201SHI

JOHNS HOPKINS UNIVERSITY, INNER HARBOR, NATIONAL AQUARIUM, SCIENCE CENTER, WALTERS MUSEUM, SYMPHONY.

Near Park & Howard sts., I–83.

Located in downtown Baltimore, this stately Victorian inn is convenient to all business and tourist attractions. Built in 1880, the entire structure has been restored to its original grandeur, and it now provides a delightful blend of Southern hospitality and European elegance. The inn is near Inner Harbor, one block from antique row, and within walking distance of museums, theater, the symphony, and fine restaurants. The entry hall leads to an ornately carved wooden staircase, and there is a charming parlor in which you may mingle over an early evening aperitif. The five-

story building, with an elevator, offers twenty-five guest suites with private baths. Some have kitchenettes. The rooms, done in mauve and grey, are tastefully furnished with authentic English antiques. All the rooms have individual heat and air-conditioning controls, telephone, and TVs. Laundry facilities, a yard, and a patio are available for your use. A Continental breakfast is served. Your host is a historian who enjoys Baltimore.

No. Rooms: 25	**Breakfast:** Continental
Singles: None	**S-Rates:** $55–$105 pb
Doubles: 25 pb	**D-Rates:** $65–$105 pb
Type: Inn	**Bldg:** 1880 Victorian

Minimum Stay: none. **Credit Card(s) Accepted:** AE, MC, V. **Open:** all year. No resident dogs. No dogs please. No resident cats. No cats please. Nonsmoking host. Guests may smoke. Children welcome. **Discounts:** none.

Reservation Contact: Bed & Breakfast Registry Ltd., Gary Winget, Box 8174, St. Paul, MN 55108; 612–646–4238.

ID: 21217BET

MEYERHOFF SYMPHONY HALL, LYRIC OPERA, THEATRE PROJECT, INNER HARBOR, NATIONAL AQUARIUM, SCIENCE CENTER, HARBORPLACE.

Near Lafayette & Mosha, I–83, I–95, I–695.

This charming, four-story, 1870 townhouse is located on a broad, tree-shaded street in the heart of historic and cultural Baltimore. It is just minutes from Meyerhoff Symphony Hall, the Lyric Opera, and the Theatre Project, and just a bit further is the Inner Harbor with the National Aquarium, Science Center, and the unique shops and restaurants of Harborplace. The house is graced with many elegant features such as a foyer floor inlaid with strips of oak and walnut, six carved marble fireplaces, twelve-foot ceilings, and a center staircase that opens to the fourth-floor skylight. The three air-conditioned guest rooms are furnished with antiques, heirloom quilts, and brass rubbings (executed by your host). Brynn's Room, on the second floor, has a queen-sized bed, private bath, and dressing area. The third-floor Blue Room has a king-sized bed which can be made into twin beds. It shares a bath with the Baltimore Room, which has twin beds plus a trundle and is decorated with posters and Baltimore memorabilia. A Continental Plus breakfast is served in the dining room. TV, telephone, and off-street parking are available. There is also a hot tub on the patio for guests' relaxation.

No. Rooms: 3	**Breakfast:** Continental Plus
Singles: None	**S-Rates:** $65 pb, $60 sb
Doubles: 1 pb, 2 sb	**D-Rates:** $65 pb, $60 sb
Type: Private townhouse	**Bldg:** 1870 Brick Victorian

Minimum Stay: none. **Credit Card(s) Accepted:** AE, MC, V. **Open:** all year. Dog in residence. No dogs please. No resident cats. No cats please.

Nonsmoking host. Guest may not smoke in residence. Children welcome.
Discounts: 10% after 3 days.

Reservation Contact: Bed & Breakfast Registry Ltd., Gary Winget, Box
8174, St. Paul, MN 55108; 612–646–4238.

BETTERTON

ID: 21610LAN

WILDLIFE REFUGE, WASHINGTON COLLEGE; SWIMMING, BOATING, CRABBING.

Near Rte. 292, Rte. 213, U.S. 301.

Betterton is a small Victorian-era resort located at the mouth of the Sassa-
fras River and the headwaters of the Upper Chesapeake Bay, eleven miles
north of Chestertown. The town has a public beach and a picnic area.
Betterton is part of Kent County, a treasury of early-American history,
beautiful old homes, and historic landmarks. This comfortable, old-
fashioned little inn has been open since 1905. There are parlor areas,
with TV, games, and reading material; sailboats, and tennis rackets are
available to guests. The fourteen guest rooms share baths. The rooms provide sleeping accommodations for at least two people. Additional meals
are available.

No. Rooms: 14	**Breakfast:** Continental Plus
Singles: 4 sb	**S-Rates:** $35 sb
Doubles: 10 sb	**D-Rates:** $40–$45 sb
Type: Inn	**Bldg:** 1905 New England clapboard

Minimum Stay: none. **Credit Card(s) Accepted:** none. **Open:** all year.
No resident dogs. A dog is allowed with restrictions. No resident cats.
No cats please. Nonsmoking host. Guests may not smoke in guest rooms.
Children welcome with restrictions. **Discounts:** none.

Reservation Contact: Bed & Breakfast Registry Ltd., Gary Winget, Box
8174, St. Paul, MN 55108; 612–646–4238.

MASSACHUSETTS

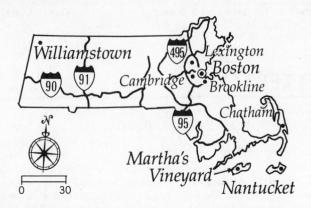

ARLINGTON

ID: 02174ORN

ON THE TRAIL OF PAUL REVERE'S RIDE; SALEM, CONCORD, LEXINGTON AND CONCORD MUSEUMS, SCIENCE CENTER, AQUARIUM.

Near Mystic & Summer sts., I–93, I–95, I–90.

This comfortable informal home, located in a residential area, is conveniently located for historic tours and commuting to Boston and Cambridge. You can relax in the living room near the fireplace. Off-street parking and laundry facilities are available. Breakfast is served in the dining room. There are two guest rooms available, one double and one single, with shared bath. Your host's interests include antique jewelry, music, and politics.

No. Rooms: 2	**Breakfast:** Continental
Singles: 1 sb	**S-Rates:** $45 sb
Doubles: 1 sb	**D-Rates:** $55sb
Type: Private home	**Bldg:** 1925 New England

Minimum Stay: none. **Credit Card(s) Accepted:** none. **Open:** all year. No resident dogs. A dog is allowed with restrictions. No resident cats. No cats please. Nonsmoking host. Guests may not smoke in guest rooms. **Discounts:** none.

Reservation Contact: Bed & Breakfast Registry Ltd., Gary Winget, Box 8174, St. Paul, MN 55108; 612–646–4238.

BARNSTABLE

CAPE COD, HISTORIC DISTRICT, BEACHES, WHALE WATCHING, SUMMER THEATER, MUSEUMS.

Near Old Kings Hwy., rtes. 6A & 132.

This 1705 Queen Anne colonial was built by one of Barnstable's founders, and has been painstakingly restored to its original appearance. Here guests can visit America's past and partake of the charm and simplicity of an earlier age but without giving up modern conveniences. Visitors will find blacksmith-made latches (rather than door knobs), eighteenth-century paneling, and wide-board pine floors. The three guest rooms have private baths. The first, originally used as a parlor and morning room (now the bath), is furnished with a double pencil-post canopy bed and other antiques. It also boasts a working fireplace and comfortable sitting area. A light, airy upstairs room has a queen-sized canopy bed and working fireplace. This room is very private and has its own staircase leading to it. The third room is actually a suite of two smaller rooms, one with an antique bed, one with a double canopy bed. A full breakfast is served in the Keeping Room in front of the ten-foot fireplace. The room is accented with the iron kettles, pots, and utensils of the eighteenth century. After breakfast, stop for a minute on the patio, surrounded by an old-fashioned perennial garden. The house is very convenient to shopping, fine restaurants, whale watching boats, and much more. Your hostess is interested in sharing travel information and cuttings from her garden with guests. Guests frequently stop in the host's barn/workshop where he makes Windsor chairs and carves birds and decoys. Both hosts are avid antiques collectors.

No. Rooms: 3	**Breakfast:** Full
Singles: None	**S-Rates:** $75–$85 pb
Doubles: 3 pb	**D-Rates:** $75–85 pb
Type: Private home	**Bldg:** 1705 Colonial

Minimum Stay: 2 nights on weekends. **Credit Card(s) Accepted:** MC, V. **Open:** all year. Resident dog. No dogs please. No resident cats. No cats please. Nonsmoking host. Guests may smoke. Children welcome with restrictions. **Discounts:** none.

Reservation Contact: Bed & Breakfast Cape Cod, Clark Diehl, Box 341, W. Hyannisport, MA 02672; 617–775–2772.

CAPE COD, BEACHES, RESTAURANTS, WHALE WATCHING, CHARTER FISHING, MUSEUMS, ANTIQUE SHOPS.

Near rtes. 6A & 132, U.S. 6.

This three-story, center-chimney colonial, circa 1800, was built as a residence and tavern by Cornelius Crocker, Jr. It enjoyed a colorful involve-

ment in Barnstable's pre-revolutionary history and the current hosts have
found numerous interesting artifacts from this period including an iron
spoon, clay pipestems, and pottery shards. The ancient post-and-beam
barn and connecting wing provide family quarters, an office, workshop,
main kitchen, pantry, and guest entrance. The house is gracious, simple,
and inviting, furnished with authentic country antiques and fine reproductions. Guests will like the three large common rooms (a Keeping Room,
Parlor, and Sitting Room) as well as the screened porch and brick terrace.
Take a quiet stroll along the brook, romp on the sprawling lawns, inspect
the gardens, or try your hand at bocce. An informal afternoon tea is
served during which your hosts can help guests get their bearings, assist
with dinner reservations, and introduce other guests. Each of the four
guest rooms has a beautiful handmade quilt, Windsor rocker, good reading lamp, interesting books, bathrobes, a lap desk, and an alarm clock.
The "Coachman" is a single room with tavern shelves, Robert Newell
lithographs, and a sun-filled east window. Appletop has a double bed,
antique pine dresser, pine floor, and marine photographs. A queen-sized,
canopy bed, pine armoire, eighteenth-century blanket chest, and a fireplace grace "Tavernside" which overlooks the garden and brook. Court-
view is a sunny front room with fireplace, queen-sized, canopy Sheraton
bed, and antique Vermont cupboard. It has views of the 1774 Court-
house, the Olde King's Highway and Saint Mary's Church. The guest
rooms share two modern baths with tub and shower. Each morning between 8:30 and 9:30 guests gather around the massive table in the Keeping Room for a family-style, Continental Plus breakfast with homemade
breads or muffins and fresh-ground coffee. The hosts are interested in
civic affairs, local history, conservation, canoeing, maritime subjects,
genealogy, and woodworking.

No. Rooms: 4	**Breakfast:** Continental Plus
Singles: 1 sb	**S-Rates:** $40–$75 sb
Doubles: 3 sb	**D-Rates:** $50–$75 sb
Type: Inn	**Bldg:** 1800 colonial

Minimum Stay: none. **Credit Card(s) Accepted:** MC, V. **Open:** all year except Christmas. No resident dogs. No dogs please. No resident cats. No cats please. Nonsmoking host. Guests may not smoke in residence. Children over 12 years welcome. **Discounts:** 6 or more nights. Some French spoken.

Reservation Contact: Bed & Breakfast Registry Ltd., Gary Winget, Box 8174, St. Paul MN 55108; 612–646–4238.

BASS RIVER ID: CAPECOD02

WALK TO BEACHES, STORES, RESTAURANTS; 10 MINUTES TO HYANNIS.

Near rtes. 28, 6, 3, & 25.

This 1829 sea captain's house is complete with a belvedere on top. The walls are painted and stenciled in warm colors, and the floors are of wide-board pumpkin pine. A crystal chandelier illuminates the formal dining room, furnished with antiques. Two guest rooms share a bath and one room has a private bath. The Hamilton is spacious and airy, with a queen-sized bed, antique furnishings, including dressing table, and walls covered in a lively colonial floral print. The Virginia Anthony is a Victorian-style room furnished with two four-poster mahogany twin beds. Lace-trimmed curtains cover the windows, and the walls are covered in a pale blue and white floral print. A raspberry velvet chair accents the color scheme. The Florilla, an exceptionally bright room, is furnished with a double bed. The color scheme of soft pastels is taken from a pleasing floral-print wall covering. A soft-pillowed rattan chair and separate dressing area with vanity table are offered. A Continental Plus breakfast of freshly baked breads and muffins is served in the dining room. The house is on an acre of beautifully landscaped shaded property, which includes holly trees and two-hundred-year-old maples. Guests are invited to make use of the shaded picnic area. A stroll along tree-lined Main Street is an enjoyable experience and an easy walk to stores and restaurants. The area has fine beaches (within walking distance), harbors for boating, recreational activity, and shopping. Fine restaurants are a short drive away. Your host is interested in crafts, painting, decorating, gardening, and cooking. Arrival/departure transportation and box lunches are available.

No. Rooms: 3	**Breakfast:** Continental Plus
Singles: None	**S-Rates:** $40 sb
Doubles: 1 pb, 2 sb	**D-Rates:** $65 pb, $55 sb
Type: Private inn	**Bldg:** 1820 Federal

Minimum Stay: none. **Credit Card(s) Accepted:** none. **Open:** all year. Dog in residence. No dogs please. No resident cats. No cats please. Nonsmoking host. Guests may not smoke in residence. Children welcome with restrictions. **Discounts:** none.

Reservation Contact: Bed & Breakfast Cape Cod, Clark Diehl, Box 341, W. Hyannisport, MA 02672; 617–775–2772.

BEDFORD

ID: 3–MINUTEMAN

CONCORD & LEXINGTON.

Near Rtes. 2, 3, 93, 128.

Bedford is in the heart of "Minuteman Country," close to high-tech firms and medical centers. Major historical buildings and sites are nearby; there are even some seventeenth-century houses amid the many eighteenth-century homes. Although built in 1934, this house, situated in the Bedford countryside, was finished with golden oak floors, wood paneling, and mantle pieces from a much older Bedford home. There are six fireplaces, and the furnishings are a mixture of antique and modern. There are three guest rooms; two have double beds, one has twin beds, and one has private bath. All the rooms have their own heat and air-conditioning. A Continental Plus breakfast is served. You are also invited to use the game room, with pool table, ping pong, and darts, as well as the library. Both hosts are employed in the textbook publishing industry. Their interests include gardening, horse racing, reading, and travel.

No. Rooms: 3	**Breakfast:** Continental Plus
Singles: None	**S-Rates:** $48–$55 pb, $45–$48 sb
Doubles: 1 pb, 2 sb	**D-Rates:** $60–$66 pb, $55–$60 sb
Type: Private home	**Bldg:** 1934 Colonial

Minimum Stay: 2 nights in season. **Credit Card(s) Accepted:** AE, MC, V. **Open:** all year. Dog in residence. No dogs please. Two resident cats. No cats please. Host smokes. Guests may smoke. Children welcome. **Discounts:** 10% for senior citizens and stays of 14 or more nights.

Reservation Contact: Bed & Breakfast in Minuteman Country, Tally & Pamela Carruthers, Box 665, Cambridge, MA 02140; 617–576–2112.

BOSTON

ID: BAY.COL.M220

BACK BAY, PRUDENTIAL CENTER, HYNES CONVENTION CENTER, COPLEY PLACE.

Near St. Botolph St., Huntington Ave.

This elegant Victorian brownstone is furnished with traditional wood, leather, family antiques, and collectibles. Two guest rooms share a bath. A charming room at the front of the house is furnished with twin beds that can be made into a king-sized bed and an antique secretary. The other guest room has a single bed. A generous, gourmet Full breakfast is served in the dining room or in the guest rooms. Other amenities include a sherry hour, light laundry and shoe-shine service, and complimentary snacks and beverages. The hosts are experts on Boston sights, restaurants, history, and culture.

No. Rooms: 2	**Breakfast:** Full
Singles: 1 sb	**S-Rates:** $65–$70 sb
Doubles: 1 sb	**D-Rates:** $75–$85 sb
Type: Private home	**Bldg:** Victorian brownstone

Minimum Stay: 2 nights. **Credit Card(s) Accepted:** none. **Open:** all year. No resident dogs. No dogs please. No resident cats. No cats please. Host smokes. Guests may smoke. Children welcome with restrictions. **Discounts:** none.

Reservation Contact: Bed & Breakfast Associates Bay Colony, Ltd., A. Kardasis & M. Mitchell, Box 166, Babson Pk. Br., Boston, MA 02157; 617–449–5302.

ID: BAY.COL.M240

ST. BOTOLPH AREA, NEAR BACK BAY.

Near Massachusetts & Huntington Aves., I–90.

St. Botolph is a landmark area of restored Victorian row houses adjacent to Boston's Back Bay. Boston is unsurpassed in the U.S. for its concentration of historical, cultural, medical, and educational centers, all within walking distance of this Victorian bow-front home built in 1881. Guests will find many little extras here, such as fresh fruit, hard candy, complimentary sherry, cut flowers in season, and clock radios. Two second-floor guest rooms and a patio apartment are available. The first room has a double and a single bed with down comforters, Victorian furnishings accented with family pictures in antique frames, easy chairs in the sitting area, and adequate lighting, particularly for reading in bed. The second room has twin beds, also with quilts and antique furnishings. These two rooms share a bath. The apartment has its own entrance, bath, and kitchen with quarry tile floor. A Murphy bed sleeps two, but a rollaway is also available. A Full breakfast is served. Your hosts interests include cooking, reading, theater, and music.

No. Rooms: 3	**Breakfast:** Full
Singles: None	**S-Rates:** $75 pb, $55–$60 sb
Doubles: 1 pb, 2 sb	**D-Rates:** $75 pb, $65–$75 sb
Type: Private home	**Bldg:** 1881 bowfront Victorian

Minimum Stay: 2 nights. **Credit Card(s) Accepted:** none. **Open:** all year. No resident dogs. No dogs please. Cat in residence. No cats please. Nonsmoking host. Guests may not smoke in residence. Children welcome with restrictions. **Discounts:** none.

Reservation Contact: Bed & Breakfast Associates Bay Colony, Ltd., A. Kardasis & M. Mitchell, Box 166, Babson Pk. Br., Boston, MA 02157; 617–449–5302.

BUNKER HILL, U.S.S. CONSTITUTION, FREEDOM TRAIL; HISTORIC DISTRICT.

Near Monument Ave., Rte. 93.

Built in 1846, this beautifully restored brick townhouse is located in the historic district, just one and one-half blocks from the Bunker Hill Monument and ten minutes from the U.S.S. Constitution. It is close to the famous Freedom Trail and a walking tour of historic sites, and a bus at the corner takes visitors to Quincy Market (Faneuil Hall) in five minutes. From the deck on top of the townhouse, guests get a panoramic view of Boston Harbor. A butler's pantry, with refrigerator for drinks and snacks, is available for guests' use. The second floor features a two-room suite, including bedroom with double bed, separated by sliding glass doors from a private living room, and a private bath. The decor is a mixture of contemporary and antique furnishings. The third-floor room also has a double bed and is comfortably furnished, and shares a bath with your hosts. Rollaway beds are available. A Continental Plus breakfast is served. Your hosts, who go out of their way to make their guests feel comfortable, can suggest nearby restaurants and provide advice on how to get around Boston easily. One of your hosts is an engineer; one, an administrative assistant. Their interests include travel, music, jogging, opera, and skiing.

No. Rooms: 2	**Breakfast:** Continental Plus
Singles: None	**S-Rates:** $48 pb, $40 sb
Doubles: 1 pb, 1 sb	**D-Rates:** $55 pb, $48 sb
Type: Private townhouse	**Bldg:** 1846 brick row house

Minimum Stay: none. **Credit Card(s) Accepted:** none. **Open:** all year. No resident dogs. No dogs please. No resident cats. No cats please. Nonsmoking host. Guests may not smoke in guest rooms. Children welcome with restrictions. **Discounts:** none. French & Turkish spoken.

Reservation Contact: Pineapple Hospitality, Inc., Judy M. Mulford, 47 N. Second St., Suite 3A, New Bedford, MA 02740; 617–990–1696.

CHARLESTOWN AREA, OLD IRONSIDES MUSEUM, FREEDOM TRAIL, CHARLESTOWN NAVAL YARD.

Near I–93, First St.

Beautiful views of Boston Harbor and the city's skyline enhance this tastefully decorated three-story townhouse located in the historic Charlestown Naval Yard. Fine antiques, art objects, fireplaces, and decks add to the charm of the home. The air-conditioned guest room on the third floor has a double bed, a desk, and a private bath. A Continental breakfast is served. Parking is available on the street or in a garage ($5). The downtown area can be reached by bus, ferry, or foot.

No. Rooms: 1	**Breakfast:** Continental
Singles: none	**S-Rates:** $66 pb
Doubles: 1 pb	**D-Rates:** $75 pb
Type: Private home	**Bldg:** Townhouse

Minimum Stay: 2 nights. **Credit Card(s) Accepted:** none. **Open:** all year. Resident dog. No dogs please. No resident cats. No cats please. Nonsmoking host. Guest may not smoke in residence. Children welcome with restrictions. **Discounts:** 10% for senior citizens and stays of 14 or more nights.

Reservation Contact: Bed & Breakfast in Minuteman Country, Tally & Pamela Carruthers, Box 665, Cambridge, MA 02140; 617–576–2112.

ID: 12–GRTBOS

CENTRAL BOSTON.

Near I–93.

Built in 1799 by General Nathaniel Austin, this grey-stone house hearkens back almost to the Revolutionary War. John Harvard lived in this area, where he was pastor of the church built by the settlers of his era. This home, a registered historic landmark, features window boxes and thick English ivy across the front to brighten its facade. The beautiful second-floor guest room is reminiscent of the eighteenth century. It has a fireplace, a four-poster bed, pumpkin pine floors, private bath, and three windows overlooking the linden trees in a small park. A second room with a trundle bed which sleeps two is available for members of the same party. There is a deck across from the room. A Full breakfast is served. Parking, a rare commodity, is included in the room rate. Your host is a retired art teacher and has an excellent collection of art books.

No. Rooms: 1	**Breakfast:** Full
Singles: None	**S-Rates:** $80 pb
Doubles: 1 pb	**D-Rates:** $80 pb
Type: Private townhouse	**Bldg:** 1799 granite

Minimum Stay: none. **Credit Card(s) Accepted:** none. **Open:** all year. No resident dogs. No dogs please. No resident cats. No cats please. Guests may not smoke in residence. Residence not appropriate for children. **Discounts:** none.

Reservation Contact: Greater Boston Hospitality, Lauren Simonelli, Box 1142, Brookline, MA 02146; 617–277–5430.

FREEDOM TRAIL, QUINCY MARKET.

Near Rte. 1, Huntington Ave.

If you're looking for the charm of old Boston, try this 1870 red-brick Victorian townhouse just minutes from major hotels, shops, and excellent restaurants. There are two guest rooms with kitchenettes, private baths, private entrances off the front foyer, and excellent views of the city. The first has a double bed and the second has a queen-sized bed. Ingredients for Full breakfasts are stocked in the kitchenettes. Parking is scarce in this neighborhood with narrow streets, so it's best not to have a car. The host is active in community affairs and enjoys travel, theater, and good restaurants.

No. Rooms: 2	**Breakfast:** Full
Singles: None	**S-Rates:** $65 pb
Doubles: 2 pb	**D-Rates:** $65 pb
Type: Private home	**Bldg:** 1870 brick Victorian

Minimum Stay: 2 nights. **Credit Card(s) Accepted:** none. **Open:** all year. No resident dogs. No dogs please. No resident cats. No cats please. Nonsmoking host. Guests may not smoke in residence. Children welcome. **Discounts:** none.

Reservation Contact: Greater Boston Hospitality, Lauren Simonelli, Box 1142, Brookline, MA 02146; 617–277–5430.

DOWNTOWN BOSTON.

Near Huntington Ave., Rte. 9, Rte. 2.

This modern luxury apartment is in a prime Boston location. Exclusive boutiques, art galleries, and fine restaurants can be found in the immediate area. The beautifully appointed air-conditioned guest room features twin beds and private bath. A Continental breakfast is served. There is a garage under the building that is available for a guest's car.

No. Rooms: 1	**Breakfast:** Continental
Singles: None	**S-Rates:** $74 pb
Doubles: 1 pb	**D-Rates:** $81 pb
Type: Private apartment	**Bldg:** 1960s modern luxury

Minimum Stay: 2 nights. **Credit Card(s) Accepted:** none. **Open:** all year. No dogs please. No cats please. Nonsmoking host. Residence not appropriate for children. **Discounts:** for extended stays.

Reservation Contact: Greater Boston Hospitality, Lauren Simonelli, Box 1142, Brookline, MA 02146; 617–277–5430.

PRUDENTIAL CENTER, COPLEY SQUARE.

Near Storrow Dr., Rte. 1.

This brownstone in an interesting downtown neighborhood has been converted into a three-story condominium with high ceilings, skylights, and very modern amenities. The furniture is a mixture of Victorian, Duncan Fife, and traditional. The air-conditioned guest room with private bath has twin beds and bay windows that overlook a pretty square. A Continental Plus breakfast is served. Your hosts have traveled extensively in Europe and Africa. Both attend the symphony and are serious walkers.

No. Rooms: 1	**Breakfast:** Continental Plus
Singles: None	**S-Rates:** $62 pb
Doubles: 1 pb	**D-Rates:** $62 pb
Type: Private home	**Bldg:** 1890 brownstone

Minimum Stay: 2 nights. **Credit Card(s) Accepted:** none. **Open:** all year. No resident dogs. No dogs please. No resident cats. No cats please. Nonsmoking host. Guests may not smoke in residence. Children welcome with restrictions. **Discounts:** none.

Reservation Contact: Greater Boston Hospitality, Lauren Simonelli, Box 1142, Brookline, MA 02146; 617–277–5430.

BEACON HILL, STATE HOUSE, BOSTON COMMON.

Near Beacon & Charles sts.

Built in 1830 and recently restored, this beautiful townhouse is in the center of Beacon Hill, a designated National Historic Area full of brick sidewalks, gas lights, and Georgian homes. It is minutes to the State House, public garden, Boston Common, excellent restaurants, and art galleries. Two of the six guest rooms have private baths and the others share two baths. One of the rooms, with twin beds, has a small kitchenette, exposed brick walls, and a patio. Another features a queen-sized bed, an unusual writing desk, separate seating area, fireplace, and bow window. All the rooms are decorated with lovely fabrics and have TVs, telephones, and air-conditioning. A Full breakfast is served as well as afternoon tea and sherry. One of the hosts is a graduate of the Restaurant School in Philadelphia and La Varenne École de Cuisine in Paris. The other works in hospital administration. Both are graduates of L'Academie de Vin in Paris and have been in the hospitality field for several years.

No. Rooms: 6	**Breakfast:** Full
Singles: None	**S-Rates:** $75–$115 sb, $75–$115 pb
Doubles: 2 pb, 4 sb	**D-Rates:** $75–$115 sb, $75–$115 pb
Type: Private home	**Bldg:** Georgian townhouse

Minimum Stay: none. **Credit Card(s) Accepted:** MC, V. **Open:** all year. No resident dogs. No dogs please. No resident cats. No cats please. Nonsmoking host. Guests may not smoke in residence. Children welcome. **Discounts:** 7th night free. French spoken.

Reservation Contact: Greater Boston Hospitality, Lauren Simonelli, Box 1142, Brookline, MA 02146; 617–277–5430.

ID: 02115CUM

PRUDENTIAL CENTER, SYMPHONY HALL, MUSEUM OF FINE ARTS, COPLEY SQUARE.

Near Massachusetts & Huntington aves., I–90, I–95, U.S. 1.

This lovely brick and brownstone townhouse is located in a quaint Victorian neighborhood just two blocks south of the Prudential Center. The little street on which the house is located is a quiet one. Symphony Hall is only two blocks away. The renowned Boston Museum of Fine Arts is six blocks away, and the Isabella Stewart Gardiner Museum is right behind it. The house has two guest rooms and a studio apartment. The guest rooms each sleep two, offer antique furnishings, and share a bath. The studio apartment has a kitchen, private bath, double bed, private entrance, and patio. A full breakfast is served. Your hospitable hosts have interests in movies, theater, music, and reading.

No. Rooms: 3	**Breakfast:** Full
Singles: None	**S-Rates:** $65 pb, $40–$45 sb
Doubles: 1 pb, 2 sb	**D-Rates:** $65 pb, $50–$65 sb
Type: Private townhouse	**Bldg:** 1881 bowfront Victorian

Minimum Stay: 2 nights. **Credit Card(s) Accepted:** none. **Open:** all year. No resident dogs. No dogs please. Cat in residence. No cats please. Nonsmoking host. Guests may not smoke in residence. Children welcome. **Discounts:** none.

Reservation Contact: Bed & Breakfast Registry Ltd., Gary Winget, Box 8174, St. Paul, MN 55108; 612–646–4238.

ID: 02116LAW

SOUTH END, COPLEY SQUARE.

Near Columbus & Dartmouth, I–90, I–93.

This brick townhouse, within walking distance to the "T" (public transit), Copley Square, and shops and restaurants, is located on a quiet residential street with brick sidewalks and old-fashioned street lamps. This 1860s house still retains its original mahogany door and marble fireplace. Two guest rooms are available. One has a double bed, white wicker furniture, an off-white rug on a pine floor, and a white-and-pastel color scheme. Your host's watercolors and weavings adorn the walls, and there is a view of the back yard and patio. The bath is shared with the host. The second room has a private entrance off the patio, private bath, and king-sized bed plus bunk beds, a wicker settee, hanging plants, and a refrigerator, toaster oven, and coffee maker. A Continental Plus breakfast is served. Your host, an artist and real estate broker who has traveled widely, enjoys skiing and sailing.

No. Rooms: 2	**Breakfast:** Continental Plus
Singles: None	**S-Rates:** $60 pb, $50 sb
Doubles: 1 pb, 1 sb	**D-Rates:** $70 pb, $60 sb
Type: Private home	**Bldg:** 1869 brick townhouse

Minimum Stay: none. **Credit Card(s) Accepted:** none. **Open:** all year. No resident dogs. No dogs please. Cat in residence. No cats please. Nonsmoking host. Guests may not smoke in residence. Children welcome. **Discounts:** none. Spanish spoken.

Reservation Contact: Bed & Breakfast Registry Ltd., Gary Winget, Box 8174, St. Paul, MN 55108; 612–646–4238.

ID: 02118CLA

NEAR BACK BAY AREA, SYMPHONY HALL, MUSEUM OF FINE ARTS, BOSTON ARENA.

Near Columbia & Massachusetts aves., I–90, I–95.

This charming nineteenth-century townhouse is located on a tree-lined street with brick sidewalks. The neighborhood is adjacent to Copley Square and the Back Bay area and is convenient to downtown Boston. The bright and spacious guest room has a private bath and opens onto a large balcony. The comfortably furnished room has hardwood floors, Oriental rugs, natural woodwork, telephone, a double and a single bed, microwave, refrigerator, and coffee maker. Framed prints decorate the walls. A Continental breakfast is served.

No. Rooms: 1	**Breakfast:** Continental
Singles: None	**S-Rates:** $69 pb
Doubles: 1 pb	**D-Rates:** $69 pb
Type: Private home	**Bldg:** 1880s brick townhouse

Minimum Stay: none. **Credit Card(s) Accepted:** none. **Open:** all year. No resident dogs. No dogs please. No resident cats. No cats please. Nonsmoking host. Guests may not smoke in residence. Children welcome. **Discounts:** none.

Reservation Contact: Bed & Breakfast Registry Ltd., Gary Winget, Box 8174, St. Paul, MN 55108; 612–646–4238.

BROOKLINE
ID: BAY.COL.M605

BROOKLINE, HISTORIC DISTRICT.

Near Beacon St. & Commonwealth Ave., rtes. 95, 1, 9.

Located in one of Brookline's finest neighborhoods, with tree-lined streets, stately homes, and a view of Boston skyscrapers, this Victorian house was built in 1900. With a subway stop at either end of the street, there is easy access to universities, downtown Boston, museums, and restaurants. The large, sunny home is across from a scenic park, complete with a bird sanctuary, duck pond, clay tennis courts, and excellent jogging paths along the Charles River. The kitchen, with its skylight and three glass walls looking onto the deck, has appeared in *Better Homes and Gardens.* Two guest rooms offer private baths, TVs, and telephones. The first room is cozy and comfortable, with windows on three sides, a queen-sized bed, dresser, night tables with lamps, easy chair, Oriental rug, maps and tour books, and a closet with a full-length mirror. The second is a large room with a double bed, desk, easy chair, Chinese rug, hardwood floor, and view of the park. For long-term stays, a table and cooking appliances are available. A Continental Plus breakfast, featuring a variety of muffins and croissants, is served. This busy household, with two children, two dogs, and a Persian cat, is not suitable for anyone unaccustomed to the sights and sounds of children and pets. Your hosts, employed in special education and psychiatric social work, are interested in cooking, reading, movies, and people.

No. Rooms: 2
Singles: None
Doubles: pb
Type: Private home

Breakfast: Continental Plus
S-Rates: $50 pb
D-Rates: $60 pb
Bldg: 1900 Victorian

Minimum Stay: none. **Credit Card(s) Accepted:** none. **Open:** all year. Dogs in residence. No dogs please. Cat in residence. No cats please. Nonsmoking host. Guests may not smoke in residence. **Discounts:** none. French & Russian spoken.

Reservation Contact: Bed & Breakfast Associates Bay Colony, Ltd., A. Kardasis & M. Mitchell, Box 166, Babson Pk. Br., Boston, MA 02157; 617–449–5302.

ID: 36–GRTBOS

HARVARD MEDICAL SCHOOL, MUSEUMS, FINE RESTAURANTS.

Near Beacon & Boylston sts., Rte. 9, I–95.

Conveniently located for driving into and out of Boston, this fine older brick Colonial, with its many antiques and books offers two lovely guest rooms with shared guest bath. The rooms, on a separate floor from the rest of the house, open onto a large patio. Both rooms are carpeted and have color TV, two large upholstered chairs, Laura Ashley linens, fresh flowers, and lovely color schemes. One has twin beds and marble-top bureaus; the other has a queen-sized bed. The breakfast menu includes such items as fresh fruit, French toast, waffles, scrambled eggs, bacon, and baked apples. The house, in a superior older neighborhood of single-family homes with beautiful lawns and shrubs and magnificent old trees, is close to the Harvard medical area and only a few minutes' walk to an express subway to downtown Boston. Parking is included in the rate. Your hosts, a real-estate broker and a computer analyst, are both Harvard graduates. They have traveled extensively and are interested in the arts and sciences. Both being native Bostonians, they are extremely knowledgeable about the city.

No. Rooms: 2	**Breakfast:** Full
Singles: None	**S-Rates:** $60 sb
Doubles: 2 sb	**D-Rates:** $62 sb
Type: Private home	**Bldg:** 1920 brick Georgian

Minimum Stay: 2 nights. **Credit Card(s) Accepted:** none. **Open:** all year. No resident dogs. No dogs please. No resident cats. No cats please. Nonsmoking host. Guests may not smoke in residence. Residence not appropriate for children. **Discounts:** none.

Reservation Contact: Greater Boston Hospitality, Lauren Simonelli Box 1142, Brookline, MA 02146; 617–277–5430.

ID: 37–GRTBOS

20 MINUTES FROM DOWNTOWN BOSTON VIA PUBLIC TRANSIT; SHOPPING, RESTAURANTS.

Near Beacon & Commonwealth.

This brick Georgian home, circa 1915, is in an outstanding neighborhood minutes from the express train (green line) to Boston. The home is filled with Oriental rugs, antiques, and magnificent art. There is one guest room with private bath and color TV. The room is decorated with designer fabrics and features a queen-sized bed, mirrored doors, and an extensive library. Guests also have the use of a den. A Full breakfast is served. Parking, which is increasingly more difficult to find in the area, is also included. Your hosts enjoy travel, reading, walking, and are interested in the history of Boston.

No. Rooms: 1	**Breakfast:** Full
Singles: None	**S-Rates:** $82 pb
Doubles: 1 pb	**D-Rates:** $82 pb
Type: Private home	**Bldg:** 1915 Georgian

Minimum Stay: 2 nights. **Credit Card(s) Accepted:** none. **Open:** all year. No resident dogs. No dogs please. No resident cats. No cats please. Nonsmoking host. Guests may not smoke in residence. Residence not appropriate for children. **Discounts:** 7th night free.

Reservation Contact: Greater Boston Hospitality, Lauren Simonelli, Box 1142, Brookline, MA 02146; 617–277–5430.

ID: 02146BEA

BEACON STREET, MUSEUMS, HARBOR; UNIVERSITIES, CONCERTS, THEATER, SUPERB RESTAURANTS.

Near Beacon & Carlton sts., Massachusetts Tpk., U.S. 1.

This brick Victorian inn is conveniently located only ten minutes from downtown Boston, and a two-minute walk to public transportation. The house features high ceilings and decorative fireplaces. Fifteen guest rooms offer twin or double beds, and private or shared baths. Continental breakfast is served. Your well-traveled host likes gourmet cooking, reading, and the arts.

No. Rooms: 15	**Breakfast:** Continental
Singles: None	**S-Rates:** $45–$55 pb, $35–$45 sb
Doubles: 8 pb, 7 sb	**D-Rates:** $55–$65 pb, $45–$55 sb
Type: Inn	**Bldg:** 1900 Victorian

Minimum Stay: none. **Credit Card(s) Accepted:** AE, DC, MC, V. **Open:** all year. No resident dogs. No dogs please. No resident cats. No cats please. Nonsmoking host. Guests may smoke. Children welcome. **Discounts:** groups, seniors.

Reservation Contact: Bed & Breakfast Registry Ltd., Gary Winget, Box 8174, St. Paul, MN 55108; 612–646–4238.

CAMBRIDGE   ID: BAY.COL.M890

HARVARD UNIVERSITY, M.I.T.

Near Massachusetts Ave., Broadway, I–93, I–95.

This classic Victorian Italianate home, built in 1854, is located in an upper-middle-class neighborhood, with a mixture of large houses, condominiums, and small townhouses. It is midway between Harvard University and central squares, about a ten-minute walk from Harvard, and a twenty-minute walk to M.I.T. The house has high ceilings, lots of art and books, and a pottery collection. It is formal but homey. The quiet guest quarters are at the back wing of the house, with large windows overlooking the garden, antique furniture, and private entry and bath. Features include a small balcony with French doors off the bedroom, a sitting room with a small sofa, a larger furnished hall, and a small kitchenette. A Continental Plus breakfast of assorted breads, muffins, and coffee cake is served in the large adjacent sitting room. Your hosts, both architects, are interested in visual arts, music, science, gardening, and sailing. They have traveled in Europe, primarily in France. The household is an active one, with three children ages four to nine.

No. Rooms: 1	**Breakfast:** Continental Plus
Singles: None	**S-Rates:** $70 pb
Doubles: 1 pb	**D-Rates:** $70 pb
Type: Private home	**Bldg:** 1854 Victorian

Minimum Stay: 2 nights. **Credit Card(s) Accepted:** none. **Open:** Jan 1 to Dec. 15. Resident dogs. A dog is allowed with restrictions. No resident cats. A cat is allowed with restrictions. Nonsmoking host. Guests may smoke. Children welcome. **Discounts:** weekly. French spoken.

Reservation Contact: Bed & Breakfast Associates Bay Colony, Ltd., A. Kardasis & M. Mitchell, Box 166, Babson Pk. Br., Boston, MA 02157; 617–449–5302.

ID: 30–GRTBOS

HARVARD UNIVERSITY, M.I.T.

Near Harvard St. & Massachusetts Ave., Rte. 2, U.S. 1.

This brick Federal-style home is located in a superb neighborhood convenient to Harvard University. The lovely home has a California-style family room and kitchen, floor-to-ceiling windows, a beautiful patio, and vegetable garden. There is one guest room, with single bed and shared bath. A Continental breakfast is served. Your host is a well-traveled public relations specialist.

No. Rooms: 1	**Breakfast:** Continental
Singles: 1 sb	**S-Rates:** $40 sb
Doubles: None	**D-Rates:** None
Type: Private home	**Bldg:** 1920 brick Federal

Minimum Stay: 2 nights. **Credit Card(s) Accepted:** none. **Open:** all year. No resident dogs. No dogs please. No resident cats. No cats please. Nonsmoking host. Guests may not smoke in residence. Residence not appropriate for children. **Discounts:** for extended stays.

Reservation Contact: Greater Boston Hospitality, Lauren Simonelli, Box 1142, Brookline, MA 02146; 617–277–5430.

CENTERVILLE   ID: CAPECOD52

CRAIGVILLE BEACH, HISTORIC AREA; 3 MILES FROM HYANNIS.

Near Rte. 28, Rte. 149, U.S. 6.

In 1830, Captain Hillman Crosby, an intercoastal sea captain, built this Cape Cod-style house for his bride. Now beautifully restored, it sits amidst tall trees, including a giant beech. The nearby private estates and duck pond lend a feeling of gracious living to this area. The inn has parlors for reading, music, or conversation, a dining area, a family-sized kitchen, and outdoor sunning areas on the well-tended grounds. Three guest rooms offer private baths. The second-floor room is done in an early American and Victorian decor with wide-board pine floors, a king-sized bed, and antique wood stove. The two first-floor rooms have double beds. One, done in blue, has a colonial decor and overlooks a private park and pond. The other, with a Victorian decor, has a view of an historic mansion and park. A sumptuous country breakfast of fresh-baked pastry, seasonal fruit, and specialties of the house is served in the dining room or on the porch between 8:00 and 10:00 A.M. First settled in the 1700s, this community has been a center for fishing, shipbuilding, and cranberry farming through the years. It has retained its nineteenth-century appearance, when many sea captains lived in Centerville along Main Street. The beauty of the area is complemented by Craigville Beach, only a half-mile away, one of the finest warm-water beaches on the Cape. Hyannis, with its fine shops, restaurants, and nightlife, is only a five-minute drive away, as is the ferry to Nantucket and Martha's Vineyard. One of your hosts has a special interest in women's education; the other has been in the corporate world for years. Both have traveled extensively.

No. Rooms: 3	**Breakfast:** Full
Singles: None	**S-Rates:** $65–$75 pb
Doubles: 3 pb	**D-Rates:** $65–$75 pb
Type: Private home	**Bldg:** 1830 Cape Cod style

Minimum Stay: 2 nights in season. **Credit Card(s) Accepted:** AE. **Open:** all year. No resident dogs. No dogs please. No resident cats. No cats please. Host smokes. Guests may not smoke in guest rooms. Children welcome with restrictions. **Discounts:** none.

Reservation Contact: Bed & Breakfast Cape Cod, Clark Diehl, Box 341, W. Hyannisport, MA 02672; 617–775–2772.

CHATHAM

ID: CAPECOD12

65 MILES OF BEACH, LIGHTHOUSE, FISHING PIER.

Near Barcliff Ave., Rte. 6.

This recently completed Cape-style house was patterned after a house built in the 1600s with wainscotting and rough plastered walls. The home also features wide-board floors, braided rugs, an upstairs skylight, beautiful furnishings, and an enormous fireplace in the family room. The decor is early American. Each of two guest rooms offers a double and a single bed, dresser, and desk. The two rooms share a bath. A Continental breakfast is served. The house is in a residential neighborhood away from noise and traffic but within walking distance to the village, churches, playhouses, beaches, and fishing pier. Chatham is one of the Cape's most picturesque towns with sixty-five miles of beach. The village shops are well-known for their charm, and their lighthouse, fish pier, and windmill all add grace to this beautiful community. The hobbies of your hosts, a college professor and a public health nurse, include walking the beaches, fishing, good books, good company, and good conversation.

No. Rooms: 2	**Breakfast:** Continental
Singles: None	**S-Rates:** $40 sb
Doubles: 2 sb	**D-Rates:** $50 sb
Type: Private home	**Bldg:** 1983 Cape Cod

Minimum Stay: 2 nights. **Credit Card(s) Accepted:** none. **Open:** all year. No resident dogs. No dogs please. Cat in residence. No cats please. Nonsmoking host. Guests may not smoke in residence. Children welcome. **Discounts:** none.

Reservation Contact: Bed & Breakfast Cape Cod, Clark Diehl, Box 341, W. Hyannisport, MA 02672; 617–775–2772.

ID: 02633VIE

CAPE COD, OCEAN VIEW, BEACH, FISHING, TENNIS, GOLF, BIKING, SHOPS, RESTAURANTS.

Near Shore & Old Harbor rds., U.S. 6.

This large, gracious colonial house is filled with furniture brought from your host's travels throughout Europe and the Orient. There are two double guest rooms and one single with shared guest bath. One has a single bed; one has twin beds, and one has a double bed; all are furnished with antiques and have Oriental rugs and TV. A Full breakfast is served on the glass-paneled porch with a view of the pond, gardens, and ocean; during inclement weather, it is served in the dining room on a large Spanish table or in front of the fireplace. On Sunday mornings, a champagne brunch is usually served. The house is located about 1,500 feet from the Chatham fish pier and a sandy beach, and areas for private sunbathing are available. It is a two-minute walk to the golf course and tennis courts, five minutes to the town center, and ten minutes to the lighthouse. Your host provides ice chests and fishing tackle and gear for those wishing to explore the long sandbar lying offshore. A two-day minimum stay is required (three days on holiday weekends.) The house is available only from May 15 until November 15. A retired newspaper and magazine editor, your host has traveled extensively through Europe, South and Central America, and the Orient, and has made four trips around the world.

No. Rooms: 3	Breakfast: Full
Singles: 1 pb	S-Rates: $60 pb
Doubles: 2 pb	D-Rates: $75 pb
Type: Private home	Bldg: 1924 New England colonial

Minimum Stay: 2–3 nights. **Credit Card(s) Accepted:** none. **Open:** May 15–Nov. 15. No resident dogs. No dogs please. No resident cats. No cats please. Host smokes. Guests may smoke. Children welcome with restrictions. **Discounts:** none. Spanish spoken.

Reservation Contact: Bed & Breakfast Registry Ltd., Gary Winget, Box 8174, St. Paul, MN 55108; 612–646–4238.

DENNISPORT

ID: CAPECOD4

CAPE COD, ON NANTUCKET SOUND.

Near rtes. 28 & 6.

In 1721 Dr. Hedge built this house in Yarmouth Port; two hundred years later, in 1921, the house was moved to its present location, three hundred feet from the beach. The house has the low ceilings and narrow stairs characteristic of its era, and a hide-away closet to escape Indians. A mixture of antiques and family heirlooms make up the decor. At the rear of the house there is a summer house with various games, a refrigerator, and TV for guests' use. Three guest rooms with king-sized beds share two baths. The Blue Room and the Rose Room also have non-working fireplaces. A Full breakfast is served of juice, fruit in season, pastry and various house specialties, and crystal and silver add a special touch. Your hosts are an archaeologist and an artist.

No. Rooms: 3	Breakfast: Full
Singles: None	S-Rates: $55–$70 sb
Doubles: 3 sb	D-Rates: $55–$70 sb
Type: Private home	Bldg: 1721 colonial

Minimum Stay: 2 nights. **Credit Card(s) Accepted:** none. **Open:** all year. Resident dog. No dogs please. No resident cats. No cats please. Host smokes. Guests may smoke in residence. Children welcome. **Discounts:** none.

Reservation Contact: Bed & Breakfast Cape Cod, Clark Diehl, Box 341, W. Hyannisport, MA 02672; 617–775–2772.

ID: 02639DEN

CAPE COD, BEACHES, SHOPPING, ANTIQUING, GOLF.

Near rtes. 28 & 134, U.S. 6.

This inn is within a short walk of beaches and a few minutes drive to Hyannis. Five sunny guest rooms, all with double or twin beds, share three baths. A Continental breakfast is served. The interests of your hosts include music and theater.

No. Rooms: 5	**Breakfast:** Continental
Singles: None	**S-Rates:** $45 sb
Doubles: 5 sb	**D-Rates:** $50 sb
Type: Private Home	**Bldg:** 1820 Cape Cod

Minimum Stay: none. **Credit Card(s) Accepted:** AE, MC, V. **Open:** all year. No resident dogs. No dogs please. No resident cats. No cats please. Nonsmoking host. Guest may not smoke in residence. Children welcome. **Discounts:** none.

Reservation Contact: Bed & Breakfast Registry Ltd., Gary Winget, Box 8174, St. Paul, MN 55108; 612–646–4238.

ID: 02639WES

CAPE COD.

Near rtes. 28, 134.

This large Cape-style house, decorated in earth tones, offers colonial furnishings. On the landscaped grounds, you will find pine groves, picnic tables, and grills for a home-like atmosphere. TV is available in the living room. There are four guest rooms; one has a double bed and private bath; one has a single bed; one has two double beds; and one has one double and two singles. You will usually find fresh flowers in your room. Continental breakfast is served, on china and silver, in the dining room. Three efficiency units (available by the week only) are also offered.

No. Rooms: 4	**Breakfast:** Continental
Singles: 1 sb	**S-Rates:** $40 pb, $35–$40 sb
Doubles: 1 pb, 2 sb	**D-Rates:** $50 pb, $50–$60 sb
Type: Private home	**Bldg:** Cape Cod

Minimum Stay: none. **Credit Card(s) Accepted:** none. **Open:** May–Oct. Dog in residence. No dogs please. Resident cat. No cats please. Nonsmoking host. Guests may smoke. Children welcome. **Discounts:** none.

Reservation Contact: Bed & Breakfast Registry Ltd., Gary Winget, Box 8174, St. Paul, MN 55108; 612–646–4238.

DUXBURY

30 MINUTES FROM BOSTON; BOUTIQUES, HISTORIC HOMES.

Near rtes 14 & 3A.

This colonial home, located on the John Alden Land Grant in the historic village of Duxbury, is a replica of an 1840s design. The house is one block from the John Alden House, built in the 1600s and near other historic homes. It is furnished with country colonial as well as country French furniture. Three guest rooms share a bath. The first is done in blue and white and has twin beds, a mahogany bureau, side tables, and an easy chair. The second has grasscloth wallpaper, a king-sized bed that can be converted into twin beds, and mahogany furniture. The third room, with a double bed, is done in a dusty rose paisley print and has country French furnishings. A Full breakfast is served. Your hosts are consultants who enjoy decorating and collecting antique cars and furniture.

No. Rooms: 3	**Breakfast:** Full
Singles: None	**S-Rates:** $60 sb
Doubles: 3 sb	**D-Rates:** $70 sb
Type: Private home	**Bldg:** Colonial

Minimum Stay: 2 nights over holidays. **Credit Card(s) Accepted:** none. **Open:** Mar.–Dec. Resident dog. No dogs please. No resident cats. No cats please. Nonsmoking host. Guests may not smoke. Children over 13 welcome. **Discounts:** none.

Reservation Contact: Pineapple Hospitality, Inc., Judy Mulford, 47 N. 2nd St., Suite 3A, New Bedford, MA 02740; 617–990–1696.

GLOUCESTER

ON WATER; PRIVATE BEACH, TENNIS, WHALE WATCHING.

Near Rte. 127, Rte. 128.

Located on the Annisquam River, this 1889 waterfront home is a delightful getaway spot less than an hour from Boston. It boasts a private beach on a warm calm ocean riverway, where swimming and boating are continuous. Since the house faces west-northwest, the sunsets are spectacular. Public tennis courts and whale-watching excursions are nearby. Gloucester, an old New England fishing village, abounds with things to do and see. There are art colonies, unique shops and galleries, fascinating museums, and restaurants serving delectable fresh seafood. If guests just want to relax, there is a beautiful grass patio and rock gardens. The four guest rooms have views of the water and primitive wood ceilings, and all are decorated with Laura Ashley fabrics. One room has twin beds, one has a queen-sized bed, and two have double beds. The rooms share two baths. A Continental breakfast is served. Your hosts, graduates of

Wentworth Institute of Technology and Cornell University, are interested in travel and antiques. The guest rooms are not available between December and April.

No. Rooms: 4	**Breakfast:** Continental
Singles: None	**S-Rates:** $60 sb
Doubles: 4 sb	**D-Rates:** $68 sb
Type: Private home	**Bldg:** 1898 traditional

Minimum Stay: none. **Credit Card(s) Accepted:** none. **Open:** May–November. No resident dogs. No dogs please. No resident cats. No cats please. Host smokes. Guests may smoke. Children welcome. **Discounts:** none. Spanish spoken.

Reservation Contact: Greater Boston Hospitality, Lauren Simonelli, Box 1142, Brookline, MA 02146; 617–277–5430.

GREAT BARRINGTON   ID: IND–2

ROUND HILL FARM
TANGLEWOOD, JACOB'S PILLOW; FALL FOLIAGE, DOWNHILL & CROSS-COUNTRY SKIING.

Round Hill Rd.

You'll find peace and quiet on a horse farm, where everything works but the guests! This lovingly maintained turn-of-the-century classic New England hilltop farmhouse, on a dirt road three miles out in the country, was designed for summer visitors. It has wrap-around porches, acres of fields and woods, and a swimming hole in the trout stream. Five double rooms with antique furnishings share three guest baths. Three rooms have private baths. Accommodations feature separate entrance and stairs and an elegant parlor. A Full breakfast is served.

No. Rooms: 8	**Breakfast:** Full
Singles: None	**S-Rates:** $80 pb, $65 sb
Doubles: 3 pb, 5 sb	**D-Rates:** $80 pb, $65 sb
Type: Inn	**Bldg:** Horse farm

Minimum Stay: none. **Credit Card(s) Accepted:** MC, V. **Open:** all year. Pets can be accommodated but not in the house. Restricted to nonsmokers only. Children under 16 not permitted. **Discounts:** none. French spoken.

Reservation Contact: Dr. and Mrs. Thomas J. Whitfield III, Round Hill Farm, 17 Round Hill Rd., Great Barrington, MA 01230; 413–528–3366.

HYANNIS

CAPE COD, BEACH, TOWN CENTER, CRANBERRY BOG.

Near Bayview St., U.S. 6.

The Cape-style home is situated beside an eighty-acre cranberry bog that has a path around it for joggers and walkers. A small, private beach is nearby and the town beach is five minutes away. Guests can walk to local restaurants, shops, and night spots as well as to the ferries to Nantucket and Martha's Vineyard. There are two guest rooms, one with a nautical motif with twin beds and the other with a double brass bed. The bath is shared with the hosts. A Continental breakfast is served Friday–Sunday; a Full breakfast is served Monday–Thursday. Possible extra services include sailing.

No. Rooms: 2	**Breakfast:** Continental or Full
Singles: None	**S-Rates:** $60–$70 sb
Doubles: 2 sb	**D-Rates:** $60–$70 sb
Type: Private home	**Bldg:** 1947 Cape-style

Minimum Stay: none. **Credit Card(s) Accepted:** none. **Open:** all year. No resident dogs. No dogs please. Cat in residence. No cats please. Nonsmoking host. Guests may not smoke in guest rooms. Children welcome. **Discounts:** none.

Reservation Contact: Bed & Breakfast Registry Ltd., Gary Winget, Box 8174, St. Paul, MN 55108; 612–646–4238.

LENOX

TANGLEWOOD, JACOB'S PILLOW.

Near Main St., U.S. 7, Rte. 183.

This early colonial house, built in 1800, is graced with interesting carvings over the door and railings of the spacious veranda. The seven guest rooms have antique furnishings, quilts, and restored wide-plank pine floors. Two have private baths. Two bathrooms are shared among the other rooms. A Continental breakfast is served in the comfortable sitting room with fireplace and period pieces. Your host is interested in music, art, drama, and travel, and collects stamps, bottles, and shells.

No. Rooms: 7	**Breakfast:** Continental
Singles: None	**S-Rates:** $50–$60 sb, $75–$100 pb
Doubles: 2 pb, 5 sb	**D-Rates:** $55–$65 sb, $75–$100
Type: Public home	pb
	Bldg: 1800 early colonial

Minimum Stay: 3 nights. **Credit Card(s) Accepted:** none. **Open:** Jan.–Oct. Dog in residence. No dogs please. Cat in residence. No cats please. Nonsmoking host. Guests may not smoke in residence. Children welcome with restrictions. **Discounts:** none.

Reservation Contact: Covered Bridge Bed & Breakfast, Diane Tremblay, Box 701, Norfolk, CT 06058; 203–542–5944.

ID: 01240GAB

TANGLEWOOD, JACOB'S PILLOW, BERKSHIRE PLAYHOUSE, NORMAN ROCKWELL MUSEUM, SHAKER MUSEUM, BARRINGTON FAIR, HISTORIC SITES AND TOWNS.

Near U.S. 7, Mass. Turnpike.

Built in 1885, this elegant Queen Anne-style house was home to novelist Edith Wharton from 1889–1890. It is located in the most historic part of Lenox and affords warmth and friendliness reminiscent of Victorian times. Furnishings, too, reflect this bygone era. Guests will find these quiet surroundings relaxing as well as convenient to the area's many cultural and seasonal activities. The fourteen guest rooms all have private baths and most have queen-sized beds. A sampling includes Mrs. Wharton's

former room; the Shakespeare Room, which has a large walnut bed with a bust of The Bard on top; and the President's Room, with presidential memorabilia and photographs. A Continental breakfast is served.

No. Rooms: 14	**Breakfast:** Continental
Singles: None	**S-Rates:** $60–$135 pb
Doubles: 14 pb	**D-Rates:** $60–$135 pb
Type: Inn	**Bldg:** 1885 Queen Anne

Minimum Stay: none. **Credit Card(s) Accepted:** AE, MC, V. **Open:** all year. No resident dogs. No dogs please. Cat in residence. No cats please. Host smokes. Guests may smoke. Children over 12 years welcome. **Discounts:** none. Spanish spoken.

Reservation Contact: Bed & Breakfast Registry Ltd., Gary Winget, Box 8174, St. Paul, MN 55108; 612–646–4238.

LEXINGTON   ID: 2–MINUTEMAN

MUNROE TAVERN, OLD BELFRY, CARY MEMORIAL LIBRARY.

Near Rtes. 1–28, 2, 93.

This Cape-style house in a quiet residential neighborhood of well-established homes adds the special personal touch of your hosts in its landscaping, decoration, handmade quilts, and needlepoint. The guest room offers twin beds, a sitting area with chair and loveseat, and private bath. Guests will also find magazines, local historical information, menus from local restaurants, and area maps. A Full breakfast is served on the enclosed porch during the summer or beside the fireplace in winter. Your hosts' interests include fishing, hunting, quilting, and needlework.

No. Rooms: 1	**Breakfast:** Full
Singles: None	**S-Rates:** $48–$51 pb
Doubles: 1 pb	**D-Rates:** $57–$63 pb
Type: Private home	**Bldg:** 1955 New England

Minimum Stay: 2 nights in season. **Credit Card(s) Accepted:** AE, MC, V. **Open:** all year. No resident dogs. No dogs please. Cat in residence. No cats please. Nonsmoking host. Guests may not smoke in guest rooms. Children welcome. **Discounts:** 10% senior citizens and stays of 14 or more nights.

Reservation Contact: Bed & Breakfast in Minuteman Country, Tally & Pamela Carruthers, Box 665, Cambridge, MA 02140; 617–576–2112.

ID: 8–MINUTEMAN

CONCORD AND CAMBRIDGE AREA.

Near I–95, rtes. 128, 2.

This large Cape-style house features early American furniture, several fireplaces, a screened porch, and is located in a suburban neighborhood with a rural feeling on the edge of a conservation area. There are two guest rooms that have traditional furnishings and share a bath. One has a double bed and the other has twin beds. A Full breakfast is served in the cozy breakfast room. Your host's knowledge of the area and local real estate make this a great place for those considering relocating here. The home is convenient to downtown Boston and the historic areas of Lexington and Concord. There is a direct subway line to Harvard and downtown Boston at nearby Alewife Station.

No. Rooms: 2	**Breakfast:** Full
Singles: None	**S-Rates:** $45 sb
Doubles: 2 sb	**D-Rates:** $59–$63 sb
Type: Private home	**Bldg:** Cape Cod

Minimum Stay: 2 nights. **Credit Card(s) Accepted:** none. **Open:** all year. Resident dog. No dogs please. No resident cats. No cats please. Nonsmoking host. Guest may not smoke in residence. Children welcome. **Discounts:** 10% for senior citizens and stays of 14 or more nights.

Reservation Contact: Bed & Breakfast in Minuteman Country, Tally & Pamela Carruthers, Box 665, Cambridge, MA 02140; 617–576–2112.

LOWELL

ID: 01851SHE

NEAR CONCORD AND LEXINGTON, UPPER HIGHLANDS AREA.

Near Rte. 3, I–495.

Lowell is the site of the only urban national park. It celebrates the city's history as the nation's first planned industrial community and as the birthplace of the industrial revolution in this country. The Upper Highlands area was developed around the turn of the century and is about two miles from the park headquarters. This Queen Anne Victorian house was built in 1893 for Fredrick Sherman, a prosperous insurance man. The house has antiques, stained glass, a friendly ghost, and a marvelous sugar maple that shades the wraparound front porch in the summer and, as your host puts it, "turns show-off" in the fall. The front parlor is filled with antiques while the back parlor has a fireplace and well-stocked bookcases. Upstairs there is a sitting room for watching TV or reading. The two guest rooms share one and a half baths with the family. The Maple Tree Room, at the front of the house, has a brass bed with a trundle hidden underneath, a large closet, rocking chair, and bookcase; it is done in beige and brown and displays Alaskan art. At the back of the house is Rose's Room, named for the daughter of the first owners. It is graced with a double sleigh bed with frilly white coverlet and pillow shams, antique dolls, and grape-colored walls. For families, the sitting room can also accommodate two people in an antique double Murphy Bed. A Continental breakfast on weekdays and a Full breakfast on weekends is served in the old-fashioned kitchen which contains many pieces of Alaskan art, on one of the large porches, or in the formal dining room with sterling silver, china, and crystal. A tandem bike is available for guests' use. After twenty-five years in Alaska, your hosts are now deeply involved in their New England community and are members of the Lowell Historical Society. One of the hosts is a computer marketing manager and the other has a masters degree in counseling psychology but currently enjoys being an innkeeper and antique dealer.

No. Rooms: 3	**Breakfast:** Continental or Full
Singles: None	**S-Rates:** $45 sb
Doubles: 3 sb	**D-Rates:** $50 sb
Type: Private home	**Bldg:** 1893 Queen Anne Victorian

Minimum Stay: 3 days in October. **Credit Card(s) Accepted:** none. **Open:** all year. No resident dogs. A dog is allowed with restrictions. No resident cats. No cats please. Nonsmoking host. Guests may not smoke in residence. Children welcome. **Discounts:** none.

Reservation Contact: Bed & Breakfast Registry Ltd., Gary Winget, Box 8174, St. Paul, MN 55108; 612–646–4238.

LYNN
ID: 01902CAR

BEACH, BOSTON AREA, MARBLEHEAD, SALEM WITCH MUSEUM, PEABODY MUSEUM, ANTIQUE SHOPS.

Near 1A & Lynnshore Dr., U.S. 1, I–93, I–95.

This large 1870 Victorian house possesses both charm and convenience. Just a few steps away a three-mile beach invites guests to relax and enjoy; while in Marblehead, ten minutes away, guests will find antique shops, Fort Sewell, Crocker Park, and Abbott Hall; and in Salem, a fifteen-minute journey, the Witch Museum, House of Seven Gables, Peabody Museum, and Pickering Wharf await guests. Bus transportation to Boston is a half block away. The house boasts four fireplaces, original fixtures, and many antiques. Three guest rooms share two baths. The first, with a working fireplace, is furnished with a double four-poster bed with down comforter and pillows and a cozy antique chair for reading or sitting by the fire. The second has a Victorian oak bed and furniture and Oriental rugs. Twin beds and antique chests and trunks grace the third room. A Continental Plus breakfast is served. Your hosts love to travel and collect antiques.

No. Rooms: 3	**Breakfast:** Continental Plus
Singles: None	**S-Rates:** $60 sb
Doubles: 3 sb	**D-Rates:** $70 sb
Type: Private home	**Bldg:** 1870 Victorian

Minimum Stay: none. **Credit Card(s) Accepted:** AE, MC, V. **Open:** all year. No resident dogs. No dogs please. No resident cats. No cats please. Nonsmoking host. Guests may not smoke in residence. Children over 5 years welcome. **Discounts:** none.

Reservation Contact: Bed & Breakfast Registry Ltd., Gary Winget, Box 8174, St. Paul, MN 55108; 612–646–4238.

MARBLEHEAD

NORTH SHORE.

Near Rte. 1A, Rte. 114.

This unusual historic home was built in 1790, with an addition made in 1812. The house, surrounded by water, has seven fireplaces. It offers a self-contained guest apartment consisting of a queen-sized hide-a-bed, well stocked kitchenette for a Full breakfast, private bath, and deck. Other amenities include a cathedral ceiling, fireplace, air-conditioning, TV, and telephone. This is a wonderful getaway spot, close to the harbor in this magnificent yachting community. You can walk to the rocky beaches and nearby antique shops. Both well-traveled hosts are career counselors interested in history. They are particularly knowledgeable about the North Shore area.

No. Rooms: 1	**Breakfast:** Full
Singles: None	**S-Rates:** $60 pb
Doubles: 1 pb	**D-Rates:** $62 pb
Type: Private home	**Bldg:** 1790 colonial

Minimum Stay: none. **Credit Card(s) Accepted:** none. **Open:** all year. Dog in residence. No dogs please. No resident cats. No cats please. Nonsmoking host. Guests may smoke. Residence not appropriate for children. **Discounts:** 7th night free.

Reservation Contact: Greater Boston Hospitality, Lauren Simonelli, Box 1142, Brookline, MA 02146; 617–277–5430.

HARBOR.

Near rtes. 1A & 114.

This charming older home offers guests the use of the entire second floor including living room with fireplace, dining room, and a private deck overlooking the harbor. The two guest rooms share a bath. One has a double bed and the other has twin beds. Your hosts enjoy sharing their knowledge of Boston and the North Shore.

No. Rooms: 2	**Breakfast:** Continental Plus
Singles: None	**S-Rates:** $75–$85 sb
Doubles: 2 sb	**D-Rates:** $75–$85 sb
Type: Private home	**Bldg:** Two-story frame

Minimum Stay: 2 nights. **Credit Card(s) Accepted:** none. **Open:** all year. No resident dogs. No dogs please. Resident cat. No cats please. Nonsmoking host. Guests may smoke in living room. Children welcome with restrictions. **Discounts:** none.

Reservation Contact: Bed & Breakfast Associates Bay Colony, Ltd., A. Kardasis & M. Mitchell, Box 166, Babson Pk. Br., Boston, MA 02157; 617–449–5302.

NANTUCKET ISLAND

ON OCEAN; SIASCONSET.

Near east side of island.

This B&B inn, located on the ocean front, has a private beach and extremely large yard. It is serenely tucked away from the summer crowds that flock to Nantucket, yet is convenient to the center of this seventeenth-century historic village. There are guest rooms with shared or private baths, suites with kitchens and one to four bedrooms, and cottages with kitchens and three to five bedrooms. Continental breakfast is served to room guests only. Laundry facilities are available. Your hosts are a teacher and a writer from New York.

No. Rooms: 8
Singles: None
Doubles: 3 pb, 5 sb
Type: Inn

Breakfast: Continental
S-Rates: $106–$117 pb, $77–$80 sb
D-Rates: $106–$117 pb, $70–$77 sb
Bldg: 1930 traditional Nantucket

Minimum Stay: 3 nights–2 weeks, depending on season and accommodations. **Credit Card(s) Accepted:** none. **Open:** May–Sept. No resident dogs. No dogs please. Cat in residence. No cats please. Nonsmoking host. Guests may smoke. Children welcome. **Discounts:** Up to 40% in May, June, Sept. French spoken.

Reservation Contact: Bed & Breakfast Registry Ltd., Gary Winget, Box 8174, St. Paul, MN 55108; 612–646–4238.

NEEDHAM

20 MINUTES FROM BOSTON.

Near Rte 9.

On the west side of Boston, this outstanding suburban neighborhood has well-manicured lawns and well-maintained homes. Parking, a rare commodity in the Boston area, is available here, but the house is also close to the "T" public transit system. The house is an outstanding example of a Royal Barry Willis house, a prominant Boston architect. It is full of nooks and crannies, characteristic of this architectural style. The house has a beautiful yard and lovely terrace for guests' use. There are three guest rooms available, one with twin beds, one with a double bed, and one with a queen-sized bed. The three rooms share a bath. A Full breakfast is served. A telephone and TV are available, and the house is air-conditioned. Your host is a retired executive who enjoys entertaining.

No. Rooms: 3	**Breakfast:** Full
Singles: None	**S-Rates:** $52 sb
Doubles: 3 sb	**D-Rates:** $52 sb
Type: Private home	**Bldg:** Royal Barry Wills

Minimum Stay: 2 nights. **Credit Card(s) Accepted:** none. **Open:** all year. No resident dogs. No dogs please. No resident cats. No cats please. Nonsmoking host. Smoking not permitted. Children welcome. **Discounts:** 7th night free.

Reservation Contact: Greater Boston Hospitality, Lauren Simonelli, Box 1142, Brookline, MA 02146; 617–277–5430.

NEWTON

ID: NEW–ENG–1

NEAR NEWTON CAMPUS OF BOSTON COLLEGE; 20 MINUTES N.W. OF BOSTON.

Near Centre St. & Rte. 30, I–90, I–95.

This colonial home is on a quiet cul-de-sac in an upper-middle-class residential neighborhood is near Boston College's Newton campus. The beautifully decorated home has a living room with fireplace, elegant dining room, and a recently remodeled kitchen. The guest room features a double bed, the host's original artwork, and private bath. A Continental Plus breakfast is served. Your hosts are college graduates who have traveled extensively. They enjoy music, theater, and gourmet cooking.

No. Rooms: 1	**Breakfast:** Continental Plus
Singles: None	**S-Rates:** $39 pb
Doubles: 1 pb	**D-Rates:** $55 pb
Type: Private home	**Bldg:** 1950s colonial

Minimum Stay: 2 nights. **Credit Card(s) Accepted:** none. **Open:** all year. No resident dogs. No dogs please. Cat in residence. No cats please. Host smokes. Guests may not smoke in guest rooms. Children welcome. **Discounts:** none. French spoken.

Reservation Contact: New England Bed & Breakfast, Inc., John and Margo Gardiner, 1045 Centre St., Newton Centre, MA 02159; 617–244–2112.

ID: NEW–ENG–2

15 MINUTES FROM BOSTON.

Near Rte. 9, I–95.

Located in a convenient suburb northwest of Boston, this 1920s stucco home, across the street from the "T," the subway into Boston, provides a pleasant haven after a busy day in the city. A small shopping area in the village is also nearby. The house has one guest room with twin beds and a bath shared with one other person. A Continental Plus breakfast is served. Your host, a grandparent twenty-eight times, likes to knit, sew, and, of course, talk about those wonderful grandchildren.

No. Rooms: 1	**Breakfast:** Continental Plus
Singles: None	**S-Rates:** $36 sb
Doubles: 1 sb	**D-Rates:** $49 sb
Type: Private home	**Bldg:** 1920s New England stucco

Minimum Stay: none. **Credit Card(s) Accepted:** none. **Open:** all year. No resident dogs. A dog is allowed with restrictions. Cat in residence. A cat is allowed with restrictions. Nonsmoking host. Guests may not smoke in guest rooms. Children welcome with restrictions. **Discounts:** none.

Reservation Contact: New England Bed & Breakfast, Inc., John and Margo Gardiner, 1045 Centre St., Newton Centre, MA 02159; 617–244–2112.

ID: NEW–ENG–4

CONVENIENT TO CONCORD AND LEXINGTON.

Near Beacon St. & Rte. 30, I–90.

The Waban section of Newton is a quiet residential area near routes 9, 128, and I–95. From here, it is an easy drive north to historic Concord and Lexington. The "T" offers easy access to downtown Boston. The house has three guest rooms; one with a double bed, one with twin beds. One of the rooms is a large suite with a king-sized bed and private bath; the other two rooms share a bath. Your host, working on a Ph.D. in art history, enjoys cooking and redecorating, and has traveled a good deal.

No. Rooms: 3	**Breakfast:** Continental Plus
Singles: None	**S-Rates:** $60 pb, $36 sb
Doubles: 1 pb, 2 sb	**D-Rates:** $60 pb, $55 sb
Type: Private home	**Bldg:** 1940

Minimum Stay: none. **Credit Card(s) Accepted:** none. **Open:** all year. No resident dogs. No dogs please. Cat in residence. No cats please. Nonsmoking host. Guests may not smoke in residence. Children welcome with restrictions. **Discounts:** none.

Reservation Contact: New England Bed & Breakfast, Inc., John and Margo Gardiner, 1045 Centre St., Newton Centre, MA 02159; 617–244–2112.

ID: NEW–ENG–5

BOSTON COLLEGE.

Near I–90, I–95.

This beautiful English Tudor-style home was designed and built by an architect as a show place for other homes he built in the area. The distinctive copper roof with fieldstone, wood, and brick construction makes the house a local landmark. Two guest rooms offer private baths. One is a former maid's quarters that has been renovated and features double bed and separate entrance to afford additional privacy for guests. The other is a lovely, quiet room with black-walnut twin beds. Near the "T," the house, with large screened porch, backyard, and garden, is about twenty minutes from downtown Boston and offers off-street parking. One of your hosts is a social service director; the other is a travel consultant. They also operate a Reservation Service Organization. Both are college graduates who have traveled extensively and enjoy books, music, theater, and cooking. Dinner and area tours are available.

No. Rooms: 2	**Breakfast:** Continental Plus
Singles: None	**S-Rates:** $39 pb
Doubles: 2 pb	**D-Rates:** $52 pb
Type: Private home	**Bldg:** 1935 English Tudor

Minimum Stay: none. **Credit Card(s) Accepted:** none. **Open:** all year. No resident dogs. No dogs please. No resident cats. No cats please. Non-smoking host. Guests may not smoke in residence. Children welcome with restrictions. **Discounts:** none.

Reservation Contact: New England Bed & Breakfast, Inc., John and Margo Gardiner, 1045 Centre St., Newton Centre, MA 02159; 617–244–2112.

ID: 108–GRTBOS

BOSTON COLLEGE, PINE MANOR.

Near Rte. 9, I–95.

This excellent suburban home, custom-designed by an outstanding architect, provides a quiet, restful spot after a busy day in the city. Large windows open out onto a garden and beautifully landscaped yard. The guest room offers lovely dark mahogany furniture, double bed, hardwood floor, ample closet space, good lighting, and private bath. A Full breakfast, including homemade peach preserves, is served in the dining room or, in summer, on a glass-enclosed porch overlooking the pretty yard. The well-educated college librarian host is extremely pleasant and attentive. She has traveled widely but, as a native Bostonian, she is well-acquainted with Boston activities.

No. Rooms: 1	**Breakfast:** Full
Singles: None	**S-Rates:** $52 pb
Doubles: 1 pb	**D-Rates:** $58 pb
Type: Private home	**Bldg:** 1948 custom design

Minimum Stay: 2 nights. **Credit Card(s) Accepted:** none. **Open:** all year. No resident dogs. No dogs please. No resident cats. No cats please. Nonsmoking host. Guests may not smoke in residence. Residence not appropriate for children. **Discounts:** none.

Reservation Contact: Greater Boston Hospitality, Lauren Simonelli, Box 1142, Brookline, MA 02146; 617–277–5430.

NORTH FALMOUTH ID: CAPECOD51

CAPE COD, FERRY TO MARTHA'S VINEYARD, 15 MINUTES FROM WOODS HOLE.

Near rtes. 6 & 28.

Falmouth is a historic community that dates back to when the Cape was settled. Today lovely shops surround the old village green. Woods Hole, a port from which many deep-sea explorers have sailed, is 15 minutes away, and Falmouth harbor offers a passenger ferry to Martha's Vineyard. The first part of this Cape Cod colonial was built in 1793. Although additions were made over the years, the property has been restored and now reflects the early American country style of its origin. Your hosts are antique dealers and have filled the house with their collection from years of finding, preserving, and restoring. There are two guest suites with private baths. Both have double four-poster canopy beds, fireplaces, wide board floors, and sitting areas where a Full breakfast is served.

No. Rooms: 2	**Breakfast:** Full
Singles: None	**S-Rates:** $85 pb
Doubles: 2 pb	**D-Rates:** $85 pb
Type: Private home	**Bldg:** 1793 colonial

Minimum Stay: 2 nights. **Credit Card(s) Accepted:** none. **Open:** all year. No resident dogs. No dogs please. No resident cats. No cats please. Nonsmoking host. Guests may not smoke in residence. Residence is not appropriate for children. **Discounts:** none.

Reservation Contact: Bed & Breakfast Cape Cod, Clark Diehl, Box 341, W. Hyannisport, MA 02672; 617–775–2772.

ID: CAPECOD46

CAPE COD, HISTORIC WIANNO DISTRICT, EAST BAY, NANTUCKET SOUND.

Near Rte. 6.

Built in 1872, "Blink Bonnie" (Beautiful View), as this home is known, is located in the historic Wianno District, an area dotted with waterfront estates reflecting the shingle-style architecture of the late 19th century. The Osterville village center, a leisurely ten-minute walk away, is a charming grouping of small shops. The house is a blend of turn-of-the-century shingle-style architecture and Classical Revival, the latter additions completed in 1932. The manor home and its windmill water tower are both listed in the National Register of Historic Places. The house sits on a hill looking over Osterville's East Bay and Nantucket Sound. Guests will enjoy the short walk to the beach and the use of the estate's private tennis court. Beach roses skirt the edge of the excellent sandy beach, and the waters here are Cape Cod's warmest. Each of the three guest rooms has a water view. The first is a large room with a double bed adorned with an antique headboard. There is also a small refrigerator, bureau, and closet. A separate sitting room adjoins the room and it can accommodate an additional person. Together these rooms comprise the International Suite. The Santa Fe Room has twin beds, a bureau, desk, closet, and sitting area. The rooms share a private stairway and bath. A Continental Plus breakfast is served. Your hosts, a semi-retired surgeon and an artist, are interested in real estate development and love to travel.

No. Rooms: 3	**Breakfast:** Continental Plus
Singles: 1 sb	**S-Rates:** $45–$80 sb
Doubles: 2 sb	**D-Rates:** $65–$80 sb
Type: Private home	**Bldg:** Shingle-style and Classical Revival

Minimum Stay: 2 days. **Credit Card(s) Accepted:** none. **Open:** May–Oct. No resident dogs. No dogs please. Resident cat. No cats please. Host smokes. Guest may smoke in designated areas. Children welcome with restrictions. **Discounts:** family.

Reservation Contact: Bed & Breakfast Cape Cod, Clark Diehl, Box 341, W. Hyannisport, MA 02672; 617–775–2772.

PLYMOUTH
ID: BOGGILLIS

HISTORIC AREA, BEACHES.

Near rtes. 123, 3A & 3.

This antique carriage house dates back to 1743. From the back window, there is a view of two lovely landscape acres and several hundred-foot blue spruce trees. Three guest rooms share a guest bath. One of the rooms has twin beds, a dresser, an antique rocking chair, table, and clock radio. Another has a queen-sized bed with handmade quilt, antique

dresser, and white antique chair. This room overlooks patches of blueber-
ries (available for picking in season). The third has a pineapple double
bed with a handmade quilt, antique dresser, rocking chair, and table. A
Full breakfast is served on the enclosed back porch or in the formal dining
room with fireplace. Queen Anne furnishings, candles, and fresh flowers.
Use of living room with TV available. The hosts have local interests and
enjoy antiques.

No. Rooms: 3	**Breakfast:** Full
Singles: 1 sb	**S-Rates:** $38 sb
Doubles: 2 sb	**D-Rates:** $50 sb
Type: Private home	**Bldg:** 1743 carriage house

Minimum Stay: none. **Credit Card(s) Accepted:** none. **Open:**
May–Nov. Host's dog is not allowed in guest areas. No dogs please. No
resident cats. No cats please. Nonsmoking host. Guests may not smoke
in guest rooms. Children welcome. **Discounts:** none.

Reservation Contact: Be Our Guest, Bed & Breakfast, Ltd., Mary Gill,
Box 1333, Plymouth, MA 02360; 617–837–9867.

REHOBOTH   ID: 02769PER

GOLF, BIKING, TENNIS, CLAM BAKES, HAY & SLEIGH RIDES, CROSS-COUNTRY SKIING, SWIMMING, HOT-AIR BALLOON RIDES.

Near Rte. 118, U.S. 44.

Founded by the pilgrims in 1643, Rehoboth has retained much of its old
charm. Country-road excursions unveil stone walls, farms, and houses
dating back to the eighteenth-and nineteenth-centuries. This newly renovated nineteenth-century farmhouse (on the National Register of Historic
Places) is situated on four wooded acres with a brook, shaded walking
paths, flower gardens, and stone walls. The three-story house was built
in the 1820s with an addition made in 1897. Since your hosts occupy the
third floor only, you are assured absolute privacy. Relax in one of
two comfortable sitting rooms that offer a wide variety of reading material
and a game table. Furnishings are a tasteful blend of antiques and reproduction pieces. There are five guest rooms that share four baths; all sleep
at least two and are furnished with antiques. A Continental Plus breakfast
is served in the elegant dining room or on the screened porch. Afternoon
tea or sherry is also offered, and there is a refrigerator for your use. Hay
rides, sleigh rides, and even hot-air ballooning can be arranged by your
hosts, and there are tandem bicycles for your use. Golf, cross-country
skiing, polo matches, tennis, and clam bakes are also nearby. Your hosts
have interests in history, gardening, sailing, jogging, skiing, and cooking.

No. Rooms: 5	**Breakfast:** Continental Plus
Singles: None	**S-Rates:** $55–$65 pb, $40 sb
Doubles: 3 pb, 2 sb	**D-Rates:** $55–$75 pb, $40–$60 sb
Type: Inn	**Bldg:** 1826 Queen Anne Victorian

Minimum Stay: 2 days on holidays. **Credit Card(s) Accepted:** AE, MC, V. **Open:** all year. No resident dogs. No dogs please. Cat in residence. No cats please. Nonsmoking host. Guests may not smoke in residence. Children welcome. **Discounts:** none. Some French spoken.

Reservation Contact: Bed & Breakfast Registry Ltd., Gary Winget, Box 8174, St. Paul, MN 55108; 612–646–4238.

SANDWICH
ID: CAPECOD15

CAPE COD, BEACH, HERITAGE PLANTATION, GLASS MUSEUM.

Near rtes. 6A, 130.

Settled in 1637, Sandwich is the oldest town on Cape Cod. Daniel Webster was a frequent visitor to Sandwich, where he pursued his love of fishing and hunting. The village offers many attractions: a working grist mill, doll museum, glass museum, and Heritage Plantation. Set on Academy Hill, this home overlooks the village, and at the foot of the property is a pond with swans and mallards. There are three guest rooms, one with a private bath. One of the rooms, furnished with white wicker, has a queen-sized bed, writing desk, and comfortable chairs. Another room has dark pine, colonial decor, and twin beds. The third room also has twin beds and a colonial decor. Having retired from the corporate world, your hosts now enjoy golf, gardening, travel, and entertaining.

No. Rooms: 3	**Breakfast:** Continental
Singles: None	**S-Rates:** $60 pb, $60 sb
Doubles: 1 pb, 2 sb	**D-Rates:** $60 pb, $60 sb
Type: Private home	**Bldg:** Cape-style

Minimum Stay: 2 nights. **Credit Card(s) Accepted:** none. **Open:** all year. No resident dogs. No dogs please. No resident cats. No cats please. Nonsmoking host. Guests may not smoke in residence. Children welcome with restrictions. **Discounts:** none.

Reservation Contact: Bed & Breakfast Cape Cod, Clark Diehl, Box 341, W. Hyannisport, MA 02672; 617–775–2772.

STURBRIDGE/WARE
ID: 01082WIL

OLD STURBRIDGE VILLAGE, OLD DEERFIELD, AMHERST COLLEGE, BRIMFIELD ANTIQUE SHOWS, FARM MUSEUM, CARRIAGE MUSEUM.

Near rtes. 9, 32.

Built in the 1800s as a private home, this cozy little inn offers a country parlor with a welcoming fireplace, where you can gather for conversation, reading, or relaxation. There are five guest rooms with twin, double, or queen-sized beds. All offer antique furnishings and shared baths. A homemade Continental breakfast is served in the dining room Tues.–Thurs. and Sat.–Sun. (no breakfast is served Mon. and Fri.). There is an old-fashioned brook-fed swimming hole, free canoeing and tennis, croquet, badminton, a stone barbecue for outdoor cooking, and a hammock under the fir trees. Liquor is not sold at the inn, you can bring your own, and it will be graciously served in pewter goblets by the fire or on the wrap-around porch. Your hosts' interests include antiques, New England history, poetry, and family activities.

No. Rooms: 5	**Breakfast:** Continental
Singles: None	**S-Rates:** $37–$66 sb
Doubles: 5 sb	**D-Rates:** $37–$66 sb
Type: Inn	**Bldg:** 1880 Victorian

Minimum Stay: 2 nights on weekends. **Credit Card(s) Accepted:** none. **Open:** all year, except winter weekdays. No resident dogs. No dogs please. No resident cats. No cats please. Nonsmoking host. Guests may not smoke in residence. Children welcome with restrictions. **Discounts:** 10% for 7 nights.

Reservation Contact: Bed & Breakfast Registry Ltd., Gary Winget, Box 8174, St. Paul, MN 55108; 612–646–4238.

SWAMPSCOTT

ID: 01907MAR

BEACH, BOATING, WHALE-WATCHING; NEAR BOSTON, LYNN, AND HISTORIC SALEM.

Near MA 1A & MA 129, U.S. 1, I–95.

This Victorian house is in a beachfront residential neighborhood near restaurants, shops, and public transportation, and has a porch with a view of the ocean. Boating and whale-watching excursions are nearby and historic Salem is ten minutes away. The M.B.T.A. bus to Boston is a two-minute walk and the train is a five-minute walk. The home is done in a country style with a wood-burning stove and comfortable sofas. All four guest rooms have TVs and refrigerators. The first has a queen-sized bed with brass headboard, handmade quilt, antique trunk, antique rocking chair, and bureau with mirror and antique clock. The walls are papered and stenciled and the refinished hardwood floor has a large area rug. The second room, with a border print on the walls, has a pineapple spindle head and footboard on the double bed, a velvet upholstered chair, and a table and two chairs in front of a window with an ocean view. The third room has a double bed with a white metal-and-brass headboard and handmade quilt, nonworking fireplace with stenciling on the mantle, bureau, full-length mirror, and antique scatter rugs. The fourth room has a single bed, quilt rack, white stenciled bureau, and white wicker furniture. All the rooms look cozy and inviting and each has its own charm. A Continental breakfast is served in the paneled dining room. Bicycles are available and there is an area guests may use for cookouts. Arrival/departure transportation is also available. One of your hosts is an artist and craftsman who enjoys biking and camping. The other is a teacher, lobster fisherman, and diver.

No. Rooms: 4	**Breakfast:** Continental
Singles: 1 sb	**S-Rates:** $45–$58 sb
Doubles: 3 sb	**D-Rates:** $50–$64 sb
Type: Private home	**Bldg:** 1917 Victorian

Minimum Stay: 2 days on holidays. **Credit Card(s) Accepted:** AE, MC, V. **Open:** all year. No resident dogs. No dogs please. No resident cats. No cats please. Nonsmoking host. Guests may not smoke in residence. Children over 4 years welcome. **Discounts:** 25% weekly.

Reservation Contact: Bed & Breakfast Registry Ltd., Gary Winget, Box 8174, St. Paul, MN 55108; 612–646–4238.

TRURO

ID: 02666PAR

CAPE COD, NINE MILES FROM PROVINCETOWN SAND DUNES, WHALE WATCHES, NATIONAL SEASHORE, TENNIS, GOLF.

Near Rte. 6A, U.S. 6.

This spacious 1820s full-size Cape Cod-style house is furnished with family antiques and has a comfortable parlor where you can gather for conversation or TV, and a screened porch and large private yard for relaxing. A buffet Continental breakfast is served in the formal dining room. Three comfortable guest rooms are available; all sleep two, are furnished with antiques, and share two baths. There is ample parking; refrigerator space, laundry facilities, and beach towels are available. Truro is an unspoiled little town with a beautiful bay, dunes, and ocean beaches two miles away. It is only nine miles from Provincetown's quaint shops, restaurants, and nightlife. Your charming New England host, a native of the area, can offer invaluable advice on how to make the most of your stay.

No. Rooms: 3
Singles: None
Doubles: 3 pb
Type: Private home

Breakfast: Continental
S-Rates: $48 sb
D-Rates: $55 sb
Bldg: 1815 old Cape

Minimum Stay: none. **Credit Card(s) Accepted:** none. **Open:** all year. No resident dogs. No dogs please. Cat in residence. No cats please. Nonsmoking host. Guests may smoke. Residence not appropriate for children. **Discounts:** none.

Reservation Contact: Bed & Breakfast Registry Ltd., Gary Winget, Box 8174, St. Paul, MN 55108; 612–646–4238.

VINEYARD HAVEN

ID: 02568CAP

MARTHA'S VINEYARD, BEACH, SHOPS, RESTAURANTS.

Near Main and Union sts.

This B&B is located in the heart of town just one block from the ferry, making it an ideal location for guests without cars. However, if you bring your car, there is ample private parking and a locked garage is available for storing bicycles. Walk to the beach, excellent shops, and restaurants. Built in 1843, this former sea captain's house has been meticulously restored and elegantly furnished. Guests are surrounded by flowers, 18th-century antiques, early American oil paintings, Oriental rugs, graceful mouldings, Count Rumford fireplaces, and hand-stenciled walls. The eight richly appointed guest rooms have period reproduction wallpapers, velvet wing chairs, hand-sewn quilts, and private baths. Several have working fireplaces and four-poster beds with white lace canopies. Guests will also find fresh flowers and complimentary sherry in their rooms. Continental breakfast is served in the formal dining room or in the garden. (Note: If you plan to take the ferry from Woods Hole and bring your car, call 617–540–2022 for a car reservation well in advance of your trip.)

No. Rooms: 8	**Breakfast:** Continental
Singles: None	**S-Rates:** $55–$140 pb
Doubles: 8 pb	**D-Rates:** $55–$140 pb
Type: Inn	**Bldg:** 1843 Victorian

Minimum Stay: none. **Credit Card(s) Accepted:** AE, MC, V. **Open:** all year. No resident dogs. No dogs please. No resident cats. No cats please. Nonsmoking host. Guests may smoke. Children over 12 years welcome. **Discounts:** none.

Reservation Contact: Bed & Breakfast Registry Ltd., Gary Winget, Box 8174, St. Paul, MN 55108; 612–646–4238.

WEST BARNSTABLE   ID: 02668HON

CAPE COD, SANDY NECK BEACH; WHALE WATCHES, BICYCLING TRAILS, GOLF, CRAFT & ANTIQUE SHOPS.

Near Rte. 6A, U.S. 6.

This restored rambling Cape farmhouse, circa 1820, is located across from the great salt marshes of Cape Cod, where the colonists' cattle used to graze. The house has many lovely antiques, a wrap-around screened porch, and a spacious new Great Room. Your hosts have tried to make their three guest rooms epitomize everyone's fantasy of the ideal country inn. They offer king- or queen-sized beds, Victorian furnishings, and private baths. On the bedside table, there are tins of fresh homemade cookies, crystal wine glasses, a tray, and corkscrew. There is also a tape player in each room with a wide selection of audio cassettes. In the baths, a decanter of bath oils, selection of English toiletries, and two thick terry cloth robes can be found. A Full country breakfast and afternoon tea are served. West Barnstable is conveniently situated between historic Sandwich and bustling Hyannis. The town is still quite pastoral, with horses and sheep grazing nearby. Arrival/departure transportation, picnic lunches, bicycles, and area tours are available. Your hosts are interested in hockey, fishing, golf, boating, and art.

No. Rooms: 3	**Breakfast:** Full
Singles: None	**S-Rates:** $75–$105 pb
Doubles: 3 pb	**D-Rates:** $75–$105 pb
Type: Private home	**Bldg:** 1820 rambling Cape Cod

Minimum Stay: 2 days on weekends. **Credit Card(s) Accepted:** AE, MC, V. **Open:** all year. Two dogs in residence. No dogs please. No resident cats. No cats please. Nonsmoking host. Guests may smoke. Children welcome with restrictions. **Discounts:** weekly.

Reservation Contact: Bed & Breakfast Registry Ltd., Gary Winget, Box 8174, St. Paul, MN 55108; 612–646–4238.

WEST HARWICH
ID: 02671SUN

CAPE COD, BEACH, GOLF, FALL CRANBERRY FESTIVAL, CONSERVATION AREA.

Near Rte. 28, U.S. 6.

This turn-of-the-century Victorian Cape Cod home comes highly recommended by former guests. The two living rooms are furnished with antiques and Oriental rugs, cable TV, and mahogany drop-leaf table for games. You may also lounge on the wrap-around porch, with wicker furniture, overlooking the pool. Six guest rooms with twin, queen-sized, or double beds are offered; all the rooms have private baths and sitting rooms. A Full gourmet, Irish breakfast is served in the formal dining room, complete with antique crystal, bone china, and fine table linens. Tea, wine, and cheese are served in the living room in the late afternoon along with lots of good conversation. Your warm and gracious hosts are interested in antiques, electronics, ocean technology, cooking, gardening, and sea stories.

No. Rooms: 6	**Breakfast:** Full
Singles: None	**S-Rates:** $75 pb
Doubles: 6 pb	**D-Rates:** $75 pb
Type: Inn	**Bldg:** 1900 Victorian

Minimum Stay: 2 nights. **Credit Card(s) Accepted:** AE, MC, V. **Open:** all year. Dog in residence. No dogs please. No resident cats. No cats please. Nonsmoking host. Guests may smoke. Children welcome with restrictions. **Discounts:** none.

Reservation Contact: Bed & Breakfast Registry Ltd., Gary Winget, Box 8174, St. Paul, MN 55108; 612–646–4238.

WHATELY
ID: PV21–BERK

SMITH COLLEGE, MT. HOLYOKE COLLEGE, AMHERST COLLEGE, UNIVERSITY OF MASSACHUSETTS, OLD DEERFIELD VILLAGE.

Near rtes. 91, 5, 10.

Built in 1870, this wonderful New England farmhouse has been in the family for generations. It has fourteen large antique-furnished rooms, as well as three porches furnished with antique rockers, wicker furniture, and beautiful ferns. A swimming pool is available for guests' use, and biking is very popular along the scenic country roads. A large yard is available for croquet and badminton. The five guest rooms, which share two baths, are furnished with antiques and lovely linens and towels, and they have a view of the surrounding fields and meadows. Two have twin beds, one has a double bed, one has a king-sized bed, and one has a single bed. A Full breakfast is served. Whately is just fifteen minutes northwest of Amherst, where Emily Dickinson's home is located, and just south of historic Deerfield, the last outpost on New England's frontier when it was settled in 1669. The picturesque village maintains twelve museums and a research library. Bicyclists can get information on six tours, ranging from five to thirty miles and covering all areas of the Pioneer Valley—from mellow farm fields and quiet streams and woods, to the area's many fascinating attractions. The area also has factory outlets and mill stores where visitors can find clothing, fabrics, shoes, furniture, and carpets. Your host, a widely traveled registered nurse with an avid interest in art, can offer many other suggestions for touring this lovely part of the country.

No. Rooms: 5
Singles: 1 sb
Doubles: 4 sb
Type: Private home

Breakfast: Full
S-Rates: $35 sb
D-Rates: $60–$65 sb
Bldg: 1870 New England farmhouse

Minimum Stay: none. **Credit Card(s) Accepted:** none. **Open:** all year. Dog in residence. No dogs please. No resident cats. No cats please. Nonsmoking host. Guests may not smoke in guest rooms. Children welcome with restrictions. **Discounts:** none.

Reservation Contact: Berkshire Bed & Breakfast Homes, Eleanor Hebert, Box 211, Williamsburg, MA 01096; 413–268–7244.

WILLIAMSTOWN   ID: M4–COVBR

WILLIAMS COLLEGE, CLARK ART INSTITUTE, SUMMER THEATER, TACONIC TRAIL STATE PARK.

Near Rtes. 7 & 2.

Williamstown is not only a beautiful New England town, but a cultural and educational center as well. It is the home of Williams College and the Sterling and Francine Clark Art Institute. Fine restaurants, antique shops, and ski areas abound. Within an hour's drive is Tanglewood, Jacob's Pillow, Berkshire Theater Festival, Marlboro Music Festival, Hancock Shaker Village, and the Performing Arts Center and the racetrack in Saratoga, New York. This early 1900s farmhouse is located two miles from the center of Williamstown on fifty acres of land, with panoramic views of New York, Vermont, and Massachusetts. The house is set back on a winding road bordered by a split-rail fence and many fruit and nut trees. There are two large barns, a sugar house, a greenhouse, a pond filled with trout, a canoe, rowboat, raft, and diving board. The resident farm animals consist of cows, sheep, pigs, turkeys, geese, ducks, chickens, and pheasants, and there are also labrador retrievers bred by your hosts. Two of the four guest rooms have antique oak furniture with double beds, comforters, and marble-topped bureaus. One of these rooms has a view of Vermont, while the other provides a three-state view from a large picture window. The other two rooms have twin beds, a bureau, and commode. One has a view of the rock garden and the other of the New York mountains. The bath is shared. A Continental Plus breakfast is served in the dining room, with a crackling fire in the hearth during the winter months and on the large screened porch with a tristate view in the summer. Your hosts, a nurse and a teacher, enjoy traveling, fishing, hiking, gardening, and cross-country skiing on their own trails. Reservations will not be accepted for Thanksgiving or Christmas.

No. Rooms: 4	**Breakfast:** Continental Plus
Singles: 1 sb	**S-Rates:** $30–$40 sb
Doubles: 3 sb	**D-Rates:** $55–$65 sb
Type: Private home	**Bldg:** 1920 country farmhouse

Minimum Stay: 2 nights on weekend. **Credit Card(s) Accepted:** none. **Open:** all year, except some holidays. Dog in residence. No dogs please. No resident cats. No cats please. Nonsmoking host. Guests may not smoke in residence. Children welcome. **Discounts:** none.

Reservation Contact: Covered Bridge Bed & Breakfast, Diane Tremblay, Box 701, Norfolk, CT 06058; 203–542–5944.

MICHIGAN

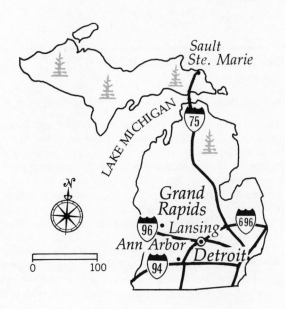

ANN ARBOR

ID: AA–1–MI

UNIVERSITY OF MICHIGAN.

Near I–94, U.S. 23, Huron River Dr., Maple Rd.

Built in 1859, this two-story farmhouse in a rural area of Ann Arbor has many quaint architectural features. Guests can relax on the screened porch which has wicker furniture and a garden view. There are four guest rooms. One has twin beds with handmade patchwork quilts and a private bath. A second has a double bed, sitting room, and private bath. Two other rooms, one with a double bed and one with a single bed, share a bath. A Continental breakfast is served. Your host, a school administrator, likes to garden, collect antiques, and raise German shorthair pointers.

No. Rooms: 4	**Breakfast:** Continental
Singles: 1 sb	**S-Rates:** $50 pb, $45 sb
Doubles: 2 pb, 1 sb	**D-Rates:** $50 pb, $45 sb
Type: Private home	**Bldg:** Farmhouse

Minimum Stay: none. **Credit Card(s) Accepted:** MC, V. **Open:** all year. Resident dog. Guest dogs allowed in kennel. No resident cats. No cats please. Nonsmoking host. Guest may smoke in residence. Children welcome. **Discounts:** none.

Reservation Contact: Bed & Breakfast in Michigan, Diane Shields, Box 1731, Dearborn, MI 48121; 313–561–6041.

ID: 48104URB

UNIVERSITY OF MICHIGAN, DOWNTOWN ATTRACTIONS.

Near Washtenaw Ave. & Huron Parkway, I–94, U.S. 23, U.S. 12.

This brick ranch house, located on a quiet, tree-lined street, is only ten minutes from the University of Michigan and downtown Ann Arbor. The 127-acre meadowland park next door is a great spot for jogging, walking, or bird-watching. A TV and VCR are available in the sitting room and books and magazines can be found in the living room. The three guest rooms share a bath with the family. The first room, decorated in pink and cream with lace curtains and old-fashioned wallpaper, features a double bed and maple furniture. The second room, done in yellow, peach, and white, has a large Amish quilt covering one wall, a queen-sized bed, and an attached sitting room with TV and telephone. The third room is furnished with antiques and has twin brass beds with down quilts, a stained-glass window, and original artwork. The Full breakfast includes homemade jams and preserves. Your hosts like jazz, old movies, and gardening.

No. Rooms: 3	**Breakfast:** Full
Singles: None	**S-Rates:** $45 sb
Doubles: 3 sb	**D-Rates:** $55–$70 sb
Type: Private home	**Bldg:** 1950 ranch

Minimum Stay: 2 nights. **Credit Card(s) Accepted:** none. **Open:** all year. No resident dogs. No dogs please. Cat in residence. No cats please. Nonsmoking host. Guests may not smoke in guest rooms. Children over 12 years welcome. **Discounts:** none.

Reservation Contact: Bed & Breakfast Registry Ltd., Gary Winget, Box 8174, St. Paul, MN 55108; 612–646–4238.

BLOOMFIELD HILLS

ID: BL–2–MI

30 MINUTES FROM DETROIT.

Near I–696, Telegraph & Long Lake rds.

A flower-filled entrance way leads to this three-story townhouse. In summer one can enjoy the view of the golf course from the deck; in winter, sit by the cozy fire in the white marble fireplace. Two guest rooms with twin beds share a bath. A Continental Plus breakfast is served.

No. Rooms: 2	Breakfast: Continental Plus
Singles: None	S-Rates: $45 sb
Doubles: 2 sb	D-Rates: $50 sb
Type: Private home	Bldg: Townhouse

Minimum Stay: none. Credit Card(s) Accepted: MC, V. Open: all year. No resident dogs. No dogs please. No resident cats. No cats please. Nonsmoking host. Guests may not smoke in residence. Children welcome. Discounts: weekly.

Reservation Contact: Bed & Breakfast in Michigan, Diane Shields, Box 1731, Dearborn, MI 48121; 313–561–6041.

CASEVILLE   ID: C–1–MI

SAGINAW BAY, THUMB AREA, SWIMMING, BOATING, FISHING.

Near Rte. 25.

This waterfront location on Saginaw Bay offers swimming, boating, and fishing. Guests will enjoy sitting by the stone fireplace in the paneled living room with beamed ceiling. Bicycles are available, and your host sometimes takes guests fishing in his boat. There are two guest rooms. One has a double bed and private bath. The other is a loft with four beds that can be used by children or parties traveling together. The rooms are not rented separately to unrelated parties. Continental breakfast is served on the glassed-in porch which has a view of Lake Huron.

No. Rooms: 2	Breakfast: Continental
Singles: None	S-Rates: $45 pb
Doubles: 1 pb, 1 sb	D-Rates: $45 pb, plus $10 per
Type: Private home	person

Minimum Stay: none. Credit Card(s) Accepted: none. Open: all year. No resident dogs. No dogs please. No resident cats. No cats please. Nonsmoking host. Guests may not smoke in residence. Children welcome with restrictions. Discounts: none.

Reservation Contact: Bed & Breakfast in Michigan, Diane Shields, Box 1731, Dearborn, MI 48121; 313–561–6041.

ID: DB–3–MI

FORD HEADQUARTERS, GREENFIELD VILLAGE.

Near U.S. 12, U.S. 24, I–94.

This cozy brick bungalow is decorated with antiques in traditional country-colonial style. Two guest rooms, one with a queen-sized bed and one with twin beds, share a bath. Complimentary welcome beverages are served before the fireplace in winter and in the garden in summer. Free arrival/departure transportation from the Amtrak station is available.

No. Rooms: 2
Singles: None
Doubles: 2 sb
Type: Private home

Breakfast: Continental Plus
S-Rates: $40 sb
D-Rates: $45 sb
Bldg: Brick bungalow

Minimum Stay: none. **Credit Card(s) Accepted:** MC, V. **Open:** all year. Dog in residence. Nonsmoking host. Guests may not smoke in residence. **Discounts:** 7th night free.

Reservation Contact: Bed & Breakfast in Michigan, Diane Shields, Box 1731, Dearborn, MI 48121; 313–561–6041.

GRAND RAPIDS

ID: GR.RAPID243

CONVENTION CENTER, BEACHES, MUSEUMS; HERITAGE HILL HISTORIC DISTRICT.

Near Wealthy & Cherry sts., U.S. 131, 196.

Built in 1908 by a furniture-maker, this stucco and brick home (listed on the National Register of Historic Places) still has some original furnishings and features oak, mahogany, birch, and gumwood. The dining room is paneled in oak and richly decorated in royal blue. The guest room is furnished with twin four-poster antique beds and family antiques. A Continental Plus breakfast is served. Your hosts' interests include gardening, reading, needlecraft, and community and church activities.

No. Rooms: 1
Singles: None
Doubles: 1 pb
Type: Private home

Breakfast: Continental Plus
S-Rates: $40–$45 pb
D-Rates: $55 pb
Bldg: 1908 stucco and brick

Minimum Stay: none. **Credit Card(s) Accepted:** MC, V. **Open:** all year. No resident dogs. No dogs please. Cat in residence. No cats please. Nonsmoking host. Guests may not smoke in residence. Residence not appropriate for children. **Discounts:** special packages.

Reservation Contact: Bed & Breakfast of Grand Rapids, Dorothy Stout, 455 College St. SE, Grand Rapids, MI 49503; 616–451–4849.

ID: GR.RAPID455

HERITAGE HILL HISTORIC DISTRICT.

Near Wealthy & Cherry sts., U.S. 131, 196.

This lovely craftsman-style home, built in 1893 and listed on the National Register of Historic Places, has a solarium with a working fountain. The house has recently been completely restored and is furnished with antique and traditional pieces. The two guest rooms have double beds and private baths. The Rose Room is filled with antiques, from the walnut bed and floral rug to several other family treasures. The Green Room has a brass bed and antique pieces. A Continental Plus breakfast is served. Your hosts' interests include reading, travel, sailing, and restoring antiques.

No. Rooms: 2
Singles: None
Doubles: 2 pb
Type: Private home

Breakfast: Continental Plus
S-Rates: $40–$45 pb
D-Rates: $50 pb
Bldg: 1893 craftsman

Minimum Stay: none. **Credit Card(s) Accepted:** MC, V. **Open:** all year. No resident dogs. No dogs please. No resident cats. No cats please. Non-smoking host. Guests may not smoke in residence. Residence not appropriate for children. **Discounts:** none. Some German spoken.

Reservation Contact: Bed & Breakfast of Grand Rapids, Dorothy Stout, 455 College St. SE, Grand Rapids, MI 49503; 616–451–4849.

ID: GR.RAPIDS516

CONVENTION CENTER, GERALD R. FORD PRESIDENTIAL MUSEUM; HERITAGE HILL HISTORIC DISTRICT.

Near Wealthy & Cherry sts., U.S. 131, 196.

The Heritage Hill Historic District is one of the largest urban historical districts in the United States. With 1,300 homes dating from the 1840s to the turn-of-the-century, it boasts sixty-two different styles of architecture. It is adjacent to downtown entertainment, cultural events, shopping, and the convention center. This twenty-room Georgian Revival, built in 1889, has ten bedrooms, a ballroom, a curved staircase, two-story bay and circular windows, and fluted two-story pilasters. Listed on the National Register of Historic Places, this marvelous home is decorated with traditional and antique furnishings. The two guest rooms have double beds and shared bath. The Blue Room has a large semicircular bay window used as a sitting area, with a Queen Anne settee and blue Chinese antique rug. The other room has a four-poster bed, antique walnut and butternut chest, and writing table. A Continental Plus breakfast is served. Your hosts are interested in antiques, decorating, politics, and community activities. They also enjoy walking, traveling, and collecting.

No. Rooms: 2
Singles: None
Doubles: 2 sb
Type: Private home

Breakfast: Continental Plus
S-Rates: $40–$45 sb
D-Rates: $55 sb
Bldg: 1889 Georgian revival

Minimum Stay: none. **Credit Card(s) Accepted:** AE, MC, V. **Open:** all year. No resident dogs. No dogs please. No resident cats. No cats please. Nonsmoking host. Guests may not smoke in residence. Residence not appropriate for children. **Discounts:** occasional.

Reservation Contact: Bed & Breakfast of Grand Rapids, Dorothy Stout, 455 College St. SE, Grand Rapids, MI 49503; 616–451–4849.

ROCHESTER

MEADOWBROOK HALL, SILVERDOME, PINE KNOB.

Near I–75, Adams & Rochester rds.

This 145-year-old farmhouse is close to Meadowbrook Hall, the home of the Dodge family. Also nearby is Metropark with its bike and cross-country ski trails. Two guest rooms share a bath. One has antique furnishings and a double bed adorned with a handmade quilt. The other has a single bed. Guests can watch the birds that gather outside the large picture window in the dining room where a Continental breakfast is served.

No. Rooms: 2
Singles: 1 sb
Doubles: 1 sb
Type: Private home

Breakfast: Continental
S-Rates: $35 sb
D-Rates: $40 sb
Bldg: Farmhouse

Minimum Stay: none. **Credit Card(s) Accepted:** MC, V. **Open:** all year. No resident dogs. No dogs please. No resident cats. No cats please. Non-smoking host. Guests may not smoke in residence. Children welcome with restrictions. **Discounts:** weekly.

Reservation Contact: Bed & Breakfast in Michigan, Diane Shields, Box 1731, Dearborn, MI 48121; 313–561–6041.

MINNESOTA

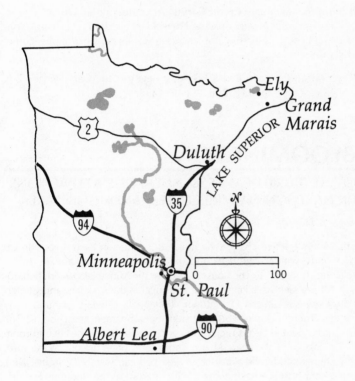

ALBERT LEA

ID: 56007NEV

HELMER MYRE STATE PARK.

Near I–90, I–35.

This lovely home, located in a quiet neighborhood, has a nicely land-scaped front yard and large backyard with flower and vegetable gardens. The family room is at your disposal for TV watching or chatting. There are two spacious carpeted guest rooms, with double beds, desks, rocking chairs, large chests and closets, bookcases, reading lamps, and shared guest bath. A Full breakfast is served in the breakfast area overlooking the vegetable gardens. Additional meals, arrival/departure transporta-tion, area tours, and child care are available. The interests of your excep-tionally hospitable hosts include gardening, travel, photography, sewing, and crafts.

No. Rooms: 2	**Breakfast:** Full
Singles: None	**S-Rates:** $20 sb
Doubles: 2 sb	**D-Rates:** $25 sb
Type: Private home	**Bldg:** 1961

Minimum Stay: none. **Credit Card(s) Accepted:** none. **Open:** all year. No resident dogs. No dogs please. No resident cats. No cats please. Nonsmoking host. Guests may not smoke in residence. Children welcome. **Discounts:** none.

Reservation Contact: Bed & Breakfast Registry Ltd., Gary Winget, Box 8174, St. Paul, MN 55108; 612–646–4238.

BLOOMINGTON   ID: 55438OAK

CANTERBURY DOWNS, MINNEAPOLIS ATTRACTIONS, RICHARDSON NATURE CENTER, ANDERSON LAKE.

Near I–94 & Bush Lake Rd., I–35W.

This very attractive chalet-style house on Anderson Lake is surrounded by woods, with a large deck and spacious yard lending a quiet, rustic, relaxing atmosphere. The house is close to the Minnesota River, Richardson Nature Center, biking, hiking and jogging trails, skiing, and Canterbury Downs racetrack. Downtown Minneapolis is twenty minutes away by car. There are two wood-paneled, open-beamed guest rooms. The first has a double bed, sitting room, and private bath. The second room has a single bed and shared bath. Both rooms open directly to the yard. A Continental Plus breakfast is served. You can watch TV in the living area. Your host is a bacteriologist with interests in the Audubon Society, Minnesota history, biking, tennis, cross-country skiing, squash, badminton, hiking, sailing, and reading. She has gone on bike tours both in the U.S. and the Republic of China, and has climbed to Mt. Everest's base camp.

No. Rooms: 2	**Breakfast:** Continental Plus
Singles: 1 sb	**S-Rates:** $35 pb, $25 sb
Doubles: 1 pb	**D-Rates:** $35 pb
Type: Private home	**Bldg:** 1960 Chalet style

Minimum Stay: none. **Credit Card(s) Accepted:** none. **Open:** all year. No resident dogs. Guests may bring dog. Resident cats. Guests may bring cat. Nonsmoking host. Guests may not smoke in residence. Children welcome. **Discounts:** none. German spoken.

Reservation Contact: Bed & Breakfast Registry Ltd., Gary Winget, Box 8174, St. Paul, MN 55108; 612–646–4238.

DULUTH

ID: 55812ELL

INTERNATIONAL PORT, UNIVERSITY OF MINNESOTA–DULUTH, MUSEUMS, MARATHON.

Near London Rd. & Superior St., U.S. 61, I–35.

Indulge yourself in the elegance of this 1890 Victorian home originally built for real estate tycoon Elley Holliday. In the 1800s, when Duluth exploded into thriving metropolis, the predominant architectural style was one of material extravagance and prosperity. This charming Queen Anne home is graced with gentle curves, beveled and stained-glass windows, a turreted porch, balconies, and many other embellishments. Relax in the spacious parlor which is furnished with Oriental rugs, period antiques, and a grand piano. Five guest rooms are available. The Ellery Suite, decorated in rust and cream, features an ornate, queen-sized brass bed, mahogany dresser, a sitting room with a day bed, a balcony, and private bath. Lilla's Room is done in blue and white with an antique white iron double bed. Daisy's Room has a peach-and-white color scheme and a queen-sized brass bed with a handmade quilt. The Thomas Wall Room boasts a bedside fireplace, sunny bay window, a walnut double bed, and private bath. The Sleeping Porch is a sunny room filled with wicker furniture that offers a view of the birch woods. A hearty country breakfast is served in the dining room or in the privacy of your room. Your hosts enjoy gardening, films, and antiques, and one is a violinist.

No. Rooms: 5	**Breakfast:** Full
Singles: None	**S-Rates:** $65–$70 pb, $45–$55 sb
Doubles: 2 pb, 3 sb	**D-Rates:** $70–$75 pb, $50–$60 sb
Type: Inn	**Bldg:** 1890 Queen Anne Victorian

Minimum Stay: none. **Credit Card(s) Accepted:** MC, V. **Open:** all year. Dog in residence. No dogs please. No resident cats. No cats please. Nonsmoking host. Guests may not smoke in residence. Children are welcome with restrictions. **Discounts:** midweek.

Reservation Contact: Bed & Breakfast Registry Ltd., Gary Winget, Box 8174, St. Paul, MN 55108; 612–646–4238.

ELY

ID: 55731BRO

SUPERIOR NATIONAL FOREST, HIDDEN VALLEY SKI AREA; HIKING, CROSS-COUNTRY SKIING.

Near rtes. 169, 1.

Surrounded by Norwegian pines and spruce trees, this brick and stone home has a living room with high beamed ceiling, a large fireplace, rustic furniture, a sunny dining area, galley kitchen, and sauna. Of the three guest rooms, one has a double bed, one has twin beds, and the third offers a single bed. The rooms are furnished with antiques and there is a shared bath. You have a choice of a Continental Plus or Full breakfast.

Besides the enchanting natural surroundings, the area offers a Voyageur's Visitor Center, nature trails, interpretive center, excellent restaurants, a free summer Northwoods nights program, a week-long festival in July, and great walleye, trout, and bass fishing. A challenging nine-hole golf course is adjacent to the home, and a newly finished two hundred-mile snowmobile trail from Grand Rapids to Ely is nearby. Arrival/departure transportation is always available; additional meals and area tours are sometimes available. Your host, a writer, is interested in music, literature, and camping.

No. Rooms: 3	**Breakfast:** Full or Continental Plus
Singles: 1 sb	**S-Rates:** $20 sb
Doubles: 2 sb	**D-Rates:** $30 sb
Type: Private home	**Bldg:** 1954 brick and stone

Minimum Stay: none. **Credit Card(s) Accepted:** none. **Open:** all year. No resident dogs. No dogs please. Cat in residence. No cats please. Non-smoking host. Guests may smoke. Children welcome. **Discounts:** none. French spoken.

Reservation Contact: Bed & Breakfast Registry Ltd., Gary Winget, Box 8174, St. Paul, MN 55108; 612–646–4238.

EXCELSIOR
ID: 55331MUR

CHANHASSEN THEATRE, ANTIQUE SHOPS, BOUTIQUES, ARBORETUM, LAKE MINNETONKA SCENIC BOAT RIDES AND BEACHES.

Near MN 7, MN 101, I–494.

Guests will find terraced gardens, extensive landscaping, and walking paths leading down to the lake at this attractive rambler just outside of the town center. The papered and wainscotted guest room has a private bath and opens onto a balcony overlooking a lovely wooded area. A Full breakfast is served. Area tours and arrival/departure transportation are available. Your hosts, both in education, enjoy gardening and reading.

No. Rooms: 1	**Breakfast:** Full
Singles: None	**S-Rates:** $40–$50 pb
Doubles: 1 pb	**D-Rates:** $40–$50 pb
Type: Private home	**Bldg:** 1900s Rambler

Minimum Stay: none. **Credit Card(s) Accepted:** none. **Open:** all year. No resident dogs. Guest may bring dog. No resident cats. Guest may bring cat. Nonsmoking host. Guests may smoke. Children welcome. **Discounts:** none.

Reservation Contact: Bed & Breakfast Registry Ltd., Gary Winget, Box 8174, St. Paul, MN 55108; 612–646–4238.

GRAND MARAIS

ID: 55604KIL

CULTURAL CENTER OF THE NORTH SHORE, LUTSEN SKI AREA, BOUNDARY WATERS CANOE AREA, SUPERIOR NATIONAL FOREST; ON LAKE SUPERIOR.

Near U.S. 61.

You'll drift off to sleep to the sound of waves breaking on the shore and awaken to hear birds singing in the nearby woods at this beautifully situated home on the wooded north shore of Lake Superior. There is a private beach for quiet walks, or you can build a driftwood fire and roast hot dogs and marshmallows next to the water. Nearby (five hundred feet away) is a small deep-canyon river for exploring or fishing for brook and rainbow trout. Lake trout, coho, and chinook salmon from Lake Superior are available from shore or chartered boat. The house has a lovely living room with a fireplace and cozy dining room with round oak table. Nearly all the rooms have a captivating view of Lake Superior. There are two guest rooms, one with a queen-sized bed and one with twin beds; both share a bath. A two-room suite, with fireplace, eight-foot picture window, kitchenette, dining area, queen-sized bed, double and single hide-a-beds, TV, private bath, and entrance is also available. A Full or Continental breakfast is served in the dining room or in your suite if you like. (Full before 8 A.M., Continental after 8 A.M.). Other perks include sherry in the rooms, a take-home bottle of quality, home-made wine (the Gitchi Gumee Winery), and a photo taken and sent home to you. Bus arrival/departure transportation and area tours are available. Your very congenial, well-traveled hosts enjoy wine-making, photography, printing, sewing, cooking, and church activities.

No. Rooms: 3	**Breakfast:** Full or Continental
Singles: None	**S-Rates:** $40 pb, $25 sb
Doubles: 1 pb, 2 sb	**D-Rates:** $40 pb, $25 sb
Type: Private home	**Bldg:** 1927 rustic board & batten

Minimum Stay: none. **Credit Card(s) Accepted:** none. **Open:** all year. No resident dogs. No dogs please. No resident cats. No cats please. Non-smoking host. Guests may not smoke in residence. Children welcome with restrictions. **Discounts:** none.

Reservation Contact: Bed & Breakfast Registry Ltd., Gary Winget, Box 8174, St. Paul, MN 55108; 612–646–4238.

HENDRICKS
ID: 56136TRI

WORKING FARM, HUNTING, CROSS-COUNTRY SKIING, PIONEER MUSEUM.

Near MN 19 & MN 271, U.S. 75.

A good stop between the Twin Cities and the Black Hills, this southwestern Minnesota farm offers city dwellers a change of pace and the sights and sounds of nature. Two guest rooms are available. The first has a double bed, queen-sized hide-a-bed, enough space for a rollaway or crib, and a private bath. The second has a double bed and shared bath. In both rooms guests can snuggle under the comfort of homemade quilts. Guests are welcome to use the living room and yard for relaxing. A Continental Plus breakfast is served.

No. Rooms: 2	**Breakfast:** Full
Singles: None	**S-Rates:** $35 pb, $35 sb
Doubles: 1 pb, 1 sb	**D-Rates:** $45 pb, $45 sb
Type: Private home	**Bldg:** 1800s farmhouse

Minimum Stay: none. **Credit Card(s) Accepted:** none. **Open:** all year. No resident dogs. No dogs please. No resident cats. No cats please. Non-smoking host. Guests may not smoke in residence. Children welcome. **Discounts:** none.

Reservation Contact: Bed & Breakfast Registry Ltd., Gary Winget, Box 8174, St. Paul, MN 55108; 612–646–4238.

MELROSE

NEAR BOYHOOD HOMES OF CHARLES LINDBERGH
AND SINCLAIR LEWIS; SWIMMING, BOATING,
FISHING.

Near I–94, Rte. 4, U.S. 71.

This spacious, recently restored Victorian home has a guest rooms with
a double bed. You are invited to use the small private balcony or share
the large porch, yard, and TV room with your hosts. A Continental breakfast is served in the dining room or kitchen as desired. Melrose is an at-

tractive town on the banks of the Sauk River. The glacial hills and lakes
provide scenic drives. Nearby are the boyhood homes of Charles Lindbergh and Sinclair Lewis. Your hosts, a science teacher and a freelance
feature writer, share interests in travel, reading, antiques, crafts, nature,
and bird-watching.

No. Rooms: 1	**Breakfast:** Continental
Singles: None	**S-Rates:** $28 sb
Doubles: 1 sb	**D-Rates:** $30 sb
Type: Private home	**Bldg:** 1903 Victorian

Minimum Stay: none. **Credit Card(s) Accepted:** none. **Open:** all year.
No resident dogs. No dogs please. Cat in residence. No cats please. Non-
smoking host. Guests may smoke. Children welcome. **Discounts:** none.
German spoken.

Reservation Contact: Bed & Breakfast Registry Ltd., Gary Winget, Box 8174, St. Paul, MN 55108; 612–646–4238.

MINNEAPOLIS

ID: 55405EVE

GUTHRIE THEATER, WALKER ART CENTER, ART INSTITUTE, CHILDREN'S THEATER, DOWNTOWN AREA.

Near Hennepin & Franklin, I–94, I–35W.

This spacious 1890s neoclassical house has a highly embellished well-preserved Victorian interior, original dark oak woodwork, corner parlor fireplace and antique Victorian furnishings throughout, including the four guest rooms. All guest rooms have double beds; two have an additional single bed. The bath is shared. A Continental Plus breakfast is served in the formal dining room or in your room, if preferred. The third-floor guest area has a sitting alcove, with table and chairs, small refrigerator for snacks, and coffeemaker. Complimentary coffee, tea, and cocoa, as well as current magazines and Twin Cities information, and a private phone are available for your use. The house is six blocks from the Guthrie Theater, Walker Art Center, and the Minneapolis Lake District. It is on a direct bus line to the downtown area, and within walking distance of many cafés and fine restaurants. Your very cordial hosts, whose interests include running, antiques, travel, the arts, and cooking, make this one of the area's most popular B&Bs.

No. Rooms: 4	**Breakfast:** Continental Plus
Singles: None	**S-Rates:** $20–$25 sb
Doubles: 4 sb	**D-Rates:** $30–$35 sb
Type: Private home	**Bldg:** 1897 neoclassical revival

Minimum Stay: none. **Credit Card(s) Accepted:** none. **Open:** all year. Host's dog is not allowed in guest areas. No dogs please. No resident cats. No cats please. Nonsmoking host. Guests may not smoke in residence. Children welcome. **Discounts:** child under 3 free.

Reservation Contact: Bed & Breakfast Registry Ltd., Gary Winget, Box 8174, St. Paul, MN 55108; 612–646–4238.

ID: 55409JIB

THEATER, CONCERTS, MUSEUMS, METRODOME SPORTS EVENTS, BEACH, BOATING, TENNIS, ANTIQUES.

Near 50th & Logan, I–35W, I–94.

This Early-1900s Victorian home, on a tree-lined residential street, offers large yard, patio, and screened front porch. The living-room fireplace adds to the home's handsome traditional decor. The one spacious guest room features a queen-sized bed, desk, chairs, TV, air-conditioning, private bath, and walk-in closet. Your very thoughtful hosts serve a delicious Continental Plus breakfast in the formal dining room. The house is near excellent area restaurants, specialty and antique shops, Lake Harriet's beaches, bike paths, sailing, tennis, and the wonderful rose garden. The direct downtown bus line is only one block away. Arrival/departure transportation, child care, laundry facilities, bicycles, and cots are available. Your hosts' interests include tennis, sailing, canoeing, skiing, swimming, and theater.

No. Rooms: 1	**Breakfast:** Full
Singles: None	**S-Rates:** $40 pb
Doubles: 1 pb	**D-Rates:** $45 pb
Type: Private home	**Bldg:** 1920s Victorian

Minimum Stay: none. **Credit Card(s) Accepted:** none. **Open:** all year. No resident dogs. No dogs please. No resident cats. No cats please. Nonsmoking host. Guests may not smoke in guest rooms. Children welcome with restrictions. **Discounts:** none.

Reservation Contact: Bed & Breakfast Registry Ltd., Gary Winget, Box 8174, St. Paul, MN 55108; 612–646–4238.

ID: 55409MAT

10 MINUTES FROM DOWNTOWN; BEACH, SWIMMING, HIKING; ORCHESTRA HALL, GUTHRIE THEATER.

Near Lyndale Ave. & 46th St.

This charming old neighborhood is within walking distance to lovely Lake Harriet, which offers a swimming beach, rose garden, walking and biking paths, tennis courts, and summer concerts; and is ten minutes from downtown attractions, shops, and restaurants. The two-story stucco house offers one guest room with a queen-sized bed and shared bath. The room boasts a patchwork quilt, desk, built-in closet, breakfast area, TV, and wood floors. A Continental breakfast is served. Additional meals, arrival/departure transportation, and area tours are available.

No. Rooms: 1	**Breakfast:** Continental
Singles: none	**S-Rates:** $50 sb
Doubles: 1 sb	**D-Rates:** $55 sb
Type: Private home	**Bldg:** Two-story stucco

Minimum Stay: none. **Credit Card(s) Accepted:** none. Resident dog. No dogs please. No resident cats. No cats please. Nonsmoking host. No smoking allowed. Residence not appropriate for children. **Discounts:** none.

Reservation Contact: Bed & Breakfast Registry, Gary Winget, Box 8174, St. Paul, MN 55108; 612–646–4238.

ID: 55410LIN

GUTHRIE THEATER, WALKER ART CENTER, MINNEAPOLIS MUSEUM OF ART, ORCHESTRA HALL, CONVENTION CENTER; TWO BLOCKS FROM LAKE HARRIET.

Near 36th & Xerxes, I–35W, I–94.

This stately Victorian home, two blocks from lovely Lake Harriet, is located in one of the most desirable areas of the city. Lake Harriet offers beaches, boating, outdoor concerts, the rose garden, and rides on an old trolley car, as well as walking, jogging and biking trails. There is good public transportation to and from downtown Minneapolis. The spacious house occupies a double lot and has a comfortable screened front porch. You are also welcome to use the downstairs den, which has a gas fireplace and TV. There are three guest rooms plus a sleeping porch overlooking the backyard, which are available in summer. All rooms sleep two. A Continental breakfast is served. One of your hosts is a community education coordinator; the other is in business.

No. Rooms: 3	**Breakfast:** Continental
Singles: None.	**S-Rates:** $35–$50 sb
Doubles: 3 sb	**D-Rates:** $40–$60 sb
Type: Private home	**Bldg:** 1908 Victorian

Minimum Stay: none. **Credit Card(s) Accepted:** none. **Open:** all year. No resident dogs. No dogs please. No resident cats. No cats please. Nonsmoking host. Guests may not smoke in residence. Children welcome. **Discounts:** none.

Reservation Contact: Bed & Breakfast Registry Ltd., Gary Winget, Box 8174, St. Paul, MN 55108; 612–646–4238.

ID: 55401SHA

NICOLLET MALL SHOPPING, BUSINESS DISTRICT, RIVERPLACE, ST. ANTHONY MAIN, FINE RESTAURANTS.

Near Hennepin & First sts., I–94, I–35W.

This attractive high-rise apartment is conveniently located for downtown business and shopping. Guests will also want to visit Riverplace and St. Anthony Main, just across the river, with their variety of fine shops and restaurants. The doorman building offers guest parking, an outdoor pool, and a beautiful courtyard. The guest room has a double bed, abundant drawer and closet space, and a private bath. Guests are welcome to use the TV in the adjoining room as well as the living room. A Continental Plus breakfast is served. Your host's interests include theater, art, music, and literature.

No. Rooms: 1	**Breakfast:** Continental Plus
Singles: None	**S-Rates:** $40 pb
Doubles: 1 pb	**D-Rates:** $50 pb
Type: Private apartment	**Bldg:** 1960 high-rise

Minimum Stay: none. **Credit Card(s) Accepted:** none. **Open:** all year. No resident dogs. No dogs please. No resident cats. No cats please. Non-smoking host. Guests may not smoke in residence. Children welcome with restrictions. **Discounts:** none.

Reservation Contact: Bed & Breakfast Registry Ltd., Gary Winget, Box 8174, St. Paul, MN 55108; 612–646–4238.

ID: 55408LIN

GUTHRIE THEATER, WALKER ART CENTER, MINNEAPOLIS INSTITUTE OF ART, CHILDREN'S THEATER, LAKE OF THE ISLES.

Near Hennepin & Franklin sts., I–94, I–35W, U.S. 12.

This 1896 Victorian home has the carved wood, inlaid floors, and leaded glass typical of the Queen Anne period. The house is conveniently located in the pleasant lake area of the city, four blocks from both the exciting uptown area and lovely Lake of the Isles. Bus lines to downtown and the University of Minnesota are a block away and the airport is 20 minutes away. Three guest rooms share a bath. Two rooms have queen-sized brass beds and the third has a full-sized four-poster bed, antique dresser, and access to a three-season porch. All rooms have tables and chairs, ceiling fans, and reading lamps. A Full breakfast is served on weekends and Continental breakfast is served during the week. Your hosts enjoy travel, history, murder mysteries, needlecraft, and antiques.

No. Rooms: 3	**Breakfast:** Continental or Full
Singles: None	**S-Rates:** $50–$60 sb
Doubles: 3 sb	**D-Rates:** $50–$60 sb
Type: Private home	**Bldg:** 1896 Queen Anne

Minimum Stay: none. **Credit Card(s) Accepted:** AE. **Open:** all year. No resident dogs. No dogs please. No resident cats. No cats please. Non-smoking host. Guests may not smoke in residence. Children are welcome with restrictions. **Discounts:** none. Swedish spoken.

Reservation Contact: Bed & Breakfast Registry Ltd., Gary Winget, Box 8174, St. Paul, MN 55108; 612–646–4238.

ID: 55410YOR

LAKE HARRIET, LAKE CALHOUN, 15 MINUTES FROM DOWNTOWN MINNEAPOLIS.

Near France & 50th sts., I–94, I–35, Rte. 100.

This cottage-style house is located in the beautiful Linden Hills area of the city. Guests have easy access to the beaches of Lake Calhoun and Lake Harriet, to tennis courts, and to jogging, walking, and bicycle trails. There are two guest rooms which share a bath. The York Room has a queen-sized bed, dressers, easy chair, and ample closet space. The Castleford Room has twin beds and similar furnishings. A Full breakfast is served in the dining room or on the porch. Child care, arrival-departure transportation, and dinners are available. Your English-born hosts are well acquainted with the tradition of bed and breakfast and they love to meet new people.

No. Rooms: 2	**Breakfast:** Full
Singles: None	**S-Rates:** $25 sb
Doubles: 2 sb	**D-Rates:** $35–$45 sb
Type: Private home	**Bldg:** 1942 cottage

Minimum Stay: none. **Credit Card(s) Accepted:** none. **Open:** all year. No resident dogs. No dogs please. No resident cats. No cats please. Non-smoking host. Guests may not smoke in residence. Children welcome. **Discounts:** none.

Reservation Contact: Bed & Breakfast Registry Ltd., Gary Winget, Box 8174, St. Paul, MN 55108; 612–646–4238.

ID: 55419CRE

MINNEHAHA CREEK, LAKE HARRIET, SOUTH MINNEAPOLIS PLANETARIUM; THEATER, CONCERTS, SPORTS EVENTS.

Near Lyndale & 54th sts., I–35W, I–94.

This country French-style home, with large sunken living room, offers fireplace, comfortable furnishings, antiques, a piano, and French doors opening to a screened porch for your warm-weather relaxation. Two pleasant guest rooms feature king-sized and twin beds. One has a private bath and one a shared bath. A Full breakfast is served in the formal dining room furnished with antique reproductions. Arrival/departure transportation, area tours, child care, laundry facilities, skiis, and canoes are available. The house is two blocks from a direct downtown bus route. Your cordial host, who has raised a large family, has hosted many foreign students. She is interested in gardening, jogging, cross-country skiing, and sewing.

No. Rooms: 2
Singles: None
Doubles: 1 pb, 1 sb
Type: Private home

Breakfast: Full
S-Rates: $30 pb, $25 sb
D-Rates: $35 pb, $40 sb
Bldg: 1929 country French

Minimum Stay: none. Credit Card(s) Accepted: none. Open: all year. No resident dogs. No dogs please. No resident cats. No cats please. Non-smoking host. Guests may not smoke in guest rooms. Children welcome. Discounts: 7th night free.

Reservation Contact: Bed & Breakfast Registry Ltd., Gary Winget, Box 8174, St. Paul, MN 55108; 612–646–4238.

NEW HOPE

ID: 55427OLE

MINNEAPOLIS SUBURB; MEDICINE LAKE, GOLF COURSES, CROSS-COUNTRY SKI TRAILS.

Near County rds. 18 & 9, I–494, I–94.

Nowhere will you find better or warmer hospitality than at this lovely suburban home, an attractive L-shaped rambler, located in a quiet residential neighborhood only fifteen minutes from downtown Minneapolis. There is one very private guest room on the lower level with private bath, king-sized bed, telephone, color TV, radio, and central air-conditioning. You are invited to enjoy the adjacent recreation room, with wet bar, small refrigerator, and electric fireplace. There is also a lovely landscaped yard and patio. Guests staying a week or more, even get their laundry done! The house is only two blocks to a lovely park with full facilities; two miles from Medicine Lake, where guests can swim, fish or skate; two miles from groomed cross-country ski trails; and within five miles of four golf courses. Your hosts enjoy a wide range of interests and have traveled both in the U.S. and abroad.

No. Rooms: 1
Singles: None
Doubles: 1 pb
Type: Private home

Breakfast: Continental
S-Rates: $30 pb
D-Rates: $35 pb
Bldg: 1970 rambler

Minimum Stay: none. Credit Card(s) Accepted: none. Open: all year. No resident dogs. No dogs please. No resident cats. No cats please. Host smokes. Guests may not smoke in guest rooms. Children welcome. Discounts: none.

Reservation Contact: Bed & Breakfast Registry Ltd., Gary Winget, Box 8174, St. Paul, MN 55108; 612–646–4238.

NORTHFIELD

ID: 55057LOG

WEEKEND GET-AWAY; ST. OLAF COLLEGE, CARLTON COLLEGE, CROSS-COUNTRY SKIING, HIKING, JESSE JAMES DAYS.

Near MN 3 & MN 19.

Although the exterior of this cozy log cabin retains its 1856 facade, the interior has been transformed into charming and comfortable accommodations. Decorated in a color scheme of rose and dark blue, the cabin consists of a main-floor bedroom with double bed graced with a handmade quilt, a writing desk, tables, lamps, and bookcase. The upstairs parlor, furnished with antiques and a braided rug, provides an intimate spot for private chats. A delicious Continental Plus breakfast is served by a cook of French training. Dinners are also available. Northfield is a great weekend get-away spot only an hour away from Minneapolis and St. Paul.

No. Rooms: 1	**Breakfast:** Continental Plus
Singles: None	**S-Rates:** $65 pb
Doubles: 1 pb	**D-Rates:** $70 pb
Type: Private cottage	**Bldg:** 1856 log cabin

Minimum Stay: none. **Credit Card(s) Accepted:** none. **Open:** all year. No resident dogs. No dogs please. No resident cats. No cats please. Non-smoking host. Guests may not smoke in residence. Residence not appropriate for children. **Discounts:** none.

Reservation Contact: Bed & Breakfast Registry Ltd., Gary Winget, Box 8174, St. Paul, MN 55108; 612-646-4238.

ID: 55057THO

ST. OLAF COLLEGE, CARLETON COLLEGE; CROSS-COUNTRY SKIING, SKYDIVING, HIKING, JESSE JAMES DAYS, WEEKEND GETAWAY.

Near Rte. 3, Rte. 19, I-35.

This two-story farmhouse with large yard and garden, provides a quiet, scenic country setting. It has a sitting room, with fireplace and TV for your enjoyment. There are two guest rooms, one with double bed and sliding glass doors to a screened porch; the other is a wood-paneled room with twin beds and shared bath. The furnishings are early-American. A Continental Plus breakfast is served. Additional meals, arrival/departure transportation, and area tours are available. Your knowledgeable hosts can direct you to the best hiking and cross-country ski trails in the area. Their interests include gardening, music, cross-country skiing, rugmaking, and farming.

No. Rooms: 2	**Breakfast:** Continental Plus
Singles: None	**S-Rates:** $30 sb
Doubles: 2 sb	**D-Rates:** $40 sb
Type: Private home	**Bldg:** 1977 rustic farmhouse

Minimum Stay: none. **Credit Card(s) Accepted:** none. **Open:** all year. Dog in residence. No dogs please. No resident cats. No cats please. Non-smoking host. Guests may not smoke in residence. Children welcome. **Discounts:** none. Spanish spoken.

Reservation Contact: Bed & Breakfast Registry Ltd., Gary Winget, Box 8174, St. Paul, MN 55108; 612–646–4238.

PLYMOUTH
ID: 55441HIN

SWIMMING, FISHING, SKATING ON MEDICINE LAKE, MINNEAPOLIS ATTRACTIONS.

Near Medicine Lake Dr., Rte. 55.

Near Medicine Lake, this attractive suburban condominium features a deck, outdoor pool, tennis courts, and a picnic area. A beach and boat rentals are nearby. There is one bright and cheerful guest room which overlooks the nature preserve. It has a double bed, color TV, and a telephone. A Continental breakfast is served in the dining area. Additional meals, arrival/departure transportation, and area tours are usually available. Your host's interests include theater, music, and participant sports.

No. Rooms: 1	**Breakfast:** Continental
Singles: None	**S-Rates:** $25 sb
Doubles: 1 sb	**D-Rates:** $35 sb
Type: Private condominium	**Bldg:** 1979 Tudor

Minimum Stay: none. **Credit Card(s) Accepted:** none. **Open:** all year. No resident dogs. No dogs please. No resident cats. No cats please. Non-smoking host. Guests may not smoke in residence. Residence not appropriate for children. **Discounts:** none.

Reservation Contact: Bed & Breakfast Registry Ltd., Gary Winget, Box 8174, St. Paul, MN 55108; 612–646–4238.

RAY
ID: 56669BUN

NORTHERN MINNESOTA; VOYAGEURS NATIONAL PARK, LAKE KABETOGAMA, 30 MILES FROM INTERNATIONAL FALLS.

Near U.S. 53 & Lake Kabetogama.

This attractive, contemporary home, surrounded by twenty wooded acres, is located only a half mile from the entry point to Voyageurs Na-

tional Park and Lake Kabetogama Visitors' Center. There are two large decks for bird watching, reading, or barbecuing; satellite TV is available in the living room. The three carpeted guest rooms have Thomasville furniture and color TVs. Two have king-sized beds and one has twin beds; one has a private bath while the other two rooms share a guest bath. A Continental breakfast is served.

No. Rooms: 3
Singles: None
Doubles: 2 pb, 1 sb
Type: Inn

Breakfast: Continental
S-Rates: $60 pb, $48 sb
D-Rates: $75 pb, $60 sb
Bldg: 1984 rustic ranch

Minimum Stay: none. **Credit Card(s) Accepted:** MC, V. **Open:** all year. Host's dog is not allowed in guest areas. No dogs please. No resident cats. No cats please. Nonsmoking host. Guests may smoke. Children welcome. **Discounts:** 10% weekdays.

Reservation Contact: Bed & Breakfast Registry Ltd., Gary Winget, Box 8174, St. Paul, MN 55108; 612–646–4238.

ST. FRANCIS
ID: 55070PIN

45 MINUTES FROM TWIN CITIES, ON THE RUM RIVER; CANOEING, HIKING, CROSS-COUNTRY SKIING.

Near MN 47 & County 9, MN 65.

Country solitude and outdoor recreation welcome guests to this wooded area along the wild and scenic Rum River. There are eighteen acres of woods and meadows and two ponds around which guests can enjoy numerous outdoor activities. During the summer, test your skills at canoeing and river tubing, take a hayride through the countryside, or enjoy a hike along the paths; in the winter you can skate on the pond, cross-country ski, and enjoy a sleigh ride. The six guest rooms, with double or twin beds, share two baths. A Full, family-style breakfast is served. Your hosts grow their own vegetables, grind wheat for flour, and keep farm animals. They are also interested in photography.

No. Rooms: 6	**Breakfast:** Full
Singles: None	**S-Rates:** $20–$22 sb
Doubles: 6 sb	**D-Rates:** $40–$44 sb
Type: Private home	**Bldg:** 1972 Rambler

Minimum Stay: none. **Credit Card(s) Accepted:** none. **Open:** all year. Dog in residence. Guest may bring dog. Cat in residence. Guest may bring cat. Nonsmoking host. Guests may not smoke in residence. Children welcome. **Discounts:** 10% after 4 days. German spoken.

Reservation Contact: Bed & Breakfast Registry Ltd., Gary Winget, Box 8174, St. Paul, MN 55108; 612–646–4238.

ST. PAUL   ID: 55102MIL

CIVIC CENTER, DOWNTOWN ATTRACTIONS, FORT SNELLING, LANDMARK CENTER, MISSISSIPPI RIVERBOAT TOURS, AREA HOSPITALS.

Near Fort Rd. & St. Clair, I–94, I–35E, I–494.

Located on a quiet, well-kept residential street, this tastefully furnished home is easily accessible to downtown St. Paul and attractions. The two guest rooms share a bath. The first room, decorated in peach tones, is furnished with a double four-poster bed with a fluffy down quilt, matching curtains, and antique dresser. The other has a single bed with a beige down comforter and an antique dresser. Both open onto a comfortable sitting room exclusively for guests' use and a solarium. Guests also have a private entrance. A Continental breakfast is served in the downstairs dining room. Arrival/departure transportation is available. Your cordial and thoughtful hosts have interests in spectator sports, reading, gardening, bird-watching, and music.

No. Rooms: 2	**Breakfast:** Continental Plus
Singles: 1 sb	**S-Rates:** $25 sb
Doubles: 1 sb	**D-Rates:** $30 sb
Type: Private home	**Bldg:** 1912 brick

Minimum Stay: none. **Credit Card(s) Accepted:** none. **Open:** all year. Dog in residence. No dogs please. No resident cats. No cats please. Nonsmoking host. Guests may not smoke in residence. Residence not appropriate for children. **Discounts:** none. Slovak spoken.

Reservation Contact: Bed & Breakfast Registry Ltd., Gary Winget, Box 8174, St. Paul, MN 55108; 612–646–4238.

STATE CAPITOL; COLLEGES OF ST. THOMAS & ST. CATHERINE, SCIENCE MUSEUM.

Near St. Clair & Fairview, I–94, I–35E.

This warm and inviting home, attractively furnished, has refinished wood-work and floors and a comfortable sitting room and porch for a guest's relaxation. The house is conveniently located for most attractions and it is only one block from the bus line to downtown St. Paul or Minneapolis (a twenty-minute ride). The guest room has a single bed, well-stocked bookcases, desk, dresser, and large closet. Your charming host makes guests feel welcome and at home. She has traveled through Europe, the Soviet Union, Australia, Israel, India, and the United States. Her other interests include art, dance, reading, writing, photography, and skiing.

No. Rooms: 1	**Breakfast:** Continental Plus
Singles: 1 sb	**S-Rates:** $25 pb
Doubles: None	**D-Rates:** None
Type: Private home	**Bldg:** 1913 wood frame

Minimum Stay: none. **Credit Card(s) Accepted:** none. **Open:** all year. No resident dogs. No dogs please. Cat in residence. No cats please. Non-smoking host. Guests may not smoke in guest rooms. Residence not appropriate for children. **Discounts:** none.

Reservation Contact: Bed & Breakfast Registry Ltd., Gary Winget, Box 8174, St. Paul, MN 55108; 612–646–4238.

SHOREWOOD

MINNEAPOLIS ATTRACTIONS, CHANHASSAN DINNER THEATRE, OLD LOG THEATRE, RENNAISANCE FESTIVAL, EXCELSIOR ANTIQUE SHOPS, CANTERBURY DOWNS; TENNIS, SWIMMING, NATURE TRAILS.

Near hwys. 7 & 41, I–494.

This exquisite cottage, near the main house, is situated on twelve private wooded acres, with lake, nature trails, flower gardens, private clay tennis court, and private heated pool—truly a magnificent setting. The cottage has a bedroom with adjacent sitting room done in French-country decor. Laura Ashley fabrics cover the sofa, easy chair, ottoman, and twin beds. Other special touches include Oriental rugs, remote-control satellite television, a balcony overlooking the dining area, a wet bar, and large windows with a view of the woods. The dining area is furnished with antiques, including a wood-burning stove. The cottage has a private entrance, central heat and air-conditioning, and private bath. A Full gourmet breakfast is served on a table set with fine linens, china, crystal, and silver. You can canoe on the lake and relax in the heated pool after a game of tennis. In winter, you can cross-country ski from the door to explore the historic town of Excelsior, with its many fine shops and restaurants. Other area activities include boating, fishing, sightseeing on Lake Minnetonka, Canterbury Downs Racetrack, Valleyfair, the Renaissance Festival, and several dinner theaters. Arrival/departure transportation and area tours are available. Your gracious hosts are interested in tennis, travel, gardening, music, languages, and sports.

No. Rooms: 1	**Breakfast:** Full
Singles: None	**S-Rates:** $95 pb
Doubles: 1 pb	**D-Rates:** $95 pb
Type: Private cottage	**Bldg:** Country cottage

Minimum Stay: none. **Credit Card(s) Accepted:** AE, MC, V. **Open:** all year. Dog in residence. No dogs please. No resident cats. No cats please. Nonsmoking host. Guests may smoke. Residence not appropriate for children. **Discounts:** none. German & Japanese spoken.

Reservation Contact: Bed & Breakfast Registry Ltd., Gary Winget, Box 8174, St. Paul, MN 55108; 612–646–4238.

MISSISSIPPI

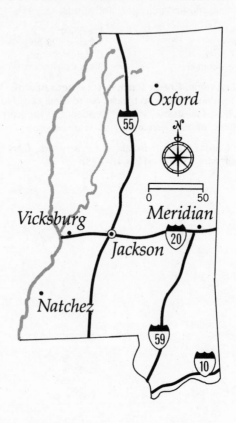

JACKSON

ID: 10–MS–LTD

CENTRAL BUSINESS & GOVERNMENT.

Near I–55, I–20.

Step back a century into a world of sparkling chandeliers and finely crafted furnishings. This inn offers eleven guest rooms with private baths. A Continental breakfast is served on gleaming china and silver. Join quiet conversations in the library and musical evenings around the grand piano in the parlor.

No. Rooms: 11	**Breakfast:** Continental
Singles: None	**S-Rates:** $65–$95 pb
Doubles: 11 pb	**D-Rates:** $75–$105 pb
Type: Inn	**Bldg:** 19th-century

Minimum Stay: none. **Credit Card(s) Accepted:** none. **Open:** Jan. 1 to Nov. 30. No resident dogs. No dogs please. No resident cats. No cats please. Nonsmoking host. Guests may not smoke in residence. Children welcome. **Discounts:** none.

Reservation Contact: Lincoln, Ltd. Bed & Breakfast, Barbara Lincoln Hall, Box 3479, Meridian, MS 39303; 601–482–5483.

LORMAN   ID: MPG–2–SOUTH

25 MILES NORTH OF NATCHEZ.

Near U.S. 61, U.S. 84.

This beautifully restored antebellum mansion is full of antiques and treasures from around the world. The Greek Revival house, built in 1857, is located on a one-hundred-acre Christmas tree plantation. Four guest rooms, offer double beds, antique furnishings, and private baths. A full plantation breakfast is served. Your hosts, a retired army colonel and his wife, have lived all over the world.

No. Rooms: 4	**Breakfast:** Full
Singles: None	**S-Rates:** $75 pb
Doubles: 4 pb	**D-Rates:** $90 pb
Type: Inn	**Bldg:** 1857 Greek Revival

Minimum Stay: none. **Credit Card(s) Accepted:** none. *Open:* all year. No resident dogs. No dogs please. No resident cats. No cats please. Guests may smoke. Children welcome: **Discounts:** none. French & German spoken.

Reservation Contact: Southern Comfort Bed & Breakfast, Susan Morris & Helen Heath, 2856 Hundred Oaks, Baton Rouge, LA 70808; 504–346–1928.

MERIDIAN   ID: 13–MS.LTD

COUNTRY MUSIC FESTIVAL, COLLECTOR'S FAIR, TREES OF CHRISTMAS TOUR.

Near Hwy. 19, I–20, Rte. 59.

This Victorian home in Meridian was built in 1890 and features outstanding stained glass, hand-carved woodwork, and antique furnishings. Two guest rooms feature Victorian decor. One has a double canopy bed, antique furnishings, lace curtains, and a private bath with footed tub; the other has a carved rosewood double bed, dresser, and lace curtains, and looks out on the porch. The bath is shared with the family. A full country breakfast is served, and dinner is available with advance arrangements. Your hosts are interested in older homes, antiques, and gourmet cooking.

Meridian is the site of the Jimmie Rodgers Memorial Festival, a festival of country music and a week of related events during the last week of May. In the first two weeks of December, the Meridian Restorations Foundation presents an annual Trees of Christmas Tour. Both traditional and contemporary interpretations of the Christmas tree make Christmas more meaningful for the thousands who view the trees in the various tour homes. On the third Saturday of each month, artists from all over the state exhibit and sell their arts and crafts at the Collector's Fair at the Frank Cochran Center.

No. Rooms: 2	**Breakfast:** Full
Singles: None	**S-Rates:** $65 pb, $55 sb
Doubles: 1 pb	**D-Rates:** $65 pb, $65 sb
Type: Private home	**Bldg:** 1890 Victorian

Minimum Stay: none. **Credit Card(s) Accepted:** none. **Open:** all year, except Christmas. Dog in residence. A dog is allowed with restrictions. No resident cats. A cat is allowed with restrictions. Nonsmoking host. Guests may not smoke in guest rooms. Residence not appropriate for children. **Discounts:** none.

Reservation Contact: Lincoln, Ltd. Bed & Breakfast, Barbara Lincoln Hall, Box 3479, Meridian, MS 39303; 601–482–5483.

ID: 18–MS.LTD

COLLECTOR'S FAIR, JIMMY RODGERS MEMORIAL FESTIVAL.

Near Popular Springs Dr., I–20, I–59.

This country bungalow is located in an older established neighborhood of fine homes with beautiful grounds and large over-hanging oak trees. The house is furnished with antiques and complementary accent pieces. The two carpeted guest rooms are on the first floor and share a guest bath. The first room has French furniture and a double bed with a spread that matches the drapes. The other room, also with a double bed, is furnished with country oak antiques. A full breakfast is served on the large brick patio surrounded by flowering beds. A sample menu features eggs Mornay, ham or bacon, grits, muffins, jelly, fruit or juice, and coffee or tea. Additional meals, arrival/departure transportation, and child care are available. Your host enjoys cooking, gardening, decorating, all types of handiwork, and entertaining. She is the founder and leader of a local preservation movement, which includes the restoration of two historic properties.

No. Rooms: 2
Singles: None
Doubles: 2 sb
Type: Private townhouse

Breakfast: Full
S-Rates: $45 sb
D-Rates: $45 pb
Bldg: 1920 country bungalow

Minimum Stay: none. **Credit Card(s) Accepted:** none. **Open:** all year. No resident dogs. No dogs please. No resident cats. No cats please. Non-smoking host. Guests may not smoke in residence. Children welcome. **Discounts:** none.

Reservation Contact: Lincoln, Ltd. Bed & Breakfast, Barbara Lincoln Hall, Box 3479, Meridian, MS 39303; 601–482–5483.

NATCHEZ   ID: LINDEN–MS

HISTORIC DISTRICT.

Near Quitman and Melrose, U.S. 61, U.S. 84.

Begun by James Moore in 1792 as a small two-story cottage with two rooms and a hallway on each floor, this lovely Federal-style home has developed into the sizeable estate it is today. Additions were made between 1818 and 1849, including the one-story extensions on both sides of the original building, the ninety-eight-foot front gallery, and the front doorway that features an exquisite fanlight. The doorway was made famous when it was used in the filming of *Gone with the Wind.* This dwelling has remained in the same family since 1949, and the current family is the sixth generation to reside there. Seven guest rooms offer private baths. One room offers furniture made almost exclusively in Natchez at the turn of the nineteenth century. A second room, all period furnishings, including a king-sized four-poster bed, bedside tables, and large wing chairs. The bed hangings and window treatments are eighteenth-century reproduction fabrics. Chippendale furnishings prevail in a fourth room. The four-poster double bed is draped in an eighteenth-century repro-

duction fabric as are the windows. Another room has a mixture of Chippendale and Federal furniture. A Full plantation breakfast of grits, ham, eggs, homemade biscuits, orange juice, and coffee or tea is served. The interests of your host include preservation and restoration projects, and studying and collecting antiques. She has also traveled extensively.

No. Rooms: 7	**Breakfast:** Full
Singles: None	**S-Rates:** $75 pb
Doubles: 7 pb	**D-Rates:** $75 pb
Type: Private home	**Bldg:** 1790 Federal

Minimum Stay: none. **Credit Card(s) Accepted:** AE, MC, V. **Open:** all year. No resident dogs. No dogs please. No resident cats. No cats please. Host smokes. Guests may not smoke in guest rooms. Children welcome with restrictions. **Discounts:** none.

Reservation Contact: Natchez Pilgrimage Tours, Box 347, Natchez, MS 39120; 800–647–6742.

ID: MELROSE–MS

NATIONAL HISTORIC LANDMARK.

Near U.S. 61, U.S. 84.

This stately mansion, built in 1841–45 by John Thompson McMurran, is a classical blend of Greek Revival and Georgian architecture. The house stands majestically amidst moss-draped magnolias on an eighty-four-acre estate. Of special interest is the museum-quality furniture, stately woodwork, silver-trimmed faux bois doors, and Italian marble fireplaces. The drawing room features skillful carvings of scrolls and delicate flowers on the original rosewood furniture. Also original are the brocatelle draperies, French gilt mirrors, and the chandelier. The six guest rooms, all with central heat and air-conditioning, contain the original furniture. One room has a queen-sized mahogany four-poster bed, beautiful armoire, dresser, secretary, and bookcase; another has a four-poster double bed; a third has twin sleigh beds. Three guest rooms share a bath, and the other three have private baths. There is also a second-floor apartment in the dairy building that consists of a bedroom with double bed, bath, and sitting room. Its furnishings are a mixture of antiques and reproductions, and it has central air-conditioning, too. The guest house has a bedroom with twin beds, a sitting room, TV, telephone, kitchen, utility room, bath, car port, and front gallery. A full Southern breakfast is served.

No. Rooms: 6	**Breakfast:** Full
Singles: None	**S-Rates:** $80 sb
Doubles: 3 sb, 3 pb	**D-Rates:** $100 sb, $100 pb
Type: Private home	**Bldg:** 1845 Greek Revival

Minimum Stay: none. **Credit Card(s) Accepted:** AE, MC, V. **Open:** all year. No resident dogs. No dogs please. No resident cats. No cats please. Host smokes. Guests may not smoke in residence. Children welcome. **Discounts:** none.

Reservation Contact: Natchez Pilgrimage Tours, Box 347, Natchez, MS 39120; 800–647–6742.

ID: MONMOUTH–MS

Near U.S. 61, U.S. 84.

Built in 1818, this magnificent Greek Revival mansion is located on twenty-six beautifully landscaped acres. There are nineteen guest rooms with private baths, central heat and air-conditioning, TV, telephones, and authentic period furnishings. There are king- and queen-sized beds as well as doubles and singles. Several rooms have fireplaces. Guests are welcome to a guided tour of the house and to stroll the grounds after a day of sightseeing. A Full Southern breakfast is served.

No. Rooms: 19	**Breakfast:** Full
Singles: 5 pb	**S-Rates:** $75–$150 pb
Doubles: 15 pb	**D-Rates:** $75–$150 pb
Type: Private hotel	**Bldg:** 1818 Greek Revival

Minimum Stay: none. **Credit Card(s) Accepted:** AE, MC, V. **Open:** all year. No resident dogs. No dogs please. No resident cats. No cats please. Nonsmoking host. Guests may not smoke in residence. Residence not appropriate for children. **Discounts:** none.

Reservation Contact: Natchez Pilgrimage Tours, Box 347, Natchez, MS 39120; 800–647–6742.

ID: 29–MS.LTD

HISTORIC DISTRICT, PILGRIMAGE TOURS, FOLK ART.

Near Rte. 84.

This elegant one-hundred-fifty-year-old Greek Revival raised cottage on the National Register received the American Automobile Association's 1985 Four-Diamond Award. Located in a quiet residential area three blocks from Main Street in the heart of Natchez-Upon-the-Hill Historic District, this home's beautifully maintained exterior is virtually unchanged from its original circa-1835 appearance. The yard offers a lovely garden, play equipment for children, including a swinging locally handcrafted wooden horse, and hammock. A wide veranda room, formerly an enclosed porch, stretches across the rear ground floor of the house and serves as a gathering room for guests. The five air-conditioned guest rooms feature handsome antiques or reproductions, bed canopies, and hangings done in fine fabrics with patterns true to the period, and private baths. Trundles under the high antique beds can accommodate children. On the ground floor, four of the guest rooms are reached from a wide hallway, and one can also be reached from the veranda room. The fifth guest room is on the second floor, as are the dining room, formal and informal living rooms, office, kitchen, and breakfast room. A Full family-style breakfast of ham, eggs, grits, biscuits, homemade preserves, juice, and coffee is served around a nineteenth-century table. Very early risers can serve themselves in the veranda room. When the antique grandfather clock in the entry hall strikes five, complimentary drinks are served in the family room, and new arrivals can gather around a television to view a video cassette on the history of Natchez. Guests will also enjoy the spring and fall pilgrimage tours of the local antebellum mansions and gardens. Child care, arrival/departure transportation, and area tours are available. Your host, a former Texan, offers a taste of true Southern hospitality.

No. Room: 5	**Breakfast:** Full
Singles: None	**S-Rates:** $70 pb
Doubles: 5 pb	**D-rates:** $75 pb
Type: Private Home	**Bldg:** 1835 Greek Revival

Minimum Stay: none. **Credit Card(s) Accepted:** none. **Open:** all year. Dog in residence. No dogs please. No resident cats. No cats please. Host smokes. Guests may smoke. Children welcome. **Discounts:** none.

Reservation Contact: Lincoln, Ltd. Bed & Breakfast, Barbara Lincoln Hall, Box 3479, Meridian, MS 39303; 601–482–5483.

ID: 31–MS.LTD

ANTEBELLUM MANSIONS, NATCHEZ TRACE, LIVING HISTORY PROGRAM, MISSISSIPPI MEDICINE SHOW.

Near Lower Woodville Rd., hwys. 61 & 84.

This home is in a semirural wooded area on the outskirts of Natchez, very close to a half-dozen antebellum mansions that can be toured. Three miles from the Mississippi River, it is convenient to the downtown area and all tourist attractions. The guest quarters consist of a small cottage that opens onto a flagstone patio, with a small fish pool, table, chairs and umbrella, all in the shade of two enormous oak trees. No other houses are in sight, so it feels like the country even though it is within the city limits. The bedroom/sitting room has oak floors and fireplace, cathedral ceiling, and white walls with cypress trim. There is a double bed plus a single futon. The small kitchen, overlooking the woods, has a refrigerator, sink, and two burners. The bathroom has a deep old-fashioned tub and shower. Guests will also find literature on the area and a walking-tour guidebook. A Continental Plus breakfast is served. Both hosts are graduates of Yale University School of Architecture. One is interested in photography, cars, boats, sailing, and running; the other enjoys gardening, writing, and painting.

No. Rooms: 1	**Breakfast:** Continental Plus
Singles: None	**S-Rates:** $45 pb
Doubles: 1 pb	**D-Rates:** $45 pb
Type: Private home	**Bldg:** 1940s modern

Minimum Stay: none. **Credit Card(s) Accepted:** none. **Open:** Sept. 1–Aug. 15. No resident dogs. No dogs please. No resident cats. A cat is allowed with restrictions. Nonsmoking host. Guests may smoke. Children welcome. **Discounts:** weekly. French & Japanese spoken.

Reservation Contact: Lincoln, Ltd. Bed & Breakfast, Barbara Lincoln Hall, Box 3479, Meridian, MS 39303; 601–482–5483.

OXFORD
ID: 23–MS.LTD

FAULKNER COUNTRY, UNIVERSITY OF MISSISSIPPI.

Near Rte. 6.

This homey museum-like showplace, conveniently located near downtown Oxford and the University of Mississippi, is an ideal place to stay during the Faulkner conference held each August at the university. The 1836 house, on the National Register, was the first house built in Oxford, and traces of the log cabin still can be seen. The antebellum house is built of native heart pine and furnished with Empire and Victorian antiques. Other treasures include the first diploma awarded by the university in 1851; in the attic, one-hundred-fifty years of fashions are displayed on mannequins. Two guest rooms offer double beds and private baths. A Continental Plus breakfast is served on the balcony or back lawn. In chilly weather, a roraring fire in the family room is popular with guests. Your host, who is widely traveled, is active in civic affairs, both within Oxford and throughout the state. Should you care to see Rowen Oaks, your host will be happy to take you and share a considerable knowledge of Faulkner.

No. Rooms: 2	**Breakfast:** Continental Plus
Singles: None	**S-Rates:** $45–$65 pb
Doubles: 2 pb	**D-Rates:** $45–$65 pb
Type: Private townhouse	**Bldg:** Antebellum

Minimum Stay: none. **Credit Card(s) Accepted:** none. **Open:** all year. No resident dogs. No dogs please. No resident cats. No cats please. Nonsmoking host. Guests may not smoke in guest rooms. Children are welcome with restrictions. **Discounts:** none.

Reservation Contact: Lincoln, Ltd. Bed & Breakfast, Barbara Lincoln Hall, Box 3479, Meridian, MS 39303; 601–482–5483.

VICKSBURG
ID: 27–MS.LTD

HISTORICAL ATTRACTIONS.

Near Clay and Cherry sts., I-20, Hwy. 61.

This 1830 Greek Revival home is in the oldest part of town near several local attractions. All nine rooms are full of beautiful period antiques, and all have private baths, heat, air-conditioning, and TVs. Several rooms have queen-sized canopy beds and fireplaces. A Full breakfast is served.

Guests are welcome to enjoy the pool, hot tub, patio, and yard in this very private setting. Honeymooners and anniversary celebrants are given a complimentary bottle of champagne in a silver wine cooler and can have breakfast served in the room if they choose.

No. Rooms: 9	**Breakfast:** Full
Singles: None	**S-Rates:** $60–$100 pb
Doubles: 9 pb	**D-Rates:** $65–$105 pb
Type: Private townhouse	**Bldg:** 1830 Greek Revival

Minimum Stay: none. **Credit Card(s) Accepted:** AE, MC, V. **Open:** all year. No resident dogs. Guests may bring dog. No resident cats. Guests may bring cat. Nonsmoking host. Guests may smoke. Children welcome. **Discounts:** AAA Members.

Reservation Contact: Lincoln, Ltd. Bed & Breakfast, Barbara Lincoln Hall, Box 3479, Meridian, MS 39303; 601–482–5483.

MISSOURI

BRANSON

SCHOOL OF THE OZARKS, TABLE ROCK LAKE, & STATE PARK.

Near Hwy. 65.

This elegant turn-of-the-century home, completely restored and redecorated, is located in downtown Branson and overlooks the town and nearby bluffs. The entire home is furnished with antiques, and a spacious parlor is available for guests. The house has seven guest rooms with private baths, and twin and double beds. Your host is interested in interior design.

No. Rooms: 7	**Breakfast:** Continental
Singles: None	**S-Rates:** None
Doubles: 7 pb	**D-Rates:** $45–$60 pb
Type: Private Home	**Bldg:** 1900s

Minimum Stay: none. **Credit Card(s) Accepted:** none. **Open:** all year. No resident dogs. No dogs please. No resident cats. No cats please. Non-smoking host. Guests may smoke. Residence not appropriate for children. **Discounts:** none.

Reservation Contact: Ozark Mountain Country Bed & Breakfast, Linda Johnson & Kay Cameron, Box 295, Branson, MO 65726; 417–334–4720.

HARTVILLE

ID: 6566–FRI

LAURA INGALLS WILDER HOME & MUSEUM, AMISH COMMUNITY, MARK TWAIN NATIONAL FOREST; HEART OF THE SCENIC OZARKS.

Near Rte. 5, Rte. 38, U.S. 60.

This 1890s Victorian house has been completely restored, retaining absolute authenticity throughout. Inconspicuous additions of modern heating, central air-conditioning, and plumbing are the only modifications. The furnishings are period pieces, many of which are third- and fourth-generation family heirlooms. You have a choice of four bedrooms, one on the first floor and three on the second floor. All have double or queen-sized beds, antique furnishings, and shared baths. The wainscoted dining room, furnished in oak, is where you are served tea or wine and homemade breads on arrival and a hearty Full breakfast each morning. Additional meals and area tours are available. Reservations are not accepted during the Christmas holidays. Your hosts, a former vice president of Burlington Northern and his wife, have interests in conservation, history, travel, historic preservation, "railroadiana," and forestry.

No. Rooms: 4	**Breakfast:** Full
Singles: None	**S-Rates:** $30 sb
Doubles: 4 sb	**D-Rates:** $35 sb
Type: Private home	**Bldg:** 1895 Victorian

Minimum Stay: none. **Credit Card(s) Accepted:** none. **Open:** all year, except Christmas. No resident dogs. No dogs please. No resident cats. A cat is allowed with restrictions. Nonsmoking host. Guests may not smoke in residence. Residence not appropriate for children. **Discounts:** 5% after 2 nights.

Reservation Contact: Bed & Breakfast Registry Ltd., Gary Winget, Box 8174, St. Paul, MN 55108; 612–646–4238.

INDEPENDENCE

ID: KS–STADIUM

MISSOURI RIVER, STADIUM.

Near I–435, I–70.

This beautifully decorated English-style, two-story home offers wonderful views of the Missouri River and the Kansas City skyline. There are two guest rooms, one with a private bath. One has twin beds and the other has a double bed and fireplace. The furnishings are a mixture of period and contemporary. A Full breakfast is served on the patio or in the dining room.

No. Rooms: 2
Singles: None
Doubles: 1 pb, 1 sb
Type: Private home

Breakfast: Full
S-Rates: $45 pb, $45 sb
D-Rates: $55 pb, $55 sb
Bldg: Two-story English-style

Minimum Stay: none. **Credit Card(s) Accepted:** none. **Open:** all year. No resident dogs. No dogs please. No resident cats. No cats please. Non-smoking host. Guest may not smoke in residence. Children welcome with restrictions. **Discounts:** none.

Reservation Contact: Bed & Breakfast Kansas City, Edwina Monroe, Box 14781, Lenexa, KS 66215; 913–888–3636.

KANSAS CITY

ID: KS–DA61

COUNTRY CLUB PLAZA.

Near Main & Oak sts.

Built for William Rockhill Nelson's gardener, this "cottage" has a bedroom with king-sized bed, sitting room (for which a double bed is available), and private bath. A Full breakfast is served in the dining room or on the spacious front porch. Convenient to all the best attractions of Kansas City, the house is near the Nelson Art Gallery and within walking distance to Country Club Plaza.

No. Rooms: 1
Singles: None
Doubles: 1 pb
Type: Private home

Breakfast: Full
S-Rates: $55 pb
D-Rates: $60 pb
Bldg: 1900s stone

Minimum Stay: none. **Credit Card(s) Accepted:** none. **Open:** all year. No resident dogs. No dogs please. No resident cats. No cats please. Host smokes. Guests may not smoke in guest rooms. Children welcome with restrictions. **Discounts:** none.

Reservation Contact: Kansas City Bed & Breakfast, Diane Kuhn, Box 14781, Lenexa, KS 66215; 913–268–4214.

ID: KS–HA36

HYDE PARK AREA.

Near Main & Grillon sts.

This lovely Queen Anne-style house was built in 1887. Located in Hyde Park, it is near Westport, Country Club Plaza, and the downtown area, and is only a one-block walk to public transportation. Two guest rooms offer double beds; one has a private bath and one shares a bath. One of the rooms boasts a magnificent antique walnut bed and a private screened porch. A Full breakfast is served. Your host is a retired social worker.

No. Rooms: 2	**Breakfast:** Full
Singles: None	**S-Rates:** $35 pb, $35 sb
Doubles: 1 pb, 1 sb	**D-Rates:** $40 pb, $40 sb
Type: Private home	**Bldg:** Queen Anne

Minimum Stay: none.**Credit Card(s) Accepted:** none. **Open:** all year. No resident dogs. No dogs please. Cat in residence. No cats please. Host does not smoke in guest areas. Guests may not smoke in guest rooms. Residence not appropriate for children. **Discounts:** none.

Reservation Contact: Kansas City Bed & Breakfast, Diane Kuhn, Box 14781, Lenexa, KS 66215; 913–268–4214.

ID: KS–HYDE

HYDE PARK AREA.

Near Main St. & Gillham Rd.

This stunning Georgian home was built in 1913 by a former Kansas City mayor. The third-floor guest suite consists of a bedroom with a double bed, a living room with a hide-a-bed, game table, and cable TV, and a private bath. A Continental breakfast is served in the first-floor breakfast room.

No. Rooms: 1	**Breakfast:** Continental
Singles: None	**S-Rates:** $40 pb
Doubles: 1 pb	**D-Rates:** $50 pb
Type: Private home	**Bldg:** Georgian colonial

Minimum Stay: none. **Credit Card(s) Accepted:** none. **Open:** all year. No resident dogs. No dogs please. No resident cats. No cats please. Non-smoking host. Guests may smoke in residence. Children welcome. **Discounts:** none.

Reservation Contact: Bed & Breakfast Kansas City, Edwina Monroe, Box 14781, Lenexa, KS 66215; 913–888–3636.

ID: KS–ke32

KANSAS CITY MUSEUM.

Near Independence Ave., I–70.

Large comfortable residence near the Kansas City Museum is only minutes from I–70, ideal for long-distance travelers. Two guest rooms offer double beds and share a guest bath. Additional space is available for children with sleeping bags on the third floor. A crib is also available. A Full breakfast is served. One of your hosts, though retired, stays busy gardening and redecorating; the other does catering for small parties. Arrival/departure transportation is available.

No. Rooms: 2	**Breakfast:** Full
Singles: None	**S-Rates:** $30 sb
Doubles: 2sb	**D-Rates:** $35 sb
Type: Private home	**Bldg:** 1900s

Minimum Stay: none. **Credit Card(s) Accepted:** none. **Open:** all year. No resident dogs. A dog is allowed with restrictions. No resident cats. A cat is allowed with restrictions. Host smokes. Guests may not smoke in residence. Children welcome. **Discounts:** none.

Reservation Contact: Kansas City Bed & Breakfast, Edwina Monroe, Box 14781, Lenexa, KS 66215; 913–888–3636.

ID: KS–TUDOR

COUNTRY CLUB PLAZA.

Near I–70, I–35.

This two-story English Tudor home is located eight blocks from Country Club Plaza, a shopping center full of interesting shops and restaurants. There are two guest rooms, one with a king-sized bed and one with a double bed, that share a bath. Guests may use the hot tub on the deck. A Continental breakfast is served either on the deck or in the breakfast room. Your host is an interior decorator.

No. Rooms: 2	**Breakfast:** Continental
Singles: None	**S-Rates:** $55 sb
Doubles: 2 sb	**D-Rates:** $55–$60 sb
Type: Private home	**Bldg:** English Tudor

Minimum Stay: none. **Credit Card(s) accepted:** none. **Open:** all year. No resident dogs. No dogs please. No resident cats. No cats please. Non-smoking host. Guests may not smoke in residence. Residence not appropriate for children. **Discounts:** none.

Reservation Contact: Bed & Breakfast Kansas City, Edwina Monroe, Box 14781, Lenexa, KS 66215; 913–888–3636.

ID: KS–WH60

COUNTRY CLUB PLAZA, HISTORIC AREA.

Near Wornall & Ward Pwy., I–29, I–35.

Situated in a wooded residential area on the site of the Civil War Battle of Westport, this English Tudor residence is just two blocks south of Country Club Plaza, with excellent stores and fine restaurants. Buses to the downtown convention center are easily accessible. Guests can enjoy pleasant evening strolls through this historic area. The house has one upstairs guest room with private bath and balcony. Your host, a retired professor, is interested in travel and history.

No. Rooms: 1	Breakfast: Full
Singles: None	S-Rates: $53 pb
Doubles: 1 pb	D-Rates: $58 pb
Type: Private home	Bldg: English Tudor

Minimum Stay: none. **Credit Card(s) Accepted:** none. **Open:** all year. No resident dogs. No dogs please. No resident cats. No cats please. Non-smoking host. Guests may not smoke in residence. Residence not appropriate for children. **Discounts:** none.

Reservation Contact: Kansas City Bed & Breakfast, Edwina Monroe, Box 14781, Lenexa, KS 66215; 913–888–3636.

KIMBERLING CITY

ID: OZARK105

TABLE ROCK LAKE, OZARK MOUNTAINS.

Near Rte. 13, Rte. 86, U.S. 65.

This contemporary brick home offers a spectacular view of Table Rock Lake and the Ozark Mountains. Guests have use of the sitting area, game room, and library. Two guest rooms, offering double beds and a shared guest bath, open onto a private patio and are rented only to a family or couples traveling together. A Full breakfast is served as well as a complimentary snack upon arrival. Your host is a teacher at the School of the Ozarks.

No. Rooms: 2	Breakfast: Full
Singles: None	S-Rates: $55 sb
Doubles: 2 sb	D-Rates: $55 sb
Type: Private Home	Bldg: 1984 modern brick

Minimum Stay: none. **Credit Card(s) Accepted:** none. **Open:** all year. No resident dogs. No dogs please. No resident cats. No cats please. Non-smoking host. Guests may not smoke in guest rooms. Children welcome. **Discounts:** none.

Reservation Contact: Ozark Mountain Country Bed & Breakfast, Linda Johnson & Kay Cameron, Box 295, Branson, MO 65726; 417–334–4720.

LEBANON

ID: OZARK217

OZARK MOUNTAINS.

Near I–44.

This three-story Victorian home is furnished with antiques. The three second-floor guest rooms share a bath. The largest of the rooms has two double beds and can accommodate four persons. A Full country breakfast is served.

No. Rooms: 3
Singles: None
Doubles: 3 sb
Type: Private home

Breakfast: Full
S-Rates: $35–$50 sb
D-Rates: $35–$50 sb
Bldg: Victorian

Minimum Stay: none. Credit Card(s) Accepted: none. Open: all year. No resident dogs. No dogs please. No resident cats. No cats please. Non-smoking host. Guests may not smoke in residence. Children welcome with restrictions. Discounts: none.

Reservation Contact: Ozark Mountain Country Bed & Breakfast, Linda Johnson & Kay Cameron, Box 295, Branson, MO 65726; 417–334–4720.

MARIONVILLE
ID: OZARK 210

20 MILES FROM SPRINGFIELD.

Near Hwy. 60.

This Victorian home has been restored to its original splendor with antique furnishings, stained-glass windows, parquet floors, and Victorian reproduction wallpaper imported from Paris. Watch rare white squirrels frolic on the grounds, enjoy the fireplace and TV in the parlor, or relax in the library or the upstairs sitting room. The five guest rooms have double beds; two have private baths. The Honeymoon Suite, done in white, is furnished with a lace canopy bed and Oriental rug and has a private screened balcony. Other rooms include the Gold Coast Room, the Elizabethan Room, Turkish Corners, and the Wild Wild West Room. A hearty, Full country breakfast is served in the formal dining room or on the screened porch.

No. Rooms: 5
Singles: None
Doubles: 2 pb, 3 sb
Type: Inn

Breakfast: Full
S-Rates: $40–$65
D-Rates: $40–$65
Bldg: 1890s Victorian

Minimum Stay: none. Credit Card(s) Accepted: None. Open: all year. Resident dog. No dogs please. No resident cats. No cats please. Host smokes. Guests may smoke in common areas only. Residence not appropriate for children under 15. Discounts: none.

Reservation Contact: Ozark Mountain Country Bed & Breakfast, Linda Johnson & Kay Cameron, Box 295, Branson, MO 65726; 417–334–4720.

PARKVILLE

ID: KS–CO22

INDOOR POOL.

Near I–29.

This unusual earth-integrated home is located on eighty-eight acres of land with three ponds for fishing. Four guest rooms offer private baths and private entrances. Three have double beds and one has twin beds. A Full breakfast is served either in bed, by the pool, or in the dining room. Guests are invited to use the indoor pool, exercise room, and jogging path. One of your hosts is a teacher; the other is in the agricultural business.

No. Rooms: 4	**Breakfast:** Full
Singles: None	**S-Rates:** $55 pb
Doubles: 4 pb	**D-Rates:** $60 pb
Type: Private home	**Bldg:** Contemporary ranch

Minimum Stay: none. **Credit Card(s) Accepted:** none. **Open:** all year. Dog in residence. No dogs please. No resident cats. No cats please. Non-smoking host. Guests may not smoke in guest rooms. **Discounts:** long-term.

Reservation Contact: Kansas City Bed & Breakfast, Edwina Monroe, Box 14781, Lenexa, KS 66215; 913–888–3636.

MONTANA

BILLINGS

DEACONESS & ST. VINCENT HOSPITALS, CANCER CENTER; DOWNTOWN SHOPPING.

Between 7th & 8th aves., N., I–90.

This historic home, built between 1912 and 1914, is set in the heart of the medical corridor, minutes from downtown Billings and two miles from the airport. There are seven guest rooms with shared guest baths. Most rooms have double beds and antique furnishings; one room is a single. A Continental Plus breakfast is served; additional meals and kitchen privileges are available. Child care and arrival/departure transportation can also be arranged. Your host is an area native who does everything possible to make guests comfortable.

No. Rooms: 7
Singles: 1 sb
Doubles: 6 sb
Type: Private home

Breakfast: Continental Plus
S-Rates: $20 sb
D-Rates: $24–$36 sb
Bldg: 1913 craftsman

Minimum Stay: none. **Credit Card(s) Accepted:** none. **Open:** all year. No resident dogs. A dog is allowed with restrictions. No resident cats. A cat is allowed with restrictions. Host smokes. Guests may smoke. Children welcome. **Discounts:** weekly.

Reservation Contact: Bed & Breakfast Western Adventure, Paula Deigert, Box 20972, Billings, MT 59104; 406–259–7993.

BOZEMAN

MONTANA STATE UNIVERSITY.

Near I–90, 3rd & Curtis sts.

Built in 1906, this colonial revival home is located in the Bon Ton historic district. It has a large front porch with swing and is comfortably furnished with turn-of-the-century antiques and interesting pieces collected from your hosts' European travels. There are three guest rooms on the second floor, two of which share a bath. The third has a queen-sized bed and private shower. A Full breakfast is served in the dining room or on the sun deck. One of your hosts is a professor at the university and the other is an interior designer and weaver.

No. Rooms: 3	**Breakfast:** Full
Singles: None	**S-Rates:** $35 pb, $30 sb
Doubles: 1 pb, 2 sb	**D-Rates:** $40 pb, $35 sb
Type: Private home	**Bldg:** 1906 colonial revival

Minimum Stay: none. **Credit Card(s) Accepted:** none. **Open:** all year. No resident dogs. No dogs please. Resident cat. No cats please. Non-smoking host. Guests may not smoke in residence. Children welcome with restrictions. **Discounts:** none.

Reservation Contact: Bed & Breakfast Western Adventure, Paula Deigert, Box 20972, Billings, MT 59104; 406–259–7993.

POLSON

ON FLATHEAD LAKE.

Near Hwy. 35.

This handsome Alpine country two-story home is decorated inside and out with cedar and quarried rock. Custom windows allow views of the peninsular beach that sits between Starvation Bay and Bootlegger Bay. Gravel beaches, rock gardens, and boardwalks adorn the property. This is an excellent spot for bird watchers; look for the ospreys and golden eagles that frequent the area. There are four guest rooms available.

No. Rooms: 4	**Breakfast:** Full
Singles: None	**S-Rates:** $70–$90
Doubles: 4	**D-Rates:** $75–$95
Type: Private home	**Bldg:** Alpine country

Minimum Stay: none. **Credit Card(s) Accepted:** none. **Open:** all year. Resident dog. No dogs please. No resident cats. No cats please. Host smokes. Guests may not smoke in guest rooms. Children welcome with restrictions. **Discounts:** none.

Reservation Contact: Bed & Breakfast Western Adventure, Paula Diegert, Box 20972, Billings, MT 59104; 406–259–7993.

NEBRASKA

GRAND ISLAND

STUHR MUSEUM; HORSE RACING, SWIMMING.

Near I–80, Hwy. 34.

Guests will find clean fresh air in this rural residential area, safe for jogging or biking at any time of the day or night, located on a semiprivate lake available for swimming. The house is part of a twenty-year-old subdivision about three miles from town and away from city traffic. Its appeal is in the peaceful quiet atmosphere it affords guests, yet there are many activities in Grand Island. Your hosts gladly share TV viewing with their guests. One guest room is available, with double bed, dresser, chairs, closet, and private bath. A Continental breakfast is served. A real-estate broker and a legal secretary, your hosts like traveling and enjoy theater, concerts, swimming, and church activities.

No. Rooms: 1	**Breakfast:** Continental
Singles: None	**S-Rates:** None
Doubles: 1 pb	**D-Rates:** $35 pb
Type: Private home	**Bldg:** 1980 salt box

Minimum Stay: none. **Credit Card(s) Accepted:** none. **Open:** all year. No resident dogs. No dogs please. No resident cats. No cats please. Non-smoking host. Guests may not smoke in residence. Children welcome with restrictions. **Discounts:** none.

Reservation Contact: Bed & Breakfast of the Great Plains, Rose Ann Foster, Box 2333, Lincoln, NE 68502; 402–423–3480.

GRETNA

SCHRAMM PARK STATE RECREATION AREA.

Near Hwy. 31, I–80.

This ranch home is one-half mile north of Schramm Park State Recreation Area, site of the state's first fish hatchery, popular with Nebraskans for over a century. Now the home of the exceptional Ak-Sar-Ben Aquarium and World-Herald Theater, the park is open from sunrise to sunset for picnics and hiking. It is located on ten acres of land, including a spring-fed creek. The guest room has a double bed, oak dresser with mirror, and clothes rack. From the family room, with double hide-a-bed, recliner, TV, stereo, and wood-burning stove, guests can walk out to the patio. You may choose between a Continental and a Full breakfast. Your hosts are an attorney and his wife.

No. Rooms: 2	**Breakfast:** Full or Continental
Singles: None	**S-Rates:** $35 sb
Doubles: 2 sb	**D-Rates:** $45 sb
Type: Private home	**Bldg:** Ranch

Minimum Stay: none. **Credit Card(s) Accepted:** none. **Open:** all year. No resident dogs. No dogs please. Cat in residence. No cats please. Non-smoking host. Guests may smoke. Children welcome. **Discounts:** none.

Reservation Contact: Bed & Breakfast of the Great Plains, Rose Ann Foster, Box 2333, Lincoln, NE 68502; 423–3480.

KENNARD

DE SOTO BEND WILDLIFE REFUGE, FT. ATKINSON STATE PARK; 15 MILES NORTHWEST OF OMAHA.

Near Hwy. 31, I–80, Hwy. 30.

Many of the houses in this area of dairy and thoroughbred-racing farms date back to the early 1900s. This large attractive farmhouse, built in 1890, has been totally renovated, but it has retained the original woodwork and stained glass. The house is on four acres of beautiful timbered land, a perfect place for those who relish the peace of the country. Flower gardens and patio flowers provide bright summertime color, and an old tree swing hangs from an eighty-year-old sycamore. The guest room is decorated with antique furniture, and the double bed is a high framed spindle dressed in white eyelet. On the windows are handmade curtains, and a rocking chair is tucked in the corner. A Full breakfast, consisting of egg dishes, several kinds of muffins, homemade jams, juice, a fresh fruit bowl, and coffee or tea, is served. One of your hosts enjoys canning and freezing produce from the garden, needlework, sewing, stenciling, and entertaining; the other is interested in computer work, skiing, tennis, electronics, and woodworking.

No. Rooms: 1	**Breakfast:** Full
Singles: None	**S-Rates:** $30 pb
Doubles: 1 pb	**D-Rates:** $35 pb
Type: Private home	**Bldg:** 1890 farmhouse

Minimum Stay: none. **Credit Card(s) Accepted:** none. **Open:** all year, except Christmas. Dog in residence. No dogs please. Cat in residence. No cats please. Nonsmoking host. Guests may not smoke in guest rooms. Children welcome with restrictions. **Discounts:** none.

Reservation Contact: Bed & Breakfast of the Great Plains, Rose Ann Foster, Box 2333, Lincoln, NE 68502; 402–423–3480.

NORTH PLATTE

ID: GP106NE

ANTIQUE SHOPS, HISTORICAL MUSEUM, RODEOS, COMMUNITY PLAYHOUSE.

Near I–80.

In 1897, when Mr. Beeler, an attorney, discovered that the railroad was going through North Platte rather than Wallace, he decided he would have to move to North Platte. His wife, however, was reluctant to leave her house, so it was cut into four sections and moved by team and hay-rack to its present location. Over the years it has undergone extensive remodeling, and in 1984 it suffered a devastating fire, which led to extensive rebuilding. Now, it is open as a B&B inn. Four newly decorated guest rooms offer antique furnishings, some with hand-sewn quilts, and one with a private bath. Two of the rooms have queen-sized beds, one has a double bed, and one has a single. The guests' sitting room has an antique white iron and brass crib that doubles as a settee and is filled with pillows. It also has a wicker rocker, chaise lounge, and many plants. Outdoors, guests will find a redwood deck with antique white wrought-iron patio furniture, picnic table, and soothing spa. A hearty Full breakfast is served, which might consist of fresh fruit, homemade bread, jams, omelets, French toast, or even quiche. The food is delicious, the service friendly, and the home immaculate. Your hosts enjoy stained glass, antiques, and entertaining. North Platte is a lovely town on Interstate 80. Nearby visitors will find golf, cross-country skiing, lakes for fishing and water sports, the Lincoln County Historical Museum, rodeos, community theater, and antiques.

No. Rooms: 4	**Breakfast:** Full
Singles: 1 sb	**S-Rates:** $40 pb, $35 sb
Doubles: 1 pb, 2 sb	**D-Rates:** $45 pb, $40 sb
Types: Private home	**Bldg:** 1897

Minimum Stay: none. **Credit Card(s) Accepted:** AE, MC, V. **Open:** all year. No resident dogs. A dog is allowed with restrictions. No resident cats. No cats please. Nonsmoking host. Guests may not smoke in guest rooms. Children welcome. **Discounts:** weekly.

Reservation Contact: Bed & Breakfast of the Great Plains, Rose Ann Foster, Box 2333, Lincoln, NE 68502; 402–423–3480.

LINCOLN
ID: GP104NE

STATE CAPITOL; UNIVERSITY OF NEBRASKA, STATE MUSEUM OF SCIENCE, STATE MUSEUM OF HISTORY, CHILDREN'S ZOO, NATIONAL ROLLERSKATING MUSEUM.

Near I–180.

In 1914, a retiring banker built his new home in the Jacobean revival style. Located in the historic Near South neighborhood, the house is just minutes from the University of Nebraska, the Sunken Gardens, the Children's Zoo, and the capitol. There are eight guest rooms, each with a private bath. All are furnished with antiques and have unique characteristics such as fireplaces or sun rooms. Breakfast consists of a hot entree such as quiche or natural grain French toast, fruit, fresh-squeezed orange juice, muffins or pastries, and coffee or tea. A glass of wine awaits each guest on arrival.

No. Rooms: 8	**Breakfast:** Full
Singles: None	**S-Rates:** $40–$50 pb
Doubles: 8 pb	**D-Rates:** $45–$55 pb
Type: Inn	**Bldg:** 1914 Jacobean revival

Minimum Stay: none. **Credit Card(s) Accepted:** AE, MC, V. **Open:** all year. No resident dogs. No dogs please. No resident cats. No cats please. Nonsmoking host. Guests may smoke in residence. Children welcome with restrictions. **Discounts:** Stays of more than 2 nights.

Reservations Contact: Bed & Breakfast of the Great Plains, Rose Ann Foster, Box 2333, Lincoln, NE 68502; 402–423–3480.

OMAHA

JOSLYN ART MUSEUM, OLD MARKET, ORPHEUM THEATRE, CENTRAL PARK MALL, UNION PACIFIC MUSEUM, CITY AUDITORIUM.

Near I–480.

Built in 1894, this handsome home on Omaha's historic Gold Coast reminds one of a European chateau. It features a grand oak entrance hall and staircase and an inviting living room with fireplace, grand piano, and walls of books. The seven spacious guest rooms are furnished with antiques. One has a delicate iron bedstead and antique cotton embossed bedspread; others have walnut beds and dressers, embroidered linens, and quilts. All are air-conditioned, two have fireplaces, and one has a sun porch. Fresh-squeezed orange juice, fruit, pastries, and steaming croissants with jellies are served for breakfast. The dining room is done in walnut and elegant fabric.

No. Rooms: 7	**Breakfast:** Continental
Singles: None	**S-Rates:** $50 pb, $40 sb
Doubles: 2 pb, 5 sb	**D-Rates:** $60 pb, $50 sb
Type: Private home	**Bldg:** 1894 mansion

Minimum Stay: none. **Credit Card(s) Accepted:** AE, MC, V. **Open:** all year. No resident dogs. A dog is allowed with restrictions. No resident cats. No cats please. Guests may smoke in residence. Children welcome with restrictions. **Discounts:** weekly.

Reservation Contact: Bed & Breakfast of the Great Plains, Rose Ann Foster, Box 2333, Lincoln, NE 68502; 402–423–3480.

NEVADA

LAS VEGAS

ID: INTNAT238

Near Eastern & Flamingo sts., I–15.

Many travelers prefer the quiet of a residential neighborhood to the noisy activity of the Strip. This comfortable L-shaped home partially surrounds the large swimming pool, and a roof overhang provides shade for the patio. Visitors often have the luxury of having an entire pool to themselves. Two carpeted guest rooms are available with double and twin beds, handmade quilts, complete bedroom set, chairs, and table. One has a private bath; one has a shared bath. One has a view of the pool, while the other looks out over the fruit trees. A Full breakfast is served. Laundry facilities and refrigerator space are available. Visitors should not overlook the many scenic attractions close to Las Vegas, such as spectacular Red Rock. Your host, a school librarian, likes animals.

No. Rooms: 2
Singles: None
Doubles: 1 pb, 1 sb
Type: Private home

Breakfast: Full
S-Rates: $52 pb, $42 sb
D-Rates: $58 pb, $48 sb
Bldg: 1960 ranch

Minimum Stay: 2 nights. **Credit Card(s) Accepted:** none. **Open:** all year. No resident dogs. No dogs please. Cats in residence. No cats please. Nonsmoking host. Guests may not smoke in guest rooms. Children welcome. **Discounts:** 10% weekly; family.

Reservation Contact: Bed & Breakfast International—California, Jean Brown, 1181-B Solano Ave., Albany, CA 94706; 415–525–4569.

VIRGINIA CITY

ID: 89440PAL

COMSTOCK LODE, MINING & WILD WEST
MUSEUMS, ANNUAL CAMEL RACE.

Near B & Union sts., Rte. 341.

Built about 1875, this Pleasant little country inn offers beautiful, elegant gardens. Both the interior and the exterior have been completely renovated. There are six guest rooms with king-sized or double beds; one has a private bath, and the others share a bath. A Full breakfast is served. Virginia City has become one of the few surviving examples of Old West life as it was in pioneer days.

No. Rooms: 6
Singles: None
Doubles: 1 pb, 5 sb
Type: Inn

Breakfast: Full
S-Rates: $45–$65 pb, $45–$65 sb
D-Rates: $45–$65 pb, $45–$65 sb
Bldg: 1875

Minimum Stay: 2 nights. **Credit Card(s) Accepted:** none. **Open:** all year. No resident dogs. No dogs please. Cat in resident. No cats please. Nonsmoking host. Guests may not smoke in residence. Children welcome. **Discounts:** none.

Reservation Contact: Bed & Breakfast Registry Ltd., Gary Winget, Box 8174, St. Paul, MN 55108; 612–646–4238.

NEW HAMPSHIRE

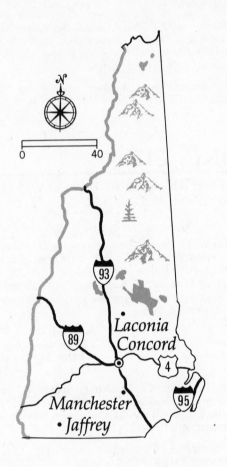

0   40

93

89

Laconia
Concord

4

Manchester
• Jaffrey

95

GLEN

ID: 03839BER

SKIIERS' PARADISE; HIKING, CLIMBING, SIGHTSEEING,
MT. WASHINGTON VALLEY.

Near Rte. 16, U.S. 302.

This cozy little inn, built in the early 1890s, has nine cheerful guest rooms,
with double or twin beds, and private or shared baths. A second-floor
sitting room provides a nice place to curl up with a good book, watch
television, or socialize with other guests. The third floor has a Finnish
sauna. A short stroll through the pines leads you to the swimming pool,

and there is also a children's playground. The more ambitious guest can follow the trail to the top of Mount Washington. A hearty breakfast is served, and the inn also specializes in superb Continental cuisine for those seeking a special dinner in an atmosphere of old-world charm. If you spend three nights at the inn, you will be pampered with a champagne breakfast in bed on the third morning. Besides excellent downhill and cross-country skiing, the area offers a spring Mountain Fest with hot-air balloon and glider demonstrations, a summer Arts Jubilee, summer theater, and brilliant fall foliage set against snowcapped Mount Washington.

No. Rooms: 9	**Breakfast:** Full
Singles: None	**S-Rates:** $60–$85 pb, $50–$75 sb
Doubles: 2 pb, 7 sb	**D-Rates:** $70–$95 pb, $60–$85 sb
Type: Inn	**Bldg:** 1890s Victorian

Minimum Stay: 2 days on holidays. **Credit Card(s) Accepted:** AE, MC, V. **Open:** all year. No resident dogs. No dogs please. No resident cats. No cats please. Nonsmoking host. Guests may not smoke in guest rooms. Children welcome with restrictions. **Discounts:** none.

Reservation Contact: Bed & Breakfast Registry Ltd., Gary Winget, Box 8174, St. Paul, MN 55108; 612–646–4238.

HAMPTON
ID: 03842CUR

3 MILES FROM EXETER, 6 MILES FROM OCEAN.

Near Rte. 101, Exeter Rd., I–95.

This house was built by the host's father, a master craftsman who also built many antique reproductions. It is located in a quiet country neighborhood three miles from the historicl town of Exeter and six miles from Atlantic beaches. There are three guest rooms with twin canopy beds, a queen-sized bed, or a double canopy bed. A Full breakfast is served. Your hosts are interested in travel, tennis, skiing, gardening, and crafts.

No. Rooms: 3	**Breakfast:** Full
Singles: None	**S-Rates:** $50 pb, $45 sb
Doubles: 2 pb, 1 sb	**D-Rates:** $60 pb, $50 sb
Type: Private home	**Bldg:** 1952 Custom Cape

Minimum Stay: none. **Credit Card(s) Accepted:** MC, V. **Open:** all year. No resident dogs. No dogs please. No resident cats. No cats please. Nonsmoking host. Guest may not smoke in residence. Children welcome with restrictions. **Discounts:** 10% more than 2 nights.

Reservation Contact: Bed & Breakfast Registry Ltd., Gary Winget, Box 8174, St. Paul, MN 55018; 612–646–4238.

HAMPTON BEACH
ID: NH530–PINE

BEACH, RESTAURANTS, SHOPS.

Near I–95, Rte. 51E.

Built in the 1900s as a private home, this inn reflects earlier periods with carefully chosen antiques and decorator touches. Relax in the parlor with fireplaces, in the glassed-in porch, or on the wraparound deck. Games, TV, and a library are also available. The long hall that leads to the guest rooms is a gallery of Victorians. Each of the ten guest rooms, all with private baths, is tastefully decorated with added touches of vintage shawls, hats, and purses. A Continental Plus breakfast is served. Although the inn is in an uncongested part of Hampton Beach, it is directly across from the beach and within walking distance of restaurants, shops, and other attractions. Free parking is provided.

No. Rooms: 10	**Breakfast:** Continental Plus
Singles: 1 pb	**S-Rates:** $45–$85 pb
Doubles: 9 pb	**D-Rates:** $69–$85 pb
Type: Inn	**Bldg:** 1900s

Minimum Stay: none. **Credit Card(s) Accepted:** AE, MC, V. **Open:** mid-May–mid-Oct. Resident dog. No dogs please. No resident cats. No cats please. Nonsmoking host. Guests may not smoke in residence. Residence is not appropriate for children. **Discounts:** 10% before June 24 & after Sept. 6.

Reservation Contact: Pineapple Hospitality, Judy M. Mulford, 47 N. Second St., Suite 3A, New Bedford, MA 02740; 617–990–1696.

HILLSBORO
ID: N.H.B&B–#3

HOMESTEADS OF PRESIDENT FRANKLIN PIERCE AND NATHANIEL HAWTHORNE, HILLSBORO CENTER.

Near Rtes. 5, 202, 9.

This rural Cape-style solar home with open living space invites the outdoors in. In the winter, guests can cross-country ski from the back door across the fields to the marked trails of nearby Fox Forest State Park. The country setting—roads and fields and a nearby fishing brook and stone arch bridge—is ideal for hikers and artists. The guest suite consists of a country-cottage bedroom with wall stenciling patterns by Moses Eaton, an early-nineteenth-century stenciler. It has a king-sized bed and maple furniture. Adjoining it is a studio/sitting room and private bath. A hearty Full breakfast is served in the sun room, overlooking the fields and woods. There are always birds to observe at the window feeders. Your hosts' enjoy canoeing, bird watching, hiking, and painting.

No. Rooms: 1	**Breakfast:** Full
Singles: None	**S-Rates:** None
Doubles: 1 pb	**D-Rates:** $65 pb
Type: Private home	**Bldg:** 1982 Cape Cod

Minimum Stay: none. **Credit Card(s) Accepted:** none. **Open:** all year. Dog in residence. No dogs please. No resident cats. No cats please. Non-smoking host. Guests may not smoke in guest rooms. Children welcome with restrictions. **Discounts:** weekly.

Reservation Contact: New Hampshire Bed & Breakfast, Martha Dorais, RFD 3, Box 53, Laconia, NH 03246; 603–279–8348.

JACKSON   ID: 03846NES

BLACK, CRANMORE, & WILDCAT MTS. SKI AREAS; SLEIGH & HAY RIDES, GROOMED CROSS-COUNTRY TRAILS, HORSEBACK RIDING, SWIMMING.

Near Dinsmore Rd., U.S. 302, Rte. 16.

This enchanting seventeen-room 150-year-old colonial farmhouse is nestled on sixty-five secluded acres on the banks of the sparkling Ellis River. This delightful little inn, which has been completely refurbished, seems to offer something for everyone. You can swim in the pool; relax in the gazebo; hike some sixteen miles of trails; challenge a new friend to a game of badminton, volleyball, or croquet; or saddle up for horseback riding. In fall, there are hay wagon rides and a spectacular foliage display. In winter, you will find some of the best Alpine skiing in New England just minutes away. Cross-country skiing begins at the door, or you may

want to connect onto the Jackson Ski Touring Foundation network of groomed trails. Afterward, snuggle by the fire or while away the evening on an old-fashioned sleigh ride. Or just curl up with a good book in the comfort of the inn's parlor or take advantage of the extensive video film library. There are ten guest rooms in the inn, six of which have private baths, and all are furnished with antiques. An additional five rooms with shared baths have recently been created in what was formerly the carriage house. These are available during summer and fall only. There are also three cottages available; a studio, a one bedroom with loft, and a two-bedroom. A Full country breakfast is served.

No. Rooms: 15	**Breakfast:** Full
Singles: 2 pb, 2 sb	**S-Rates:** $40–$50 pb, $45–$50 sb
Doubles: 4 pb, 7 sb	**D-Rates:** $60–$95 pb, $65–$75 sb
Type: Inn	**Bldg:** 1880s colonial

Minimum Stay: 2 nights on weekends. **Credit Card(s) Accepted:** MC, V. **Open:** all year. Dog in residence. A dog is allowed with restrictions. Cat in residence. No cats please. Nonsmoking host. Guests may not smoke in guest rooms. Children welcome. **Discounts:** none.

Reservation Contact: Bed & Breakfast Registry Ltd., Gary Winget, Box 8174, St. Paul, MN 55108; 612–646–4238.

JAFFREY
ID: 03452LIL

MONADNOCK MOUNTAIN, SKIING, SKATING, FISHING, SWIMMING, HIKING.

Near U.S. 202 & NH 124.

Built in the early 1800s on a high hill surrounded by fifty acres of meadow and woodland, this serene farm inn offers spectacular views. One side overlooks Gilmore Pond, Pack Monadnock, and Temple Mountain. On another side, majestic Mt. Monadnock rises up. The land was originally settled by Thomas Dutton in the 1770s, and remained in the family until Lyman Sawtell purchased it in 1876, and sold it in 1888 to Joseph E. Gay, a copper-mining executive from New York. Mr. Gay turned the farm into a show place and people came from miles around to see his latest innovations. The house was one of the first to have electricity and, by installing a windmill, Mr. Gay was able to pump water from the pond into the house. The area offers attractions for all seasons: skating in winter, trout fishing in spring, swimming in summer. There is cross-country and Alpine skiing nearby. Hike the many trails of Mt. Monadnock, or just sit beside the fire with a cup of hot mulled cider. The inn offers six guest rooms with shared bath. The Gilmore Pond Room is done in green and wicker and has twin beds. The Monadnock Room, in rust with oak furnishings, has a king-sized and a twin bed. The Blue Room has mahogany furnishings and twin beds while the Brown Room, also with mahogany furnishings, has a king-sized bed. The large Family Room has a king-sized bed and three twin beds. A Full breakfast of fresh farm eggs, homemade breads, and syrup from the nearby sugar mill is served. Besides farming, your hosts have interests in travel and real estate.

No. Room: 6	**Breakfast:** Full
Singles: None	**S-Rates:** $55 pb, $50 sb
Doubles: 2 pb, 4 sb	**D-Rates:** $65 pb, $60 sb
Type: Private home	**Bldg:** 1800s colonial

Minimum Stay: 2 nights on weekends during foliage season. **Credit Card(s) Accepted:** none. **Open:** all year. Host's dog is not allowed in guest areas. No dogs please. Host's cat is not allowed in guest areas. No cats please. Nonsmoking host. Guests may not smoke in guest rooms. Children are welcome with restrictions. **Discounts:** none.

Reservation Contact: Bed & Breakfast Registry Ltd., Gary Winget, Box 8174, St. Paul, MN 55108; 612–646–4238.

JEFFERSON
ID: 03583JEF

SANTA'S VILLAGE, SIX GUN CITY, COG RAILROAD, MT. WASHINGTON.

Near U.S. 2 & NH 115.

Located in the heart of the North Country, this Victorian inn overlooks the Presidential Range of the White Mountains. It captures the charm of a gracious era gone by with many antiques throughout the house. Guests receive footwarmers in the evening along with their nightly tea—an English tradition. Guests may watch TV in the lounge, visit on the wrap-around porch, or stroll over the three acres of grounds. There are six guest rooms. One is a large room with a cupola and a hand-painted antique double bed. Another has a bed with a carved headboard and an old spinning wheel. Two of the rooms can accommodate three people, the others accommodate two. Additional meals and arrival/departure transportation are sometimes available. Area attractions include hiking, skiing, swimming, golf, the Cog Railway, Santa's Village, and Six Gun City. Your hosts lived in London for six years and are interested in travel, outdoor activities, art, hockey, and basketball.

No. Rooms: 6	**Breakfast:** Full
Singles: None	**S-Rates:** $33–$41 sb
Doubles: 6 sb	**D-Rates:** $35–$45 sb
Type: Inn	**Bldg:** 1896 Victorian

Minimum Stay: none. **Credit Card(s) Accepted:** MC, V. **Open:** all year. No resident dogs. No dogs please. No resident cats. No cats please. Nonsmoking host. Guest may not smoke in residence. Children welcome. **Discounts:** 10% weekly. Dutch & French spoken.

Reservation Contact: Bed & Breakfast Registry Ltd., Gary Winget, Box 8174, St. Paul, MN 55108; 612–646–4238.

LACONIA

GUNSTOCK SKI AREA, LAKE WINNEPESAUKE BEACHES.

Near Rtes. 3 & 93.

Built in 1903, this large Victorian home offers backyard and barbecue facilities, a piano in the living room, fireplace, TV, phone, and laundry facilities. The house is located four miles from Gunstock Ski Area and the beaches of Lake Winnepesauke. Three pleasant guest rooms offer double beds and shared bath, one of which overlooks the greenhouse. A Full breakfast is served. Your host, a Radcliffe graduate, has traveled throughout Europe and enjoys music and art. Lunch and arrival/departure transportation are available.

No. Rooms: 4	**Breakfast:** Full
Singles: None	**S-Rates:** $40–$45 sb
Doubles: 3 sb	**D-Rates:** $45–$50 sb
Type: Private home	**Bldg:** 1903 Victorian

Minimum Stay: none. **Credit Card(s) Accepted:** MC. **Open:** all year. No resident dogs. No dogs please. No resident cats. No cats please. Non-smoking host. Guests may not smoke in guest rooms. Children welcome with restrictions. **Discounts:** weekly. Greek spoken.

Reservation Contact: New Hampshire Bed & Breakfast, Martha Dorias, RFT 3, Box 53, Laconia, NH 03246; 603–279–8348.

MANCHESTER

MASSABESIC LAKE, MCINTYRE SKI AREA.

Near Mammoth Rd., I–93.

This contemporary split-level home in a well-kept residential neighborhood is only three miles from the heart of the city yet surrounded by greenery. Within a two-mile radius is Massabesic Lake for sailing and boating, the country club for golf and tennis, horseback riding, hiking trails, and McIntyre Ski Area. Restaurants and theaters are also nearby. In the enclosed backyard, guests will find a built-in swimming pool and small flower garden. Three guest rooms are available. The first, with private bath, has a double bed, new oak bedroom furniture, including a bachelor chest, and a dresser with a leaded glass mirror. The bookcase headboard holds a portable telephone, clock radio, and books; doors fold down to form a writing desk or snack table in bed. The entertainment unit holds a remote control TV and VCR. The walk-in closet is complete with a washer/dryer and fold-down ironing board. The second room is done in blue tones with coordinated headboards and curtains. Furnishings consist of two white bureaus and a loveseat. The third room has birch-paneled walls, a single bed, and matching spread and curtains. Behind louvered doors is a bureau, lamp, and TV. The last two rooms share a bath. A Full breakfast is served in the dining room, which overlooks the pool and yard. Your friendly host, who takes pride in her surroundings and enjoys sharing the comfort of her home with guests, is a dental assistant who likes tennis, gardening, jogging, biking, cross-country skiing, and sewing. Arrival/departure transportation and lunch are also available.

No. Rooms: 3	**Breakfast:** Full
Singles: 1sb	**S-Rates:** $40 pb, $40 sb
Doubles: 1 pb, 1 sb	**D-Rates:** $50 pb, $50 sb
Type: Private home	**Bldg:** 1963 split-level

Minimum Stay: none. **Credit Card(s) Accepted:** None. **Open:** all year. No resident dogs. A dog is allowed with restrictions. No resident cats. Guests may bring cat. Nonsmoking host. Guests may smoke. Children welcome. **Discounts:** weekly.

Reservation Contact: New Hampshire Bed & Breakfast, Martha Dorias, RFD 3, Box 53, Laconia, NH 03246; 603–279–8348.

NORTHWOOD ID: 03261COM

NEAR CAPITOL AND HISTORIC COAST.

Near U.S. 4, U.S. 202.

A favorite spot for honeymoons or romantic weekends, this large contemporary home with spacious rooms is situated in a beautiful wooded area on a large lake. It is a quiet, peaceful spot great for bird-watching and observing small wildlife. Guests can swim in the lake or lounge on the deck, private dock, or screened porch. There is a grill available for guests who like outdoor cooking. The house is furnished in an eclectic style with many antiques and collections. Guests are invited to use the living room with TV. There are three guest rooms available, one with a private bath; the other two rooms share a bath. The first room has antique twin beds, a bureau, chairs, chest, a view of the lake and mountains, and access to the lake just outside the door. The second has twin beds, chairs, antique bureaus, secretary, a view of the lake and woods, and access to the woods outside the door. The third room has a queen-sized bed, two bureaus, chairs, private bath, and view of the woods and garden. A Full breakfast is served in the dining room which overlooks the lake. Your hosts' interests include golf, sailing, tennis, birding, gardening, photography, fishing, and bridge.

No. Rooms: 3	**Breakfast:** Full
Singles: None	**S-Rates:** $24–$30 pb, $25–$30 sb
Doubles: 1 pb, 2 sb	**D-Rates:** $35–$48 pb, $35–$48 sb
Type: Private home	**Bldg:** 1979 contemporary

Minimum Stay: none. **Credit Card(s) Accepted:** none. **Open:** all year except holidays. No resident dogs. A dog is allowed with restrictions. No resident cats. A cat is allowed with restrictions. Nonsmoking host. Guests may not smoke in guest rooms. Children are welcome with restrictions. **Discounts:** none.

Reservation Contact: Bed & Breakfast Registry Ltd., Gary Winget, Box 8174, St. Paul, MN 55108; 612–646–4238.

RINDGE

MT. MONADNOCK, SKI AREAS, CATHEDRAL OF THE PINES, ARTS CENTER.

Near U.S. 202, NH 119.

In a Currier and Ives corner of New Hampshire this small New England inn is located on a tree farm on a 1,400-foot hill providing a view of three states. The hundred acres of hardwoods are spectacular at foliage time and 12 acres of Christmas trees supply year-round greenery. Although secluded in the midst of a forest and off the beaten track, the inn is very accessible. There are woodland trails on the property for hiking, snow-shoeing, cross-country skiing, and bird-watching, and a natural pond for swimming. The five simply furnished guest rooms have twin, double, or king-sized beds. One room can accommodate three people. There are two shared baths. The house has a fireplace around which guests can gather and TV is available. Breakfast is served in the old-fashioned, eat-in kitchen. Area activities include antiquing and climbing Mt. Monadnock. Fine restaurants are nearby. The host, a graduate of the University of Toronto and Cornell University, has traveled most of the world. Her interests include skiing, restoring old homes, and photography.

No. Rooms: 5	**Breakfast:** Continental
Singles: None	**S-Rates:** $25–$30 sb
Doubles: 5 sb	**D-Rates:** $50–$50 sb
Type: Private home	**Bldg:** 1850 colonial

Minimum Stay: none. **Credit Card(s) Accepted:** none. **Open:** May–Nov. No resident dogs. No dogs please. Cat in residence. No cats please. Nonsmoking host. Guests may not smoke in residence. Residence not appropriate for children. **Discounts:** none. Dutch, French, and German spoken.

Reservation Contact: Bed & Breakfast Registry Ltd., Gary Winget, Box 8174, St. Paul, MN 55108; 612–646–4238.

STRAFFORD

SOUTHEASTERN NEW HAMPSHIRE.

Near Rte. 101B.

This restored eighteenth-century colonial home is located in Bow Lake's completely unspoiled country setting. The lake provides boating, swimming, and fishing; in winter, cross-country skiing, snowmobiling, and snowshoeing are at your door. The house is about twenty-five minutes from the University of New Hampshire, Concord, and Portsmouth. Perhaps the most impressive characteristics of this 1780 home are the enclosed heated swimming pool and tennis courts. The five guest rooms, which share a bath, have a mixture of antique and contemporary furnishings. Three have double beds; one has a twin bed. Your hosts, an airline pilot and a flight attendant, are interested in Olympic-class bicycling, water sports, ice skating, and travel.

No. Rooms: 5	**Breakfast:** Continental
Singles: 1 sb	**S-Rates:** $55 sb
Doubles: 4 sb	**D-Rates:** $55 sb
Type: Private home	**Bldg:** 1780 colonial

Minimum Stay: none. **Credit Card(s) Accepted:** none. **Open:** all year. Dog in residence. No dogs please. Cat in residence. No cats please. Host smokes. Guests may smoke. Children welcome with restrictions. **Discounts:** none.

Reservation Contact: Pineapple Hospitality, Inc., Judy M. Mulford, 47 N. Second St., Suite 3A, New Bedford, MA 02740; 617–990–1696.

NEW JERSEY

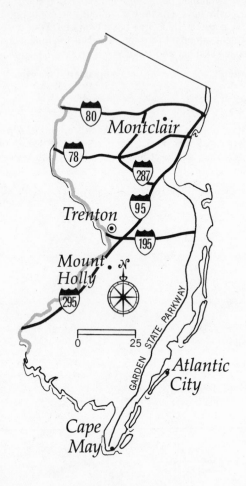

MOUNT HOLLY

ID: 08060ISA

DELAWARE VALLEY, 30 MINUTES FROM
PHILADELPHIA, TRENTON, FORT DIX & MCGUIRE AIR
FORCE BASE.

Near Rtes. 541 & 537, NJ Turnpike, U.S. 206.

This three-story Georgian house, Circa 1832, is steeped in history. The
house is within walking distance of the business district and government
buildings, and its location provides a pleasant getaway from Philadelphia
and Trenton. Mount Holly, the county seat, is enjoying a burst of revital-

ization through its efforts toward historic preservation. Four guest rooms are available. The Cottage has a double bed, antique furniture, a working fireplace, and framed antique quilt pieces. The Amish Room is furnished with a five-poster antique bed, marble dresser, a blanket chest, and Amish watercolors. A third room has a queen-sized canopy bed, a Queen Anne highboy, a captain's chest, and an 1840 tapestry. The Franklin Room is furnished with an antique spool bed, a Chippendale dresser, and a Franklin stove. A Continental Plus breakfast is served. The hosts are both involved in the field of education.

No. Rooms: 4	**Breakfast:** Continental Plus
Singles: 1 sb	**S-Rates:** $50–$55 pb, $45–$50 sb
Doubles: 1 pb, 2 sb	**D-Rates:** $60–$65 pb, $55–$60 sb
Type: Private Home	**Bldg:** 1832 Georgian

Minimum Stay: 2 days weekends. **Credit Card(s) Accepted:** none. **Open:** Summers, weekends Sept.–May. No resident dogs. No dogs please. No resident cats. No cats please. Nonsmoking host. Guests may not smoke in guest rooms. Children welcome. **Discounts:** long stays.

Reservation Contact: Bed & Breakfast Registry Ltd., Gary Winget, Box 8174, St. Paul, MN 55108; 612–646–4238.

RIDGEWOOD

ID: 07450GLE

MEADOWLANDS SPORTS AND RACING ARENA, GARDEN STATE ARTS CENTER; 35 MINUTES FROM NEW YORK CITY.

Near Glen & Maple aves., rtes. 3, 17.

With its tree-lined streets, this suburban community of 25,000 maintains the image of a village, yet it is only thirty-five minutes from New York via car or public transportation. Secaucus, a shoppers' paradise, with outlets for almost everything, is twenty minutes away, and the Meadowlands Sports and Racing Arena is twenty miles to the south. The two-story traditionally furnished Colonial home offers two air-conditioned guest rooms, (one with twin beds, one with a single bed) which share a guest bath. The second room, however, is used only for a third member of the same party. A Continental breakfast is served in the dining room or on a screened porch overlooking the heavily wooded backyard. Your hosts, who have lived and traveled in Europe and throughout the United States, enjoy cooking, tennis, racquetball, and sailing.

No. Rooms: 2	**Breakfast:** Continental
Singles: 1 sb	**S-Rates:** $40 sb
Doubles: 2 sb	**D-Rates:** $50 sb
Type: Private home	**Bldg:** Stone

Minimum Stay: none. **Credit Card(s) Accepted:** none. **Open:** all year. Dog is residence. No dogs please. No resident cats. No cats please. Nonsmoking host. Guests may smoke. Children welcome with restrictions. **Discounts:** none.

Reservation Contact: Bed & Breakfast Registry Ltd., Gary Winget, Box 8174, St. Paul, MN 55108; 612–646–4238.

NEW MEXICO

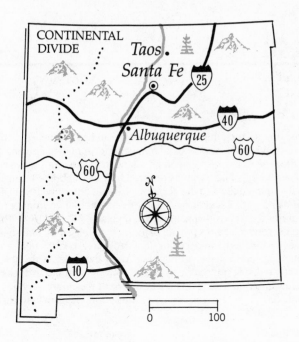

ALBUQUERQUE

ID: ROC–TRAFALG

HORSEBACK RIDING, HIKING, TENNIS, GOLF.

Near Tramway, McNaul, I–40, I–25.

This contemporary ranch house, in a very private setting on the outskirts of Albuquerque, is twenty minutes from downtown and historic Old Town. Completely furnished with English antiques, the residence features a lovely garden, two patios, swimming pool, and Jacuzzi. The guest room has a queen-sized bed, sun room and hot tub adjoining a private patio, and private bath. A Full breakfast is served. Your well-traveled British host enjoys bowling, racquetball, and swimming.

No. Rooms: 1	**Breakfast:** Full
Singles: None	**S-Rates:** $35 pb
Doubles: 1 pb	**D-Rates:** $45 pb
Type: Private home	**Bldg:** 1972 ranch

Minimum Stay: none. **Credit Card(s) Accepted:** none. **Open:** all year. Dog in residence. No dogs please. No resident cats. No cats please. Nonsmoking host. Guests may not smoke in guest rooms. Children welcome with restrictions. **Discounts:** weekly.

MESILLA

N.M.S.U., MESILLA PLAZA, GOLF, SWIMMING, BIKING.

Near I–10, I–25.

Situated on one acre, this inn is a miniresort offering a variety of activities. There is a swimming pool with a large patio for sunning, a putting green, horseshoes, and bicycles (including a tandem). The inn is a five-minute walk from Mesilla Plaza with its restored buildings and interesting shops, and a five-minute drive to the N.M.S.U. campus and downtown Las Cruces. Sunland Park Racetrack is a forty-five-minute drive from here. The inn features a parlor with a game table, fireplace, TV, and VCR. The thirteen guest rooms features private baths, and are elegantly furnished with antiques, brass beds, and ceiling fans. All have central heat and air-conditioning, and twelve rooms open onto balconies with tables and chairs for relaxing and enjoying the view. A Full gourmet breakfast is served in the atrium. There is also a gourmet restaurant serving classic Continental cuisine. Arrival/departure transportation from Las Cruces airport is available.

No. Rooms: 13	**Breakfast:** Full
Singles: 2 pb	**S-Rates:** $45 pb
Doubles: 11 pb	**D-Rates:** $50–$75 pb
Type: Inn	**Bldg:** 1985 southwestern pueblo

Minimum Stay: none. **Credit Card(s) Accepted:** AE, MC, V. **Open:** all year. Dog in residence. A dog is allowed with restrictions. No resident cats. No cats please. Nonsmoking host. Guests may smoke. Children are welcome with restrictions. **Discounts:** none.

Reservation Contact: Meson de Mesilla, Chuck Walker, 1803 Avenida De Mesilla, Box 1212, Mesilla, NM 88046; 505–525–9212.

SANTA FE

PLAZA AREA, SHOPS, RESTAURANTS.

Near I–25, NM 68.

Located within walking distance of the Plaza, galleries, shops, and restaurants, this Victorian inn offers six guest rooms with double, twin, or queen-sized beds. One of the options is a two-story carriage house with a double hide-a-bed, fireplace, queen-sized bed, antiques, wicker, and a kitchenette. Four of the rooms have private baths and two rooms share a bath. A Continental breakfast is served. Your host likes travel, the arts, and decorating.

No. Rooms: 6	**Breakfast:** Continental
Singles: None	**S-Rates:** $70–$110 pb, $55 sb
Doubles: 4 pb, 2 sb	**D-Rates:** $80–$115 pb, $65 sb
Type: Inn	**Bldg:** Victorian

Minimum Stay: none. **Credit Card(s) Accepted:** MC, V. **Open:** all year. No resident dogs. No dogs please. No resident cats. No cats please. Non-smoking host. Guests may not smoke in residence. Children welcome with restrictions. **Discounts:** none.

Reservation Contact: Bed & Breakfast Rocky Mountains, Kate Peterson Winters, Box 804, Colorado Springs, CO 80901; 719–630–3433.

ID: ROC–45

GALLERY AREA.

Near I–25, Canyon Rd.

This abobe-style house offers one guest room with wooden beams, kiva fireplace, hardwood floors, brass double bed, quilts, writing desk, and adjacent private bath with heated towel rack. A Full breakfast is served. The house is five minutes from the art galleries of Canyon Road and ten minutes from shops at the Plaza. Your host enjoys weaving, photography, interior design, and travel.

No. Rooms: 1	**Breakfast:** Full
Singles: None	**S-Rates:** $55 pb
Doubles: 1 pb	**D-Rates:** $65 pb
Type: Private home	**Bldg:** Adobe style

Minimum Stay: none. **Credit Card(s) Accepted:** MC, V. **Open:** all year. No resident dogs. No dogs please. Resident cat. No cats please. Host smokes. Guests may smoke in residence. Children welcome with restrictions. **Discounts:** none.

Reservation Contact: Bed & Breakfast Rocky Mountains, Kate Peterson Winters, Box 804, Colorado Springs, CO 80901; 719–630–3433.

ID: ROC–46

GALLERIES, SHOPS, HISTORIC SITES, TAOS PLAZA, TAOS PUEBLO, KIT CARSON STATE PARK, TAOS SKI VALLEY, ARTS FESTIVAL, WHITE-WATER RAFTING, INDIAN CELEBRATIONS.

Near U.S. 64, Rte. 3.

La Loma Plaza, a historic niche in the heart of Taos, is the secluded setting for this gracious old adobe home. The house was purchased in 1921 by

W. Herbert "Buck" Duton, one of the six founders of the Taos Art Society. He added a studio in which he worked until his death in 1936. The studio sign still remains. With its kiva fireplaces, beamed vigas, cedar latillas, and massive adobe walls, this home tastefully combines the ambiance and warmth of the past with modern conveniences. The enclosed garden patios, fragrant with lilacs in spring and summer, are surrounded by high adobe walls that preserve a sense of time and history, as well as privacy. Two guest suites with private baths are available. Suite A features an airy, expansive living room with wood-burning stove, color cable TV, a Persian rug, and contemporary works of art. The downstairs bedroom has a double bed, sunny windows, and greenery. The upstairs bedroom has a king-sized bed, expansive view of the Plaza and Taos Mountain, beside fireplace, and screened sun porch with lovely sunset views. Suite B offers a large warm living room, over a hundred years old, with a southwest decor. The bedroom, with double bed and fireplace, has a private entry to an enclosed patio. Candles and fresh flowers are always found in both suites. Breakfast includes a fruit plate, farm-fresh eggs, ham, bacon or sausage, homemade muffins, and freshly ground coffee. Arrival/departure transportation and dinners are available. Your host, a sculptor and a realtor, try to make each guest's stay a memorable one.

No. Rooms: 2	**Breakfast:** Full
Singles: None	**S-Rates:** $70 pb
Doubles: 2 pb	**D-Rates:** $70 pb
Type: Private home	**Bldg:** 1850s southwestern adobe

Minimum Stay: 2 days on weekends. **Credit Card(s) Accepted:** none. **Open:** all year. No resident dogs. No dogs please. No resident cats. No cats please. Host smokes. Guests may not smoke in guest rooms. Children welcome with restrictions. **Discounts:** weekly.

Reservation Contact: Bed & Breakfast-Rocky Mountains, Kate Peterson Winters, Box 804, Colorado Springs, CO 80901; 719–630–3433.

ID: ROC–55

TAOS MOUNTAIN.

Near S. Pueblo Dr., Rte. 64, Rte. 3.

This adobe-style house is located one mile from a historic plaza, within five minutes of Taos Pueblo, art galleries, restaurants, and Kit Carson State Park. Outdoor hot tub, TV in the common room, and patio and yard for guests' use are offered. Guests may also enjoy the main house with wood-beamed ceilings and fireplace. The three guest rooms, with fireplaces, adjoin the main house and are decorated with southwestern furniture, oils, lithographs, sculptures, and pottery. Each has twin beds that can be made into king-sized beds, individual thermostats, and a full view of Taos Mountain. One has a private bath, while the other two share a bath. A Continental breakfast is served.

No. Rooms: 4	**Breakfast:** Continental
Singles: None	**S-Rates:** $35–$75 pb, $30–$40 sb
Doubles: 2 pb, 2 sb	**D-Rates:** $52–$95 pb, $45–$58 sb
Type: Private home	**Bldg:** 1956 southwestern adobe

Minimum Stay: none. **Credit Card(s) Accepted:** none. **Open:** all year. No resident dogs. No dogs please. No resident cats. No cats please. Nonsmoking host. Guests may not smoke in residence. Children welcome. **Discounts:** none.

Reservation Contact: Bed & Breakfast-Rocky Mountains, Kate Peterson Winters, Box 804, Colorado Springs, CO 80901; 719–630–3433.

ID: ROC–68

SKIING, HIKING.

Near NM 68 & 3.

Situated in a rural residential area, this two hundred-year-old adobe-style home is located just five minutes from a shopping plaza. There are seven guest rooms with private baths. One room, decorated with Espinoza pieces and lovely art work, has a king-sized bed, hot tub, fireplace, and skylight. Another option is an apartment with a small kitchenette, double bed, queen-sized hide-a-bed, twin beds, and fireplaces. A third room, with a double bed, has a "courting balcony" and fireplace. A gourmet Full breakfast is served. Your host has an interest in the arts and travel.

No. Rooms: 7	**Breakfast:** Full
Singles: None	**S-Rates:** $50–$90 pb
Doubles: 7 pb	**D-Rates:** $55–$95 pb
Type: Inn	**Bldg:** 1788 Adobe

Minimum Stay: none. **Credit Card(s) Accepted:** MC, V. **Open:** all year. No resident dogs. No dogs please. Resident cats. No cats please. Nonsmoking host. Guests may smoke in common rooms. Children welcome. **Discounts:** none.

Reservation Contact: Bed & Breakfast Rocky Mountains, Kate Peterson Winters, Box 804, Colorado Springs, CO 80901; 719–630–3433.

NEW YORK

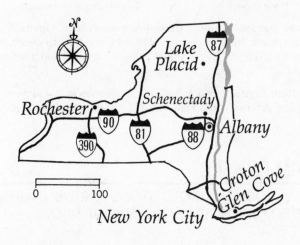

BLUEBERRY HILL

ID: LS-BLUEBERRY

REVERE COPPER & BRASS, HAMILTON COLLEGE,
S.U.N.Y. UTICA/ROME, GOLF; UTICA AREA;
HISTORICAL SITES, OUTLET AND ANTIQUE SHOPS.

Near I–90, Rte. 20.

This spacious Greek Revival house, built in 1828, is accented by rose-covered stone fences, gardens, and two hundred-year-old maple trees. Its sixty acres afford a spectacular view of the Mohawk Valley in all seasons, as well as an opportunity to walk or cross-country ski through wooded trails and view the wildlife on nearby ponds and streams. The furnishings are a combination of antique and traditional. One of the two guest rooms is a large, airy room overlooking mountains and valley, with king-sized bed, done in tones of beige and old rose; the second is done in yellow and white, with crisp curtains and Colonial-style twin beds. The rooms can be used as a suite since they have a connecting vanity. The cozy country kitchen, with exposed beams and a brick hearth fireplace, enhance the informal atmosphere while guests enjoy a delicious full breakfast. One of your hosts owns a wholesale-food distributing business, is a member of the school board, and collects antique bottles; the other is a homemaker and public-health nurse interested in the history of the Mohawk Valley and gardening. Frankfort Hill is convenient to all central New York Leatherstocking areas, historical sites, forts, museums, antique and outlet shops, fine restaurants, and several colleges.

No. Rooms: 2	**Breakfast:** Full
Singles: None	**S-Rates:** $40 pb, $35 sb
Doubles: 1 pb, 1 sb	**D-Rates:** $40 pb, $35 sb
Type: Private home	**Bldg:** 1828 Greek Revival

Minimum Stay: none. **Credit Card(s) Accepted:** none. **Open:** all year. Dog in residence. No dogs please. Cat in residence. No cats please. Non-smoking host. Guests may not smoke in guest rooms. Children welcome. **Discounts:** 10% weekly.

Reservation Contact: Bed & Breakfast Leatherstocking, Floranne Mc-Craith, 389 Brockway Rd., Frankfort, NY 13340; 315–733–0040.

COBLESKILL   ID: LS–GABLES

S.U.N.Y. COBLESKILL, OLD STONE FORT, BLENHEIM BRIDGE, SHARON SPRINGS; ANTIQUE SHOWS, CRAFT FAIRS.

Near W. Main St. & Washington Ave., I–88.

Built in 1880, this Victorian Gothic brick home and adjacent family homestead are located in the heart of the lovely village of Cobleskill. They boast unique architectural beauty, with Queen Anne towers, Gothic gables, and wood ornaments. Country warmth and charm with traditional and antique furnishings are enhanced by the creative display of crafts by local artists. Seven rooms with double or twin beds (one of which is a suite with private bath) are available. The other rooms share two baths. One of your hosts is an expert in food preservation, nutrition, and human development; the other is an economist and management consultant. The region offers the natural beauty of fertile valleys, majestic caverns, rolling hills, and much early architecture. The Old Stone Fort, originally a limestone church erected in 1772, was fortified during the Revolution and now houses an historical museum. The Blenheim Bridge is the world's longest single span wooden covered bridge of its kind. Nearby is the beautifully restored and furnished Lansing Manor House, built in 1819.

No. Rooms: 7	**Breakfast:** Continental
Singles: 1 sb	**S-Rates:** $70 pb, $35–$45 sb
Doubles: 1 pb, 5 sb	**D-Rates:** $70 pb, $45–$50 sb
Type: Inn	**Bldg:** 1880 Victorian Gothic

Minimum Stay: none. **Credit Card(s) Accepted:** MC, V. **Open:** all year. No resident dogs. No dogs please. No resident cats. No cats please. Non-smoking host. Guests may not smoke in guest rooms. Children welcome. **Discounts:** 10% weekly for seniors.

Reservation Contact: Bed & Breakfast Leatherstocking, Floranne Mc-Craith, 389 Brockway Rd., Frankfort, NY 13340; 315–733–0040.

CROTON-ON-HUDSON

ID: US–36

VAN CORTLANDT MANOR.

Near Rte. 9, Taconic Pkwy.

This large Victorian dwelling is set on a cliff overlooking the Hudson River. On the grounds are a small apple orchard and thirty-five-foot in-ground swimming pool. Municipal tennis courts are within walking distance, and the home is convenient to Van Cortlandt Manor. West Point is twenty minutes away, and New York City is accessible via the Metro North train. The house is furnished with many Victorian antiques and has a fireplace and a piano. Four guest rooms share two baths, offer double or twin beds, and antique furnishings. There is also a ground-level apartment with kitchen, bedroom with double bed, single hide-a-bed in the living room, and private bath; and a guest suite with a cast-iron bed, Hepplewhite armoire, cheval mirror, sitting room with fireplace and queen-sized sofa bed, and a private bath. A Full breakfast is served on the patio beside the pool or in the sun room. Bicycles, TV, off-street parking, and laundry facilities are available. Your host is a psychologist.

No. Rooms: 6	**Breakfast:** Full
Singles: None	**S-Rates:** $60 pb, $35 sb
Doubles: 2 pb, 4 sb	**D-Rates:** $60–$125 pb, $50 sb
Type: Private home	**Bldg:** 1889 Victorian

Minimum Stay: 2 nights on weekends.**Credit Card(s) Accepted:** none. **Open:** all year. No resident dogs. No dogs please. No resident cats. No cats please. Nonsmoking host. Guests may not smoke in residence. Children welcome with restrictions. **Discounts:** weekly. French spoken.

Reservation Contact: Bed & Breakfast U.S.A., Ltd., Barbara Notarius, Box 606, Croton-on-Hudson, NY 10520; 914–271–6228.

FAIRPORT

ID: ROCH.WOODS

ROCHESTER AREA, ANTIQUE SHOPS.

Near Rte. 31, I–90, NYS Thruway.

On the edge of the woods, this contemporary home offers peace and quiet, and deer and racoons can be seen among the trees. It is located in an area called Egypt, one of the earliest settlements in the county. Now, however, it has lost its identity and become part of Fairport and Perinton. Fairport, on the banks of the old Erie Canal, is a good area for antiques and auction lovers. The house is decorated with old country pine antiques that work well with the contemporary architecture. Amenities include a fireplace, TV, patio, air-conditioning, laundry facilities, and bicycles. Two guest rooms share a guest bath; the first is a large room with twin, antique pine beds, pine dresser, loveseat, and handwoven Mexican rug. An alcove contains a full-sized crib, and a small refrigerator is available. The other room, done with blue-green plaid wallpaper, has an antique pine double bed, two chests, a desk, and two comfortable chairs.

A room tucked into the upper level of the house can be used for extra guests, usually children. It has a queen-sized hide-a-bed and extra sofa and chairs. Guests are served a Full breakfast. Child care, dinner, and arrival/departure transportation are available. One of your hosts is a professor; the other is a Registry Service Organization manager. They like travel and have hosted many exchange students.

No. Rooms: 3	**Breakfast:** Full
Singles: None	**S-Rates:** $40 sb
Doubles: 3 sb	**D-Rates:** $45 sb
Type: Private home	**Bldg:** 1976 country contemporary

Minimum Stay: none. **Credit Card(s) Accepted:** none. **Open:** all year. No resident dogs. No dogs please. Cat in residence. No cats please. Non-smoking host. Guests may not smoke in residence. Children welcome. **Discounts:** none.

Reservation Contact: Bed & Breakfast Rochester, Beth Kinsman, Box 444, Fairport, NY 14450; 716–223–8877.

GLEN COVE
ID: LI–GCB

THEODORE ROOSEVELT'S HOME, N.Y. TECHNICAL INSTITUTE, C.W. POST UNIVERSITY, OYSTER BAY; OUTDOOR CONCERTS.

Near NY–107, Northern Blvd., Rte. 25A, I–495.

This huge Victorian house, with completely renovated ground-level quarters in stunning contemporary design with atria and large windowed walls, overlooks the exquisitely landscaped gardens, fish pond, and swimming pool. There are two guest rooms with private baths. One retains its Victorian charm, with papered floral walls in yellow and white,

brass double bed, Tiffany lamp, and loveseat. The second room has a country decor with scrubbed pine armoire, double bed, TV, and a magnificent black-and-white marble bathroom complete with bidet, heated towel racks, and lighted make-up mirror. Continental breakfast is served. The house, in an upper-middle-class area known for its Victorian homes, is one-and-a-half miles from the beach, two blocks from the Long Island Railroad, and close to Theodore Roosevelt's home in Sagamore Hill. Your French hosts, who designed and renovated part of the house and gardens, enjoy gourmet cooking.

No. Rooms: 2	**Breakfast:** Continental
Singles: None	**S-Rates:** $68–$72 pb
Doubles: 2 pb	**D-Rates:** $68–$72 pb
Type: Private home	**Bldg:** 1800s Victorian

Minimum Stay: none. **Credit Card(s) Accepted:** none. **Open:** Jan. 1 to Nov. 30. No resident dogs. No dogs please. No resident cats. No cats please. Nonsmoking host. Guests may not smoke in residence. **Discounts:** none. French spoken.

Reservation Contact: Bed & Breakfast of Long Island, Naomi Kavee, Box 392, Old Westbury, NY 11568; 516–334–6231.

KENMORE   ID: 14223EIS

NIAGARA FALLS, FORT ERIE, AMUSEMENT PARK, SCIENCE MUSEUM.

Near Rte. 384, I–290, I–90.

This attractive suburban home is conveniently located for area attractions. The guest room offers double bed plus double hide-a-bed and shared bath. You are welcome to use other rooms for TV and relaxation. A Full breakfast is served. Additional meals, arrival/departure transportation, area tours, and child care are available. Your hosts are interested in fishing, reading, gymnastics, music, and needlework.

No. Rooms: 1	**Breakfast:** Full
Singles: None	**S-Rates:** $30 sb
Doubles: 1 sb	**D-Rates:** $35 sb
Type: Private home	**Bldg:** Tudor

Minimum Stay: none. **Credit Card(s) Accepted:** none. **Open:** all year, except Christmas. No resident dogs. No dogs please. No resident cats. A cat is allowed with restrictions. Nonsmoking host. Guests may not smoke in residence. Children welcome. **Discounts:** none.

Reservation Contact: Bed & Breakfast Registry Ltd., Gary Winget, Box 8174, St. Paul, MN 55108; 612–646–4238.

LAKE PLACID

ID: 12946INT

SKI AREAS, BOBSLEDDING, SKATING, SWIMMING, SAILING, HIKING, GOLF, JOHN BROWN FARM, SANTA'S WORKSHOP.

Near Mirror Lake Dr., Hwy. 86.

This small lodge, with country atmosphere, sits on a hill between Mirror Lake and Lake Placid in the beautiful Adirondack Mountains area. The twelve guest rooms have twin and double beds; some have balconies, terraces, or scenic views. All have private baths. For families, there is a two-room suite separated by French doors and opening to a private terrace. A Full breakfast is served in the dining room; Continental breakfast is available in your room. You may mingle or watch TV in the main sitting room with fireplace. Area tours and childcare are available; special packages are available for golf, sailing, and skiing.

No. Rooms: 12	**Breakfast:** Full
Singles: None	**S-Rates:** $47–$67 pb
Doubles: 12 pb	**D-Rates:** $70–$130 pb
Type: Inn	**Bldg:** 1906 Victorian

Minimum Stay: special weekends. **Credit Card(s) Accepted:** MC, V. **Open:** all year. No dogs please. No cats please. Guests may smoke. Children welcome. **Discounts:** weekly.

Reservation Contact: Bed & Breakfast Registry Ltd., Gary Winget, Box 8174, St. Paul, MN 55108; 612–646–4238.

LITTLE VALLEY

ID: 14755NAP

CHAUTAUQUA AREA, ALLEGANY STATE PARK, HOLIDAY VALLEY SKI AREA, COCKAIGNE SKI AREA, SENECA-IROQUOIS NATIONAL MUSEUM.

Near rtes. 242 & 353, 17.

This beautifully renovated one-hundred-fifty-five-year-old former stagecoach inn is set on early east-west pioneer route in a hilly, scenic area of western New York. It is located on seven-and-half acres with fruit-producing orchards. The house offers a family room with fireplace and a well-stocked library. The three guest rooms have twin, single, or double beds, easy chairs, and night stands and share a guest bath. One of the rooms opens onto an upstairs porch. A Full breakfast is served in either the dining room, family room, or kitchen, or on the patio in summer. Your hosts are interested in cooking, sewing, antiques, and ceramics. Additional meals, arrival/departure transportation, and area tours are available.

No. Rooms: 3
Singles: 1 sb
Doubles: 2 sb
Type: Private home.

Breakfast: Full
S-Rates: $25 sb
D-Rates: $35 sb
Bldg: 1830 colonial

Minimum Stay: none. **Credit Card(s) Accepted:** none. **Open:** all year. No resident dogs. No dogs please. No resident cats. No cats please. Non-smoking host. Guests may not smoke in guest rooms. Children welcome with restrictions. **Discounts:** monthly.

Reservation Contact: Bed & Breakfast Registry Ltd., Gary Winget, Box 8174, St. Paul, MN 55108; 612–646–4238.

MANHASSET
ID: LI–SM

JONES BEACH, HEMPSTEAD HARBOR.

Near I–495, L.I. Expressway, Northern Blvd.

Built in 1840, this colonial building is one of the oldest in the area. It boasts a huge dining room with three chandeliers, original carved fire-place, and a table that can comfortably seat 30. There are four air-conditioned guest rooms available, three with double beds and one with a single bed. There is also a sitting room with TV for guests to use. From this residence, guests can walk to the Long Island railroad or to local res-taurants and movies. A short ride takes one to quiet beaches and luxuri-ous shops and designer boutiques.

No. Rooms: 4
Singles: 1 pb
Doubles: 2 pb, 1 sb
Type: Private home

Breakfast: Continental Plus
S-Rates: $65 pb
D-Rates: $70–$75 pb, $70 sb
Bldg: 1840 colonial

Minimum Stay: none. **Credit Card(s) Accepted:** none. **Open:** all year. No resident dogs. No dogs please. No resident cats. No cats please. Non-smoking host. Guests may not smoke in residence. Children welcome. **Discounts:** monthly.

Reservation Contact: Bed & Breakfast of Long Island, Naomi Kavee, Box 392, Old Westbury, NY 11568; 516–334–6231.

MATTITUCK, LONG ISLAND

ID: 11952MAT

LONG ISLAND, BOATING, BEACHES, THEATER, SHOPPING, WINERIES.

Near NY 25 & Love Ln.

This spacious Queen Anne home, located on Long Island's North Fork, offers easy access to many public beaches. Unlike the South Fork, the largely undeveloped North Fork has many farms and wineries (available for tours). Mattituck itself contains a library, theater, churches, a general store that offers old-fashioned shopping, and a boating inlet in the center of town. The house sits on a stunning piece of property beautifully landscaped with a variety of evergreens, holly trees, and assorted perennials. Guests can enjoy the serenity of the surroundings on the wraparound porch. Meticulously restored and furnished with American antiques, the house makes a wonderful retreat. There are seven guest rooms, two with queen-sized beds, three with double beds, and two with single beds. One of the rooms, furnished with an inlaid, freestanding full-length mirror and velvet drapes in beige, burgundy, and green, has a private bath. Another room, furnished with two Victorian wing chairs upholstered with a beautiful tapestry fabric, provides a separate dressing room. A third room offers lovely views of the gardens, and one of the single rooms contains some attractive artwork and a hundred-year-old bureau. Guests are served Continental breakfast in the main parlor furnished with cafe tables and chairs. The house is convenient to both the Mattituck stations of the Long Island Rail Road and the Sunrise Bus Line which run directly to and from midtown Manhattan. Arrival/departure transportation and area tours are available.

No. Rooms: 7	**Breakfast:** Continental
Singles: 2 sb	**S-Rates:** $70–$75 pb, $60–$65 sb
Doubles: 2 pb, 3 sb	**D-Rates:** $80–$85 pb, $70–$75 sb
Type: Public inn	**Bldg:** 1907 Queen Anne Victorian

Minimum Stay: none. **Credit Card(s) Accepted:** none. **Open:** all year. No resident dogs. No dogs please. No resident cats. No cats please. Guests may not smoke in guest rooms. Children welcome. **Discounts:** 10% weekly.

Reservation Contact: Bed & Breakfast Registry Ltd., Gary Winget, Box 8174, St. Paul, MN 55108; 612–646–4238.

MAYVILLE

ID: 14725MIC

CHAUTAUQUA INSTITUTE, GOLF, SWIMMING, BOATING.

Near Rte. 17, I–90.

This attractive home with well-manicured lawn features canal-front property leading to Chautauqua Lake and large enclosed porch. Three guest rooms, all with twin beds, share a bath. Continental breakfast is served. Your hosts are interested in travel, sewing, teaching, and handiwork.

No. Rooms: 3	**Breakfast:** Continental
Singles: 1 sb	**S-Rates:** $30 sb
Doubles: 2 sb	**D-Rates:** $35 sb
Type: Private Home	**Bldg:** Cottage

Minimum Stay: none. **Credit Card(s) Accepted:** none. **Open:** all year. No resident dogs. A dog is allowed with restrictions. No resident cats. A cat is allowed with restrictions. Nonsmoking host. Guests may not smoke in residence. Children welcome. **Discounts:** none.

Reservation Contact: Bed & Breakfast Registry Ltd., Gary Winget, Box 8174, St. Paul, MN 55108; 612–646–4238.

NEW YORK CITY

ID: N.WORLD#1

WASHINGTON SQUARE, COOPER UNION, NEW YORK UNIVERSITY, THE NEW SCHOOL FOR SOCIAL RESEARCH, MAC DOUGAL ALLEY, WASHINGTON MEWS; GREENWICH VILLAGE.

Near Bleecker St. & 7th Ave.

Greenwich Village is one of the most charming and neighborly areas of the city, filled with sidewalk cafés, quaint little restaurants, boutiques, and delicatessens galore. From Washington Square North, visitors can see the fine old homes from Henry James' days; there are blocks upon blocks of wonderful townhouses. This guest room is in an 1890s Queen Anne revival building on a tree-lined street in the heart of the historic district. The apartment has been completely renovated with exposed brick walls, refinished wood trim, and antique pressed tin ceilings. The room has a double bed, TV, air-conditioning, and a western exposure with a view of the local rooftops. Transportation is excellent with the #1 subway and the 8th Avenue and crosstown M-13 bus. Your host, a music scholar and world traveler, has an interest in historic renovation and is very knowledgeable about village history and New York attractions.

No. Rooms: 1	Breakfast: Continental
Singles: None	S-Rates: $50 sb
Doubles: 1 sb	D-Rates: $65 sb
Type: Private apartment	Bldg: 1890s Queen Anne revival

Minimum Stay: 2 nights. **Credit Card(s) Accepted:** none. **Open:** all year. No resident dogs. No dogs please. Cat in residence. No cats please. Nonsmoking host. Guests may smoke. Residence not appropriate for children. **Discounts:** none.

Reservation Contact: New World Bed & Breakfast, Laura Tilden, 150 5th Avenue, #711, New York, NY 10011; 212–675–5600/ 800–443–3800.

ID: N.WORLD#2

RESTAURANTS, CABARETS, ART GALLERIES; NEAR CHINATOWN, TRIBECA.

Near West Broadway & Canal St., Holland Tunnel.

Originally a warehouse district north of City Hall, TriBeCa (Triangle Below Canal) is now the newest art colony in New York City, populated by those driven out of SoHo by rising rents. It offers large loft spaces, with lots of windows, light, and air, as well as restaurants, cabarets, and art galleries. This is an area tourists rarely get to know but one which New Yorkers value as an eclectic district close to Chinatown and SoHo. This guest room is large and sunny, with a double bed and a mixture of modern and antique wood furniture, typical of artists' loft spaces. An early settler of the area, your host, in fashion merchandising is well-traveled, friendly, and informed about the area.

No. Rooms: 1	Breakfast: Continental
Singles: None	S-Rates: $60 sb
Doubles: 1 sb	D-Rates: $75 sb
Type: Private loft	Bldg: 1890s

Minimum Stay: 2 nights. **Credit Card(s) accepted:** none. **Open:** all year. No resident dogs. No dogs please. No resident cats. No cats please. Nonsmoking host. Guests may smoke. Children welcome with restrictions. **Discounts:** none.

Reservation Contact: New World Bed & Breakfast, Laura Tilden, 150 5th Avenue, #711, New York, NY 10011; 212–675–5600/ 800–443–3800.

INEXPENSIVE RESTAURANTS, UNUSUAL CABARETS, ART GALLERIES; EAST VILLAGE.

Near 1st Ave. & 10th St., FDR Dr.

The East Village is a conglomeration of Hispanics, Ukranians, punk rockers, and artists—the new Bohemia. There are unusual clothing stores, boutiques with leather goods and jewelry, record stores, a wide variety of good, inexpensive restaurants, unusual cabarets and art galleries, and two spectacular Italian bakeries. The neighborhood is exciting and vibrant but probably best appreciated by the more adventurous traveler. This 1860s late Greek Revival house has three guest rooms that offer simple homey old-fashioned basics with a shared guest bath. One of the rooms has a single bed, one has twin beds, and one has a double bed. Your host assures spotlessly clean and comfortable surroundings for guests and serves a full breakfast. She is a native New Yorker who knows her neighborhood well and loves her city. She can also be very helpful with budget travel tips for city visitors.

No. Rooms: 3	**Breakfast:** Full
Singles: 1 sb	**S-Rates:** $40 sb
Doubles: 2 sb	**D-Rates:** $60 sb
Type: Private Home	**Bldg:** 1860s late Greek Revival

Minimum Stay: 2 nights. **Credit Card(s) Accepted:** none. **Open:** all year. No resident dogs. No dogs please. Cat in residence. No cats please. Nonsmoking host. Guests may not smoke in residence. Children welcome with restrictions. **Discounts:** none.

Reservation Contact: New World Bed & Breakfast, Laura Tilden, 150 5th Avenue, #711, New York, NY 10011; 212–675–5600/ 800–443–3800.

ANTIQUE SHOPS, NEW YORK UNIVERSITY, ASTOR PLACE THEATER, COOPER UNION, CAFÉS; GREENWICH VILLAGE.

Near Broadway & 11th St.

A huge artist's loft space, this accommodation is special and deluxe in every way. The guest room is very private with a full wall of closets, king-sized brass bed, several plants, sixteen-foot ceiling, and private bath with sunken tub and bidet. It is on a street lined with antique shops, just three blocks from New York University. Your French host, a professional artist, has traveled extensively and understands the needs of travelers for privacy and comfort.

No. Rooms: 1

Singles: None

Doubles: 1 pb

Type: Private loft

Breakfast: Continental

S-Rates: $75

D-Rates: $90 pb

Bldg: 1890s

Minimum Stay: 2 nights. **Credit Card(s) Accepted:** none. **Open:** Sept. 1 to June 30. No resident dogs. No dogs please. No resident cats. No cats please. Nonsmoking host. Guests may smoke. Residence not appropriate for children. **Discounts:** none. French spoken.

Reservation Contact: New World Bed & Breakfast, Laura Tilden, 150 5th Avenue, #711, New York, NY 10011; 212–675–5600/ 800–443–3800.

ID: N.WORLD#6

CENTRAL PARK, LINCOLN CENTER, BROADWAY THEATERS, VISITORS' INFORMATION OFFICE, SHOPPING, RESTAURANTS; MIDTOWN WEST AT COLUMBUS CIRCLE.

Near Broadway & 59th St., Lincoln Tunnel.

This luxury high-rise with doorman is perfectly located for travelers with business along Corporate Row. It is close to many things visitors love about New York. Central Park is across the street, Lincoln Center is six blocks away, the Visitors' Information Office is on the corner, and Broadway theaters are three blocks away. Fine stores and restaurants abound. The guest room is large and sunny with a western exposure, king-sized bed, and large closet. Your friendly and helpful host is a self-employed consultant and world traveler who makes frequent trips to England.

No. Rooms: 1

Singles: None

Doubles: 1 sb

Type: Private apartment

Breakfast: Continental

S-Rates: $65 pb

D-Rates: $80 pb

Bldg: 1950s modern luxury

Minimum Stay: 2 nights. **Credit Card(s) Accepted:** none. **Open:** all year. No resident dogs. No dogs please. No resident cats. No cats please. Host smokes. Guests may smoke. Children welcome. **Discounts:** none.

Reservation Contact: New World Bed & Breakfast, Laura Tilden, 150 5th Avenue, #711, New York, NY 10011; 212–675–5600/ 800–443–3800.

ID: N.WORLD#8

COLUMBIA UNIVERSITY, MUSEUM OF NATURAL HISTORY, HAYDEN PLANETARIUM, RIVERSIDE CHURCH; UPPER WEST SIDE.

Near 93rd & Central Park W., Hudson Pkwy.

This well-located apartment building with twenty-four-hour doorman is opposite Central Park. It is near Columbia University, the Museum of Natural History, Hayden Planetarium, and eclectic shopping and dining establishments along Columbus Avenue. The apartment has a quiet charm and casual and comfortable atmosphere. The guest room offers twin beds, air-conditioning, TV, and private bath. Continental breakfast is served in a lovely nook. Your hosts are a hospitable couple with varied interests.

No. Rooms: 1
Singles: None
Doubles: 1 pb
Type: Private apartment

Breakfast: Continental
S-Rates: $65 pb
D-Rates: $75 pb
Bldg: 1930s modern

Minimum Stay: 2 nights. **Credit Card(s) Accepted:** none. **Open:** all year. No resident dogs. No dogs please. No resident cats. No cats please. Nonsmoking host. Guests may smoke. Children welcome. **Discounts:** none.

Reservation Contact: New World Bed & Breakfast, Laura Tilden, 150 5th Avenue, #711, New York, NY 10011; 212–675–5600/ 800–443–3800.

ID: N.WORLD#10

GUGGENHEIM, COOPER-HEWITT, JEWISH, METROPOLITAN MUSEUMS, INTERNATIONAL CENTER OF PHOTOGRAPHY, GRACIE MANSION; UPPER EAST SIDE.

Near 86th St. & 2d Ave.

The Yorkville area of the Upper East Side is a traditional German neighborhood, with good restaurants, lovely side streets, and excellent transportation. It is an easy walk to East River Park and Gracie Mansion, the mayor's home. This apartment, in a high-rise building, is very secure, with a twenty-four hour doorman. The one available guest room, furnished as a den, has two twin beds, TV, stereo, air-conditioning, and private bath. It provides a great view in a beautiful setting. Your charming host, a high-school teacher, will give you a warm welcome.

No. Rooms: 1
Singles: None
Doubles: 1 pb
Type: Private apartment

Breakfast: Continental
S-Rates: $60 pb
D-Rates: $75 pb
Bldg: 1970s modern high rise

Minimum Stay: none. **Credit Card(s) Accepted:** none. **Open:** all year. No resident dogs. No dogs please. No resident cats. No cats please. Non-smoking host. Guests may not smoke in residence. Children welcome with restrictions. **Discounts:** none.

Reservation Contact: New World Bed & Breakfast, Laura Tilden, 150 5th Ave., #711, New York, NY 10011; 212–675–5600/ 800–443–3800.

ID: N.WORLD#11

CENTRAL PARK SOUTH, LINCOLN CENTER, CARNEGIE HALL, ROCKEFELLER CENTER, 5TH AVE. SHOPPING.

Near 59th St. & 7th Ave.

This modern apartment building situated across from Central Park is two blocks from Carnegie Hall and Fifth Avenue shopping and four blocks from Broadway theaters. With the business person in mind, the guest room is complete with desk, telephone, single bed, and private bath. Your hosts, who are in the garment business, are knowledgeable about the city.

No. Rooms: 1	**Breakfast:** Continental
Singles: 1 pb	**S-Rates:** $65 pb
Doubles: None	**Bldg:** Modern apartment
Type: Private home	

Minimum Stay: 2 nights. **Credit Card(s) Accepted:** none. **Open:** all year. No resident dogs. No dogs please. Resident cat. No cats please. Nonsmoking host. Guests may not smoke in residence. Residence is not appropriate for children. **Discounts:** none.

Reservation Contact: New World Bed & Breakfast, Laura Tilden, 150 5th Ave., #711, New York, NY 10011; 212–675–5600/ 800–443–3800.

ID: N.WORLD#12

LINCOLN CENTER, CENTRAL PARK, TAVERN ON THE GREEN.

Near Broadway & 66th St.

You'll have a spectacular view of the Manhattan skyline from this 46th-floor apartment. Central Park and the excellent shops and restaurants of Columbus Ave. are less than two blocks away. The guest room has a double bed, modern furnishings, and private bath. Your hosts, originally from Germany, have traveled extensively.

No. Rooms: 1	Breakfast: Continental
Singles: None	S-Rates: $70 pb
Doubles: 1 pb	D-Rates: $85 pb
Type: Private home	Bldg: Skyscraper.

Minimum Stay: 2 nights. **Credit Card(s) Accepted:** none. **Open:** all year. No resident dogs. No dogs please. No resident cats. No cats please. Nonsmoking host. Guests may smoke in residence. Children welcome. **Discounts:** none. German spoken.

Reservation Contact: New World Bed & Breakfast, Laura Tilden, 150 5th Ave., #711, New York, NY 10011; 212–675–5600/ 800–443–3800.

ID: US–037

WEST SIDE, RIVERSIDE PARK.

Near Riverside Dr., low 70s.

On the West Side near Riverside Park two unhosted apartments are available in an 1886 townhouse. One has a double bed, love seat, and marble bath. The other has a queen-sized bed plus a small hide-a-bed and a fantastic view. Both apartments are stocked for a Continental breakfast.

No. Rooms: 2	Breakfast: Continental
Singles: None	S-Rates: $100 pb
Doubles: 2 pb	D-Rates: $110 pb
Type: Unhosted apartment	Bldg: Townhouse

Minimum Stay: 2 nights. **Credit Card(s) Accepted:** MC, V. **Open:** all year. No resident dogs. No dogs please. No resident cats. No cats please. Guests may smoke in residence. Children welcome. **Discounts:** none.

Reservation Contact: Bed & Breakfast U.S.A., Ltd., Barbara Notarius, Box 606, Croton-on-Hudson, NY 10520; 914–271–6228.

ID: 1CITYLIGHTS

UPPER EAST SIDE.

Near 85th St., First Ave.

This four-story townhouse on the Upper East Side is a haven of grace and hospitality. The second-floor living room is decorated with rare Chinese antiques, delicate silk sofas, an intricately carved coffee table, and has an imposing wood-burning fireplace and tall French windows flanked by palms. The guest suite comprises two bedrooms, two baths, a living room with queen-sized sofa bed, and kitchen facilities for light snacks. One of the bedrooms has a double bed and the other, which faces the garden, has a queen-sized bed. There is also a wood-burning fireplace and an adjoining dressing room. A third room features a king-sized circular bed, wood-burning fireplace, dressing room, and bath. A Continental breakfast is served. Your host is an English lady in the theater. This extraordinary accommodation is located in one of Manhattan's most exclusive areas and is convenient to transportation, museums, restaurants, and Gracie Mansion.

No. Rooms: 3	**Breakfast:** Continental
Singles: None	**S-Rates:** $60–$175 pb
Doubles: 3 pb	**D-Rates:** $65–$175 pb
Type: Private home	**Bldg:** Townhouse.

Minimum Stay: none. **Credit Card(s) Accepted:** none. **Open:** all year. No resident dogs. No dogs please. No resident cats. No cats please. Nonsmoking host. Guests may not smoke. Children welcome with restrictions. **Discounts:** none.

Reservation Contact: City Lights Bed & Breakfast, Ltd., Dee Staff, Box 20355, Cherokee Station, New York, NY 10028; 212–737–7049.

ID: 2CITYLIGHTS

CENTRAL PARK, TAVERN ON THE GREEN, CARNEGIE HALL, COLISEUM, 57TH ST. GALLERIES.

Near 57th St., 8th Ave.

Situated in the heart of Manhattan is this oversized, beautifully appointed studio apartment. It consists of sitting room, dining area, full kitchen, queen-sized bed, TV, stereo, telephone, and an incomparable view of Central Park. The luxurious high-rise building features health-club facilities with swimming pool and tennis courts on the roof. There is also twenty-four hour doorman service and a concierge. The apartment is unhosted, but items for a Continental breakfast are stocked. From this location, guests can enjoy Central Park's summer theater, concerts, and winter skating. The theater district is within walking distance as are the 57th Street galleries, Lincoln Center, and wonderful Fifth Avenue stores. For nearby deluxe dining there are two landmark restaurants, The Russian Tea Room and Tavern-on-the-Green. The apartment's owner is a well-traveled television executive who enjoys music, literature, theater, and sports.

No. Rooms: 1	**Breakfast:** Continental
Singles: None	**S-Rates:** $100 pb
Doubles: 1 pb	**D-Rates:** $145 pb
Type: Private apartment	**Bldg:** 1980s luxury high rise.

Minimum Stay: 2 nights. **Credit Card(s) Accepted:** none. **Open:** all year. No resident dogs. No dogs please. No resident cats. No cats please. Nonsmoking host. Guests may not smoke in residence. Children welcome. **Discounts:** none. French & Spanish spoken.

Reservation Contact: City Lights Bed & Breakfast, Ltd., Dee Staff, Box 20355, Cherokee Station, New York, NY 10028; 212–737–7049.

OFF-BROADWAY THEATER, NEW YORK UNIVERSITY, ART GALLERIES, OUTDOOR CAFS, WASHINGTON SQUARE.

Near Barrow St.

This apartment is in a neighborhood typical of Greenwich Village, with interesting old townhouses and brownstones. One can even find a stable used in Revolutionary times that is now an elegant home. Within walking distance are off-Broadway theaters, art galleries, dance studios, outdoor cafés, and New York University. The apartment is delightfully "villagey" both inside and out. Guests use a double hide-a-bed when the apartment is hosted; unhosted there is also a bedroom with double bed. A Continental breakfast is served. Your hospitable and interesting host is a freelance writer who has traveled extensively.

No. Rooms: 1	**Breakfast:** Continental
Singles: None	**S-Rates:** $55 sb
Doubles: 1 sb	**D-Rates:** $65 sb
Type: Private apartment	**Bldg:** Victorian

Minimum Stay: 2 nights. **Credit Card(s) Accepted:** none. **Open:** all year. No resident dogs. No dogs please. No resident cats. No cats please. Nonsmoking host. Guests may not smoke in guest rooms. Children welcome with restrictions. **Discounts:** none. German & French spoken.

Reservation Contact: City Lights Bed & Breakfast, Ltd., Dee Staff, Box 20355, Cherokee Station, New York, NY 10028; 212–737–7049.

UPPER WEST SIDE.

Near Riverside Dr., 84th St.

This lovely pre-war building is reminiscent of the elegance of a bygone era. The elevator has an ornate brass door and attendant, and the building has a doorman. Via the Broadway bus, the location is very accessible to the theater district and Lincoln Center, and the building boasts many celebrities. Three blocks to the south is *Zabar's,* a delicatessen known for gourmet delicacies from every corner of the globe. On Sunday mornings, theatrical and literary celebrities as well as plain folk can be found crowded around the various counters purchasing lox, bagels, and other choice morsels for Sunday brunch. The eleventh-floor apartment overlooks a tree-lined street of brownstones. It is comfortably furnished and has one large guest room with double bed and private adjacent bath. A Continental breakfast is served. Your unusually gracious and hospitable host is a university administrator who has traveled extensively.

No. Rooms: 1	**Breakfast:** Continental
Singles: None	**S-Rates:** $60 pb
Doubles: 1 pb	**D-Rates:** $70 pb
Type: Private apartment	**Bldg:** Pre-War

Minimum Stay: 2 nights. **Credit Card(s) Accepted:** none. **Open:** all year. No resident dogs. No dogs please. No resident cats. Nonsmoking host. Guests may not smoke in guest rooms. Children welcome. **Discounts:** over 10 nights. French & German spoken.

Reservation Contact: City Lights Bed & Breakfast, Ltd., Dee Staff, Box 20355, Cherokee Station, New York, NY 10028; 212–737–7049.

ID: 5CITYLIGHTS

JACOB JAVITS CONVENTION CENTER; CHELSEA AREA.

Near 23rd St., 8th Ave.

From this air-conditioned pre-war co-op apartment, one can walk north to the Jacob Javits Convention Center or south to historic Gramercy Park and Greenwich Village. The sunny apartment is furnished with a combination of rare antiques and fine contemporary pieces. You are welcome to relax in the living room. The guest room is done in pastel colors, and the double bed is a comfortable futon on a platform, creating a unique use of space. There is also a loveseat. A Continental breakfast is served; guests also have kitchen privileges. Child care is available. The "Hollywood" bathroom features double sinks and a Jacuzzi. Your extremely gracious host is a fashion editor for a well-known journal. Her hobbies include horseback riding and clothing and jewelry design.

No. Rooms: 1	**Breakfast:** Continental
Singles: None	**S-Rates:** $55 sb
Doubles: 1 sb	**D-Rates:** $65 sb
Type: Private apartment	**Bldg:** Pre-War

Minimum Stay: 2 nights. **Credit Card(s) Accepted:** none. **Open:** all year. No resident dogs. No dogs please. Cat in residence. No cats please. Nonsmoking host. Guests may not smoke in residence. Children welcome with restrictions. **Discounts:** after 10 days. French & Italian spoken.

Reservation Contact: City Lights Bed & Breakfast, Ltd., Dee Staff, Box 20355, Cherokee Station, New York, NY 10028; 212–737–7049.

ID: 6CITYLIGHTS

CENTRAL PARK, LINCOLN CENTER, CARNEGIE HALL, FIFTH AVE. SHOPPING, COLUMBUS CIRCLE.

Near Central Park S., 59th St.

This stretch along Central Park South is undoubtedly one of New York's finest locations. Just outside this pre-war, doorman apartment building you will find horse-drawn carriages, perfect for a leisurely ride through the park and down Fifth Avenue. Carnegie Hall, Lincoln Center, and the stores along Fifth Avenue are only a walk away. You can also get pamphlets and advice from the New York Convention and Visitors Bureau at Columbus Circle. The apartment offers a sense of charm and grace, with sculpture, rare art, and antique collections. The guest room features electrically controlled twin beds that together form a king-sized bed, color TV, and private bath. A Continental breakfast is served in the beautiful dining room overlooking Central Park. Your host, a highly cultivated philanthropist, is well traveled and very gracious.

No. Rooms: 1	**Breakfast:** Continental
Singles: None	**S-Rates:** $75 pb
Doubles: 1 pb	**D-Rates:** $85 pb
Type: Private apartment	**Bldg:** 1930s Pre-War

Minimum Stay: 2 nights. **Credit Card(s) Accepted:** none. **Open:** all year. No resident dogs. No dogs please. No resident cats. No cats please. Nonsmoking host. Guests may not smoke in guest rooms. Children welcome with restrictions. **Discounts:** after 10 nights. German & French spoken.

Reservation Contact: City Lights Bed & Breakfast, Ltd., Dee Staff, Box 20355, Cherokee Station, New York, NY 10028; 212–737–7049.

ID: 7CITYLIGHTS

METROPOLITAN MUSEUM OF ART, WHITNEY MUSEUM, GUGGENHEIM MUSEUM, FRICK COLLECTION; UPPER EAST SIDE.

Near 79th St., 2nd Ave.

This deluxe pre-war co-op apartment, with doorman and elevator attendant, is within walking distance of many major art museums, Central Park, shops, and restaurants featuring every imaginable type of cuisine. Three blocks to the east, guests will come upon the East River, where they can walk along the promenade and watch the boats pass. A few blocks to the north is Gracie Mansion, the mayor's residence. The air-conditioned apartment is furnished with antiques and collectibles from the world over and early-American and Degas prints. The spacious, bright and airy guest room, is furnished with a queen-sized bed with hand-carved Victorian headboard and handmade quilt, an exquisite Queen Anne desk, antique chest, round and drop-leaf tables, hurricane lamps, and antique window shutters. A cot is also available. A Continental breakfast is served. Your host, who teaches at a well-known theater academy, enjoys taking guests on a tour of the city when time permits. She is well-traveled and her interests include the arts, horses, and literature.

No. Rooms: 1	**Breakfast:** Continental
Singles: None	**S-Rates:** $55 sb
Doubles: 1 sb	**D-Rates:** $65 sb
Type: Private apartment	**Bldg:** 1930s Pre-War

Minimum Stay: 2 nights. **Credit Card(s) Accepted:** none. **Open:** all year. No resident dogs. No dogs please. No resident cats. No cats please. Host smokes. Guests may smoke. Children welcome. **Discounts:** after 10 nights. Spanish & Hebrew spoken.

Reservation Contact: City Lights Bed & Breakfast, Ltd., Dee Staff, Box 20355, Cherokee Station, New York, NY 10028; 212–737–7049.

ID: 8CITYLIGHTS

MUSEUM OF NATURAL HISTORY, HAYDEN PLANETARIUM, NEW YORK HISTORICAL SOCIETY, CENTRAL PARK; UPPER WEST SIDE.

Near 81st St., Columbus Ave.

The entire street is lined with eighteenth- and nineteenth-century brownstones and townhouses recently refurbished and gentrified. The old wood, glass, and brass have had their original shine restored. This Victorian brownstone offers a self-contained air-conditioned studio apartment, with fully equipped kitchen and terrace overlooking the garden. It is furnished in an electic manner, with some antiques, TV, telephone, fireplace, and a queen-sized platform bed. The family occupies the other two floors of the house. Items for a Continental breakfast are provided. From the apartment, you can walk to the Museum of Natural History, Hayden Planetarium, and Central and Riverside parks. Your host is an interior designer and real-estate broker with interests in the arts and sports.

No. Rooms: 1	**Breakfast:** Continental
Singles: None	**S-Rates:** $95 pb
Doubles: 1 pb	**D-Rates:** $95 pb
Type: Private townhouse	**Bldg:** 1800s Victorian

Minimum Stay: 2 nights. **Credit Card(s) Accepted:** none. **Open:** all year. Nonsmoking host. Guests may smoke. Children welcome with restrictions. **Discounts:** none.

Reservation Contact: City Lights Bed & Breakfast, Ltd., Dee Staff, Box 20355, Cherokee Station, New York, NY 10028; 212–737–7049.

GRACIE MANSION, GUGGENHEIM MUSEUM, JEWISH MUSEUM, COOPER-HEWITT MUSEUM; UPPER EAST SIDE.

Near 89th St., 1st Ave.

In this Victorian brownstone is a delightful guest room decorated in subtly coordinated Liberty of London prints, including the wall covering. The prints, coupled with fine English antiques, produce a cozy and elegant effect. The room has a double bed. Adjoining the guest room is an unusual balcony/library overlooking a rotunda-like dining area where Continental plus breakfast is served. The balcony is furnished with a sumptuous soft leather sofa, nestled into built-in bookshelves covering the entire wall. A large color TV is also available. Guests can walk to Gracie Mansion, several art museums, and alongside the East River. Catch the 86th Street bus for all points west or the 86th Street subway to Broadway. Your English hosts are most creative.

No. Rooms: 1	**Breakfast:** Continental
Singles: None	**S-Rates:** $60 pb
Doubles: 1 pb	**D-Rates:** $75 pb
Type: Private townhouse	**Bldg:** 1800s Victorian brownstone

Minimum Stay: 2 nights. **Credit Card(s) Accepted:** none. **Open:** all year. **Discounts:** none.

Reservation Contact: City Lights Bed & Breakfast, Ltd., Dee Staff, Box 20355, Cherokee Station, New York, NY 10028; 212–737–7049.

MUSEUM OF NATURAL HISTORY, HAYDEN PLANETARIUM; UPPER WEST SIDE.

Near Columbus Ave., West 80s.

This nicely refurbished apartment in a lovely old building is located in an exciting, recently gentrified area, with good transportation to Lincoln Center and the theater district. The apartment has a fireplace and is furnished with a medley of antiques, collectibles, and contemporary pieces. All the rooms are spacious and the color schemes interesting. The guest room has a double bed, white lacquered furniture, and private bath. A Continental breakfast is served. Your lively, intelligent host is an art collector and co-owner of an advertising agency.

No. Rooms: 1	**Breakfast:** Continental
Singles: 1 pb	**S-Rates:** $60 pb
Doubles: None	**D-Rates:** $70 pb
Type: Private apartment	**Bldg:** Turn-of-the-century

Minimum Stay: 2 nights. **Credit Card(s) Accepted:** none. **Open:** all year. No resident dogs. No dogs please. No resident cats. No cats please.

Nonsmoking host. Guests may not smoke in guest rooms. Residence is not appropriate for children. **Discounts:** none.

Reservation Contact: City Lights Bed & Breakfast, Ltd., Dee Staff, Box 20355, Cherokee Station, New York, NY 10028; 212–737–7049.

ID: 11CITYLIGHTS

GREENWICH VILLAGE.

Near University Pl. & 11th St.

Many 19th-century commercial buildings in Greenwich Village have been converted to artists' lofts. The guest room in this particular loft has 14-foot ceilings and is furnished, like the loft itself, with exquisite taste. As a centerpiece it has a king-sized bed covered with a custom-designed bedspread which subtly reflects the colors of the unit. The bathroom has a sumptuously tiled sunken bath flanked by delicate palms. The plank floors are covered with Oriental rugs and the walls are aquamarine color. To reach the guest room one passes through your host's studio filled with etchings, prints, paintings, and various tools of the trade. The kitchen, where a Continental Plus breakfast is served, is contemporary, a charming counterpoint to the 19-century architecture and decor. The loft is situated on a street filled with galleries, antique shops, boutiques, and restaurants.

No. Rooms: 1	**Breakfast:** Continental Plus
Singles: None	**S-Rates:** $65–$75
Double: 1 pb	**D-Rates:** $75–$85
Type: Private home	**Bldg:** Loft

Minimum Stay: none. **Credit Card(s) Accepted:** none. **Open:** all year. No resident dogs. No dogs please. No resident cats. No cats please. Nonsmoking host. Guests may not smoke in residence. Children welcome. **Discounts:** 10% for 8 or more nights.

Reservation Contact: City Lights Bed & Breakfast, Dee Staff, Box 20355, Cherokee Station, New York, NY 10028; 212–737–7049.

ID: 12CITYLIGHTS

WASHINGTON SQUARE, OFF-BROADWAY THEATER, SIDEWALK CAFÉS, NEW YORK UNIVERSITY, COOPER UNION, WASHINGTON MEWS, MAC DOUGAL ALLEY; GREENWICH VILLAGE.

Near 5th Ave., Washington Square Park.

This Washington Square restored townhouse has a modern exterior and elevator, but the interior retains its Victorian charm. The vast living room features high French windows, a wood-burning fireplace, and carefully selected antiques. When hosted, the apartment has one cozy guest room with single bed and shared bath. Unhosted, there are two single rooms plus a double hide-a-bed in the living room. A Continental breakfast is provided. Your host is a freelance writer. Midtown attractions are only minutes away via the subway, and there are also convenient crosstown and midtown buses.

No. Rooms: 3
Singles: 2 sb
Doubles: 1 sb
Type: Private townhouse

Breakfast: Continental
S-Rates: $55–$100 sb
D-Rates: $65–$100 sb
Bldg: Victorian

Minimum Stay: 2 nights. **Credit Card(s) Accepted:** none. **Open:** all year. No resident dogs. No dogs please. No resident cats. No cats please. Host smokes. Guests may smoke. Children welcome. **Discounts:** none.

Reservation Contact: City Lights Bed & Breakfast, Ltd., Dee Staff, Box 20355, Cherokee Station, New York, NY 10028; 212–737–7049.

ID: 14CITYLIGHTS

GREENWICH VILLAGE.

Near 11 St. & 7th Ave.

This Victorian townhouse in the West Village can be used as a two-bedroom, unhosted apartment. The spacious rooms retain many of the original architectural details such as wedding-cake ceiling trim and early-Dutch fireplace tiles. The rooms are decorated with a blend of contemporary comfort and Victorian grandeur. As a hosted facility, there is one guest room with a queen-sized bed and private bath. The guest room is separated from the rest of the apartment by means of sliding oak doors. Breakfast is served in the dining room which is furnished with interesting antiques and has a glass ceiling.

No. Rooms: 1
Singles: None
Doubles: 1 pb
Type: Private home

Breakfast: Continental
S-Rates: $75 pb
D-Rates: $85 pb
Bldg: Townhouse

Minimum Stay: none. **Credit Card(s) Accepted:** none. **Open:** all year. No resident dogs. No dogs please. No resident cats. No cats please. Non-smoking host. Guests may smoke in designated areas. Children welcome with restrictions. **Discounts:** none.

Reservation Contact: City Lights Bed & Breakfast, Dee Staff, Box 20355, Cherokee Station, New York, NY 10028; 212–737–7049.

LINCOLN CENTER.

Near West 60s, Broadway.

In this plush high-rise apartment building with doorman and concierge, guests can see the Chagall paintings from the apartment windows. The large terrace overlooks the entire Lincoln Center complex. The apartment is beautifully furnished with antiques. A large kitchen with lots of counter space, living room with hide-a-bed, rounded alcove with desk, chairs, and telephone, and terrace off the living room are featured. One bedroom offers a queen-sized bed, and another features a single bed; both have private baths. Continental breakfast is provided, although the apartment is unhosted. The owner has been a successful costume designer and editor.

No. Rooms: 2	**Breakfast:** Continental
Singles: 1 pb	**S-Rates:** $80 pb
Doubles: 1 pb	**D-Rates:** $150 pb
Type: Private apartment	**Bldg:** Luxury

Minimum Stay: 2 nights. **Credit Card(s) Accepted:** none. **Open:** all year. No resident dogs. No dogs please. No resident cats. No cats please. Nonsmoking host. Guests may not smoke in guest rooms. **Discounts:** none.

Reservation Contact: City Lights Bed & Breakfast, Ltd., Dee Staff, Box 20355, Cherokee Station, New York, NY 10028; 212–737–7049.

COLUMBIA UNIVERSITY, ST. JOHN THE DIVINE CHURCH, BARNARD COLLEGE, UNION THEOLOGICAL SEMINARY, GRANT'S TOMB; UPPER WEST SIDE.

Near Riverside Dr., Broadway.

This Victorian townhouse offers one guest room, with spectacular wood paneling, carved ceiling, bay windows, and sliding doors. Delightfully and imaginatively furnished, it boasts a view of Riverside Park. There is a single Shaker-style bed, a single hide-a-bed, and shared bath. The country kitchen, filled with sophisticated cooking devices, reflects your host's career as a food writer and consultant.

No. Rooms: 1	**Breakfast:** Continental
Singles: None	**S-Rates:** $50 sb
Doubles: 1 sb	**D-Rates:** $65 sb
Type: Private townhouse	**Bldg:** Victorian

Minimum Stay: 2 nights. **Credit Card(s) Accepted:** none. **Open:** all year. No resident dogs. No dogs please. No resident cats. No cats please. Nonsmoking host. Guests may smoke. Children welcome. **Discounts:** none.

Reservation Contact: City Lights Bed & Breakfast, Ltd., Dee Staff, Box 20355, Cherokee Station, New York, NY 10028; 212–737–7049.

ID: 17CITYLIGHTS

COLUMBUS CIRCLE, LINCOLN CENTER.

Near Central Park West & 62nd St.

At the southernmost end of Central Park West is this elegant, rambling apartment maintained in its original Art Deco Style. The two guest rooms, like the rest of the apartment, are spacious. One has a queen-sized bed with a black-lacquer headboard and chests and built-in floor-to-ceiling cabinets. The other has a single bed and similar decor. Breakfast is served in the formal dining room or in the sun-drenched solarium overlooking the park. From this location one can walk to Columbus Circle, Lincoln Center, and Fifth Avenue shops. The host is a business executive who is also involved in the arts.

No. Rooms: 2	**Breakfast:** Continental
Singles: 1 pb	**S-Rates:** $75 pb
Doubles: 1 pb	**D-Rates:** $85 pb
Type: Private home	**Bldg:** Apartment building

Minimum Stay: none. **Credit Card(s) Accepted:** none. **Open:** all year. No resident dogs. No dogs please. No resident cats. No cats please. Non-smoking host. Guests may not smoke. Children welcome with restrictions. **Discounts:** none.

Reservation Contact: City Lights Bed & Breakfast, Dee Staff, Box 20355, Cherokee Station, New York, NY 10028; 212–737–7049.

ID: 32CITYLIGHTS

BLOOMINGDALE'S, ALEXANDER'S, CHRISTIE'S, SOTHEBY PARKE BERNET, BERGDORF GOODMAN, F.A.O. SCHWARZ; UPPER EAST SIDE.

Near Upper 50s, 3d Ave.

This contemporary apartment building is conveniently located for the business traveler as well as the tourist. The walls of the living room are covered with exciting and eclectic works of art. The spacious guest room offers restful decor and is free of street noise. It has a double bed, TV, telephone, air-conditioning, and a private bath. A Continental Plus breakfast is served. You will find exclusive shops and galleries a short distance away. Your host is an art dealer/consultant who has traveled widely.

No. Rooms: 1	**Breakfast:** Continental Plus
Singles: None	**S-Rates:** $60 pb
Doubles: 1 pb	**D-Rates:** $65 pb
Type: Private apartment	**Bldg:** 1960s contemporary

Minimum Stay: none. **Credit Card(s) Accepted:** none. **Open:** all year. No resident dogs. No dogs please. No resident cats. No cats please. Host does not smoke in guest areas. Residence not appropriate for children. **Discounts:** none.

Reservation Contact: City Lights Bed & Breakfast, Ltd., Dee Staff, Box 20355, Cherokee Station, New York, NY 10028; 212–737–7049.

ID: 33CITYLIGHTS

METROPOLITAN MUSEUM OF ART; UPPER EAST SIDE.

Near Lower 80s, 3d Ave.

This twenty-fifth floor apartment in a high-rise building with doorman offers one delightfully decorated guest room with double bed. Other amenities include air-conditioning, TV, telephone, laundry facilities, and the use of a bicycle. The bath is shared with your host although the apartment is also available unhosted. A Continental breakfast is served. Your host is a fashion executive with interests in theater and the arts.

No. Rooms: 1	**Breakfast:** Continental
Singles: None	**S-Rates:** $55–$100 sb
Doubles: 1 sb	**D-Rates:** $65–$100 sb
Type: Private apartment	**Bldg:** 1970s high rise

Minimum Stay: none. **Credit Card(s) Accepted:** none. **Open:** all year. Cat in residence. Nonsmoking host. Guest may not smoke in residence. Children welcome. **Discounts:** none.

Reservation Contact: City Lights Bed & Breakfast, Ltd., Dee Staff, Box 20355, Cherokee Station, New York, NY 10028; 212–737–7049.

ID: 34CITYLIGHTS

UPPER WEST SIDE.

Near West End Ave. & 85th St.

Famous for large rooms, high ceilings, and thick, sound-proof walls, West End Avenue apartments have a special place in the hearts of New Yorkers. This unhosted, one-bedroom apartment is sumptuously decorated in the French traditional style. The bedroom is furnished with a queen-sized, four-poster bed, mahogony chests, and a chaise lounge. The apartment also has a living room, a full-sized dining room with an antique étagère displaying a collection of fine china, and a fully equipped, eat-in kitchen. The location is convenient to Lincoln Center, midtown theaters, and the Jacob Javits Center.

No. Rooms: 1	**Breakfast:** None
Singles: None	**S-Rates:** $135 pb
Doubles: 1 pb	**D-Rates:** $150 pb
Type: Private home	**Bldg:** 1900 apartment building

Minimum Stay: none. **Credit Card(s) Accepted:** none. **Open:** all year. No resident dogs. No dogs please. No resident cats. No cats please. Nonsmoking host. Guests may not smoke. Children welcome with restrictions. **Discounts:** none.

Reservation Contact: City Lights Bed & Breakfast, Dee Staff, Box 20355, Cherokee Station, New York, NY 10028; 212–737–7049.

ID: 35CITYLIGHTS

TRIBECA.

Near Harrison St.

New high-rise building with doorman is located in one of the city's most exciting areas. The Statute of Liberty, as well as many recently restored pre-revolutionary houses and newly erected high-rises may be viewed from the terrace. The area is filled with ethnic restaurants, posh new eateries, and many shops. It is convenient to the Wall Street area and the World Trade Center. The unhosted apartment has one bedroom with a queen-sized bed, color cable TV, and black lacquered furnishings. Staples for a Continental breakfast are provided. The owner is a sales representative with interests in sports, finance, and history.

No. Rooms: 1	**Breakfast:** Continental
Singles: None	**S-Rates:** $50 sb
Doubles: 1 sb	**D-Rates:** $65 sb
Type: Private apartment	**Bldg:** 1970s contemporary

Minimum Stay: none. **Credit Card(s) Accepted:** none. **Open:** all year. Cat in residence. Host smokes. Guest may smoke. Children welcome. **Discounts:** none.

Reservation Contact: City Lights Bed & Breakfast, Ltd., Dee Staff, Box 20355, Cherokee Station, New York, NY 10028; 212–737–7049.

ID: 10024BER

HISTORICAL SOCIETY, MUSEUM OF NATURAL HISTORY, HAYDEN PLANETARIUM; UPPER WEST SIDE.

Near Central Park W., 97th St.

Located on a quiet tree-lined street in Manhattan's upper west side, this brick apartment building is convenient to many area attractions. There is one guest room available with queen-sized bed and private bath.

Guests may use the kitchen for preparing light meals. Your congenial host, director of a cooking school, is interested in photography and travel.

No. Rooms: 1	**Breakfast:** Continental
Singles: None	**S-Rates:** $88 pb
Doubles: 1 pb	**D-Rates:** $113 pb
Type: Private apartment	**Bldg:** 1950s brick

Minimum Stay: 2 nights. **Credit Card(s) Accepted:** none. **Open:** all year. No resident dogs. No dogs please. No resident cats. No cats please. Nonsmoking host. Guests may not smoke in residence. Older children are welcome with restrictions. **Discounts:** none.

Reservation Contact: Bed & Breakfast Registry Ltd., Gary Winget, Box 8174, St. Paul, MN 55108; 612–646–4238.

NEW YORK– BROOKLYN

ID: 13CITYLIGHTS

BROOKLYN MUSEUM, BOTANICAL GARDENS, ZOO.

Near 8th Ave. Carroll St.

Formerly a famous mansion, this landmark Brooklyn brownstone is one-half block from Prospect Park. The house retains many original antiques, Oriental rugs, marble sinks, and all its old Victorian accessories. The two spacious, beautifully furnished guest rooms share a bath. Each consists of a bed/sitting room: one has a double bed, while the other has twin beds. A Continental breakfast is left on a tray in the lovely foyer. Your host is a travel writer. The house is an easy walk from the Brooklyn Museum and the Botanical Gardens and about thirty-five minutes from midtown Manhattan.

No. Rooms: 2	**Breakfast:** Continental
Singles: None	**S-Rates:** $60 sb
Doubles: 2 sb	**D-Rates:** $70 sb
Type: Private mansion	**Bldg:** Brownstone

Minimum Stay: 2 nights. **Credit Card(s) Accepted:** none. **Open:** all year. No resident dogs. No dogs please. No resident cats. No cats please. Nonsmoking host. Guests may not smoke in residence. Children welcome. **Discounts:** none.

Reservation Contact: City Lights Bed & Breakfast, Ltd., Dee Staff, Box 20355, Cherokee Station, New York, NY 10028; 212–737–7049.

PITTSFORD
ID: ROCH.HOLLOW

HIKING & BIKING TRAILS, ANTIQUING, COLLEGES; ROCHESTER AREA.

Near Rte. 490, I–90, NYS Thruway.

This brick colonial, tucked into a hollow between two hills, is situated on the edge of one of the prettiest county parks. The area is in a hamlet known as Bushnel's Basin, on the banks of the Erie Canal. The surroundings are woodsy, with a small pond and many large trees; however, it is only twenty minutes from downtown Rochester. There are two guest rooms in this air-conditioned house, one with a double bed and one with twin beds. They are furnished with large mirrored dressers, nightstands, lamps, and large closets. Their windows offer a view of the woods. The two rooms share a guest bath. A Full breakfast is served. Your host, an author and lecturer, is well-traveled. She is currently working on a book on early New England gravestone carvers.

No. Rooms: 2	**Breakfast:** Full
Singles: None	**S-Rates:** $45 sb
Doubles: 2 sb	**D-Rates:** $45 sb
Type: Private home	**Bldg:** 1984 brick colonial

Minimum Stay: none. **Credit Card(s) Accepted:** none. **Open:** all year. No resident dogs. No dogs please. Cat in residence. No cats please. Non-smoking host. Guests may not smoke in residence. Children welcome. **Discounts:** none.

Reservation Contact: Bed & Breakfast Rochester, Beth Kinsman, Box 444, Fairport, NY 14450; 716–223–8877.

PITTSTOWN
ID: 12185TOW

SARATOGA SPRINGS, SKI AREAS, SCENIC DRIVES, WILLIAMSTOWN, MA.

Near Rte. 7, I–90

This lovely colonial home, in a beautiful country setting, offers spacious grounds and garden. The house is furnished with colonial antiques throughout. You are welcome to use the entire house; the large fireplace in the family room is particularly inviting in winter as is the shady screened porch in summer. Two guest rooms feature double beds, antique furnishings, and shared bath. A Full breakfast is served in the dining room or country kitchen as preferred. Your host's interests include singing, classical music, skiing, and sewing. Child care, additional meals (including picnic lunches), arrival/departure transportation, and area tours are available.

No. Rooms: 2	**Breakfast:** Full
Singles: None	**S-Rates:** $25 sb
Doubles: 2 sb	**D-Rates:** $35 sb
Type: Private home	**Bldg:** Colonial

Minimum Stay: none. **Credit Card(s) Accepted:** none. **Open:** all year. No resident dogs. No dogs please. No resident cats. No cats please. Non-smoking host. Guests may not smoke in residence. Children are allowed with restrictions. **Discounts:** none.

Reservation Contact: Bed & Breakfast Registry Ltd., Gary Winget, Box 8174, St. Paul, MN 55108; 612–646–4238.

RICHFIELD SPRINGS   ID: LS-JONATHAN

COLGATE UNIVERSITY, BASEBALL HALL OF FAME, FARMERS' MUSEUM, FENIMORE HOUSE, MT. OSTEGO SKI AREA.

Near Rte. 28, Rte. 80, U.S. 20.

Built by a wealthy family in 1883, this Victorian Stick/Eastlake-style house still maintains its beautiful cherry woodwork, doors, and staircase. The seventeen-room house is three stories high with a four-story tower. It has been restored and is now filled with fine antiques, art, and Oriental rugs; there is also a library. Three guest rooms are available, two with private baths. The Rose Room, actually a suite consisting of a bedroom with queen-sized bed, sitting room with TV, and private bath, is beautifully furnished with antiques. The Gold Room, with a queen-sized canopied bed and private bath, is a large corner room also furnished with antiques. The Blue Room offers a double bed, large bay window, and shared bath. A Full breakfast is served. Both well-traveled hosts are accomplished painters interested in gardening and restoration of old houses. One operates a drama school; the other, an Emily Dickinson scholar, is deeply involved in literature. Additional meals are available. The house is located on Main Street in an area of large well-maintained nineteenth-century homes, near Cooperstown, the Baseball Hall of Fame, the Farmers' Museum, Colgate University, and a major antique center.

No. Rooms: 3	**Breakfast:** Full
Singles: None	**S-Rates:** $55–$65, pb, $42 sb
Doubles: 2 pb, 1 sb	**D-Rates:** $55–$65, pb, $42 sb
Type: Private home	**Bldg:** 1883 Victorian

Minimum Stay: none. **Credit Card(s) Accepted:** MC, V. **Open:** all year. Dog in residence. No dogs please. No resident cats. No cats please. Non-smoking host. Guests may not smoke in guest rooms. Children welcome. **Discounts:** weekly.

Reservation Contact: Bed & Breakfast Leatherstocking, Floranne McCraith, 389 Brockway Rd., Frankfort, NY 13340; 315–733–0040.

ROCHESTER

ART GALLERIES, BOUTIQUES, RESTAURANTS.

Near Rte. 490 & Monroe Ave.

This turn-of-the-century Tudor home is located near boutiques, restaurants, antique shops, and the fascinating Park Avenue area. It allows easy access to museums, concerts, colleges, and the business section. The house has high ceilings, a sunny informal living room, a formal dining room, and a front porch with comfortable chairs. There are two guest rooms with private baths. The Regency Room, done in blue, gold, and champagne, features Italian provincial furniture and a king-sized bed covered with a satin comforter. It has an eight-foot, padded window seat, two easy chairs, and a triple dresser topped with gilt-framed mirrors. The Coventry Room has a homespun feeling with its braided rug, hobnail lamps, and mahogany furniture. The yellow roses on the wallpaper match the moire shades and drapes and give the room a cheerful glow. Furnishings include two beds, a highboy, dressing table, tub chairs, and an ornately carved antique table. A Full breakfast is served in the remodeled kitchen. Your hosts have traveled extensively and enjoy music, photography, art, and architecture.

No. Rooms: 2	**Breakfast:** Full
Singles: None	**S-Rates:** $45–$50 pb
Doubles: 2 pb	**D-Rates:** $55 pb
Type: Private home	**Bldg:** 1900 Tudor

Minimum Stay: none. **Credit Card(s) Accepted:** none. **Open:** all year. No resident dogs. No dogs please. No resident cats. No cats please. Nonsmoking host. Guests may not smoke in residence. Children welcome with restrictions. **Discounts:** $5 less if more than 1 night.

Reservation Contact: Bed & Breakfast Rochester, Beth Kinsman, Box 44, Fairport, NY 14450; 716–223–8877.

EAST SIDE, HIGHLAND PARK, EASTMAN HOUSE OF PHOTOGRAPHY.

Near Winton Rd.

In a quiet, residential neighborhood with wide lawns and generous setbacks, this house is a five-minute bus ride from the center of the city. There are two guest rooms with private baths. The Lilac Room has a king-sized bed with the famous Rochester lilacs printed on the bedding. The Cherry Room is furnished with a double bed, rocker, comfortable chair, and a small round table. Both rooms are air-conditioned. Your host is gaining quite a reputation for his Dutch-oven pancakes served with pear-ginger or strawberry sauce.

No. Rooms: 2	**Breakfast:** Full
Singles: None	**S-Rates:** $45–$55 pb
Doubles: 2 pb	**D-Rates:** $55–$60 pb
Type: Private home	**Bldg:** Tri-level

Minimum Stay: none. **Credit Card(s) Accepted:** none. **Open:** all year. No resident dogs. No dogs please. No resident cats. No cats please. Non-smoking host. Guests may not smoke in residence. Children welcome. **Discounts:** $5 less for more than 1 night.

Reservation Contact: Bed & Breakfast Rochester, Beth Kinsman, Box 444, Fairport, NY 14450; 716–223–8877.

ROME
ID: LS-97

FORT STANWICK, ERIE CANAL VILLAGE, DELTA LAKE.

Near rtes. 69 & 49, Black River Blvd., Turin Rd.

This attractive split-level home has a tasteful blend of antiques and collectibles and offers three guest rooms, one with a private half-bath. One of the rooms has twin beds, one a double bed, and the third has a single bed. A Full breakfast is served. Your hosts have interests in travel, decorating, history, and golf. This location is near Fort Stanwick, Delta Lake, Erie Canal Village, and a cheese museum.

No. Rooms: 3	**Breakfast:** Full
Singles: 1 sb	**S-Rates:** $35–$45 sb
Doubles: 2 sb	**D-Rates:** $45 sb
Type: Private home	**Bldg:** Split-level

Minimum Stay: none. **Credit Card(s) Accepted:** MC, V. **Open:** all year. No resident dogs. No dogs please. No resident cats. No cats please. Non-smoking host. Guests may not smoke in residence. Children welcome with restrictions. **Discounts:** weekly rates.

Reservation Contact: Bed & Breakfast Leatherstocking, Floranne McCraith, 389 Brockway Rd., Frankfort, NY 13340; 315–733–0040.

SAYVILLE
ID: LI–SS

ON BAY, FISHING, BOATING, HORSEBACK RIDING.

Near I–495, Montauk Hwy.

Situated on the water directly opposite Fire Island, this contemporary home is furnished with beautiful antiques, brass beds, Tiffany lamps, oak pieces, and Oriental rugs. The two guest rooms have a separate entrance and are on a separate floor for greater privacy. They have double beds and share a bath. There is a bulkhead to accommodate guests' boats. Two golf courses, tennis courts, hiking areas, and horseback riding are nearby, and it is a short walk to excellent restaurants. Your hosts, an interior designer and a teacher and landscaper, are world travelers and enjoy sailing.

No. Rooms: 2	**Breakfast:** Full
Singles: None	**S-Rates:** $65 sb
Doubles: 2 sb	**D-Rates:** $70 sb
Type: Private home	**Bldg:** Contemporary

Minimum Stay: surcharge for 1 night stay. **Credit Card(s) Accepted:** none. **Open:** all year. No resident dogs. No dogs please. No resident cats. No cats please. Nonsmoking host. Guests may not smoke in residence. Children welcome with restrictions. **Discounts:** none.

Reservation Contact: Bed & Breakfast of Long Island, Naomi Kavee, Box 392, Old Westbury, NY 11568; 516–334–6231.

SCHENECTADY
ID: 12309GRA

SARATOGA PERFORMING ARTS CENTER, RACETRACK, SPA, CONGRESS PARK & CASINO, HISTORIC WALKING TOURS, POLO, GOLF, SWIMMING.

Near rtes. 7E & 146, I–87, I–90.

This charming house, near the bank of the Mohawk River, is located on a scenic winding road. From the patio you can watch rabbits, squirrels, and many birds in the exceptionally large and private yard. You can also use the available bikes to take advantage of the picturesque trail winding along the river. The house is very tastefully furnished, with several unusually beautiful pieces from Japan, where your host lived for several years. There are three guest rooms, one with double bed and the others with single beds; one has a fireplace and private entrance, and the rooms share two baths. TV is available in the sitting room. A Full breakfast is served in the dining area or on the patio. Saratoga offers the Arts Center, the July home of the New York City Ballet and the August home of the Philadelphia Orchestra; and the Saratoga Race Course. You may also want to try the mineral-water baths at one of the many spas in the area or visit the petrified gardens. Arrival/departure transportation and area tours are available. Your very cordial host has a wide range of interests encompassing the arts, travel, biking, and skiing. She also makes delicious blueberry muffins.

No. Rooms: 2	**Breakfast:** Full
Singles: 2 sb	**S-Rates:** $35 sb
Doubles: 1 sb	**D-Rates:** $45 sb
Type: Private home	**Bldg:** 1930 Dutch colonial

Minimum Stay: none. **Credit Card(s) Accepted:** none. **Open:** all year, except holidays. No resident dogs. Guests may bring dog. No resident cats. Guests may bring cat. Nonsmoking host. Guests may smoke. Children welcome. **Discounts:** none.

Reservation Contact: Bed & Breakfast Registry Ltd., Gary Winget, Box 8174, St. Paul, MN 55108; 612–646–4238.

SEVERANCE

LAKE GEORGE AREA; ADIRONDACK MOUNTAINS, FORT TICONDEROGA.

Near Rte. 74, I–87.

This lovely old farmhouse is located on two acres of rolling hills and wooded area, which backs up to state-owned mountain land. There are four guest rooms with twin or double beds. Sinks are in two of the guest rooms but they all share a bath. A Full country breakfast is served. Living room with TV is available for your use, as is a screened porch. Many restaurants and shops are nearby, and the Lake George resort area is only forty-five minutes away. Child care, additional meals, arrival/departure transportation, and area tours are available. Your hosts' interests include cars, coins, glass, and antiques.

No. Rooms: 4	**Breakfast:** Full
Singles: None	**S-Rates:** $27 sb
Doubles: 4 sb	**D-Rates:** $39 sb
Type: Private home	**Bldg:** 1850s farmhouse

Minimum Stay: none. **Credit Card(s) Accepted:** none. **Open:** May 16–Oct. 31. No resident dogs. No dogs please. No resident cats. No cats please. Nonsmoking host. Guests may not smoke in guest rooms. Children welcome. **Discounts:** none.

Reservation Contact: Bed & Breakfast Registry Ltd., Gary Winget, Box 8174, St. Paul, MN 55108; 612–646–4238.

SOUTHOLD

ON WATER.

Near Youngs Ave., Rte. 25.

This contemporary home directly on the beach allows boat owners to pull right up to the house. The deck overlooking the water is lined with potted geraniums. Two-story-high windows with water views grace the living and dining rooms. There are two guest rooms that share a guest bath. The first, with a water view, is furnished with queen-sized bed, wicker chair, chest, TV, and plants; the other, similarly furnished, has twin beds. A Continental Plus breakfast is served. Windsurfers and sailboats are available for rental nearby. This locale is a short drive to wineries and wine-tasting tours. Guests can pick their own fruit and vegetables at nearby farm stands and are invited to the July Fourth barbecue.

No. Rooms: 2	**Breakfast:** Continental Plus
Singles: None	**S-Rates:** $68 sb
Doubles: 2 sb	**D-Rates:** $75 sb
Type: Private home	**Bldg:** 1983 contemporary

Minimum Stay: 2 days for July 4th holiday. **Credit Card(s) Accepted:** none. **Open:** all year. Dog in residence. No dogs please. No resident cats. No cats please. Nonsmoking host. Guests may not smoke in guest rooms. Children welcome with restrictions. **Discounts:** none.

Reservation Contact: Bed & Breakfast of Long Island, Naomi Kavee, Box 392, Old Westbury, NY 11568; 516–334–6231.

WEST SHOKAN
ID: US–217

HIKING, SWIMMING, BIKING, SKIING.

Near rtes. 28A & 28W.

This farm, dating back to the 1840s, is on fifteen acres of woods and meadows with a cool running stream, twelve miles from Woodstock. Local activities include hiking, biking, swimming, fishing, and cross-country skiing. Winery tours and horseback riding are within thirty miles. You are welcome to use the spacious living room with wood-burning stove, game table, cable TV, and VCR. Two guest rooms share a guest bath; one has an antique Colonial double bed and fireplace, and the other is furnished with four twin beds. A full country breakfast is served either in the antique-filled dining room' or on the screened porch. One of your hosts is a teacher and farmer who enjoys cooking and fishing; the other, a bookkeeper, is interested in cooking, baking, canning, and local lore.

No. Rooms: 2	**Breakfast:** Full
Singles: None	**S-Rates:** $40 sb
Doubles: 2 sb	**D-Rates:** $45–$55 sb
Type: Private home	**Bldg:** 1840 farmhouse

Minimum Stay: 2 nights. **Credit Card(s) Accepted:** MC, V. **Open:** all year. No resident dogs. No dogs please. Cat in residence. No cats please. Host smokes. Guests may smoke. Children welcome. **Discounts:** weekly.

Reservation Contact: Bed & Breakfast U.S.A., Ltd., Barbara Notarious, Box 606, Croton-on-Hudson, NY 10520; 914–271–6228.

WESTBURY

HOFSTRA UNIVERSITY, ADELPHI UNIVERSITY, CLARK GARDENS, JONES BEACH, ROOSEVELT RACEWAY, AVIATION MUSEUM, WESTBURY MUSIC FAIR.

Near Ellison Ave., Northern State Pkwy., Long Island Pkwy.

This Cape Cod-style house is in a beautifully maintained residential neighborhood, in a quiet suburb convenient to the Long Island Railroad and all cultural activities on the north shore. Two guest rooms share a bath. One is a large pine-paneled room, with twin beds, couch, antique dresser, coffee table, and lamps; the other is furnished with a single bed, day bed with foam mattress, chaise, desk, and coffee table. A Full breakfast is served. Your host enjoys theater, music, travel, and historic homes.

No. Rooms: 2	**Breakfast:** Full
Singles: None	**S-Rates:** $50 sb
Doubles: 2 sb	**D-Rate:** $60 sb
Type: Private home	**Bldg:** 1940s Cape Cod

Minimum Stay: none. **Credit Card(s) Accepted:** none. **Open:** all year. No resident dogs. No dogs please. No resident cats. No cats please. Nonsmoking host. Guests may not smoke in guest rooms. Children welcome with restrictions. **Discounts:** after 7 days. Italian spoken.

Reservation Contact: Bed & Breakfast of Long Island, Naomi Kavee, Box 392, Old Westbury, NY 11568; 516–334–6231.

NORTH CAROLINA

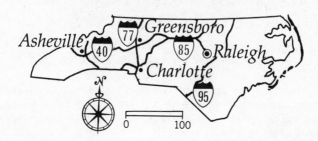

ASHEVILLE

ID: 28801FLI

BLUE RIDGE, MTNS., PISGAH NATIONAL FOREST, BILTMORE MANSION & GARDENS, FOLK ART CENTER, ANTIQUE AUTOMOBILE MUSEUM.

Near Flint St., I–240, I–40, I–26.

Built in 1915, this very graceful house is currently on the National Register and featured on the Montford Historic District's walking tour. Most of the structures in the district date from the late nineteenth and early twentieth centuries, when Asheville changed rather rapidly from a village to a busy mountain city. This house, built on a half acre, is beautifully landscaped with garden and small fish pond. A large deck out back and a spacious front porch are available for your use. There are eight guest rooms, all with beautifully refinished pine floors, turn-of-the-century furnishings, double beds, air-conditioning, and private baths. There is also a gracious sitting room where you can gather for conversation. A second inn next door with similar furnishings provides four additional guest rooms. A Full Southern-style breakfast is served in the dining room. The interests of your very cordial hosts are travel, antiques, auctions, and the mountains.

No. Rooms: 8	**Breakfast:** Full
Singles: None	**S-Rates:** $50 pb
Doubles: 8 pb	**D-Rates:** $65 pb
Type: Inn	**Bldg:** 1915 prairie

Minimum Stay: none. **Credit Card(s) Accepted:** AE, DIS, MC, V. **Open:** all year. No resident dogs. No dogs please. No resident cats. No cats please. Host smokes. Guests may smoke. Children welcome with restrictions. **Discounts:** none.

Reservation Contact: Bed & Breakfast Registry Ltd., Gary Winget, Box 8174, St. Paul, MN 55108; 612–646–4238.

ASHEVILLE

BILTMORE HOUSE AND GARDENS, CIVIC CENTER, THOMAS WOLFE MEMORIAL, FOLK ART CENTER, SMOKY MOUNTAINS NATIONAL PARK.

Near Baltimore Ave. & Meadow Rd.

This lovely English Tudor home is surrounded by oak, maple, and pine trees and has a shady deck with an outdoor Jacuzzi. The house is decorated with many fine oak antiques and hand-made items. A baby grand piano adorns the living room. The three guest rooms have double beds; two rooms share a bath and one has a private bath. A Full breakfast is served in the dining room or on the patio. Ricotta pancakes, four-cheese and herb quiche, or vegetarian brunch torte might be served, topped off with home-baked goodies, fruits, and freshly ground coffee. Afternoon refreshments are also served.

No. Rooms: 3	**Breakfast:** Full
Singles: none	**S-Rates:** $60–$75 pb, $50–$60 sb
Doubles: 1 pb, 2 sb	**D-Rates:** $65–$85 pb, $55–$70 sb
Type: Inn	**Bldg:** English Tudor

Minimum Stay: none. **Credit Card(s) Accepted:** none. **Open:** all year. No resident dogs. No dogs please. Resident cat. No cats please. Non-smoking host. Guests may not smoke. Children over 11 welcome. **Discounts:** none.

Reservation Contact: Bed & Breakfast Registry, Gary Winget, Box 8174, St. Paul, MN 55108; 612–646–4238.

CHARLOTTE

MINT MUSEUM OF ART.

Near I–77, I–85.

Built in the style of an 1840s English manor house, this B&B inn offers deluxe service, attention to details, and elegant surroundings. Private bedroom suites are decorated in the style of European palaces. The inn has two splendidly furnished sitting rooms, an Empire-style formal dining room, and an informal English pub-style parlor suitable for afternoon tea—all completed in period antiques. A Continental or full English breakfast is served in the privacy of each of the five available suites. Limousine service via a Rolls Royce Silver Shadow is available for to and from the airport. Other amenities on the eleven acres of lawns and gardens include an Olympic-size swimming pool, Jacuzzi, lawn croquet, and tennis courts.

No. Rooms: 4	**Breakfast:** Full
Singles: None	**S-Rates:** $116–$406 pb
Doubles: 4 pb	**D-Rates:** $116–$406 pb
Type: Inn	**Bldg:** English manor

Minimum Stay: none. **Credit Card(s) Accepted:** none. **Open:** all year. Dog in residence. Guests may bring dog. No resident cats. Guests may bring cat. Host smokes. Guests may smoke. Children welcome. **Discounts:** none.

Reservation Contact: Bed & Breakfast Registry Ltd., Gary Winget, Box 8174, St. Paul, MN 55108; 612–646–4238.

CURRIE
ID: 28435BEL

MOORE'S CREEK BATTLEGROUND, HISTORIC WILMINGTON; 30 MINUTES FROM OCEAN.

Near rtes. 421 & 210.

This exceptional one-hundred-forty-five-year-old Georgian country home is on a sixty-acre lot, part of a thousand-acre corn, soybean, and tobacco farm. The air-conditioned home offers large picturesque gardens, an enormous wrap-around screened porch, and antique furnishings. Other amenities include use of the TV, yard, bicycles, and laundry facilities. Three guest rooms, two with double beds and one with single bed, share a guest bath. You may choose the type of breakfast you prefer, complete with garden-fresh fruits and vegetables and homemade sausage. Complimentary homemade wine is also offered. You can even pick some of the grapes, peanuts, and vegetables from the abundant garden. The house is twenty minutes from historic Wilmington and thirty minutes from the ocean; Moore's Creek Battleground is one mile away. Additional meals, child care, arrival/departure transportation, and area tours are available by arrangement. One of your hosts is a doctor of education; the other is a retired farm supply merchant. Their interests include gardening, old cars and homes, swimming, horses, and antiques.

No. Rooms: 3	**Breakfast:** Full
Singles: 1 sb	**S-Rates:** $25 sb
Doubles: 2 sb	**D-Rates:** $35 sb
Type: Private home	**Bldg:** 1845 Georgian

Minimum Stay: none. **Credit Card(s) Accepted:** none. **Open:** all year. No resident dogs. No dogs please. No resident cats. No cats please. Non-smoking host. Guests may not smoke in guest rooms. Children welcome. **Discounts:** none.

Reservation Contact: Bed & Breakfast Registry Ltd., Gary Winget, Box 8174, St. Paul, MN 55108; 612–646–4238.

GLENVILLE

ID: 28736MOU

GREAT SMOKEY MTNS., BREVARD MUSIC CENTER, APPALACHIAN TRAIL.

Near Rte. 107, U.S. 64.

At an altitude of 4,200 feet, this wonderful Dutch colonial house over-looking a lake, provides a spectacular panoramic view of seven mountain ranges. This location, though secluded and peaceful, is only minutes away from Brevard Music Center and the excellent shops and restaurants in Cashiers and Highlands. Trails abound, from the Appalachian Trail to quiet nature walks threading through waterfalls, coves, and rushing streams, and there are an endless number of scenic drives to enjoy. Boating, fishing, whitewater rafting, and horseback riding. The house has three guests rooms, a single and two doubles, with comfortable furnishings and a shared guest bath. A Full breakfast is served. Your cordial, well-traveled hosts are interested in art, flying, and horseback riding.

No. Rooms: 3	**Breakfast:** Full
Singles: 1 sb	**S-Rates:** $20 sb
Doubles: 2 sb	**D-Rates:** $36 sb
Type: Private home	**Bldg:** Dutch colonial

Minimum Stay: none. **Credit Card(s) Accepted:** none. **Open:** summer and fall. No resident dogs. No dogs please. Cat in residence. No cats please. Nonsmoking host. Guests may not smoke in residence. Residence is not appropriate for children. **Discounts:** none.

Reservation Contact: Bed & Breakfast Registry Ltd., Gary Winget, Box 8174, St. Paul, MN 55108; 612–646–4238.

GREENSBORO

ID: 27415GRE

HISTORICAL MUSEUM, BLANDWOOD MANSION, GUILFORD NATIONAL BATTLEGROUND, OUTLET STORES.

Near N. Elm & Bessemer sts., I–85, U.S. 70.

Built in 1905, this charming Stick-Style house has been carefully renovated and air-conditioned for your comfort and is conveniently located on a park in the historic district, only three minutes from downtown Greensboro. In addition to a gracious living area with two fireplaces, you are free to use the separate dining area as well as the guest kitchen. You can enjoy a dip in the pool on a summer afternoon or a roaring fire on wintery evenings. Five guest rooms, all of which sleep at least two, offer private or shared baths. A Continental breakfast of fresh orange juice and home-made breads is served in the morning. Your gracious hosts are interested in sailing, wood carving, and painting.

No. Rooms: 5
Singles: None
Doubles: 3 pb, 2 sb
Type: Private home

Breakfast: Continental
S-Rates: $35 pb, $30 sb
D-Rates: $40–$55 pb, $35 sb
Bldg: 1905 Stick Style

Minimum Stay: none. **Credit Card(s) Accepted:** AE, MC, V **Open:** all year. No resident dogs. No dogs please. No resident cats. No cats please. Host smokes. Guests may smoke in residence. Children welcome. **Discounts:** none.

Reservation Contact: Bed & Breakfast Registry Ltd., Gary Winget, Box 8174, St. Paul, MN 55108; 612–646–4238.

NEW BERN

ID: 28560NEW

TRYON PALACE, GOLF, CROATAN NATIONAL FOREST.

Near Broad & George sts., U.S. 70, U.S. 17.

This brick colonial, a replica of an 18th-century home, is one block from Tryon Palace, the only building in the U.S. to serve as both a royal palace and a colonial governor's mansion. There are daily tours of Tryon Palace and three other of historic New Bern's 18th-century residences. Nearby are championship golf courses, sailing, and other water sports. Pamilco Sound and Cape Hatteras National Seashore are about 30 miles away. The house boasts mantels carved by Elijah Taylor, the original owner and builder; a large, formal parlor with a baby grand piano; a fully stocked library; and a sweeping staircase with a mahogany handrail that curves continuously up to the third floor. The six guest rooms have private baths. One of the rooms, done in navy and rose, has twin mahogany four-poster beds and wing chairs. Another room, done in forest green and rose, boasts a queen-sized four-poster bed, fireplace, carved oak table, Sheraton chairs, and a walk-in closet. The other rooms are similarly decorated and furnished with double or queen-sized beds. A Full, plantation-style breakfast includes specialties such as sautéed apple crepes and wine jelly. Afternoon tea is served daily from 3 to 5 P.M. and complimentary champagne is provided for special occasions. The interests of your hosts include antiques, restoration, and aviation. Arrival/departure transportation is available.

No. Rooms: 6
Singles: None
Doubles: 6 pb
Type: Inn

Breakfast: Full
S-Rates: $55 pb
D-Rates: $75 pb
Bldg: 1923 brick colonial

Minimum Stay: none. **Credit Card(s) Accepted:** AE, MC, V. **Open:** all year. Dog in residence. A dog is allowed with restrictions. Cat in residence. A cat is allowed with restrictions. Nonsmoking host. Guests may smoke. Children welcome. **Discounts:** 15% senior citizens.

Reservation Contact: Bed & Breakfast Registry Ltd., Gary Winget, Box 8174, St. Paul, MN 55108; 612–646–4238.

THOMASVILLE
ID: 27360CAR

WINSTON-SALEM AREA, R.J. REYNOLDS ESTATE, MUSEUM OF EARLY DECORATIVE ARTS, OLD SALEM, WHITAKER PARK, NATURE SCIENCE CENTER, DINNER THEATER.

Near Rte. 68, I–85.

Convenient to most attractions in the Winston-Salem area, this gracious country home has a sitting room with TV, living room with large organ, and a patio for your enjoyment. There are two guest rooms: one is pleasant and comfortable, with a queen-sized double bed, chair, dresser, and bookcases; the other is a bit more formal in appearance and has a double bed, chest, and rocking chair. A full breakfast is served in the dining room or on the patio. Additional meals, arrival/departure transportation, and area tours are available. Your well-traveled, cordial hosts are interested in square dancing, music, gardening, and church activities.

No. Rooms: 2	**Breakfast:** Full
Singles: None	**S-Rates:** $25 sb
Doubles: 2 sb	**D-Rates:** $30 sb
Type: Private home	**Bldg:** 1955 Ranch

Minimum Stay: none. **Credit Card(s) Accepted:** none. **Open:** all year. No resident dogs. No dogs please. No resident cats. No cats please. Non-smoking host. Guests may not smoke in guest rooms. Children welcome. **Discounts:** none.

Reservation Contact: Bed & Breakfast Registry Ltd., Gary Winget, Box 8174, St. Paul, MN 55108; 612–646–4238.

TRYON
ID: 28782CAR

NATIONAL PARKS, BLUE RIDGE MTNS., FALL FOLIAGE, BIRD-WATCHING, HIKING, FISHING.

Near I–26.

This graceful hundred-year-old house offers screened porch, patio, ivy walkways, living room with TV, and piano. Four guest rooms feature twin, double, or single beds and shared bath. All rooms are handsomely decorated. Continental breakfast is served. Arrival/departure transportation, water skiing, hot tub, and horseback riding are available. Your host's interests include horses, snow and water skiing, antiques, music, and art.

No. Rooms: 4	**Breakfast:** Continental
Singles: 1 sb	**S-Rates:** $35 sb
Doubles: 3 sb	**D-Rates:** $45 sb
Type: Inn	**Bldg:** 1880s

Minimum Stay: none. **Credit Card(s) Accepted:** none. **Open:** all year. No resident dogs. No dogs please. Cat in residence. No cats please. Non-

smoking host. Guests may not smoke in residence. Children welcome
with restrictions. **Discounts:** none.

Reservation Contact: Bed & Breakfast Registry Ltd., Gary Winget, Box
8174, St. Paul, MN 55108; 612–646–4238.

ID: 28782MIL

CARL SANDBURG HOME, BLUE RIDGE MTNS.; THEATER, CONCERTS, CRAFTS.

Near Rte. 108, I–26.

This charming little stone country inn on three-and-a-half acres features
lovely porches overlooking lawns, pastures, and the Pacoet River, which
flows through the property. You are welcome to mingle in the spacious
living room with its glowing fireplace. Eight very fine guest rooms feature
with double, twin, or king-sized beds, air-conditioning, and private baths.
Two-bedroom suites are also available. You also have kitchen privileges.
A Continental breakfast, consisting of specialty breads and muffins, is
served. This is a perfect spot for quiet relaxation amidst the beauty and
attractions of the area.

No. Rooms: 8	**Breakfast:** Continental
Singles: None	**S-Rates:** $50 pb
Doubles: 8 pb	**D-Rates:** $65 pb
Type: Inn	**Bldg:** Stone

Minimum Stay: none. **Credit Card(s) Accepted:** none. **Open:** all year.
No resident dogs. No dogs please. No resident cats. No cats please. Host
smokes. Guests may smoke. Children welcome. **Discounts:** none.

Reservation Contact: Bed & Breakfast Registry Ltd., Gary Winget, Box
8174, St. Paul, MN 55108; 612–646–4238.

NORTH DAKOTA

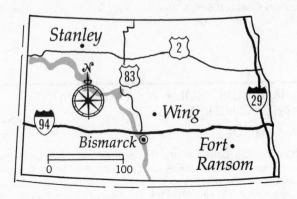

FORT RANSOM

RODEOS, CRAFT FAIRS, FISHING, HUNTING.

Near Rte. 27, Rte. 1.

This contemporary split-level home with relaxed atmosphere is in a beautiful open area. The area boasts many agricultural activities as well as rodeos, craft fairs, deer, pheasant, goose, and duck hunting, and fishing lakes are within a thirty-minute drive. One of the guest rooms, on the second floor, is done in mauve and rose with an antique decor. It has a double bed, dressers, and an east window for morning sunshine. The downstairs bedroom, done in tones of blue and purple has a double waterbed, dresser, and private bath. There is also a second-floor den with queen-sized hide-a-bed to accommodate children, if necessary. A Full breakfast is served; additional meals, laundry facilities, child care, and area tours are available. One of your hosts, who likes fishing, hunting, and boating, can even provide car repair; your other host, a nurse, enjoys all crafts, the outdoors, movies, and opera.

No. Rooms: 2	**Breakfast:** Full
Singles: None	**S-Rates:** $20–$25 pb
Doubles: 2 pb	**D-Rates:** $30–$35 pb
Type: Private home	**Bldg:** 1984 split-level

Minimum Stay: 2 nights. **Credit Card(s) Accepted:** AE, MC, V. **Open:** all year. Dog in residence. A dog is allowed with restrictions. No resident cats. Guests may bring cat. Nonsmoking host. Guests may not smoke in guest rooms. Children welcome. **Discounts:** none. Ukrainian spoken.

Reservation Contact: Old West Bed & Breakfast, Marlys Prince, Box 211, Regent, ND 58650; 701–563–4542.

LIDGERWOOD

ID: KALER–WEST

SOUTHEASTERN N.D., CHAHINKAPA PARK, FORT SISSETON.

Near I–29.

Guests will enjoy seeing birds and deer in this picturesque setting, and there are walking trails through a grove. Lake Elsie offers excellent fishing and swimming just 15 minutes away, and golf and tennis are available in town. Fort Sisseton, South Dakota, where pow-wows are held during the summer and fall, is an hour away. Four guest rooms plus a children's room share a bath. The Full breakfast includes eggs Dakota and home-made rolls. Your hosts enjoy gardening and square dancing and they have traveled to Spain, Switzerland, and Japan.

No. Rooms: 4		**Breakfast:** Full	
Singles: None		**S-Rates:** $25 sb	
Doubles: 4 sb		**D-Rates:** $30 sb	
Type: Private home		**Bldg:** Farmhouse	

Minimum Stay: none. **Credit Card(s) Accepted:** none. **Open:** all year. No resident dogs. Guest dogs permitted outside. No resident cats. Guest cats permitted outside. Nonsmoking host. Guests may smoke in residence. Children welcome. **Discounts:** none.

Reservation Contact: Old West Bed & Breakfast, Marlys Prince, Box 211, Regent, ND 58650; 701–563–4542.

MINOT

ID: BB0009–WEST

STATE FAIR, NORSK HOSTEFEST.

Near U.S. rtes. 2 & 83.

This two-story frame house offers a well-shaded yard with patio, table, lounge chairs, fountain, and flowers. There is also a recreation room with a pool table that guests are welcome to use. Two air-conditioned guest rooms share a bath. One has a queen-sized bed and multi-colored carpeting, while the other has a double bed and white carpeting. Both rooms have a private entrance. A self-serve breakfast is provided. Your hosts, who have traveled to all the states west of the Mississippi, enjoy hunting, woodworking, masonry, and archery.

No. Rooms: 2		**Breakfast:** Continental	
Singles: None		**S-Rates:** $25 sb	
Doubles: 2 sb		**D-Rates:** $35 sb	
Type: Private home		**Bldg:** Frame two-story	

Minimum Stay: none. **Credit Card(s) Accepted:** none. **Open:** all year. No resident dogs. No dogs please. No resident cats. No cats please. Nonsmoking host. Guests may smoke in designated areas. Children welcome. **Discounts:** weekly and for children under 12.

Reservation Contact: Old West Bed & Breakfast, Marlys Prince, Box 211, Regent, ND 58650; 701–563–4542.

STANLEY

RODEOS, HORSEBACK RIDING, SWIMMING, FISHING, HUNTING.

Near Rte. 8.

This ranch-style home is located in the Little Knife River Valley. With the closest neighbors a mile-and-a-half away, it is a place where you can get a true taste of country life. Settled by ranchers in the 1890s and homesteaded in the early 1900s, the area is close to Lake Sakakawea, with swimming, fishing, and boating, and fifteen miles from Fort Berthold Indian Reservation. The area is perfect for hiking and horseback riding in the hills and coulees. Upland game birds, white-tailed deer, and other small wildlife afford a good opportunity to photograph or hunt in season. During many summer weekends there are rodeos and Indian powwows. The ranch features a spacious yard, ideal for guests' relaxation. The guest quarters consist of two large bedrooms, private bath, and family room, with fireplace, pool table, games, and semiprivate entry. A homemade Continental breakfast is served; additional meals, arrival/departure transportation, and area tours are available. One of your hosts is interested in archaeaology and enjoys hunting, photography, and looking for Indian artifacts; your other host likes gardening, needlework, and public speaking. They both like to travel.

No. Rooms: 2	**Breakfast:** Continental Plus
Singles: None	**S-Rates:** $25 sb
Doubles: 2 sb	**D-Rates:** $30 sb
Type: Private home	**Bldg:** 1976 ranch style

Minimum Stay: none. **Credit Card(s) Accepted:** none. **Open:** all year. No resident dogs. No dogs please. No resident cats. No cats please. Nonsmoking host. Guests may not smoke in guest rooms. Residence not appropriate for children. **Discounts:** none.

Reservation Contact: Old West Bed & Breakfast, Marlys Prince, Box 211, Regent, ND 58650; 701–563–4542.

WING

MITCHEL LAKE, HAYSTACK BUTTE.

Near hwys. 36 & 14.

This contemporary ranch house is located on an active grain farm and ranching operation. There is good fishing in Mitchel Lake, and Haystack Butte is an ideal hiking spot. It is a forty-five minute drive to the capitol, heritage center, and Garrison Dam. The spaciousness of the house invites easy, comfortable living. Patio doors open to a deck overlooking the yard with trees and flower beds. Family pictures and paintings add an interesting touch to the interior, and the family room, with fireplace and hot tub, is available to guests. The two guest rooms share a bath. One room has gray carpeting, red curtains, double bed, mirrored dresser, lamp, towel bars, and closet; the second is done in green, with an antique maple bedroom set, doll bed, and dolls. A Full breakfast of juice, bacon, eggs, popovers, and jam is served. Your hosts enjoy politics, photography, quilting, and writing. They have traveled to the Caribbean, Mexico, Canada, and throughout the U.S.

No. Rooms: 2	**Breakfast:** Full
Singles: None	**S-Rates:** $20 sb
Doubles: 2 sb	**D-Rates:** $25 sb
Type: Private home	**Bldg:** 1983 ranch

Minimum Stay: none. **Credit Card(s) Accepted:** none. **Open:** all year. Dog in residence. No dogs please. Cat in residence. No cats please. Nonsmoking host. Guests may not smoke in residence. Children welcome. **Discounts:** none.

Reservation Contact: Old West Bed & Breakfast, Marlys Prince, Box 211, Regent, ND 58650; 701–563–4542.

OHIO

LAKE ERIE

Cleveland

90

Akron

80

75

71

77

70

Columbus

Cincinnati

N

0   50

BETHEL

ID: 6–OHIO

EAST FORK STATE PARK, KINGS ISLAND, BEACH.

Near Rte. 125.

This 1906 restored farmhouse is situated on 12 acres of land. Although the location provides rustic surroundings, it is only 30 minutes from Cincinnati. There is a pleasant creek to sit by, the area is good for hiking, and guests will enjoy relaxing on the wrap-around front porch. Three guest rooms with double beds share a bath. The rooms are furnished with antiques. A Full breakfast of the guests' choice is served in the eat-in kitchen or on the vine-covered back porch. Telephone, TV, and laundry facilities are available. Your host is an antique dealer and community leader. She loves sewing and refinishing furniture.

No. Rooms: 3	Breakfast: Full
Singles: None	S-Rates: $35 sb
Doubles: 3 sb	D-Rates: $40 sb
Type: Private home	Bldg: 1906 farmhouse

Minimum Stay: none. **Credit Cards Accepted:** MC, V. **Open:** all year. Resident dog. No dogs please. Resident cat. No cats please. Nonsmoking host. Guests may smoke in living room. Children welcome. **Discounts:** none.

Reservation Contact: Ohio Valley Bed & Breakfast, Nancy Cully, 6876 Taylor Mill Rd., Independence, KY 41051; 606–356–7865.

CANFIELD

ID: 44406SHI

FISHING, SWIMMING, NATURE WALKS; NEAR YOUNGSTOWN.

Near U.S. 62, U.S. 224, I–76, I–80.

This contemporary home is located on five secluded acres yet is easily accessible from the turnpike. Cleveland and Pittsburg are about one-and-a-half hours away, and Akron is about forty-five minutes away. The very spacious house has an unusually attractive and distinctive design, with several decks and a massive stone chimney. You can swim or fish in the private lake or enjoy quiet nature walks. There are conference rooms for small business meetings, an intercom system, and room phones. The exercise room is equipped with a whirlpool, exercise bike, and ping pong, pool, and card tables. There are four second-floor guest rooms, all of which sleep two. Guests are served a Continental Plus breakfast in addition to lunch. Other amenities include kitchen and laundry privileges, TV, four fireplaces, a wood-burning stove, bicycles, and fishing equipment. Your host enjoys travel, cooking, reading, fishing, and swimming.

No. Rooms: 4	**Breakfast:** Continental Plus
Singles: None	**S-Rates:** $89 pb
Doubles: 4 pb	**D-Rates:** $129 pb
Type: Private home	**Bldg:** 1985 contemporary design

Minimum Stay: none. **Credit Card(s) Accepted:** MC, V. **Open:** all year. Dog in residence. No dogs please. No resident cats. No cats please. Non-smoking host. Guests may smoke. Residence not appropriate for children. **Discounts:** weekly.

Reservation Contact: Bed & Breakfast Registry Ltd., Gary Winget, Box 8174, St. Paul, MN 55108; 612–646–4238.

CINCINNATI
ID: 2–OHIO

PLEASANT RIDGE, KING'S ISLAND, CINCINNATI GARDENS.

Near I–75, I–74, Montgomery Rd., Norwood Lateral.

Convenient to downtown, Cincinnati Gardens, Kings Island, and shopping, this spacious Tudor home is situated on a gas-lit street lined with large shade trees in a secluded residential area. Tennis and golf are nearby. There are two Spanish-motif guest rooms with reading lights and ample drawer and closet space. One has a king-sized waterbed and the other has a queen-sized waterbed. Guests may use the patio, and off-street parking, TV, telephone, arrival/departure transportation, and area tours are also available. A Continental breakfast is served. Your host, currently in hotel management, loves sports, travel, music, and theater.

No. Rooms: 2	**Breakfast:** Continental
Singles: None	**S-Rates:** $25 sb
Doubles: 2 sb	**D-Rates:** $30 sb
Type: Private home	**Bldg:** Tudor

Minimum Stay: none. **Credit Card(s) Accepted:** MC, V. **Open:** all year. No resident dogs. No dogs please. No resident cats. No cats please. Host smokes. Guests may smoke in residence. Children welcome with restrictions. **Discounts:** none.

Reservation Contact: Ohio Valley Bed & Breakfast, Nancy Cully, 6876 Taylor Mill Rd., Independence, KY 41051; 606–356–7865.

ID: 3–OHIO

UNIVERSITY OF CINCINNATI, ZOO, XAVIER UNIVERSITY, TAFT ART MUSEUM.

Near I–75, I–471, I–71, I–275.

Though located on a private shaded street in an exclusive neighborhood, this turn-of-the-century Victorian stone mansion is near public transportation and I–75. Ample parking is available in the circular driveway. You can enjoy the lovely yard, deck, and an unusual fountain large enough for wading and sunning. Entry, through the wrought-iron gates, leads to a large hallway, with natural woodwork, tiled floor, stained glass, and sweeping staircase. Furnishings are an interesting blend of antiques and Art-Deco. There are two second-floor guest rooms. One has Wedgewood wood tiles, double bed, sofa, reading lights, and private bath; the other, a corner room, has double bed, antiques, and a bath shared with your hosts. A Full breakfast is served. TV and laundry facilities, additional meals, arrival/departure transportation, and area tours are available. One of your hosts is in advertising, and the other owns a clothing store. They both travel and enjoy cooking.

No. Rooms: 2	**Breakfast:** Full
Singles: None	**S-Rates:** $50 pb, $45 sb
Doubles: 1 pb, 1 sb	**D-Rates:** $55 pb, $50 sb
Type: Private home	**Bldg:** 1900 Victorian stone

Minimum Stay: none. **Credit Card(s) Accepted:** none. **Open:** all year. Dog in residence. Guests may bring dog. No resident cats. No cats please. Nonsmoking host. Guests may not smoke in guest rooms. Children welcome with restrictions. **Discounts:** none.

Reservation Contact: Ohio Valley Bed & Breakfast, Nancy Cully, 6876 Taylor Mill Rd., Independence, KY 41051; 606–356–7865.

ID: 5–OHIO

UNIVERSITY OF CINCINNATI, CINCINNATI REDS, CINCINNATI BENGALS, KING'S ISLAND.

Near I–75, I–471, I–74, I–71.

This large frame house, built in 1910, is on a lovely tree-lined street in the Gaslight District, centrally located near the university, zoo, several hospitals, major league baseball and football, and the racetrack. Good public bus transportation is accessible. The house is filled with antiques and has an inviting stairway. Three second-floor guest rooms share a guest bath. All have antique furnishings, fans, and ample closet and drawer space. Two rooms have a double and a single bed plus a view of the street and neighboring mansions. A third has a double bed and fireplace. A typical breakfast might include spinach quiche with bacon, homemade muffins, organic oatmeal, fresh fruit, juice, and coffee. A snack bar with refrigerator and microwave is located in the guest area. Arrival/departure transportation, and area tours are available. Your host, a former restauranteur, enjoys cooking, playing bridge, and collecting antiques, and will be happy to direct you to the local attractions.

No. Rooms: 2	**Breakfast:** Full
Singles: None	**S-Rates:** $50 sb
Doubles: 3 sb	**D-Rates:** $50 sb
Type: Private home	**Bldg:** 1910 large frame

Minimum Stay: none. **Credit Card(s) Accepted:** none. **Open:** all year.

No resident dogs. No dogs please. Cat in residence. No cats please. Host smokes. Guests may not smoke in guest rooms. Children welcome with restrictions. **Discounts:** none.

Reservation Contact: Ohio Valley Bed & Breakfast, Nancy Cully, 6876 Taylor Mill Rd., Independence, KY 41051; 606–356–7865.

CLEVELAND
ID: PVT–001

CASE WESTERN RESERVE UNIVERSITY, SEVERANCE HALL, CLEVELAND PLAYHOUSE.

Near I–271, I–90.

This Tudor-style home on a historic boulevard of beautiful homes and mansions is located one mile from the cultural center of Cleveland. This house was built in the 1920s and is listed on the National Register of Historic Places; it boasts ornate ceilings and cornices, beautiful woodwork, leaded and stained-glass windows, and antique furnishings. There are two guest rooms with double beds and private baths. Other amenities include a fireplace, TV, telephone, off-street parking, and use of the yard. A Full breakfast is served. Your well-traveled hosts enjoy boating, cross-country skiing, reading, and music.

No. Rooms: 2	**Breakfast:** Full
Singles: None	**S-Rates:** $50 pb
Doubles: 2 pb	**D-Rates:** $60 pb
Type: Private townhouse	**Bldg:** 1921 Tudor style

Minimum Stay: none. **Credit Card(s) Accepted:** none. **Open:** all year. Dog in residence. No dogs please. No cats please. Nonsmoking host. Guest may not smoke in guest rooms. Children welcome. **Discounts:** for extended stays.

Reservation Contact: Private Lodgings, Inc., Roberta Cahen, Box 18590, Cleveland, OH 44118; 216–321–3213.

ID: PVT–002

HISTORIC DISTRICT.

Near I–271, I–90.

This historic boulevard is lined with large homes and mansions built in the 1920s. The house is near Cleveland's cultural center, museums, universities, and medical facilities. It has natural wood, original art, Oriental rugs, antiques, and collectibles. Guests will want to stroll the landscaped yard with reflecting pool and gardens. Two guest rooms with private baths are available. One has a single bed and the other has a double hide-a-bed. A Continental Plus breakfast is served and arrival/departure transportation is available. Your host is an art collector who is interested in public radio and television and travel.

No. Rooms: 2
Singles: 1 pb
Doubles: 1 pb
Type: Private home

Breakfast: Continental Plus
S-Rates: $50 pb
D-Rates: $60 pb
Bldg: 1925

Minimum Stay: none. **Credit Card(s) Accepted:** none. **Open:** all year. Resident dog. No dogs please. No resident cats. No cats please. Non-smoking host. Guests may smoke in residence. Children welcome with restrictions. **Discounts:** weekly.

Reservation Contact: Private Lodgings, Inc., Roberta Cahen, Box 18590, Cleveland, OH 44118; 216–321–3213.

NEW RICHMOND

ID: 1–OHIO

30 MINUTES TO CINCINNATI; GRANT'S BIRTHPLACE, OHIO RIVER.

Near I–275, OH Rte. 52

At this restored, seventy-year-old farmhouse guests will find a shaded patio for watching birds and wildlife as well as a pond for fishing. This secluded spot surrounded by wooded natural beauty is 30 minutes from Cincinnati. One of the two guest rooms is a nicely appointed suite with a queen-sized bed, sitting room with fireplace, private bath, and private entrance. The second guest room has a double bed and shared bath. A seven-course country breakfast is served. Your host enjoys birdwatching, waterskiing, gardening, and raising sheep.

No. Rooms: 2
Singles: None
Doubles: 1 pb, 1 sb
Type: Private home

Breakfast: Full
S-Rates: $75 pb, $35 sb
D-Rates: $75 pb, $35 sb
Bldg: 1910 farmhouse

Minimum Stay: none. **Credit Card(s) Accepted:** MC, V. **Open:** all year. No resident dogs. No dogs please. No resident cats. No cats please. Host smokes. Guest may smoke in residence. Children welcome with restrictions. **Discounts:** none.

Reservation Contact: Ohio Valley Bed & Breakfast, Nancy Cully, 6876 Taylor Mill Rd., Independence, KY 41051; 606–356–7865.

OKLAHOMA

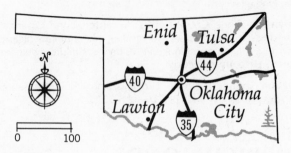

TULSA

ID: OZARK401

PHILBROOK ARTS CENTER, UNIVERSITY OF TULSA.

Near I–44.

This five-level home is located on a half-acre at the edge of Tulsa and overlooks the city's skyline. The home features ten-foot ceilings, crown moldings, antiques, a grand piano in the living room, balconies, and a spacious deck. The two guest rooms have color cable TV, telephones, private balconies, and private baths. One has a queen-sized Queen Anne bed and the other has twin beds. A Full breakfast is served in the dining room or on the deck. Free transportation is provided to and from the airport, and guests may enjoy a spin around the neighborhood on a bicycle built for two.

No. Rooms: 2
Singles: None
Doubles: 2 pb
Type: Private home

Breakfast: Full
S-Rates: $45–$50 pb
D-Rates: $45–$50 pb
Bldg: Contemporary 5-level

Minimum Stay: none. **Credit Card(s) Accepted:** none. **Open:** all year. Resident dog. No dogs please. No resident cats. No cats please. Non-smoking host. Guests may not smoke in residence. Children welcome with restrictions. **Discounts:** none.

Reservation Contact: Ozark Mountain Country Bed & Breakfast, Linda Johnson & Kay Cameron, Box 295, Branson, MO 65726; 417–334–4720.

OREGON

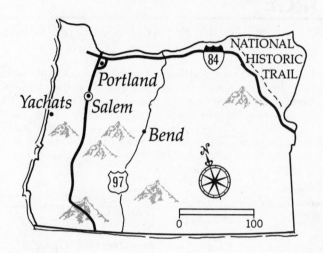

BEND

ID: LARA

MT. BACHELOR SKIING, FISHING, BIKING, WHITE-WATER RAFTING.

Near Congress & Louisiana sts.

This spacious house, built by a Bend pioneer in 1910, has a large lawn and sheltered patio for your relaxation as well as a living room with fireplace and a formal dining room. The prime location offers easy access to downtown shopping and restaurants while retaining a secluded atmosphere. The home overlooks Drake Park and Mirror Pond and is adjacent to the main road to Mt. Bachelor. The guest rooms are spacious and include queen-sized beds and private baths. Amenities for your use include TV, telephone, sauna, hot tub, and off-street parking. The hearty Full breakfast consists of fresh fruit, juice, omelets or quiche, Belgian waffles with fruit and whipped cream, and coffee. Your host, a teacher, is also a licensed raft guide and a skier.

No. Rooms: 5	**Breakfast:** Full
Singles: None	**S-Rates:** $45 pb
Doubles: 5 pb	**D-Rates:** $55 pb
Type: Private home	**Bldg:** 1910

Minimum Stay: none. **Credit Card(s) Accepted:** AE, MC. **Open:** all year. No resident dogs. No dogs please. No resident cats. No cats please. Nonsmoking host. Guests may not smoke in guest rooms. Children welcome. **Discounts:** after five nights.

Reservation Contact: Lara House Bed & Breakfast, Cheryl Hukari, 640 NW Congress, Bend, OR 97701; 503–388–4064.

BRIDLE VAIL/COLUMBIA GORGE

ID: LH–307–OR

PARKS, HIKING TRAILS, WATERFALLS, RESTAURANTS.

Near I–84.

Crafted out of rough lumber and knotty pine, this country lodge was built in the 1920s to accommodate travelers on the Columbia River Highway. Now refurbished, the lodge has two upstairs guest rooms that share a bath. Each room has a double bed plus a day bed that would be suitable for a child. A Full breakfast is served and there is a large common room available for guests' use. The lodge is near parks, hiking trails, waterfalls, and the unsurpassed beauty of the Columbia River Gorge. Your hosts are interested in travel and antiques.

No. Rooms: 2	**Breakfast:** Full
Singles: None	**S-Rates:** $45 sb
Doubles: 2 sb	**D-Rates:** $45 sb
Type: Private home	**Bldg:** Country lodge

Minimum Stay: none. **Credit Card(s) Accepted:** none. **Open:** all year. No resident dogs. No dogs please. No resident cats. No cats please. Non-smoking host. Guests may not smoke in residence. Children welcome. **Discounts:** none.

Reservation Contact: Pacific Bed & Breakfast Agency, Irmgard Castleberry, 701 N.W. 60th, Seattle, WA 98107; 206–784–0539.

CANNON BEACH

ID: 312A–NW

COASTAL AREA.

Near Hwy. 101.

Guests can listen to the surf from the wooded setting of this contemporary home. Two cheerful guest rooms share a bath. One of the rooms has a king-sized bed, traditional furniture with some antiques, carpeting, lots of closet space, and a view of the woods and landscaping. The other room has a queen-sized bed plus a single bed and furnishings similar to the first room. A Full breakfast is served. Your host, a teacher, enjoys antiques, reading, and arts and crafts.

No. Rooms: 2	**Breakfast:** Full
Singles: None	**S-Rates:** $60 sb
Doubles: 2 sb	**D-Rates:** $60 sb
Type: Private home	**Bldg:** Contemporary

Minimum Stay: none. **Credit Card(s) Accepted:** none. **Open:** all year. No resident dogs. No dogs please. No resident cats. No cats please. Non-smoking host. Guests may not smoke in residence. Children welcome with restrictions. **Discounts:** none.

Reservation Contact: Northwest Bed & Breakfast, Inc., L. Friedman & G. Shaich, 610 SW Broadway, #606, Portland, OR 97205; 503–243–7616.

COOS BAY
ID: C–1–PLUS

OREGON DUNES, COOS-CURRY MUSEUM, SHORE ACRES & CAPE ARGO STATE PARKS.

Near Coos River Hwy., Hwy. 101.

This rustic cabin in a rural setting is close to a state park and thirty minutes from ocean beaches. It is located on a river with a beach. The residence is furnished with country antiques and quilts. The brick fireplace will keep you warm on chilly evenings and an antique wood cooking stove and small kitchen are at your convenience for preparing a full breakfast (ingredients are provided). A double bed with beautiful bedding, a sitting area, and private bath with a tin tub are offered. You will find fresh flowers in your room and mints beside the bed. The cabin provides peace, quiet, and privacy, although your hosts are close by to meet any needs you may have. One of your hosts enjoys collecting old cars; the other likes to cross-stitch and garden.

No. Rooms: 1	**Breakfast:** Full
Singles: None	**S-Rates:** $60 pb
Doubles: 1 pb	**D-Rates:** $60 pb
Type: Private cottage	**Bldg:** 1945 rustic

Minimum Stay: 2 days. **Credit Card(s) Accepted:** none. **Open:** all year. Dog in residence. A dog is allowed with restrictions. Cat in residence. No cats please. Nonsmoking host. Guests may not smoke in guest rooms. Children welcome with restrictions. **Discounts:** weekly.

Reservation Contact: Pacific Bed & Breakfast Agency, Irmgard Castleberry, 701 N.W. 60th, Seattle, WA 98107; 206–784–0539.

GOLD BEACH
ID: C–23–PLUS

BEACHES, WHALE WATCHING, WINDSURFING, JET-BOAT RIDES, FISHING.

Near Hwy. 101, Hunter Creek Rd.

From this house, high in the Siskiyou foothills, no other residences can be seen. Ocean beaches are nearby, and Rogue River, with its jet-boat trips and fishing, is only five miles away. This location is a wonderful marriage of house and grounds; it is beautifully serene and colorful with wild and cultivated flowers and shrubs, as well as all kinds of trees. Now and then deer wander down the hill or rabbits pop out and make an appearance. At times you can even hear the ocean in the distance. The gazebo, set amidst myrtlewood, pine, cedar, hemlock, and oak, houses a hot tub. The house is furnished with antiques and has a wood-burning stove, perfect for nestling around on cold, rainy nights. There is also a good library with books to suit nearly every taste, and five wooded, hilly acres to explore. The first spacious guest room has cedar paneling and is decorated with antiques. It has an antique double bed, fresh flowers on the marble-topped chest of drawers, an antique desk, two easy chairs, and bookshelves lined with books of regional interest. The second room has cedar-paneled walls lined with books, a single Hollywood bed, easy chair, and sliding glass doors leading to a secluded garden. The rooms are air-conditioned, and bathrobes, slippers, sherry, and night snack are provided. A Full breakfast, which might consist of a casserole or eggs with bacon, sausage, ham, and cheese, as well as fruit, homemade breads, and coffee or tea, is served. Your well-traveled host enjoys gardening, reading, weaving, and antiques.

No. Rooms: 2	**Breakfast:** Full
Singles: 1 sb	**S-Rates:** $40 sb
Doubles: 1 sb	**D-Rates:** $45 sb
Type: Private home	**Bldg:** 1980 ranch

Minimum Stay: none. **Credit Card(s) Accepted:** none. **Open:** all year, except Christmas. No resident dogs. No dogs please. No resident cats. No cats please. Nonsmoking host. Guests may not smoke in guest rooms. Children welcome. **Discounts:** none.

Reservation Contact: Pacific Bed & Breakfast Agency, Irmgard Castleberry, 701 N.W. 60th, Seattle, WA 98107; 206–784–0539.

GOVERNMENT CAMP   ID: 97028FAL

MT. HOOD NATIONAL FOREST, MULTROPOR SKI BOWL.

Near U.S. 26.

This rustic little inn is located in the Mount Hood National Forest across from the Multropor Ski Bowl and near cross-country ski trails. Guests will enjoy the wonderful mountain views, wrap-around decks, and the Great Room with its oak furnishings and wood-burning stove. There are four guest rooms with private baths. Cat Ballou has a king-sized bed, French doors, family antiques, and a Silver City ghost town painting. Sophia, done in soft blues, peach, and ecru, has twin beds, parquet floors, and French doors. Safari, with a queen-sized bed, is filled with toy stuffed animals and furnished with an antique trunk and rattan furniture. The Master room has a French country decor with soft white carpets, a four-poster cherry bed, and a Victorian love seat and rocker. This room also boasts a Jacuzzi for two and a Finish sauna and has sliding glass doors open to a private deck overlooking the forest. A Full breakfast is served.

No. Rooms: 4	Breakfast: Full
Singles: None	S-Rates: $70–$95 pb
Doubles: 4 pb	D-Rates: $70–$95 pb
Type: Inn	Bldg: Wood frame

Minimum Stay: none. **Credit Card(s) Accepted:** MC, V. **Open:** all year. No resident dogs. No dogs please. No resident cats. No cats please. Non-smoking host. Guests may not smoke in residence. Children welcome. **Discounts:** groups only.

Reservation Contact: Bed & Breakfast Registry, Gary Winget, Box 8174, St. Paul, MN 55108; 612–646–4238.

LINCOLN CITY

ID: 97367LIN

TWENTY MIRACLE MILES, ANTIQUES, ART GALLERIES; SWIMMING, SAILING, CRABBING.

Near Rte. 18, U.S. 101.

Two blocks from the beach, this attractive home provides a refreshing, rustic atmosphere. It has two decks for relaxing and sunbathing, and many amenities, including mats, umbrellas, kits and beach games for sea-side fun, bicycles, sailboat, color TV, laundry and refigerator facilities, and off-street parking. Two cheerful guest rooms are in a private wing of the house. One offers double bed and shared bath; the other features double bed plus bunk beds and private bath with double sink. A Continental Plus breakfast is served. This scenic area offers a wide variety of activities, with swimming, boating, fishing, crabbing, and clamming. There are also antique and specialty shops, restaurants, art galleries, hiking in Devil's Lake State Park, beautiful drives, and crafts of all types, including glass-blowing. Additional meals, arrival/departure transportation, area tours, and child care are available. Your hosts enjoy sailing, square dancing, music, and painting.

No. Rooms: 2	Breakfast: Continental Plus
Singles: None	S-Rates: $35 pb, $35 sb
Doubles: 1 pb, 1 sb	D-Rates: $45 pb, $40 sb
Type: Private cottage	Bldg: Rustic

Minimum Stay: none. **Credit Card(s) Accepted:** none. **Open:** all year. Dog in residence. Guests may bring dog. No resident cats. A cat is allowed with restrictions. Nonsmoking host. Guests may not smoke in residence. Children welcome. **Discounts:** none.

Reservation Contact: Bed & Breakfast Registry Ltd., Gary Winget, Box 8174, St. Paul, MN 55108; 612–646–4238.

PORT ORFORD

ID: 97465HOM

BEACH, JET BOAT RIDES, HISTORIC LIGHTHOUSE, WHALE WATCHING.

Near U.S. 101.

Port Orford was founded in 1851 by Captain William Tichenor, who named the settlement after a look-alike town in southern England. This modern two-story home, in an exceptional location, affords unobstructed views of miles of impressive seascapes and forested mountains sloping to the sea. The house is just a short block from a natural deep-water harbor, with access to miles of secluded beaches for agate and driftwood hunters. It is also near some excellent salmon rivers. This part of the coast is a favorite with scuba divers and surfers. Whale-watching season runs from October to May, and the Oregon Islands National Wildlife Refuge is just offshore. The house has two guest rooms with ocean views and private baths. Both rooms have queen-sized beds with locally crafted myrtlewood headboards. Your hosts, a teacher and a carpenter, enjoy weaving and fiber arts, home building, and their personal computer.

No. Rooms: 2	**Breakfast:** Full
Singles: None	**S-Rates:** $50–$55 pb
Doubles: 2 pb	**D-Rates:** $50–$55 pb
Type: Private home	**Bldg:** 1985 contemporary

Minimum Stay: none. **Credit Card(s) Accepted:** MC, V. **Open:** all year, except holidays. No resident dogs. No dogs please. Cat in residence. No cats please. Nonsmoking host. Guests may not smoke in residence. Residence not appropriate for children. **Discounts:** none.

Reservation Contact: Bed & Breakfast Registry Ltd., Gary Winget, Box 8174, St. Paul, MN 55108; 612–646–4238.

PORTLAND

ID: P–2–PLUS

15 MINUTES FROM DOWNTOWN.

Near Pacific Hwy. & 64th, I–5.

This Cape Code-style home is furnished with traditional and antique furniture. You are welcome to use the living room or join your hosts in the family room with its wood-burning stove and TV. From this area you can walk out to the private garden surrounded by an eight-foot ivy hedge. The two second-floor guest rooms, which share a bath, are very private, since your hosts' quarters are on the main floor. One room, done in yellow with a flowered wallpaper, has a double bed, dresser, and vanity; the other has twin beds with rose dust ruffles, a desk, and built-in dresser. Arrival/departure transportation and additional meals are available. A Full breakfast, which might include potato pancakes with applesauce or waffles with jam or syrup, is served. Your hosts like gardening, canning, sewing, and rock collecting. Reservations will not be accepted during the last two weeks of December or on holidays.

No. Rooms: 2	**Breakfast:** Full
Singles: None	**S-Rates:** $30 sb
Doubles: 2 sb	**D-Rates:** $40 sb
Type: Private home	**Bldg:** 1939 Cape Cod

Minimum Stay: none. **Credit Card(s) Accepted:** none. **Open:** all year. No resident dogs. No dogs please. No resident cats. No cats please. Non-smoking host. Guests may not smoke in guest rooms. Children welcome with restrictions. **Discounts:** none.

Reservation Contact: Pacific Bed & Breakfast Agency, Irmgard Castleberry, 701 N.W. 60th, Seattle, WA 98107; 206–784–0539.

ID: NE–011–PAC

TEN MINUTES TO DOWNTOWN BUSINESS AND SHOPPING.

Near I–5, NE 22nd.

Fit for a king or queen, this stately mansion features an elegant, open staircase, enormous public rooms, priceless antiques, hand-painted murals, stained-glass windows, hardwood floors, Oriental rugs, mahogany woodwork, and the original light fixtures. The six guest rooms have queen-sized or double beds. One room has a canopy bed, and two rooms have private baths. A Continental breakfast is served. This enchanting residence is only ten minutes from downtown Portland. Your hosts' hobbies include art, music, travel, and restoring antiques.

No. Rooms: 6	**Breakfast:** Continental
Singles: None	**S-Rates:** $60 pb, $47–$58 sb
Doubles: 2 pb, 4 sb	**D-Rates:** $65 pb, $47–$58 sb
Type: Private home	**Bldg:** 1921 mansion

Minimum Stay: none. **Credit Card(s) Accepted:** MC, V. **Open:** all year. No resident dogs. No dogs please. No resident cats. No cats please. Non-smoking host. Guests may not smoke in residence. Children welcome with restrictions. **Discounts:** none.

Reservation Contact: Pacific Bed & Breakfast, Irmgard Castelberry, 701 NW 60th St., Seattle, WA 98107; 206–784–0539.

ID: NE–015–PAC

SHOPPING, RESTAURANTS.

Near I–5, 28th Ave.

This English-style home is nicely situated on a tree-lined street in a historic neighborhood close to shopping and restaurants. A baby grand piano sits in the antique-filled living room, and the dining room boasts gleaming wood floors and mahogany woodwork. One of the guest rooms has a double bed, fireplace, TV, dressing room, and private bath. The other is a suite with a king-sized bed, a single bed, a double hide-a-bed, private bath, and use of the kitchenette. A Full breakfast is served. Your hosts enjoy antiques, gardening, and travel, and speak some French and Spanish. Dinner and child care are available.

No. Rooms: 2	**Breakfast:** Full
Singles: None	**S-Rates:** $45–$50 pb
Doubles: 2 pb	**D-Rates:** $50–$55 pb
Type: Private home	**Bldg:** English masonry

Minimum Stay: none. **Credit Card(s) Accepted:** none. **Open:** all year. No resident dogs. No dogs please. No resident cats. No cats please. Non-smoking host. Guests may not smoke in residence. Children welcome. **Discounts:** none.

Reservation Contact: Pacific Bed & Breakfast, Irmgard Castleberry, 701 NW 60th St., Seattle, WA 98107; 206–784–0539.

ID: 371A–TRAVUN

LADDS ADDITION.

Near Hawthorne & Harrison, I–84, I–205, I–5.

This English Tudor home is located in Ladds Addition, a quiet and beautiful historic area on the National Registry, with rose and rhododendron gardens, tree-lined streets, and gracious homes. The air-conditioned home has outstanding landscaping and an elegant yet comfortable decor. It is ideal for anyone with allergies, since it has an electronic air cleaner. There are three professionally decorated guest rooms. The two second-floor rooms share a bath, while the main-floor guest room has private bath. One of the upstairs rooms, done in green and white with gold carpeting, has a single bed with a velveteen spread, white marble table, lamps, and chair; the other room has pale peach walls, white carpeting, double bed, a dresser, rocker, night tables, and clock radio. The room on the main floor has a double bed, desk, two lamps, large mirrors, and a platform rocker. Your host enjoys travel, landscape gardening, gourmet cooking, theater, and entertaining.

No. Rooms: 3	**Breakfast:** Full
Singles: 1 sb	**S-Rates:** $45 pb, $35 sb
Doubles: 1 pb, 1 sb	**D-Rates:** $45 pb, $35 sb
Type: Private home	**Bldg:** 1925 English Tudor

Minimum Stay: none. **Credit Card(s) Accepted:** none. **Open:** all year. No resident dogs. No dogs please. Cat in residence. No cats please. Non-smoking host. Guests may not smoke in residence. Residence not appropriate for children. **Discounts:** none. Norwegian spoken.

Reservation Contact: Northwest Bed & Breakfast, Inc., L. Friedman &

G. Shaich, 610 SW Broadway, #606, Portland, OR 97205; 503–243–7616.

ID: 408A–NW

PART OF SCENIC DRIVE.

Near 50th & Alameda, I–84, I–205, I–5.

Frank Lloyd Wright designed this home, built in 1910, with the same design of stained glass and oak exhibited in the Smithsonian Institute. Also noteworthy is the beautifully maintained old-fashioned garden of fragrant roses and herbs. There are three guest rooms with double beds and shared guest bath. The first has a walnut bedroom set, armoire with mirror, an Amish quilt, two lamps, and a satin-covered chair. Another room offers Roman shades with Afghan fabric and rugs, a hundred-year-old quilt, chest, TV, lamps, and walnut bedroom set. The third room provides wonderful views of the city with three walls of windows, and includes a chest and lamps. A Full breakfast is served. Your host, an avid opera and concert fan, has traveled throughout the world and enjoys gardening, weaving, hiking, and reading.

No. Rooms: 3	**Breakfast:** Full
Singles: None	**S-Rates:** $30–$45 sb
Doubles: 3 sb	**D-Rates:** $30–$45 sb
Type: Private home	**Bldg:** 1910 Federal

Minimum Stay: none. **Credit Card(s) Accepted:** none. **Open:** all year. No resident dogs. No dogs please. No resident cats. No cats please. Non-smoking host. Guests may not smoke in residence. Children welcome. **Discounts:** none.

Reservation Contact: Northwest Bed & Breakfast, Inc., L. Friedman & G. Shaich, 610 SW Broadway, #606, Portland, OR 97205; 503–243–7616.

ID: 97214GAR

5 MINUTES FROM DOWNTOWN, THEATER, CONCERT HALL, RESTAURANTS.

Near U.S. 30, I–5, I–80.

This beautiful English Tudor home, located in historic Ladd's Addition, is just five minutes from downtown Portland, theaters, concert halls, and fine restaurants. There are two guest rooms with private baths, walk-in closets, floor-to-ceiling mirrors, TVs, and telephones. Guests are allowed light kitchen privileges for coffee, tea, and wine and cheese. The house has central air-conditioning and electronic air cleaners. A Continental Plus breakfast is served on the patio, weather permitting.

No. Rooms: 2	**Breakfast:** Continental Plus
Singles: None	**S-Rates:** $33 pb
Doubles: 2 pb	**D-Rates:** $43 pb
Type: Private home	**Bldg:** 1920s English Tudor

Minimum Stay: none. **Credit Card(s) Accepted:** none. **Open:** all year. No resident dogs. No dogs please. Cat in residence. No cats please. Non-smoking host. Guests may not smoke in residence. Children are welcome with restrictions. **Discounts:** none.

Reservation Contact: Bed & Breakfast Registry Ltd., Gary Winget, Box 8174, St. Paul, MN 55108; 612–646–4238.

WILSONVILLE
ID: A–14–PLUS

ANTIQUE SHOPS, MUSEUM, WINERIES; 12 MILES SOUTH OF PORTLAND.

Near Stafford Rd., I–5.

This contemporary house is situated in a quiet, pastoral setting, edged by tall fir trees, two miles from Interstate 5, in a neighborhood that includes Christmas-tree farms and pastures for sheep, show horses, and llamas. It is five miles from the historic settlement of Aurora and close to antique shops, a museum, and Washington County wineries. Enjoy a stroll across the laws and over the creek bridges, where the trees are full of birds, and an occasional deer or racoon can be seen. The home is beautifully decorated with lovely Victorian antiques, including a well-tuned pump organ. You will find a formal dining room and country French kitchen. The nicely furnished guest suite consists of a large room with double bed and picture window overlooking the garden and creek, a smaller room with a single bed, and a sitting room with color TV. A private bath and private entrance are featured. A Full breakfast is served with your morning paper in the sunroom amidst wicker and ferns. A typical breakfast includes juice, fresh fruit (in season from your hosts' garden and orchard), local farm-fresh eggs, sausage, homemade muffins or cinnamon rolls, and freshly ground coffee. One of your well-traveled hosts is a retired oil-company executive, who enjoys gardening, travel, tennis, and woodworking; the other host is a retired teacher with interests in antiques, decorating, baking, genealogy, and local history.

No. Rooms: 2	**Breakfast:** Full
Singles: 1 sb	**S-Rates:** $40 pb, $40 sb
Doubles: 1 pb	**D-Rates:** $45 pb, $45 sb
Type: Private home	**Bldg:** 1984 conventional

Minimum Stay: none. **Credit Card(s) Accepted:** none. **Open:** all year. No resident dogs. No dogs please. No resident cats. No cats please. Non-smoking host. Guests may not smoke in guest rooms. Children welcome with restrictions. **Discounts:** none.

Reservation Contact: Pacific Bed & Breakfast Agency, Irmgard Castle-berry, 701 N.W. 60th, Seattle, WA 98107; 206–784–0539.

YACHATS

ID: 97498ORE

SUISLAW NATIONAL FOREST, NATIONAL DUNES, HECETA LIGHTHOUSE, SEA LION CAVES; 9 MILES SOUTH OF YACHATS.

Near U.S. 101, Rte. 34.

This secluded little inn is nestled on the high cliffs of the Pacific. You have daylight access to a unique two-story glassed-in look-out tower for coastal viewing, seasonal whale watching, and the observation of beautiful surf action during winter coastal storms. You can enjoy ocean views from the private deck and bonfires on the beach, and evenings can be spent in front of the fireplace in the candlelit living room. Three guest rooms offer private baths and double beds. A Continental breakfast is served.

No. Rooms: 3	**Breakfast:** Continental
Singles: None	**S-Rates:** $40–$60 pb
Doubles: 3 pb	**D-Rates:** $46–$66 pb
Type: Inn	**Bldg:** 1962 contemporary

Minimum Stay: 2 days on weekends. **Credit Card(s) Accepted:** none. **Open:** all year. No resident dogs. No dogs please. No resident cats. No cats please. Nonsmoking host. Guests may not smoke in residence. Children welcome with restrictions. **Discounts:** for long stays.

Reservation Contact: Bed & Breakfast Registry Ltd., Gary Winget, Box 8174, St. Paul, MN 55108; 612–646–4238.

PENNSYLVANIA

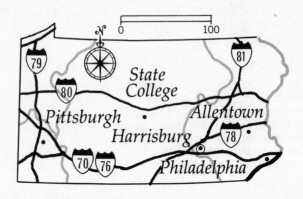

ALLENTOWN

ID: OAK–TREE–PA

LEHIGH VALLEY.

Near I–78, Rte. 9, Cedar Crest Blvd.

One of the oldest homes in the area, this location is near local colleges and hospitals. It offers a guest suite consisting of an upstairs bedroom with a double and two twin beds, a private bath, and a downstairs sitting room. The two rooms are joined by a staircase that is separate from the family quarters. There are fans, but no air-conditioning. Your hosts like to travel and have interests in education and current events.

No. Rooms: 1	**Breakfast:** Guest's choice
Singles: None	**S-Rates:** $50 pb
Doubles: 1 pb	**D-Rates:** $60 pb
Type: Private home	**Bldg:** Brick

Minimum Stay: none. **Credit Card(s) Accepted:** MC, V. **Open:** all year. No resident dogs. No dogs please. Resident cats. No cats please. Non-smoking host. Guests may not smoke in residence. Children welcome with restrictions. **Discounts:** none.

Reservation Contact: Bed & Breakfast of Southeast Pennsylvania, Patricia & Ruth Morrison, 146 W. Philadelphia Ave., Boyertown, PA 19512; 215–367–4688.

BOALSBURG

PENN STATE, BOAL MANSION, COLUMBUS CHAPEL, LOCAL CRAFTS.

Near Rte. 322.

At the foot of Tussey Mountain lies the quaint village of Boalsburg, reportedly the birthplace of Memorial or Decoration Day, since graves in the old cemetary were decorated at least five years prior to the passing of the official ordinance. It was once a stagecoach stop along the King's Highway to the west. Many of the houses are built of native stone with deeply recessed windows and doors with delicate fan lights above. Building of this wonderful farm home began around 1872, with the last addition made in the early 1900s. The home, which now sits in the middle of a contemporary neighborhood, is filled with family treasures and antiques. Your hosts have been meticulous in its restoration, and each large room has a character all its own. There are two guest rooms with antique furnishings, double beds, and family quilts. One room has a view of the woods, stream, and mountain range in the background; the other has a hide-a-bed that can accommodate a third person. The guest rooms share a bath. During the week, a Continental Plus breakfast is served; on weekends a Full breakfast is offered. One of your hosts is a special-education teacher; the other runs his own distributing business. Both enjoy meeting people, antiquing, reading, and church activities. The residence is within walking distance of the 28th Division shrine, Boal Mansion, Columbus Chapel, and downtown Boalsburg's country shops.

No. Rooms: 2　　　　　**Breakfast:** Continental Plus or Full
Singles: None　　　　　**S-Rates:** $28 sb
Doubles: 2 sb　　　　　**D-Rates:** $35–$45 sb
Type: Private home　　　**Bldg:** 1800s Victorian

Minimum Stay: none. **Credit Card(s) Accepted:** none. **Open:** all year. No resident dogs. No dogs please. Cat in residence. No cats please. Non-smoking host. Guests may not smoke in guest rooms. Children welcome with restrictions. **Discounts:** none.

Reservation Contact: Rest & Repast Bed & Breakfast Service, Linda Feltman & Brent Peters, Box 126, Pine Grove Mills, PA 16868; 814–238–1484.

CHESTER COUNTY

30 MINUTES FROM AMISH COUNTRY; VALLEY FORGE NATIONAL PARK, ANDREW WYETH MUSEUM.

Near Rte. 30, Pennsylvania Tpk., Rte. 202.

This charming rural homestead nestles in a hollow of Chester County. Attached to the home is a greenhouse with a hot tub at your disposal.

Two guest rooms share a bath. One room has a queen-sized four-poster bed, working fireplace, and louvered French doors leading to the brick patio; the other, also with a queen-sized four-poster bed, has a wood-burning stove, desk, chair, Iranian rugs, and bookcases. A Full breakfast is served. Arrival/departure transportation is available from the train station. Your hosts are avid travelers, freshwater fishermen, sailors, and computer enthusiasts.

No. Rooms: 2	**Breakfast:** Full
Singles: None	**S-Rates:** $45 sb
Doubles: 2 sb	**D-Rates:** $55 sb
Type: Private home	**Bldg:** Post-and-beam colonial

Minimum Stay: $5 surcharge for 1 night stay. **Credit Card(s) Accepted:** V. **Open:** all year. Dog in residence. No dogs please. No resident cats. No cats please. Nonsmoking host. Guests may not smoke in residence. Children welcome. **Discounts:** none.

Reservation Contact: Bed & Breakfast of Philadelphia, Box 630, Chester Springs, PA 19425; 215–827–9650.

CHICORA
ID: 16025LES

MORAINE STATE PARK, MC CONNELL'S MILL, ALLEGHENY RIVER, PITTSBURGH.

Near U.S. 442, Rte. 68, Rte. 38.

Surrounded by one hundred acres of beautiful rolling hills, this captivating hand-built stone house invites hikes and secluded picnics. There is also a one-acre lake for fishing and swimming. All furnishings are handcrafted. There are two guest rooms; one has twin beds, the other has a double bed, and both share a guest bath. Cots are available for children. In hand-crafted Shaker decor, the guest quarters feature hardwood floors, cherry paneling, handwoven rugs, and a beautiful view of the countryside. A Full breakfast is served. The house is isolated at the end of a rough one-mile dirt lane yet conveniently located just fifteen miles south of I–80. Moraine State Park is to its west and the Allegheny River to its east. Additional meals, arrival/departure transportation, area tours, and child care are sometimes available. Your well-traveled hosts have interests in wood-working, weaving, architecture, and spinning.

No. Rooms: 2	**Breakfast:** Full
Singles: None	**S-Rates:** $30 sb
Doubles: 1 pb, 1 sb	**D-Rates:** $40 sb
Type: Private home	**Bldg:** 1983 stone and solar

Minimum Stay: none. **Credit Card(s) Accepted:** MC, V. **Open:** all year. No resident dogs. No dogs please. No resident cats. No cats please. Nonsmoking host. Guests may not smoke in residence. Children welcome. **Discounts:** none.

Reservation Contact: Bed & Breakfast Registry Ltd., Gary Winget, Box 8174, St. Paul, MN 55108; 612–646–4238.

COWANSVILLE

ID: P–GARROTT

ARMSTRONG COUNTY, ALLEGHENY RIVER, ANTIQUES.

Near Rte. 268.

Celebrate the seasons surrounded by 40 acres of fields, groves of trees, and gardens in this hundred-year-old farmhouse. Every room is furnished with antiques and collectibles, and the library contains a wealth of material on art, architecture, restoration, gardening, and nature. The spacious living room has a fireplace and French doors. In the summer guests can sit on the front porch or fish or swim from the dock. Three guest rooms share two baths. One is done in spruce green and is furnished with twin beds, a hand-painted rush-seat chair, and a reading lamp. Another has hand-stenciled floors complemented by colorful braided rugs, antique furnishings, oil paintings, and framed needlepoint. Floral wallpaper and hand-hooked rugs adorn a third room furnished with a large writing desk, comfortable chair, washstand, dresser, and a high-back, queen-sized oak bed. A Full breakfast is served in the dining room which is furnished with Queen Anne chairs and a large pine table. A welcome snack is also provided. Your host, an educator and counselor, is an avid gardener, bird watcher, astronomer, photographer, and cross-country skier.

No. Rooms: 3	**Breakfast:** Full
Singles: None	**S-Rates:** $50 sb
Doubles: 3 sb	**D-Rates:** $60 sb
Type: Private home	**Bldg:** 1884 Farmhouse

Minimum Stay: none. **Credit Card(s) Accepted:** none. **Open:** all year. Resident dog. No dogs please. No resident cats. No cats please. Host smokes. Guests may smoke downstairs. Children welcome with restrictions. **Discounts:** none.

Reservation Contact: Pittsburgh Bed & Breakfast, Judy Antico, 2190 Ben Franklin Dr., Pittsburgh, PA 15237; 412–367–8080.

EAST GREENVILLE

ID: F2–PA

GOSHENHOPPEN FOLK FESTIVAL.

Near Rte. 29.

This lovely Victorian brick house was the home of the town miller, and the old grist mill is still on the property, in perfect condition. The house, furnished with antiques, is in a rural setting on eight acres of land leading down to the riverbank of a well-known state-stocked trout stream. You are welcome to fish; but a license is required. On the second floor, there are two guest rooms with double beds; one has a private bath. Another second-floor room has a single bed. On the third floor are three rooms, each with twin beds. The bath is shared with the second-floor guest rooms. Third-floor rooms are available only in summer. A Full breakfast is served on the screened porch during the summer and beside the bay window in the kitchen at other times. Your hosts, a retired couple, are active in the Chamber of Commerce and mental-health organizations.

No. Rooms: 6	**Breakfast:** Full
Singles: 1 sb	**S-Rates:** $35 pb, $35 sb
Doubles: 1 pb, 4 sb	**D-Rates:** $50 pb, $45 sb
Type: Private home	**Bldg:** Victorian brick

Minimum Stay: 2 days on holidays. **Credit Card(s) Accepted:** none. **Open:** all year. Dog in residence. No dogs please. No resident cats. No cats please. Nonsmoking host. Guests may not smoke in residence. Children welcome with restrictions. **Discounts:** family rates available.

Reservation Contact: Bed & Breakfast of Southeast Pennsylvania, Joyce Stevenson, Box 278, RD #1, Barto, PA 19504; 215–845–3526.

ELKIN PARK   ID: 19117MAN

INDEPENDENCE NATIONAL HISTORIC PARK, INDEPENDENCE HALL, LIBERTY BELL, HISTORIC HOMES AND SHOPS.

Near Township & York rds., Pennsylvania Tkp.

This exquisite house is on a heavily wooded lot in one of Philadelphia's older, elegant suburbs. It has a sheltered flagstone patio overlooking a running brook, a wonderfully quiet and peaceful spot for reading or relaxing. There is also a den with TV that opens onto a redwood deck, also overlooking the brook. The two delightful second-floor guest rooms offer double or twin beds and Victorian decor; one has a private bath, and one has a shared bath. A Continental Plus breakfast is served in the dining room or on the patio. Shops, restaurants, and public transportation to downtown Philadelphia are just a few blocks away. The homes of Betsy Ross, Edgar Allan Poe, and Dolly Madison are in this area. Society Hill, within walking distance of Independence Hall, an area of restored eighteenth- and nineteenth-century homes and shops is accessible. Independence National Historic Park, with its graceful fountains, landscaping, and tree-lined walks, Ben Franklin's home and press, and the Graff House are other local points of interest. Your charming and very cordial hosts would be happy to guide you to many local attractions. Arrival/departure transportation, additional meals, and area tours are often available.

No. Rooms: 2	**Breakfast:** Continental Plus
Singles: None	**S-Rates:** $40 pb, $40 sb
Doubles: 1 pb, 1 sb	**D-Rates:** $45 pb, $45 sb
Type: Private home	**Bldg:** 1954 contemporary

Minimum Stay: none. **Credit Card(s) Accepted:** none. **Open:** all year. Dog in residence. No dogs please. Cat in residence. No cats please. Host smokes. Guests may smoke. Children welcome. **Discounts:** none.

Reservation Contact: Bed & Breakfast Registry Ltd., Gary Winget, Box 8174, St. Paul, MN 55108; 612–646–4238.

EPHRATA
ID: 17522MIL

LOCAL CRAFTS & ANTIQUES, AMISH & MENNONITE AREAS, WORKING WATER MILLS, COVERED BRIDGES, OUTLET STORES PENNSYLVANIA DUTCH COUNTRY.

Near Academy & Main sts., U.S. 322, U.S. 30.

Beautifully restored, this 1763 stone inn is furnished with antiques and handmade furnishings to create a very romantic, candlelit environment. As you pass through the doorway, you enter a world of eighteenth-century charm, albeit with modern comforts and conveniences. Gardens, great room, tavern room, and library are available to you. Almost every room in the inn has a fireplace, which burns daily during the cool months. There are four guest rooms plus a four-room suite; all sleep at least two and have working fireplaces and private baths. The four-room Cloister Suite consists of a kitchen with dining area, parlor with fireplace, upstairs bedroom with a queen-sized canopy bed, and another bedroom with two single beds. The bath has a whirlpool and shower. A Full all-you-can-eat breakfast is served in the dining room. You are also served tea and a bedtime snack. Dinner is served nightly at 7:30 P.M. for an extra charge. The inn was built by members of the Ephrata Cloister, a unique eighteenth-century Protestant monastic society. The Cloister, now a state museum, is in a little valley that the historic inn overlooks. The inn is also near Lancaster County's largest farmers' market, the Pennsylvania Farm Museum, one of the East Coast's great antique and craft markets, and the historic town of Lititz. Ephrata is central to the nineteenth-century farms of the Old Order Mennonite and Amish, who pursue their daily activities as their forbears did a hundred years ago with horse and wagon. Your gracious host is a director of the local arts center and is interested in flower gardening and antiquarian subjects.

No. Rooms: 8	**Breakfast:** Full
Singles: None	**S-Rates:** $50–$135 pb
Doubles: 8 pb	**D-Rates:** $60–$145 pb
Type: Inn	**Bldg:** 1763 German stone inn

Minimum Stay: 2 nights on weekends. **Credit Card(s) Accepted:** AE, MC, V. **Open:** all year. No resident dogs. Guests may bring dog. No resident cats. Guests may bring cat. Nonsmoking host. Guests may not smoke in guest rooms. Children welcome. **Discounts:** weekly.

Reservation Contact: Bed & Breakfast Registry Ltd., Gary Winget, Box 8174, St. Paul, MN 55108; 612–646–4238.

GREENSBURG

ALLEGHENY MOUNTAINS, LAUREL HIGHLANDS, SETON HILL, ST. VINCENT COLLEGE, WESTMORELAND MUSEUM.

Near rtes. 119 & 30, Pennsylvania Tpk.

Nestled in the foothills of the Allegheny Mountains, just two miles east of Greensburg, is this lovely 1848 Georgian home. Listed in *Historic Places in Western Pennsylvania,* it still possesses the original Egyptian Revival interior woodwork. Large living areas furnished with antiques, as well as the gardens and porches, are available for your use. Four large corner guest rooms with two shared baths are available. One room has a double bed, fireplace, and furnishings from the 1870s; another similar room has twin beds; the third, done in Vermont maple, and the fourth, in an elegant French Provincial style, also have twin beds. A Full breakfast is served. The property, located in the western section of the Laurel Highlands Recreational Area, contains many scenic and historical sites. Seton Hill and St. Vincent colleges are a few minutes away, as are Labrobe, Westmoreland, and Jeannette hospitals. Excellent restaurants, antique shops, golf, and the Westmoreland Museum of Art are nearby. Your hosts, retired professionals, are interested in social work, law, business, gardening, golf, history, and antiques.

No. Rooms: 4	**Breakfast:** Full
Singles: None	**S-Rates:** $40–$55 sb
Doubles: 4 sb	**D-Rates:** $50–$65 sb
Type: Private home	**Bldg:** 1848 Georgian

Minimum Stay: none. **Credit Card(s) Accepted:** AE. **Open:** all year. Dog in residence. No dogs please. No resident cats. No cats please. Nonsmoking host. Guests may not smoke in guest rooms. Children welcome with restrictions. **Discounts:** 10% weekly.

Reservation Contact: Pittsburgh Bed & Breakfast, Judy Antico, 2190 Ben Franklin Dr., Pittsburgh, PA 15237; 412–367–8080.

HOLTWOOD

LANCASTER COUNTY, AMISH COUNTRY.

Near PA 372 & 272.

This country cottage is located on a winding, tree-lined lane. It has a living room with a hide-a-bed, large stone fireplace, TV, VCR, and stained-glass windows; a bedroom with a double bed; a complete kitchen in an alcove off the dining area; and a private bath with shower. There are two decks for sitting outside and an enclosed sun porch which may also be used for children with sleeping bags. A ramp provides good handicapped access. Seven-hundred-acre Muddy Run Park is nearby, and Baltimore and

Gettysburg are about 90 minutes away. Your hosts are a psychologist and a teacher.

No. Rooms: 1	**Breakfast:** Continental
Singles: None	**S-Rates:** $65 pb
Doubles: 1 pb	**D-Rates:** $65 pb
Type: Private home	**Bldg:** Rustic cottage

Minimum Stay: 2 nights on holiday weekends. **Credit Card(s) Accepted:** MC, V. **Open:** all year. No resident dogs. No dogs please. No resident cats. No cats please. Nonsmoking host. Guests may smoke in living room. Children welcome. **Discounts:** weekly.

Reservation Contact: Bed & Breakfast of Southeast Pennsylvania, Patricia Sedor & Ruth Morrison, 146 W. Philadelphia Ave., Boyertown, PA 19512; 215–367–4688.

KENNETT SQUARE   ID: MYERS–PA

LONGWOOD GARDENS, BRANDYWINE RIVER MUSEUM, WINTERHUR, VALLEY FORGE NATIONAL PARK, HAGLEY MUSEUM, FRANKLIN MINT; BRANDYWINE VALLEY.

Near U.S. 202, I–95.

Once a tannery, this historically certified Pennsylvania stone farm house was originally built in 1760, with additions made in the 1830s. The house, furnished with antiques, has a formal Williamsburg decor. The parlor has a fireplace, baby grand piano, and spiral stairwell. The guest room has a magnificent canopied double bed, country French armoire, and private bath; the windows look out onto the rolling pasture. A Full breakfast of homemade delicacies is served by the pool, patio, or in front of the fire in the dining room. Your host, a registered nurse, can also prepare special diet breakfasts. She teaches piano, and is interested in stenciling, and crafts.

No. Rooms: 1	**Breakfast:** Full
Singles: None	**S-Rates:** $50 pb
Doubles: 1 pb	**D-Rates:** $60 pb
Type: Private home	**Bldg:** 1760 stone farmhouse

Minimum Stay: none. **Credit Card(s) Accepted:** none. **Open:** all year. Dog in residence. No dogs please. No resident cats. No cats please. Nonsmoking host. Guests may not smoke in guest rooms. Children welcome. **Discounts:** monthly.

Reservation Contact: Bed & Breakfast of Philadelphia, Louise Mullen, Box 630, Chester Springs, PA 19425; 215–688–1633.

ID: 19348KAN

MUSEUM OF NATURAL HISTORY, HAGLEY MUSEUM, WINTERTHUR, MUSEUM AND GARDENS, BRANDYWINE BATTLEFIELD, LONGWOOD GARDENS.

Near U.S. 1, Rte. 82, U.S. 202.

This cozy home away from home is on a quiet tree-lined residential street, convenient to all area attractions. You have access to the entire house, with its comfortable living room, porch, and yard for leisure hours. There are four guest rooms, one with twin beds, one with double bed, one with king-sized bed, and one with a sofa bed. They are all tastefully furnished and share a guest bath. A Full breakfast is served. The Brandywine Valley offers visitors a wealth of attractions, all within a few miles, and an opportunity to step back into America's past. Longwood is perhaps the world's greatest pleasure garden. Winterthur is the vast estate of Henry Francis du Pont, where you will find depictions of Americana between 1650 and 1850. The Hagley Museum allows you to reenter the world of nineteenth-century American industry. At the Brandywine River Museum, you will find three generations of Wyeth paintings. Additional meals and child care are sometimes available. Nonsmokers preferred. Your thoughtful and generous host is interested in travel, reading, and meeting new people.

No. Rooms: 4	**Breakfast:** Full
Singles: 1 sb	**S-Rates:** $40–$50 sb
Doubles: 3 sb	**D-Rates:** $50–$55 sb
Type: Private home	**Bldg:** 1953 brick and stone

Minimum Stay: none. **Credit Card(s) Accepted:** none. **Open:** all year. No resident dogs. No dogs please. No resident cats. No cats please. Nonsmoking host. Guests may not smoke in residence. Children welcome. **Discounts:** none.

Reservation Contact: Bed & Breakfast Registry Ltd., Gary Winget, Box 8174, St. Paul, MN 55108; 612–646–4238.

ID: 19348MEA

LONGWOOD GARDENS, WINTERTHUR MUSEUM AND GARDENS, BRANDYWINE RIVER MUSEUM, CHADDS FORD WINERY, HAGLEY MUSEUM, NEMOURS MUSEUM, PHILIPS MUSHROOM MUSEUM, ANTIQUE SHOPS, SKIING; 20 MILES NORTHWEST OF WILMINGTON, DELAWARE, 50 MILES SOUTHWEST OF PHILADELPHIA.

Near U.S. 1 & PA. 82, U.S. 202.

Guests will drive down a picturesque country lane to this beautiful house built in 1836 on a 245-acre farm. It is filled with lovely family antiques and warm hospitality. During the summer, guests are welcome to swim in the pool and pick fresh vegetables from the garden. In winter, relax in the hot tub in the solarium. Guests are also welcome to see the milking operation, gather eggs, take a hayride, or enjoy the game room with pool and ping-pong tables, Trivial Pursuit, and a bar. The second floor is devoted entirely to guests and each of the five guest rooms has a TV. One room has Chippendale furniture, a queen-sized canopy bed with a handmade Amish quilt, and an 1840 cradle. Another room has a queen-sized sleigh bed with a handmade quilt and lots of pillows and a fireplace. A third room has a Laura Ashley motif and features twin beds with matching ruffled spreads and has antique wedding gowns hanging on one wall. Fresh flowers adorn each room, even in the winter months. A Full country breakfast of homemade breads and jellies, fresh fruit in season, fresh eggs (any style, including your host's famous fresh mushroom omelet), and delicious corn fritters is served. This feast can be enjoyed in the spacious dining room with a blazing fire or on the screened porch, or you can luxuriate with breakfast in bed. Your host loves to entertain and will gladly serve dinner with advance notice. As a long-time resident, she will be happy to help with touring plans or arrange for sleigh rides, carriage rides, or even hot-air-balloon rides. The Brandywine Valley, in historic Chester County, offers visitors a wealth of attractions, all within a few miles. Longwood is perhaps the world's greatest pleasure garden and is sure to delight anyone who likes exquisite flowers, majestic trees, and opulent architecture.

No. Rooms: 5
Singles: None
Doubles: 3 pb, 2 sb
Type: Private Home

Breakfast: Full
S-Rates: $55 pb, $40 sb
D-Rates: $65 pb, $50 sb
Bldg: 1836 Traditional

Minimum Stay: none. **Credit Card(s) Accepted:** none. **Open:** all year. Dog in residence. No dogs please. No resident cats. No cats please. Non-smoking host. Guests may not smoke in guest rooms. Children welcome. **Discounts:** 10% for families.

Reservation Contact: Bed & Breakfast Registry Ltd., Gary Winget, Box 8174, St. Paul, MN 255108; 612–646–4238.

LANDIS STORE
ID: F5–PA

CROSS-COUNTRY SKIING, BIKING, ANTIQUE AND CRAFT SHOPS.

Near Rte. 100.

The village of Landis Store has only four dwellings, one of which houses a very good restaurant, and Within a ten-mile radius, antique and craft shops abound. The city of Boyertown is also nearby. This cottage is completely hidden from the road and reminds one of the English Cotswolds with its acres of woodland. It has been skillfully decorated by your host using antiques, handmade furniture, and quilts. The first-floor sitting room has a wood-burning stove, bay window, and refrigerator. Hand-hewn stairs lead to a bedroom with double bed and a Laura Ashley-decorated bathroom with four-foot Victorian tub. A Continental breakfast is served. Your hosts have traveled widely and are involved in making furniture and quilts.

No. Rooms: 1	**Breakfast:** Continental Plus
Singles: None	**S-Rates:** $40 pb
Doubles: 1 pb	**D-Rates:** $50 pb
Type: Private cottage	**Bldg:** English Cotswold style

Minimum Stay: $5 surcharge for one-night stay. **Credit Card(s) Accepted:** none. **Open:** all year. No resident dogs. No dogs please. Three resident cats. No cats please. Nonsmoking host. Guests may not smoke in guest rooms. Residence not appropriate for children. **Discounts:** none.

Reservation Contact: Bed & Breakfast of Southeast Pennsylvania, Joyce Stevenson, Box 278, RD #1, Barto, PA 19504; 215-845-3526.

MERCER ID: P-STRANAHAN

THIEL, WESTMINSTER, GROVE CITY COLLEGES, SLIPPERY ROCK UNIVERSITY, ANTIQUES, SPECIALTY SHOPS.

Near rtes. 58 & 258, I–79, I–80.

At this 150-year-old Colonial Empire-style home, you will find a peaceful night's rest amidst antiques and cherished family heirlooms. The first of the two guest rooms has antique Victorian furniture, double bed, and ceiling fan; the second room offers a working fireplace, two double beds, and a hand-braided rug. The beds in both rooms are dressed in white coverlets and pillow shams for a romantic touch. Guests in both rooms will find a small box of sweets from the local candy store left on their pillows at night. The first room has a private bath, while the second shares a bath. After a delicious breakfast chosen from one of several menus, your host will arrange for a guided tour of the area or plan a map, highlighting local sites based on your particular interests. Mercer is a light industrial town situated within a farming region in northwestern Pennsylvania. One of your hosts is a member of the fourth generation to practice law in Mercer County; he is also a golfer and jogger. Your other host has a business background in sales and administration and enjoys antiquing, needlework, brisk walks, and aerobics. Both are active in community affairs and volunteer work.

No. Rooms: 2	**Breakfast:** Full
Singles: None	**S-Rates:** $45 pb, $45 sb
Doubles: 1 pb, 1 sb	**D-Rates:** $50 pb, $50 sb
Type: Private home	**Bldg:** 1840 Empire

Minimum Stay: none. **Credit Card(s) Accepted:** none. **Open:** all year. No resident dogs. No dogs please. No resident cats. No cats please. Nonsmoking host. Guests may not smoke in residence. Children welcome. **Discounts:** none.

Reservation Contact: Pittsburgh Bed & Breakfast, Judy Antico, 2190 Ben Franklin Dr., Pittsburgh, PA 15237; 412–367–8080.

MERCERSBURG

ID: D–BL.RIDGE

TUSCARORA MOUNTAINS, ANTIQUES, BATTLEFIELDS.

Near rtes. 16 & 75, I–81.

Near the birthplace of President James Buchanan, this historical manor offers guests the use of a sun room, swimming pool, barbecue grill, picnic tables, games, tennis courts, fishing equipment, patio, and kitchen and laundry facilities. Three of the five guest rooms have private baths; two share a bath. The rooms are furnished with oak antiques and Oriental rugs. Two have double beds, two have queen-sized beds, and one has a king-sized bed. Your host, a broker, offers discounts to area antique shops. Dinner and area tours are also available.

No. Rooms: 5	**Breakfast:** Full
Singles: None	**S-Rates:** $65 pb, $55 sb
Doubles: 3 pb, 2 sb	**D-Rates:** $65 pb, $55 sb
Type: Private home	**Bldg:** Manor

Minimum Stay: none. **Credit Card(s) Accepted:** none. **Open:** all year. Dog in residence. A dog is allowed with restrictions. Cat in residence. A cat is allowed with restrictions. Host smokes. Guests may not smoke in guest rooms. Children welcome with restrictions. **Discounts:** 10% for seniors.

Reservation Contact: Blue Ridge Bed & Breakfast, Rita Duncan, Rte. 2, Box 3895, Berryville, VA 22611; 703–955–1246.

NEW HOPE

ID: 18938WED

WASHINGTON CROSSING MEMORIAL BUILDING, PLAYHOUSE, ART COLONY, ANTIQUES, FINE SHOPS AND RESTAURANTS; BUCKS COUNTY.

Near Rte. 32, Hwy. 202.

Built in 1870, this lovely B&B inn is situated on one acre of beautifully landscaped grounds with a gazebo. The house has a wrap-around veranda and large parlor with period furnishings, where you can mingle with other guests or just relax. There are 12 guest rooms with a variety of double and single beds; all are furnished with antiques and offer private or shared baths. Also available are a 1899 carriage house with a fireplace in the living room, a kitchenette, and a second-floor bedroom with deck; and a revival stone manor house with additional guest rooms. There is turndown service in the evening, and you will find mints on your pillows, and fresh flowers and a carafe of Amaretto in your rooms. A Continental

breakfast is served in a glass-enclosed porch or in the guest room, as preferred. You can wander through the narrow old streets and enjoy early
Pennsylvania architecture, art galleries, and charming shops. New Hope
is also a famed artists' town. In addition, there are boat excursions, fine
dining and nightlife, festivals, and antiques. Your hosts can offer guidance
and place your theater or dining reservations. Their interests include travel, gardening, interior design, preservation, antiques, computers, and biking.

No. Rooms: 12
Singles: None
Doubles: 10 pb, 2 sb
Type: Inn

Breakfast: Continental
S-Rates: $75–$110 pb, $55–$85 sb
D-Rates: $80–$125 pb, $60–$85 sb
Bldg: 1870 Victorian

Minimum Stay: 2 days on weekends. **Credit Card(s) Accepted:** none.
Open: all year. Dog in residence. No dogs please. No resident cats. No
cats please. Nonsmoking host. Guests may not smoke in residence. Children welcome with restrictions. **Discounts:** Mon.–Thur. French & Dutch
spoken.

Reservation Contact: Bed & Breakfast Registry Ltd., Gary Winget, Box
8174, St. Paul, MN 55108; 612–646–4238.

PHILADELPHIA

SOCIETY HILL AREA, INDEPENDENCE HALL, HISTORIC AREA.

Near I–95, U.S. 30.

This attractive, 19th-century townhouse is in the Society Hill section of the city. The modern, open floor plan of the present interior makes one forget that this historic building has been housing Philadelphia families for almost 200 years. The living room opens onto a patio and garden where guests can escape the hustle and bustle of the outside streets. Four spacious, air-conditioned guest rooms share two baths. A Continental breakfast is served. Within easy walking distance are Independence Hall, the historic area, choice restaurants, and the activities at Penn's Landing. Local buses, which pass by the door, conveniently transport guests to places such as the Academy of Music and the Philadelphia Museum of Art. Your host, an author who specializes in consumer research, can offer valuable shopping tips.

No. Rooms: 4	**Breakfast:** Continental
Singles: None	**S-Rates:** $60–$65 sb
Doubles: 4 sb	**D-Rates:** $65–$70 sb
Type: Private home	**Bldg:** 1800s townhouse

Minimum Stay: $5 surcharge for 1 night stay. **Credit Card(s) Accepted:** none. **Open:** all year. No resident dogs. No dogs please. No resident cats. No cats please. Host smokes. Guests may smoke. Children welcome. **Discounts:** none.

Reservation Contact: Bed & Breakfast of Philadelphia, Box 630, Chester Springs, PA 19425; 215–827–9650.

PITTSBURGH

UPPER ST. CLAIR, CARNEGIE MUSEUM OF NATURAL HISTORY, SCAIFE ART MUSEUM, PLANETARIUM, PHIPPS CONSERVATORY.

Near Rte. 19, Boyce-Johnston Rd., I–79, I–70.

On this land, where George Washington assembled his troops to put down the Whiskey Rebellion in 1794, there now stands a sedate Colonial home. A park is next door and stores and restaurants are nearby. You are welcome to stroll through the two acres of tall oaks, orchard, and gardens, or to play the Steinway in the living room or just relax with the latest periodicals. The guest room has a double bed and private bath, a fireplace, many antiques, crystal chandelier, and French doors leading to a private porch overlooking a small pond. You'll will find fruit and fresh flowers, plus other thoughtful touches, such as a hair dryer, toiletries, terry robes, and luggage racks. The room is air-conditioned and has ample closet space. You are served a Full breakfast in the antique-filled dining room. Afternoon tea is served on bone china with silver on the porch in summer or by the hearth in winter. Public transportation is good. Additional meals, arrival/departure transportation, and area tours are available. One of your hosts was a gourmet caterer; the other is a research scientist. Both enjoy entertaining, antiques, gardening, theater, music, art, and travel.

No. Rooms: 1	**Breakfast:** Full
Singles: None	**S-Rates:** None
Doubles: 1 pb	**D-Rates:** $45 pb
Type: Private home	**Bldg:** 1930s colonial

Minimum Stay: none. **Credit Card(s) Accepted:** none. **Open:** all year. No resident dogs. No dogs please. Cat in residence. No cats please. Nonsmoking host. Guests may smoke. Residence not appropriate for children. **Discounts:** none.

Reservation Contact: Pittsburgh Bed & Breakfast, Judy Antico, 2190 Ben Franklin Dr., Pittsburgh, PA 15237; 412–367–8080.

POTTERS MILLS
ID: PA–POTTER

ALLEGHENY MOUNTAINS.

Near rtes. 322 & 144, I–80.

This three-story red brick seventeen-room farmhouse, listed on the National Register of Historic Places and located in a rural area in the Allegheny Mountains, was begun in 1790, with the last addition completed in the late 1800s. The current owners purchased the house in 1979 and have completed extensive renovation on the entire first and second floors. The Allison Room, the largest of the six guest rooms, has twin beds, double hide-a-bed, and fireplace. The Lincoln Room, with twin beds, has family furnishings dating back to the early 1900s. The Peach, Blue, and Green rooms have antique furnishings and double beds. Four of the guest rooms share two baths and two rooms have private baths. A Full breakfast is served, prepared with fresh eggs, ham from the farm's own hogs, and grits or hashbrowns. Additional meals are available. One of your hosts is a partner in a local high-tech firm; the other teaches gifted children. Both enjoy their farm, with its beef cattle, pigs, chickens, rabbits, goats, and horses. Their other hobbies include refinishing antiques, painting, and cooking.

No. Rooms: 6	**Breakfast:** Full
Singles: None	**S-Rates:** $27–$40 sb
Doubles: 4 sb, 2 pb	**D-Rates:** $30–$40 sb, $45–$50 pb
Type: Private home	**Bldg:** 1790s

Minimum Stay: on holidays, for special events. **Credit Card(s) Accepted:** none. **Open:** all year. Dog in residence. No dogs please. Cat in residence. No cats please. Nonsmoking host. Guests may not smoke in residence. Children welcome. **Discounts:** weekday family rates.

Reservation Contact: Rest & Repast Bed & Breakfast Service, Linda Felt-man & Brent Peters, Box 126, Pine Grove Mills, PA 16868; 814–238–1484.

REINHOLDS

ID: SPRINGWOODS–PA

PENNSYLVANIA DUTCH COUNTRY.

Near Rte. 897, Pennsylvania Tpk.

Straddling the county line of Berks and Lancaster is this enlarged and re-stored Civil War frame farmhouse. On a hillside, without any other hous-es in sight, you can enjoy the grottoes, waterfalls, and walks along the streams, and terrace shaded by a copper beech tree. There is also a swim-ming pool, and bicycles are available. Golf is only five minutes away. A sitting room with TV is offered. The second-floor guest room has dou-ble bed and private bath. There is also a foam mattress that can accom-modate a child. The other room, also with a private bath, has brass twin beds plus a hide-a-bed. A Full breakfast of your choice is served. The house is convenient to Amish country and the antique emporiums of Ad-amstown. Your hosts are avid gardeners and proud of the work they have done on their property.

No. Rooms: 2	**Breakfast:** Full
Singles: None	**S-Rates:** $65 pb
Doubles: 2 pb	**D-Rates:** $65 pb
Type: Private home	**Bldg:** Civil War Farmhouse

Minimum Stay: 2 nights on holidays. **Credit Card(s) Accepted:** none. **Open:** all year. Dog in residence. No dogs please. Cat in residence. No cats please. Nonsmoking host. Guests may not smoke in guest rooms. Children welcome with restrictions. **Discounts:** none.

Reservation Contact: Bed & Breakfast of Southeast Pennsylvania, Joyce Stevenson, Box 278, RD #1, Barto, PA 19504; 215–845–3526.

SCHELLSBURG

ID: P–MILLSTONE

COVERED BRIDGES, 1806 LOG CHURCH, OLD BEDFORD VILLAGE, VILLAGE OPERA HOUSE, FORT BEDFORD MUSEUM.

Near rtes. 30 & 220.

A white picket fence encloses the beautifully landscaped grounds on which this Georgian-style inn is situated. The stone fireplace on its pil-lared porch is just perfect for roasting marshmallows or just enjoying the cool mountain air. In the living room, you will find a Victorian couch, lace curtains, and a large library. There are two guest rooms with double beds, antique furnishings, and shared bath. One of these rooms has a woodburning fireplace and an alcove with space for a twin bed, crib, or rollaway. Two rooms on the third floor have double beds and private baths. Breakfast is served at an antique oak table that can seat twelve. Area attractions include covered bridges, an 1806 log church, Shawnee Game Farm, Coral Caverns, Old Bedford Village, Crawford's Wildlife Museum, and Storyland. Your hosts' interests include history, travel, gardening, and crafts.

No. Rooms: 4	**Breakfast:** Continental Plus
Singles: None	**S-Rates:** $40–$55 sb, $60 pb
Doubles: 2 sb, 2 pb	**D-Rates:** $45–$60 sb, $65 pb
Type: Private home	**Bldg:** 1922 Georgian stone

Minimum Stay: none. **Credit Card(s) Accepted:** none. **Open:** all year. No resident dogs. No dogs please. No resident cats. No cats please. Non-smoking host. Guests may not smoke in guest rooms. Children welcome with restrictions. **Discounts:** none.

Reservation Contact: Pittsburgh Bed & Breakfast, Judy Antico, 2190 Ben Franklin Dr., Pittsburgh PA 15237; 412–367–8080.

SPRUCE CREEK   ID: PA–EDEN–CROFT

PENN STATE, BELLEFONTE.

Near rtes. 45, 22, 453.

This early 1800s stone house is located in a farm community near Spruce Creek, where Jimmy Carter used to come to fish for trout. Set in a valley with the mountain range surrounding the area, the residence has two guest rooms and a bathroom shared with the family. One room offers twin beds, wide pine floors, and throw rugs; the other has a double bed with canopy and fireplace. A Continental breakfast is served. One of your hosts is a public relations director; the other is a cattle farmer. Reservations are not accepted from January through May.

No. Rooms: 2	**Breakfast:** Continental
Singles: None	**S-Rates:** $26–$42 sb
Doubles: 2 sb	**D-Rates:** $32–$42 sb
Type: Private home	**Bldg:** 1800s stone farmhouse

Minimum Stay: special weekends. **Credit Card(s) Accepted:** none. **Open:** Mar. 1 to Dec. 31. Dog in residence. No dogs please. No resident cats. No cats please. Host smokes. Guests may not smoke in guest rooms. Residence not appropriate for children. **Discounts:** none.

Reservation Contact: Rest & Repast Bed & Breakfast Service, Linda Feltman & Brent Peters, Box 126, Pine Grove Mills, PA 16868; 814–238–1484.

STATE COLLEGE

PENN STATE.

Near I–80, U.S. 322, PA 26.

Located off a private lane a few minutes from the main house, this unique octagonal structure offers two guest rooms with double beds and private baths. There is a deck off the living room, TV, wood-burning stove, and telephone. The house is located on wooded acreage inviting walks and cross-country skiing. It is about six miles from State College. Your hosts, one an author and instructor at Penn State, are both involved in a local dance company.

No. Rooms: 2	**Breakfast:** Continental Plus
Singles: None	**S-Rates:** $55–$60 pb
Doubles: 2 pb	**D-Rates:** $55–$60 pb
Type: Private home	**Bldg:** Octagonal

Minimum Stay: 2 nights on peak weekends. **Credit Card(s) Accepted:** none. **Open:** all year. No resident dogs. No dogs please. No resident cats. No cats please. Nonsmoking host. Guests may not smoke in residence. Children welcome with restrictions. **Discounts:** 10% for more than 2 nights depending on day.

Reservation Contact: Rest & Repast Bed & Breakfast Service, Linda Feltman & Brent Peters, Box 126, Pine Grove Mills, PA 16868; 814–238–1484.

TYRONE

ANTIQUES, STATE PARKS, RAYSTONE DAM.

Near U.S. 220 & 22.

This Victorian home offers three guest rooms plus a well-stocked library, formal dining room, parlor, and breakfast room. Two of the guest rooms, one with a queen-sized half-canopy bed and the other with a double half-canopy bed and a balcony, share a bath. The third room has a king-sized bed with a velvet headboard and full canopy, a Victorian sitting couch, and private bath ensuite. There is also a small refrigerator for storing wine and cheese or other snacks. A Continental breakfast is served. Your hosts have lived in several areas of the country.

No. Rooms: 3	**Breakfast:** Continental
Singles: None	**S-Rates:** $35 sb
Doubles: 1 pb, 2 sb	**D-Rates:** $55 pb, $45 sb
Type: Private home	**Bldg:** 1890 Victorian

Minimum Stay: none except on special Penn State weekends. **Credit Card(s) Accepted:** none. **Open:** all year. No resident dogs. No dogs please. No resident cats. No cats please. Host smokes. Guests may smoke in residence. Children welcome with restrictions. **Discounts:** none.

Reservation Contact: Rest & Repast Bed & Breakfast Service, Linda Feltman & Brent Peters, Box 126, Pine Grove Mills, PA 16868; 814–238–1484.

WASHINGTON CROSSING

ID: WALN–PA

ANTIQUES, BARGE RIDES, SESAME PLACE, PEDDLER'S VILLAGE, TYLER STATE PARK; BUCKS COUNTY.

Near Pennsylvania & NJ tpks., I–95.

At the end of a long drive, bordered by century-old trees, stands this 1682 fieldstone farmhouse, built by Nicolas Waln, who accompanied William Penn in his fleet of twenty-three ships to our shores. Handmade Pennsylvania Dutch quilts, pine floors, and beamed ceilings abound in this house, and there is a two-hundred-and-fifty-year-old walk-in fireplace. Two guest rooms offer double canopied beds, warm colonial prints, and furniture handcrafted by your host. A Full breakfast is served in front of the fireplace. Sample menus include waffles, sour-cream breakfast rolls, omelets, and garden-fresh fruits. Arrival/departure transportation and area tours are available; horseback riding is nearby.

No. Rooms: 2	**Breakfast:** Full
Singles: None	**S-Rates:** $55 sb
Doubles: 2 sb	**D-Rates:** $60 sb
Type: Private home	**Bldg:** 1682 fieldstone farmhouse

Minimum Stay: $5 surcharge for one-night stay. **Credit Card(s) Accepted:** none. **Open:** all year. No resident dogs. No dogs please. No resident cats. No cats please. Nonsmoking host. Guests may not smoke in residence. Children welcome with restrictions. **Discounts:** monthly. French & German spoken.

Reservation Contact: Bed & Breakfast of Philadelphia, Box 630, Chester Springs, PA 19425; 215–827–9650.

WAYNE

ID: BROOKFERNPA

DEVON HORSE SHOW, VALLEY FORGE NATIONAL PARK, BRYN MAWR & HAVERFORD COLLEGES, VILLANOVA UNIVERSITY.

Near 202 & Pennsylvania Tpk.

This private home in a prestigious suburb was built in 1760. You are invited to use the swimming pool, patio, yard, and TV. There are four guest rooms, two with private baths and two with a shared bath. A Full breakfast is served in the formal dining room, on the patio, or by the pool.

Your hosts, an investment counselor and his wife, are history buffs who enjoy antiques.

No. Rooms: 4	**Breakfast:** Full
Singles: None	**S-Rates:** $60 pb, $50 sb
Doubles: 2 pb, 2 sb	**D-Rates:** $65 pb, $55 sb
Type: Private home	**Bldg:** 1760 Victorian

Minimum Stay: 2 nights for special events. **Credit Card(s) Accepted:** none. **Open:** all year. No resident dogs. No dogs please. Cat in residence. No cats please. Nonsmoking host. Guests may not smoke in guest rooms. Children welcome. **Discounts:** monthly.

Reservation Contact: Bed & Breakfast of Philadelphia, Box 630, Chester Springs, PA 19425; 215–827–9650.

YORK
ID: 17402MUN

APPALACHIAN MTNS., NATIONAL SCENIC TRAIL, JULY DUTCH DAYS FESTIVAL, WOODWARD CAVE, PENN STATE AND BUCKNELL UNIVERSITIES.

Near U.S. 30, Rte. 74, I–83.

This beautiful pre-Civil War Pennsylvania Dutch farmhouse offers an inviting wide front porch. The house is surrounded by farmland, has an old mill at one side of the property, and is furnished throughout with antiques. Two guest rooms offer private baths and double beds. A choice of breakfasts is served in the dining room. There is a sitting room for guests, but you are also invited to share the family room. Your well-traveled hosts are movie buffs who enjoy shopping for antiques, swimming, walks in the country, and racquetball.

No. Rooms: 2	**Breakfast:** Full
Singles: None	**S-Rates:** $40–$45 pb
Doubles: 2 pb	**D-Rates:** $46–$65 pb
Type: Private home	**Bldg:** 1850 farmhouse

Minimum Stay: none. **Credit Card(s) Accepted:** none. **Open:** all year. No resident dogs. No dogs please. No resident cats. No cats please. Nonsmoking host. Guests may not smoke in residence. Children welcome. **Discounts:** after 5 days.

Reservation Contact: Bed & Breakfast Registry Ltd., Gary Winget, Box 8174, St. Paul, MN 55108; 612–646–4238.

RHODE ISLAND

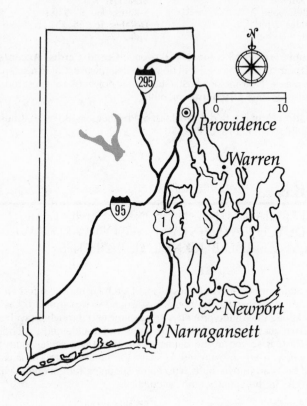

BRISTOL

ID: 02809JOS

COLT STATE PARK, COGGLESHALL FARM, MUSEUMS; 13 MILES FROM NEWPORT.

Near R.I. 114 & Hope St., I–195, R.I. 24.

The Joseph Reynolds House, circa 1693, claims to be the oldest three-story building in New England. The house was modeled after the grand country mansions popular in England at the time. Since the house was passed on from generation to generation until 1930 much of its original detail has remained intact. The home was chosen to be the headquarters for the Marquis de Lafayette for three weeks in 1778 while he planned the Battle of Rhode Island. The cannon ball that hit the house when the British attacked from the harbor is a prized relic. While staying here, Lafayette was visited by George Washington, Thomas Jefferson, and Rochambeau. During the 19th century the house was a stop on the underground railroad. Four guest rooms in the main house share two baths. A separate structure that used to be the summer kitchen is also available. It has a living room, fully equipped kitchen, and can accommodate seven people. The guest rooms share two baths. A Full breakfast is served in the great room, and the keeping room is available for guests to relax in. Bristol offers many attractions. Colt State Park, two blocks away, is a 500-acre waterfront park for walking, swimming, sailing, riding, picnicing, biking, and fishing. Next to the park is Coggleshall farm, an 18th-century working farm museum. Bristol also has the Haffenraffer Museum of anthropology, the Herreschoff Museum of sailing, and the Blithewold museum house and arboretum.

No. Rooms: 7		**Breakfast:** Full	
Singles: None		**S-Rates:** $30 sb	
Doubles: 7 sb		**D-Rates:** $40–$120 sb	
Type: Inn		**Bldg:** 1693 frame	

Minimum Stay: none. **Credit Card(s) Accepted:** MC, V. **Open:** all year. No resident dogs. No dogs please. No resident cats. No cats please. Nonsmoking host. Guests may not smoke in residence. Children are welcome with restrictions. **Discounts:** winter.

Reservation Contact: Bed & Breakfast Registry Ltd., Gary Winget, Box 8174, St. Paul, MN 55108; 612–646–4238.

MIDDLETOWN   ID: 02840LIN

NEWPORT MANSIONS, TENNIS HALL OF FAME, ART GALLERIES, MUSIC FESTIVALS, CLIFF WALK; SURFING, SWIMMING, SAILING.

Near Purgatory Rd. & Walcott Ave., Rte. 138.

The beach is only two blocks away from this pleasant house in a quiet residential neighborhood. It is one-and-a-half miles from famous Bellevue Avenue with its historic mansions, and two miles from Newport Harbor's fine restaurants and boutiques. You are welcome to use the large yard and deck as well as the living room for TV or reading. There are four guest rooms with twin or double beds. One has a private bath; the others share a bath. The rooms can accommodate one to three people. A Continental breakfast is served in the dining room or on the deck. Arrival/departure transportation, additional meals, area tours, and child care are sometimes available. Your hosts enjoy gardening, stained glass, needlework, travel, reading, and swimming.

No. Rooms: 4	**Breakfast:** Continental
Singles: None	**S-Rates:** $66–$80 pb, $60–$73 sb
Doubles: 1 pb, 3 sb	**D-Rates:** $83–$97 pb, $73–$86 sb
Type: Private home	**Bldg:** Split-level

Minimum Stay: 2 nights on holiday weekends. **Credit Card(s) Accepted:** none. **Open:** all year. No resident dogs. No dogs please. No resident cats. No cats please. Nonsmoking host. Guests may smoke. Children welcome. **Discounts:** 10% Nov.–April.

Reservation Contact: Bed & Breakfast Registry Ltd., Gary Winget, Box 8174, St. Paul, MN 55108; 612–646–4238.

NARRAGANSETT   ID: RI–213

AUDUBON PRESERVE, 30 MINUTES FROM NEWPORT.

Near Rte. 1, I–95.

This contemporary home is on an unspoiled landscape has a bird sanctuary directly in front of it. Two guest rooms are available. One has twin beds, a wicker rocker, dresser, and mirror; the other is furnished with a double bed, wash basin, brass lamps, wicker rocker, and table. A Full breakfast is served. The hosts enjoy tennis, biking, golf, and gardening.

No. Rooms: 2	**Breakfast:** Full
Singles: None	**S-Rates:** $65 sb
Doubles: 2 sb	**D-Rates:** $75 sb
Type: Private home	**Bldg:** Contemporary

Minimum Stay: none. **Credit Card(s) Accepted:** none. **Open:** all year. Resident dog. No dogs please. No resident cats. No cats please. Nonsmoking host. Guests may not smoke in residence. Children welcome with restrictions. **Discounts:** none.

Reservation Contact: Bed & Breakfast Rhode Island, Joy Meiser & Cynthia Poyant, Box 3291, Newport, RI 02840; 401–849–1298.

NEWPORT   ID: RI121PINE

VIEW OF NEWPORT BAY, POINT DISTRICT, SHOPPING, RESTAURANTS.

Near Washington St.

Built in 1810, this three-story, Federal-style home faces Newport Bay. The four guest rooms have antique furnishings, Oriental rugs, contemporary art, and private baths. All but one have water views. Two have double beds, one has twin beds, and one, on the third floor, has both a double and a single bed. A Continental breakfast is served. Your hosts, a physician and an antique dealer, enjoy downhill and cross-country skiing, golf, tennis, and sailing.

No. Rooms: 4	**Breakfast:** Continental
Singles: None	**S-Rates:** $65–$75 pb
Doubles: 4 pb	**D-Rates:** $75–$85 pb
Type: Private home	**Bldg:** 1810 Federal-style

Minimum Stay: 2 nights on holiday weekends. **Credit Card(s) Accept-**

ed: none. **Open:** Memorial Day–mid-Oct. No resident dogs. No dogs please. No resident cats. No cats please. Nonsmoking host. Guests may not smoke in residence. Children welcome with restrictions. **Discounts:** none.

Reservation Contact: Pineapple Hospitality, Inc. Judy M. Mulford, 100 Cottage St., New Bedford, MA 02740; 617–990–1696.

ID: RI–127

MANSIONS, BEACHES, JAZZ FESTIVAL, BOATING.

Near Chestnut, Walnut, rtes. 114 & 138.

This late Colonial house is one block from the bay and within walking distance of all major attractions. A small, complete neighborhood store is at the corner. The house, a blend of period and contemporary design, was built in 1850; a new wing was added in 1976 to create a spacious living area. You have the use of the delightful downstairs sitting room and dining room. If your hosts are given adequate notice, they usually acknowledge anniversaries and birthdays. One of the two guest rooms, bright and sunny, overlooks the gardens in two directions; it is furnished with a double bed and highboy and has a sitting area with wing chairs and desk. This room shares a bath with your hosts. The fireplace and mantle give the second room a cozy, quiet atmosphere; a camelback sofa, small rocker, and good reading lamp make up the sitting area. Antique books fill an oak bookcase and are available for browsing. A Full breakfast is served. Your well-traveled hosts, owners of a flower shop, have a variety of interests including civic affairs, gardening, knitting, designing quilts, sewing, and collecting cookbooks.

No. Rooms: 2	**Breakfast:** Full
Singles: None	**S-Rates:** $70 pb, $65 sb
Doubles: 1 pb, 1 sb	**D-Rates:** $70 pb, $65 sb
Type: Private home	**Bldg:** 1850 late colonial

Minimum Stay: 2 nights on summer weekends. **Credit Card(s) Accepted:** none. **Open:** all year, except holidays. Dog in residence. No dogs please. No resident cats. No cats please. Nonsmoking host. Guests may smoke in residence. Children welcome with restrictions. **Discounts:** weekly.

Reservation Contact: Bed & Breakfast of Rhode Island, Joy Meiser & Cynthia Poyant, Box 3291, Newport, RI 02840; 401–849–1298.

HISTORIC AREA.

Near Parket & Narragansett Sts., Rte. 114, Rte. 138.

This shingle-style Victorian house is located in Newport's famous mansion area of quiet streets bordered by turn-of-the-century summer cottages belonging to some of the nation's wealthiest families. This house, built in 1886, offers a unique combination of antique charm and modern comfort. The three-story cathedral entry hall, paneled entirely in chestnut, is a breathtaking reminder of the grandeur and craftsmanship of another era. There are eight guest rooms, four with private baths. Many of the rooms offer brass beds and fireplaces. There is also a third-floor suite consisting of two bedrooms and bath, ideal for families. A Continental Plus breakfast is served.

No. Rooms: 8
Singles: None
Doubles: 4 pb, 4 sb
Type: Private home

Breakfast: Continental Plus
S-Rates: $135–$145 pb, $70–$105 sb
D-Rates: $135–$145 pb, $70–$105 sb
Bldg: 1886 Victorian

Minimum Stay: 2 nights in season. **Credit Card(s) Accepted:** MC, V. **Open:** all year. Dog in residence. No dogs please. Cat in residence. No cats please. Host smokes. Guests may smoke. Children welcome. **Discounts:** weekly.

Reservation Contact: Bed & Breakfast of Rhode Island, Joy Meiser & Cynthia Poyant, Box 3291, Newport, RI 02840; 401–849–1298.

PAWTUCKET

NORTHEAST OF PROVIDENCE.

Near I–95.

Located in a quiet residential neighborhood, this Cape-style home features detailed moldings and fireplace mantels, a front door with a bull's eye glass window, traditional furnishings, and Oriental rugs. The two rooms, both with twin beds, share a bath. One has pineapple headboards and overlooks the rose garden; the other has an antique lion's claw bureau. Your hosts like walking, biking, and travel.

No. Rooms: 2
Singles: None
Doubles: 2 sb
Type: Private home

Breakfast: Continental
S-Rates: $50 sb
D-Rates: $55 sb
Bldg: Cape style

Minimum Stay: none. **Credit Card(s) Accepted:** none. **Open:** all year. No resident dogs. No dogs please. No resident cats. No cats please. Host smokes. Guests may smoke on first floor. Residence not appropriate for children. **Discounts:** weekly.

Reservation Contact: Bed & Breakfast Rhode Island, Joy Meiser & Cynthia Poyant, Box 3291, Newport, RI 02840; 401–849–1298.

PROVIDENCE

BROWN UNIVERSITY, RHODE ISLAND SCHOOL OF DESIGN.

Near Angell & Hope sts., I–95, I–195.

The historic preservation district is a quiet, tree-lined oasis of stately Victorian homes a few blocks from Brown University's main artery. You are within walking distance of Brown's theaters and athletic facilities as well as the museum and galleries of the Rhode Island School of Design. Tasteful furnishings and artwork create an atmosphere of refinement in this 1880 home. You can relax in the music room with its antique furnishings, rugs, and grand piano, or in the library with its book-lined walls, TV, fireplace, and comfortable furniture. There are three carpeted guest rooms with private baths. The first is a very large room with twin beds, desk, bureau, sitting area, fireplace, and bay window; the second room also has twin beds, bureau, chairs, and closet; the third room has a double bed, desk, chairs, closet, and bath with tub but no shower. A Full breakfast is served on a lace-covered table in the sunny formal dining room graced with hanging plants and palms. Choose from juices, cereal, eggs with ham or sausage, home-baked goods, croissants, coffee, tea, and espresso. With advance notice your hosts will try to accommodate special requests. One of your hosts has degrees in economics and art and enjoys boat restoration, antiques, and cooking; the other, with degrees in music and voice, is interested in opera, musical comedy, and antiques.

No. Rooms: 3	**Breakfast:** Full
Singles: None	**S-Rates:** $50–$60 pb
Doubles: 3 pb	**D-Rates:** $55–$65 pb
Type: Private home	**Bldg:** 1880 Victorian

Minimum Stay: none. **Credit Card(s) Accepted:** none. **Open:** Sept. to June. No resident dogs. A dog is allowed with restrictions. Cats in residence. No cats please. Nonsmoking host. Guests may not smoke in residence. Children welcome with restrictions. **Discounts:** weekly. French spoken.

Reservation Contact: Bed & Breakfast of Rhode Island, Joy Meiser & Cynthia Poyant, Box 3291, Newport, RI 02840; 401–849–1298.

BROWN UNIVERSITY, RHODE ISLAND SCHOOL OF DESIGN; EAST SIDE.

Near N. Main & Hope sts., I–95.

This colonial home is within easy walking distance of boutiques, restaurants, banks, churches, and synagogues. Brown University and Rhode Island School of Design are a mile away; the city center is a mile-and-a-half away. The house offers a sitting room with TV, telephone, and balcony for your use. There are three guest rooms with shared guest bath. Two rooms have double brass beds; one has brass and iron twin beds. Contemporary and impressionist art is displayed throughout the house, and the furnishings are a combination of antiques and fine antique reproductions. A Continental breakfast is served. Your university-educated host is currently doing painting conservation and restoration.

No. Rooms: 3	**Breakfast:** Continental
Singles: None	**S-Rates:** $70 sb
Doubles: 3 sb	**D-Rates:** $70 sb
Type: Private home	**Bldg:** 1921 colonial

Minimum Stay: 2 nights in summer. **Credit Card(s) Accepted:** none. **Open:** all year. Resident dog. No dogs please. Cat in residence. No cats please. Host smokes. Guests may not smoke in guest rooms. Residence is not appropriate for children. **Discounts:** weekly.

Reservation Contact: Bed & Breakfast of Rhode Island, Joy Meiser & Cynthia Poyant, Box 3291, Newport, RI 02840; 401–849–1298.

TIVERTON

25 MINUTES FROM NEWPORT.

Near I–95, R.I. 24.

This cozy cottage offers a combined living room/dining room/kitchen on the first floor. On the second floor you'll find the sleeping quarters with pineapple twin beds, old-fashioned nightstand, and bureau. A Continental Plus breakfast is served. Your hosts enjoy bridge, tennis, biking, gardening, and animals.

No. Rooms: 1	**Breakfast:** Continental Plus
Singles: None	**S-Rates:** $55–$65 pb
Doubles: 1 pb	**D-Rates:** $55–$65 pb
Type: Private home	**Bldg:** Cottage

Minimum Stay: 2 nights. **Credit Card(s) Accepted:** none. **Open:** all year. Resident dog. No dogs please. Resident cat. No cats please. Nonsmoking host. Guests may not smoke in residence. Residence is not appropriate for children. **Discounts:** weekly.

Reservation Contact: Bed & Breakfast Rhode Island, Joy Meiser & Cynthia Poyant, Box 3291, Newport, RI 02840; 401–849–1298.

WARREN

BAY QUEEN CRUISES, STATE PARKS, SAKOMMET VINEYARDS, PRUDENCE ISLAND FERRY, BATTLESHIP COOE, FALL RIVER MILL SHOPS, MUSEUMS.

Near rtes. 114 & 103, I–195, U.S. 6.

Warren, formerly a summer community, is now becoming a desirable year-round area, because of its proximity to Fall River, Providence, and Newport. The historic Water Street district is being renovated with many new shops, galleries, and restaurants. The house, located on Touisset Point, which juts out into Mt. Hope Bay, is buffered from town by dairy and produce farms and nurseries. A large wrap-around screened porch welcomes visitors to the Dutch Colonial house. Guests enter their own living room, with fireplace, extensive library, games, and puzzles. The two carpeted guest rooms share a guest bath. One is a light, airy room with windows facing south and west, and a double and a single bed with homemade quilts. The second room overlooks the garden and has a mahogany four-poster double bed, crocheted afghan, and built-in bookcase. A Full breakfast might include Portuguese sweetbreads and sausage (a local specialty), homemade pastries and jams, and fresh produce from the neighboring farms. Your host's coffee cake won a blue ribbon at the county fair! She enjoys reading, gardening, croquet, and cribbage.

No. Rooms: 2	**Breakfast:** Full
Singles: None	**S-Rates:** $50 sb
Doubles: 2 sb	**D-Rates:** $55 sb
Type: Private home	**Bldg:** 1930 Dutch colonial

Minimum Stay: none. **Credit Card(s) Accepted:** none. **Open:** all year. No resident dogs. No dogs please. Cat in residence. No cats please. Non-smoking host. Guests may not smoke in residence. Children welcome. **Discounts:** weekly.

Reservation Contact: Bed & Breakfast of Rhode Island, Joy Meiser & Cynthia Poyant, Box 3291, Newport, RI 02840; 401–849–1298.

WESTERLY

WATCH HILL, MYSTIC SEAPORT, BEACHES.

Near Rte. 1, I–95, U.S. 1.

This home is located on a tree-lined road just minutes from the beach and Watch Hill's shops, harbor, and mansions. Mystic Seaport is only ten miles away. Stone pillars mark the entry drive to this little inn, and a huge stone porch wraps around three sides of this three-story home. Because the house is on a hill, there is a magnificent view of Block Island Sound. You are welcomed in the living room and invited to enjoy the large stone fireplace, oversized sofa, and down-filled cushions. The house has twelve guest rooms, ten with shared baths, two with private baths. The rooms offer an intriguing blend of antique, wrought-iron, and wicker furnishings. A Continental Plus breakfast is served in the large sun room. Area tours, arrival/departure transportation, and child care are available. Both hosts have extensive experience in broadcasting and enjoy tennis, jogging, and theater. Minimum stay of two nights during weekends in season and three nights on holiday weekends is required.

No. Rooms: 12	**Breakfast:** Continental Plus
Singles: None	**S-Rates:** $45–$60 sb
Doubles: 2 pb, 10 sb	**D-Rates:** $65–$80 sb
Type: Inn	**Bldg:** 1910

Minimum Stay: 2 nights on summer weekends. **Credit Card(s) Accepted:** none. **Open:** all year. Dog in residence. No dogs please. No resident cats. No cats please. Nonsmoking host. Guests may not smoke in guest rooms. Children welcome. **Discounts:** weekly, off season.

Reservation Contact: Bed & Breakfast of Rhode Island, Joy Meiser & Cynthia Poyant, Box 3291, Newport, RI 02840; 401–849–1298.

ID: 02891HEN

MYSTIC SEAPORT, AQUARIUM, MISQUAMICUT STATE BEACH.

Near RI 1A, U.S. 1, I–95.

Guests will enjoy this especially attractive home located on a salt pond with the ocean just beyond. The furnishings are elegant but comfortable with several antique pieces and many books accenting a generally contemporary setting. A pleasant feature of this house is the many porches and terraces with water views. There are two guest rooms with private baths. The first is a very large room with two double beds, antique furnishings, and views in three directions. The other room has a four-poster double bed and a deck with a water view. A Continental Plus breakfast is served. The house is fifteen minutes from Mystic Seaport and Aquarium and about ten minutes from Misquamicut State Beach. Your host is a designer and painter whose interests include art history, architecture, travel, gardening, and reading.

No. Rooms: 2	**Breakfast:** Continental Plus
Singles: None	**S-Rates:** $70 pb
Doubles: 2 pb	**D-Rates:** $85 pb
Type: Private Home	**Bldg:** 1920

Minimum Stay: none. **Credit Card(s) Accepted:** none. **Open:** all year. No resident dogs. No dogs please. No resident cats. No cats please. Nonsmoking host. Guests may not smoke in residence. Children welcome. **Discounts:** none.

Reservation Contact: Bed & Breakfast Registry Ltd., Gary Winget, Box 8174, St. Paul, MN 55108; 612–646–4238.

WICKFORD

UNIVERSITY OF RHODE ISLAND, GRADUATE SCHOOL OF OCEANOGRAPHY.

Near Rte. 1A, U.S. 1.

Located on a tree-lined street, this former dairy farm is surrounded by two-and-a-half acres of fields, flower gardens, stone fences, and barns. Historic Wickford, with its eighteenth- and nineteenth-century homes and antique and specialty shops, is only a mile away. The house is one mile from the water, where Narragansett Bay offers ample opportunities for swimming, boating, and fishing. The University of Rhode Island, Graduate School of Oceanography, and Newport are within a fifteen-minute drive. The main section of this Colonial-style house was built in 1854, but legend has it that the smaller part was brought to this site by oxcart in the 1700s. Three guest rooms share a guest bath. Two of the rooms have double beds, one has twin beds, and they all feature beautiful antique furniture and handmade spreads. A Continental Plus breakfast of home-baked goods is served. Both hosts are oceanographers and can suggest out-of-the-way places to explore, as well as provide you with an extensive list of available nature walks and beachcombing expeditions. There is a two-night minimum stay on weekends during the summer, and a three-night minimum on holiday weekends.

No. Rooms: 3	**Breakfast:** Continental Plus
Singles: None	**S-Rates:** $40–$50 sb
Doubles: 3 sb	**D-Rates:** $40–$50 sb
Type: Private home	**Bldg:** 1854 colonial farmhouse

Minimum Stay: 2 nights on weekends. **Credit Card(s) Accepted:** none. **Open:** all year. Dog in residence. No dogs please. No resident cats. No cats please. Nonsmoking host. Guests may not smoke in guest rooms. Children welcome. **Discounts:** none.

Reservation Contact: Bed & Breakfast of Rhode Island, Joy Meiser & Cynthia Poyant, Box 3291, Newport, RI 02840; 401–849–1298.

SOUTH CAROLINA

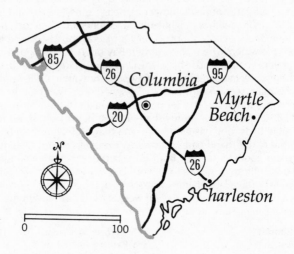

CHARLESTON

ID: CHAS–GIBBS

HISTORIC DISTRICT.

Near Rte. 17, I–26.

Built in 1850, this elegant home is in a residential neighborhood but within walking distance of all major attractions. Because of its beautiful woodwork, furnishings, and famous rose garden, this house is often included in historical tours. The second-floor guest room, furnished with antiques, has a double bed and private bath. A Continental breakfast is served. Your well-traveled host is a licensed tour guide in Charleston.

No. Rooms: 1
Singles: None
Doubles: 1 pb
Type: Private home

Breakfast: Continental
S-Rates: $65 pb
D-Rates: $75 pb
Bldg: 1850

Minimum Stay: none. **Credit Card(s) Accepted:** none. **Open:** all year. Dog in residence. No dogs please. No resident cats. No cats please. Non-smoking host. Guests may smoke. Residence not appropriate for children. **Discounts:** none.

Reservation Contact: Charleston Society Bed & Breakfast, Eleanor Rogers, 84 Murray Blvd., Charleston, SC 29401; 803–723–4948.

HISTORIC AREA, RESTAURANTS, SHOPS, MUSEUMS, FORTS, NAVAL MUSEUM.

Near Wentworth St., I–26, U.S. 17.

This Greek Revival-style dwelling, built in 1838, with four columns and large classic garden, has been restored to mint condition and is furnished with American eighteenth-century antiques. The house, listed in the *Charlestown Historic Architecture Inventory,* is located near the College of Charleston, in the heart of the historic area, and within walking distance of restaurants, churches, shops, and museums. There are three suites and one guest room available. Two of the suites consist of two bedrooms each; all accommodations have private baths, air-conditioning, and sleeping space for at least two people. A Full breakfast is served. Your hosts are retired interior designers who have restored and decorated many plantations and historic houses. They are well-informed about American history and the history of the area.

No. Rooms: 6	**Breakfast:** Full
Singles: None	**S-Rates:** $75–$120 pb
Doubles: 6 pb	**D-Rates:** $75–$120 pb
Type: Private home	**Bldg:** 1838 Greek Revival-style

Minimum Stay: none. **Credit Card(s) Accepted:** none. **Open:** all year. No resident dogs. No dogs please. No resident cats. No cats please. Nonsmoking host. Guests may not smoke in residence. Children welcome with restrictions. **Discounts:** none.

Reservation Contact: Historic Charleston Bed & Breakfast, Charlotte Fairey, 43 Legare St., Charleston, SC 29401; 803–722–6606.

HISTORIC DISTRICT.

Near King St., Broad St., I–26, Hwy. 17.

This Williamsburg-style house, built before 1715, and centrally located in the historic district, is the oldest frame house in Charleston. At one time the oldest drugstore in the country was housed in this building, which was saved from destruction by the Preservation Society in 1963, restored, and returned to its original use as a private residence. Its three guest rooms, limited to one family or group at a time, offer an opportunity to experience Colonial living. The rooms have cypress floors, heavy beams, and antique furnishings. One has two twin beds; each of the other two rooms has a single bed. One of the rooms has a fireplace, and another serves as a sitting room, with windowseats, and table and chairs for your Continental breakfast. The three rooms share a bath. Your host is interested in historic preservation and gardening.

No. Rooms: 3	**Breakfast:** Continental
Singles: 2 sb	**S-Rates:** $15–$70 sb
Doubles: 1 sb	**D-Rates:** $60–$75 sb
Type: Private home	**Bldg:** 1715 Williamsburg style

Minimum Stay: none. **Credit Card(s) Accepted:** none. **Open:** all year. No resident dogs. No dogs please. No resident cats. No cats please. Non-smoking host. Guests may not smoke in residence. Children welcome. **Discounts:** none.

Reservation Contact: Historic Charleston Bed & Breakfast, Charlotte Fairey, 43 Legare St., Charleston, SC 29401; 803–722–6606.

ID: 3–CHARLEST

CITY MARKET AREA, WHITE POINT GARDENS.

Near Broad, King, Legare & Tradd sts., I–26, U.S. 17.

This Charleston house, built in an orange grove in the 1770s, retains its eighteenth-century moldings and paneling in rooms recently adapted for twentieth-century living. The kitchen building, tucked behind the Georgian-style house, serves as the bed-and-breakfast unit. It is self-contained with its own central heating and air-conditioning. It consists of a ground-floor sitting room, with built-in kitchen unit (oven, surface cooking unit, refrigerator, and sink) and an upstairs bedroom and bath. Furnishings are primarily Southern antiques, such as a mahogany Empire double sleigh bed and a white iron-and-brass single bed. Breakfast specialties include homemade coffee cakes and breads as well as fruit; the refrigerator is fully stocked with such staples as milk, eggs, and butter. Your host has lived in Germany, traveled extensively, and enjoys cooking, sewing, interior design, and gardening.

No. Rooms: 1	**Breakfast:** Continental Plus
Singles: None	**S-Rates:** $80–$115 pb
Doubles: 1 pb	**D-Rates:** $80–$115 pb
Type: Private home	**Bldg:** 1779 Charleston Single

Minimum Stay: none. **Credit Card(s) Accepted:** none. **Open:** all year. No resident dogs. No dogs please. No resident cats. No cats please. Non-smoking host. Guests may not smoke in residence. Children welcome with restrictions. **Discounts:** none. German, French spoken.

Reservation Contact: Historic Charleston Bed & Breakfast, Charlotte Fairey, 43 Legare St., Charleston, SC 29401; 803–722–6606.

HISTORIC DISTRICT.

Near Broad St., Meeting St. (Four Corners of Law), I–26.

This bed-and-breakfast unit, an original kitchen house for the eighteenth-century Federal-style home built by Daniel Ravenel, is the oldest residential property in the city to remain continuously in the same family. The location, in the center of the historic district, is excellent. The unit has two bedrooms, two baths, a living room, and eat-in kitchen. The kitchen is completely stocked with wine, fresh fruits, milk, juice, eggs, cereal, coffee cake or croissants, coffee, and tea. Your hosts have interests in reading, interior design, and history.

No. Rooms: 2	**Breakfast:** Full
Singles: None	**S-Rates:** $75–$85 pb
Doubles: 2 pb	**D-Rates:** $75–$85 pb
Type: Private home	**Bldg:** 1790 Federal style

Minimum Stay: none. **Credit Card(s) Accepted:** none. **Open:** all year. No resident dogs. No dogs please. No resident cats. No cats please. Nonsmoking host. Guests may smoke. Children welcome with restrictions. **Discounts:** none.

Reservation Contact: Historic Charleston Bed & Breakfast, Charlotte Fairey, 43 Legare St., Charleston, SC 29401; 803–722–6606.

HISTORIC DISTRICT, 10 MILES FROM BEACHES & PLANTATIONS.

Near I–26, Hwy. 17, Meeting, Broad, East Bay.

Built in 1720, the Robert Brewton House is now a national historic landmark. The interior reflects renovations from various periods: American colonial, early Georgian, late Georgian, and American Federal. The domestic slave quarters, the kitchen house, and the original carriage house have now been combined to create the current carriage house which consists of a living room, dining room, modern kitchen, two bedrooms (one with a queen-sized bed and one with twin beds), dressing area, bath, and private entrance. The unit is rented only to members of the same party. The backyard has been newly landscaped and the garden, originally designed by Loutrel Briggs, has been restored with additions. Ingredients for a Continental breakfast are provided. Street parking is limited to two hours, but there is a metered city lot one block from the house. Your hosts, who live in a separate structure, enjoy travel, gardening, interior design, and music.

No. Rooms: 2	**Breakfast:** Continental
Singles: None	**S-Rates:** $100 pb
Doubles: 2 sb	**D-Rates:** $110 sb
Type: Private home	**Bldg:** 1720 carriage house

Minimum Stay: 2 nights during high season. **Credit Card(s) Accepted:** AE, MC, V. **Open:** all year. No resident dogs. No dogs please. No resident cats. No cats please. Nonsmoking host. Guests may smoke in residence. Children welcome with restrictions. **Discounts:** none.

Reservation Contact: Historic Charleston Bed & Breakfast, Charlotte Fairey, 43 Legare St., Charleston, SC 29401; 803–722–6606.

ID: 29401PAL

HISTORIC DISTRICT, HARBOR & FORT SUMTER, HISTORIC HOMES & CHURCHES, YACHT TOURS, HORSE-DRAWN CARRIAGES.

Near Broad & Battery sts., I–26.

This lovely old mansion in historic Charleston, overlooking the harbor and Fort Sumter, has shaded porches running along each of its three stories, a beautifully landscaped yard with gardens, and a swimming pool. The twenty-seven room 1840 house is furnished with family antiques. There are two guest rooms with private baths. Nearby are the Charleston Museum, Fort Sumter, and Boone Hall.

No. Rooms: 2	**Breakfast:** Continental
Singles: None	**S-Rates:** $90 pb
Doubles: 2 pb	**D-Rates:** $95 pb
Type: Private home	**Bldg:** 1840

Minimum Stay: none. **Credit Card(s) Accepted:** none. **Open:** all year. No resident dogs. No dogs please. No resident cats. No cats please. Nonsmoking host. Guests may not smoke in residence. Children welcome. **Discounts:** none.

Reservation Contact: Bed & Breakfast Registry Ltd., Gary Winget, Box 8174, St. Paul, MN 55108; 612–646–4238.

ID: 29401SWO

HISTORIC DISTRICT.

Near Meeting & Broad sts., I–26.

This exceptional little inn is located in Charleston's historic residential district. You will experience quiet elegance in the six guest rooms, all with private baths, color TV, central heat and air-conditioning, and antique furnishings. Each room has a double and single bed; some have four-poster canopies, fireplaces, and private entrances. A Full breakfast is served. Additional meals and area tours are available. Your charming host provides personal service.

No. Rooms: 6	**Breakfast:** Full
Singles: None	**S-Rates:** $75–$90 pb
Doubles: 6 pb	**D-Rates:** $90–$105 pb
Type: Inn	**Bldg:** 1800 inn

Minimum Stay: 2 nights May–June. **Credit Card(s) Accepted:** AE, MC, V. **Open:** all year. No resident dogs. No dogs please. No resident cats. No cats please. Nonsmoking host. Guests may not smoke in guest rooms. Children welcome with restrictions. **Discounts:** none.

Reservation Contact: Bed & Breakfast Registry Ltd., Gary Winget, Box 8174, St. Paul, MN 55108; 612–646–4238.

SULLIVAN'S ISLAND
ID: 29842PAL

CHARLESTON AREA; HISTORIC FORT MOULTRIE, VISITOR CENTER, LIGHTHOUSE, BEACH.

Near SC703, I–26, U.S. 17.

This recently renovated 1880s home offers an excellent example of typical island architecture, with its broad front, columned portico with double French doors, pine floors, and high ceilings. A large fireplace in the Great Room and large old-fashioned kitchen add to the ambience. Sand beaches are a short walk from front gates. Five guest rooms offer both single and double beds in each room, private baths, and individually controlled heating and cooling systems. Continental breakfast is served in the dining room or on the screened porch. Sullivan's Island is situated near the entrance to Charleston harbor, about twelve miles away. Your personable hosts are interested in travel, woodworking, and sewing. Child care and arrival/departure transportation, bikes, volleyball, and other games are available.

No. Rooms: 5	**Breakfast:** Continental
Singles: None	**S-Rates:** $60 pb
Doubles: 5 pb	**D-Rates:** $60 pb
Type: Private home	**Bldg:** 1880s island architecture

Minimum Stay: none. **Credit Card(s) Accepted:** none. **Open:** all year. Dog in residence. Guests may bring dog. No resident cats. No cats please. Host smokes. Guests may smoke. Children welcome. **Discounts:** none. Spanish spoken.

Reservation Contact: Bed & Breakfast Registry Ltd., Gary Winget, Box 8174, St. Paul, MN 55108; 612–646–4238.

SOUTH DAKOTA

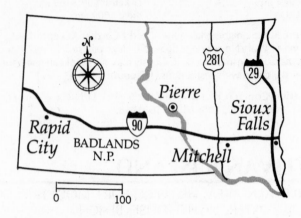

BERESFORD

ID: 57004RYG

30 MILES SOUTH OF SIOUX FALLS.

Near I–29, U.S. 18.

In this lovely home, built in 1916, you get the royal treatment. The spacious house has a large porch and yard for your warm-weather enjoyment. Three guest rooms offer double beds, rocking chairs, desk, and black and white TV; one of the rooms has private bath. Additional cots are available for children. A Full breakfast, including homemade bread and jam, is served in the dining room. It is a short walk to the local park, pool, restaurants, and old-fashioned popcorn wagon. The town of Beresford, formerly a major Northwestern Railroad town, celebrated its centennial in July of 1984. Nearby Sioux Falls, believed to be one of the midwest's most beautiful cities, offers the excellent Great Plains Zoo, tree-shaded parks, and a modern downtown shopping area with fine restaurants and several excellent malls. Additional meals, arrival/departure transportation, area tours, and child care are available. Your well-traveled, hospitable hosts are interested in history, genealogy, education, games, and music.

No. Rooms: 3	**Breakfast:** Full
Singles: None	**S-Rates:** $30 pb, $25 sb
Doubles: 1 pb, 2 sb	**D-Rates:** $40 pb, $35 sb
Type: Private home	**Bldg:** 1916 two-story clapboard

Minimum Stay: none. **Credit Card(s) Accepted:** none. **Open:** all year. No resident dogs. A dog is allowed with restrictions. No resident cats. A cat is allowed with restrictions. Nonsmoking host. Guests may not smoke in guest rooms. Children welcome. **Discounts:** none.

Reservation Contact: Bed & Breakfast Registry Ltd., Gary Winget, Box 8174, St. Paul, MN 55108; 612–646–4238.

CANOVA
ID: 57321SKO

MITCHELL CORN PALACE, PIONEER MUSEUM.

Near I–90, U.S. 81.

This large antique-furnished farmhome has a yard and porch for outdoor relaxation and is located near a swimming pool, tennis courts, and golf course. There are five guest rooms with queen-sized, double, or twin beds; one has a private bath while the others share a bath. A Full breakfast and dinner are served, family-style, in the dining room. Canova is forty miles from Mitchell, where you can tour the world's only palace made of corn. Your hosts' interests include fishing, gardening, and cooking. For families, the rate drops after the first night.

No. Rooms: 5	**Breakfast:** Full
Singles: None	**S-Rates:** $28 pb, $28 sb
Doubles: 1 pb, 4 sb	**D-Rates:** $56 pb, $56 sb
Type: Private home	**Bldg:** Farmhouse

Minimum Stay: none. **Credit Card(s) Accepted:** none. **Open:** all year. No resident dogs. Guests may bring dog. No resident cats. Guests may bring cat. Nonsmoking host. Guests may smoke. Children welcome. **Discounts:** 2nd night.

Reservation Contact: Bed & Breakfast Registry Ltd., Gary Winget, Box 8174, St. Paul, MN 55108; 612–646–4238.

MITCHELL
ID: 57301HEI

FISHING, SWIMMING, BOATING.

Near I–90, SD 37.

Nestled among the hills overlooking the James River Valley, this contemporary home is located at the beginning of a state canoe trail and near the James River which offers swimming, boating, and fishing. Guests can use the game room with pool table, darts, bar, and fireplace, or watch television in the living room. The four wood-paneled guest rooms share two baths; two have single beds, one a double, and one has twin beds. All have central heat and air-conditioning. A Full breakfast is served and other meals are available. Your hosts are interested in hunting, gardening, fishing, canoeing, and reading; they have traveled widely in the United States and abroad.

No. Rooms: 4	**Breakfast:** Full
Singles: 1 sb	**S-Rates:** $23 sb
Doubles: 3 sb	**D-Rates:** $29 sb
Type: Private home	**Bldg:** 1961 tri-level

Minimum Stay: none. **Credit Card(s) Accepted:** none. **Open:** all year. Host's dog is not allowed in guest areas. Guest may bring dog. Host's cat is not allowed in guest areas. Guest may bring cat. Nonsmoking host. Guests may not smoke in guest rooms. Children welcome. **Discounts:** families. Some Spanish spoken.

Reservation Contact: Bed & Breakfast Registry Ltd., Gary Winget, Box 8174, St. Paul, MN 55108; 612–646–4238.

TENNESSEE

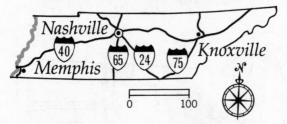

Nashville • Memphis • Knoxville • 40 65 24 75

0   100

KNOXVILLE

ID: 37922MOU

SMOKY MOUNTAIN NATIONAL PARK, UNIVERSITY OF TENNESSEE, APPALACHIA MUSEUM.

Near Campbell Station Rd., I–40, I–75.

Located just two-and-a-half miles from Interstates 40 and 75, this Cape Cod-style house has a quiet country setting. It is warmly furnished with antiques, ceiling fans, and other country accents. You can relax on the deck overlooking the wooded backyard. There are two guest rooms with private baths, antique furnishings, and double beds. In both rooms, you will find homemade cookies as well as a basket of area brochures. A Full breakfast might include fruit compote, an omelet, homemade muffins or bread, and coffee or tea. One of your hosts is an insurance software consultant who enjoys photography and sailing; the other is an accountant with interests in cooking and needlework.

No. Rooms: 2	**Breakfast:** Full
Singles: None	**S-Rates:** $45 pb
Doubles: 2 pb	**D-Rates:** $45 pb
Type: Private home	**Bldg:** 1982 Cape Cod

Minimum Stay: none. **Credit Card(s) Accepted:** none. **Open:** all year. Dog in residence. No dogs please. No resident cats. No cats please. Host smokes. Guests may smoke in common areas only. Children welcome with restrictions. **Discounts:** none.

Reservation Contact: Mountain Breeze B&B, Brad & Cindy Rogers, 501 Mountain Breeze Ln., Knoxville, TN 37922; 615–966–3917.

MEMPHIS

ID: 38105LOW

UNIVERSITY OF TENNESSEE COLLEGE OF MEDICINE, CIVIC CENTER, ZOO, MEMPHIS MUSEUM, STADIUM.

Near Poplar, Madison, I–40, I–55.

According to a former director of the Memphis Heritage Society, this is one of the twelve most outstanding homes in Memphis and it is on the National Register of Historic Places. The first floor has spacious formal

rooms, with fifteen-foot ceilings, mahogany woodwork, large mantles, and two large porches. The 1899 Queen Anne-style house is air-conditioned and has a one-acre yard plus ample off-street parking. TV can be viewed in the sun room. Five guest rooms are furnished in the style of the period. All have fireplaces, wall sconces, ceiling fans, and queen-sized beds; four rooms have private baths. The house is near a large medical center, located between the downtown and midtown areas. It is one mile from the Mississippi River, close to all tourist attractions, and convenient to the expressway. One of your hosts is a professor at Memphis State University; the other teaches in the Memphis public-school system. They are interested in coins, stamps, languages, and literature.

No. Rooms: 5	**Breakfast:** Continental
Singles: None	**S-Rates:** $50 pb, $50 sb
Doubles: 4 pb, 1 sb	**D-Rates:** $50 pb, $50 sb
Type: Private mansion	**Bldg:** 1899 Queen Anne

Minimum Stay: none. **Credit Card(s) Accepted:** none. **Open:** all year. No resident dogs. A dog is allowed with restrictions. No resident cats. No cats please. Nonsmoking host. Guests may smoke. Children welcome with restrictions. **Discounts:** AARP, weekly. Russian & French spoken.

Reservation Contact: Bed & Breakfast Registry Ltd., Gary Winget, Box 8174, St. Paul, MN 55108; 612–646–4238.

TEXAS

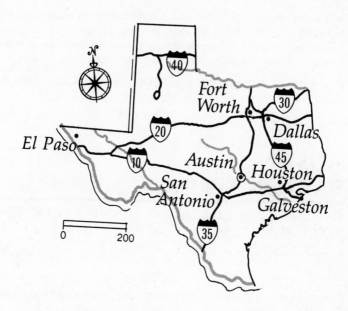

AUSTIN

ID: 78705BRO

UNIVERSITY OF TEXAS, CAPITOL BUILDING.

Near 34th and Guadalupe sts., I–35.

Located in the heart of Austin, this 1920s house sits on three-quarters of an acre in a residential neighborhood. Large oaks and lush landscaping surround the house and three porches and a patio serve as a gathering spot for guests. The rooms are furnished with antiques, antique reproductions, and a pleasant mix of artwork. There are two guest rooms in the main house as well as a cottage and a carriage house. The Blue Room has a four-poster queen-sized bed, a white wicker sofa, and a private porch. The Rose Room has twin pine beds. These two rooms share a bath. The cottage consists of a living area, a bedroom with double bed, a private porch, and a private bath. The carriage house, over the garage, can accommodate up to four people. It has a double bed, queen-sized hide-a-bed a large room with a kitchen, and a private bath. A Continental Plus breakfast is served. The hosts enjoy golf, boating, music, and art.

No. Rooms: 4	**Breakfast:** Continental Plus
Singles: None	**S-Rates:** $65 pb, $49 sb
Doubles: 2 pb, 2 sb	**D-Rates:** $65 pb, $49 sb
Type: Inn	**Bldg:** 1922 Clapboard

Minimum Stay: 2 days on holidays. **Credit Card(s) Accepted:** AE, MC, V. **Open:** all year. No resident dogs. No dogs please. Cat in residence. Guest may bring cat. Nonsmoking host. Guests may not smoke in residence. Children welcome. **Discounts:** 15% after 5 days.

Reservation Contact: Bed & Breakfast Registry Ltd., Gary Winget, PO Box 8174, St. Paul, MN 55108; 612–646–4238.

AUSTIN/ BARTON SPRINGS   ID: CLIFFSIDETX

CAPITOL TOUR, L.B.J. LIBRARY, UNIVERSITY OF TEXAS, BERGSTROM AIR FORCE BASE, BARTON CREEK MALL.

Near Rte. 290W, Loop 360, I–35, Hwy. 183.

This efficiency apartment is adjacent to your host's ranch-style home, located on two wooded acres, just within the city limits in the southwestern portion of Austin, near Barton Springs Creek. You can listen to the owls and mourning doves and watch the antics of the racoons and opossums when they are fed in the evening. There is a double hide-a-bed as well as a pull-out chair that can accommodate a third person. The kitchenette has a small refrigerator, coffee-maker, toaster, and electric skillet. Breakfast items are stocked in the refrigerator. The private bath has a shower but no tub. Your hosts, an attorney and a social worker, enjoy travel and family activities.

No. Rooms: 1	**Breakfast:** Full
Singles: None	**S-Rates:** $45 pb
Doubles: 1 pb	**D-Rates:** $50 pb
Type: Private apartment	**Bldg:** Ranch

Minimum Stay: 2 nights. **Credit Card(s) Accepted:** none. **Open:** all year. Dog in residence. No dogs please. No resident cats. No cats please. Nonsmoking host. Guests may not smoke in guest rooms. Children welcome. **Discounts:** none. Spanish spoken.

Reservation Contact: Bed & Breakfast Texas Style, Ruth Wilson, 4224 W. Red Bird Ln., Dallas, TX 75237; 214–298–8586.

BELTON

ANTIQUE & CRAFT SHOPS, HOT-AIR BALLOONING.

Near I–35, Main St. & 6th Ave.

This lovely Queen Anne Victorian has five air-conditioned guest rooms, two with private baths. The four upstairs rooms are named after the seasons. Spring has a four-poster twin beds while, Summer has a king-sized bed and white wicker furniture; the color scheme in both rooms is one of soft greens. Fall is furnished with a brass double bed, a handmade quilt and dust ruffle, and rocking chairs. Winter boasts a corner cupola where poinsettias are displayed and a queen-sized brass bed. The fifth down-

stairs room is graced with a fireplace, beautiful furniture (including an armoire), a small sitting area, and a double bed. A Continental Plus breakfast is served.

No. Rooms: 5
Singles: None
Doubles: 2 pb, 3 sb
Type: Private home

Breakfast: Continental Plus
S-Rates: $50 pb, $40 sb
D-Rates: $50 pb, $40 sb
Bldg: 1893 Queen Anne Victorian

Minimum Stay: none. **Credit Card(s) Accepted:** MC, V. **Open:** all year. No resident dogs. No dogs please. No resident cats. No cats please. Non-smoking host. Guests may not smoke in residence. Children welcome. **Discounts:** none.

Reservation Contact: Bed & Breakfast Texas Style, Ruth Wilson, 4224 W. Red Bird Ln., Dallas, TX 75237; 214–298–8586.

DALLAS

WHITE ROCK LAKE AREA, SOUTHERN METHODIST UNIVERSITY, SHOPPING.

Near I–30, I–635, Lawther Ave. & Mockingbird Ln.

Located on White Rock Lake, this contemporary home is in one of the most secluded and little-known areas of Dallas. Its fine furnishings and collectibles are tastefully displayed. There are two guest rooms with private baths. One of the rooms is done in yellow and has a four-poster double bed, and the other has a single bed, TV, and sitting area. A Full breakfast is served. A bike is available for riding around the lake and walking and jogging trails are nearby. Your hostess, a musician and business woman, likes to fish and read.

No. Rooms: 2	**Breakfast:** Full
Singles: 1 pb	**S-Rates:** $50 pb
Doubles: 1 pb	**D-Rates:** $60 pb
Type: Private home	**Bldg:** Contemporary

Minimum Stay: none. **Credit Card(s) Accepted:** MC, V. **Open:** all year. No resident dogs. No dogs please. Resident cat. No cats please. Non-smoking host. Guests may not smoke in residence. Residence is not appropriate for children. **Discounts:** none.

Reservation Contact: Bed & Breakfast Texas Style, Ruth Wilson, 4224 W. Red Bird Ln., Dallas, TX 75237; 214–298–8586.

PRESTONWOOD, GALLERIA, SIX FLAGS OVER TEXAS, UNIVERSITY OF TEXAS.

Near Hillcrest, Arapaho, I–635, U.S. 75.

Just east of Richardson and west of Carrollton, this contemporary home in north Dallas is close to Prestonwood and the Galleria shopping center and fifteen minutes south of Southfork Ranch. There are two air-conditioned guest rooms with private baths. One, with twin beds, displays an antique fan; the other room has a double bed. A Full country breakfast is served, including Jalepeña muffins, especially for first-time visitors to Texas. There is off-street parking, and you are welcome to use the TV, piano, and fireplace. Laundry facilities are available. Your hosts, active in the Methodist church and community activities, enjoy travel, weekend gardening, refinishing furniture, and painting both in oil and watercolors.

No. Rooms: 2	**Breakfast:** Full
Singles: None	**S-Rates:** $40 pb
Doubles: 2 pb	**D-Rates:** $45 pb
Type: Private home	**Bldg:** 1979 modern

Minimum Stay: none. **Credit Card(s) Accepted:** none. **Open:** all year.

Dog in residence. A dog is allowed with restrictions. No resident cats. A cat is allowed with restrictions. Nonsmoking host. Guests may smoke. Children welcome. **Discounts:** weekly, monthly.

Reservation Contact: Bed & Breakfast Texas Style, Ruth Wilson, 4224 W. Red Bird Ln., Dallas, TX 75237; 214–298–8586.

ID: IRIS–TX

SIX FLAGS OVER TEXAS, UNIVERSITY OF DALLAS, COTTON BOWL, STATE FAIR PARK.

Near Swiss & Munger, U.S. 75, I–30, Loop 635.

This Frank Lloyd Wright prairie-style home is located in the historic preservation district close to downtown Dallas. This two-story red-brick home is furnished with many antiques. There are two guest rooms with private baths. One has a double bed with canopy and iris coverlet. The bath has a pedestal sink and tub but no shower. The other room, with king-size canopy bed and connecting bath, overlooks the pool and treetops. Both rooms are air-conditioned. A Full breakfast is served on a tray with fresh flowers in your room. Your host is a gourmet cook, so a typical menu might consist of eggs Benedict, homemade breads, and cheese. Additional meals and area tours are available. You are welcome to relax in the yard, on the patio, or by the pool, fireplace, or TV. Your well-traveled hosts have entertained guests from many parts of the world and enjoy gardening and cooking.

No. Rooms: 2	**Breakfast:** Full
Singles: None	**S-Rates:** $60 pb
Doubles: 2 pb	**D-Rates:** $75 pb
Type: Private home	**Bldg:** 1920s prairie-style

Minimum Stay: none. **Credit Card(s) Accepted:** none. **Open:** all year. No resident dogs. No dogs please. Cat in residence. No cats please. Nonsmoking host. Guests may not smoke in residence. Children welcome with restrictions. **Discounts:** weekly.

Reservation Contact: Bed & Breakfast Texas Style, Ruth Wilson, 4224 W. Red Bird Ln., Dallas, TX 75237; 214–298–8586.

EL PASO
ID: VIEW–TX

UNIVERSITY OF TEXAS, CIVIC CENTER, MUSEUM OF ART.

Near I–10, Rim Rd. & Mesa.

Perched high above the city, this impressive home provides views of Mexico and three states. There are three guest rooms with private baths. The first, done in pale greens, has a king-sized water bed and antique chairs and armoire. The second, which overlooks the pool, has a double bed and Mexican artifacts. The third room is downstairs and has a private entrance, double bed, and a view of the garden. A Full southwestern-style breakfast is served in the breakfast nook or in the landscaped courtyard. High tea may also be served, depending on the guests' schedule. The pool and cabana are in the back courtyard.

No. Rooms: 3	**Breakfast:** Full
Singles: None	**S-Rates:** $110 pb
Doubles: 3 pb	**D-Rates:** $120 pb
Type: Private home	**Bldg:** Spanish

Minimum Stay: none. **Credit Card(s) Accepted:** none. **Open:** all year. No resident dogs. No dogs please. Resident cat. No cats please. Non-smoking host. Guests may not smoke in residence. Children welcome. **Discounts:** none.

Reservation Contact: Bed & Breakfast Texas Style, Ruth Wilson, 4224 W. Red Bird Ln., Dallas, TX 75237; 214–298–8586.

FORT STOCKTON   ID: RANCH–TX

BIG BEND NATIONAL PARK, UNIVERSITY OF TEXAS, WINERY.

Near Ligon Rd., I–10.

This west Texas ranch is twenty-seven miles east of Fort Stockton and one hour north of Big Bend National Park. Fort Davis Observatory is thirty minutes away, and vineyards and the newest Texas winery are only three miles away. Your host promises you a firsthand look at the vineyards and a complimentary glass of St. Genevieve's wine. The ranch consists of four sections, 640 acres each. There are two well-appointed guest houses, with king-sized beds, air-conditioning, antique dressers, carpeting, small refrigerators, and private baths. One guest house also has twin beds and a room with pool table and two large sofas. A Full breakfast, served in the main house, might consist of an egg and cheese casserole or a Mexican dish, such as of *huevos rancheros.* Dinner is also available. Your host, a rancher, is a member of the Daughters of the American Revolution and enjoys bridge and traveling.

No. Rooms: 2	**Breakfast:** Full
Singles: None	**S-Rates:** $40 pb
Doubles: 2 pb	**D-Rates:** $50 pb
Type: Private cottage	**Bldg:** 1890s Texas ranch

Minimum Stay: none. **Credit Card(s) Accepted:** none. **Open:** all year. No resident dogs. No dogs please. No resident cats. No cats please. Non-smoking host. Guests may smoke. Children welcome. **Discounts:** weekly, monthly.

Reservation Contact: Bed & Breakfast Texas Style, Ruth Wilson, 4224 W. Red Bird Ln., Dallas, TX 75237; 214–298–8586.

FORT WORTH

ID: UNIVERSITY–TX

MUSEUMS, BOTANICAL GARDENS, ZOO.

Near I–35, University & White Settlement Rd.

Five minutes from downtown, this guest cottage is convenient to the famous museums of Fort Worth. Situated behind the main house, it consists of a sitting area with a piano, sofa, and chairs, a bedroom with twin beds and designer linens, a kitchen, and bath (shower only). Ingredients for a Continental breakfast are stocked, and there is off-street parking. Your hosts are an investment banker and a chef.

No. Rooms: 1
Singles: None
Doubles: 1 pb
Type: Private home

Breakfast: Continental
S-Rates: $65 pb
D-Rates: $65 pb
Bldg: Frame & brick cottage

Minimum Stay: none. **Credit Card(s) Accepted:** MC, V. **Open:** all year. No resident dogs. No dogs please. No resident cats. No cats please. Non-smoking host. Guests may not smoke in residence. Residence is not appropriate for children. **Discounts:** none.

Reservation Contact: Bed & Breakfast Texas Style, Ruth Wilson, 4224 W. Red Bird Ln., Dallas, TX 75237; 214–298–8586.

GALVESTON

ID: VA.PT.INN

BEACH, SEAWALL AMUSEMENTS, STRAND, RAILROAD MUSEUM.

Near Broadway, U.S. 45S.

This neo-Mediterranean home, built in 1907, has been meticulously restored to its original beauty. It is centrally located, just one block off Broadway, in an historic area known as the Silk Stocking District, convenient to the beach, seawall amusements, and the Strand. Family antiques are found in the five guest rooms that overlook the beautiful gardens. All rooms but one have their own screened porches. Four rooms have double-, queen-, or king-sized beds and one has a single bed; the master bedroom has a fireplace and private bath. A Continental Plus breakfast is served with cold ham, cheese, fresh fruit, and hot breads. Cheese and biscuits are served in the afternoon. Bicycles are available, as is the exercise equipment in the basement. Your hosts are interested in gardening, sailing, cooking, Galveston, and European antiques.

No. Rooms: 5
Singles: 1 sb
Doubles: 1 pb, 3 sb
Type: Inn

Breakfast: Continental Plus
S-Rates: $85–$125 pb, $65–$75 sb
D-Rates: $85–$125 pb, $85–$125 sb
Bldg: 1907 Neo-Mediterranean

Minimum Stay: none. **Credit Card(s) Accepted:** none. **Open:** all year. Dog in residence. No dogs please. No resident cats. No cats please. Non-

smoking host. Guests may not smoke in residence. Residence not appropriate for children. **Discounts:** none. Spanish spoken.

Reservation Contact: Bed & Breakfast Society of Texas, Pat Thomas, 8880–B2 Bellaire Blvd., #296, Houston, TX 77036; 713–771–3919.

HOUSTON   ID: BAROQUE–TX

ASTRODOME, RICE UNIVERSITY, UNIVERSITY OF HOUSTON, GALLERIA MALL, MUSEUMS.

Near I–10, U.S. 90, Voss Rd., Westheimer & San Felipe.

Twenty minutes from downtown Houston and near the Galleria Mall, this home offers two guest rooms. One has a four-poster double bed with lots of lace and pillows in pink and white and a private bath. The other room has twin beds accented with colorful spreads and teddy bears. A Continental breakfast is served in the atrium where a fountain adds an exotic touch. Your hosts, an architect and a travel guide, have traveled extensively.

No. Rooms: 2	**Breakfast:** Continental
Singles: None	**S-Rates:** $40 pb, $40 sb
Doubles: 1 pb, 1 sb	**D-Rates:** $50 pb, $50 sb
Type: Private home	**Bldg:** Townhouse

Minimum Stay: none. **Credit Card(s) Accepted:** MC, V. **Open:** all year. No resident dogs. No dogs please. No resident cats. No cats please. Host smokes. Guests may smoke. Children welcome with restrictions. **Discounts:** none.

Reservation Contact: Bed & Breakfast Texas Style, Ruth Wilson, 4224 Red Bird Ln., Dallas, TX 75237; 214–298–8586.

UNIVERSITY OF HOUSTON, GULF BEACHES, SHOPPING.

Near Bellfort, Broadway, I–45S.

Very near I–45 South, the Gulf Freeway, is this lovely two-story colonial-style house in a quiet neighborhood near the University of Houston, shops, and restaurants, and close to Gulf beaches. Antique furnishings make this air-conditioned home very special. An upstairs sun room overlooks the wooded backyard, a small bayou, deck, and swimming pool. Three guest rooms feature private baths. The downstairs room offers a double bed, rocking chair, and bookcase filled with books. The upstairs room has antique twin beds and matching vanity and a room with a double bed and antique accessories overlooking the front yard. Your host, a wonderful cook, serves a full breakfast, made to accommodate your taste whenever possible. Arrival/departure transportation is available. A skilled musician and antique dealer, she is well-acquainted with the Gulf Coast area, and is available for tours. Your co-host is a retired florist, as the abundance of flowers around the house will attest to.

No. Rooms: 3	**Breakfast:** Full
Singles: None	**S-Rates:** $30 pb
Doubles: 3 pb	**D-Rates:** $35 pb
Type: Private home	**Bldg:** 1967 colonial

Minimum Stay: none. **Credit Card(s) Accepted:** none. **Open:** all year. No resident dogs. No dogs please. No resident cats. No cats please. Non-smoking host. Guests may not smoke in guest rooms. Children welcome. **Discounts:** none.

Reservation Contact: Bed & Breakfast Society of Texas, Pat Thomas, 8880–B2 Bellaire Blvd., #296, Houston, TX 77036; 713–771–3919.

NEAR DOWNTOWN HOUSTON, GALLERIA AREA.

Near 11th St., I–10, Loop 610 S.

In this charming home, you will enjoy the atmosphere of the 1890s. Ride a bicycle built for two, enjoy the authentic player piano, or just relax on the comfortable wicker furniture. This dwelling, built in 1886, part of a restored Victorian neighborhood, has three guest rooms with private baths. The romantic Blue Room has a queen-sized bed, lace curtains, and antique vanity; the Turret Room, with antique furnishings and hand-crocheted spread, has a double bed. Downstairs there is a suite with a double bed, sitting room with TV and hide-a-bed, and a private entrance.

A Full home-baked breakfast is served in the formal dining room, on the deck, or in the guest room, as desired. One of your hosts is a marketing manager for an oil company; the other is an RSO owner and antique dealer interested in people, travel, and cooking.

No. Rooms: 3	**Breakfast:** Full
Singles: None	**S-Rates:** $40 pb
Doubles: 2 sb, 1 pb	**D-Rates:** $50 pb
Type: Private home	**Bldg:** 1886 Victorian

Minimum Stay: none. **Credit Card(s) Accepted:** MC, V. **Open:** all year. Dog in residence. No dogs please. No resident cats. No cats please. Nonsmoking host. Guests may not smoke in residence. Children welcome with restrictions. **Discounts:** 10% after 1 week. Spanish spoken.

Reservation Contact: Bed & Breakfast Society of Texas, Pat Thomas, 8880–B2 Bellaire Blvd., #296, Houston, TX 77036; 713–771–3919.

ID: TX–WOODFOREST

HOUSTON SHIP CHANNEL, SAN JACINTO MONUMENT, BATTLESHIP TEXAS.

Near Woodforest Blvd., I–10, Loop 610, Rte. 59N.

This contemporary home, in the eastern section of Houston, is a decorator's delight. The house is near the San Jacinto Monument and the Battleship Texas in an attractive suburban community. The lovely furnishings and accessories provide a pleasant atmosphere that you will find difficult to leave. The Getaway Room was built especially for bed & breakfast, over the garage and away from the main house. Both private and beautiful, it has a queen-sized bed and private bath with clawfoot tub; it is decorated with Laura Ashley prints, linens, and china. There are also two guest rooms in the house proper, one with a double four-poster bed and private bath; the other has a single bed, wing chair, and private bath. Arrival/departure transportation and area tours are available. A Full breakfast is served. Your host, an interior designer, is interested in travel, decorating, meditation, and entertaining.

No. Rooms: 3	**Breakfast:** Full
Singles: 1 pb	**S-Rates:** $25 pb
Doubles: 2 pb	**D-Rates:** $35 pb
Type: Private home	**Bldg:** 1974 contemporary

Minimum Stay: none. **Credit Card(s) Accepted:** none. **Open:** all year. No resident dogs. No dogs please. No resident cats. No cats please. Nonsmoking host. Guests may not smoke in guest rooms. Children welcome with restrictions. **Discounts:** none.

Reservation Contact: Bed & Breakfast Society of Texas, Pat Thomas, 8880–B2 Bellaire Blvd., #296, Houston, TX 77036; 713–771–3919.

HOUSTON/PASADENA

M.O. ANDERSON MEDICAL CENTER, SAN JACINTO MONUMENT, L.B.J. SPACE CENTER; SOUTHEAST QUADRANT OF CITY.

Near Flynn, Pasadena Blvd., I–45, Hwy. 3.

This two-story colonial home is in a quiet well-maintained neighborhood in the southeast quadrant of the Houston metroplex, close to Anderson Medical Center, Galveston, and the bay area. It is also accessible to downtown Houston (twenty-five minutes), the ship channel, Hobby Airport, University of Houston, and the Astrodome. The two spacious air-conditioned guest rooms and guest bath take up the entire second-floor of the house. The rooms offer large double beds and comfortable furnishings. The breakfast menu includes *huevos rancheros,* refried beans, tortillas, fresh fruit, and coffee or tea. Additional meals, child care, and arrival/departure transportation are available. Your host, an office manager who loves pets, will also supply a cooler and picnic basket, and give you use of the kitchen to prepare a picnic lunch.

No. Rooms: 2	**Breakfast:** Full
Singles: None	**S-Rates:** $35 sb
Doubles: 2 sb	**D-Rates:** $40 sb
Type: Private home	**Bldg:** 1966 colonial

Minimum Stay: none. **Credit Card(s) Accepted:** none. **Open:** all year. Dog in residence. A dog is allowed with restrictions. Cat in residence. A cat is allowed with restrictions. Nonsmoking host. Guests may smoke. Children welcome. **Discounts:** families of hospital patients.

Reservation Contact: Bed & Breakfast Texas Style, Ruth Wilson, 4224 W. Red Bird Ln., Dallas, TX 75237; 214–298–8586.

JACKSONVILLE

EAST TEXAS, TEXAS STATE RAILROAD, LAKE PALESTINE.

Near hwys. 84, 79, 69.

On this farm guests can relax with the smell of pine woods and watch an assortment of wildlife including deer, raccoons, oppossum, armadillos, and a variety of birds. The rustic, unhosted house has two guest rooms plus a full kitchen. One of the rooms has a Jenny Lind queen-sized bed plus a trundle bed, quilts, chests, an antique trunk, floor-length mirror, and a deck. The other room has a double bed with a hand-crocheted canopy, a white wicker rocking chair, and a treadle sewing machine. The bath has a shower and clawfoot tub. The house also has a TV and telephone. There is a pond on the farm and fishing poles for guests' use. A Continental self-serve breakfast is provided.

No. Rooms: 2	**Breakfast:** Continental
Singles: None	**S-Rates:** $40 pb
Doubles: 2 pb	**D-Rates:** $50 pb
Type: Private farm	**Bldg:** Farmhouse

Minimum Stay: none. **Credit Card(s) Accepted:** MC, V. **Open:** all year. No resident dogs. No dogs please. No resident cats. No cats please. Non-smoking host. Guests may not smoke in residence. Children welcome. **Discounts:** none.

Reservation Contact: Bed & Breakfast Texas Style, Ruth Wilson, 4224 W. Red Bird Ln., Dallas, TX 75237; 214–298–8586.

SAN ANTONIO
ID: BULLIS–HS

NEAR DOWNTOWN, FORT SAM HOUSTON; RESTAURANTS.

Near Broadway, Grayson, U.S. 35, U.S. 81.

This elegant little inn is found in a seventy-six-year-old mansion designed and built by noted Texas architect Harvey Page for Cavalry General John L. Bullis and his family. The interior of the home consists of deep rich oak staircases and wall paneling. Large chandeliers are located in the foyer and parlor areas. Unique geometrically patterned wood floors, marble fireplaces, and decorative fourteen-foot ceilings enhance the downstairs area, giving it a feeling of spaciousness. A wide veranda surrounds the house. There are six second-floor guest rooms, all with high ceilings. Four have fireplaces and five have French doors that, when open, bring in the cool breezes characteristic of San Antonio nights. All rooms, however, are provided with air-conditioning and heating units. There are two

guest bathrooms; two of the rooms have a connecting bath and may be used as a suite, and on the first floor one guest room has a fireplace and private bath. A Continental breakfast is served in the parlor, on the veranda, or in the guest room. Off-street parking is available. One of your hosts is an artist.

No. Rooms: 7	**Breakfast:** Continental
Singles: None	**S-Rates:** $39 pb, $22–$33 sb
Doubles: 1 pb, 6 sb	**D-Rates:** $45 pb, $28–$39 sb
Type: Private home	**Bldg:** 1909 neoclassical

Minimum Stay: none. **Credit Card(s) Accepted:** MC, V. **Open:** all year. No resident dogs. No dogs please. No resident cats. No cats please. Host smokes. Guests may smoke. Children welcome. **Discounts:** none.

Reservation Contact: Bed & Breakfast Society of Texas, Pat Thomas, 8880–B2 Bellaire Blvd., #296, Houston, TX 77036; 713–771–3919.

ID: COURTYARDTX

MEDICAL CENTER, ALAMO, RIVER WALK, ART MUSEUM, LA VILLITA, TEXAS RANGER MUSEUM, ZOO; WEST SIDE OF CITY.

Near Wurzbach Rd., Babcock, I–35, I–410, I–10.

This modern Spanish-style house is conveniently located near a medical center in a well-maintained neighborhood of upper-middle-class homes. The air-conditioned house has three guest rooms that share a guest bath. The first room has a queen-sized bed and double dresser; in the second rooms, pretty crewel pillows accent twin beds; the third room features a double bed, desk, cane chair, and antique clock. A Full breakfast is served. Arrival/departure transportation and area tours are available. Your host is a retired court reporter and choir soloist who enjoys bridge, needlework, swimming, and racquetball.

No. Rooms: 3	**Breakfast:** Full
Singles: None	**S-Rates:** $40 sb
Doubles: 3 sb	**D-Rates:** $45 sb
Type: Private home	**Bldg:** 1973 modern Spanish

Minimum Stay: none. **Credit Card(s) Accepted:** none. **Open:** all year. Dog in residence. A dog is allowed with restrictions. No resident cats. No cats please. Nonsmoking host. Guests may not smoke in guest rooms. Children welcome. **Discounts:** weekly, monthly.

Reservation Contact: Bed & Breakfast Texas Style, Ruth Wilson, 4224 W. Red Bird Ln., Dallas, TX 75237; 214–298–8586.

KING WILLIAM HISTORIC DISTRICT, RIVER WALK, ALAMO, DOWNTOWN.

Near I–35, I–10, S. St. Mary's, S. Alamo.

Dating from around 1850, the King William Historic District is an eclectic neighborhood that is now 95 percent restored. This turn-of-the-century house has four air-conditioned guest rooms with queen-sized beds, hand-crocheted bedspreads or quilts, and private baths. The Blue Room has a white iron bed, a white wicker rocker, lace curtains, and a kitchenette with microwave and small refrigerator. The other rooms are done in

aqua, peach, or red. A Continental Plus breakfast is served. Your host's hobbies include travel, dancing, gardening, water sports, and cooking.

No. Rooms: 4	**Breakfast:** Continental Plus
Singles: None	**S-Rates:** $60–$70 pb
Doubles: 4 pb	**D-Rates:** $60–$70 pb
Type: Private home	**Bldg:** Post-Victorian

Minimum Stay: none. **Credit Card(s) Accepted:** AE, MC, V. **Open:** all year. Resident dog. No dogs please. No resident cats. No cats please. Host smokes. Guests may smoke in residence. Children welcome. **Discounts:** weekly.

Reservation Contact: Bed & Breakfast Hosts of San Antonio, Lavern & Vicky Campbell, 166 Rockhill, San Antonio, TX 78209; 512–824–8036.

ID: 2–SANANTON

FORT SAM HOUSTON.

Near I–35, I–37, I–10, Broadway, N. New Braunfels Ave.

Edwin Terrell was a lawyer and statesman who served as ambassador and plenipotentiary to Belgium under the presidency of Benjamin Harrison in the early 1890s. While in Europe Mr. Terrell fell in love with the castles and chateaus in Belgium and France, and on his return to Texas in 1894 he commissioned architect Alfred Giles to design this home. The central hall is a distinctive feature of this home's design since all the major rooms open off of it. The staircase, with harp-shaped newel posts, is an architectural highlight as is the inlaid border of the parquet floor. The library features an outstanding molded brickwork fireplace, and the parlor's most striking feature is its round front window. The formal dining room shows rich woodwork, and the oval end of the room boasts curved windows and a carved mantel. There are nine guest rooms, six with private baths. The Yellow Rose Room has a magnificent antique Victorian double bed of carved walnut, while the octagonal Colonial Room has a fireplace and is furnished entirely with maple. In addition to the king-sized bed in the Terrell Room, there is a single bed in the attached sun room/TV area. A king-sized canopy bed graces the Giles Suite with fireplace, reading corner, and attached sun room which can accommodate a single bed or a crib. The sunny Oval Room features window seats in front of curved windows. All of the above rooms are on the second floor and have private baths. On the third floor the former ball room has been converted into a conference center. There are also two guest rooms on this floor: the Tower Room, which can accommodate three people, and the Moffat Room, which is furnished with an antique double bed and two single beds. These rooms share a bath. The fourth-floor room, done in red, white, and blue, provides a marvelous view of the city and is furnished with a magnificent Victorian double bed plus a single bed and a potbellied stove. A Full breakfast is served. Guests enjoy the front porch and large yard with a variety of plants and trees. The hosts, who purchased the home in 1986, have done extensive restoration. They also enjoy photography, reading, and crafts.

No. Rooms: 9	**Breakfast:** Full
Singles: None	**S-Rates:** $50–$65 pb, $50 sb
Doubles: 6 pb, 2 sb	**D-Rates:** $65–$75 pb, $65 sb
Type: Inn	**Bldg:** Castle

Minimum Stay: none. **Credit Card(s) Accepted:** none. **Open:** all year. No resident dogs. No dogs please. No resident cats. No cats please. Nonsmoking host. Guests may not smoke in residence. Children welcome with restrictions. **Discounts:** none.

Reservation Contact: Bed & Breakfast Hosts of San Antonio, Lavern & Vicky Campbell, 166 Rockhill, San Antonio, TX 78209; 512–824–8036.

HISTORIC AREA.

Near Austin Hwy., N. New Braunfels Ave., I–35.

This large home is built in the Mediterranean mode of the late 1920s. Recently constructed and separate from the main house is a charming upstairs guest apartment, with private entrance and off-street parking. It consists of a living/kitchen area, with wide-plank pine floors, hand-hewn beamed cathedral ceiling, woodburning fireplace, and central heat and air-conditioning. The bedroom has a queen-sized canopy bed plus a trundle for a third person. The apartment is furnished with the owner's collection of country and primitive antiques. French doors open onto a large covered deck overlooking the picturesque courtyard, swimming pool, and gardens. The kitchen is generously stocked for a Continental Plus breakfast. Your host can help you plan your tour.

No. Rooms: 1	**Breakfast:** Continental Plus
Singles: None	**S-Rates:** $90 pb
Doubles: 1 pb	**D-Rates:** $90 pb
Type: Private apartment	**Bldg:** 1980 Mediterranean style

Minimum Stay: 2 nights. **Credit Card(s) Accepted:** MC, V. **Open:** all year. Host's dog is not allowed in guest areas. No dogs please. No resident cats. No cats please. Nonsmoking host. Guests may not smoke in residence. Residence not appropriate for children. **Discounts:** none.

Reservation Contact: Bed & Breakfast Hosts of San Antonio, Lavern & Vicky Campbell, 166 Rockhill, San Antonio, TX 78209; 512–824–8036.

ALAMO, CONVENTION CENTER, RIVER WALK, RIVER CENTER.

Near I–10, I–35, I–37, S. Alamo, E. Guenther, Mission Rd.

Antiques and Mexican folk art decorate the interior of this 1881 Victorian located in the King William Historic District. Guests are welcome to use the front porch equipped with swings and rockers, the library, and the grand piano. The three-room guest suite has 14-foot ceilings, a queen-sized bed, fireplace, central heat and air-conditioning, ceiling fans, TV, telephone, and private bath. A Full breakfast is served which sometimes includes homemade tortillas. Guests can walk or take a ten-cent trolley ride to downtown, the Alamo, the convention center, River Walk, and River Center. Your host likes musicals, tea, and porch parties (to which guests are welcome). She is an aficionado of classical and avant-garde dance and travels to Mexico, South America, and Europe.

No. Rooms: 1	**Breakfast:** Full
Singles: None	**S-Rates:** $85
Doubles: 1 pb	**D-Rates:** $105
Type: Private home	**Bldg:** 1881 Victorian

Minimum Stay: 2 nights. **Credit Card(s) Accepted:** AE, MC, V. **Open:** all year. No resident dogs. No dogs please. No resident cats. No cats please. Nonsmoking host. Guests may not smoke in residence. Children welcome with restrictions. **Discounts:** 10% for 3 or more week nights; 10% for 6 nights or more.

Reservation Contact: Bed & Breakfast of San Antonio, Lavern & Vicky Campbell, 166 Rockhill, San Antonio, TX 78209; 512–824–8036.

SEABROOK
ID: TX–SEABROOK

SAILING, FISHING, JOHNSON SPACE CENTER; ON WATER.

Near Rte. 146, U.S. 45.

This cheerful air-conditioned Cape Cod-style waterfront cottage provides the perfect blend of casual comfort and the excitement of Texas coastal activity. Verandas on two levels offer beautiful sea views that go on and on. Watch ships in the distance and colorful shrimp boats unloading their catch across the way. You have a choice of two bedrooms with private baths or an upstairs loft with two double beds and a single. One bedroom has a lovely water view, some antique furnishings, and nautical accessories; the other has handsome Victorian Eastlake furniture. A Continental Plus breakfast is served. Nearby attractions include deep-sea fishing, sailboat rental, the Johnson Space Center, and dining in the numerous waterfront restaurants. One of your hosts is an architect; the other is a tour guide available for trips to nearby Galveston.

No. Rooms: 3	**Breakfast:** Continental Plus
Singles: None	**S-Rates:** $30–$40 pb, $30–$40 sb
Doubles: 2 pb, 1 sb	**D-Rates:** $40–$50 pb, $40–$50 sb
Type: Private home	**Bldg:** 1932 Cape Cod cottage

Minimum Stay: none. **Credit Card(s) Accepted:** none. **Open:** all year. No resident dogs. No dogs please. No resident cats. No cats please. Nonsmoking host. Guests may not smoke in guest rooms. Children welcome with restrictions. **Discounts:** none.

Reservation Contact: Bed & Breakfast Society of Texas, Pat Thomas, 8880–B2 Bellaire Blvd. #296, Houston, TX 77036; 713–771–3919.

TEMPLE
ID: DOME–TX

CENTRAL TEXAS.

Near I–35, Rte. 53, 363.

Just north of Temple, this unique house was designed by your hosts' architect son. The structure is a concrete dome with almost 5,000 square feet of living space. Stepping into the living room is like entering a cathedral, but the most interesting feature is the 200 house plants that grow over the second-floor balcony. There are two guest rooms with private baths. One has a king-sized bed with an heirloom, crocheted lace spread, an antique dresser and vanity, and collections of eyeglasses, miniatures, and dolls. The other room boasts a colorful country quilt on a double bed. The Full country breakfast includes locally made German sausage. Your hosts are active in neighborhood and church activities.

No. Rooms: 2	**Breakfast:** Full
Singles: None	**S-Rates:** $65 pb
Doubles: 2 pb	**D-Rates:** $65 pb
Type: Private home	**Bldg:** Concrete dome

Minimum Stay: none. **Credit Card(s) Accepted:** MC, V. **Open:** all year. No resident dogs. No dogs please. No resident cats. No cats please. Non-smoking host. Guests may not smoke in residence. Children welcome. **Discounts:** none.

Reservation Contact: Bed & Breakfast Texas Style, Ruth Wilson, 4224 W. Red Bird Ln., Dallas, TX 75237; 214–298–8586.

WACO
ID: LAKESIDE–TX

TEXAS RANGER MUSEUM, BAYLOR UNIVERSITY, BRAZOS RIVER, ZOO, ART CENTER, WACO LAKE, GOLF.

Near I–35, Lakeshore Dr. & China Spring.

This contemporary home offers one guest room with a duck motif, double bed, and shared bath. The large deck, where a Continental Plus breakfast is served, overlooks a pond and trees. Golf fans can tee off right next door at the country club. One of the hosts is an avid golfer; the other is a teacher who also writes a newspaper column and enjoys travel and gourmet cooking.

No. Rooms: 1	**Breakfast:** Continental Plus
Singles: None	**S-Rates:** $40 sb
Doubles: 1 sb	**D-Rates:** $45 sb
Type: Private home	**Bldg:** Contemporary

Minimum Stay: none. **Credit Card(s) Accepted:** MC, V. **Open:** all year. Resident dog. No dogs please. Resident cat. No cats please. Host smokes. Guests may smoke in residence. Children welcome. **Discounts:** none.

Reservation Contact: Bed & Breakfast Texas Style, Ruth Wilson, 4224 W. Red Bird Ln., Dallas, TX 75237; 214–298–8586.

UTAH

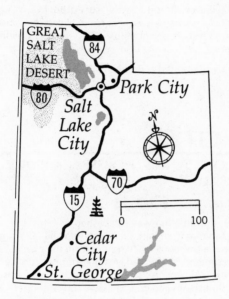

CEDAR CITY

ID: ROC-720

BRYCE CANYON NATIONAL PARK, ZION NATIONAL PARK, SOUTHERN UTAH STATE COLLEGE, BRAITHWAITE ART GALLERY; RODEOS, SKIING.

Near I–15.

Built in 1898, this home bears the name of its original owner, John S. Woodbury, a prominent mayor, educator, and businessman during Cedar City's formative years. This Victorian boasts spacious lawns, and its large redwood deck offers perfect summertime tanning or a place to relax while sipping a cool drink. All four guest rooms have private baths. The Peach Room, the largest, is an ideal honeymoon suite with its queen-sized bed and sitting room. Rustic oak and natural touches accent the Beige Room, which has a double bed. The Ivory Room is graced with dusty rose, cranberry, and ivory lace and twin beds. The Rose Room, in delicate pink and crisp white, has a double bed and clawfoot tub. A Full breakfast is served in the dining room. The house is a three-minute walk from the Utah Shakespearean Festival; it is also centrally located to southern Utah's national parks and ski resorts.

No. Rooms: 4
Singles: None
Doubles: 4 pb
Type: Inn

Breakfast: Full
S-Rates: $40–$65 pb
D-Rates: $40–$65 pb
Bldg: Victorian

Minimum Stay: none. **Credit Card(s) Accepted:** MC, V. **Open:** all year. No resident dogs. No dogs please. No resident cats. No cats please. Non-smoking host. Guests may not smoke in residence. Children welcome. **Discounts:** none.

Reservation Contact: Bed & Breakfast Rocky Mountains, Kate Peterson Winters, Box 804, Colorado Springs, CO 80901; 719–630–3433.

PARK CITY
ID: ROC–32

SKIING, GOLF, TENNIS, HORSEBACK RIDING, HIKING, HOT-AIR BALLOONS.

Near I–80, Rte. 224, Rte. 248.

Built in 1893, this little inn was established as housing for local miners seeking their fortunes from Park City's ore-rich hills. The large living room with fireplace is a gathering place for guests in the evening when complimentary refreshments are served. An outdoor hot tub welcomes guests back after a day of skiing. All seven guest rooms have private baths and offer antique furnishings and down pillows and comforters. A Full country breakfast is served. Skiers will find the inn is within an easy walk of the town lift servicing the Park City Ski Area. They also have the opportunity to ski home. Historic Main Street, with its many restaurants, shops, galleries, and bus stops, is only one block away.

No. Rooms: 7
Singles: None
Doubles: 7 pb
Type: Inn

Breakfast: Full
S-Rates: $35–$150 pb
D-Rates: $40–$155 pb
Bldg: 1893 Victorian

Minimum Stay: 4–6 days on holidays. **Credit Card(s) Accepted:** AE, MC, V. **Open:** all year. Dog in residence. No dogs please. No resident cats. No cats please. Nonsmoking host. Guests may not smoke in guest rooms. Children welcome. **Discounts:** Groups of 8 or more.

Reservation Contact: Bed & Breakfast—Rocky Mountains, Kate Peterson Winters, Box 804, Colorado Springs, CO 80901; 719–630–3433.

ST. GEORGE
ID: ROC–770

ZION NATIONAL PARK, BRYCE CANYON.

Near I–15.

Located diagonally across from Brigham Young's winter home, this house has an interesting history. It was built about 1873 by Edwin Woolley, a local judge and merchant. It was rumored that he hid polygamist men in the attic and that there was a secret door that these men used to get in and out of the building. When the house was renovated, the little door and other evidence substantiating these rumors was found. There are nine guest rooms, all with private baths. A sampling of the rooms includes Melissa, a large romantic room on the second floor decorated in antique American oak. It has a queen-sized bed with a lace canopy, a fireplace, and a Chippendale love seat. Harriet has a tiny private balcony and is furnished with European antiques, a queen-sized bed, a settee that opens to a bed. Sarah, a large, primitive pine room on the first floor, boasts a fireplace flanked by church pews, a queen-sized bed in the main room, a single bed on the sun porch, and a private entrance. The other rooms have queen-sized or double beds. A Full, gourmet breakfast is served and picnic lunches are available with prior arrangement. Your hosts enjoy gardening, cooking, and decorating.

No. Rooms: 9	**Breakfast:** Full
Singles: None	**S-Rates:** $25–$70 pb
Doubles: 9 pb	**D-Rates:** $25–$70 pb
Type: Inn	**Bldg:** 1870s frame

Minimum Stay: none. **Credit Card(s) Accepted:** MC, V. **Open:** all year. No resident dogs. No dogs please. No resident cats. No cats please. Nonsmoking host. Guests may not smoke in residence. Children welcome. **Discounts:** none.

Reservation Contact: Bed & Breakfast Rocky Mountains, Kate Peterson Winters, Box 804, Colorado Springs, CO 80901; 719–630–3433.

SALT LAKE CITY   ID: ROC–SALT

ALTA & SNOWBIRD SKI AREAS.

Near I–15, I–80.

Surrounded by a small quarter-horse breeding and training farm, this turn-of-the-century inn is set among tall spruce trees. Four guest suites have telephones, TVs, country vistas, and private baths. The Pony Suite consists of three bedrooms, two with queen-sized beds, one with a double bed, a living room, and kitchen. The other three have queen-sized beds and one has a kitchen. A Continental breakfast is served.

No. Rooms: 6	**Breakfast:** Continental
Singles: None	**S-Rates:** $60–$70 pb, $60–$70 sb
Doubles: 3 pb, 3 sb	**D-Rates:** $60–$70 pb, $60–$70 sb
Type: Inn	**Bldg:** 1903 farmhouse

Minimum Stay: none. **Credit Card(s) Accepted:** MC, V. **Open:** all year. No resident dogs. No dogs please. No resident cats. No cats please. Nonsmoking host. Guests may not smoke in residence. Children welcome. **Discounts:** none.

Reservation Contact: Bed & Breakfast Rocky Mountains, Kate Winters, Box 804, Colorado Springs, CO 80901; 719–630–3433.

VERMONT

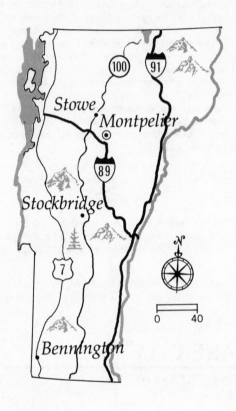

BARTON

ID: 05822LAF

DAIRY FARM, HIKING, SWIMMING, CROSS-COUNTRY SKIING, SNOWMOBILE TRAILS.

Near Rte. 16, I–91.

This secluded rural home on a working dairy farm offers a quiet, scenic getaway. The Cape-style house, built in 1921, has two guest rooms, with private entrances, double beds, and shared guest bath. Cots and cribs are available for additional members of your party. A Full breakfast is served, usually pancakes with that wonderful Vermont maple syrup. Because this is a dairy farm, it offers a great opportunity for city-dwelling families to get a hands-on taste of farm life. The winter months also provide miles of cross-country ski trails—and it's a lovely place for quiet walks.

No. Rooms: 2	**Breakfast:** Full
Singles: None	**S-Rates:** $25 sb
Doubles: 2 sb	**D-Rates:** $35 sb
Type: Private home	**Bldg:** 1921 Cape Cod

Minimum Stay: none. **Credit Card(s) Accepted:** none. **Open:** all year. No resident dogs. Guests may bring dog. Cat in residence. Guests may bring cat. Nonsmoking host. Guests may not smoke in guest rooms. Children welcome. **Discounts:** weekly.

Reservation Contact: Bed & Breakfast Registry Ltd., Gary Winget, Box 8174, St. Paul, MN 55108; 612–646–4238.

BENNINGTON
ID: VT801

MOUNT SNOW.

Near Rte. 7.

Built in 1774, this colonial house is the oldest in the village. It is furnished with many antiques and has its own exercise room and hot tub. There are five guest rooms. Three have double beds and one has twin beds; these four rooms share a bath. The fifth room has a queen-sized bed, sitting room, and private bath. A Full breakfast is served. Mount Snow is 30 minutes away.

No. Rooms: 5	**Breakfast:** Full
Singles: None	**S-Rates:** $33 sb
Doubles: 1 pb, 4 sb	**D-Rates:** $75 pb, $48 sb
Type: Private home	**Bldg:** 1774 colonial

Minimum Stay: none. **Credit Card(s) Accepted:** MC, V. **Open:** all year. Dog in residence. No dogs please. Cat in residence. No cats please. Nonsmoking host. Guests may not smoke in residence. Children welcome. **Discounts:** none.

Reservation Contact: Vermont Bed & Breakfast, Jane Torbert Zurn, Box One, East Fairfield, VT 05448; 802–827–3827.

DERBY LINE
ID: VT202

CLOSE TO CANADA; OPERA HOUSE, SHOPS, RESTAURANTS.

Near I–91.

Filled with antiques, this elegant Victorian home is close to the Canadian border and is a short walk from shops and restaurants. A library and an opera house are also nearby. There are five guest rooms with private baths. Two rooms, one with a fireplace, have twin beds. A third room has a queen-sized bed, and the other two have double beds. A Full breakfast is served.

No. Rooms: 5
Singles: None
Doubles: 5 pb
Type: Private home

Breakfast: Full
S-Rates: $35 pb
D-Rates: $45–$50 pb
Bldg: Victorian

Minimum Stay: none. **Credit Card(s) Accepted:** MC, V. **Open:** all year. No resident dogs. No dogs please. No resident cats. No cats please. Non-smoking host. Guests may not smoke in residence. Children welcome. **Discounts:** none.

Reservation Contact: Vermont Bed & Breakfast, Jane Torbert Zurn, Box One, East Fairfield, VT 05448; 802–827–3827.

EAST BURKE
ID: 05832LEW

SKI AREAS, HIKING, BIKING, BEACHES, BOATING, LYNDON STATE COLLEGE, FALL FOLIAGE, MAPLE MUSEUM; NORTHEAST VERMONT.

Near U.S. 5, Rte. 114.

This completely remodeled 1840s farmhouse is on twenty-seven acres of apple trees, blackberries, and family gardens. The house still has its exposed beams and two fireplaces. You are welcome to join the family in the evening, or you can enjoy the privacy of the living room. There are two guest rooms and a guest suite; each sleeps at least two, and one

has a private bath. There are several ski areas nearby, and you will find many hiking and biking opportunities, two state beaches, and beautiful Lake Willoughby, often compared with Switzerland's Lake Lucerne. This is a quiet, rural area of small, picturesque villages. One of your hosts is a civil engineer and land surveyor.

No. Rooms: 3	**Breakfast:** Continental
Singles: None	**S-Rates:** $38 pb, $38 sb
Doubles: 1 pb, 2 sb	**D-Rates:** $50 pb, $50 sb
Type: Private home	**Bldg:** 1840s

Minimum Stay: none. **Credit Card(s) Accepted:** none. **Open:** all year. Dog in residence. No dogs please. Cat in residence. No cats please. Non-smoking host. Guests may not smoke in guest rooms. Children welcome. **Discounts:** 7th night free.

Reservation Contact: Bed & Breakfast Registry Ltd., Gary Winget, Box 8174, St. Paul, MN 55108; 612–646–4238.

EAST FAIRFIELD   ID: VTB104

ONE AND A HALF HOURS FROM MONTREAL, 30 MINUTES FROM STOWE.

Near rtes. 36, 108.

Fairfield lies on an undulating upland plateau in the northwest corner of Vermont. Favored by abundant streams and rivers, fertile meadows, and productive hardwood forests, it possesses a long and proud tradition of productivity. This delightful guest cottage sits on the bank of a lovely brook and waterfall on the edge of the village. Skiing, swimming, hiking, fishing, sightseeing, antiques, auctions, interesting restaurants, and one of the finest American museums provides day-trip excursions. Or you can just enjoy the beautiful snow and cozy nights of winter, gathering maple sugar with draft horses in early spring, the wildflowers and lushness of summer, or the brilliant foliage of autumn. There are three upstairs bedrooms, one with a double bed, one with twin beds, and one with a single bed and a youth bed. The living room is located in the east wing of the cottage and has a comfortable double hide-a-bed. Other amenities include TV, radio, off-street parking, and use of the patio, yard, and laundry facilities. Because the cottage is unhosted, no breakfast is served.

No. Rooms: 3	**Breakfast:** None
Singles: None	**S-Rates:** $35–$50 pb
Doubles: 2 pb	**D-Rates:** $35–$50 pb
Type: Private cottage	**Bldg:** 1870

Minimum Stay: 2 nights. **Credit Card(s) Accepted:** MC, V. **Open:** all year. Guests may bring dog. Guests may bring cat. Guests may smoke. Children welcome. **Discounts:** weekly.

Reservation Contact: Vermont Bed & Breakfast, Jane Torbert Zurn, Box One, East Fairfield, VT 05448; 802–827–3827.

HUNTINGTON

ID: VTB102

DOWNHILL & CROSS-COUNTRY SKIING, HIKING; GREEN MOUNTAINS.

Near I–89.

Located in the foothills of the Green Mountains, this marvelously quaint and rustic log cabin provides spectacular views and wide vistas. There are many easily accessible walking trails, downhill and cross-country skiing are nearby, but what makes this cabin special is its quiet and solitude. The stone fireplace, many handcrafted artifacts, and shelves of books give it a particularly cozy atmosphere. Not only are the walls made of log, but so is the double bed in one of the two guest rooms. The second guest room also has log walls, a double bed, crib, and bureau. You are welcome to use the TV. A Full breakfast is served. Your hosts are owners of a ski center. One is a social worker; the other is a tennis professional. They enjoy hiking, skiing, and tennis.

No. Rooms: 2	**Breakfast:** Full
Singles: None	**S-Rates:** $45 sb
Doubles: 2 sb	**D-Rates:** $55 sb
Type: Private home	**Bldg:** 1973 log cabin

Minimum Stay: none. **Credit Card(s) Accepted:** MC, V. **Open:** all year. Dog in residence. No dogs please. Cat in residence. No cats please. Non-smoking host. Guests may not smoke in residence. Children welcome. **Discounts:** none.

Reservation Contact: Vermont Bed & Breakfast, Jane Torbert Zurn, Box One, East Fairfield, VT 05448; 802–827–3827.

JERICHO

ID: VTB100

GREEN MOUNTAINS, SKIING, SHELBURNE MUSEUM.

Near I–89, U.S. Z.

Although built in 1978, this salt-box Colonial home was authentically designed with special attention to details of the past. Wide plank floors are found throughout the house as is wrought-iron hardware. Stenciling adorns the living room, formal dining room, and master bedroom, creating an atmosphere of genuine New England country living. There are three guest rooms, with queen-sized or double beds; one has a private bath. A Full breakfast is served. This home, located in the foothills of the Green Mountains, offers three major ski areas within a forty-five minute drive. The Shelburne Museum is also in the area. Your hosts are interested in genealogy, church activities, and their two little granddaughters.

No. Rooms: 3
Singles: None
Doubles: 1 pb, 2 sb
Type: Private home

Breakfast: Full
S-Rates: $55 pb, $30 sb
D-Rates: $65 pb, $50 sb
Bldg: 1978 salt box

Minimum Stay: 2 nights. **Credit Card(s) Accepted:** none. **Open:** all year, except Christmas. Discounts: none.

Reservation Contact: Vermont Bed & Breakfast, Jane Torbert Zurn, Box One, East Fairfield, VT 05448; 802–827–3827.

MIDDLETOWN SPRINGS   ID: VT501

GREEN MOUNTAIN NATIONAL FOREST, ST. CATHERINE STATE PARK, CASTLETON STATE COLLEGE.

Near Rte. 7.

This 1870 Italianate Victorian is listed on the National Register of Historic Places. It offers four guest rooms. Two have queen-sized beds and private baths. One with twin beds and another with a queen-sized bed share a bath. A Full breakfast is served.

No. Rooms: 4
Singles: None
Doubles: 2 pb, 2 sb
Type: Private home

Breakfast: Full
S-Rates: $50 pb, $50 sb
D-Rates: $56 pb, $56 sb
Bldg: 1870 Italianate Victorian

Minimum Stay: none. **Credit Card(s) Accepted:** MC, V. **Open:** all year. Dog in residence. No dogs please. No resident cats. No cats please. Non-smoking host. Guests may not smoke in residence. Children welcome. **Discounts:** none.

Reservation Contact: Vermont Bed & Breakfast, Jane Torbert Zurn, Box One, East Fairfield, VT 05448; 802–827–3827.

STOCKBRIDGE   ID: 05772DUR

DOWNHILL & CROSS-COUNTRY SKIING, ANTIQUE SHOPS, HIKING.

Near Rte. 100, U.S. 4, I–89.

This house, built in 1780 was the first to be erected in Stockbridge. It is on two scenic acres twelve miles from Killington and Pico ski areas and thirty miles from Sugarbush. Cross-Country skiing can be found at Trail Head, a quarter-mile away, or Mountain Meadow, twelve miles away. The house has antique furnishings and a lovely common room for your use. There are seven guest rooms that can accommodate two to five adults. The rooms are furnished with dressers, nightstands, lamps, quilts, and rocking chairs. Two rooms have private baths; the other rooms share two and a half baths. The family quarters are separate. A Full breakfast is served in the dining room.

No. Rooms: 7	**Breakfast:** Full
Singles: None	**S-Rates:** $60–$75 pb, $60 sb
Doubles: 2 pb, 5 sb	**D-Rates:** $80–$100 pb, $70 sb
Type: Inn	**Bldg:** 1780 colonial

Minimum Stay: ski season. **Credit Card(s) Accepted:** none. **Open:** all year. No resident dogs. No dogs please. No resident cats. No cats please. Nonsmoking host. Guests may not smoke in residence. Children welcome with restrictions. **Discounts:** none.

Reservation Contact: Bed & Breakfast Registry Ltd., Gary Winget, Box 8174, St. Paul, MN 55108; 612–646–4238.

STOWE

ID: 05672SKI

MT. MANSFIELD, ALPINE SLIDE; GOLF, TENNIS, SWIMMING, HIKING, HORSEBACK RIDING, SKI AREAS; GREEN MOUNTAINS.

Near rtes. 100 & 108.

This inviting little country inn is surrounded by green hemlock and spruce trees in the ski capital of the east and prides itself on Mount Mansfield, Vermont's highest peak. The inn provides a view of the ski runs from its windows and, after a day on the slopes, it's only a short return drive or ski back to the inn. You find delicious meals, good conversation, and all the warmth and informality of an old-fashioned ski lodge. The ten guest rooms, with shared or private baths, are large, comfortable, colorful, and spotlessly clean. A Full breakfast and dinner (all you can eat) are served during the winter months (Modern American Plan); Continental breakfast is served during the other months. Besides skiing, this charming New England town offers golf, tennis, swimming, hiking, and horseback riding.

A trout stream and twenty-eight wooded acres are available. Your hosts, in business since 1941, truly enjoy their guests and go out of their way to ensure a pleasant stay.

No. Rooms: 10
Singles: None
Doubles: 5 pb, 5 sb
Type: Inn

Breakfast: Continental
S-Rates: $50 pb, $40 sb
D-Rates: $55–$75 pb, $55–$75 sb
Bldg: 1940 colonial

Minimum Stay: none. **Credit Card(s) Accepted:** none. **Open:** all year. No resident dogs. No dogs please. No resident cats. No cats please. Non-smoking host. Guests may smoke. Children welcome. **Discounts:** none.

Reservation Contact: Bed & Breakfast Registry Ltd., Gary Winget, Box 8174, St. Paul, MN 55108; 612–646–4238.

WALDON
ID: VT108

LINDON OUTING SKI AREA.

Near I–91.

This post-and-beam house offers five guest rooms. One has a queen-sized and double bed with a private bath; one has a double bed and private bath. The other three, with double or queen-sized beds, share a bath. A Full breakfast is served.

No. Rooms: 5
Singles: None
Doubles: 2 pb, 3 sb
Type: Private home

Breakfast: Full
S-Rates: $40–$60 pb, $40 sb
D-Rates: $45–$65 pb, $45 sb
Bldg: Post and beam

Minimum Stay: none. **Credit Card(s) Accepted:** MC, V. **Open:** all year. Dog in residence. No dogs please. Cat in residence. No cats please. Non-smoking host. Guests may not smoke in residence. Children welcome. **Discounts:** none.

Reservation Contact: Vermont Bed & Breakfast, Jane Torbert Zurn, Box One, East Fairfield, VT 05448; 802–827–3827.

WILMINGTON
ID: 05363RED

SOUTHWESTERN VERMONT SKI AREAS, CROSS-COUNTRY TRAILS, GREEN MOUNTAINS; HIKING, SWIMMING, BOATING, HORSEBACK RIDING.

Near rtes. 100 & 9.

This fine old colonial home, recently redecorated, is furnished with an-tiques. There is a lounge with fireplace where you can mingle with other guests. During warmer months, you will also find spacious and well-groomed lawns, flower and vegetable gardens, evergreens and old maple trees. The five guest rooms have king-sized, double, or twin beds with shared or private baths. A Full gourmet breakfast with a choice of entrées is served in the dining room or on the canopied veranda. There is an old-fashioned country fair in August and many art and craft festivals. Children will love the Maple Grove Honey Museum. Beaches and hiking trails abound. You will also enjoy the Mt. Snow Playhouse and Michael's Theater. Additional meals are available.

No. Rooms: 5	**Breakfast:** Full
Singles: None	**S-Rates:** $75 pb, $75 sb
Doubles: 4 pb, 1 sb	**D-Rates:** $75 pb, $75 sb
Type: Inn	**Bldg:** Colonial

Minimum Stay: 2 nights. **Credit Card(s) Accepted:** none. **Open:** all year. Dog in residence. No dogs please. Cat in residence. No cats please. Nonsmoking host. Guests may not smoke in residence. Children welcome. **Discounts:** none.

Reservation Contact: Bed & Breakfast Registry Ltd., Gary Winget, Box 8174, St. Paul, MN 55108; 612–646–4238.

VIRGINIA

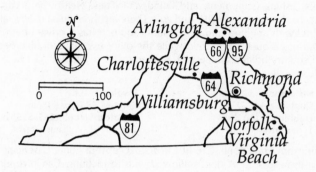

ARLINGTON

15 MINUTES FROM WASHINGTON, D.C.

Near Jefferson Davis Hwy. & 23rd St.

This attractive Dutch colonial is two blocks from restaurants and only 15 minutes from Washington via subway. The home is furnished with antiques and wicker throughout and there is a lovely yard with gardens for guests to use. There are six guest rooms available. Four have queen-sized beds and two have single beds. One of the single rooms has a private bath; the other rooms share two baths. Most of the rooms are furnished with antiques and hand made quilts. A Continental Plus breakfast is served.

No. Rooms: 6	**Breakfast:** Continental Plus
Singles: 1 pb, 1 sb	**S-Rates:** $40 pb, $40 sb
Doubles: 4 sb	**D-Rates:** $50 sb
Type: Private home	**Bldg:** Dutch colonial

Minimum Stay: none. **Credit Card(s) Accepted:** none. **Open:** all year. No resident dogs. No dogs please. No resident cats. No cats please. Nonsmoking host. Guests may smoke. Children welcome. **Discounts:** 10% after 7 days.

Reservation Contact: Bed & Breakfast Registry, Gary Winget, Box 8174, St. Paul, MN 55108; 612–646–4238.

BERRYVILLE

HUNT COUNTRY, APPALACHIAN TRAIL.

Near rtes. 340 & 7.

This recently built colonial-style home is located in a rural area in the foothills of the Blue Ridge Mountains near Harpers Ferry, Charlestown, and the Appalachian Trail. The house, in Virginia hunting country, features a yard and patio, fireplace, wood-burning stove, and amenities like bikes, fishing equipment, and laundry facilities. Nearby you can find horseback riding, canoeing, and golf. There are three guest rooms, all furnished with antiques and ceiling fans, and one has a private bath. One room has a queen-sized bed while the other two have double beds. A Full country breakfast is served. Area tours are available. Your host is an RSO manager.

No. Rooms: 3	**Breakfast:** Full
Singles: None	**S-Rates:** $35 pb, $35 sb
Doubles: 1 pb, 2 sb	**D-Rates:** $60 pb, $45–$55 sb
Type: Private home	**Bldg:** 1978 Williamsburg

Minimum Stay: none. **Credit Card(s) Accepted:** none. **Open:** all year. Dog in residence. A dog is allowed with restrictions. Cat in residence. A cat is allowed with restrictions. Host smokes. Guests may smoke. Children welcome with restrictions. **Discounts:** none.

Reservation Contact: Blue Ridge Bed & Breakfast, Rita Duncan, Rte. 2, Box 3895, Berryville, VA 22611; 703–955–1246.

CHARLOTTESVILLE ID: GUE–AUBURN

MONTICELLO, ASH LAWN.

Near U.S. 250, U.S. 29, I–64.

This antebellum cottage is located on a scenic horse farm that was part of the original Jefferson plantation. The main house was originally built by Thomas Jefferson for one of his overseers. Just six miles east of the city, it is conveniently located between Jefferson's Monticello home and Ash Lawn, the home of President James Monroe. The cottage has a sitting area with fireplace and four-poster bed, and a bedroom with twin beds and connecting bath with shower. Both rooms have private entrances. A Continental Plus breakfast is served on the porch or near the pool. You are welcome to use the swimming pool, and horseback riding is available at an extra charge. Your hosts, a gentleman farmer and his wife, recently returned from Columbia, South America, and are interested in painting and horse training.

No. Rooms: 2	**Breakfast:** Continental Plus
Singles: None	**S-Rates:** $100 sb
Doubles: 2 sb	**D-Rates:** $100 sb
Type: Private cottage	**Bldg:** 1810 brick

Minimum Stay: none. **Credit Card(s) Accepted:** none. **Open:** all year. Dog in residence. No dogs please. No resident cats. No cats please. Nonsmoking host. Guests may not smoke in residence. Children welcome with restrictions. **Discounts:** none. Spanish & French spoken.

Reservation Contact: Guesthouses Bed & Breakfast, Inc., Mary Hill Caperton, Box 5737, Charlottesville, VA 22905; 804–979–7264.

UNIVERSITY OF VIRGINIA, MONTICELLO, ASH LAWN, MONTPELIER.

Near Rugby Rd., U.S. 250, U.S. 29, I-64.

This charming early twentieth-century white-frame house, with pleasant tree-shaded yard, is within walking distance of the University of Virginia. The university, designed by Thomas Jefferson as an academic village, boasts classical pavilions, sweeping lawns, gardens, and serpentine walls. The house, originally built as a summer cottage for the daughter of a university professor, is attractively furnished in the style of a country house, and you are free to use the beautifully decorated parlor and yard. Three guest rooms are available: one has twin beds and a sitting room with a double hide-a-bed and TV; another has a single bed, small screened

porch, and sink. These two rooms share a bath. The third room has a queen-sized bed and private bath. A Continental breakfast is served. Your host, an interior designer born in England, maintains interests in travel, gardening, reading, and restoration.

No. Rooms: 3
Singles: 1 sb
Doubles: 1 pb, 1 sb
Type: Private home

Breakfast: Continental
S-Rates: $48 pb, $48 sb
D-Rates: $60 pb, $60 sb
Bldg: 1921 cottage

Minimum Stay: $4 surcharge for one-night stay. **Credit Card(s) Accepted:** none. **Open:** all year. No resident dogs. No dogs please. No resident cats. No cats please. Host smokes. Guests may not smoke in guest rooms. Children welcome with restrictions. **Discounts:** none.

Reservation Contact: Guesthouses Bed & Breakfast, Inc., Mary Hill Caperton, Box 5737, Charlottesville, VA 22905; 804–979–7264.

SKYLINE DRIVE, BLUE RIDGE PARKWAY, MONTICELLO, ASH LAWN, UNIVERSITY OF VIRGINIA.

Near U.S. 29, U.S. 250, I–64.

This immaculately maintained split-level ranch home is on a horse farm seven miles northwest of Charlottesville. You may enter the private lower-level entrance, where you have the seclusion of your own suite. It consists of sitting room with fireplace, TV, double hide-a-bed, and comfortable chairs, and two bedrooms with adjoining bath. One room has antique twin beds, while the other has a double bed and wicker furnishings. A Full farm-style breakfast is served in the dining room or on the sun porch overlooking the rolling pastures. Your hosts have an old-fashioned doctor's buggy in which they give rides, time and weather permitting. This consistently popular home has been earning wonderful reviews for several years. One of your hosts, educated in Europe, raises horses, and enjoys entertaining and fox hunting; your other host is a retired army major.

No. Rooms: 3	**Breakfast:** Full
Singles: None	**S-Rates:** $56 sb
Doubles: 3 sb	**D-Rates:** $56–$60 sb
Type: Private home	**Bldg:** 1966 brick ranch

Minimum Stay: $4 surcharge for one-night stay. **Credit Card(s) Accepted:** none. **Open:** all year. Dog in residence. No dogs please. No resident cats. No cats please. Host smokes. Guests may not smoke in guest rooms. Children welcome with restrictions. **Discounts:** none. German spoken.

Reservation Contact: Guesthouses Bed & Breakfast, Inc., Mary Hill Caperton, Box 5737, Charlottesville, VA 22905; 804–979–7264.

BLUE RIDGE PARKWAY, MONTICELLO, UNIVERSITY OF VIRGINIA.

Near I–64, U.S. 250 & 29.

Located on a 150-acre farm just west of Charlottesville, this two-hundred-year-old log cabin offers spectacular views of the Blue Ridge Mountains. It is furnished with American antiques and has a double bed, hide-a-bed, microwave, refrigerator, wood-burning stove, and bath with shower. Your Continental breakfast arrives in a picnic basket. A children's play set and a tennis court are available. Your hosts are an active family interested in sports, gardening, and woodworking.

No. Rooms: 1
Singles: None
Doubles: 1 pb
Type: Private home

Breakfast: Continental
S-Rates: $80 pb
D-Rates: $80 pb
Bldg: 1700s log cabin

Minimum Stay: none. **Credit Card(s) Accepted:** none. **Open:** all year.
No resident dogs. No dogs please. No resident cats. No cats please. Non-smoking host. Guests may not smoke in residence. Children welcome.
Discounts: none.

Reservation Contact: Guesthouses Bed & Breakfast, Inc., Mary Hill Caperton, Box 5737, Charlottesville, VA 22905; 804–979–7264.

ID: GUE–WAYSIDE

BLUE RIDGE PARKWAY, SKYLINE DRIVE, UNIVERSITY OF VIRGINIA, WINTERGREEN SKI RESORT.

Near Rugby Rd., U.S. 250, U.S. 29.

This one-story white brick house furnished with American antiques is located on a quiet elegant street near the university, within walking distance of restaurants. Two guest rooms are available. A room with double bed and a room with a single share a bath with guests of the same party. Off-street parking, a fireplace, TV in the cozy study, and a yard are all at your disposal. A Full breakfast is served. Your interesting, gracious, and well-traveled host has lived in most South American countries, as well as California and New York, and is interested in civics and bridge. The lawns and gardens attest to her talent for gardening.

No. Rooms: 2	**Breakfast:** Full
Singles: 1 sb	**S-Rates:** $48 sb
Doubles: 1 sb	**D-Rates:** $56–$60 sb
Type: Private home	**Bldg:** 1935 brick colonial

Minimum Stay: $4 surcharge for one-night stay. **Credit Card(s) Accepted:** none. **Open:** all year. No resident dogs. No dogs please. No resident cats. No cats please. Nonsmoking host. Guests may not smoke in guest rooms. Children welcome with restrictions. **Discounts:** none. Spanish spoken.

Reservation Contact: Guesthouses Bed & Breakfast, Inc., Mary Hill Caperton, Box 5737, Charlottesville, VA 22905; 804–979–7264.

FLINT HILL

ID: A–BL.RIDGE

CANOEING, HIKING, HORSEBACK RIDING, CAVERNS.

Near Rte. 340.

This 1807 Georgian stone home was one of the original seven stone houses in Rappahannock County. Its stone walls are two feet thick and the beams are thirty-two feet long. The two guest rooms, with double beds and shared guest bath, are air-conditioned, filled with lovely antiques, and provide wonderful views. The rooms have TVs and a selection of over one thousand video tapes. A Full breakfast is served. There is a cocktail hour, and cognac and chocolates are served before bed. The house is adjacent to Shenandoah National Park, Skyline Drive, and the Appalachian Trail. Canoeing, hiking, tennis, horseback riding, hunting, caverns, and outstanding restaurants are nearby. Arrival/departure transportation, dinner, and area tours are available. Your host is a retired announcer for the Voice of America.

No. Rooms: 1	Breakfast: Full
Singles: None	S-Rates: $70–$100 sb
Doubles: 1 sb	D-Rates: $70–$100 sb
Type: Private home	Bldg: 1807 Georgian stone

Minimum Stay: none. **Credit Card(s) Accepted:** none. **Open:** all year. No resident dogs. A dog is allowed with restrictions. No resident cats. No cats please. Nonsmoking host. Guests may not smoke in residence. Residence not appropriate for children. **Discounts:** none.

Reservation Contact: Blue Ridge Bed & Breakfast, Rita Duncan, Rt. 2, Box 3895, Berryville, VA 22611; 703–955–1246.

LURAY
ID: SHENANDO–L–RUF

SHENANDOAH VALLEY, LURAY CAVERNS, SKYLINE DRIVE.

Near I–211, Jackson Hwy.

Situated in the foothills of the Blue Ridge and Massanutten Mountains is this stately manor, built over two hundred years ago. Guests can enjoy mountain views from the outdoor porches, relax by the fireplace, or participate in the many nearby sports activities, including tennis, golf, swimming, skiing, and canoeing. There are four guest rooms with private baths and fireplaces. A Continental Plus breakfast is served in the Victorian dining room. The house is on an 18-acre estate where Arabian horses graze in the pasture.

No. Rooms: 4	Breakfast: Continental Plus
Singles: 2 pb	S-Rates: $65 pb
Doubles: 2 pb	D-Rates: $75 pb
Type: Inn	Bldg: 1739 manor house

Minimum Stay: none. **Credit Card(s) Accepted:** MC, V. **Open:** all year. No resident dogs. No dogs please. No resident cats. No cats please. Nonsmoking host. Guests may not smoke in residence. Children welcome with restrictions. **Discounts:** none. German & Russian spoken.

Reservation Contact: Shenandoah Valley B&B Reservations, Patricia Kollar, Box 634, Woodstock, VA 22664; 703–459–8241.

MT. JACKSON

ID: 22842WID

SHENANDOAH VALLEY, CAVERNS, HIKING, SUMMER THEATER, HARPER'S FERRY NATIONAL PARK, CIVIL WAR HISTORY, 2 HOURS FROM WASHINGTON, D.C.

Near U.S. 11 & VA 263, I–81.

This 1830s colonial is perched on seven acres overlooking the Shenandoah Mountains. Guests are welcomed in a ten-by-fifteen-foot center hall with an English oval bar and antique library table. Beside the hall is the living room, with fireplace, done in warm melon shades. All seven guest rooms have working fireplaces; five have private baths and two rooms share a bath. The Verbena Room, named for its burgundy flowered wallpaper, features an eight-foot-high, heavily scrolled Lincoln bed, an ornate partner's desk, a high English armchair, ruffled curtains, and an antique quilt. The Marigold Room is enhanced by its sunny glow from the southern exposure and mountain view. Twin pineapple poster beds, primitive paintings, an eight-foot armoire, and two comfortable chairs make this a popular room. The Sweet William Room is done in shades of mauve and pink. It has 1920s furniture, a well-stocked bookcase, and many needlecrafts on the walls. The Full country breakfast is served in the dining room. Following that, guests may relax beside the sixteen-by-thirty-two-foot swimming pool, rock and daydream on the side veranda, or picnic along the Shenandoah River. Your host's interests include crafts, cooking, and gardening.

No. Rooms: 7	**Breakfast:** Full
Singles: None	**S-Rates:** $50–$70 pb, $45 sb
Doubles: 5 pb, 2 sb	**D-Rates:** $60–$70 pb, $55 sb
Type: Public Inn	**Bldg:** 1830 Colonial

Minimum Stay: none. **Credit Card(s) Accepted:** MC, V. **Open:** all year. No resident dogs. No dogs please. Cat in residence. A cat is allowed with restrictions. Nonsmoking host. Guests may not smoke in guest rooms. Children welcome. **Discounts:** none.

Reservation Contact: Bed & Breakfast Registry Ltd., Gary Winget, Box 8174, St. Paul, MN 55108; 612–646–4238.

NORFOLK

ID: TIDEWATER#1

OLD DOMINION UNIVERSITY, NAVAL BASE; LARCHMONT AREA.

Near I–64.

Enormous magnolia trees lining the street and Norfolk's oldest giant sequoia make this an especially beautiful part of the city. It is convenient for those visiting Old Dominion University or the naval base, and it is a ten-minute drive to the downtown waterfront. This spacious traditional home is tastefully furnished with antiques and family pieces. Two bright and airy guest rooms with double beds share a bath with your hosts. A Full breakfast is served. One of your hosts is a teacher; the other is a retired clothing store owner.

No. Rooms: 2	**Breakfast:** Full
Singles: None	**S-Rates:** $30 sb
Doubles: 2 sb	**D-Rates:** $35 sb
Type: Private home	**Bldg:** 1920s traditional

Minimum Stay: $5 surcharge for one-night stay. **Credit Card(s) Accepted:** none. **Open:** all year. No resident dogs. No dogs please. Cat in residence. No cats please. Nonsmoking host. Guests may not smoke in guest rooms. Children welcome with restrictions. **Discounts:** none.

Reservation Contact: Bed & Breakfast of Tidewater Virginia, Ashby Wilcox & Susan Hubbard, Box 3343, Norfolk, VA 23514; 804–627–1983.

ID: TIDEWATER #3

CHRYSLER MUSEUM; GHENT AREA.

Near Rte. 44 Expwy.

Built in 1905, this townhouse is in Norfolk's picturesque Ghent section, a designated historic area in which stately homes grace tree-lined streets. The Chrysler Museum, a jewel in Norfolk's crown, is only a few blocks away, and the new Waterside downtown marketplace is within walking distance. Across the street is a small boat harbor and a branch of the Elizabeth River. The third-floor guest room, with twin beds and private bath, overlooks the water. Your hosts, natives of the area who lived abroad for several years, are deeply involved in community affairs, and one has served as a member of the school board.

No. Rooms: 1	**Breakfast:** Continental
Singles: None	**S-Rates:** $40 pb
Doubles: 1 pb	**D-Rates:** $45 pb
Type: Private home	**Bldg:** 1905 traditional

Minimum Stay: 3 nights. **Credit Card(s) Accepted:** none. **Open:** all year. Dog in residence. No dogs please. No resident cats. No cats please. Guests may smoke in residence. Residence not appropriate for children. **Discounts:** none.

Reservation Contact: Bed & Breakfast of Tidewater Virginia, Ashby Wilcox & Susan Hubbard, Box 3343, Norfolk, VA 23514; 804–627–1983.

RAWLEY SPRINGS

GEORGE WASHINGTON NATIONAL FOREST, SWITZER DAM, JAMES MADISON UNIVERSITY.

Near rtes. 847 & 33W, I–81.

Nature lovers and romantics will relish this home beside Dry River. It has wide porches and three terraces for reading or relaxing in a quiet spot. Because it borders George Washington National Forest, it has a park-like setting; options for walking abound. The fifty-foot living room has beamed ceiling, large stone fireplace, and double windows with lovely views. Fresh fruit and flowers are found in the four guest rooms, which feature queen-sized or double beds; one room has a private bath and the rest shared baths. A Continental Plus breakfast is served. Your host is a teacher and writer.

No. Rooms: 4
Singles: None
Doubles: 1 pb, 3 sb
Type: Private home

Breakfast: Continental Plus
S-Rates: $40 pb, $40 sb
D-Rates: $50 pb, $50 sb
Bldg: 1925 lodge

Minimum Stay: none. **Credit Card(s) Accepted:** none. **Open:** all year, except Christmas week. Dog in residence. No dogs please. No resident cats. No cats please. Nonsmoking host. Guests may not smoke in guest rooms. Children welcome. **Discounts:** none.

Reservation Contact: Shenandoah Valley B&B Reservations, Patricia Kollar, Box 634, Woodstock, VA 22664; 703–459–8241.

STAUNTON

MARY BALDWIN COLLEGE, STUART HALL PREP SCHOOL, GYPSY HILL PARK, BLUE RIDGE PARKWAY.

Near U.S. 11, I–81, I–64.

Family antiques are showcased in this elegant turn-of-the-century modified Georgian home, with its wrap-around veranda and spacious grounds. It is adjacent to the two-hundred-acre Gypsy Hill Park and is only four blocks from Mary Baldwin College. The house has three guest rooms with double or king-sized beds and private baths. Two of the rooms are air-conditioned and have private entrances. A Continental breakfast of house specialties is served in the formal dining room. Afternoon tea is also served. Both hosts are involved in musical activities in the community, and both have traveled extensively in England.

No. Rooms: 3
Singles: None
Doubles: 3 pb
Type: Private home

Breakfast: Continental
S-Rates: $35 pb
D-Rates: $45–$50 pb
Bldg: 1912 modified Georgian

Minimum Stay: 3 days for July 4th holiday. **Credit Card(s) Accepted:**

none. **Open:** all year. No resident dogs. No dogs please. No resident cats. No cats please. Nonsmoking host. Guests may not smoke in residence. Children welcome. **Discounts:** 10% after 3d day.

Reservation Contact: Shenandoah Valley B&B Reservations, Patricia Kollar, Box 634, Woodstock, VA 22664; 703–459–8241.

VIRGINIA BEACH
ID: TIDEWATER#4–GLA

NAVAL BASE, 2 BLOCKS TO OCEAN.

Near I–64.

This two-story beach house, located in a residential resort area, has three guest rooms that share one bath. One room has an extra-long, four-poster double bed, Oriental rugs, desk, chair, and air conditioner. The second has twin beds, two chests, and a ceiling fan. The third is a single room suitable for a child. A Continental Plus breakfast is served. The house is less than two blocks from the ocean. Your host enjoys people, the arts, and travel.

No. Rooms: 3	**Breakfast:** Continental Plus
Singles: 1 sb	**S-Rates:** $25–$50 sb
Doubles: 2 sb	**D-Rates:** $45–$55 sb
Type: Private home	**Bldg:** Shingle beach house

Minimum Stay: none. **Credit Card(s) Accepted:** none. **Open:** all year. Dog in residence. No dogs please. No resident cats. No cats please. Nonsmoking host. Guests may smoke in residence. Children welcome with restrictions. **Discounts:** off season rates.

Reservation Contact: Bed & Breakfast of Tidewater Virginia, Ashby Willcox & Susan Hubbard, Box 3343, Norfolk, VA 23514; 804–627–1983.

ID: TIDEWATER#5

ON LINKHORN BAY.

Near I–64, Expwy. 44.

Overlooking Linkhorn Bay, in one of Virginia Beach's prettiest neighborhoods, is this home, furnished with antiques, some brought from an antebellum South Carolina plantation. Your host's own needlepoint is featured. The beautiful lawn and garden slope down to the water, where there is a pier for relaxing; if you would like to try crabbing, you can do that, too! Many porches and sitting areas are also available. The first-floor guest room is furnished with twin beds and private bath. A Full breakfast is served. Your hosts enjoy art, travel, and gardening.

No. Rooms: 1
Singles: None
Doubles: 1 pb
Type: Private home

Breakfast: Full
S-Rates: $40–$50 pb
D-Rates: $45–$55 pb
Bldg: 1920s cottage

Minimum Stay: 2 nights. **Credit Card(s) Accepted:** none. **Open:** all year. No resident dogs. No dogs please. No resident cats. No cats please. Nonsmoking host. Guests may not smoke in residence. Children welcome with restrictions. **Discounts:** none.

Reservation Contact: Bed & Breakfast of Tidewater Virginia, Ashby Willcox & Susan Hubbard, Box 3343, Norfolk, VA 23514; 804–627–1983.

ID: 23452TRA

BUSCH GARDENS, VIRGINIA BEACH SEASHORE STATE PARK.

Near Rosemont & Beach Blvd., I–64, U.S. 13.

The large yard, patio, comfortable den with fireplace, and pool table make this modern two-story home a pleasant place for you to relax. There is one guest room with double bed, private bath, radio, and TV. The room has a lovely view overlooking the golf course. Conveniently located, the house is one block from a recreation center with a pool, five miles from Virginia Beach Seashore State Park, and one hour from Busch Gardens and historic Jamestown. Additional meals and arrival/departure transportation are available. Your hosts' hobbies are golf, fishing, and dancing.

No. Rooms: 1
Singles: None
Doubles: 1 pb
Type: Private home

Breakfast: Continental
S-Rates: $30 pb
D-Rates: $35 pb
Bldg: 1980 modern

Minimum Stay: none. **Credit Card(s) Accepted:** none. **Open:** all year, except Christmas. No resident dogs. A dog is allowed with restrictions. No resident cats. A cat is allowed with restrictions. Host smokes. Guests may not smoke in guest rooms. Residence not appropriate for children. **Discounts:** none.

Reservation Contact: Bed & Breakfast Registry Ltd., Gary Winget, Box 8174, St. Paul, MN 55108; 612–646–4238.

WILLIAMSBURG
ID: 9–VA–TREE

COLONIAL WILLIAMSBURG, JAMESTOWN, YORKTOWN.

This air-conditioned brick colonial is situated in a wooded residential area, four miles from Colonial Williamsburg. It has a guest suite with private entrance, two bedrooms, and private bath. A Continental breakfast is served.

No. Rooms: 2	**Breakfast:** Continental
Singles: None	**S-Rates:** $56 pb
Doubles: 2 pb	**D-Rates:** $70 pb
Type: Private home	**Bldg:** Colonial style

Minimum Stay: 2 nights. **Credit Card(s) Accepted:** none. **Open:** all year. No resident dogs. No dogs please. No resident cats. No cats please. Nonsmoking host. Guests may not smoke in residence. Children welcome. **Discounts:** none.

Reservation Contact: The Travel Tree, J. Proper & S. Zubkoff, Box 838, Williamsburg, VA 23187; 804–253–1571.

ID: 133–VA–TRE

3 MILES FROM HISTORIC AREA.

Near I–64.

This rambler, located in a wooded, residential area three miles from the historic district, has one spacious guest room with a king-sized bed, private entrance, and private bath. A Continental breakfast is served. The host is a retired real estate broker.

No. Rooms: 1	**Breakfast:** Continental
Singles: None	**S-Rates:** $48 pb
Doubles: 1 pb	**D-Rates:** $60 pb
Type: Private home	**Bldg:** Rambler

Minimum Stay: 2 nights. **Credit Card(s) Accepted:** none. **Open:** all year. Dog in residence. No dogs please. No resident cats. No cats please. Nonsmoking host. Guests may not smoke in residence. Children welcome. **Discounts:** none.

Reservation Contact: The Travel Tree, J. Proper & S. Zubkoff, Box 838, Williamsburg, VA 23187; 804–253–1571.

WIRTZ
ID: 24184MAN

ROANOKE AREA, BLUE RIDGE PARKWAY, SMITH MOUNTAIN LAKE.

Near VA 122 & Rte. 116, U.S. 220.

Situated on 90 acres in the beautiful Piedmont region of southwest Virginia, this picturesque country estate combines old-world charm with modern comforts. It is convenient to Roanoke, Smith Mountain Lake recreational area, and the Blue Ridge Parkway. The property invites hiking, cross-country skiing, and picnicking, as well as fishing and canoeing on five spring-fed ponds. Should you decide to just relax in the sun room, parlor, or hot tub, reading material is available from the extensive library. There are three guest rooms with private baths and a separate three-bedroom cottage. One of the rooms is decorated with Victorian antiques, rose-colored woodwork, floral balloon-style curtains, a walnut double bed, and tapestry parlor chairs. The library is just outside the door and there is a private stairway leading up to the room. The second room, decorated in the Williamsburg style, features blue woodwork, candlewick swag curtains, a queen-sized bed with a crocheted canopy, and French doors which lead to a private balcony. The garden-level suite has a brass double bed, an ornate inlaid wardrobe, a private porch with wicker furniture, and a full kitchen. The cottage has rustic decor, fireplace, and a fantastic view. A Full breakfast is served. The hosts are interested in art, music, outdoor activities, antiques, nutrition, and travel.

No. Rooms: 6	**Breakfast:** Full
Singles: None	**S-Rates:** $50–$70 pb
Doubles: 5 pb	**D-Rates:** $50–$70 pb
Type: Private home	**Bldg:** 1820 Federal-style

Minimum Stay: none. **Credit Card(s) Accepted:** MC, V. **Open:** all year. No resident dogs. No dogs please. No resident cats. No cats please. Non-smoking host. Guests may not smoke in residence. Children over 12 years welcome. **Discounts:** 10% to seniors. Some German spoken.

Reservation Contact: Bed & Breakfast Registry Ltd., Gary Winget, Box 8174, St. Paul, MN 55108; 612–646–4238.

WOODSTOCK
ID: SHENANDO–W–S

MUSEUMS, ANTIQUE SHOPS, WAYSIDE THEATER, NEW MARKET BATTLEFIELD, CAVERNS.

Near U.S. 11, I–81.

This luxurious Victorian home provides a marvelous setting for weddings and other special occasions. The inn is located in the foothills of beautiful Massanutten Mountain, twenty-five minutes from Skyline Drive in historic Shenandoah county. The double sitting rooms are graced with massive stone fireplaces. The Great Room, also with a large fireplace, is elegantly furnished with a grand piano, mahogany empire sofa, and an antique walnut buffet. There are twelve fireplaces throughout the home. The eight guest rooms have double or twin beds and private baths. A Full gourmet breakfast, prepared by a European chef, is served. At this home an additional fee is charged to set the fireplace or to use the whirlpool. Additional meals are available for groups. Both of your hosts enjoy travel, antiques, art, music, gourmet cooking, and interesting people.

No. Rooms: 8	**Breakfast:** Full
Singles: None	**S-Rates:** $65–$95 pb
Doubles: 8 pb	**D-Rates:** $65–$95 pb
Type: Inn	**Bldg:** Victorian

Minimum Stay: none. **Credit Card(s) Accepted:** none. **Open:** all year.

No resident dogs. No dogs please. Cat in residence. No cats please. Non-smoking host. Guests may not smoke in guest rooms. Children welcome with restrictions. **Discounts:** none. German & Hungarian spoken.

Reservation Contact: Shenandoah Valley B&B Reservations, Patricia Kollar, Box 634, Woodstock, VA 22664; 703–459–8241.

WASHINGTON

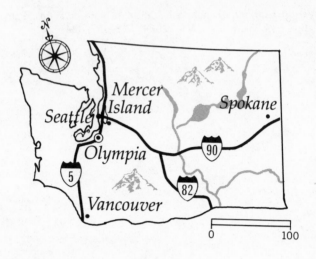

MERCER ISLAND

ID: MI–I–PAC

LAKE WASHINGTON BEACHES.

Near I–90.

This elegant contemporary home is furnished with antiques and offers two guest rooms with a shared bath. The Pink Room has double canopy bed with seventy-five yards of fabric cascading down from the ceiling and sliding glass doors to the patio. The Brown Room features early American furniture and has a four-poster double bed. Between the rooms is a sitting room with TV, a small refrigerator, and a telescope for star gazing. A Continental Plus breakfast is served in the dining room beneath an elaborate crystal chandelier.

No. Rooms: 2	**Breakfast:** Continental Plus
Singles: None	**S-Rates:** $50 sb
Doubles: 2 sb	**D-Rates:** $55 sb
Type: Private home	**Bldg:** Contemporary

Minimum Stay: none. **Credit Card(s) Accepted:** none. **Open:** all year. No resident dogs. No dogs please. No resident cats. No cats please. Non-smoking host. Guests may not smoke in residence. Children welcome with restrictions. **Discounts:** none.

Reservation Contact: Pacific Bed & Breakfast, Irmgard Castleberry, 701 NW 60th St., Seattle, WA 98107; 206–784–0539.

COSMOPOLIS
ID: COS–1–PAC

OLYMPIC NATIONAL FOREST; WHALE WATCHING, SALMON FISHING, BEACHES, GOLF, TENNIS.

Near hwys. 101 & 105.

Nestled in wooded seclusion adjoining a golf course, tennis courts, and a park, this turn-of-the-century home was originally constructed by lumber baron Neil Cooney. Between March and May in this area whale watchers can observe forty-five-ton gray whales return from Baja. Only 15 minutes away are beaches where guests can try fishing or clam digging. In the evening, relax in front of the fireplace in the large parlor or unwind in the whirlpool or sauna. Five of the nine guest rooms have private baths, and one room has a fireplace and windows on three sides. All the rooms have double beds. A Continental Plus breakfast is served.

No. Rooms: 9	**Breakfast:** Continental Plus
Singles: None	**S-Rates:** $60–$65 pb, $50–$55 sb
Doubles: 5 pb, 4 sb	**D-Rates:** $60–$65 pb, $50–$55 sb
Type: Inn	**Bldg:** 1908

Minimum Stay: 2 nights on weekends in season. **Credit Card(s) Accepted:** MC, V. **Open:** all year. No resident dogs. No dogs please. No resident cats. No cats please. Nonsmoking host. Guests may not smoke in residence. Children welcome with restrictions. **Discounts:** none.

Reservation Contact: Pacific Bed & Breakfast, Irmgard Castleberry, 701 NW 60th St., Seattle, WA 98107; 206–784–0539.

INDIANOLA
ID: 133–NW

ON PUGET SOUND.

Near I–5, Hwy. 3.

From this exceptionally beautiful country home in a rural setting on Puget Sound, one enjoys views of downtown Seattle, Mt. Rainier, and Bainbridge Island. There are three carpeted guest rooms with wood-paneled walls. One room features a private bath with Jacuzzi, a skylight, and a water view. The other two rooms share a bath. A Full breakfast is served. Your hosts' interests encompass world affairs, travel, animal breeding, and needlework.

No. Rooms: 3	**Breakfast:** Full
Singles: None	**S-Rates:** $75 pb, $60 sb
Doubles: 1 pb, 2 sb	**D-Rates:** $75 pb, $60 sb
Type: Private home	**Bldg:** Western cedar

Minimum Stay: none. **Credit Card(s) Accepted:** none. **Open:** all year. Resident dog. No dogs please. No resident cats. No cats please. Nonsmoking host. Guests may not smoke in residence. Children welcome. **Discounts:** none.

Reservation Contact: Northwest Bed & Breakfast, Inc., L. Friedman & G. Shaich, 610 SW Broadway, #606, Portland, OR 97205; 503–243–7616.

ISSAQUAH

CASCADE RANGE; THIRTY MINUTES FROM SEATTLE.

Near I–90.

This quaint, hundred-year-old town is close to the Cascade Range, a winery, and a spectacular waterfall. The two-story log house, surrounded by lawns, flower beds, and stately evergreens, has four guest rooms. The Strawberry Room and the Fern Room have queen-sized beds and private baths. The Rose Room, with a queen-sized bed, and the Daisy Room, with a double and a single bed, share a bath. A Full breakfast is served.

No. Rooms: 4
Singles: None
Doubles: 2 pb, 2 sb
Type: Private home

Breakfast: Full
S-Rates: $50 pb, $45 sb
D-Rates: $50 pb, $45 sb
Bldg: 1986 log

Minimum Stay: 2 nights. **Credit Card(s) Accepted:** none. **Open:** all year. No resident dogs. No dogs please. Resident cat. No cats please. Nonsmoking host. Guests may not smoke in residence. Children welcome with restrictions. **Discounts:** none.

Reservation Contact: Pacific Bed & Breakfast, Irmgard Castleberry, 701 NW 60th St., Seattle, WA 98107; 206–784–0539.

MERCER ISLAND

2 BLOCKS TO BEACH.

Near I–90.

This lovely contemporary cedar home filled with antiques provides a great view of Lake Washington. A one-bedroom apartment can accommodate two parties of two. One half of the apartment offers sleeping quarters, kitchen, and private bath; the other half offers guest room with double bed, antiques, and private bath. Other amenities include off-street parking and use of the patio, yard, and TV. The house is two blocks from a beach and five miles from the center of Seattle. Your host, from Germany, is a gourmet cook who enjoys travel and antiques.

No. Rooms: 2
Singles: None
Doubles: 2 pb
Type: Private home

Breakfast: Continental Plus
S-Rates: $35–$40 pb
D-Rates: $40–$45 pb
Bldg: 1975 contemporary

Minimum Stay: 2 nights. **Credit Card(s) Accepted:** none. **Open:** all year. No resident dogs. No dogs please. No resident cats. No cats please.

Nonsmoking host. Guests may not smoke in residence. Children welcome. **Discounts:** none. German spoken.

Reservation Contact: Pacific Bed & Breakfast, Irmgard Castleberry, 701 NW 60th St., Seattle, WA 98107; 206–784–0539.

OLYMPIA
ID: 98506PUG

TOLMIE STATE PARK, PUGET SOUND; BOATING.

Near Marvin Rd. & 56th, I–5.

This cozy waterfront guest cottage is only five hundred feet from Tolmie State Park's hiking trails, picnic grounds, and beach activities. Puget Sound is at your doorstep, and this location offers a panoramic view. The cedar cottage has two bedrooms, one with a double bed and one with twin beds. Both have glass doors that open onto a porch where you are greeted with fresh sea air and the scent of the apple, fig, and fir trees, and lilacs and roses. A Continental Plus breakfast is served on a silver tray, and the table is set with linen, china, silver, and fresh flowers. Your hosts can suggest a variety of activities. Birdwatchers can visit Nisqually National Wildlife Refuge and hike the trails or take a guided raft trip. Boat rentals, scuba diving, and fishing are also nearby. One of your hosts, a former forest engineer, is interested in scuba diving and backpacking; your other host enjoys the arts, writing, theater, and dance.

No. Rooms: 2	**Breakfast:** Continental Plus
Singles: None	**S-Rates:** $55–$70 pb
Doubles: 2 pb	**D-Rates:** $55–$70 pb
Type: Private cottage	**Bldg:** 1930s cedar

Minimum Stay: 2 nights on holidays. **Credit Card(s) Accepted:** MC, V. **Open:** all year. No resident dogs. A dog is allowed with restrictions. Host's cat is not allowed in guest areas. A cat is allowed with restrictions. Nonsmoking host. Guests may smoke. Children welcome. **Discounts:** 7th night free.

Reservation Contact: Bed & Breakfast Registry Ltd., Gary Winget, Box 8174, St. Paul, MN 55108; 612–646–4238.

SEATTLE
ID: ABA–1–PAC

CONVENIENT LOCATION.

Near 8th Ave., NW, I–5.

This traditional house, in a quiet residential neighborhood, is close to a beach and only ten minutes from the city center. A fully furnished ground-level apartment is available, with one bedroom with double bed, kitchen, cable TV, and private bath. There is daily maid service, and a

Continental breakfast is provided. Your host, an engineer, is interested in travel, photography, and music.

No. Rooms: 1	**Breakfast:** Continental
Singles: None	**S-Rates:** $40 pb
Doubles: 1 pb	**D-Rates:** $40–$45 pb
Type: Private home	**Bldg:** 1914

Minimum Stay: 2 nights. **Credit Card(s) Accepted:** AE, MC, V. **Open:** all year. No resident dogs. No dogs please. No resident cats. No cats please. Nonsmoking host. Guests may not smoke in residence. Children welcome with restrictions. **Discounts:** none. German spoken.

Reservation Contact: Pacific Bed & Breakfast, Irmgard Castleberry, 701 NW 60th St., Seattle, WA 98107; 206–784–0539.

BH–1–PAC

BEACON HILL AREA.

Near I–5.

Built in 1910, this home in the Beacon Hill area features fine woodwork, beamed ceilings, huge windows, and private decks that overlook Elliott Bay, the Olympic Mountains, and the downtown area. The house is decorated with antiques, Navajo weavings, and art work from many Latin American countries. Guests are welcome to read or watch TV in the large parlor with tiled fireplace. Four guest rooms share two baths. The largest room has a queen-sized bed, built-in wardrobe, window seats, and a sitting area. Another room has an antique four-poster queen-sized bed and private view. The third room also has a queen-sized bed, and the fourth is a single. A Continental Plus breakfast is served. Your hosts enjoy travel, art, music, and antiques collecting.

No. Rooms: 4	**Breakfast:** Continental Plus
Singles: 1 sb	**S-Rates:** $25–$40 sb
Doubles: 3 sb	**D-Rates:** $45 sb
Type: Private home	**Bldg:** Queen Anne

Minimum Stay: none. **Credit Card(s) Accepted:** MC, V. **Open:** all year. No resident dogs. No dogs please. No resident cats. No cats please. Nonsmoking host. Guests may not smoke in residence. Children welcome with restrictions. **Discounts:** none.

Reservation Contact: Pacific Bed & Breakfast, Irmgard Castleberry, 701 NW 60th St., Seattle, WA 98107; 206–784–0539.

ID: CH–8–PAC

12 BLOCKS FROM DOWNTOWN.

Near I–5, Broadway, 15th E.

This Victorian home is on a tree-lined street twelve blocks from the downtown area and one block from bus transportation. There is a parlor with a window seat, books, TV, and telephone. The two guest rooms have double beds and private baths. A Continental breakfast is served. Your hosts' interests include music, art, travel, and teaching.

No. Rooms: 2	**Breakfast:** Continental
Singles: None	**S-Rates:** $30 pb
Doubles: 2 pb	**D-Rates:** $38 pb
Type: Private home	**Bldg:** Victorian

Minimum Stay: none. **Credit Card(s) Accepted:** none. **Open:** all year. No resident dogs. No dogs please. No resident cats. No cats please. Nonsmoking host. Guests may not smoke in residence. Children welcome. **Discounts:** none.

Reservation Contact: Pacific Bed & Breakfast, Irmgard Castleberry, 701 NW 60th St., Seattle, WA 98107; 206–784–0539.

ID: CH–9–PAC

CAPITOL HILL AREA.

Near I–5.

Capitol Hill is a fine old established neighborhood with large turn-of-the-century homes, city parks, shops, and restaurants. The atmosphere, urban yet tranquil, is cherished by city dwellers and is close to the downtown area and the University of Washington. This Queen Anne-style home, filled with antiques, has four second-floor guest rooms that share two baths; three of them have queen-sized beds, and one has twin beds. A Continental Plus breakfast is served in the dining room, library, or on the patio. Your recently retired host, bought and remodeled this house, built in 1914, to fulfill her dream of owning a B&B.

No. Rooms: 4	**Breakfast:** Continental Plus
Singles: None	**S-Rates:** $48 sb
Doubles: 4 sb	**D-Rates:** $65 sb
Type: Private home	**Bldg:** 1914 Queen Anne

Minimum Stay: 2 nights. **Credit Card(s) Accepted:** none. **Open:** all year. No resident dogs. No dogs please. No resident cats. No cats please. Nonsmoking host. Guests may not smoke in residence. Residence not appropriate for children. **Discounts:** none.

Reservation Contact: Pacific Bed & Breakfast, Irmgard Castleberry, 701 NW 60th St., Seattle, WA 98107; 206–784–0539.

QUEEN ANNE AREA.

Near I–5.

Built eighty-five years ago, this lovely Victorian home has a view of Puget Sound, the Olympic Mountains, and the ferry traffic. It has an old-fashioned country decor with pieces collected by your host. The three guest rooms, one with private deck, share a bath; two rooms have double beds, and one has two double beds. A Continental Plus breakfast is served in the dining room or on the sun porch. Transportation is excellent, since the house is located directly on the local bus line. Your host likes collecting and restoring antiques.

No. Rooms: 3	**Breakfast:** Continental Plus
Singles: None	**S-Rates:** $45 sb
Doubles: 3 sb	**D-Rates:** $50 sb
Type: Private home	**Bldg:** 1900 Victorian

Minimum Stay: 2 nights. **Credit Card(s) Accepted:** none. **Open:** all year. No resident dogs. No dogs please. No resident cats. No cats please. Nonsmoking host. Guests may not smoke in residence. Children welcome. **Discounts:** none.

Reservation Contact: Pacific Bed & Breakfast, Irmgard Castleberry, 701 NW 60th St., Seattle, WA 98107; 206–784–0539.

QUEEN ANNE AREA.

Near I–5.

This very elegant brick colonial-style home on top of Queen Anne Hill is surrounded by formal English gardens. One of the three guest rooms features a sitting area and private deck with a view of downtown, Puget Sound, and the mountains. All the rooms are furnished with fine period antiques and have double beds. One has a private bath; the other two rooms share a bath. You will also find fresh flowers and fruit in your room. The house is within walking distance of bus lines and Seattle Center, site of the 1962 World's Fair. Nearby is a jogging track. During the week, the Continental Plus breakfast is self-service, but on weekends a delicious home-cooked meal is served. Your hosts have two children and enjoy collecting antiques and gardening.

No. Rooms: 3	**Breakfast:** Continental Plus
Singles: None	**S-Rates:** $45 pb, $45 sb
Doubles: 1 pb, 2 sb	**D-Rates:** $50 pb, $50 sb
Type: Private home	**Bldg:** 1928 brick colonial

Minimum Stay: 2 nights. **Credit Card(s) Accepted:** none. **Open:** all year. No resident dogs. No dogs please. No resident cats. No cats please. Nonsmoking host. Guests may not smoke in residence. Children welcome. **Discounts:** none.

Reservation Contact: Pacific Bed & Breakfast, Irmgard Castleberry, 701 NW 60th St., Seattle, WA 98107; 206–784–0539.

ID: 98112PEN

UNIVERSITY OF WASHINGTON, VOLUNTEER & INTERLAKEN PARKS, ARBORETUM.

Near Interlaken Blvd. & Crescent Dr., I–5.

A charming Tudor-style home, filled with antiques, is located in a quiet, older residential neighborhood near public transportation, the University of Washington, downtown, hospitals, and museums. Three second-floor guest rooms share a bath and offer antique furnishings and double or king-sized beds. Your European host, a language instructor at a local college, enjoys preparing gourmet breakfasts.

No. Rooms: 3	**Breakfast:** Continental Plus
Singles: None	**S-Rates:** $40 sb
Doubles: 3 sb	**D-Rates:** $45 sb
Type: Private townhouse	**Bldg:** 1921 Tudor-style

Minimum Stay: 2 nights on weekends. **Credit Card(s) Accepted:** none. **Open:** all year. Dog in residence. A dog is allowed with restrictions. Cat in residence. A cat is allowed with restrictions. Nonsmoking host. Guest may not smoke in guest rooms. Children welcome with restrictions. **Discounts:** $5/day after 1 week. German & French spoken.

Reservation Contact: Bed & Breakfast Registry Ltd., Gary Winget, Box 8174, St. Paul, MN 55108; 612–646–4238.

ID: 98112WOL

UNIVERSITY OF WASHINGTON, SEATTLE UNIVERSITY, SEATTLE ART MUSEUM.

Near 23d Ave. East & E. Prospect, I–5.

This stately brick house is in a quiet, exclusive neighborhood of lovely old mansions, beautiful gardens, and tree-lined streets. The house is elegantly furnished and accessories demonstrate an eye for detail. There are three guest rooms. One has a private bath, the other two share a bath. All the newly decorated, color-coordinated rooms sleep two. You may also enjoy the fireplace, TV, patio, and yard. A Continental Plus breakfast is served. Your host, retired from the University of Washington, is interested in the performing and visual arts, needlepoint, gardening, and travel.

No. Rooms: 3	**Breakfast:** Continental Plus
Singles: None	**S-Rates:** $40 pb, $30 sb
Doubles: 1 pb, 2 sb	**D-Rates:** $45 pb, $35 sb
Type: Private home	**Bldg:** 1923 brick traditional

Minimum Stay: 2 nights. **Credit Card(s) Accepted:** none. **Open:** all year. No resident dogs. No dogs please. No resident cats. No cats please. Nonsmoking host. Guests may not smoke in residence. Children welcome with restrictions. **Discounts:** none.

Reservation Contact: Bed & Breakfast Registry Ltd., Gary Winget, Box 8174, St. Paul, MN 55108; 612–646–4238.

SPOKANE   ID: 99223SOU

SPOKANE FALLS, RIVERFRONT PARK, OPERA HOUSE, CONVENTION CENTER.

Near Grand Blvd. & 43d St., I–90.

Bright, cheerful, and attractive this house is located in a quiet upper-class residential area. There are two guest rooms with private baths and double beds. Bicycles and a football table are available for your enjoyment. A Full breakfast, which might include huckleberry pancakes, the house specialty, is served in the dining room. You will want to visit Riverfront Park with its carousel, the Opera House, and the many fine shops and restaurants only ten minutes away. Your extremely cordial hosts have interests in skiing, reading, swimming, boating, dog breeding, and racquetball.

No. Rooms: 2	**Breakfast:** Full
Singles: None	**S-Rates:** $20 pb
Doubles: 2 pb	**D-Rates:** $28 pb
Type: Private home	**Bldg:** 1960 contemporary

Minimum Stay: 2 nights. **Credit Card(s) Accepted:** none. **Open:** all year. Dog in residence. Guests may bring dog. No resident cats. No cats please. Nonsmoking host. Guests may not smoke in residence. Children welcome. **Discounts:** none.

Reservation Contact: Bed & Breakfast Registry Ltd., Gary Winget, Box 8174, St. Paul, MN 55108; 612–646–4238.

VASHON ISLAND
ID: 98070SWA

BEACHES, HIKING, HORSEBACK RIDING, BIKING, BOATING, FISHING, ANTIQUE SHOPS, ART GALLERIES, FERRY TO SEATTLE & TACOMA.

Near Bank Rd., 99th Ave., SW.

This extraordinary replica of an fourteenth-century English inn (the land-mark Crown Inn of Chiddingfold, Surrey, south of London) was designed by your host to be as authentic as possible, even to the point of using old timbers and rustic hardware. The inn has a massive fireplace and lead-ed windows and is furnished throughout with English antiques, including many seventeenth- and eighteenth-century period pieces. Three beautiful guest rooms feature double beds and beautiful antique furnishings; one has a private bath and the other two share a bath. A Full breakfast is served in the formal dining room. You will enjoy unspoiled, uncrowded beaches, and the waters of Puget Sound support one of the most exciting concentrations of sea life on earth. Swimming, surfing, beachcombing, sailing, fishing, hiking, horseback riding, and biking are available. There are also many nearby art galleries, festivals, shops, and restaurants.

No. Rooms: 3	**Breakfast:** Full
Singles: None	**S-Rates:** $85 pb, $65 sb
Doubles: 1 pb, 2 sb	**D-Rates:** $85 pb, $65 sb
Type: Private home	**Bldg:** 1976 authentic half-timber

Minimum Stay: none. **Credit Card(s) Accepted:** MC, V. **Open:** all year. No resident dogs. No dogs please. No resident cats. No cats please. Non-smoking host. Guests may not smoke in residence. Children welcome with restrictions. **Discounts:** none.

Reservation Contact: Bed & Breakfast Registry Ltd., Gary Winget, Box 8174, St. Paul, MN 55108; 612–646–4238.

WASHOUGAL
ID: 118–NW

STEELHEAD FISHING ON WASHOUGAL RIVER.

Near Hwy. 14 & 6th St., Hwy. 205, I–84.

An area of exceptional beauty, with snow-capped mountains, pine for-ests, golden wheat fields, and fascinating rock formations, Washougal is the home of Pendleton Woolen Mills' Seconds Shop. Mt. St. Helens, Mt. Adams, and the ski slopes of Mt. Hood in Oregon are all within easy ac-cess. The area is a favorite with fishermen, hunters, hikers, and white-water rafters. Maryhill Museum houses an interesting collection of Rodin sculptures, Russian icons, and Indian artifacts. Goldendale Observatory, the largest in the nation, is available for public use. This contemporary ranch-style home in a party-like setting has a deck overlooking the Washougal River. Steelhead fishing is as close as your backyard. Two guest rooms share a guest bath. The first attractively decorated room has a king-sized bed, two dressers, antique table, lamps, and chair; the second is similarly furnished with double bed and solid maple bedroom set. Your hosts particularly welcome families with children, and sleeping bags are available for those who wish to rough it outdoors on summer nights. A Full breakfast is served in the dining room with a picturesque view of the river. Arrival/departure transportation, dinner, and picnic lunches are available. Your gracious hosts are interested in travel, especially to Alaska, as well as gardening, gourmet cooking, and handicrafts.

No. Rooms: 2	**Breakfast:** Full
Singles: None	**S-Rates:** $35 sb
Doubles: 2 sb	**D-Rates:** $45 sb
Type: Private home	**Bldg:** 1971 ranch

Minimum Stay: none. **Credit Card(s) Accepted:** none. **Open:** all year. No resident dogs. No dogs please. No resident cats. No cats please. Non-smoking host. Guests may not smoke in residence. Children welcome. **Discounts:** none.

Reservation Contact: Northwest Bed & Breakfast, Inc., L. Friedman & G. Shaich, 610 SW Broadway #609, Portland, OR 97205; 503–243–7616.

WEST VIRGINIA

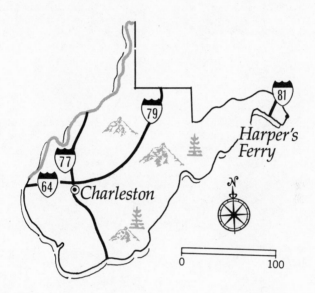

MIDDLEWAY

ID: E–BL.RIDGE

HARPER'S FERRY, FACTORY OUTLETS.

Near Rte. 340.

Large stone house built in 1800 is close to Harper's Ferry, Summit Point Raceway, Shepardstown, and Winchester. Canoeing, hiking, and antique shops are also nearby. In one of the oldest settlements in West Virginia, the house has five air-conditioned guest rooms with double beds and private baths. The rooms have antique furnishings, hardwood floors, and oriental rugs; some have fireplaces. A Full country breakfast is served and area tours are available.

No. Rooms: 5	**Breakfast:** Full
Singles: None	**S-Rates:** $55–$120 pb
Doubles: 5 pb	**D-Rates:** $55–$120 pb
Type: Private home	**Bldg:** 1800 stone

Minimum Stay: none. **Credit Card(s) Accepted:** none. **Open:** all year. No resident dogs. No dogs please. No resident cats. No cats please. Host smokes. Guests may not smoke in guest rooms. Children welcome. **Discounts:** none.

Reservation Contact: Blue Ridge Bed & Breakfast, Rita Duncan, Rte. 2, Box 3895, Berryville, VA 22611; 703–955–1246.

WISCONSIN

BANGOR

ID: 54614WOO

BOATING, FISHING, SKIING, HUNTING, ART & CRAFT
SHOWS, JULY RIVERFEST, OCTOBERFEST, CRANBERRY
FESTIVAL, APPLE FESTIVAL.

Near Rte. 162, I–90.

Built on a hillside, this attractive double A-frame has a deck overlooking
the beautiful Coulee region of Wisconsin. The home is in a wooded area,
part of a nine-hundred acre cattle ranch adjacent to three-thousand acres
of state forest—an ideal spot for anyone seeking peace and quiet. The
house is decorated in a casual style with antiques and treasures from your
hosts' world travels. Guest have only to step out the door to take advantage of the many hiking and cross-country ski trails. This location also
offers many area festivities, such as the July Riverfest, Folk Arts and Crafts
Show in September, and the Octoberfest. There are three guest rooms.
Two have double beds with hand-stitched quilts and form part of a suite
that includes a living room and bath, ideal for two couples traveling together. Your hosts will not book strangers into these two rooms at the
same time. The third guest room has a single bed, seaside motif, and pri-

vate bath. Your hosts can provide you with a candlelight dinner in the cozy balcony dining room. There is also a remote hilltop enclosed gazebo for year-round use. It is available for camping, picnics, or quiet evenings under the stars. A Full breakfast is served. Additional meals and nature tours are available. One of your hosts manages his own business as well as the ranch. The other is owner and manager of a dance school. They have traveled to the Far East, India, Nepal, New Zealand, and Australia. Their interests include bonsai, hiking, hunting, skiing, and farming.

No. Rooms: 3	**Breakfast:** Full
Singles: 1 pb	**S-Rates:** $40 pb
Doubles: 2 pb	**D-Rates:** $60 pb
Type: Private home	**Bldg:** 1967 double A-frame

Minimum Stay: none. **Credit Card(s) Accepted:** none. **Open:** all year. No resident dogs. No dogs please. No resident cats. No cats please. Non-smoking host. Guests may smoke. Children welcome. **Discounts:** none.

Reservation Contact: Bed & Breakfast Registry Ltd., Gary Winget, Box 8174, St. Paul, MN 55108; 612–646–4238.

EGG HARBOR
ID: 54209BAR

DOOR COUNTY, SUMMER THEATER, MUSIC FESTIVALS, ARTISAN SHOPS & GALLERIES, BEACHES, BOATING, FISHING, GOLF, TENNIS, CROSS-COUNTRY SKIING.

Near Rte. 42 & County E.

Door County is striking for its variety and contrasts. The two-hundred-and-fifty-mile shoreline varies from steep limestone bluffs and plunging cliffs to placid sand beaches and lush pine forests. Outstanding plays are presented by the Peninsula Players, America's oldest professional summer theater group. The Peninsula Music Festival gives an annual series of concerts, and the local artists and craftsmen exhibit their work in various shops and galleries. For at least one meal, visitors will want to try the legendary Door County Fish Boil, a tasty local tradition cooked outdoors over a roaring fire. This spacious contemporary house of rustic red-cedar siding is on a lovely Door County farm. There is a large yard, with picnic table and lawn chairs, several big shade trees, and enough open space for sunning. It is secluded from the tourist scene yet close to area attractions. You are welcome to relax in the spacious living room or in the den for TV, music, and reading. Four guest rooms on the second floor share two baths. There is also a four-bedroom guest cottage available, with seven double beds, kitchen, fireplace, and two baths. It is ideal for large families or groups getting together for a weekend of golf, fishing, or cross-country skiing. A Full farm breakfast is served in the spacious country kitchen/dining room, where you are always welcome to stop off for a cup of tea, cold drink, or snack. Lunch, child care, laundry facilities, arrival/departure transportation, and area tours are available. Your very hospitable hosts, one of whom is a graduate home economist, go out of their way to meet your every need. Their interests include hunting and gardening.

No. Rooms: 4	**Breakfast:** Full
Singles: None	**S-Rates:** $45–$75 sb
Doubles: 4 sb	**D-Rates:** $45–$75 sb
Type: Private home	**Bldg:** Contemporary

Minimum Stay: none. **Credit Card(s) Accepted:** MC, V. **Open:** all year. Host's dog is not allowed in guest areas. Guests may bring dog. No resident cats. No cats please. Nonsmoking host. Guests may not smoke in residence. Children welcome. **Discounts:** none.

Reservation Contact: Bed & Breakfast Registry Ltd., Gary Winget, Box 8174, St. Paul, MN 55108; 612–646–4238.

ELLISON BAY   ID: 54210COU

FRONTAGE ON EUROPE LAKE, WASHINGTON ISLAND FERRY DOCK.

Near Rte. 42.

This cedar ranch-style house is located on fifty-three acres adjacent to Newport State Park. The house has a large wooded yard with many flowers and offers a quiet, peaceful setting minutes from shops, galleries, and restaurants. You can swim, canoe, picnic, or cross-country ski at Europe Lake, one block away from the house. There are two guest rooms available, both with double beds and shared guest bath. One is done in blue and white, with a dressing table and sitting area. The other, yellow and white, has an antique maple headboard and dressing table. A Full country breakfast is served on the sun deck. Child care, additional meals, arrival/departure transportation, and area tours are available. Your hosts' interests include gardening, crafts, volunteer work, hunting, and diving.

No. Rooms: 2	**Breakfast:** Full
Singles: None	**S-Rates:** $40 sb
Doubles: 2 sb	**D-Rates:** $42 sb
Type: Private home	**Bldg:** 1969 cedar ranch

Minimum Stay: none. **Credit Card(s) Accepted:** none. **Open:** January thru October. Dog in residence. No dogs please. Cat in residence. No cats please. Host smokes. Guests may smoke. Children welcome with restrictions. **Discounts:** none. Swedish spoken.

Reservation Contact: Bed & Breakfast Registry Ltd., Gary Winget, Box 8174, St. Paul, MN 55108; 612–646–4238.

GREENDALE

MILWAUKEE AREA; SYMPHONY, BALLET, ZOO, MUSEUMS, THEATER, GRAND AVENUE MALL, BOERNER BOTANICAL GARDENS, NEW DEAL VILLAGE, RESTAURANTS.

Near I–894, I–94, I–43, Grange Ave. & 76th St.

This comfortable contemporary home is situated on a two-acre wooded lot in historic Greendale. Guests are only 15 minutes from all the attractions of downtown Milwaukee and will find hiking, biking, golfing, tennis, skiing, horseback riding, and the famed Boerner Botanical Gardens in the nearby Parkland area. History buffs will delight in Roosevelt's New Deal Village. After a day of business or sightseeing, guests can relax in an intimate room with a fireplace, giant chess board, and a wide variety of books, or on the patio where trees, birds, squirrels, and an occasional doe can be seen. The two second-floor guest rooms with private baths overlook the woods and are graced with original art works and wildflowers in season. One of the rooms has a double bed and the other a king-sized bed. A Continental Plus breakfast is served which includes a fresh fruit dish with a special dressing. Your host is an artist and former teacher whose interests include travel, conservation, and nature.

No. Rooms: 2	**Breakfast:** Continental Plus
Singles: None	**S-Rates:** $40–$50 pb
Doubles: 2 pb	**D-Rates:** $45–$55 pb
Type: Private home	**Bldg:** Contemporary

Minimum Stay: none. **Credit Card(s) Accepted:** MC, V. **Open:** all year. Resident dog. No dogs please. Resident cat. No cats please. Nonsmoking host. Guests may not smoke in residence. Children welcome. **Discounts:** weekly.

Reservation Contact: Bed & Breakfast of Milwaukee, Inc., Barbara Gardner, 320 E. Buffalo St., Milwaukee, WI 53202; 414–271–2337.

JANESVILLE

BELOIT COLLEGE, SWISS FESTIVALS, WATER-SKI SHOWS; 35 MILES SOUTH OF MADISON.

Near Rte. 11, I–90.

This Victorian house with high ceilings, maple floors, and antique furnishings is situated on lovely grounds that boast stone and shrubbery landscaping, many trees, a raspberry patch, flower and vegetable gardens, and a patio where you can view it all. There are four guest rooms, three with antique furnishings and queen-sized beds, one with twin beds. Two have private baths and the other two share a bath. You are welcome to join your hosts beside the fire in the living room and watch TV. A Full breakfast is served on the screened porch or in the dining room. The

house is five blocks from the center of town, an easy walk to tennis courts, old town restorations, golf courses, bike, hiking, and cross-country ski trails, beach, or pool. There are also tours of the General Motors nearby. Your hosts can provide guidance and directions. Their interests are travel, spectator sports, gardening, cooking, and sewing. Arrival/departure transportation and area tours are available.

No. Rooms: 4
Singles: None
Doubles: 2 pb, 2 sb
Type: Private home

Breakfast: Full
S-Rates: $35 sb
D-Rates: $45–$55 sb
Bldg: Victorian

Minimum Stay: none. **Credit Card(s) Accepted:** MC, V. **Open:** all year. No resident dogs. No dogs please. No resident cats. No cats please. Non-smoking host. Guests may smoke. Children welcome. **Discounts:** business, senior citizens, and stays of more than 2 nights.

Reservation Contact: Bed & Breakfast Registry Ltd., Gary Winget, Box 8174, St. Paul, MN 55108; 612–646–4238.

KIEL
ID: 53042LAR

ROAD AMERICA, CEDAR LAKE, LAKE WINNEBAGO, KETTLE MORAINE STATE FOREST, STOELTING HOUSE, WADE HOUSE; FISHING, HIKING, SWIMMING, CROSS-COUNTRY SKIING.

On Sheboygan River near Rte. 57, Rte. 149, U.S. 43.

This stately Georgian house is located on an acre of land that slopes down to the shore of the Sheboygan River. You will find many large trees, flowering bushes, and flower and vegetable gardens on the grounds. The house, built in 1924, is beautifully furnished, and the living room has a fireplace and Steinway grand piano. TV is available in the sun room. There are two guest rooms, each with double beds, dressers, desks, book-

cases, dressing tables, and easy chairs; the two rooms share a guest bath. A Full breakfast, including homegrown strawberries and raspberries in season, homemade jams and rolls, and samples from the area's excellent butcher and cheese shops, is served in the dining room. Kiel and the surrounding area enjoy numerous reminders of a colorful past, such as the historic Stoelting House overlooking the Sheboygan River and the Wade House in nearby Greenbush, built during the mid-1800s to serve as a stagecoach stop and Civil War recruitment center. Both are now open to the public. Your delightful hosts know the area well and can suggest many things to see and do. Your hosts (one a retired editor/publisher) enjoy reading, writing, art, music, and gardening, and are involved in community organizations. The guest rooms are not available from December to April 1.

No. Rooms: 2	**Breakfast:** Full
Singles: None	**S-Rates:** $30–$35 sb
Doubles: 2 sb	**D-Rates:** $40–$45 sb
Type: Private home	**Bldg:** 1924 Georgian

Minimum Stay: none. **Credit Card(s) Accepted:** none. **Open:** April 2–Nov. No resident dogs. No dogs please. No resident cats. No cats please. Nonsmoking host. Guests may not smoke in guest rooms. Children welcome with restrictions. **Discounts:** none.

Reservation Contact: Bed & Breakfast Registry Ltd., Gary Winget, Box 8174, St. Paul, MN 55108; 612–646–4238.

LA FARGE

ID: 54639TRI

HOUSE ON THE ROCK, FRANK LLOYD WRIGHT MUSEUM, CIRCUS WORLD, AMISH COMMUNITY & CHEESE FACTORY.

Near Rte. 82 & County D, U.S. 14.

This cozy cottage is the ideal spot for relaxing and unwinding in the peaceful beauty of a rural setting. It has a double bed in the bedroom and hide-a-bed in the living room; it also offers a single bed and portable crib, so it can easily accommodate four adults and two children. The many windows provide views of the woods and fields, where much wild-life can be observed, and the house is joined on two sides by an organic garden and orchard. You are welcome to explore all eighty-five acres. The cottage is fully equipped, right down to the kitchen utensils. A Full breakfast is served, and you can prepare other meals if you like, although three nearby towns offer a good selection of restaurants. The area boasts a wide variety of activities throughout the year, with many ethnic festivals, parades, and celebrations taking place during spring, summer, and fall. Near the farm are the Mississippi and Kickapoo rivers, Wildcat State Park, many small lakes with beaches, trout-fishing streams, canoe rentals, picnic facilities, guided hiking and biking trails, cross-country ski trails, and a downhill ski area. Your hosts are interested in gardening, spinning, embroidery, reading, and music.

No. Rooms: 1	**Breakfast:** Full
Singles: None	**S-Rates:** $60 pb
Doubles: 1 pb	**D-Rates:** $86 pb
Type: Private cottage	**Bldg:** Cedar

Minimum Stay: none. **Credit Card(s) Accepted:** none. **Open:** all year. No resident dogs. No dogs please. No resident cats. No cats please. Non-smoking host. Guests may smoke in residence. Children welcome. **Discounts:** 10% after 7 nights.

Reservation Contact: Bed & Breakfast Registry Ltd., Gary Winget, Box 8174, St. Paul, MN 55108; 612–646–4238.

LODI

ID: 53555LAK

WISCONSIN DELLS, DEVIL'S HEAD SKI RESORT; BOATING, FISHING.

Near Rte. 60, I–90.

This attractive contemporary home, with one-hundred feet of water frontage, has two nicely decorated guest rooms that share a bath. One has twin beds and TV, and the other has a single bed. A Continental breakfast is served during the week, and a Full breakfast is served on weekends in the dining area or on the deck overlooking a lagoon. A park with tennis courts is two blocks away. The Wisconsin Dells, Devil's Head, and Cascade ski areas are within a twenty-five minute drive. Your hosts enjoy boating, fishing, gardening, bird-watching, travel, and painting.

No. Rooms: 2	**Breakfast:** Continental/Full
Singles: 1 sb	**S-Rates:** $25 sb
Doubles: 1 sb	**D-Rates:** $35 sb
Type: Private home	**Bldg:** 1980 modern

Minimum Stay: none. **Credit Card(s) Accepted:** none. **Open:** all year. No resident dogs. No dogs please. No resident cats. No cats please. Non-smoking host. Guests may smoke. Children welcome. **Discounts:** none.

Reservation Contact: Bed & Breakfast Registry Ltd., Gary Winget, Box 8174, St. Paul, MN 55108; 612–646–4238.

MILWAUKEE   ID: BOE–MILWK

EAST SIDE, ART MUSEUM, GRAND AVENUE MALL, SUMMERFEST PARK; 3 BLOCKS FROM LAKE FRONT.

Near I–94, I–794, I–43, Wisconsin Ave. & Van Buren St.

Located in the center of the east side, a renewed and exciting downtown Milwaukee, this 1896 home is within walking distance of many attractions. The lake front and art museum are three blocks away, the theater district is six blocks away, and even Summerfest Park is within walking distance. The house is Tudor-style with Victorian details and is now protected as part of a National Register Historic District. Although the exterior has been preserved, the home has a unique contemporary interior. Two air-conditioned guest rooms with double beds and private baths are available. Guests have use of the general living space and, during the summer, will enjoy the garden and terrace with beautiful flowers and a view of the city. A Continental Plus breakfast is served. Your host is an architect.

No. Rooms: 2	**Breakfast:** Continental Plus
Singles: None	**S-Rates:** $55–$65 pb
Doubles: 2 pb	**D-Rates:** $60–$70 pb
Type: Private home	**Bldg:** 1896 modified Tudor

Minimum Stay: none. **Credit Card(s) Accepted:** MC, V. **Open:** all year. No resident dogs. No dogs please. Resident cats. No cats please. Non-smoking host. Guest may not smoke in residence. Children welcome with restrictions. **Discounts:** weekly.

Reservation Contact: Bed & Breakfast of Milwaukee, Inc., Barbara Gardner, 320 E. Buffalo St., Milwaukee, WI 53202; 414–271–2337.

ID: GAR–1–MILWK

HISTORIC 3RD WARD.

Near N. Water St., E. Buffalo, I–43, I–94.

This unique accommodation is located on the ninth floor of a warehouse in the historic third ward. This area, the major nineteenth- and early twentieth-century wholesale and manufacturing district in Milwaukee, has both architectural and historic interest for visitors. It is currently undergoing dynamic change as warehouses are being converted to condominiums, artist's studios and shops. Set in the midst of downtown activity, this two-story penthouse is an oasis of peace and tranquility with exquisite city and lake views in all directions. You are within walking distance of downtown Milwaukee, the fruit and vegetable district, several small restaurants, and the lakefront. There is easy bus, train, and freeway access. The guest apartment is one flight up from your hosts' quarters. It includes living area, kitchen, bedroom, and full bath. There is a queen-sized canopy bed and also a queen-sized hide-a-bed in the living room. Other amenities include a desk, telephone, alarm clock, hair dryer, curling iron, electric shoe polisher, color TV, bicycles, indoor parking, air-conditioning, and door-to-door airport limo service. A patio, rooftop garden, and stone walkway surround this unusual home. Guests have use of the tree-filled solarium and whirlpool spa. In the solarium, either a Full or Continental breakfast is served with sterling silver, fine china, fresh flowers, and a newspaper. Your hosts are a business owner and an interior designer. Their interests include politics, sports, the arts, bridge, cooking, and travel.

No. Rooms: 1	**Breakfast:** Full or Continental
Singles: None	**S-Rates:** $80 pb
Doubles: 1 pb	**D-Rates:** $85 pb
Type: Private home	**Bldg:** 1922 warehouse loft

Minimum Stay: none. **Credit Card(s) Accepted:** MC, V. **Open:** all year. No resident dogs. No dogs please. No resident cats. No cats please. Non-smoking host. Guests may not smoke in residence. Children welcome. **Discounts:** none.

Reservation Contact: Bed & Breakfast of Milwaukee, Inc., Barbara Gardner, 320 E. Buffalo St., Milwaukee, WI 53202; 414–271–2337.

ID: MOS–1–MILWK

OGDEN HOUSE
HISTORIC DISTRICT.

Near Lake Dr., North Ave., Prospect, Ling Mem. Dr., I–43, I–45, I–94.

Greater Milwaukee has an exciting array of attractions suited to many tastes, among them fine food, sports, theater, music, the arts, diverse shopping, colleges and universities, museums, parks, a nationally ranked zoo, and architectural treasures. On the National Registry of Historic

Homes, this 1916 house is located in an historic district of Milwaukee near the lakefront and on a bluff among many fine old mansions. It is within walking distance of small shopping areas, two major hospitals, and an art museum. The Federal-style house has three floors and a large central entrance. The two guest rooms have Queen Anne furniture and private baths. One of the rooms has a four-poster queen-sized bed and an adjoining sitting room with fireplace; the other, also with queen-sized bed, has a view of the water tower. A Continental Plus breakfast is served in the dining room on heirloom china. Your host enjoys needlepoint and quilting.

No. Rooms: 2	**Breakfast:** Continental Plus
Singles: None	**S-Rates:** $60–$70 pb
Doubles: 2 pb	**D-Rates:** $65–$75 pb
Type: Private home	**Bldg:** 1916 Federal

Minimum Stay: none. **Credit Card(s) Accepted:** MC, V. **Open:** all year. No resident dogs. No dogs please. No resident cats. No cats please. Host smokes. Guests may not smoke in guest rooms. Children welcome with restrictions. **Discounts:** none.

Reservation Contact: Bed & Breakfast of Milwaukee, Inc., Barbara Gardner, 320 E. Buffalo St., Milwaukee, WI 53202; 414–271–2337.

ID: WIN–1–MILWK

UNIVERSITY OF WISCONSIN—MILWAUKEE.

Near Capitol, Downer, I–43, I–94.

This Tudor-style house, with leaded windows, beamed ceilings, and large fireplace, is in the vicinity of Lake Michigan and the University of Wisconsin's Milwaukee campus. The house is in an attractive residential neighborhood with interesting shops and is close to the center of the city. The guest room has twin beds with private bath. There is handicapped access. Your hosts, a professor of French and his wife, are interested in literature, tennis, skating, and skiing. They have traveled widely in Europe.

No. Rooms: 1	**Breakfast:** Continental Plus
Singles: None	**S-Rates:** $35–$40 pb
Doubles: 1 pb	**D-Rates:** $45 pb
Type: Private home	**Bldg:** 1921 Tudor

Minimum Stay: none. **Credit Card(s) Accepted:** MC, V. **Open:** all year. No resident dogs. No dogs please. Cat in residence. No cats please. Non-smoking host. Guests may not smoke in residence. Residence not appropriate for children. **Discounts:** weekly. French & Spanish spoken.

Reservation Contact: Bed & Breakfast of Milwaukee, Inc., Barbara Gardner, 320 E. Buffalo St., Milwaukee, WI 53202; 414–271–2337.

MT. HOREB

ID: 53572LAI

HOUSE ON THE ROCK, FRANK LLOYD WRIGHT'S
TALIESIN; HANDCRAFTS, FISHING, SKIING.

Near Rte. 92, U.S. 18, U.S. 151.

Mt. Horeb is a small, picturesque village in a hilly, wooded, scenic section
of Wisconsin. It is just a short drive to Spring Green, where you will find
two Frank Lloyd Wright buildings: Hillside School and Taliesin. Hillside
School is open to the public from June to late fall, with tours every hour.
Taliesin is open to the public on a limited basis for special tours, and most
of the building is visible from the highway. Not far from there and in dramatic contrast to Wright's style, stands the House on the Rock. Visitors
can also see Unity Chapel, built in 1886 for use by the Wright family;
its simple interior was designed by him. The B&B house, built in 1900,
offers one sunny guest room, with Victorian furnishings, many windows,
walk-in closet, and adjoining bath. Your host has interests in cycling, skiing, and literature.

No. Rooms: 1	**Breakfast:** Continental Plus
Singles: None	**S-Rates:** $20–$25 sb
Doubles: 1 sb	**D-Rates:** $22–$27 sb
Type: Private townhouse	**Bldg:** 1900 Victorian

Minimum Stay: none. **Credit Card(s) Accepted:** none. **Open:** all year.
No resident dogs. No dogs please. No resident cats. No cats please. Nonsmoking host. Guests may smoke. Residence not appropriate for children. **Discounts:** none.

Reservation Contact: Bed & Breakfast Registry Ltd., Gary Winget, Box
8174, St. Paul, MN 55108; 612–646–4238.

NEILLSVILLE

ID: 54456STU

SKI AREAS, HIKING, HUNTING, CROSS-COUNTRY
SKIING, ANTIQUING.

Near U.S. 10, Rte. 73, U.S. 12.

This cozy, well-preserved 1880s house is filled with family antiques and
surrounded by a yard of flowers and pine trees. There are three guest
rooms, one with a double and single bed and private bath. The other two
have double beds and share a bath. A Continental Plus breakfast is
served. The area has excellent hunting and fishing. Brouce Mound and
Powers Bluff ski areas are just minutes away. You will find many antique
shops and fine restaurants in the area. Your host's interests include quilting, crocheting, and antiques.

No. Rooms: 3	**Breakfast:** Continental Plus
Singles: None	**S-Rates:** $30 pb, $30 sb
Doubles: 1 pb, 2 sb	**D-Rates:** $35 pb, $35 sb
Type: Private home	**Bldg:** 1880s

Minimum Stay: none. **Credit Card(s) Accepted:** none. **Open:** all year. No resident dogs. No dogs please. No resident cats. A cat is allowed with restrictions. Nonsmoking host. Guests may not smoke in guest rooms. Children welcome with restrictions. **Discounts:** after two nights.

Reservation Contact: Bed & Breakfast Registry Ltd., Gary Winget, Box 8174, St. Paul, MN 55108; 612–646–4238.

OXFORD

ID: 53952LEN

DELLS ATTRACTIONS, ANTIQUES, FLEA MARKETS, SKIING, BOAT EXCURSIONS.

Near Rte. 82, U.S. 51, I–90.

This lovely contemporary home is located in the beautiful Wisconsin Dells. The house is a rough cedar structure with a landscaped yard that has a pond and a fountain. There is a whirlpool for your relaxation as well as a fireplace. The three inviting guest rooms have private baths. One has a king-sized waterbed, balcony, TV, and phone. Another has two double beds, and the third has one double bed. A Continental Plus breakfast is served on the patio, in the dining area, or in bed, as you prefer. There are boat trips through the Dells plus many other amusements and recreations. Additional meals, arrival/departure transportation, area tours, and laundry facilities are available. There is good handicapped access. Your very cordial host enjoys music, antiques, tennis, and fine restaurants.

No. Rooms: 3	**Breakfast:** Continental Plus
Singles: None	**S-Rates:** $25 pb
Doubles: 3 pb	**D-Rates:** $35 pb
Type: Private home	**Bldg:** 1971 contemporary

Minimum Stay: none. **Credit Card(s) Accepted:** none. **Open:** December through October. No resident dogs. Guests may bring dog. No resident cats. Guests may bring cat. Nonsmoking host. Guests may smoke. Residence not appropriate for children. **Discounts:** none.

Reservation Contact: Bed & Breakfast Registry Ltd., Gary Winget, Box 8174, St. Paul, MN 55108; 612–646–4238.

SPARTA

ID: 54656JUS

BIKE TRAILS, WEEKEND FESTIVALS, AMISH COMMUNITY.

Near I–90 & Hwy. 27.

Built by the host's grandfather, this traditional farmhouse is located on a two-hundred-acre dairy farm with ten miles of cross-country ski trails, hiking trails, and mountain bike trails. The Sparta bike trail is also nearby. The house is furnished with family antiques, has refinished maple floors and woodwork, a piano for guests' pleasure, and a front and back porch and many plants. Three guest rooms share a bath. The first has a double bed, green floral wallpaper, antique maple furniture, Laura Ashley linens, and a ceiling fan. The second is done in blue and cream and has a double and a single bed, an antique oak commode, and an antique trunk. The third, done in mauve and cream, is furnished with a double bed and re-production maple furniture. A Full breakfast is served. Your host enjoys photography and interior decorating.

No. Rooms: 3	**Breakfast:** Full
Singles: None	**S-Rates:** $53 sb
Doubles: 3 sb	**D-Rates:** $67 sb
Type: Private home	**Bldg:** Frame farmhouse

Minimum Stay: none. **Credit Card(s) Accepted:** MC, V. **Open:** all year. No resident dogs. No dogs please. No resident cats. No cats please. Non-smoking host. Guests may not smoke in residence. Children welcome. **Discounts:** 15% after 4 days.

Reservation Contact: Bed & Breakfast Registry, Gary Winget, Box 8174, St. Paul, MN 55108; 612–646–4238.

WAUKESHA

ID: MCS–1–MILWK

WESTERN SUBURB OF MILWAUKEE.

Near Broadway, Racine, I–94, Rte. 59.

This home and its grounds have been called the showplace of Waukesha. On one acre of landscaped grounds are over thirty trees, rose and vegetable gardens, and a grape orchard. The chalet-style house, a striking white stucco with royal blue trim, was built in 1915, and it had been occupied by the same family until the current owners purchased it in 1986. An antique roll-top desk, heirloom clock, original light fixtures and sconces, wainscoting, and staircase all add to the atmosphere of old-world charm. The air-conditioned guest room has a queen-sized brass bed, antique oak dresser, and floral wallpaper; it overlooks the backyard and shares a bath with the family. A Continental breakfast is served on the leaded glass-enclosed porch during the summer or at the oak table in the wainscoted dining room in colder months. The house is close to the interstate, shopping, golf, and a public pool. Your hosts, a writer and an electrical engineer, have lived in South America and traveled extensively.

No. Rooms: 1	**Breakfast:** Continental
Singles: None	**S-Rates:** $30–$35 sb
Doubles: 1 sb	**D-Rates:** $35–$40 sb
Type: Private home	**Bldg:** 1915 chalet

Minimum Stay: none. **Credit Card(s) Accepted:** none. **Open:** all year. No resident dogs. No dogs please. No resident cats. No cats please. Non-smoking host. Guests may not smoke in residence. Children welcome. **Discounts:** none. Spanish & Portuguese spoken.

Reservation Contact: Bed & Breakfast of Milwaukee, Inc., Claudette McShane, Box 1822, Milwaukee, WI 53187; 414–544–0060.

WAUSAU   ID: 54401ROS

DELLS OF THE EAU CLAIRE, LEIGH YAWKEY WOODSON ART MUSEUM, HISTORICAL SOCIETY, CROSS-COUNTRY SKIING.

Near Rte. 29, U.S. 51.

Situated in the Andrew Warren Historic District, this little inn is one of sixty-one historic properties listed on the National Register of Historic Places. The earliest houses in the district date from the 1870s, just after the arrival of the railroad, an event that transformed Wausau from a temporary lumber camp into a city of diverse industries and interests. This two-and-a-half story stucco and brick inn offers eight guest rooms with double beds and private baths. Four rooms have fireplaces. On the third floor, there is a sitting room where you can socialize with other guests, watch TV, or play chess or cards. A Continental breakfast is served there or in your room. Within walking distance from the inn are the Wausau Mall, Washington Square complex, antique shops, boutiques, restaurants, and Leigh Yawkey Woodson Art and Historical Society museums. Picturesque Dells of the Eau Claire with nature trails, rock climbing, fishing, canoeing, and picnic areas is a short drive away. Your hosts purchased this building in 1985 and have labored tirelessly to restore it to its 1900 charm for your enjoyment.

No. Rooms: 8	**Breakfast:** Continental
Singles: None	**S-Rates:** $53 pb
Doubles: 8 pb	**D-Rates:** $60 pb
Type: Inn	**Bldg:** 1908 prairie school

Minimum Stay: none. **Credit Card(s) Accepted:** MC, V. **Open:** all year. No resident dogs. No dogs please. No resident cats. No cats please. Host smokes. Guests may smoke. Children welcome. **Discounts:** none.

Reservation Contact: Bed & Breakfast Registry Ltd., Gary Winget, Box 8174, St. Paul, MN 55108; 612–646–4238.

WHITEFISH BAY

ID: EWI–1–MILWK

NORTHERN SUBURB OF MILWAUKEE.

Near Hampton Rd., Santa Monica Blvd., I–93, I–94.

This colonial home, in a well-maintained north shore suburb of fine older homes, affords easy access to downtown. It is twelve blocks from Lake Michigan and three miles from a shopping area. Jogging and biking trails are half a mile away. The home furnishings are a combination of antique and traditional. There is one guest room, with double bed, air-conditioning, and TV. A screened porch with a view of the backyard makes a pleasant setting for Continental breakfast during summer months. Your host, an assistant professor, has traveled throughout the country and enjoys long-distance biking, cross-country skiing, and sailing.

No. Rooms: 1	**Breakfast:** Continental
Singles: None	**S-Rates:** $30–$35 sb
Doubles: 1 sb	**D-Rates:** $35–$40 sb
Type: Private home	**Bldg:** 1949 colonial

Minimum Stay: none. **Credit Card(s) Accepted:** none. **Open:** all year, except Christmas, Thanksgiving. No resident dogs. No dogs please. No resident cats. No cats please. Nonsmoking host. Guests may not smoke in guest rooms. Children welcome with restrictions. **Discounts:** weekly.

Reservation Contact: Bed & Breakfast of Milwaukee, Inc., Claudette McShane, Box 1822, Milwaukee, WI 53187; 414–544–0060.

WHITEWATER

ID: 53190GRE

SOUTHERN KETTLE MORRAINE, WHITEWATER LAKES, HIKING, CROSS-COUNTRY SKIING, BIKE TRAILS, HORSEBACK RIDING; 90 MINUTES FROM CHICAGO, 30 MINUTES FROM MILWAUKEE.

Near U.S. 12, WI 20, WI 67.

The Kettle Morraine area offers a wealth of outdoor activities in a serene country setting. The University of Wisconsin–Whitewater and Old World Wisconsin are nearby, and its proximity to Chicago (90 minutes) and Milwaukee (30 minutes) make it a perfect weekend get-away from city life. To help guests get acquainted your hosts frequently stage wine-tastings, sing-alongs, and talks by local historians around a wood-burning stove. The six guest rooms share two baths. Grandma's Room has pine-plank flooring, embroidered curtains, hooked rugs, and a double bed with hand-stitched quilts. Forest colors, nature books and photos, and a queen-sized bed lend character to the Morraine Room. The Enos Hazzard Room, named after a previous owner, is done in blue and white and contains a double bed, a single bed, and photos and antiques from past and present owners. Antique birds-eye maple furniture and double bed grace the Maple Room which provides a view of the garden. Facing west, the Sunset Room is furnished with a double bed with quilts and an antique wardrobe. In all the rooms guests will find sweets on their pillows. Among the breakfast treats served are cheese omelets, potato pancakes, sausage, baked apples, and home-baked breads and pastries. Your hosts' hobbies include music, antiques, food, wine, gardening, photography, and quilting.

No. Rooms: 6	**Breakfast:** Full
Singles: None	**S-Rates:** $40–$45 sb
Doubles: 6 sb	**D-Rates:** $45–$50 sb
Type: Private home	**Bldg:** 1848 frame farmhouse

Minimum Stay: none. **Credit Card(s) Accepted:** MC, V. **Open:** all year. Dog in residence. No dogs please. No resident cats. No cats please. Nonsmoking host. Guests may not smoke in guest rooms. Children are welcome with restrictions. **Discounts:** none.

Reservation Contact: Bed & Breakfast Registry Ltd., Gary Winget, Box 8174, St. Paul, MN 55108; 612–646–4238.

WYOMING

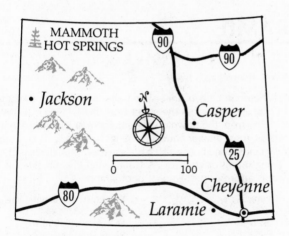

JACKSON HOLE

ID: ROC–50

GRAND TETON NATIONAL PARK, JACKSON HOLE SKI
AREA.

Near Rte. 22, U.S. 89.

Rustic yet elegant, this open-beam mountain home features large windows with views of mountains and streams. The four-story wood-sided house has a two-story living room with balcony and a large stucco fireplace and winding stairway. Hundreds of large pine, fir, and spruce trees surround the dwelling, which, although less than a mile from the village, is very secluded. Grand Teton National Park is ten miles away. There are six guest rooms with private baths and double, twin, or queen-sized beds. A Continental breakfast is served, and area tours are available. Your hosts, a builder and a teacher, are long-time residents of the area. They are also river and mountain outfitters and guides who have traveled widely.

No. Rooms: 6	**Breakfast:** Continental
Singles: None	**S-Rates:** $40–$65 pb
Doubles: 6 pb	**D-Rates:** $50–$75 pb
Type: Inn	**Bldg:** Woodside mountain dwelling.

Minimum Stay: 2 days. **Credit Card(s) Accepted:** MC, V. **Open:** all year. No resident dogs. No dogs please. No resident cats. No cats please. Nonsmoking host. Guests may not smoke in residence. Children welcome with restrictions. **Discounts:** weekly.

Reservation Contact: Bed & Breakfast Western Adventure, Paula Deigert, Box 20972, Billings, MT 59104; 406–259–7993.

LARAMIE

ID: ROC–30

UNIVERSITY OF WYOMING.

Near 9th & Ivinson sts., I–80.

This post-Victorian Queen Anne-style house is located in the oldest section of Laramie, just across the street from the University of Wyoming and six blocks from the downtown area. There are six guest rooms with shared baths; most offer antique furnishings, double beds, and sinks. The beautifully landscaped house also has a sun room, sun deck, and spacious living/dining room for your use. A Continental Plus breakfast is served. Your host is a former professional photographer.

No. Rooms: 6	**Breakfast:** Continental Plus
Singles: None	**S-Rates:** $33–$43
Doubles: 6 sb	**D-Rates:** $40–$50 sb
Type: Public home	**Bldg:** 1910 Queen Anne-style

Minimum Stay: none. **Credit Card(s) Accepted:** AE, MC, V. **Open:** all year. No resident dogs. No dogs please. Cat in residence. No cats please. Nonsmoking host. Guests may not smoke in guest rooms. Children welcome with restrictions. **Discounts:** none.

Reservation Contact: Bed & Breakfast Western Adventure, Paula Deigert, Box 20972, Billings, MT 59104; 406–259–7993.

CANADA

ALBERTA

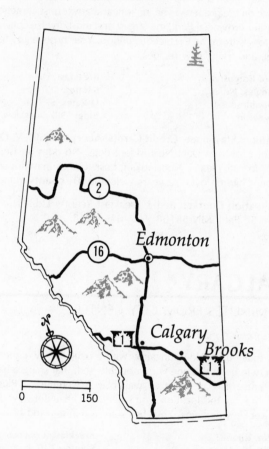

BROOKS

DINOSAUR PROVINCIAL PARK, WILDLIFE CENTER, LAKE NEWELL, FISHING, HUNTING.

Near Trans-Canada Hwy.

A crackling fire in the gathering room welcomes guests in this beautifully decorated little inn just outside the town of Brooks. There are four air-conditioned guest rooms with private baths. One, in rose and blue, has twin beds with quilts and shams, country lace curtains, dresser, and reading lamp. Another has a peach-and-blue color scheme, peach carpeting, a queen-sized bed, and antique dresser and chair. The other two have four-poster double beds. A Full country breakfast is served in the solarium. Picnic lunches and candlelight dinners are available by reservation. There are heated kennels, facilities to clean birds and fish, and freezer storage on the property. The inn is near many tourist attractions including Dinosaur Provincial Park, the largest and most diverse collection of dinosaur fossils from the Cretaceous period. Your hosts enjoy fishing, skiing, travel, and trying new recipes.

No. Rooms: 4	**Breakfast:** Full
Singles: None	**S-Rates:** $60 pb
Doubles: 4 sb	**D-Rates:** $75 pb
Type: Inn	**Bldg:** 1987 Bungalow

Minimum Stay: none. **Credit Card(s) Accepted:** MC, V. **Open:** all year except Christmas Day. No resident dogs. No dogs please. No resident cats. No cats please. Nonsmoking host. Guests may not smoke in residence. Children over 10 years welcome. **Discounts:** none.

Reservation Contact: Bed & Breakfast Registry Ltd., Gary Winget, Box 8174, St. Paul, MN 55108; 612–646–4238.

CALGARY   ID: ALB–2

20 MINUTES FROM CITY CENTER.

Near Trans-Canada 1.

This spacious hillside bungalow with a patio has two guest rooms, one with twin beds and one with a double bed, that share a bath. A hide-a-bed and rollaway are also available. A Continental Plus breakfast is served. From this location, you will have a beautiful view of the city and the Rocky Mountains. Your hosts are a minister and his wife.

No. Rooms: 2	**Breakfast:** Continental Plus
Singles: None	**S-Rates:** $40 sb
Doubles: 2 sb	**D-Rates:** $50 sb
Type: Private home	**Bldg:** Bungalow

Minimum Stay: none. **Credit Card(s) Accepted:** none. **Open:** all year. No resident dogs. No dogs please. No resident cats. No cats please. Nonsmoking host. Guest may not smoke in residence. Children welcome. **Discounts:** none.

Reservation Contact: Alberta Bed & Breakfast, June Brown, Box 15477, M.P.O., Vancouver, BC; 604–682–4610.

EDMONTON

5 MINUTES FROM CITY CENTER.

Near hwys. 16 & 2.

This historical red-brick home was built in 1910 for James Gibbons who fought in the 1885 Riel Rebellion. There is one upstairs guest room with a double bed and private bath. A Continental Plus breakfast is served. Your hosts are musicians with the Edmonton Symphony Orchestra.

No. Rooms: 1	**Breakfast:** Continental Plus
Singles: None	**S-Rates:** $30 pb
Doubles: 1 pb	**D-Rates:** $40 pb
Type: Private home	**Bldg:** Three-story brick

Minimum Stay: none. **Credit Card(s) Accepted:** none. **Open:** all year. No resident dogs. No dogs please. Resident cats. No cats please. Non-smoking hosts. Guests may not smoke in residence. Residence not appropriate for children. **Discounts:** none.

Reservation Contact: Alberta Bed & Breakfast, June Brown, Box 15477, M.P.O., Vancouver, BC; 604–682–4610.

BRITISH COLUMBIA

FULFORD HARBOUR

ID: WESTON

SALT SPRING ISLAND, RUCKLE PARK, WESTON LAKE, MARINA, PUBS, RESTAURANTS, CRAFT SHOPS.

Near Fulford-Ganges Rd., Beaver Pt. Rd.

Fulford Harbour is a quaint, hundred-year-old country village four miles away from Ruckle Park's 1,200 beautiful waterfront acres. Weston Lake provides excellent swimming and fishing and guests will find restaurants, pubs, craft shops, a marina, and a ferry terminal in the village proper. This gabled country house on a ten-acre farm provides beautiful views of Lake Weston and the surrounding countryside. Stroll the woodlands and pastures, relax on the garden terrace, or enjoy books, games, satellite TV, and VCR in the lounge. There are three guest rooms. The Petit Point Room overlooks the lake and has a double bed with down comforter and pillow shams, oak bedside tables and mirror, a provincial loveseat with petit-point upholstery, and petit point mounted in antique frames adorning the walls. The Sailboat Room overlooks the garden, woodland, and pasture and has a brass double bed, an antique rocking chair, and is decorated with a sailing theme including the work of a local artist. The Eskimo

Room, also overlooking the garden, has twin beds, a loveseat, and features Canadian Eskimo and Indian art. The Full breakfast includes fresh farm eggs and various house specialities. Your hosts were both born on the southern coast of British Columbia and have explored the Pacific Northwest extensively by sailboat, bicycle, and kayak. One had a career in social services and international development, and the other works as a criminal justice administrator.

No. Rooms: 3	**Breakfast:** Full
Singles: None	**S-Rates:** $50–$57 pb, $38–$44 sb
Doubles: 1 pb, 2 sb	**D-Rates:** $60–$69 pb, $48–$56 sb
Type: Private home	**Bldg:** Gabled country house

Minimum Stay: 2 nights on holiday weekends. **Credit Card(s) Accepted:** MC, V. **Open:** all year. Resident dog. Guest dogs allowed outdoors. Resident cat. No cats please. Nonsmoking host. Guests may not smoke in residence. Residence not appropriate for children. **Discounts:** 10% weekly.

Reservation Contact: Town & Country Bed & Breakfast in B.C. Canada, Helen Burich & Pauline Scoten, Box 46544, Station G, Vancouver, BC V6R 4G6; 604–731–5942.

NORTH VANCOUVER   ID: GRANDMAN

20 MINUTES FROM DOWNTOWN VANCOUVER.

Near Trans Canada Hwy.

This stately granite home, circa 1914, retains the character of its past. The first of the three guest rooms overlooks Grand Boulevard and has a view of surrounding mountains. It is furnished with mahogany antiques and has a queen-sized bed. The adjoining sitting room has a queen-sized hide-a-bed and fireplace. This room also has a private bath. The Sunset Room offers a great city view, a queen-sized brass bed, and a single bed. The Valley Room, furnished with oak antiques, has a double bed, a queen-sized bed, and faces the boulevard and the Lynn Valley Mountains. The second and third rooms share a bath. A Continental Plus breakfast is served in the dining room. Guests are welcome to use other areas of the house as well as the garden and patio. Your hosts enjoy antiques and renovation.

No. Rooms: 3	**Breakfast:** Continental Plus
Singles: None	**S-Rates:** $60 pb, $40–$50 sb
Doubles: 1 pb, 2 sb	**D-Rates:** $70 pb, $50–$60 sb
Type: Private home	**Bldg:** 1910 stone

Minimum Stay: 2 nights. **Credit Card(s) Accepted:** none. **Open:** all year. Resident dog. No dogs please. No resident cats. No cats please. Host smokes. Guests may smoke on the main floor. Children welcome. **Discounts:** 7th night free.

Reservation Contact: Town & Country Bed & Breakfast in B.C., Canada,

Helen Burich & Pauline Scoten, Box 46544, Station G, Vancouver, BC, V6R 4G6; 604–731–5942.

15 MINUTES FROM DOWNTOWN VANCOUVER, HORSESHOE BAY, 5 MINUTES FROM GROUSE MOUNTAIN.

Near Trans Canada, Capilano Rd.

This charming, picture-perfect home is surrounded by a half-acre, prize-winning English garden. Guests will find peace and seclusion only 15 minutes from downtown Vancouver and two blocks from major bus routes; Grouse Mountain and other tourist attractions are also nearby. Three guest rooms and two self-contained cottages are offered. In one of the rooms delicate peach tones are enhanced by white wool carpeting, moire wall covering, antique mahogany furniture, a queen-sized brass bed, leaded-pane windows facing the garden, and a private bath. Another room, also with a queen-sized bed, is done in rose and overlooks the stream and fountain. A third room, in soft shades of green, has iron-and-brass twin beds, antique furniture, and original art. The two beautifully appointed cottages reflect country elegance. One of them can accommodate six people, and the other accommodates two. Breakfast is served in the kitchen around a large pine table that seats ten. Your hosts' interests include travel, gardening, photography, and books. They are long-time residents of the area and can advise guests on routes, ferries, places of interest, restaurants, etc. Their guest book is full of favorable comments.

No. Rooms: 5	**Breakfast:** Full
Singles: None	**S-Rates:** $60–$70 pb, $50 sb
Doubles: 5	**D-Rates:** $70–$80 pb, $60 sb
Type: Private home	**Bldg:** English cottage

Minimum Stay: none **Credit Card(s) Accepted:** MC, V. **Open:** all year. No resident dogs. Dogs permitted in cottages only. Resident cat. Cats permitted in cottages only. Nonsmoking host. Guests may smoke on deck and patio only. Children welcome. **Discounts:** 6 or more nights. German spoken.

Reservation Contact: Town & Country Bed & Breakfast in B.C. Canada, Helen Burish & Pauline Scoten, Box 46544, Station G, Vancouver, BC V6R 4G6; 604–731–5942.

SORRENTO

ID: PHILLIPS

ADAM'S RIVER SALMON RUN, WHITE LAKE, SWIMMING, BOATING, GOLF, CROSS-COUNTRY SKIING, ICE FISHING; ON WATER.

Near Trans Canada Hwy., Hwy. 97B.

This attractive log home, actually a remodeled barn, is situated on sixteen acres of land with one-thousand feet of waterfront on White Lake. Boats are available, and there is a picnic area at the lake's edge. There are two guest rooms with double beds and private baths. A crib is also available. Your hospitable hosts invite you to share the garden, patio, and TV room. Breakfast is served between 8:00 and 9:00 A.M. The house is in the heart of a fast-growing recreational area, with hiking, fishing, swimming, and boating. It is close to a golf course, Salmon Arm, and the famous Adam's River salmon run. In winter, cross-country skiing and ice fishing are offered. The roads are paved. Additional meals are available. Check in before 9:00 P.M. and check out before 11:00 A.M.

No. Rooms: 2	**Breakfast:** Full
Singles: None	**S-Rates:** $25 pb
Doubles: 2 pb	**D-Rates:** $35 pb
Type: Private Home	**Bldg:** Log

Minimum Stay: none. **Credit Card(s) Accepted:** none. **Open:** all year. A dog is allowed with restrictions. A cat is allowed with restrictions. Children welcome. **Discounts:** none.

Reservation Contact: Town & Country Bed & Breakfast in B.C. Canada, Helen Burich & Pauline Scoten, Box 46544, Station G, Vancouver, BC V6R 4G6; 604–731–5942.

SURREY

REDWOOD PARK, PEACE ARCH PARK, FORT
LANGLEY, CLOVERDALE RODEO, SURREY FARM FAIR;
HARNESS RACING, GOLF, FISHING.

Near 104th Ave. & Hwy. 1A, Trans Canada Hwy.

This attractive duplex on one-third acre is located on a quiet residential street. Guest facilities consist of a kitchen, living room, dining room, two bedrooms, and a bath. One of the bedrooms has a king-sized waterbed; the other has a double bed and antique furnishings. A Full breakfast is served. Your hosts enjoy reading, gardening, cooking, travel, and opera.

No. Rooms: 2	**Breakfast:** Full
Singles: None	**S-Rates:** $45 sb
Doubles: 2 sb	**D-Rates:** $50 sb
Type: Private home	**Bldg:** 1950s modern

Minimum Stay: none. **Credit Card(s) Accepted:** none. **Open:** all year. Dog in residence. A dog is allowed with restrictions. No resident cats. No cats please. Nonsmoking host. Guests may not smoke in guest rooms. Children welcome. **Discounts:** weekly.

Reservation Contact: Bed & Breakfast Registry Ltd., Gary Winget, Box 8174, St. Paul, MN 55108; 612–646–4238.

VANCOUVER

STANLEY PARK, SEAWALL, GROUSE MOUNTAIN.

Near Trans Canada Hwy., Hwy. 99, Marine Dr. & Lonsdale.

This large Tudor home, built in 1906, is close to bus routes, local shopping and attractions, Stanley Park, and the Seawall. There are three upstairs guest rooms with color TV and double beds. One has a private bath and the other two share a bath. Two rooms have a beautiful view of Vancouver Harbour and the city lights. Guests will enjoy the game room for billiards and darts. A Full breakfast is served.

No. Rooms: 3	**Breakfast:** Full
Singles: None	**S-Rates:** $70 pb, $60 sb
Doubles: 1 pb, 2 sb	**D-Rates:** $70 pb, $60 sb
Type: Private home	**Bldg:** 1906 Tudor

Minimum Stay: none. **Credit Card(s) Accepted:** none. **Open:** all year. No resident dogs. No dogs please. No resident cats. No cats please. Nonsmoking host. Guests may not smoke in residence. Children welcome. **Discounts:** none.

Reservation Contact: Alberta Bed & Breakfast, June Brown, Box 15477, M.P.O., Vancouver, BC V6B 5B2; 604–682–4610.

OCEANFRONT, HORSESHOE BAY, GROUSE MOUNTAIN; 15 MINUTES TO DOWNTOWN.

Near hwys, 1, 99, Marine Dr. & Ferndale Ave.

Guests are welcomed to this beautiful waterfront home with a basket of fruit and fresh flowers. Situated on a quiet cul-de-sac in an exclusive area of the city, the house, with Spanish architecture accented by antique stained-glass windows, affords a panoramic view of Vancouver's busy harbor. Three guest rooms are available. The first, with private bath, is furnished with a queen-sized bed and designer sofa. A private patio leads to the beach. A second room is done with a Laura Ashley motif in pale peach and blue. The color scheme is reflected in the wallpaper, custom draperies, and bedcovers. There is a king-sized bed as well as a single bed in this room. The third room is decorated in soft tones of green with Austrian sheers and matching spreads on the double and single beds. The second and third rooms share a bath. A Full breakfast is served in the formal dining room overlooking the sea. Expect white linen, silver service, and homemade specialties. After breakfast guests can sit at the water's edge, watch the seals from the patio, go sailing or fishing, or golf at the spectacular oceanside Gleneagles Course. Your hosts, former teachers, are knowledgeable about local history, commerce, and sights. They will gladly direct guests to Stanley Park, hiking trails, sea walks, skiing areas, and shopping bargains—all within five miles of this delightful spot.

No. Rooms: 3	**Breakfast:** Full
Singles: None	**S-Rates:** $60–$65 pb, $40–$45 sb
Doubles: 1 pb, 2 sb	**D-Rates:** $60–$65 pb, $52–$56 sb
Type: Private home	**Bldg:** Spanish

Minimum Stay: none. **Credit Card(s) Accepted:** MC. V. **Open:** all year. Resident dogs. No dogs please. No resident cats. No cats please. Non-smoking hosts. Guests may smoke outside only. Children welcome with restrictions. **Discounts:** none.

Reservation Contact: Town & Country Bed & Breakfast in B.C. Canada, Helen Burich & Pauline Scoten, Box 46544, Station G, Vancouver, BC V6R 4G6; 604–731–5942.

QUEEN ELIZABETH PARK, VAN DUSEN GARDENS, UNIVERSITY OF BRITISH COLUMBIA; SHOPPING, RESTAURANTS.

Near Granville St. & 58th Ave. W.

This home offers Bed & Breakfast with Viennese charm. You are invited to relax in the secluded garden, on the patio, or in the sauna, or you can watch TV in the cozy den. One guest suite is available, with twin beds,

down comforters, and private bath. A double hide-a-bed is also available
if needed. A Full Viennese breakfast is served from 7:30 to 9:30 A.M.,
and laundry facilities are available by arrangement. The house is well-
located on the popular westside, one block from the Granville bus stop,
ten minutes from the airport, and fifteen minutes from downtown Vancouver. You will find many attractions nearby, including excellent shopping and restaurants, Queen Elizabeth Park, Van Dusen Gardens, and the
University of B.C. Arrival and departure times are flexible but should be
arranged beforehand.

No. Rooms: 1	**Breakfast:** Full
Singles: None	**S-Rates:** $40 pb
Doubles: 2 pb	**D-Rates:** $60–$65 pb
Type: Private home	

Minimum Stay: none. **Credit Card(s) Accepted:** none. **Open:** all year,
except Christmas. No resident dogs. No dogs please. No resident cats.
No cats please. Nonsmoking host. Guests may not smoke in residence.
Children welcome. **Discounts:** none. German spoken.

Reservation Contact: Town & Country Bed & Breakfast in B.C. Canada,
Helen Burich & Pauline Scoten, Box 46544, Station G, Vancouver, BC
V6R 4G6; 604–731–5942.

ID: SHAUGHNES

RESTAURANTS, MUSEUMS, THEATERS, BEACHES.

Near Granville St. & 16th Ave.

This elegant 1914 Victorian mansion, in a central but private location,
invites you to enjoy the grandeur of years gone by. There are two guest
rooms, one with a single bed and one with a double, and shared bath;
a cot is also available. Breakfast time is flexible and is served on a tray
in your room. You are invited to share the garden and patio overlooking
the city and mountains. Off-street parking and laundry facilities are available. In one of the city's finest and oldest residential areas, this home
is close to bus lines, downtown Vancouver, beaches, Stanley Park, and
other attractions.

No. Rooms: 2	**Breakfast:** Continental Plus
Singles: 1 sb	**S-Rates:** $50 sb
Doubles: 1 sb	**D-Rates:** $55 sb
Type: Private home	**Bldg:** 1914 Victorian

Minimum Stay: none. **Credit Card(s) Accepted:** none. **Open:** all year.
No resident dogs. No dogs please. No resident cats. No cats please. Nonsmoking host. Guests may not smoke in residence. Children welcome
with restrictions. **Discounts:** none.

Reservation Contact: Town & Country Bed & Breakfast in B.C. Canada,
Helen Burich & Pauline Scoten, Box 46544, Station G, Vancouver, BC
V6R 4G6; 604–731–5942.

ID: STORWICK

VAN DUSEN GARDENS, QUEEN ELIZABETH PARK, UNIVERSITY OF BRITISH COLUMBIA; SHAUGHNESSY AREA.

Near Granville St. & King Edward Ave. W., Hwy. 99.

Centrally located on a quiet tree-lined street in the Shaughnessy residential area of the city, this gracious home has three large upstairs guest rooms. Two rooms have double beds and one has twin beds. There is a shared guest bath, enclosed staircase, and a guest telephone. You are invited to share the main floor den with TV as well as the delightful flower garden, patio, and sun deck. This is an ideal location for those traveling without a car or not wishing to drive—the downtown direct bus route is nearby. Cross-town connections are a block away, and there is easy access to Highway 99, the airport, and train station. The location is also convenient to the University of B.C., Granville Island Market, Queen Elizabeth Park, Van Dusen Gardens, and ocean beaches. Your hosts are ardent salmon fishermen. Breakfast is served between 7:30 and 9:30 A.M. You are requested to check in before 9:00 P.M. and check out by 11:00 A.M. Laundry facilities are available by arrangement.

No. Rooms: 3	**Breakfast:** Full
Singles: None	**S-Rates:** $40 sb
Doubles: 3 sb	**D-Rates:** $50–$55 sb
Type: Private home	

Minimum Stay: none.**Credit Card(s) Accepted:** none.**Open:** all year. No resident dogs. No dogs please. No resident cats. No cats please. Non-smoking host. Guests may not smoke in residence. **Discounts:** off-season.

Reservation Contact: Town & Country Bed & Breakfast in B.C. Canada, Helen Burich & Pauline Scoten, Box 46544, Station G, Vancouver, BC V6R 4G6; 604–731–5942.

VICTORIA

ID: ALB–4

BEACONHILL PARK, PROVINCIAL MUSEUM; TWO BLOCKS FROM BEACH.

Near Trans Canada Hwy., Hwy. 17, May & Cook sts.

From this 1911 Victorian home guests can walk to the Empress Hotel for high tea. The beach and ocean walking paths are two blocks away, tennis courts are across the street, and Beaconhill Park and the Provincial Museum are also nearby. There are three guest rooms with color TV and shared bath. Two rooms have queen-sized beds and one has twin beds. A Full breakfast is served. Other amenities include off-street parking and use of the patio and yard.

No. Rooms: 3	**Breakfast:** Full
Singles: None	**S-Rates:** $55 sb
Doubles: 3 sb	**D-Rates:** $55 sb
Type: Private home	**Bldg:** 1911 Victorian

Minimum Stay: none. **Credit Card(s) Accepted:** none. **Open:** all year. No resident dog. No dogs please. No resident cat. No cats please. Non-smoking host. Guests may not smoke in residence. Residence is not appropriate for children. **Discounts:** none.

Reservation Contact: Alberta Bed & Breakfast, June Brown, Box 15477, M.P.O., Vancouver, BC V6B 5B2; 604–682–4610.

ID: LAIRD

BEACON HILL PARK, PARLIAMENT BUILDINGS, CRYSTAL GARDENS, PROVINCIAL MUSEUM.

Near Government & Simcoe sts.

This charming 1912 Heritage-style home is conveniently located in the historical James Bay neighborhood, close to the home of Emily Carr, West Coast artist and author. The three upstairs guest rooms, two with twin beds and one with a double bed, share a bath. One room has a fireplace and opens onto a balcony. You are invited to have tea on the veranda and to enjoy the garden and living quarters. A Full breakfast is served from 8:00 to 9:00 A.M.; a Continental breakfast is served in your room if preferred. The house is just one block from Beacon Hill Park and a fifteen-minute walk to downtown, Parliament buildings, Crystal Gardens, the cruise ship *Princess Marguerite,* and the *M. V. Coho* ferry to Port Angeles, Washington. There is also easy access to all other ferries.

No. Rooms: 2	**Breakfast:** Full
Singles: None	**S-Rates:** $40 sb
Doubles: 2 sb	**D-Rates:** $55 sb
Type: Private home	**Bldg:** 1912 Heritage style

Minimum Stay: none. **Credit Card(s) Accepted:** none. **Open:** all year. Resident dogs. No dogs please. No resident cats. No cats please. Non-smoking host. Guests may not smoke in residence. Residence not appropriate for children. **Discounts:** none

Reservation Contact: Town & Country Bed & Breakfast in B.C. Canada, Helen Burich & Pauline Scoten, Box 46544, Station G, Vancouver, BC V6R 4G6; 604–731–5942.

VICTORIA/SIDNEY   ID: PEGGYCOVE

BUTCHART GARDENS, VICTORIA'S SIGHTS; ON OCEAN.

Near Rte. 17.

This beautiful home on the ocean offers fishing at your doorstep, evening strolls on the beach, and views of the setting sun while you relax on the deck. Two guest rooms offer queen-sized beds, private patios with ocean views, and private baths. You are also invited to use the common room with its large stone fireplace, TV, and Ping-Pong table. A canoe and rowboat are also available. Your friendly host serves a Full breakfast from 8:00 to 10:00 A.M. This house offers country living with many interesting walks, yet it is within easy access of many of Victoria's sights. Boats and the Saturday night fireworks display can be viewed from the front balcony. While breakfasting on the sun deck, you can watch sea lions at play, soaring eagles, and, with a little luck, a pod of killer whales may appear. Arrival/departure times are by arrangement.

No. Rooms: 2	**Breakfast:** Full
Singles: None	**S-Rates:** $90–$105 pb
Doubles: 2 pb	**D-Rates:** $90–$105 pb
Type: Private home	

Minimum Stay: none. **Credit Card(s) Accepted:** none.**Open:** all year. Guests may bring dog. Guests may bring cat.**Discounts:** none. German spoken.

Reservation Contact: Town & Country Bed & Breakfst in B.C. Canada, Helen Burich & Pauline Scoten, Box 46544, Station G, Vancouver, BC, V6R 4G6; 604–731–5942.

WHISTLER

BLACKCOMB & WHISTLER MOUNTAINS, SKIING.

Near Hwy. 99, Nancy Greene Dr.

Whistler Village, with its mountains and lush forests, attracts visitors from all over the world. The craggy Blackcomb and Whistler mountains provide some of the longest vertical ski runs on the continent, and this picturesque town is nestled between them. In addition to skiing, the area offers hiking, horseback riding, swimming, biking, golf, tennis, canoeing, fishing, and windsurfing. This Alpine inn offers a sitting room with wood-burning stove and a sun deck with a mountain view. Six guest rooms, all with private baths, have double or twin beds with down comforters. A Continental breakfast is served. Your French and German hosts provide European hospitality.

No. Rooms: 6	**Breakfast:** Continental
Singles: None	**S-Rates:** $59–$85 pb
Doubles: 6 pb	**D-Rates:** $59–$86 pb
Type: Inn	**Bldg:** Alpine inn

Minimum Stay: none. **Credit Card(s) Accepted:** AE, MC, V. **Open:** all year. No resident dogs. No dogs please. No resident cats. No cats please. Nonsmoking host. Guests may not smoke in residence. Inn is not appropriate for children. **Discounts:** on ski packages.

Reservation Contact: Alberta Bed & Breakfast, June Brown, Box 15477, M.P.O., Vancouver, BC V6B 5B2; 604–682–4610.

WHITE ROCK

SANDCASTLE DAY; THEATER, SHOPS, RESTAURANTS, BEACHES.

Near Marine Dr. & 152 St., Hwy. 99.

Perched above the beach, with a beautiful view of the water and Gulf Islands, is this attractive home with two guest rooms. One has a double bed and one a single; they share a guest bath. Your hospitable hosts invite you to share the view from the living room, patio, and deck. There is an enclosed garden and patio off the guest rooms, as well as a TV and telephone for your use. Even breakfast is served with a view between 7:00 and 9:30 A.M. The house is on a bus route, twenty-five minutes from downtown Vancouver, and five minutes from the U.S. border. White Rock has live theater, Sandcastle Day (featuring a sandcastle-building contest), shopping malls, restaurants, waterfront shops, tennis courts, parks, and the famous warm beaches. Your hosts request arrival prior to 8:00 P.M. and departure by 11:00 A.M.

No. Rooms: 2
Singles: 1 sb
Doubles: 1 sb
Type: Private home

Breakfast: Continental Plus
S-Rates: $28 sb
D-Rates: $38 sb
Bldg: Oceanfront

Minimum Stay: none. **Credit Card(s) Accepted:** None. **Open:** all year. No dogs please. No cats please. Nonsmoking host. Guests may not smoke in residence. Children welcome. **Discounts:** none.

Reservation Contact: Town & Country Bed & Breakfast in B.C. Canada, Helen Burich & Pauline Scoten, Box 46544, Station G, Vancouver, BC, V6R 4G6; 604–731–5942.

NEW BRUNSWICK

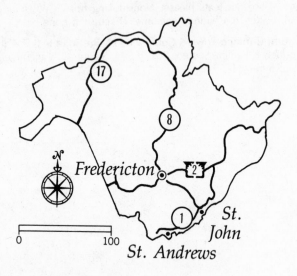

FREDERICTON

ID: E3B3JBAC

BEAVERBROOK ART GALLERY, BOYCE FARMERS MARKET, ST. JOHN RIVER.

Near Charlotte & Saunders sts., Trans Canada.

This home, built in 1929, is gradually undergoing restoration and acquiring period furnishings. Located in downtown Fredericton, it is within walking distance of federal, provincial, and municipal government offices, parks, tennis courts, art galleries, the Playhouse, Boyce Farmers Market, downtown shopping, the St. John River, and the Green. Three guest rooms share two guest baths. One is furnished with antique double bed, dresser, and area rugs; another has a four-poster double bed and walnut bedroom set; and a third has a single bed, dresser, and area rugs. A Full breakfast is served on the porch, weather permitting. Your hosts enjoy gardening and home restoration.

No. Rooms: 3	**Breakfast:** Full
Singles: 1 sb	**S-Rates:** $28 sb
Doubles: 2 sb	**D-Rates:** $35 sb
Type: Private home	**Bldg:** 1929

Minimum Stay: none. **Credit Card(s) Accepted:** none. **Open:** all year. No resident dogs. No dogs please. No resident cats. No cats please. Nonsmoking host. Guests may not smoke in residence. Children welcome with restrictions. **Discounts:** none. English & French spoken.

Reservation Contact: Back Porch Bed and Breakfast, Patrick & Wendy Beggs, 266 Northumberland St., Fredericton, NB E3B 3J6; 506–454–6875.

ST. ANDREW

ID: EOG2XPAN

PANSY PATCH

ALGONQUIN GOLF COURSE, HUNTSMAN MARINE LABORATORY & AQUARIUM, ENGLISH & IRISH IMPORT SHOPS.

Near Rte. 127, Rte. 1.

This picturesque house, complete with turret, is one of the most photographed in New Brunswick. On the ground floor you will find one of the largest rare and out-of-print books shops in the maritime provinces as well as a well-stocked antique shop. Just a few blocks away is the center of St. Andrews, with shops offering the finest in English and Irish woolens, china, crystal, and other fine imports. Also nearby are the championship Algonquin Golf Course, a swimming beach, the Huntsman Marine Laboratory and Aquarium, and many excellent examples of eighteenth-century architecture. This home offers four guest rooms that share two guest baths. Three of the rooms have double beds; one has twin beds. All the beds have fluffy comforters and pillow shams, and the rooms are furnished with antiques and afford fine views of Passamaquoddy Bay. A Full breakfast, with an ever-changing menu, is served.

No. Rooms: 4
Singles: None
Doubles: 4 sb
Type: Private home

Breakfast: Full
S-Rates: $55–$65 sb
D-Rates: $65 sb
Bldg: 1912 English cottage

Minimum Stay: none. **Credit Card(s) Accepted:** AE, MC, V. **Open:** May 15–Oct. 1. No dogs please. No resident cats. No cats please. Children welcome with restrictions. **Discounts:** none. English & French spoken.

Reservation Contact: Pansy Patch, Kathleen & Michael Lazare, 59 Carleton St., Box 349, St. Andrew, NB E0G 2X0; 506–529–3834 or 203–354–4181.

NOVA SCOTIA

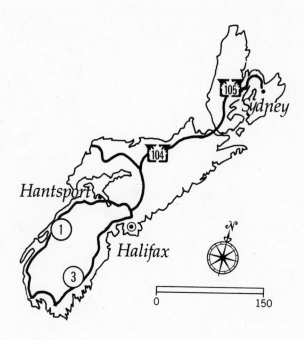

SYDNEY

ID: B1P2ZPHI

WENTWORTH PARK, CABOT TRAIL, FORTRESS OF LOUISBOURG, MINERS MUSEUM.

Near rtes. 4 & 105.

Originally built for the town miller, this one-hundred-and-seventy-five-year-old Victorian home now overlooks picturesque Wentworth Park, with its quaint duck ponds and free Sunday concerts. The house is centrally located in Sydney, and the Newfoundland ferry, Cabot Trail, the Fortress of Louisbourg, and the Miners Museum of Glace Bay are all easily accessible. There are five guest rooms, four of which have double beds; one has twin beds. The two baths are shared. Breakfast is served in the family dining room.

No. Rooms: 5	**Breakfast:** Full
Singles: None	**S-Rates:** $28 sb
Doubles: 5 sb	**D-Rates:** $33 sb
Type: Private home	**Bldg:** 1810s Victorian

Minimum Stay: none. **Credit Card(s) Accepted:** none. **Open:** all year. Children welcome.**Discounts:** none.

Reservation Contact: Phillips B&B, Ken & Jean Phillips, 148 Crescent St., Sydney, NS B1P 2Z8; 902–539–7172.

ONTARIO

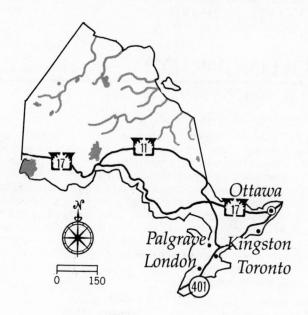

ALLISTON

ID: #3ONTARIO

HILLS OF MULMUR, HOCKLEY VALLEY.

Near Hwy. 89, Hwy. 27.

This beautifully restored and modernized Victorian farmhouse dates from 1874 when it was the local post office for an Irish community. You are invited to enjoy the patio, large yard, fireplace, and TV. Your hosts will provide transportation for hikers to the Hills of Mulmur or Hockley Valley. Two guest rooms offer double beds, antique furnishings, view of the countryside, and shared guest bath. A Full breakfast is served; other meals, as well as child care, arrival/departure transportation, and area tours, are available. Your hosts are globe-trotters from England who raise prize cattle.

No. Rooms: 2
Singles: None
Doubles: 2 sb
Type: Private home

Breakfast: Full
S-Rates: $30 sb
D-Rates: $45 sb
Bldg: 1874 brick Victorian

Minimum Stay: none. **Credit Card(s) Accepted:** none. **Open:** all year.

No resident dogs. No dogs please. No resident cats. No cats please. Non-smoking host. Guests may not smoke in guest rooms. Children welcome with restrictions. **Discounts:** weekly.

Reservation Contact: Country Host, Grace Cronin, RR #1, Palgrave, ON, LON 1PO; 519–941–7633.

COLLINGWOOD   ID: ONTARIO#10

SKIING, WASAGA BEACH, HIKING.

Near hwys. 24, 91, & 26.

An 1857 red-brick restored Victorian mansion on twenty-five acres of land is three miles from famous Bruce Trail for hikers and nature lovers. This is a quiet place, with trails for walking and magnificent views, yet Collingwood, with its many different attractions, is only 20 minutes away. Many craft and antique shops are also nearby. This is a four-season area, with downhill and cross-country skiing, snowmobiling, and ice fishing during the winter months, and boating, swimming, golfing, and fishing in summer. This home offers a self-contained apartment in a private wing of the second floor. The apartment consists of a kitchen, sitting room with double hide-a-bed, bedroom with double bed, private bath, and private entrance. Your well-educated widely traveled hosts enjoy horses, country living, nature, and people.

No. Rooms: 1	**Breakfast:** Full
Singles: None	**S-Rates:** $35 pb
Doubles: 1 pb	**D-Rates:** $50 pb
Type: Private home	**Bldg:** 1857 red-brick Victorian

Minimum Stay: none. **Credit Card(s) Accepted:** none. **Open:** all year. Dog in residence. No dogs please. No resident cats. No cats please. Non-smoking host. Guests may not smoke in guest rooms. Children welcome.

Discounts: weekly.

Reservation Contact: Country Host, Grace Cronin, RR #1, Palgrave, ON, L0N 1P0; 519–941–7633.

COURTENAY

COMOX VALLEY, SKIING, FISHING, BOATING.

Near Hwy. 19, Hilton Rd.

Comox Valley is a year-round recreation area with skiing, fishing, boating, and a ferry to Powell River. This home, one of the oldest in the valley, sits on an acre of land in a park-like setting overlooking Comox Bay and the mainland mountain. Guests can play croquet, badminton, and horseshoes on the lawn, or relax on the deck. Three guest rooms share two baths. Two have double beds and one has twin beds. All have luggage racks and are nicely furnished. A Full breakfast is served on the deck. Your hosts, a pharmacist and a teacher, enjoy cross stitch, photography, cooking, gardening, and travel.

No. Rooms: 3	**Breakfast:** Full
Singles: None	**S-Rates:** $40 sb
Doubles: 3 sb	**D-Rates:** $53 sb
Type: Private home	**Bldg:** Two-story

Minimum Stay: none. **Credit Card(s) Accepted:** none. **Open:** all year. Resident dog. No dogs please. No resident cats. No cats please. Nonsmoking host. Guests may not smoke in residence. Children welcome with restrictions. **Discounts:** none.

Reservation Contact: Town & Country Bed & Breakfast in B.C. Canada, Helen Burich & Pauline Scoten, Box 46544, Station G, Vancouver, BC V6R 4G6; 604–731–5942.

ILDERTON

LONDON AREA, STRATFORD SHAKESPEARE FESTIVAL, ANTIQUES, CRAFT SHOPS.

Near hwys. 401, 4, 7.

Settled in the 1800s, this rural area is dotted with woods, cultivated fields, and prosperous farms. Ten minutes from London, this brick farmhouse set in a large yard surrounded by evergreens and maples offers two guest rooms with a shared bath. Decorated in a color scheme of rose and blue, the first room has a double bed, vanity with carved mirror, chest of drawers, night table, upholstered chair, table, lamps, and a beautiful hooked rug over the hardwood floor. The second room has a brass single bed with comforter, a dresser, mirror, antique trunk, and a stuffed-animal collection. Olive drapes compliment the gold wallpaper and carpeting. A

Full breakfast is served. Your hosts collect antiques and antique tractors and are knowledgeable about the history of the area.

No. Rooms: 2	**Breakfast:** Full
Singles: 1 sb	**S-Rates:** $25 sb
Doubles: 1 sb	**D-Rates:** $30 sb
Type: Private home	**Bldg:** 1880 brick farmhouse

Minimum Stay: none. **Credit Card(s) Accepted:** none. **Open:** all year. Resident dog. No dogs please. No resident cats. No cats please. Non-smoking host. Guests may not smoke in residence. Children welcome. **Discounts:** 7th night free.

Reservation Contact: London Area Bed & Breakfast Association, Serena Warren, 720 Headley Dr., London, ON N6H 3V6; 519–471–6228.

KIMBERLEY
ID: ONTARIO#2

BEAVER VALLEY, KIMBERLEY AND BLUE MOUNTAIN SKI AREAS.

Near Grey Co. Rd. #13, Hwy. 10.

This spacious bungalow, with its in-ground pool, provides a view of the craggy, heavily wooded Niagara Escarpment on all sides. It is a quarter mile from Bruce Trail, which has particular appeal for hikers, naturalists, bicyclists, and bird- and nature-lovers nine months of the year. Although it is a peaceful setting, nestled in the valley of a farming community, a variety of activities are only a short drive away, and local festivals are scheduled year-round. The house has three guest rooms, two with double beds, and one with twin beds. The rooms are nicely furnished and have a view of the Escarpment. They share a bath. A Full breakfast is served, and child care, additional meals, arrival/departure transportation, and area tours are available. Your hosts will also do transfers to and from Bruce Trail for hikers. Former secondary-school teachers, they are now local historians, and one is a wood carver.

No. Rooms: 3	**Breakfast:** Full
Singles: None	**S-Rates:** $35 sb
Doubles: 3 sb	**D-Rates:** $45–$50 sb
Type: Private home	**Bldg:** 1960 brick bungalow

Minimum Stay: none. **Credit Card(s) Accepted:** none. **Open:** all year. No resident dogs. No dogs please. No resident cats. No cats please. Non-smoking host. Guests may not smoke in guest rooms. Children welcome with restrictions. **Discounts:** weekly. Some French spoken.

Reservation Contact: Country Host, Gráce Cronin, RR #1, Palgrave, ON, L0N 1P0; 519–941–7633.

LONDON

SOUTHWESTERN ONTARIO, ANTIQUES, THEATER, SPRINGBANK PARK, UNIVERSITY OF WESTERN ONTARIO.

Near hwys. 401, 4, 22; Wellington & Grand.

In old South London, amidst many heritage homes and buildings, stands this attractive Victorian home. It boasts a turret with curved-glass window panes, a living room with fireplace, and a dining room with a beamed ceiling. Three guest rooms share two baths. The first has a black wrought-iron double bed with patchwork quilt, a bentwood rocker, antique dressing table, mirror, and doll collection. The second room, done in russet and beige, has turned maple twin beds with woven spreads and matching drapes. The third room, done in green and white, has a double bed with a wicker headboard and chairs. A Continental breakfast is served. Your host is an interior designer who enjoys tennis, cycling, crossword puzzles, and travel.

No. Rooms: 3	**Breakfast:** Continental
Singles: None	**S-Rates:** $30 sb
Doubles: 3 sb	**D-Rates:** $45 sb
Type: Private home	**Bldg:** Victorian

Minimum Stay: none. **Credit Card(s) Accepted:** MC. **Open:** all year. No resident dogs. No dogs please. No resident cats. No cats please. Host smokes. Guests may smoke in residence. Children welcome with restrictions. **Discounts:** 7th night free.

Reservation Contact: London Area Bed & Breakfast Association, Anne Humberstone, 194 Elmwood Ave. East, London, ON N6C 1K2; 519–439–9196.

SPRINGBANK PARK; GOLF, THEATER.

Near Rtes. 401 & 4.

This air-conditioned home is situated in prestigious residential West London, near Springbank Park and the Thames Valley Golf Course, and ten minutes from Theatre London. Bus service is at the door. The house has a sun room for relaxation and three guest rooms with twin or double beds and shared bath. Your host is coordinator of a bed & breakfast association.

No. Rooms: 3	**Breakfast:** Full
Singles: None	**S-Rates:** $25 sb
Doubles: 3 sb	**D-Rates:** $35 sb
Type: Private home	

Minimum Stay: none. **Credit Card(s) Accepted:** none. **Open:** all year. **Discounts:** none.

Reservation Contact: London Area Bed & Breakfast Association, Serena Warren, 720 Headley Dr., London, ON, N6H 3V6; 519–471–6228.

OTTAWA   ID: OT–DICK

GLEBE AREA, RIDEAU CANAL, DOWS LAKE; ANTIQUES, ETHNIC RESTAURANTS.

Near Bank St. & Bronson Ave., rtes. 16, 417, 31.

Built in 1915, this comfortable home is part of the beautiful Glebe area and overlooks the Rideau Canal and is just a short walk to Dows Lake. Both the canal and the lake offer canoeing and bike paths in the summer and ice-skating in the winter (the Rideau Canal claims to be the longest skating rink in the world). Guests will enjoy the Spring Festival with world-famous tulips, and Winterlude with ice sculpture, skating, and races in February. Bank Street, the main street in the Glebe, is dotted with antique stores, second hand book stores, and fine restaurants. The house has first- and second-floor porches in front and back for relaxing and viewing the water and lovely garden. The conservatory, off the living room, is filled with plants, and the spacious dining room boasts a beamed ceiling and unique Tiffany-style light fixtures. The two guest rooms share a bath. One has a double bed and a view of the canal and the other has twin beds and a view of Brown's Inlet, a small lake off the canal. The Full breakfast might include homemade biscuits and jams, bacon or sausage, eggs, pancakes or quiche, and juice and coffee. Your host enjoys gardening, flower arranging, decorating, sewing, classical music, reading, and traveling.

No. Rooms: 2	**Breakfast:** Full
Singles: None	**S-Rates:** $35 sb
Doubles: 2 sb	**D-Rates:** $45 sb
Type: Private home	**Bldg:** 1915

Minimum Stay: none. **Credit Card(s) Accepted:** none. **Open:** all year. No resident dogs. No dogs please. No resident cats. No cats please. Non-smoking host. Guests may not smoke in residence. Children welcome with restrictions. **Discounts:** none.

Reservation Contact: Ottawa Area Bed & Breakfast, Robert Rivoire, Box 4848, Station E, Ottawa, ON KS 5J1; 613–563–0161.

ID: OT–ROBERT

EMBASSY ROW.

Near Wellington, Parkdale, Provincial hwys. 16, 31, 148, 417.

This charming older home is near Embassy Row and the Ottawa River Parkway. The house is furnished with a pleasant blend of Canadian and American pieces. There are three guest rooms plus a sitting room with TV for your use. One room has a single bed; the other two have double beds. A child could be accommodated in the sitting room on a hide-a-bed. A Full country breakfast is served in the dining room, which boasts hundred-year-old chair. Your host, who spent many years in the Canadian foreign service, has traveled extensively and is knowledgeable about the arts in Ottawa.

No. Rooms: 4	**Breakfast:** Full
Singles: 1 sb	**S-Rates:** $35 sb
Doubles: 3 sb	**D-Rates:** $45 sb
Type: Private townhouse	**Bldg:** 1920s

Minimum Stay: none. **Credit Card(s) Accepted:** none. **Open:** all year. No resident dogs. No dogs please. Cat in residence. No cats please. Non-smoking host. Guests may smoke. Children welcome with restrictions. **Discounts:** weekly.

Reservation Contact: Ottawa Area Bed & Breakfast, Robert Rivoire, Box 4848, Station E, Ottawa, ON K1S 5J1; 613–563–0161.

ID: OT–WORMWORTH

PARLIAMENT HILL, RIDEAU CANAL.

Near rtes. 417, 31; Somerset St. & Bronson Ave.

In Center Town, this home is within walking distance of Wellington Street and the Parliament Buildings. The neighborhood has many good restaurants and there is excellent local shopping on Bank Street. The house features a large family room with fireplace, a formal dining room with fireplace, and a contemporary living room. Two guest rooms share a bath. One room has twin beds with wicker headboards and a writing desk. The other has a single bed, wicker chair, glass-topped table, and an adjacent sitting room with wicker furnishings. Both rooms are bright and sunny and one overlooks the street. A Full breakfast is served in the dining room or breakfast nook. Your bilingual hostess loves theater, music, and flower arranging.

No. Rooms: 2	**Breakfast:** Full
Singles: 1 sb	**S-Rates:** $35 sb
Doubles: 1 sb	**D-Rates:** $45 sb
Type: Private home	**Bldg:** Red brick

Minimum Stay: none. **Credit Card(s) Accepted:** none. **Open:** all year. No resident dogs. No dogs please. No resident cats. No cats please. Non-smoking host. Guests may not smoke in residence. Children welcome with restrictions. **Discounts:** none. French spoken.

Reservation Contact: Ottawa Area Bed & Breakfast, Robert Rivoire, Box 4848, Station E, Ottawa, ON K1S 5J1; 613–563–0161.

OWEN SOUND

GEORGIAN BAY, FISHING.

Near hwys. 6, 10, 26.

This beautifully restored Edwardian home is one of many turn-of-the-century homes in the area. Four guest rooms share three baths. Two have double beds, one has twin beds, and one has a single bed. A Full breakfast is served. Lunch, area tours, and pick-up service for Bruce Trail hikers is available. Your hosts enjoy travel.

No. Rooms: 4	**Breakfast:** Full
Singles: 1 sb	**S-Rates:** $35 sb
Doubles: 3 sb	**D-Rates:** $45 sb
Type: Private home	**Bldg:** Edwardian

Minimum Stay: none. **Credit Card(s) Accepted:** none. **Open:** all year. No resident dogs. No dogs please. No resident cats. No cats please. Non-smoking host. Guests may not smoke in residence. Children welcome with restrictions. **Discounts:** weekly.

Reservation Contact: Country Host, Grace Cronin, RR #1, Palgrave, ON L0N 1P0; 519–941–7633.

PALGRAVE

HOCKLEY VALLEY.

Near hwys. 9 & 50.

This uniquely designed home on eleven heavily wooded acres, with pond, ducks, and many birds, features a greenhouse off the large living room, paneled walls, and a circular staircase leading to the living quarters. Pleasant walks to the back of the property, which rises to 11,000 feet, provide lovely views. Two conservation areas are nearby for swimming, picnicking, and fishing in summer, and cross-country skiing in winter. Arts and crafts shops, as well as excellent restaurants, are also in the vicinity. Two guest rooms offer private baths; one has twin beds, and the other has a double bed and adjacent sun room overlooking the pond. A Full breakfast is served. Child care and lunch are available. Your hosts are avid horticulturists who also enjoy the birds that abound on the property.

No. Rooms: 2	**Breakfast:** Full
Singles: None	**S-Rates:** $35 pb
Doubles: 2 pb	**D-Rates:** $45 pb
Type: Private home	**Bldg:** 1950 architectural design

Minimum Stay: none. **Credit Card(s) Accepted:** none. **Open:** all year. Two resident dogs. No dogs please. No resident cats. No cats please. Host smokes. Guests may not smoke in guest rooms. Children welcome. **Discounts:** weekly.

Reservation Contact: Country Host, Grace Cronin, RR #1, Palgrave, ON, L0N 1P0; 519–941–7633.

TOBERMORY
ID: STEINWALD

BRUCE PENINSULA.

Near Hwy. 6, Lindsay Rd.

On the Stokes River, this location is a naturalist's paradise with many birds, a forest, seven rock ridges, and rare orchids growing wild along the Bruce Trail 100 yards away. The original log house, built in 1850, has been enlarged and restored and now includes two guest rooms with private baths. One has twin beds and the other has a double and a single bed. There is also a cabin adjacent to the house with a double and a single bed. A Full breakfast is served. Area tours and pick-up service for hikers is available. Your hosts are a retired banker and a naturalist.

No. Rooms: 3	**Breakfast:** Full
Singles: None	**S-Rates:** $35 pb
Doubles: 3 pb	**D-Rates:** $45 pb
Type: Private home	**Bldg:** 1850 log two-story

Minimum Stay: none. **Credit Card(s) Accepted:** none. **Open:** spring, summer, and fall. No resident dogs. Dogs limited to outside kennel. No resident cats. No cats please. Nonsmoking host. Guests may smoke in keeping room. Residence not appropriate for children. **Discounts:** weekly.

Reservation Contact: Country Host, Grace Cronin, RR #1, Palgrave, ON L0N 1P0; 519–941–7633.

TORONTO
ID: DOW–OPPEN

UNIVERSITY OF TORONTO.

Near Spadina & College.

This 1890 Victorian is located two blocks from the University of Toronto and close to Kensington Market. It features an enormous kitchen with period furnishings and a six-hundred-square-foot sitting room with two pianos which musicians are welcomed and encouraged to use. Five guest rooms share two baths. A Full gourmet breakfast is served. Your host is a singer and writer who speaks both English and French.

No. Rooms: 5	**Breakfast:** Full
Singles: 1 sb	**S-Rates:** $45–$50 sb
Doubles: 4 sb	**D-Rates:** $55 sb
Type: Private home	**Bldg:** 1890 Victorian

Minimum Stay: 3 nights. **Credit Card(s) Accepted:** none. **Open:** all year. Resident dogs. No dogs please. No resident cats. No cats please.

Nonsmoking host. Guests may not smoke in residence. Children welcome. **Discounts:** none.

Reservation Contact: Downtown Toronto Association of B&Bs, Susan Oppenheim, Box 190, Station B, Toronto, ON M5T 2W1; 416–977–6841.

ID: TOR–LOWTHER

UNIVERSITY OF TORONTO, ROYAL ONTARIO MUSEUM.

Near Bloor St., Avenue Rd.

Queen-Anne-style home, built in 1890, features large rooms on the first and second floors plus rooms with sloped ceilings on the third floor. There are three guest rooms; one has a private bath while the other two share a bath. The first room features twin beds and pine antiques. There is a decorative fireplace and the windows are hung with lace curtains. The second room has sloped ceilings, antique furnishings, and a queen-sized bed. The third room, with twin beds, is attractively decorated and has bookcases full of good reading material. This room overlooks the tree-lined street. The Full breakfast is a special occasion at this home, which is located in an interesting walking area with several mansions and a park with a fountain just across the street. It is just a few minutes' walk from Yorkville, the Royal Ontario Museum, Casa Loma, and the subway (from which you can travel in any direction). Your host is a well-educated, well-read film technician who has many interests. Her current focus is on the renovation, restoration, and decoration of her home.

No. Rooms: 3	**Breakfast:** Full
Singles: None	**S-Rates:** $55 pb, $40 sb
Doubles: 1 pb, 2 sb	**D-Rates:** $65 pb, $50 sb
Type: Private home	**Bldg:** Queen Anne-Romanesque

Minimum Stay: none. **Credit Card(s) Accepted:** none. **Open:** all year. No resident dogs. No dogs please. No resident cats. No cats please. Non-smoking host. Guests may not smoke in residence. Children are welcome with restrictions. **Discounts:** weekly in winter.

Reservation Contact: Metropolitan Bed & Breakfast of Toronto, Elinor Bolton, 72 Lowther Ave., Toronto, ON M5R 1C8; 416–964–2566 or 928–2833.

WIARTON

COLPOYS BAY, GATEWAY TO THE BRUCE PENINSULA.

Near Hwy. 6.

Wiarton is a small town in a valley on Colpoys Bay and is the gateway to the Bruce Peninsula. This exceptionally attractive brick Victorian home is beautifully decorated throughout with hand-carved furniture and many antiques. Four guest rooms share three baths. All the guest rooms have antique furniture and individually controlled electric heat. One has a queen-sized bed plus a day bed, two have double beds, and one has twin beds. A Full breakfast is served. Your hosts, who speak French, Danish, and German, have traveled widely and recently spent six years in Switzerland.

No. Rooms: 4	**Breakfast:** Full
Singles: None	**S-Rates:** $35 sb
Doubles: 4 sb	**D-Rates:** $45 sb
Type: Private home	**Bldg:** 1896 brick Victorian

Minimum Stay: none. **Credit Card(s) Accepted:** none. **Open:** all year. No resident dogs. No dogs please. No resident cats. No cats please. Non-smoking host. Guests may smoke downstairs. Children welcome with restrictions. **Discounts:** weekly. French, Danish, and German spoken.

Reservation Contact: Country Host, Grace Cronin, RR #1, Palgrave, ON L0N 1P0; 519–941–7633.

BRUCE PENINSULA.

Near Co. Rd. 9, Hwy. 6.

Restored by its owners, this 1889 mansion is in a heavily wooded area on eight hundred acres of land near the Cape Crocker Indian Reserve. It is a beautiful area in winter or summer, with excellent roads and lovely provincial parks. It is twelve miles from Wiarton, the gateway to the Bruce Peninsula, and forty-five minutes to the ferry to Manitoulin Island with its superb fishing. The Bruce Trail crosses the property a half-mile from the house. At the end of a tree-lined drive to the house is a large in-ground pool. There are five nicely furnished rooms with some antiques; two have private baths. Three rooms have double beds, one has two twin beds, and one has a three-quarter bed. A Full breakfast is served. Your hosts are beef and grain farmers enthusiastic about meeting new people.

No. Rooms: 5	**Breakfast:** Full
Singles: 1 sb	**S-Rates:** $35 pb, $35 sb
Doubles: 2 pb, 3 sb	**D-Rates:** $45 pb, $45 sb
Type: Private Home	**Bldg:** 1889 stone

Minimum Stay: none. **Credit Card(s) Accepted:** none. **Open:** all year.

Dog in residence. No dogs please. Cat in residence. No cats please. Non-smoking host. Guests may not smoke in guest rooms. Children welcome with restrictions. **Discounts:** weekly.

Reservation Contact: Country Host, Grace Cronin, RR #1, Palgrave, ON L0N 1P0; 519–941–7633.

QUEBEC

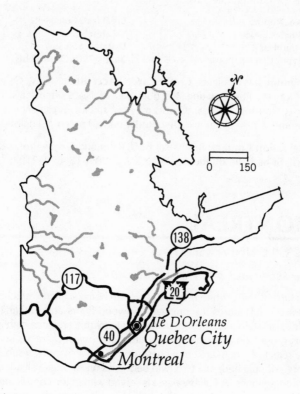

ILE D'ORLEANS

ID: G0A3WISL

BROUSSEAU B&B
12 MILES FROM QUEBEC CITY.

Near rtes. 138, 368, 40.

The Ile d'Orleans was discovered by the French in 1535 and has been farmed and inhabited by them since the early 1600s. It has always been the "garden" of Quebec City, and it is classified as an historical environment. Since it is in the middle of the St. Lawrence River, all the ships sailing to the Great Lakes or back to Europe pass in front of it. This wooden house, which is now an historic monument, was built around 1800 by a river pilot. The seventy-thousand square feet of riverfront property provides a romantic setting. You can practice your high-school French, enjoy wonderful restaurants, and easily commute to Old Quebec. The four rooms have double beds, antique furniture, private sink and toilet, and shared showers. A Continental breakfast is served at a long dining table in the main house. One of your hosts is an exhibit designer and the other owns two art-antique galleries in Old Quebec.

No. Rooms: 4
Singles: None
Doubles: 4 sb
Type: Carriage house

Breakfast: Continental
S-Rates: $58 sb
D-Rates: $58 sb
Bldg: 1790s Quebeçoise

Minimum Stay: 2 nights. **Credit Card(s) Accepted:** MC, V. **Open:** May 15–Oct. 15. Resident dog. No dogs please. No resident cats. No cats please. Nonsmoking host. Guests may not smoke in residence. Children welcome with restrictions. **Discounts:** none. French & English spoken.

Reservation Contact: Brousseau B&B, Raymond & Lyse Brousseau, 700 Royal, St-Jean, Ile d'Orleans, PQ, G0A 3W0; 418–829–3197.

MONTREAL   ID: MONTREAL–A

MC GILL UNIVERSITY.

Near Sherbrooke & Park aves., Hwy. 40.

This turn-of-the-century restored Victorian home is filled with charm and character. It features the original hardwood floors and moldings and a wide sprial staircase. A hand-carved white marble fireplace highlights the living room, and every piece of furniture and *object d'art* has been carefully selected. There are three guest rooms with a shared guest bath. One offers a double bed, one two twin beds, and one a single; all are decorated with antiques. A Full breakfast is served with color-coordinated china and linen. Your charming, well-traveled host is extremely knowledgeable about the attractions of the area and enjoys gardening and the arts. This location is Montreal's own small version of New York's Greenwich Village, near Mc Gill University, and it attracts artists, academics, and young professionals.

No. Rooms: 3
Singles: 1 sb
Doubles: 2 sb
Type: Private home

Breakfast: Full
S-Rates: $40 sb
D-Rates: $55 sb
Bldg: 1880 Victorian

Minimum Stay: none. **Credit Card(s) Accepted:** none. **Open:** all year. No resident dogs. No dogs please. No resident cats. No cats please. Nonsmoking host. Guests may smoke. Children welcome with restrictions. **Discounts:** none. English spoken.

Reservation Contact: A Downtown B&B Network, Montrealers at Home, Bob Finkelstein, 3458 Laval Ave., Montreal, PQ, H2X 3C8; 514–289–9749.

WESTMOUNT AREA.

Near Sherbrooke & Victoria sts., Hwy. 40.

Located in Westmount, the city's most prestigious residential area, is an English Tudor home built in 1900. Only ten minutes from downtown, the area contains some of the grander residences on Montreal Island. This elegant bed & breakfast home contains 5,000 square feet of magnificently detailed interiors, leaded and stained-glass windows, golden hardwood floors, three working fireplaces, and two grand skylights. Recreating the atmosphere of a bygone era, the home is furnished with fine original pieces and tasteful accessories. The two guest rooms have private baths, double beds, and fine furnishings. A Full breakfast is served in the exquisite dining room with white table linens and silverware. Both your hosts have interests in antiques, horses, and municipal politics.

No. Rooms: 2	**Breakfast:** Full
Singles: None	**S-Rates:** $75 pb
Doubles: 2 pb	**D-Rates:** $75 pb
Type: Private home	**Bldg:** 1900 English Tudor

Minimum Stay: 2 nights. **Credit Card(s) Accepted:** none. **Open:** all year. No resident dogs. No dogs please. No resident cats. No cats please. Nonsmoking host. Guests may smoke. Residence not appropriate for children. **Discounts:** none. French & English spoken.

Reservation Contact: A Downtown B&B Network, Montrealers at Home, Bob Finkelstein, 3458 Laval Ave., Montreal, PQ, H2X 3C8; 514–289–9749.

HISTORIC AREA.

Near Trans Canada Hwy., Sherbrooke & St. Denis sts.

This 90-year-old Victorian home is located in the heart of the city one block away from St. Denis Street, the main cultural throughfare of Montreal. Restaurants, cafés, bookshops, and cinemas are nearby. It overlooks Square St. Louis, the oldest park in the city. The dining room features a beautiful built-in china cabinet, and the table is hand-crafted Quebeçoise pine. Two guest rooms share a bath. One has a queen-sized bed with a handmade quilt, a collection of vintage photographs of Quebec, and a skylight. The other room has a double bed with a Quebeçoise bedstead and wardrobe, antique furnishings, and a view of the famous illuminated cross of Mount Royal. Off-street parking, TV, telephone, and patio are available for guests' use. A Full breakfast is served. Your host has traveled throughout the world and his interests range from gourmet cooking to the stock market.

No. Rooms: 2	**Breakfast:** Full
Singles: None	**S-Rates:** $45–$55 sb
Doubles: 2 sb	**D-Rates:** $45–$55 sb
Type: Private home	**Bldg:** 1900 Victorian

Minimum Stay: none. **Credit Card(s) Accepted:** none. **Open:** all year. No resident dogs. No dogs please. No resident cats. No cats please. Nonsmoking host. Guests may not smoke in residence. Children welcome with restrictions. **Discounts:** none.

Reservation Contact: A Downtown B&B Network, Montrealers at Home, Bob Finkelstein, 3458 Laval Ave., Montreal, PQ H2X 3C8; 514–289–9749.

ID: MONTREAL–D

MC GILL UNIVERSITY, HISTORIC AREA.

Near Trans Canada Hwy., Prince Arthur & University.

Mc Gill University, founded in 1829, has a full-time student population of fifteen thousand and enjoys an excellent international reputation. Many grand, old mansions dot this historic area. This charming home is located on a quiet residential street in the heart of downtown. It has traditional furnishings and many interesting works of art. The two guest rooms share a bath. The first, with twin beds, features a marble fireplace and overlooks the garden. This room also has a vanity with running water. The second room has a brass double bed, tasteful antiques, and a hand-carved wooden fireplace. Laundry facilities, TV, and telephone are available. A Full breakfast is served in the garden or solarium. Originally from Brittany, your hosts' interests include collecting Canadian art and antiques, travel, and reading.

No. Rooms: 2	**Breakfast:** Full
Singles: None	**S-Rates:** $70 sb
Doubles: 2 sb	**D-Rates:** $70 sb
Type: Private home	**Bldg:** 1890 Victorian

Minimum Stay: 2 nights. **Credit Card(s) Accepted:** none. **Open:** all year. No resident dogs. No dogs please. No resident cats. No cats please. Nonsmoking host. Guests may not smoke in residence. Children welcome. **Discounts:** none. French and Spanish spoken.

Reservation Contact: A Downtown B&B Network, Montrealers at Home, Bob Finkelstein, 3458 Laval Ave., Montreal, PQ, H2X 3C8; 514–289–9749.

MONTREAL MUSEUM OF FINE ARTS, GALLERIES, RESTAURANTS.

Near Sherbrooke & Drummond sts., Hwy. 40.

This luxury apartment in the heart of the downtown area is just blocks from the marvelous subterranean maze, ''the Underground City,'' which links the world's most extensive underground network of subways, shopping complexes, hotels, office buildings, railway stations, restaurants, and cinemas. It is also near the Montreal Museum of Fine Arts, Canada's oldest art museum. You will also want to stroll along Sherbrooke Street, Montreal's version of Fifth Avenue. The luxuriously decorated home reflects the refined tastes of its hosts. Decorated with quality antiques, this home is a delight to visit. The air-conditioned guest room features a king-sized four-poster bed, an antique library table, and built-in wardrobe. You are given a menu of gourmet breakfasts from which to choose. Your hosts, a semiretired professor of education and a homemaker, are a charming and gracious couple. Both are avid tournament bridge players who enjoy traveling (particularly to South America) and collecting antiques.

No. Rooms: 1	**Breakfast:** Full
Singles: None	**S-Rates:** $55 sb
Doubles: 1 sb	**D-Rates:** $55 sb
Type: Private apartment	**Bldg:** 1950 luxury building

Minimum Stay: 2 nights. **Credit Card(s) Accepted:**; none. **Open:** all year. Dog in residence. No dogs please. No resident cats. No cats please. Nonsmoking host. Guests may not smoke in guest rooms. Residence not appropriate for children. **Discounts:** none. English spoken.

Reservation Contact: A Downtown B&B Network, Montrealers at Home, Bob Finkelstein, 3458 Laval Ave., Montreal, PQ, H2X 3C8; 514–289–9749.

RESTAURANTS, PUBS, BOUTIQUES, ART GALLERIES; DOWNTOWN MONTREAL.

Near St. Catherine & Guy, Hwy. 40.

Located in the heart of Montreal's downtown area, this Victorian residence is surrounded by streets surging with restaurants, clubs, boutiques, and art galleries, many of which are housed in other Victorian buildings of great beauty. It is near the glamour of Crescent Street, with its nightlife and exclusive shops, the only street of Victorian townhouses in downtown Montreal that remains intact on both sides. This gracious home, lovingly restored by its owner over the past eight years to reflect its turn-of-the-century origins, is highlighted by a large skylight in the hall and a winding staircase. Original woodwork and marble are featured throughout the house. Two guest rooms, one with twin beds and one with a double bed, share a bath. A TV, laundry facilities, and bikes are available. A Full breakfast is served. Your host, who teaches biology at the University of Montreal, is interested in restoration and real estate.

No. Rooms: 2	**Breakfast:** Full
Singles: None	**S-Rates:** $55 sb
Doubles: 2 sb	**D-Rates:** $55 sb
Type: Private home	**Bldg:** 1890 Victorian

Minimum Stay: none. **Credit Card(s) Accepted:** none. **Open:** all year. No resident dogs. No dogs please. No resident cats. No cats please. Non-smoking host. Guests may smoke. Residence not appropriate for children. **Discounts:** none. French & English spoken.

Reservation Contact: A Downtown B&B Network, Montrealers at Home, Bob Finkelstein, 3458 Laval Ave., Montreal, PQ, H2X 3C8; 514–289–9749.

ID: MONTREAL–H

ALEXIS NIHON SHOPPING PLAZA, WESTMOUNT SQUARE, FORUM; WESTMOUNT AREA.

Near Sherbrooke & Atwater sts., Hwy. 20.

This Tudor-style house is located in a special area of the Downtown-Westmount area known as the "Priest Farm District." It is near the Forum, home of the famous Montreal Canadiens hockey team, Alexis Nihon Shopping Plaza, and Westmount Square, the most elegant shopping mall in town. It is also only a few blocks from stylish Greene Avenue and the Old Post Office Building now containing small high-caliber boutiques, antique shops, and a restaurant. The house is in a quiet residential area on a cul-de-sac and features interesting artifacts tastefully displayed among the clean lines of contemporary Scandinavian furniture. A working fireplace in the living room complements the decor, as do the leaded and stained-glass windows throughout the house. There are three guest rooms, two with queen-sized beds and one with twin beds, and they all share three baths. A Full, hearty Scandinavian breakfast is served featuring home-baked goodies, aromatic coffee, and even herring on request. Your host, a member of a well-known family of Swedish journalists, is an executive in a firm specializing in academic books.

No. Rooms: 3	**Breakfast:** Full
Singles: None	**S-Rates:** $55 sb
Doubles: 3 sb	**D-Rates:** $55 sb
Type: Private home	**Bldg:** 1920s Tudor

Minimum Stay: none. **Credit Card(s) Accepted:** none. **Open:** all year. No resident dogs. No dogs please. Cat in residence. No cats please. Non-smoking host. Guests may smoke. Children welcome. **Discounts:** none. English & French spoken.

Reservation Contact: A Downtown B&B Network, Montrealers at

Home, Bob Finkelstein, 3458 Laval Ave., Montreal, PQ, H2X 3C8; 514–289–9749.

ID: MONTREAL–I

SIDEWALK CAFÉS, BOUTIQUES, NIGHTSPOTS, HISTORIC SITES.

Near Sherbrooke & St. Denis sts., Hwy. 40.

A few minutes walk to Old Montreal and you are in the heart of the historic old quarter, with its boutiques, sidewalk cafés, restaurants, nightspots, and historic sites. Stroll along the boulevard facing the nineteenth-century docks of Montreal's port to Place Jacques Cartier, surrounded by houses and hotels of remarkable architectural unity. This home is an attractive and uniquely designed duplex with a secluded garden in back. The charming guest room with a queen-sized bed has traditional hand-crafted Quebeçoise furnishings. The bath is shared. A tasty Full breakfast is served, including your host's famous homemade rhubarb-strawberry jam. Your host enjoys white-water rafting, hiking, mountain climbing, bicycling, and clothing design.

No. Rooms: 1	**Breakfast:** Full
Singles: None	**S-Rates:** $55 sb
Doubles: 1 sb	**D-Rates:** $55 sb
Type: Private townhouse	**Bldg:** 1982 Quebeçoise

Minimum Stay: none. **Credit Card(s) Accepted:** none. **Open:** all year. No resident dogs. No dogs please. No resident cats. No cats please. Nonsmoking host. Guests may not smoke in residence. Residence not appropriate for children. **Discounts:** none. English & French spoken.

Reservation Contact: A Downtown B&B Network, Montrealers at Home, Bob Finkelstein, 3458 Laval Ave., Montreal, PQ, H2X 3C8; 514–289–9749.

ID: MONTREAL–6

WESTMOUNT AREA, BOUTIQUES, ART GALLERIES, RESTAURANTS.

Near Rte. 15, Sherbrooke St. W.

This three-story Victorian home is located in the Westmount area near stylish Greene Avenue with its boutiques, art galleries, and chic restaurants. Guests will want to visit Westmount Square, the underground mall. The house has much open space and antique furnishings. There are three guest rooms. One has a double bed with a canopy and a private bath; another has a king-sized bed and large balcony; and the third has twin beds. Two of the rooms share a bath. A Full breakfast is served. Your host is an art teacher interested in fashion design and travel.

No. Rooms: 3	**Breakfast:** Full
Singles: None	**S-Rates:** $70–$75 pb, $55–$65 sb
Doubles: 1 pb, 2 sb	**D-Rates:** $70–$75 pb, $55–$65 sb
Type: Private home	**Bldg:** Victorian

Minimum Stay: 2 nights on weekends. **Credit Card(s) Accepted:** AE, MC, V. **Open:** all year. No resident dogs. No dogs please. No resident cats. No cats please. Host smokes. Guests may smoke in residence. Children welcome. **Discounts:** none. French spoken.

Reservation Contact: A Bed & Breakfast á Montreal, Marian Kahn, 4912 Victoria, Montreal, PQ, H3W 2N1; 514–738–9410.

ID: MONTREAL–8

CAFÉS, FRENCH RESTAURANTS, 10 MINUTES FROM DOWNTOWN.

Near Rte. 15, Sherbrooke St. W.

West of downtown, this renovated condo is close to a subway station and several buses that can take guests downtown in ten minutes. Restaurants and cafés are nearby. The building has a small courtyard with flowers and several balconies. Some of the high points of this apartment include a 250-year-old Quebeçoise dining table, an armoire, a 1783 chest, and a stunning pink-velvet English sofa and matching chair. The guest room has a brass double bed with a white eyelet bedspread, an antique desk and chair, and a private balcony. The bath is shared. A Full breakfast is served. Your host, a potter, has interests in arts, crafts, antiques, and travel.

No. Rooms: 1	**Breakfast:** Full
Singles: None	**S-Rates:** $55 sb
Doubles: 1 sb	**D-Rates:** $55 sb
Type: Private home	**Bldg:** Renovated condo

Minimum Stay: 2 nights on weekends. **Credit Card(s) Accepted:** AE, MC, V. **Open:** all year. No resident dogs. No dogs please. No resident cats. No cats please. Nonsmoking host. Guests may smoke in residence. Residence is not appropriate for children. **Discounts:** none.

Reservation Contact: A Bed & Breakfast á Montreal, Marian Kahn, 4912 Victoria, Montreal, PQ, H3W 2N1; 514–738–9410.

ID: MONTREAL–101

ST. JOSEPH'S ORATORY, THE WAX MUSEUM, UNIVERSITY OF MONTREAL.

Near Queen Mary Rd., Hwy. 15.

This large high-ceilinged Georgian home, on landscaped grounds with a patio and garden furniture, is situated on a lovely tree-lined street. It

is furnished with some antiques and with artifacts collected on your hosts' world travels. The house is near St. Joseph's Oratory, Wax Museum, and University of Montreal. You can take the metro to the downtown area from nearby Snowdon station. There are three guest rooms, one with a single bed and two with double beds, that share a guest bath. A Full breakfast is served. Your host has degrees in music and library science and is kept busy with travel, business, and bridge.

No. Rooms: 3	**Breakfast:** Full
Singles: 1 sb	**S-Rates:** $40 (Cdn) sb
Doubles: 2 sb	**D-Rates:** $60–$65 (Cdn) sb
Type: Private home	**Bldg:** 1948 Georgian

Minimum Stay: none. **Credit Card(s) Accepted:** AE, MC, V. **Open:** all year. No resident dogs. No dogs please. No resident cats. No cats please. Nonsmoking host. Guests may not smoke in residence. Children welcome with restrictions. **Discounts:** long stays. English & French spoken.

Reservation Contact: A Bed & Breakfast á Montreal, Marian Kahn, 4912 Victoria, Montreal, PQ, H3W 2N1; 514–738–9410.

ID: MONTREAL–103

ANTIQUE SHOPS OF NOTRE DAME ST., ATWATER MARKET.

Near Notre Dame St., Atwater.

This modern townhouse is located near the Atwater Market, Old Montreal, two subway stations, and one block from the antique shops of Notre Dame Street. Some of its special features include a grand piano in the living room and a wonderful collection of plants. The guest room has a double bed, a mirrored wall, two double closets, and a needlepoint chair that reflects your host's interests. The bath is shared. A Full breakfast is served in the dining room which overlooks the garden. Other amenities include off-street parking and use of the patio and yard.

No. Rooms: 1   **Breakfast:** Full
Singles: None   **S-Rates:** $55 sb
Doubles: 1 sb   **D-Rates:** $55 sb
Type: Private home   **Bldg:** Townhouse

Minimum Stay: 2 nights on weekends. **Credit Card(s) Accepted:** AE, MC, V. **Open:** all year. Resident dog. No dogs please. Resident cat. No cats please. Host smokes. Guests may smoke. Residence not appropriate for children. French spoken. **Discounts:** None.

Reservation Contact: A Bed & Breakfast á Montreal, Marian Kahn, 4912 Victoria, Montreal, PQ, H3W 2N1; 514–738–9410.

ID: MONTREAL–104

NOTRE DAME DE GRACE.

Near Sherbrooke St., Decarie Expwy.

This large two-story home features natural oak trim, fireplaces, and Canadian furniture. Located one block from Sherbrooke Street, it is accessible to buses, shops, and restaurants. Two guest rooms share a guest bath. One has a double bed; the other, with a fireplace, has both a double and single bed. A Full breakfast is served. Your host, a teacher, enjoys travel, bridge, and backgammon.

No. Rooms: 2   **Breakfast:** Full
Singles: None   **S-Rates:** $40 sb
Doubles: 2 sb   **D-Rates:** $50 sb
Type: Private home   **Bldg:** 1915 brick Victorian

Minimum Stay: none. **Credit Card(s) Accepted:** AE, MC, V. **Open:** all year, except holiday season. No resident dogs. No dogs please. No resident cats. No cats please. Host does not smoke in guest areas. Guests may not smoke in guest rooms. Residence not appropriate for children. **Discounts:** none. French & English spoken.

Reservation Contact: A Bed & Breakfast á Montreal, Marian Kahn, 4912 Victoria, Montreal, PQ, H3W 2N1; 514–738–9410.

ID: MONTREAL–105

WESTMOUNT AREA.

Near the Boulevard, Sherbrooke St.

Overlooking the Montreal skyline and surrounded by century-old stone homes and small mansions is this enormous three-story Victorian residence, where trees, flowers, and lush lawns abound just outside your door. On the second floor is a reading/sitting area for your use. The largest of the three guest rooms has a double bed, lovely oak furniture, two

closets, wall-to-wall carpeting, and private bath. The second, also with double bed and private bath, has antique furniture and private balcony. The adjoining lounge, with fireplace, bay window, sofa, rocking chair, and foam bed, sleeps two, making it ideal for a family. The third-floor room is decorated simply with double bed and shares a bath with your hosts. A Full breakfast is served. Your hosts, a retired builder and an accountant, are interested in family activities, reading, music, politics, and entertaining.

No. Rooms: 3	**Breakfast:** Full
Singles: None	**S-Rates:** $50–$55 pb, $40 sb
Doubles: 2 pb, 1 sb	**D-Rates:** $60–$65 pb, $45 sb
Type: Private home	**Bldg:** 1880s Victorian

Minimum Stay: none. **Credit Card(s) Accepted:** AE, MC, V. **Open:** all year. No resident dogs. No dogs please. No resident cats. No cats please. Host smokes. Guests may not smoke in guest rooms. Children welcome with restrictions. **Discounts:** none. English & French spoken.

Reservation Contact: A Bed & Breakfast à Montreal, Marian Kahn, 4912 Victoria, Montreal, PQ, H3W 2N1; 514–738–9410.

ID: MONTREAL–108

DOWNTOWN MONTREAL, PLATEAU MONT ROYAL.

Near Sherbrooke St., rtes. 138 & 20.

Plateau Mont Royal is a trendy, artsy Montreal area with many renovated Victorian greystones. At its center is the lovely St. Louis Square, and its principal street is the active St. Denis, site of the ten-day jazz festival every July. This charming townhouse at St. Louis Square offers you use of the entire first floor, with guest room, private bath, living room, and indoor skylit courtyard. The guest room has a double bed, and decorations from the Far East provide a tranquil mood. It is a perfect spot for honeymooners. A Full breakfast is served. Your host, a model turned writer and actress, is a gourmet cook.

No. Rooms: 1	**Breakfast:** Full
Singles: None	**S-Rates:** $100 (Cdn.) pb
Doubles: 1 pb	**D-Rates:** $100 (Cdn.) pb
Type: Private townhouse	**Bldg:** 1920s Victorian

Minimum Stay: 2 nights. **Credit Card(s) Accepted:** AE, MC, V. **Open:** all year. Dog in residence. No dogs please. No resident cats. No cats please. Nonsmoking host. Guests may smoke. Residence not appropriate for children. **Discounts:** none. French & English spoken.

Reservation Contact: A Bed & Breakfast à Montreal, Marian Kahn, 4912 Victoria, Montreal, PQ, H3W 2N1; 514–738–9410.

ID: MONTREAL–109

ST. LOUIS SQUARE.

Near Sherbrooke St., rtes. 138 & 15.

This renovated three-story Victorian row house is three streets over from St. Denis's cafés, restaurants, shopping, and nightlift. Overlooking St. Louis Square, it is one block from must-see Prince Arthur Street. The living

room of this charming house has some fine European pieces, attractive accessories, and a fireplace. The guest rooms have double beds and private baths. A Full breakfast of crêpes, French toast, or an egg dish is served. Your European-born host maintains interests in art history, Oriental rugs, travel, and home restoration.

No. Rooms: 2	**Breakfast:** Full
Singles: None	**S-Rates:** $75 (Cdn.) pb
Doubles: 2 pb	**D-Rates:** $75 (Cdn.) pb
Type: Private townhouse	**Bldg:** 1930s Victorian stone

Minimum Stay: 2 nights. **Credit Card(s) Accepted:**; AE, MC, V. **Open:** all year. Dog in residence. No dogs please. No resident cats. No cats please. Nonsmoking host. Guests may not smoke in guest rooms. Children welcome. **Discounts:** none. English & French spoken.

Reservation Contact: A Bed & Breakfast à Montreal, Marian Kahn, 4912 Victoria, Montreal, PQ, H3W 2N1; 514–738–9410.

ID: MONTREAL–110

DOWNTOWN MONTREAL, MOUNT ROYAL PARK.

Near Cote des Neiges, Sherbrooke St.

This magnificent architectural gem opposite Mount Royal Park offers a panoramic view of the city and the St. Lawrence River. The park, ideal for joggers, is only a five-minute walk from downtown Montreal. Parking is available inside the apartment compound. The apartment has a fireplace, parquet floors, high ceilings, and lovely furnishings. The guest room has a fresh, romantic look, with double bed, Oriental rug, and modern lighting. A Continental Plus breakfast is served. Although born in Belgium, your host was raised in Montreal and is interested in business, decorating, entertaining, skiing, and travel.

No. Rooms: 1	**Breakfast:** Continental Plus
Singles: None	**S-Rates:** $65 sb
Doubles: 1 sb	**D-Rates:** $65 sb
Type: Private apartment	**Bldg:** 1920s

Minimum Stay: none. **Credit Card(s) Accepted:** AE, MC, V. **Open:** all year. No resident dogs. No dogs please. No resident cats. No cats please. Nonsmoking host. Guests may not smoke in guest rooms. Residence not appropriate for children. **Discounts:** none. French & English spoken.

Reservation Contact: A Bed & Breakfast à Montreal, Marian Kahn, 4912 Victoria, Montreal, PQ, H3W 2N1; 514–638–9410.

MONTREAL/ MT. ROYAL

ID: MONTREAL–107

10 MINUTES TO DOWNTOWN MONTREAL.

Near Graham Blvd., Rte. 15.

You will find a warm and open atmosphere in this two-story, brick, cottage-style home belonging to a grand English lady whose passions are her garden and her volunteer work. Situated in a choice section of Mount Royal, it is just ten minutes from downtown Montreal via commuter train. There is one guest room with twin beds and a shared bath. Guests may also relax in the garden. A Full breakfast is served.

No. Rooms: 1	**Breakfast:** Full
Singles: None	**S-Rates:** $35 sb
Doubles: 1 sb	**D-Rates:** $60 sb
Type: Private townhouse	**Bldg:** 1935 brick

Minimum Stay: none. **Credit Card(s) Accepted:** AE, MC, V. **Open:** all year. No resident dogs. No dogs please. Two resident cats. No cats please. Nonsmoking host. Guests may not smoke in residence. Residence not appropriate for children. **Discounts:** none. English & French spoken.

Reservation Contact: A Bed & Breakfast à Montreal, Marian Kahn, 4912 Victoria, Montreal, PQ, H3W 2N1; 514–738–9410.

MONTREAL/ WESTMOUNT

ID: MONTREAL–106

MUSEUMS, SHOPPING

Near Sherbrooke, de Maisonneuve, rtes. 10 & 15.

Located in one of the city's most prestigious residential areas, this semi-detached duplex is only ten minutes from downtown. One block away is the fabulous Westmount Square underground mall and Greene Avenue with restaurants and art galleries. This delightful home features stenciled-glass windows, oak woodwork, and fine period furnishings. There is one guest room with a double bed and shared bath. The host, a retired teacher, is active in volunteer activities which have taken her around the world.

No. Rooms: 1	**Breakfast:** Full
Singles: None	**S-Rates:** $45 (Cdn.) sb
Doubles: 1 sb	**D-Rates:** $55 (Cdn.) sb
Type: Private home	**Bldg:** 1927 brick

Minimum Stay: none. **Credit Card(s) Accepted:** AE, MC, V. **Open:** all year. No resident dogs. No dogs please. No resident cats. No cats please. Nonsmoking host. Guests may not smoke in residence. Children welcome with restrictions. **Discounts:** none. English & French spoken.

Reservation Contact: A Bed & Breakfast à Montreal, Marian Kahn, 4912 Victoria, Montreal, PQ, H3W 2N1; 514–738–9410.

QUEBEC CITY

ID: G1R3XOLD

BROUSSEAU B&B
OLD QUEBEC.

Near Ste-Anne & rue Saint Louis, rtes. 73 & 440.

A stone house that dates back to 1700 is located in the heart of the uptown section of the city, putting everything within easy walking distance. (You can park your car in the underground garage at City Hall, just across the way, for $6.00 Canadian and enjoy this very European city on foot.) The famous Chateau Frontenac and the terrace overlooking the St. Lawrence are one block away, and the best summer festival activities are held in the open air of City Hall Park right in front of the house. A charming guest apartment on the second floor offers a bedroom, living room, kitchen, dining area, and private bath. Large windows at the front of the house overlook City Hall and the park. The apartment is beautifully decorated with antiques. The bedroom has a double bed. There is also a fourth-floor loft apartment, with stone walls, beams, and wooden floors. The bedroom has a double bed, and there is a double hide-a-bed in the living room. The rooms were featured in the February 1986 issue of *Country Living.* A Continental breakfast is provided in your kitchen. Your hosts own the first-floor art and antique gallery and their son sometimes functions as tour guide.

No. Rooms: 2	**Breakfast:** Continental
Singles: None	**S-Rates:** $92 pb
Doubles: 2 pb	**D-Rates:** $92 pb
Type: Private home	**Bldg:** 1700s historical structure

Minimum Stay: 2 nights. **Credit Card(s) Accepted:** MC, V. **Open:** all year. No resident dogs. No dogs please. No resident cats. No cats please. Nonsmoking host. Guests may smoke. Children are welcome with restrictions. **Discounts:** 7th night free. French & English spoken.

Reservation Contact: Brousseau B&B, Raymond & Lyse Brousseau, 71 rue St. Anne., Old Quebec City, PQ G1R 3X4; 418–829–3197 or 418–692–1230.

ID: MONTREAL–J

LANDMARK HOME.

Near rtes. 40 & 138.

Yesterday's charm coupled with today's conveniences are found in this landmark 1671 home, facing the St. Lawrence River. Located in a typical agricultural community a short distance from Quebec City, this tranquil setting offers an attractive exterior offset by gabled windows and a split rail fence. Inside, typical Quebeçoise furnishings are teamed with the warmth and hospitality of a typical Quebeçoise home. Utilized in numerous feature films, this special dwelling attracts the attention of many passersby. One of the guest rooms is large, with twin beds, and features an unimpeded view of the beautiful St. Lawrence River. The other room, cozy and warm, has a double bed and is decorated with local handicrafts. A substantial country breakfast is prepared by a blue-ribbon chef. Your well-traveled host is a fascinating storyteller.

No. Rooms: 2	**Breakfast:** Full
Singles: None	**S-Rates:** $45 sb
Doubles: 2 sb	**D-Rates:** $55 sb
Type: Private home	**Bldg:** 1671 landmark

Minimum Stay: none. **Credit Card(s) Accepted:** none. **Open:** all year. No resident dogs. No dogs please. No resident cats. No cats please. Nonsmoking host. Guests may smoke. Children welcome. **Discounts:** none. French & English spoken.

Reservation Contact: A Downtown B&B Network, Montrealers at Home, Bob Finkelstein, 3458 Laval Ave., Montreal, PQ, H2X 3C8; 514–289–9749.

MEXICO

ACAPULCO

BEACH, WATER SKIING, FISHING, CRUISES, GOLF, HORSEBACK RIDING, RESTAURANTS, NIGHTLIFE; BALCONES DE COSTA AZUL AREA.

Near Costera Miguel Aleman & Horacio Nelson, hwys. 95 & 200.

This air-conditioned Mediterranean style trilevel home is located on a private street in the luxurious residential area of Balcones de Costa Azul. The atmosphere is very tranquil and romantic, yet it is within walking distance of Icacos Beach, and the infamous Acapulco strip. The home is in the hills, overlooking Acapulco Bay, and the city and ocean views are breathtaking. There is a private pool, poolside bar, and two terraces for meals and magnificent views. The house has two upper-level guest rooms with double beds, or twin beds that can be converted into a queen-sized bed, and private baths. A Full breakfast is served. Arrival/departure transportation, additional meals, and area tours are available for a fee. Your well-traveled hosts enjoy classical music, aquatic sports, Flamenco dancing, and puppetry.

No. Rooms: 2
Singles: None
Doubles: 2 pb
Type: Private home

Breakfast: Full
S-Rates: $40 pb
D-Rates: $40 pb
Bldg: 1974 Mediterranean

Minimum Stay: one week. **Credit Card(s) Accepted:** none. **Open:** all year, except late December. No resident dogs. No dogs please. Cat in residence. No cats please. Host smokes. Guests may smoke. Children welcome with restrictions. **Discounts:** none. English & Spanish spoken.

Reservation Contact: Bed & Breakfast Registry Ltd., Gary Winget, Box 8174, St. Paul, MN 55108; 612-646-4238.

COSTA AZUL AREA.

This modern Spanish villa is in the luxurious residential neighborhood of Costa Azul. Situated in the hills, it is within easy walking distance of the beach and main area of the city. The house is air-conditioned and offers a shaded patio, pool, breakfast terrace, maid service, kitchen privileges, and view of the city. There are two guest rooms with private baths; one has a double bed and one has twin beds. A Full breakfast is served. Arrival/departure transportation and area tours are available. Your hosts are a retired stockbroker and retired language teacher with interests in music, foreign literature, and ethnic dance.

No. Rooms: 3	**Breakfast:** Full
Singles: None	**S-Rates:** $38 pb
Doubles: 3 pb	**D-Rates:** $38 pb
Type: Private home	**Bldg:** 1984 modern Spanish

Minimum Stay: 2 nights. **Credit Card(s) Accepted:** none. **Open:** all year. No resident dogs. No dogs please. Cat in residence. No cats please. Host smokes. Guests may smoke. Children welcome with restrictions. **Discounts:** none. Spanish and English spoken.

Reservation Contact: Mi Casa—Su Casa Bed & Breakfast, Ruth Young, Box 950, Tempe, AZ 85281; 602–990–0682.

AJIJIC
ID: AJIJIV

RESTAURANTS, GOLF, TENNIS, LAKE CHAPALA; 45 MINUTES FROM GUADALAJARA.

Near Chapala Hwy., Hwy. 54.

With its large secluded garden, giant palms, fountain, and enclosed central patio with tiled roof, this house is a good example of Mexican architecture. It has colonial wood furnishings and comfortable native lounge chairs. There are four guest rooms; three have fireplaces, and one has a private bath. One has a king-sized bed; the others have queen-sized,

double, or twin beds. All have tiled floors. A Full breakfast is served. The town, originally Indian, was resettled by the Spanish in the early 1500s. Area attractions include a visit to Guadalajara, Liberta Market, Tlaquepaque and Tonala stately mansions, and the many ancient handicrafts, especially the weaving in the village of Ajijic. Your hosts speak both English and Spanish fluently and are interested in soccer, fishing, jogging, and weaving. Lunch, child care, arrival/departure transportation, and area tours are available.

No. Rooms: 4	**Breakfast:** Full
Singles: None	**S-Rates:** $15 pb, $12 sb
Doubles: 1 pb, 3 sb	**D-Rates:** $30 pb, $24 sb
Type: Private home	**Bldg:** 1850 Mexican colonial

Minimum Stay: none. **Credit Card(s) Accepted:** MC. **Open:** all year. Dog in residence. No dogs please. Cat in residence. No cats please. Nonsmoking host. Guests may smoke. Children welcome. **Discounts:** monthly. Spanish & English spoken.

Reservation Contact: Bed & Breakfast Registry Ltd., Gary Winget, Box 8174, St. Paul, MN 55108; 612–646–4238.

Fodor's Travel Guides

U.S. Guides

Alaska
American Cities
The American South
Arizona
Atlantic City & the
  New Jersey Shore
Boston
California
Cape Cod
Carolinas & the
  Georgia Coast
Chesapeake
Chicago
Colorado
Dallas & Fort Worth
Disney World & the
  Orlando Area

The Far West
Florida
Greater Miami,
  Fort Lauderdale,
  Palm Beach
Hawaii
Hawaii *(Great Travel
  Values)*
Houston & Galveston
I-10: California to
  Florida
I-55: Chicago to New
  Orleans
I-75: Michigan to
  Florida
I-80: San Francisco to
  New York

I-95: Maine to Miami
Las Vegas
Los Angeles, Orange
  County, Palm Springs
Maui
New England
New Mexico
New Orleans
New Orleans *(Pocket
  Guide)*
New York City
New York City *(Pocket
  Guide)*
New York State
Pacific North Coast
Philadelphia
Puerto Rico *(Fun in)*

Rockies
San Diego
San Francisco
San Francisco *(Pocket
  Guide)*
Texas
United States of
  America
Virgin Islands
  (U.S. & British)
Virginia
Waikiki
Washington, DC
Williamsburg,
  Jamestown &
  Yorktown

Foreign Guides

Acapulco
Amsterdam
Australia, New Zealand
  & the South Pacific
Austria
The Bahamas
The Bahamas *(Pocket
  Guide)*
Barbados *(Fun in)*
Beijing, Guangzhou &
  Shanghai
Belgium & Luxembourg
Bermuda
Brazil
Britain *(Great Travel
  Values)*
Canada
Canada *(Great Travel
  Values)*
Canada's Maritime
  Provinces
Cancún, Cozumel,
  Mérida, The
  Yucatán
Caribbean
Caribbean *(Great
  Travel Values)*

Central America
Copenhagen,
  Stockholm, Oslo,
  Helsinki, Reykjavik
Eastern Europe
Egypt
Europe
Europe *(Budget)*
Florence & Venice
France
France *(Great Travel
  Values)*
Germany
Germany *(Great Travel
  Values)*
Great Britain
Greece
Holland
Hong Kong & Macau
Hungary
India
Ireland
Israel
Italy
Italy *(Great Travel
  Values)*
Jamaica *(Fun in)*

Japan
Japan *(Great Travel
  Values)*
Jordan & the Holy Land
Kenya
Korea
Lisbon
Loire Valley
London
London *(Pocket Guide)*
London *(Great Travel
  Values)*
Madrid
Mexico
Mexico *(Great Travel
  Values)*
Mexico City & Acapulco
Mexico's Baja & Puerto
  Vallarta, Mazatlán,
  Manzanillo, Copper
  Canyon
Montreal
Munich
New Zealand
North Africa
Paris
Paris *(Pocket Guide)*

People's Republic of
  China
Portugal
Province of Quebec
Rio de Janeiro
The Riviera *(Fun on)*
Rome
St. Martin/St. Maarten
Scandinavia
Scotland
Singapore
South America
South Pacific
Southeast Asia
Soviet Union
Spain
Spain *(Great Travel
  Values)*
Sweden
Switzerland
Sydney
Tokyo
Toronto
Turkey
Vienna
Yugoslavia

Special-Interest Guides

Bed & Breakfast
  Guide: North America
  1936...On the
  Continent

Royalty Watching
Selected Hotels of
  Europe

Selected Resorts
  and Hotels of the U.S.
Ski Resorts of North
  America

Views to Dine by
  around the World